An Introduction to Large Language Models

The book offers an introduction to large language models (LLMs) that bridge foundational natural language processing (NLP) concepts with the advanced techniques underlying large language models. It offers a structured exploration of NLP evolution, from rule-based approaches to transformer architectures. Covering key principles such as tokenization, attention mechanisms, and model architectures (BERT, GPT, T5), the book explains pretraining objectives like masked and causal language modeling. It also addresses optimization techniques such as LoRA, pruning, and quantization for efficient LLM deployment. Multimodal models, including GPT-4 and PaLM-E, are explored alongside retrieval-augmented generation and AI-powered agents.

Features:

- Discusses foundational NLP concepts, theoretical depth, advanced techniques, and real-world applications.
- Covers perplexity, BLEU, ROUGE, and datasets like SuperGLUE and SQuAD for assessing LLM performance, discusses LoRA, pruning, and quantization to optimize LLM deployment in resource-constrained settings.
- Explores GPT-4, PaLM-E, and retrieval-augmented generation, expanding beyond traditional NLP models.
- Provides Python implementations for fine-tuning, classification, summarization, and conversational AI tasks.
- Highlights use cases in text generation, code generation, sentiment analysis, and multimodal AI.

This book is an invaluable textbook for students, researchers, and industry professionals seeking a deep technical understanding of LLMs and their applications.

An Introduction to Large Language Models

Joe Dhanith P. R., Geetha S. and
Sheik Abdullah A.

CRC Press
Taylor & Francis Group
Boca Raton London New York

CRC Press is an imprint of the
Taylor & Francis Group, an **informa** business
A CHAPMAN & HALL BOOK

First edition published 2027
by CRC Press
2385 NW Executive Center Drive, Suite 320, Boca Raton FL 33431

and by CRC Press
4 Park Square, Milton Park, Abingdon, Oxon, OX14 4RN

CRC Press is an imprint of Taylor & Francis Group, LLC

ISBN: 9781041094357 (hbk)
ISBN: 9781041086277 (pbk)
ISBN: 9781003650065 (ebk)

DOI: 10.1201/9781003650065

Typeset in Times
by Newgen Publishing UK

Access the Instructor and Student Resources/Support Material: www.routledge.com/9781041094357

Contents

About the Authors

Joe Dhanith P. R. is an Assistant Professor at the Vellore Institute of Technology (VIT), Chennai, with a strong academic and research background in the field of computer science. He has made notable contributions to high-impact journals, particularly in advancing the domains of natural language processing (NLP), web mining, and information retrieval. His research focuses on developing intelligent systems that enhance text understanding, knowledge extraction, and data-driven decision-making. Dr. Joe has been actively involved in mentoring students, guiding research projects, and delivering courses related to programming, machine learning, and deep learning. His work reflects a commitment to bridging theoretical foundations with practical applications, contributing to both academic research and real-world problem solving.

Geetha S. is a Professor and Associate Dean (Research) in School of Computer Science and Engineering, VIT University, Chennai Campus, India. She has received the B.E. and M.E. degrees in Computer Science and Engineering from Madurai Kamaraj University, India and Anna University of Chennai, India, and Ph.D. degree from Anna University, respectively. She has 23 years of rich teaching and research experience. She has published more than 100 papers in reputed International conferences and refereed journals. Her h-Index is 21 and i-10 index is 46. Her research interests include image processing, deep learning, feature selection, steganography, steganalysis, multimedia security, intrusion detection systems, malware detection, machine learning paradigms, and information forensics. She has given many expert lectures and keynote addresses in international and national conferences. She has organized many workshops, conferences, and FDPs. She is a recipient of University Rank and Academic Topper Award in B.E. and M.E, respectively. She is also the proud recipient of ASDF Best Academic Researcher Award 2013, ASDF Best Professor Award 2014, Research Award 2016–2020, High Performer Award 2016, from VIT University and DST – ISCA Best Poster Award 2018, Innovation Award 2022 – Cybersecurity Roadshow conducted in IISc.

Sheik Abdullah A. is working as an Associate Professor in the School of Computer Science Engineering, Vellore Institute of Technology, Chennai. He completed his Ph.D. from Anna University. He is a visiting faculty at The Institute of Mathematical Sciences IMSC Chennai and contributed and worked in computational biology, mathematical decision support models in clinical informatics, data analytics, and statistics. He is also a visiting researcher at Chennai Mathematical Institute (CMI) and is engaged in works corresponding to Timed automata and its applications. More recently, he has contributed his novelty in assessing risk factors that contribute to type II diabetes with swarm intelligence and machine learning approaches. His works correspond to real-time analysis of medical data and medical experts with the development of clinical decision support models for hospitals in rural areas. He also contributed his research intelligence in NLP, big data, knowledge-based systems, E-governance, learning analytics, and probabilistic planning algorithms. He has published over 45+ archival research papers to his credit, 15 book chapters, and a book. Being a Gold medalist (PG), he has been awarded the honorable chief minister award for the best project in E-governance.

1 Introduction to Natural Language Processing

1.1 BRIEF HISTORY OF NLP

In the early 1900s, Ferdinand de Saussure laid the groundwork for modern linguistics, shaping the way we think about language as a system. Between 1906 and 1911, while teaching courses at the University of Geneva, Saussure introduced the idea that meaning in language arises from relationships and differences between its elements. Unfortunately, he passed away in 1913 without publishing his theories. However, his colleagues Albert Sechehaye and Charles Bally compiled his notes and his students' class transcriptions to produce the seminal book Cours de Linguistique Générale in 1916. This work became the cornerstone of structural linguistics and deeply influenced future disciplines like computational linguistics and natural language processing (NLP). Saussure's concept of meaning creation through contrast and relations would later underpin efforts to teach computers how to process human language.

The 1950s brought the beginning of computational linguistics, ushering in the era of machine intelligence. Alan Turing's famous 1950 paper introduced the "Turing Test," a method for evaluating a machine's ability to exhibit human-like intelligence in conversation. Around the same time, Noam Chomsky revolutionized linguistic theory with his 1957 book *Syntactic Structures*. Chomsky introduced generative grammar, a formal framework for understanding language that was instrumental in the early development of machine translation systems. Despite these advances, early efforts struggled with challenges like ambiguity in language, which tempered the initial optimism about NLP potential.

The 1960s brought both breakthroughs and obstacles. While significant progress was made in linguistics and artificial intelligence (AI), the release of the 1966 Automatic Language Processing Advisory Committee (ALPAC) Report by the United States government dealt a major blow to NLP research. This report criticized the limited effectiveness of machine translation systems and advised halting funding for such projects, leading to an AI winter—a period of diminished interest and investment in AI technologies. Yet this decade was not without its successes. For instance, ELIZA, a conversational agent created by Joseph Weizenbaum in the mid-1960s, became famous for simulating a psychologist-patient dialogue, showcasing the potential for human–machine interaction.

DOI: 10.1201/9781003650065-1

NLP research increased once more in the 1970s as a result of theoretical developments and real-world implementations. Speech Act Theory, popularized by scholars like John Searle, explored the ways language conveys intent beyond mere words. This era also saw the development of SHRDLU by Terry Winograd, an early NLP system that allowed users to interact with a virtual world using natural language commands. Efforts to represent knowledge computationally began to take shape, as researchers worked to encode real-world concepts for more advanced semantic understanding. These milestones helped bridge linguistic theory and computer science, paving the way for the next phase of innovation.

The 1980s and 1990s marked a paradigm shift from rule-based systems to statistical models. Until the 1980s, most NLP systems relied on complex, manually written rules. However, advances in computing power and the adoption of probabilistic approaches revolutionized the field. Statistical models, capable of making probabilistic decisions, replaced rigid rule-based systems. IBM for instance developed groundbreaking statistical models for speech recognition and machine translation. Techniques like N-grams enabled the numerical analysis of linguistic patterns, offering a more flexible way to process text. In 1997, the introduction of long short-term memory (LSTM) networks added further sophistication to NLP, laying the groundwork for their use in applications like voice and text processing by the 2000s.

The 2000s brought neural networks and word embedding into the spotlight. This era saw the growing use of neural networks for language modeling—predicting the next words in a sequence based on preceding ones. Dense vector representations known as word embeddings were introduced, mapping words with similar meanings to similar numerical vectors. A major milestone came in 2013 with the publication of the Word2Vec algorithm [1], which captured semantic relationships between words with unprecedented efficiency. These innovations enabled more nuanced language understanding and fueled further advancements in NLP.

The 2010s were defined by deep learning and the emergence of transformers. recurrent neural networks (RNNs) [2] and LSTM [3] architectures became popular for capturing sequential dependencies in language, improving the contextual understanding of text. Transformer models were also introduced during this time period, which outperformed previous methods for dealing with long-range language dependencies. In 2018, Google's BERT [4] (*Bidirectional Encoder Representations from Transformers*) revolutionized NLP by enabling context-aware analysis of words in sentences. Around the same time, OpenAI's generative pretrained transformer (GPT) series demonstrated the power of transformers in generating coherent and contextually appropriate text, setting a new benchmark for conversational AI.

The 2020s ushered in the era of large language models (LLMs), built on transformer architecture. LLMs, such as GPT-3 [5] and GPT-4 [6], brought human-like text generation and understanding to applications ranging from customer support to creative writing. With the ability to process vast amounts of text and understand context at a sophisticated level, these models have become central to NLP research and applications. The combination of neural networks, deep learning, and advanced transformer models has redefined what's possible in language processing, making machines more capable than ever of understanding and generating human language [7, 8]. Figure 1.1 displays the history of NLP.

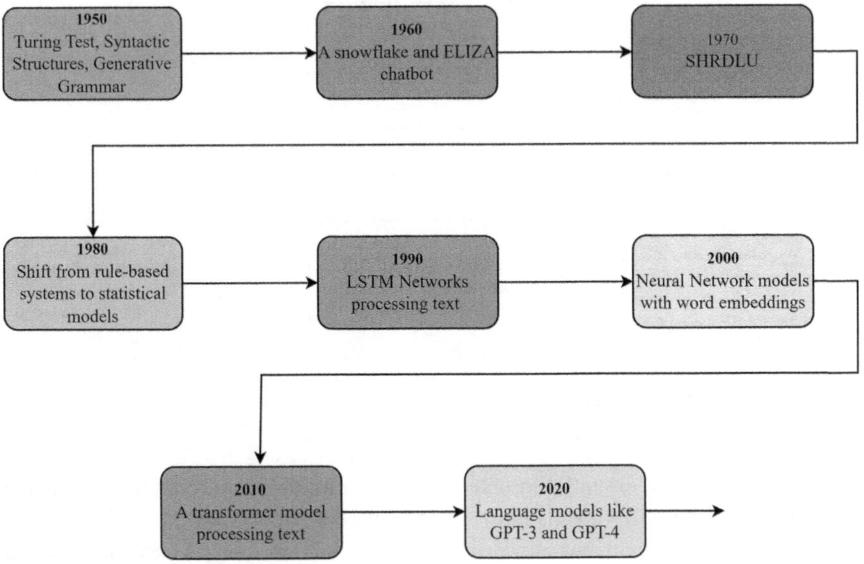

FIGURE 1.1 History of NLP.

1.2 KEY NLP TASKS

NLP is a sophisticated domain that encompasses many techniques to parse and understand human language. They vary from straightforward text preprocessing to sophisticated machine learning algorithms [9, 10].

1.2.1 Tokenization

Tokenization is a process of decomposing raw text into tokens. Tokens are either words, phrases, or sentences that assist the data scientist in knowing the context while creating an NLP model. Tokenization converts unstructured data into numerical form that is appropriate for machine learning. Through this, it becomes possible for computers to break down and analyze the meaning of the text. There are a number of tokenization types, such as word, character, and sub-word tokenization. Figure 1.2 shows the types of tokenization.

1.2.2 Stemming and Lemmatization

Stemming and lemmatization are employed to bring words down to their base or root words. Stemming method is to remove affixes from a word, but the resulting base word may or may not be accurate. Lemmatization is a more advanced NLP method that uses vocabulary and morphological analysis to give back the accurate base word, referred to as the lemma. For example, stemming would reduce "running" to "run" and "better" to "bet". Lemmatization would convert "running" to "run" and "better" to "good".

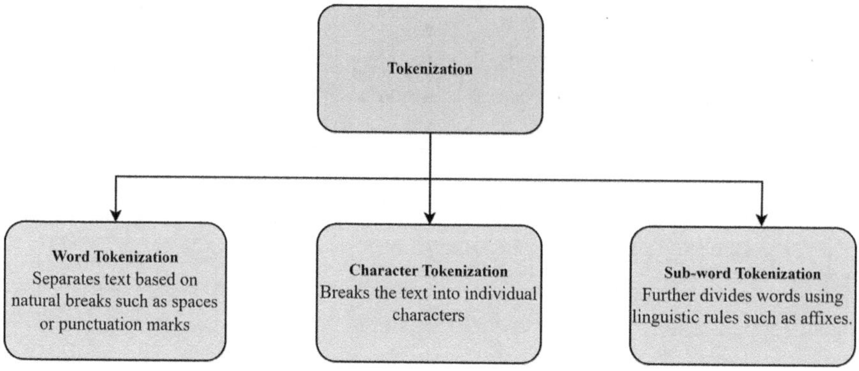

FIGURE 1.2 Types of tokenization.

Both methods are essential in text simplification and noise reduction in the data, ultimately making NLP models more accurate and efficient. Consequently, stemming and lemmatization contribute towards enhancing search queries, text analysis, and language comprehension by computers.

1.2.3 Stop Words Removal

Stop words are frequent words such as "and," "in," "the," and "is," which are not very meaningful and may generate noise in the data. Omitting these stop words from the data can significantly enhance the performance of NLP techniques, particularly in text classification tasks. It is a fundamental process of preprocessing since it reduces the data dimensionality and improves the models' efficiency.

1.2.4 Text Classification

Text classification, or document classification [4, 11], refers to the task of assigning text into predefined categories or classes based on what is stated in the text. This method is commonly applied to numerous applications, including spam filtering, sentiment analysis, and topic identification. Examples of widely popular algorithms employed in text classification include Naive Bayes, support vector machines (SVMs), and deep learning-based models such as convolutional neural networks (CNNs) and RNN.

1.2.5 Sentiment Analysis

Identification and extraction of subjective text data such as opinions, attitudes, and emotions is called sentiment analysis, emotion AI, or opinion mining. Sentiment analysis is one NLP that can be applied to customer experience measurement and measurement of brand loyalty. Sentiment analysis examines the tweets on Twitter, reviews, and other sources of text data in order to yield information that aids decision-making and performance [12].

For instance, an online movie streaming website can apply sentiment analysis to review ratings of customers and label them as highly positive, positive, neutral, negative, or highly negative. With this, the website can adapt its recommendations, which in turn improves the engagement and satisfaction levels of its customers. Generally speaking, sentiment analysis is important to improve business decisions and customer interactions. There exist several sentiment analysis types, including graded sentiment analysis, aspect-based analysis, and emotion detection.

1.2.6 Topic Modeling

Topic modeling is an unsupervised, robust text-mining method that groups words and phrases into clusters to identify hidden themes without tags or training data. It makes it easier to summarize large quantities of text, which saves time and money. Through identifying closely related words that cluster together, topic modeling offers additional insight and background.

For instance, in a 1000-document corpus where each document contains 500 words, topic modeling can cut down processing from 500,000 threads to only 2,500 threads by determining five essential topics that are found in the data. This effective method not only solves difficult problems but also improves visualization and comprehension of the text.

1.2.7 Text Summarization

Text summarization [13] is the summary of a lengthy piece of text into a shorter, clear-cut summary without losing the essential information. There are two primary methods of text summarization:

- **Extraction:** where key sentences of the original text are taken and used to develop a summary
- **Abstraction:** where the text is semantically analyzed to produce a summary that can or cannot include words from the original text

Text summarization can be used in content analysis, information extraction, and news aggregation, among others.

1.2.8 Named Entity Recognition

Named entity recognition (NER) recognizes and categorizes named entities in a piece of text into set categories, like person names, organizations, places, dates, and monetary amounts. Such an NLP technique enables companies to extract meaningful structured information from unstructured data, which can be utilized for numerous purposes, like information retrieval, data mining, and knowledge management.

For example, take the sentence shown in Figure 1.3.

"Elon Musk founded SpaceX in 2002 in California"

Through a series of steps like tokenization, parts-of-speech tagging, and chunking, NER effectively detects entities such as -

"Elon Musk" (person)
"Space-x" (organization)
"California" (location)

FIGURE 1.3 Example of NER.

Some of the various NER systems are as follows:

1. Dictionary-based systems use a predefined vocabulary and string-matching algorithms for identifying entities yet need to be updated constantly.
2. Rule-based systems apply pattern-based as well as context-based rules to derive information, based on word morphology and context.
3. Machine learning systems employ statistical patterns and feature-based representations in detecting entity names beyond the restrictions of the first two methods.
4. Deep learning methods project input data onto nonlinear representations, allowing for learning complex relationships and minimizing feature engineering efforts.

1.2.9 Machine Translation

Machine translation is the process of translating text from one human language into another automatically. NLP tools and techniques are essential for empowering machines to recognize and produce translations that reflect the meaning and context of the original text. This use of NLP has very important implications for global communication and large organizations' business operations.

1.2.10 Market Intelligence

The processing of unstructured information, for example, chatbot text, email, and forums, helps companies make sense of customer interactions.

Through the use of NLP's topic extraction function, companies are able to more clearly understand customers' questions and interests and thereby develop more specific products. Topic analysis and intent can greatly benefit market research and provide insight into trends and possibilities.

1.2.11 Intent Classification

Intent classification applies machine learning algorithms to detect text information or phrases related to a certain intent or user purpose. The process begins with data collection and labeling, model training (e.g., the BERT model), and its performance validation. Other key advantages offered through intent classification are enhanced customer service, quickened lead response time, and tailored experiences.

For instance, in customer service, a chatbot with intent classification can recognize a user's problem, like "reset password," and immediately lead them to the solution. This provides a smooth and quick resolution, improving the overall customer experience.

1.2.12 Question Answering

Question answering entails building systems that can respond to questions asked by users using natural language. Such technology has many uses in customer service, knowledge management, and search engines. Various NLP methods, including parsing, NER, and text classification, are instrumental in helping machines process and answer user questions accurately and effectively.

1.3 BASICS OF LANGUAGE MODELS

Language models are machine learning systems that use large amounts of text data to predict the next word in a sentence based on its context, facilitating tasks such as text creation and analysis. For example, in the phrase "Jenny came by the office for the keys, so I handed them to [...]," the model predicts the appropriate pronoun based on the surrounding words, such as she or her. These models prioritize word usage over grammatical rules and are essential to NLP, helping machines understand and generate language that resembles human speech. There are two types of language models one is the statistical language model and the second is the neural language model.

1.3.1 Statistical Language Models

Statistical language models use probabilities to predict the next word or phrase. These models rely on patterns found in text data and use statistical methods to calculate probabilities for words or strings. They form the basis of many NLP applications, including text prediction, machine translation, and speech recognition [14, 15].

1.3.1.1 N-Gram Models

N-gram models serve as simple yet powerful tools in language processing, designed to predict the next word in a sequence by analyzing the previous words. The number of words considered depends on the type of N-gram model used. These models assign probabilities to sequences of words, with the length of the sequence determined by the value of "n." For example, when $n = 3$, the model looks at three-word phrases such as "Are you there?" In essence, "n" indicates the amount of context required for the model to predict the upcoming word. There are several forms of N-grams: unigrams (single words), bigrams (word pairs), trigrams (word triplets), etc., each providing different levels of contextual depth to improve predictions.

The unigram model is a basic language model that focuses on individual words without considering their context. It determines the probability of each word occurring on its own. This model is useful for tasks where context is less important, such as search queries. The bigram model improves on this by evaluating the likelihood of a word based on the word that immediately precedes it. However, it only considers the preceding word and ignores the broader context. The trigram model extends this approach by looking at the two words before the current word, but still ignores any words that come before those two. A general N-gram model can extend this idea by using the last "$n - 1$" words to anticipate the next word. Figure 1.4 displays the n-gram modelling.

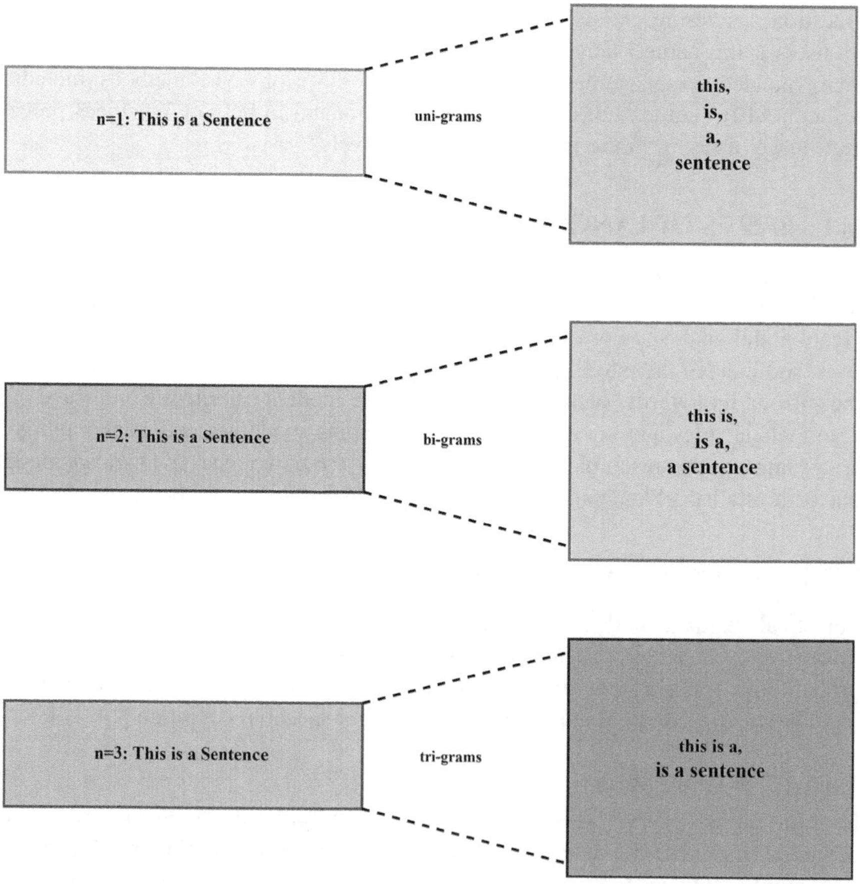

FIGURE 1.4 Examples of n-gram models.

1.3.1.2 Exponential Models

Exponential models, such as the Maximum Entropy (MaxEnt) model, are more flexible and powerful than n-gram models. They predict the probability of a word based on a variety of features, including not only the previous words but also other contextual information. MaxEnt models use an exponential function to combine these features and estimate the next word. While they are more flexible, they are also more complex and computationally expensive to train. MaxEnt models can handle a wider variety of features than n-grams, but like n-grams, they struggle with long-range dependencies due to their reliance on fixed-length context windows. Despite these limitations, they remain valuable for more sophisticated language modeling tasks.

1.3.1.3 Skip-Gram Models

Skip-gram models, primarily used for word embeddings like Word2Vec, focus on capturing the relationships between words by predicting the surrounding context for a target word. These models use neural networks to optimize the probability of context words appearing around a target word. Skip-gram models are effective for tasks such as finding similar words or clustering semantically related words. They have the advantage of capturing the semantic meaning of words and handling varying contexts better than traditional n-grams. Figure 1.5 shows the skip-gram modelling.

1.3.2 Neural Language Models

1.3.2.1 Neural Network-based Language Models (NNLMs)

NNLMs leverage neural networks to capture complex patterns and relationships in text. These models can process large vocabularies and long-range dependencies, making them more effective than traditional statistical methods [2, 16].

1.3.2.2 Recurrent Neural Networks (RNNs)

RNNs are designed to process sequences of data by handling one token at a time while maintaining a hidden state that captures contextual information. This characteristic enables RNNs to effectively model sequential data and understand long-range dependencies. For instance, RNNs are widely used in applications like sentence completion, language generation, and speech recognition, where understanding the sequence's context is crucial. However, RNNs face challenges when working with long sequences due to the vanishing and exploding gradient problems, which can hinder their ability to learn and retain information over extended periods. An example of RNN usage is in language generation, where the network predicts the next word in a sequence based on the words preceding it, such as generating a sentence in a chatbot application. Figure 1.6 shows the example of RNN language model.

1.3.2.3 Long Short-Term Memory (LSTM)

LSTM networks are an advanced variant of RNNs designed to address the vanishing gradient problem by introducing gating mechanisms. LSTMs consist of three key components: the forget gate, which determines what information to discard; the input gate, which decides what information to update; and the output gate, which generates

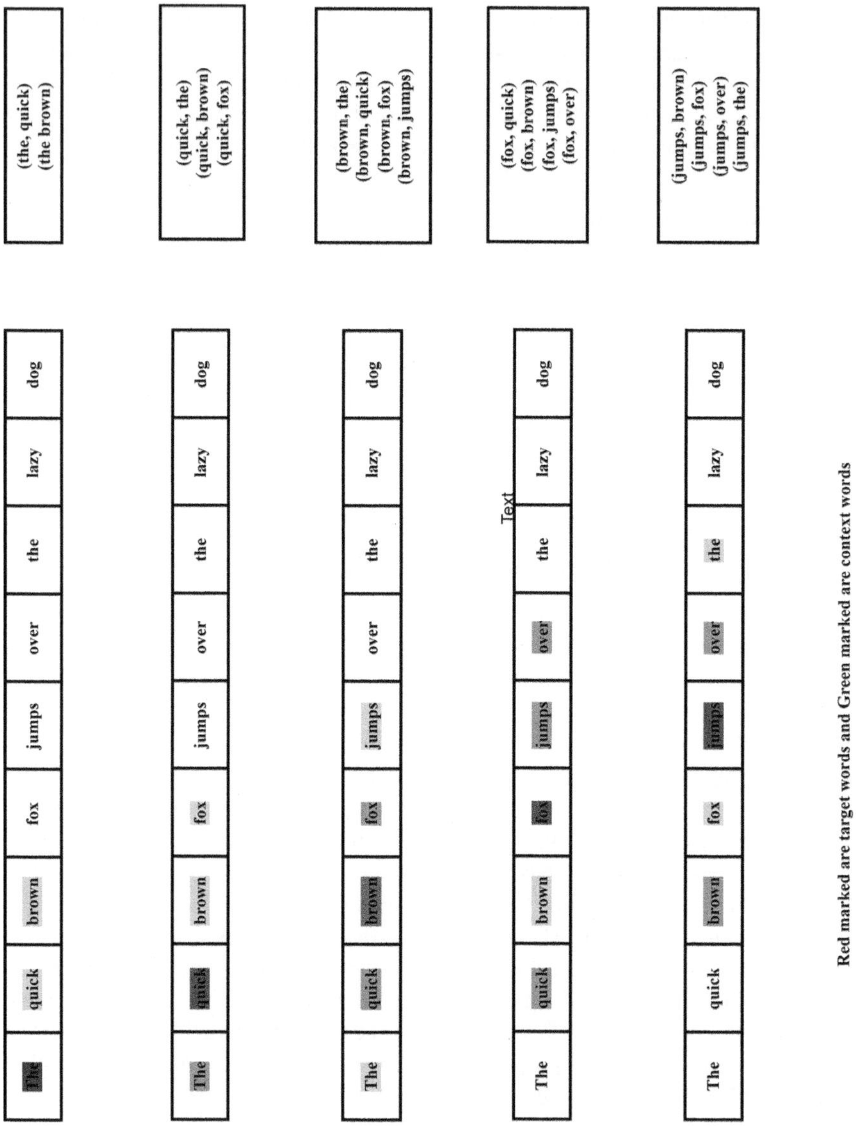

FIGURE 1.5 Example of skip-gram model.

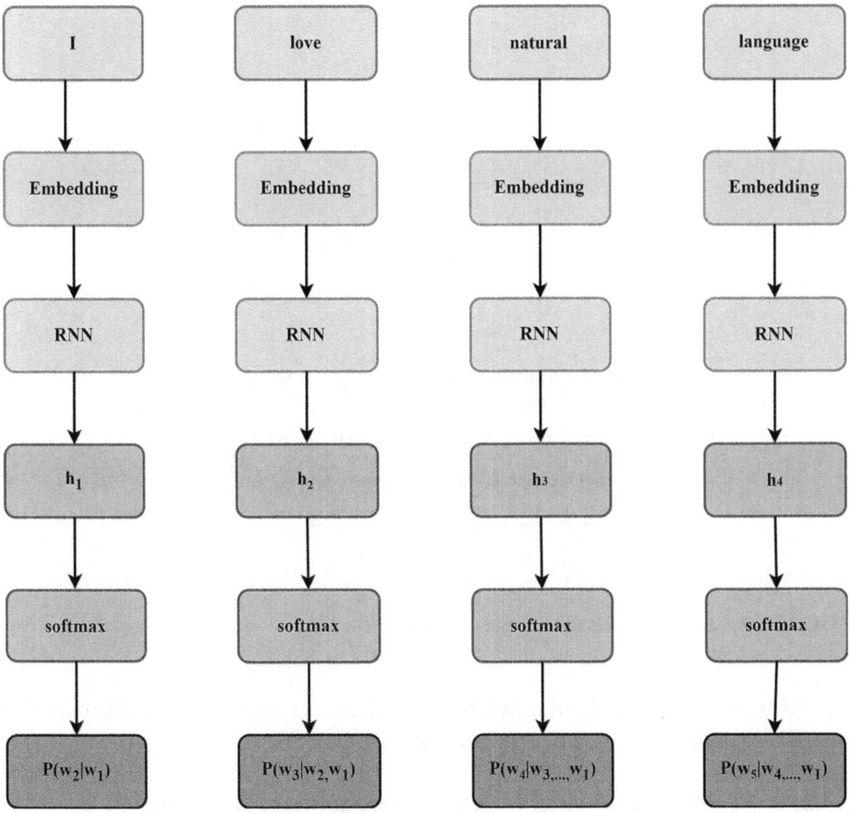

FIGURE 1.6 Example of RNN language model.

the final output for the current time step. This architecture enables LSTMs to effectively capture long-range dependencies in sequential data. LSTMs are commonly applied in tasks such as sentiment analysis, text generation, and machine translation, where understanding the context within a sequence is critical. Figure 1.7 shows the example of LSTM language model.

1.3.2.4 Transformer Models

Transformer models use self-attention mechanisms to capture dependencies between all tokens in a sequence simultaneously, unlike RNNs, which process sequences token by token. This allows for more efficient parallel processing and the ability to model long-range dependencies. Key features of transformers include self-attention, which helps to understand relationships between tokens regardless of their position in the sequence, and parallel processing, which enhances computational efficiency. Popular transformer models include BERT, which focuses on bidirectional context, GPT, which performs left-to-right causal language modeling for text generation, and T5, which treats every NLP task as a text-to-text problem. Transformers are widely

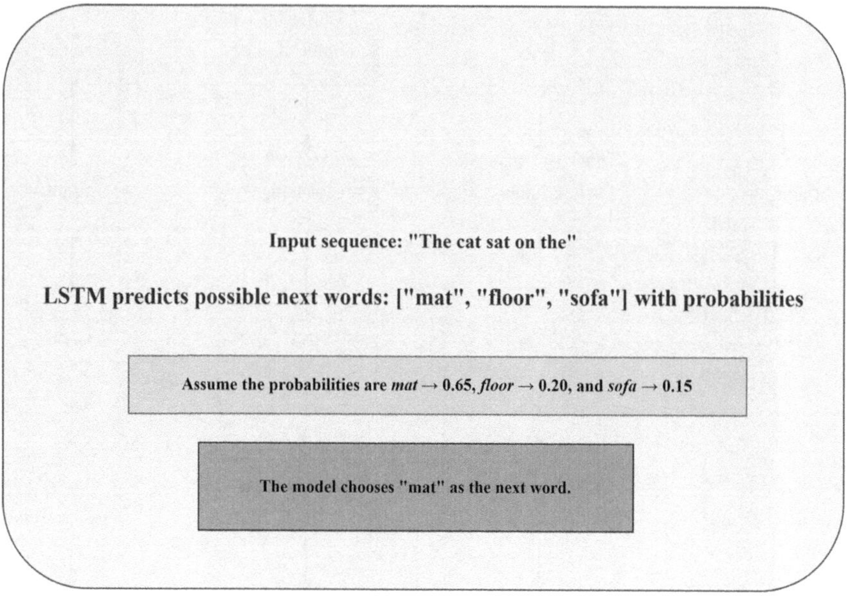

FIGURE 1.7 Example of LSTM language model.

applied in tasks like machine translation, question answering, and text summarization, where understanding and generating human-like text is essential.

1.3.2.5 Feedforward Neural Network Language Models (FNNLMs)

FNNLMs predict the next word in a sequence using a fixed-size context window. Each word is represented as a dense embedding, and the model employs feedforward layers to learn the relationships between input and output words. For example, an FNNLM might predict the next word based on the last few words in a sequence using word embeddings and a feedforward architecture. However, FNNLMs are limited by their fixed context size, which restricts their ability to capture long-term dependencies across larger sequences, making them less effective for tasks requiring a broader understanding of context.

1.3.2.6 Sequence-to-Sequence (Seq2Seq) models

Seq2Seq models combine an encoder, which processes the input, and a decoder, which generates the output, making them ideal for tasks that require input-output mapping. Seq2Seq models are widely used in applications such as machine translation, dialogue systems, and text summarization. An important advancement in Seq2Seq models is the introduction of attention mechanisms, which enhance the model by allowing the decoder to focus on the most relevant parts of the input, improving the accuracy and efficiency of generating the output.

1.4 CHALLENGES IN NATURAL LANGUAGE PROCESSING

NLP focuses on enabling machines to understand, interpret, and generate human language. Despite its advancements, NLP faces significant challenges due to the complexity, diversity, and ever-evolving nature of human language [17, 18]. Below are the key challenges in NLP, elaborated with examples and implications:

1.4.1 Ambiguity

Ambiguity in NLP is a situation where a word, phrase, or sentence can have more than one possible meaning, interpretation, or syntactic form. Ambiguity is a natural property of human language and is a major challenge for machines attempting to comprehend or produce natural language. There are various forms of ambiguity in NLP, such as lexical, syntactic, semantic, and pragmatic ambiguity.

(i) **Lexical Ambiguity:** A word has unrelated meanings (e.g., "bat" can refer to an animal or sports equipment).
(ii) **Syntactic Ambiguity:** A sentence has multiple interpretations due to its structure (e.g., "Visiting relatives can be boring" could mean visiting them is boring, or they are boring visitors).
(iii) **Semantic Ambiguity:** Context-dependent meanings lead to confusion (e.g., "He saw her duck" could refer to an action or an animal).

1.4.2 Polysemy

Polysemy in NLP is the term used when one word contains many meanings or senses, but not like in the case of homonymy (when different words with the same spelling possess wholly unrelated senses), the many meanings of a polysemous word are associated somehow. Polysemy is one of the widespread problems of NLP because the accurate understanding of a polysemous word relies largely on the environment within which the word is spoken or written. For example:

- "Bank" could mean a financial institution or the side of a river (both imply "something that holds or stores").
- "Paper" could refer to material, a newspaper, or an academic article (all involve something written).

1.4.3 Training Data

Training data consists of text inputs and their corresponding labels (e.g., sentences tagged with sentiments like "positive" or "negative"). It helps NLP models learn patterns to make predictions on new data. However, errors or biases in training data can lead to inaccurate results.

For example:

- Input: "The product quality is excellent." → Label: "Positive"
- Input: "The service was terrible." → Label: "Negative"

The model identifies patterns, such as associating words like "excellent" with positive sentiment and "terrible" with negative sentiment.

1.4.4 Data Sparsity and Quality

A major challenge in NLP is the limited availability of high-quality labeled data, especially for less-resourced languages and specialized domains. This data sparsity restricts the development of effective NLP systems, while poor data quality, including noise, biases, and inconsistencies, can negatively impact model performance. For example, if the training data contains biased or unbalanced examples, the model might incorrectly classify certain movie genres as positive or negative. If the most positive reviews are about action movies and the most negative reviews are about romantic comedies, the model may learn to associate "action" with positive sentiment and "romantic comedy" with negative sentiment. This bias could lead to inaccurate predictions when the model encounters new reviews from these genres, reflecting the inconsistencies and poor quality of the data.

1.4.5 Contextual Understanding

Contextual understanding means interpreting words based on the surrounding text. The challenge is that words can have different meanings depending on the situation, and models need to correctly identify the intended meaning. This requires considering the full context to make accurate interpretations. For example, in the sentence "She went to the bank to fish," the word "bank" should be understood as the edge of a river, not a financial institution, because of the context.

1.4.6 Misspellings

Misspelling, such as variations in spelling, can confuse NLP systems because they rely on accurate word recognition to interpret text. When words are misspelled, the system may fail to identify them correctly, leading to errors in understanding and processing. For example, the word "accommodation" is often misspelled as "acommodation" or "accomodation," causing challenges for NLP models to accurately recognize and process the intended word. This can impact the system's ability to correctly interpret the sentence or document.

1.4.7 Language Differences

Language differences can pose challenges for NLP systems, especially when dealing with multilingual data. Different languages may have unique sentence structures, vocabulary, and expressions, which can make it difficult for models to understand or translate correctly without additional processing. For example, an English speaker might say, "I need a coffee," while a French speaker would say, "J'ai besoin d'un café." Although both sentences mean the same, an NLP system would need translation to process the French version accurately, highlighting the challenge of handling different languages.

1.4.8 Tone of Voice and Inflection

Tone of voice and inflection refer to how meaning can change depending on how something is said, such as with stress on certain words or the overall emotion in a speaker's voice. NLP systems struggle with understanding these nuances, which makes tasks like sarcasm detection or identifying tone more difficult. Additionally, speech recognition algorithms may not always capture the subtleties of different accents or intonations.

Example: In the sentence "Oh, great!" if said with a rising tone, it might indicate excitement, but if said with a falling tone, it could indicate sarcasm or frustration. NLP systems might interpret this as neutral or fail to capture the tone, leading to misinterpretation.

SUMMARY

In order to enable machines to comprehend, interpret, and produce human language, the discipline of NLP, which lies at the nexus of computer science, linguistics, and artificial intelligence, is thoroughly introduced in this chapter. It starts with a brief history of NLP, detailing the early phases that relied on handcrafted linguistic rules and were dominated by rule-based systems and symbolic AI in the 1950s–1980s. This was followed by the statistical revolution in the 1990s, which brought probabilistic models like n-grams, and the deep learning era that began in the 2010s and has since seen advances in accuracy and fluency driven by neural networks and LLMs.

Part-of-speech tagging (assigning grammatical labels to words), machine translation (automatically converting text from one language to another), question answering (providing precise answers to queries), sentiment analysis (detecting emotional tone), text classification (classifying documents or messages into predefined classes), NER (identifying entities like people, places, or organizations), and summarization (condensing text while preserving key information) are some of the core applications covered in the section on key NLP tasks.

Two primary categories are used to examine the fundamentals of language models:

- Hidden Markov Models (HMMs) and n-grams are examples of statistical language models that use statistical patterns found in huge corpora to estimate the likelihood of word sequences. Despite their relative simplicity, these models include drawbacks such as limited context windows and sparse data.
- RNNs, long short-term memory networks (LSTMs), transformers, and large-scale pre-trained models like BERT and GPT are examples of neural network-based language models that better capture semantic subtleties, contextual meaning, and long-range dependencies.

Challenges in NLP are covered in the chapter's conclusion, including lexical and structural ambiguity (words or sentences having multiple meanings), context dependency (word meanings changing with surrounding text), handling idiomatic expressions, multilingual processing, limited annotated data availability for low-resource languages, domain adaptation, and ethical issues like bias, misinformation, and data privacy. These difficulties reflect the ongoing research efforts in the field and the difficulty of obtaining human-like comprehension and language generation.

QUESTIONS

1. Explain the evolution of NLP from rule-based systems to modern neural network approaches.
2. List and describe any four key NLP tasks with examples.
3. Differentiate between statistical language models and neural network-based language models.
4. What are the main challenges faced in NLP when dealing with multilingual data?
5. Explain the issue of ambiguity in NLP with suitable examples.
6. Given a sentence "I love natural language processing", compute the probability of this sentence using a **bigram statistical language model** if:
   - P(I|<s>) = 0.4
   - P(love|I) = 0.5
   - P(natural|love) = 0.3
   - P(language|natural) = 0.6
   - P(processing|language) = 0.
7. Suppose in a **unigram model**, the probabilities of words are: $P(machine) = 0.2$, $P(learning) = 0.3, P(is) = 0.25, P(fun) = 0.25$. Compute the probability of the sentence: "machine learning is fun".
8. In a neural network language model, if the input word vector is $x = [1,2]$, weight matrix $W = [[0.5, 0.2], [0.1, 0.3]]$, and bias $b = [0.1, 0.2]$, compute the hidden layer output using $h = Wx + b$.
9. A softmax layer in a neural network produces scores [2.0, 1.0, 0.1]. Compute the probability distribution after applying the softmax function.
10. Given a dataset of 1,00,000 English sentences and 5,000 Hindi sentences, explain mathematically why data imbalance is a challenge for training NLP models.
11. **Case Study – Evolution of NLP**
    In the early days, NLP used rule-based and statistical language models for tasks like translation and speech recognition, but these approaches struggled with ambiguity and context. With the growth of neural network-based models, systems improved in handling key tasks such as machine translation, sentiment analysis, and chatbots. However, challenges like ambiguity in meaning, multilingual processing, and limited understanding of context still exist. This shows how NLP has progressed from simple statistical models to advanced

neural models, while real-world applications continue to face challenges in achieving human-like understanding. Based on the case study, explain how the shift from statistical models to neural network-based models has improved NLP tasks, and discuss one key challenge that still remains.

REFERENCES

[1] T. Mikolov, K. Chen, G. Corrado, and J. Dean, "Efficient Estimation of Word Representations in Vector Space," arxiv preprint, Sep. 2013, arXiv:1301.3781.

[2] T. Mikolov, M. Karafiát, L. Burget, J. Černocký, and S. Khudanpur, "Recurrent Neural Network Based Language Model," in *Interspeech 2010*. ISCA, Sep. 2010, pp. 1045–1048, doi: 10.21437/Interspeech.2010-343.

[3] S. Jamshidi, M. Mohammadi, S. Bagheri, H. Esmaeili Najafabadi, A. Rezvanian, M. Gheisari *et al.*, "Effective Text Classification using BERT, MTM LSTM, and DT," *Data Knowl Eng*, vol. 151, p. 102306, May 2024, doi: 10.1016/j.datak.2024.102306.

[4] S. Zheng, and M. Yang, "A New Method of Improving Bert for Text Classification," in *Intelligence Science and Big Data Engineering. Big Data and Machine Learning: 9th International Conference, IScIDE 2019, Nanjing, China, October 17–20, 2019, Proceedings, Part II 9*. Springer, 2019, pp. 442–452.

[5] T. B. Brown, B. Mann, N. Ryder, M. Subbiah, J. D Kaplan, P. Dhariwal *et al.*, "Language Models are Few-Shot Learners," *Advances in Neural Information Processing Systems*, vol. 33, pp. 1877–1901, Jul. 2020.

[6] OpenAI, J. Achiam, S. Adler, S. Agarwal, L. Ahmad, I, Akkaya *et al.*, "GPT-4 Technical Report," Mar. 2024, https://doi.org/10.48550/arXiv.2303.08774.

[7] E. D. Liddy, *Natural Language Processing in Encyclopedia of Library and Information Science*, 2nd edition. Marcel Decker, Inc., 2001.

[8] J. Hirschberg, and C. D. Manning, "Advances in Natural Language Processing," *Science* (1979), vol. 349, no. 6245, pp. 261–266, Jul. 2015, doi: 10.1126/science.aaa8685.

[9] D. Jurafsky, and J. H. Martin, *Speech and Language Processing: An Introduction to Natural Language Processing, Computational Linguistics, and Speech Recognition with Language Models*, Third, 2025. https://web.stanford.edu/~jurafsky/slp3

[10] C. Manning, and H. Schütze, *Foundations of Statistical Natural Language Processing*, MIT Press, 1999.

[11] E. C. Garrido-Merchan, R. Gozalo-Brizuela, and S. Gonzalez-Carvajal, "Comparing BERT Against Traditional Machine Learning Models in Text Classification," *J Comput Cogn Eng*, vol. 2, no. 4, pp. 352–356, 2023.

[12] P. R. J. Dhanith, and K. S. S. Prabha, "A Critical Empirical Evaluation of Deep Learning Models for Solving Aspect based Sentiment Analysis," *Artif Intell Rev*, vol. 56, no. 11, pp. 13127–13186, Nov. 2023, doi: 10.1007/s10462-023-10460-0.

[13] H. Kansal, and D. Toshniwal, "Aspect based Summarization of Context Dependent Opinion Words," *Procedia Comput Sci*, vol. 35, pp. 166–175, 2014.

[14] F. Jelinek, *Statistical Methods for Speech Recognition*. The MIT Press, 2022.

[15] R. Rosenfeld, "Two Decades of Statistical Language Modeling: Where do We Go From Here?," *Proceedings of the IEEE*, vol. 88, no. 8, pp. 1270–1278, Aug. 2000, doi: 10.1109/5.880083.

[16] Y. Bengio, R. Ducharme, P. Vincent, and C. Jauvin, "A Neural Probabilistic Language Model," *J Mach Learn Res*, vol. 3, no. 6, pp. 1137–1155, 2003.

[17] D. Khurana, A. Koli, K. Khatter, and S. Singh, "Natural Language Processing: State of the Art, Current Trends and Challenges," *Multimed Tools Appl*, vol. 82, no. 3, pp. 3713–3744, Jan. 2023, doi: 10.1007/s11042-022-13428-4.

[18] E. Cambria, B. Schuller, Y. Xia, and C. Havasi, "New Avenues in Opinion Mining and Sentiment Analysis," *IEEE Intell Syst*, vol. 28, no. 2, pp. 15–21, Mar. 2013, doi: 10.1109/MIS.2013.30.

2 Linguistic Foundations and Feature Representation of NLP

Natural language processing (NLP) is based on linguistic principles that help machines process and understand human language. These principles come from traditional linguistics and include phonetics, morphology, syntax, semantics, pragmatics, and discourse analysis.

2.1 LEVELS OF LINGUISTIC ANALYSIS IN NLP

In computational linguistics and NLP, language is analyzed at different levels: the morphological level deals with the composition and form of words; the lexical level concerns the meanings and categorizations of individual words; the syntactic level looks into the syntax of sentences and grammar; the semantic level deals with interpreting the meaning of words and sentences; the discourse level examines how meaning is preserved sentence-wise for coherence and context; and the pragmatic level considers the intended sense behind language, based on context, speaker intent, and knowledge of the world. Every level is successively based on the earlier one to enable a more profound comprehension and creation of natural language [1, 2].

2.1.1 Morphology Level (ML)

The ML [3, 4] deals with the structure of words. ML is simply the study of morphemes. Morphemes are the smallest grammatical units with meaning. There are two types of morphemes as shown in Figure 2.1.

(i) **Free Morphemes** is the smallest standalone words. For example, book, run or happy.
(ii) **Bound Morphemes** is not the standalone words. It can be attached with other morphemes to give meaning. It can be either prefix or suffix of a free morpheme. For example, -s, un-, -ing.

There are two types of morphology as shown in Figure 2.2. One is inflectional morphology and second is the derivational morphology.

DOI: 10.1201/9781003650065-2

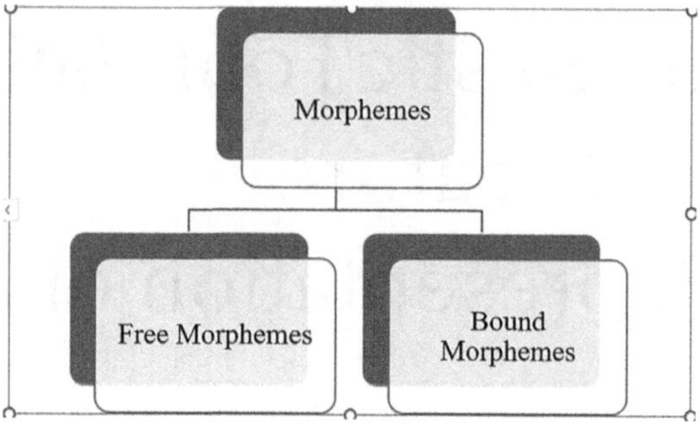

FIGURE 2.1 Morphemes.

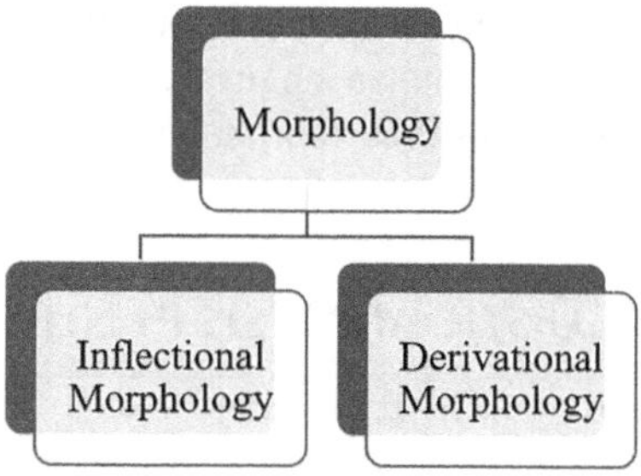

FIGURE 2.2 Morphology.

(i) **Inflectional morphology** changes the form of a word without changing its core meaning or word class. For example, run is changed to runs or running.
(ii) **Derivational morphology** forms a new word by adding prefixes or suffixes or simply merging free morphemes with inflectional morphemes. For example, un + happy = unhappy.

Some common examples at the morphological level include:

- **Stemming:** Reducing words to their root form (e.g., "running" → "run")
- **Lemmatization:** Converting words to their base form (e.g., "better" → "good").

If a word *W* has a prefix *P*, a root *R*, and a suffix *S*, then the morphological level is represented using the following Equation (2.1).

$$W = P + R + S \tag{2.1}$$

For example, the word "unhappiness" can be broken down morphologically into "un-" (a prefix), "happy" (the root), and "-ness" (a suffix).

2.1.2 Syntactic Level

Syntactic level [5, 6] is the study of the structure of a sentence. It helps to arrange words in a sentence by using the grammatical rules. Syntax helps computers to parse sentences, understand sentence components and grammatical consistency. Syntax deals with word arrangement and sentence structure according to grammatical rules.

Some common examples at the syntactic level include:

- **Parts-of-Speech (POS) Tagging** refers to the grammatical category of a word in a sentence, based on its function. Each word is assigned a POS tag that helps identify its role, such as whether it's a noun, verb, adjective, etc. "The cat sits on the mat." → (DT The) (NN cat) (VBZ sits) (IN on) (DT the) (NN mat)
- **Dependency parsing** is the process of analyzing the grammatical structure of a sentence by establishing relationships between words. Instead of breaking the sentence into phrases, it focuses on how words are connected, and which word depends on which.

For the sentence: "The boy plays football.", the example parse tree is shown below.

```
            (S)
           /   \
       (NP)   (VP)
       /  \   /  \
    DT   NN  VBZ   NN
The boy playes football
```

2.1.3 Semantic Level

In NLP, the semantic layer focuses on understanding the meaning of words, phrases, and sentences to understand the message conveyed, moving beyond syntax. This includes a number of key tasks, such as word sense disambiguation (WSD) (e.g., deciding whether "bank" refers to a financial institution or a riverbank), Named Entity Recognition (identifying names of people, places, and organizations), semantic role labeling (SRL) (e.g., "John gave Mary a book," identifying "John" as giver, "Mary" as receiver, and "book" as object), Coreference Resolution (linking "she" to "Sarah" in "Sarah went to the store. She bought milk."), and Lexical and Compositional Semantics (understanding word and word combination meanings). Semantic similarity measures are applied to assess the similarity of texts on a semantic basis. The problem can be solved using rule-based methods, machine learning models like BERT and GPT, or knowledge bases such as WordNet or DBpedia.

2.1.4 Lexical Level

Lexical semantics [7] in NLP deals with the meaning of words, their relationships, and differences in interpretation, including concepts like synonymy ("big" ≈ "large"), antonymy ("hot" vs. "cold"), hyponymy ("rose" as a type of "flower"), polysemy (several related meanings, e.g., "bank"), and homonymy (same forms with different meanings, e.g., "bat" the animal vs. the sports equipment). NLP tasks such as WSD rely on context to disambiguate meanings, while word embeddings (e.g., Word2Vec, GloVe, BERT) encode meanings as a vector space, using cosine similarity to determine semantic closeness.

2.1.5 Compositional Semantics Level

The compositional semantics [8], on the other hand, is concerned with how the meanings of words compose to create the meanings of sentences, based on Frege's Principle. This region includes predicate logic, the compositionality principle, and techniques for disambiguation to grasp whole sentences. Applications include machine translation and SRL, which identifies roles in sentences, for instance, in "John gave Mary an apple," we have John as Agent, Mary as Recipient, and Apple as Theme. Meanings of sentences can be represented formally with lambda calculus, for example, "Every student studies," $\forall x(\text{student}(x) \rightarrow \text{studies}(x))$.

2.1.6 Discourse Level

Discourse analysis in NLP studies how sentences are related to each other in a conversation or text, enabling tasks such as coreference resolution (e.g., identifying that "He" is referring to "John" in the sentence "John went to the store. He bought apples") and text summarization, which involves pulling out key information from longer writing. Cosine similarity is often used to measure semantic similarity of text vectors, calculated as the dot product of the vectors over the product of their magnitudes. NLP encompasses multiple levels of linguistics: phonology (speech recognition), morphology (lemmatization and stemming), syntax (parsing), semantics (such as named entity recognition and word embeddings), pragmatics (sentiment analysis), and discourse (coreference and summarization). A solid understanding of such layers of language enhances NLP technologies like machine translation, chatbots, and conversational systems. Modern deep learning architectures such as BERT, GPT, and T5 extend these concepts to achieve sophisticated, human-level understanding of language.

2.2 VECTOR SPACE MODEL

The vector space model (VSM) [9] is a fundamental approach in NLP and information retrieval (IR) that represents text as mathematical vectors in a multidimensional space. It is widely used in search engines, recommendation systems, and text classification tasks.

VSM converts documents and words into numerical vectors, allowing for mathematical operations such as similarity measurements, clustering, and classification. The model represents text data in a structured way, making it easier to analyze and retrieve relevant information.

Key Features of VSM

- **Vector Representation of Documents** – Each document is represented as a vector in a multi-dimensional space.
- **Dimensionality of Space** – The number of dimensions corresponds to the number of unique words in the dataset.
- **Weighting of Terms** – Words are assigned importance using term frequency (TF), inverse document frequency (IDF), and TF-IDF.
- **Similarity Measurement** – Documents are compared using mathematical similarity functions like Cosine Similarity, Euclidean Distance, and Jaccard Similarity.

2.2.1 Document Representation in VSM

Each document in a corpus is transformed into a vector, where each dimension corresponds to a unique word in the vocabulary. The position of a word in the vector depends on its frequency or importance within the document. Steps for Document Representation in VSM is given below.

2.2.1.1 Text Preprocessing

Text preprocessing includes a number of necessary steps designed to normalize and simplify the text for further analysis. First, making all text lowercase guarantees consistency, as capitalization differences are ignored. The second step includes eliminating stopwords—commonly used, meaningless words like "the," "is," and "a"—to focus on more meaningful terms. Finally, stemming or lemmatization is employed in reducing words to their core or root word form, as an example from "running" to "run." These are involved in readying the text to be further worked on effectively and accurately with various NLP tasks.

2.2.1.2 Building a Vocabulary

In order to develop a dataset for text analysis, the first step is to find all the unique words by isolating distinct terms from the text. Once the unique words are identified, every term is given a numerical index, creating a correspondence between words and their respective identifiers. This process, better referred to as tokenization and vectorization, is essential to convert text-based data into structured form suitable for machine learning and NLP tasks.

2.2.1.3 Vectorization

In order to convert each document into a numerical vector, the text is adjusted based on both word frequency and importance. This process typically involves representing each word as a feature in the vector, with the value for each feature being the occurrence (e.g., TF) and the importance (e.g., IDF, or TF-IDF) of the word relative to the document and the overall corpus. This representation as numbers makes it easy for machine learning to scan through the text information to perform processes like document categorization, grouping, and comparison.

The VSM is a successful approach to classifying, clustering, and comparing documents by expressing each document as a vector in a multidimensional space. Under this model, each document D is represented as a vector and is shown in Equation (2.2).

$$D = (w_1, w_2, \ldots., w_n) \tag{2.2}$$

where w_i is the weight of the ith term in the document. The weights w_i are typically calculated using various weighting methods, which quantifies the importance of each term based on its frequency in the document and its rarity across the entire corpus. This mathematical representation enables efficient categorization, grouping, and comparison of documents by measuring the similarity between their corresponding vectors.

2.2.2 Weighting Schemes in VSM

2.2.2.1 Binary Weighting

Binary weighting is a simple method of signaling the presence of a term in a document. Under this scheme, any term is assigned a weight of 1 if it occurs in the document and 0 if not present. This method ignores TF and focuses only on the presence of a term in the document, thus making it useful for basic text categorization and document similarity tasks where the presence of certain keywords is more important than their frequency of occurrence.

2.2.2.2 Term Frequency (TF)

TF is a metric that quantifies the frequency of a specific term or word within a given document. It reflects how often a term appears relative to the total number of words in that document, helping to capture the prominence of a term in a particular context. A higher TF value indicates that a term is more important or relevant within the document. TF is commonly used in text analysis, IR, and machine learning tasks such as document classification and search engine ranking. The TF is mathematically represented using the following Equation (2.3).

$$\text{TF} = \frac{\text{Number of items the term appears in the document}}{\text{Total number of terms in the document}} \tag{2.3}$$

2.2.2.3 Inverse Document Frequency (IDF)

IDF is a metric employed to assess the importance of a term in a collection of documents. It places higher importance on terms that are rare or unique to specific documents while reducing the value of terms that appear with high frequency in the entire collection. The reasoning in IDF is that words common in lots of documents are of less useful information, while those common in fewer documents are of more relevance. IDF is used in combination with TF to calculate TF-IDF, which helps to identify the most relevant words in a document with respect to a larger corpus. The IDF is mathematically represented using the following Equation (2.4).

$$\text{IDF} = \log\left(\frac{N}{DF}\right) \tag{2.4}$$

where N is total number of documents and DF is number of documents containing the term.

2.2.2.4 Term Frequency – Inverse Document Frequency (TF-IDF)

A combination of TF and inverse document frequency (IDF) is used to determine the relevance of a term within a specific document relative to a larger corpus. **TF-IDF** highlights terms that are both frequent in a document (high TF) and rare across other documents (high IDF), making them more informative and significant. This approach helps identify keywords or important terms, as it balances the frequency of terms with their uniqueness across the corpus, ensuring that commonly used but uninformative words are down weighted. TF-IDF is widely used in tasks like document classification, IR, and search engine ranking. The TF-IDF is mathematically represented using the following Equation (2.5).

$$\text{TF}-\text{IDF} = \text{TF} \times \text{IDF} \tag{2.5}$$

2.2.2.5 Example of Document Representation in VSM

Consider two documents:

- D1: "Machine learning is powerful."
- D2: "Deep learning is powerful."

Step 1: Vocabulary Creation

Compute the unique words across both documents.

$$[Machine, Deep, Learning, Is, Powerful]$$

Step 2: Vector Representation

Each document is represented as a binary vector (1 for word presence, 0 for absence):

$$D1:\ [1,\ 0,\ 1,\ 1,\ 1]$$

$$D2:\ [0,\ 1,\ 1,\ 1,\ 1]$$

Here,

- "Machine" appears in D1 but not in D2 → (1,0).
- "Deep" appears in D2 but not in D1 → (0,1).
- "Learning," "Is," and "Powerful" appear in both → (1,1).

If we use **TF-IDF weighting**, each word will have a numerical value instead of just 1 or 0.

2.2.3 Similarity Measures in VSM

To evaluate and compare the relevance of documents, similarity functions are employed. These functions measure the degree of similarity between document vectors, helping to determine how closely related two documents are in terms of their content. Common similarity measures include cosine similarity, Euclidean distance, and Jaccard similarity, with cosine similarity being one of the most widely used in text analysis due to its effectiveness in handling high-dimensional, sparse data.

2.2.3.1 Cosine Similarity

Cosine similarity is a metric that measures the cosine of the angle between two document vectors in a multi-dimensional space. It quantifies how similar two documents are in terms of their direction, regardless of their magnitude. A cosine similarity value of 1 indicates that the documents are identical in terms of content distribution, while 0 means they share no similarity. This method is particularly effective in text analysis because it focuses on the orientation of the vectors rather than their length, making it robust to differences in document length or word count. The cosine similarity is formulated as follows using Equation (2.6).

$$\cos(\theta) = \frac{A \cdot B}{\|A\| \, \|B\|} \tag{2.6}$$

where A *and* B are document vectors.

2.2.3.2 Euclidean Distance

Euclidean distance is a measure applied to calculate the straight-line distance between two document vectors in an n-dimensional space. It calculates the spatial difference between documents on the basis of term weights. Lower Euclidean distance indicates higher similarity between the documents, while a higher distance shows higher dissimilarity. Although it is simple and easy to interpret, Euclidean distance is susceptible to document length and is not as powerful as cosine similarity when working with high-dimensional, sparse text data commonly found in NLP applications. The Euclidean distance is formulated as follows using Equation (2.7).

$$d(A,B) = \sqrt{\sum (A_i - B_i)^2} \tag{2.7}$$

2.2.3.3 Jaccard Similarity

Jaccard similarity is a metric that measures the *degree of overlap* between two documents by comparing the size of their intersection to the size of their union. The Jaccard similarity is formulated as follows using Equation (2.8).

$$J(A,B) = \frac{|A \cap B|}{|A \cup B|} \tag{2.8}$$

where A and B are the sets of unique terms in each document. A Jaccard similarity of 1 indicates complete overlap (identical sets), while 0 means no shared terms. This method is particularly useful for binary or set-based representations of documents, such as when using presence/absence (binary weighting) rather than TF.

2.2.4 Applications of VSM

- Search Engines (Information Retrieval) – Google and Bing use VSM to rank search results.
- Document Classification – Categorizing emails as spam or nonspam.
- Text Clustering – Grouping similar news articles.
- Recommendation Systems – Suggesting articles based on similarity.
- Semantic Text Analysis – Understanding word relationships.

2.2.5 Advantages

- Simple to implement.
- Efficient for small datasets.
- Works well with basic text retrieval.

The VSM is a foundational text representation technique used in NLP and IR. Despite its simplicity, it is still widely used for text similarity tasks. However, modern deep learning models provide more accurate results by incorporating semantic understanding and contextual meaning.

2.2.6 Topic Modeling

Topic modeling [10] is an unsupervised machine learning technique used in NLP to automatically identify topics in a collection of documents. It helps in understanding the structure of large text datasets by grouping similar words together and representing the hidden themes within the text. These techniques help organize and summarize large sets of text by extracting meaningful ideas from unstructured text data, making them helpful for applications such as search engines, recommendation systems, and text classification.

Topic modeling assumes that each document in a dataset contains multiple topics, and each topic is a distribution of words. The main goal is to find a latent structure in the text and assign probability scores to words in different topics.

For example, Consider a dataset containing three documents:

- D1: “Machine learning improves AI models.”
- D2: “A healthy diet and regular exercise improve fitness.”
- D3: “AI is revolutionizing the healthcare industry.”

A topic modeling algorithm might identify the following topics:

- Topic 1: Artificial Intelligence → Words: "Machine", "Learning", "AI", "Models"
- Topic 2: Health & Fitness → Words: "Diet", "Exercise", "Fitness", "Health"

Each document will have a probability distribution over topics, meaning that a document can belong to multiple topics.

Given a set of *documents* (*D*) *and topics* (*T*), topic modeling assigns probabilities to each *word* (*W*) occurring in different topics and is represented using the following Equations (2.9) and (2.9).

$$P(W|T) = \text{Probability of word } W \text{ given topic } T \tag{2.9}$$

$$P(T|D) = \text{Probability of topic } T \text{ given document } D \tag{2.10}$$

Each document is represented as a mixture of topics and is formulated as follows in Equation (2.11).

$$D = w_1T_1 + w_2T_2 + \ldots + w_nT_n \tag{2.11}$$

where, w_i is the weight assigned to topic T_i in document D

2.2.6.1 Common Topic Modeling Techniques

2.2.6.1.1 Latent Dirichlet Allocation (LDA)

Latent Dirichlet Allocation (LDA) [10, 11] is a common topic modeling algorithm that uses a probabilistic approach to model documents as mixtures of various topics, where every topic is defined by a word distribution. The mathematical representation of LDA is given in Equation (2.12).

$$P(T|D) = \frac{\text{Count of words in topic } T \text{ within document } D}{\text{Total words in document } D} \tag{2.12}$$

2.2.6.1.2 Latent Semantic Analysis (LSA)

Latent semantic analysis (LSA) is a dimensionality reduction technique that uses singular value decomposition to uncover relationships between words and documents, and it works very well with small datasets. The mathematical formulation of LSA is given in Equation (2.13).

$$A = U\Sigma V^T \tag{2.13}$$

where A is the Term-document matrix, U is the Words-to-concepts matrix, Σ is the Singular values, and V^T is the documents-to-concepts matrix.

2.2.6.1.3 Nonnegative Matrix Factorization (NMF)

Nonnegative matrix factorization (NMF) decomposes text data into two nonnegative matrices and extracts hidden topics in the data. NMF performs well when applied to TF-IDF weighted text representations. The mathematical formulation of NMF is available in Equation (2.14).

$$X \approx WH \tag{2.14}$$

where X is the Term-document matrix, W is the Word-topic matrix, and H is the topic-document matrix.

2.2.6.1.4 Applications of Topic Modeling

Topic modeling is a good technique for discovering hidden themes in unstructured text, which is applicable in news classification, customer sentiment analysis, research organization, recommendation system construction, and fake news detection. Techniques such as LDA, LSA, and NMF help in structuring information and improving the accuracy of search and recommendation features.

2.2.7 N-Gram Models

The N-Gram Model is a statistical technique in NLP for predicting sequences of words, often used in text prediction, language modeling, and speech recognition. It analyzes fixed-size sequences of words, such as unigrams (single words), bigrams (two-word sequences), trigrams (three-word sequences), and n-grams of higher order.

The N-Gram model estimates the probability of a word sequence using the Markov assumption, which makes prediction easier by assuming that the probability of a word depends only on the $n-1$ words preceding it. This probabilistic modeling is outlined in Equation (2.15).

$$P\left(w_n \middle| w_1, w_2, \ldots, \; w_{n-1}\right) \approx P\left(w_n \middle| w_{n-(N-1)}, \ldots, w_{n-1}\right) \tag{2.15}$$

For instance, the Bigram model determines the probability of a word based on the word that precedes it immediately, and how it's formulated is shown in Equation ().

$$P\left(w_n \middle| w_{n-1}\right) = \frac{Count(w_{n-1}, \; w_n)}{Count(w_{n-1})} \tag{2.16}$$

Challenges in N-Gram models include data sparsity, where certain word combinations may not appear in training data. Smoothing techniques such as Laplace Smoothing, Backoff, and Kneser-Ney are used to address zero probabilities and improve model performance.

2.2.7.1 Smoothing Techniques in N-Gram Models

Smoothing is applied in N-Gram models to address the problem of zero probability, where a sequence of unseen words that appeared during training appears in the test data [12]. The primary smoothing methods include:

2.2.7.1.1 Laplace Smoothing (Add-One Smoothing)

Laplace smoothing addresses zero probabilities by adding 1 to all word frequencies, ensuring that no probability is ever zero and that every possible word sequence has a nonzero probability. The mathematical representation of Laplace smoothing can be found in Equation (2.17).

$$P\left(w_n \middle| w_{n-1}\right) = \frac{Count\left(w_{n-1},\ w_n\right) + 1}{Count\left(w_{n-1}\right) + V} \tag{2.17}$$

where V is the vocabulary size, and Count $\left(w_{n-1},\ w_n\right)$ is the count of the bigram in the corpus.

For example, without smoothing, $P\left(\text{"}apple\middle|red\text{"}\right) = \frac{0}{10} = 0(Zero\ probability\ issue)$. With Laplace smoothing $(assuming\ V = 1000)$ $P\left(\text{"}apple\middle|red\text{"}\right) = \frac{0+1}{1000} = 0.00099$.

2.2.7.1.2 Add-k Smoothing (Generalized Laplace)

In Add-k Smoothing, instead of adding 1, a smaller constant value k (e.g., 0.01) is added to all word counts to smooth the probabilities, providing a more flexible approach than the standard Laplace smoothing. The mathematical formulation of Add-k smoothing is presented in Equation (2.18).

$$P\left(w_n \middle| w_{n-1}\right) = \frac{Count\left(w_{n-1},\ w_n\right) + k}{Count\left(w_{n-1}\right) + kV} \tag{2.18}$$

where if $k = 1$, this is equivalent to Laplace smoothing, and smaller values of k reduce overestimation issues.

2.2.7.1.3 Backoff Smoothing

In Backoff Smoothing, whenever a higher-order N-Gram (e.g., a Trigram) encounters a zero probability, the model uses a lower-order N-Gram (such as a Bigram or Unigram) to compute the probability. The mathematical form of Backoff smoothing can be seen in Equation (2.19).

$$P\left(w_n \middle| w_{n-2},\ w_{n-1}\right) = \begin{cases} \text{Use Trigram probability,} & \text{if available} \\ \text{Else,} & \text{use Bigram probability} \\ \text{Else,} & \text{use Unigram probability} \end{cases} \tag{2.19}$$

2.2.7.1.4 Interpolation Smoothing

Instead of completely withdrawing, Interpolation Smoothing merges probabilities from different N-Gram levels through a weighted sum, enabling the model to utilize data from various orders at the same time. The mathematical formulation of Interpolation Smoothing is expressed in Equation (2.20).

$$P\left(w_n \middle| w_{n-2},\ldots,\ w_{n-1}\right) = \lambda_1 P\left(w_n \middle| w_{n-2}\ , w_{n-1}\right) + \lambda_2 P\left(w_n \middle| w_{n-1}\right) + \lambda_3 P(w_n) \tag{2.20}$$

Where $\lambda_1, \lambda_2, \lambda_3$ are weights that sum to 1, the model combines Trigram, Bigram, and Unigram probabilities.

2.2.7.1.5 Kneser-Ney Smoothing

Kneser-Ney is identified as being among the most advanced and efficient methods for smoothing language modeling. It enhances probability estimation by focusing on the diversity of contexts where a word appears, as opposed to simply relying on its frequency of occurrence. Rather than merely counting how frequently a word is encountered, Kneser-Ney considers the number of unique contexts (previous words) a word is encountered in, and therefore produces more accurate and context-sensitive probability estimates. The mathematical derivation of Kneser-Ney smoothing is described in Equation (2.21).

$$P_{KN}\left(w_n \middle| w_{n-1}\right) = \frac{\max(Count\left(w_{n-1},\ w_n\right) - d, 0)}{Count\left(w_{n-1}\right)} + \lambda P_{KN}(w_n) \tag{2.21}$$

where d *is* a discounting factor (*typically around* 0.75), and λ is a normalization constant.

2.2.7.1.6 Additive Smoothing

Additive smoothing is a method used to avoid zero probabilities by adding a small constant α (rather than 1) to the count of each word. This ensures all word sequences have a nonzero probability while allowing more control over the degree of smoothing. The mathematical formulation of additive smoothing is provided in Equation (2.22).

$$P\left(w_n \middle| w_{n-1}\right) = \frac{Count\left(w_{n-1},\ w_n\right) + \alpha}{Count\left(w_{n-1}\right) + \alpha V} \tag{2.22}$$

where α is a small positive constant (typically 0.01 or 0.1), and V is the vocabulary size.

Smoothing operations in N-Gram models approach the problem of zero probabilities differently in terms of complexity and capability. Simple implementations such as Add-k smoothing are easy to design but have been known to lead to probability overestimation. More advanced such as Interpolation and Backoff improve on the accuracy by summing up different N-Gram levels' probabilities. Kneser-Ney smoothing is considered to be the best choice, as it considers the diversity of word contexts, though it needs more computational power. Additive Smoothing offers flexible control by allowing the tuning of smoothing strength via an adjustable parameter.

2.3 WORD EMBEDDINGS

Word embeddings are vector representations of words in numbers that capture their contextual meaning. As opposed to conventional one-hot encoding, which represents words as sparse binary vectors, word embeddings make use of dense numerical vectors to enable better generalization in NLP applications.

Types of Word Embeddings

- Sparse vs. Dense Representations
- Static vs. Contextual Embeddings

2.3.1 Word Embedding Techniques

2.3.1.1 Word2Vec

Word2Vec [13] is a prominent method based on neural networks developed by Mikolov et al. (2013) with the objective of creating dense vector representations (embeddings) of words from large text corpuses. Unlike traditional models that consider words as individual units, Word2Vec represents each word as a continuous vector in a high-dimensional space with semantically similar words closer to one another. This approach allows the model to learn deep linguistic relationships, such as analogies (e.g., king – man + woman ≈ queen), as well as similar contexts among words.

Word2Vec makes use of two core architectures:

- **Continuous Bag of Words (CBOW):** This model predicts a target word based on the surrounding context words. This architecture works efficiently and with lower datasets.
- **Skip-Gram:** This approach predicts the context words around a target word. It performs very well in larger datasets and in identifying rare word connections.

These embeddings have become indispensable in many NLP tasks, such as text classification, sentiment analysis, machine translation, and recommendation systems.

2.3.1.1.1 Skip-Gram Model

Skip-Gram model [14] predicts the context words for a specified target word. Skip-Gram model performs particularly well in acquiring sensible word representation from large sets or when solving infrequent words.

For example,

Sentence: "The cat sat on the mat."
Target word: cat
Context words: The, sat, on, the, mat

In this case, the model uses the word cat to predict its neighboring words within a certain window size, thus enabling it to comprehend how words are related based on their patterns of co-occurrence.

Training involves maximizing the likelihood of predicting context words given a target word, and this objective is mathematically represented in Equation (2.23).

$$J(\theta) = \sum_{w \varepsilon D} \sum_{c \varepsilon C(w)} \log P\left(c \middle| w; \theta\right) \tag{2.23}$$

where D is the dataset, $C(w)$ are the surrounding words, and $P\left(c \middle| w; \theta\right)$ is the probability of context word given target word. Figure 2.3 shows the architecture of skip-gram model.

2.3.1.1.2 Continuous Bag of Words (CBOW)

The CBOW model works in a different manner than the Skip-Gram model by predicting a target word based on its context neighbor words. It is generally faster and more efficient, especially with smaller data sets.

For example,

Context words: The, cat, on, the
Predicted target word: sat

Here, the model is trained to infer the most likely central word from the given context, effectively capturing both syntactic and semantic structures in language.

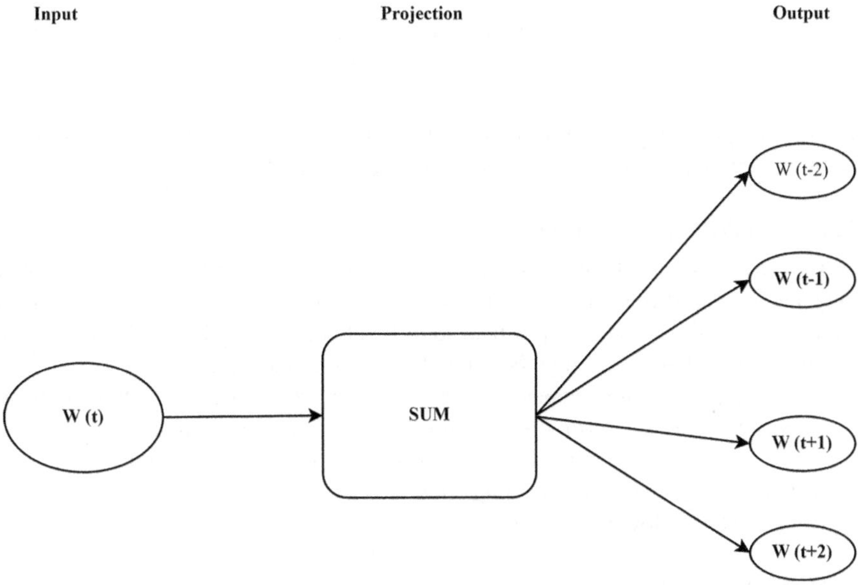

FIGURE 2.3 Skip-gram.

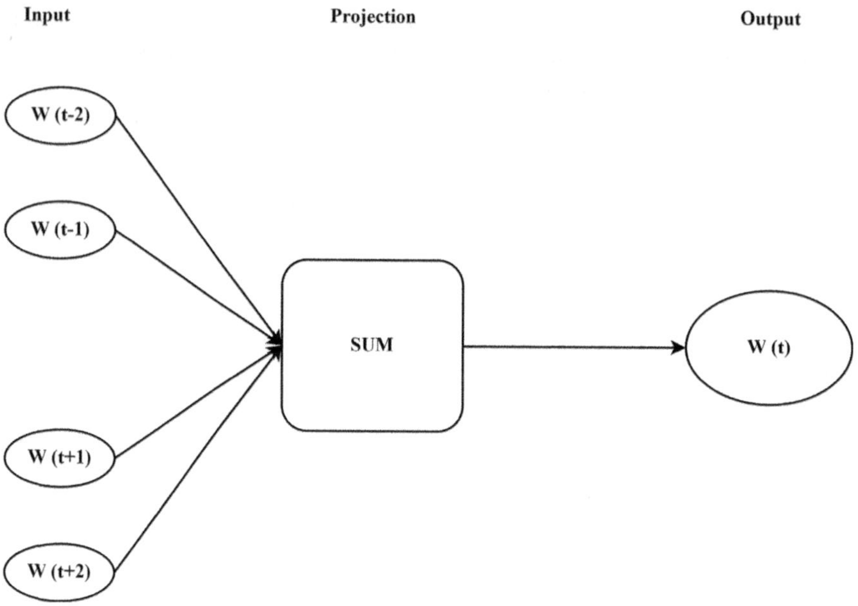

FIGURE 2.4 CBOW.

Training is aimed at maximizing the probability of accurately predicting the target word given the context words around it, and this is mathematically captured in Equation (2.24).

$$P\left(w\middle|C\right) = \frac{e^{v_w^T h}}{\sum_{w' \varepsilon V} e^{v_{w'}^T h}} \tag{2.24}$$

where h is the averaged vector of context words, v_w is the target word vector, and V is the vocabulary. Figure 2.4 shows the architecture of CBOW.

2.3.1.2 GloVe (Global Vectors)

GloVe [15], developed by Pennington and others in 2014 at Stanford, is a word embedding model that differs from Word2Vec in that it uses global word co-occurrence statistics across the whole corpus instead of local context windows. The idea behind it is that words that appear together often have similar meanings.

Words that frequently appear in the same context in a corpus show semantic relationships. GloVe constructs a word-word co-occurrence matrix that reflects global statistical relationships between words, and uses these relationships to infer embeddings that capture the meanings of words in context.

Consider the following simple corpus:

"The cat sits on the mat."
"The dog lies on the rug."

The co-occurrence matrix derived from this corpus can capture associations like how often "cat" occurs with "mat" and "dog" with "rug." GloVe then uses this matrix to create embeddings that encode these relationships, with words that occur in similar contexts often being placed near each other in the vector space.
The co-occurrence matrix might look like:

Word	The	Cat	Sits	On	Mat	Dog	Lies	Rug
The	0	2	1	2	1	2	1	1
Cat	2	0	1	1	1	0	0	0

The co-occurrence matrix is then factorized to generate low-dimensional word representations. GloVe aims to minimize the weighted least squares loss during training, with the objective of determining embeddings that best capture the relationships between words. This optimization task is mathematically represented in Equation (2.25).

$$J = \sum_{i,j} f(X_{ij})(w_i^T w_j + b_i + b_j - \log X_{ij})^2 \tag{2.25}$$

where X_{ij} is the co-occurrence count of words i and j, w_i, w_j are word vectors, b_i, b_j are biases, and $f(X_{ij})$ is a weighting function to reduce the impact of very frequent or infrequent words.

2.3.1.3 FastText

FastText [16] is an extension of Word2Vec developed by Facebook AI Research. It improves upon traditional word embeddings by incorporating subword information, making it useful for handling rare and out-of-vocabulary (OOV) words.

Instead of learning embeddings for entire words, FastText represents each word as a bag of character n-grams. This helps capture morphological variations and is particularly useful for languages with complex word structures.

Example:
Consider the word apple, which is broken into character n-grams:

$$< ap, app, ppl, ple, le >$$

where < > denote word boundaries.

The word embedding for apple is obtained by summing the embeddings of its n-grams and is formulated as follows in Equation (2.26).

$$v_{apple} = \sum_{g \in G_{apple}} v_g \tag{2.26}$$

Where G_{apple} is the set of character n-grams, and v_g is the embedding of each n-gram.

Similar to Word2Vec, FastText can be trained using Skip-gram or CBOW and is formulated as follows in Equation (2.27).

$$J = \sum_{(w,C)} \log P\left(C \middle| w\right) \tag{2.27}$$

where the probability $P\left(C \middle| w\right)$ is computed using the n-gram embeddings.

SUMMARY

Beginning with the levels of NLP in computational linguistics, which include phonology (sound systems), morphology (word formation), syntax (sentence structure), semantics (meaning), pragmatics (contextual use), and discourse (coherence across sentences), this chapter examines the linguistic and computational underpinnings of NLP. The morphology section describes how morphemes are used to create words, making a distinction between derivation (the production of new words) and inflection (grammatical modifications). Grammar structure analysis is covered by syntax and parsing, which allows machines to comprehend the relationships between words in a sentence through techniques like constituency parsing and dependency parsing. Lexical and compositional semantics focus on issues like polysemy and synonymy and examine how meaning is expressed both at the word level (lexical) and in word combinations (compositional).

The VSM, a mathematical model of text in which words or documents are represented as vectors in a multidimensional space, is next introduced in this chapter. It talks about topic modeling methods including n-gram models for capturing local word dependencies, Latent Dirichlet Allocation (LDA) for revealing hidden themes, and smoothing methods (like Laplace and Good-Turing) for handling unseen events in probabilistic models.

The article then discusses word embeddings and how dense vector representations are better than sparse representations in capturing syntactic and semantic relationships. It explains Word2Vec, which includes the Skip-Gram model, which predicts surrounding words from a target word, and the Continuous Bag of Words (CBOW) model, which predicts a word from its context. While FastText expands on Word2Vec by representing words as character n-grams, enhancing performance for rare words and morphologically rich languages, GloVe is introduced as a count-based embedding technique that makes use of global word co-occurrence statistics.

The article then discusses word embeddings and how dense vector representations are better than sparse representations in capturing syntactic and semantic relationships. It explains Word2Vec, which includes the Skip-Gram model, which predicts surrounding words from a target word, and the Continuous Bag of Words (CBOW) model, which predicts a word from its context. While FastText expands on Word2Vec by representing words as character n-grams, enhancing performance for rare words and morphologically rich languages, GloVe is introduced as a count-based embedding technique that makes use of global word co-occurrence statistics.

In order to enable more precise and context-aware language processing, the chapter ends by demonstrating how these linguistic principles and representation techniques serve as the foundation of contemporary NLP systems.

QUESTIONS

1. Explain the different levels of NLP in computational linguistics with suitable examples.
2. Define morphology. Differentiate between **inflectional** and **derivational** morphology with examples.
3. What is syntactic parsing? Compare **constituency parsing** and **dependency parsing**.
4. Explain the difference between **lexical semantics** and **compositional semantics** with an example.
5. Compare **Word2Vec, GloVe, and FastText** in terms of their working principle and advantages.
6. Given the following term frequencies in a corpus:
   - Term "data" occurs 30 times
   - Term "science" occurs 20 times
   - Term "AI" occurs 50 times

   If the total number of terms in the corpus is 500, compute the **TF** of each term.
7. In topic modelling using Latent Dirichlet Allocation (LDA), a word "cloud" appears in:
   - Topic A with probability 0.4
   - Topic B with probability 0.35
   - Topic C with probability 0.25

   Identify the most likely topic for "cloud".
8. Using an N-Gram model, compute the probability of the sentence "machine learning" using the following bigram probabilities:
   - $P(machine | <s>) = 0.3$
   - $P(learning | machine) = 0.4$
9. Suppose the bigram probability of "deep learning" is zero because it never appeared in the training corpus. Apply Laplace smoothing if:
   - Vocabulary size = 10,000
   - Count(deep, learning) = 0
   - Count(deep) = 50

   Compute the smoothed probability.
10. In a Skip-Gram Word2Vec model, if the input word vector is $x = [1, 0, 1]$, the weight matrix W is:

$$W = \begin{matrix} [[0.2, & 0.5], \\ [0.3, & 0.7], \\ [0.4, & 0.6]] \end{matrix}$$

    Compute the hidden layer output h = xW.

11. **Case Study – Word Embeddings in Sentiment Analysis**
A company wants to analyze customer reviews to understand product satisfaction. Initially, they used a simple VSM with n-grams, but the results were poor because the model could not capture word meanings and relationships (e.g., "good" vs. "great"). Later, they applied Word2Vec embeddings, where similar words were represented closely in vector space. This improved the sentiment classification accuracy because the model better understood context and semantic similarity. The same approach was extended with GloVe and FastText, where GloVe captured global word co-occurrence and FastText handled subword information, making the system effective even for misspellings or rare words. Discuss how word embeddings like Word2Vec, GloVe, and FastText overcome the limitations of traditional VSMs in NLP applications such as sentiment analysis.

REFERENCES

[1] D. Jurafsky, and J. H. Martin, *Speech and Language Processing: An Introduction to Natural Language Processing, Computational Linguistics, and Speech Recognition with Language Models*, 2025. https://web.stanford.edu/~jurafsky/slp3

[2] J. Allen, *Natural Language Understanding*, Second. Benjamin-Cummings Publishing Co., Inc., 1995.

[3] K. R. Beesley, and L. Karttunen, *Finite-State Morphology*. CSLI Publications, California, 2003.

[4] A. S. Martin Haspelmath, *Understanding Morphology*. Routledge, London, 2010, https://doi.org/10.4324/9780203776506.

[5] D. Klein, and C. D. Manning, "Accurate Unlexicalized Parsing," in *Proceedings of the 41st Annual Meeting on Association for Computational Linguistics – ACL '03*. Association for Computational Linguistics, 2003, pp. 423–430, doi: 10.3115/1075096.1075150.

[6] C. Manning, and H. Schütze, *Foundations of Statistical Natural Language Processing*. MIT Press, Cambridge, MA: May 1999.

[7] J. Pustejovsky, *The Generative Lexicon*. MIT Press, Cambridge, 1998.

[8] K. Erk, "Vector Space Models of Word Meaning and Phrase Meaning: A Survey," *Lang Linguist Compass*, vol. 6, no. 10, pp. 635–653, Oct. 2012, doi: 10.1002/lnco.362.

[9] G. Salton, A. Wong, and C. S. Yang, "A Vector Space Model for Automatic Indexing," *Commun ACM*, vol. 18, no. 11, pp. 613–620, Nov. 1975, doi: 10.1145/361219.361220.

[10] D. M. Blei, A. Y. Ng, and J. M. I. Blei, "Latent Dirichlet Allocation," *J Mach Learn Res*, vol. 3, pp. 993–1022, 2003.

[11] C. E. Shannon, "A Mathematical Theory of Communication," *Bell System Techn J*, vol. 27, no. 3, pp. 379–423, Jul. 1948, doi: 10.1002/j.1538-7305.1948.tb01338.x.

[12] S. F. Chen, and J. Goodman, "An Empirical Study of Smoothing Techniques for Language Modeling," *Comput Speech Lang*, vol. 13, no. 4, pp. 359–393, Oct. 1999, doi: 10.1006/csla.1999.0128.

[13] T. Mikolov, K. Chen, G. Corrado, and J. Dean, "Efficient Estimation of Word Representations in Vector Space," arxiv preprint, Sep. 2013, arXiv:1301.3781.

[14] T. Mikolov, I. Sutskever, K. Chen, G. Corrado, and J. Dean, "Distributed Representations of Words and Phrases and their Compositionality," in *Proceedings*

of the 27th International Conference on Neural Information Processing Systems - Volume 2 (NIPS'13), vol. 2. Curran Associates Inc., Red Hook, NY, USA, pp. 3111–3119, Oct. 2013.

[15] J. Pennington, R. Socher, and C. Manning, "Glove: Global Vectors for Word Representation," in *Proceedings of the 2014 Conference on Empirical Methods in Natural Language Processing (EMNLP)*. Association for Computational Linguistics, 2014, pp. 1532–1543, doi: 10.3115/v1/D14-1162.

[16] P. Bojanowski, E. Grave, A. Joulin, and T. Mikolov, "Enriching Word Vectors with Subword Information," *Trans Assoc Comput Linguist*, vol. 5, pp. 135–146, Dec. 2017, doi: 10.1162/tacl_a_00051.

3 Sequence Modelling with Neural Networks

Sequence modeling is the process of analyzing and predicting sequential data, where the order of elements matters. It is widely used in natural language processing (NLP), time-series forecasting, speech recognition, and other fields where data points have temporal or contextual relationships.

3.1 INTRODUCTION TO SEQUENTIAL DATA

Sequential data [1] refers to data that are arranged in some specific and useful order, whereby the position or timing of one element has a significant impact on the overall knowledge. Unlike regular (or tabular) data sets, whereby data points tend to be thought of as separate, sequential data exhibits temporal or positional relationships. This means the present element depends on one or more earlier elements.

Examples of sequential data include:

- Time series information – e.g., stock prices, weather measurements, or sensor readings.
- Text information – where the word order affects meaning and context.
- Biological sequences – like DNA or protein formations.
- Audio or speech signals – as information that changes over time and contains rhythms or tonal patterns.
- Video frames – capturing a sequence of images that convey movement and continuity.

Due to these dependencies, sequential data analysis often requires specific models such as recurrent neural networks (RNNs) [2], long short-term memory (LSTM) networks [3], Transformers [4, 5], or Hidden.

Sequence modeling is an important method in AI and deep learning that enables machines to understand and process data where the order and context matter. Its application cuts across various fields. In NLP, such models power applications like machine translation (e.g., Google Translate) and text summarization (e.g., ChatGPT).

DOI: 10.1201/9781003650065-3

In time-series forecasting, they assist in anticipating stock market trends and weather patterns by learning from historical patterns. Voice assistants such as Siri and Alexa use sequence models to interpret voice commands, while music generation software creates new melodies based on learned sequences. Sequence models in healthcare and bioinformatics assist in detecting anomalies in ECG readings and analyzing DNA for genetic data. In business and finance analytics, they uncover trends of fraudulent activity and tailor recommendations by simulating customer behavior. These diverse applications highlight the key significance of sequence modeling in deciphering and predicting sequential data across industries.

Sequential dependencies modeling is inherently challenging because of the temporal or positional nature of data, which creates several challenges that affect both learning efficacy and computational cost. One such challenge is the long-term dependencies, which require models to keep track of information over a large number of steps—for example, mapping "book" to "was amazing" in a sentence—something the traditional RNNs struggle with, but LSTMs and Transformers are designed to do. A further problem is the exploding and vanishing gradient during training, which makes it harder for deep RNNs to learn from long sequences, commonly leading them to forget previous inputs. Variable-length sequences bring a further complication because applications like chatbots have to handle short as well as long inputs; padding, truncation, and attention mechanisms are ways to cope with this. Noisy data, which is common in areas such as healthcare (e.g., noisy ECG signals), requires models capable of identifying meaningful patterns in the presence of signal disturbances. Finally, computational complexity becomes an issue, especially with long inputs such as movie scripts—efficient models like Transformers alleviate this by enabling parallel processing and shortening training time. All these challenges highlight the need for robust, scalable models in sequence modeling tasks.

3.2 RECURRENT NEURAL NETWORKS (RNNS)

RNNs [6] are a category of neural networks adapted to sequence modeling, in which the temporal order of the data matters. Unlike regular feed-forward networks, RNNs have cycles (recurrent links), which allow past information to be used in the computations at the present time steps.

3.2.1 Architecture of RNNs

RNNs are designed for sequential data processing by maintaining an internal memory of past inputs. The key feature of RNNs is that they can process sequences of varying lengths by propagating information across time steps. This feature makes them well-suited for applications that require contextual understanding over time. The architecture of RNN is shown in Figure 3.1.

In RNNs, each time step's computation consists of two essential tasks: modifying the hidden state and producing the output.

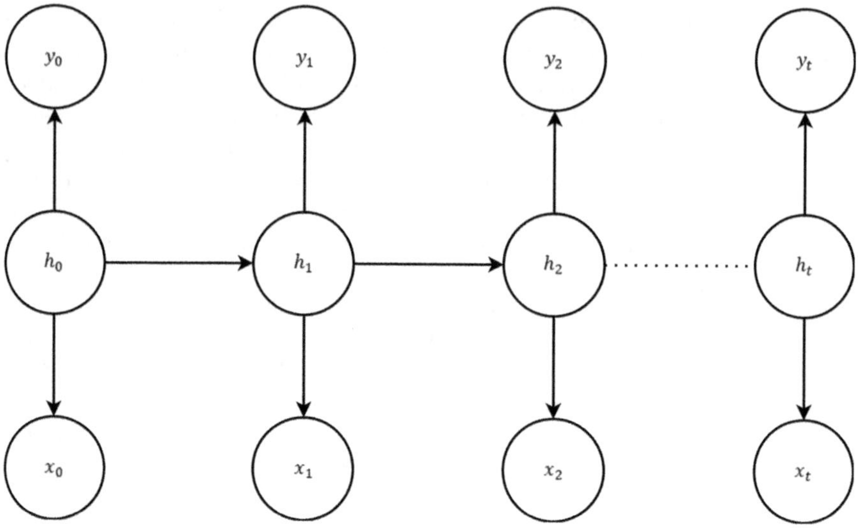

FIGURE 3.1 RNN.

The hidden state at time step t is updated based on the input at the current time step x_t and previous time step hidden state h_{t-1} and is formulated using the following Equation (3.1).

$$h_t = \sigma(U.x_t + W.h_{t-1} + b) \tag{3.1}$$

where h_t is the hidden state at time t, x_t is the input at time t, h_{t-1} is the hidden state from the previous time step, U, V are the weight matrices, and b is the bias term, and σ is activation function.

The concealed state h_t permits the network to transfer information from earlier time steps, which allows it to understand the temporal relationships within the sequence.

After the hidden state is modified, the output at the time step t is produced and is formulated in Equation (3.2).

$$y_t = V.h_t + c \tag{3.2}$$

where y_t is output at time t, V is the output weight matrix, and C is the output bias.

This formulation allows the network to retain information across time steps, effectively modeling temporal dependencies.

3.2.2 Types of Sequence Modelling Architectures in RNNs

RNNs can be categorized into various architectures based on the relationship between input and output sequences. *One-to-One* architecture maps a single input to a single output, as seen in tasks like image classification. *One-to-Many* generates a sequence of outputs from a single input, such as in image captioning. *Many-to-One* processes

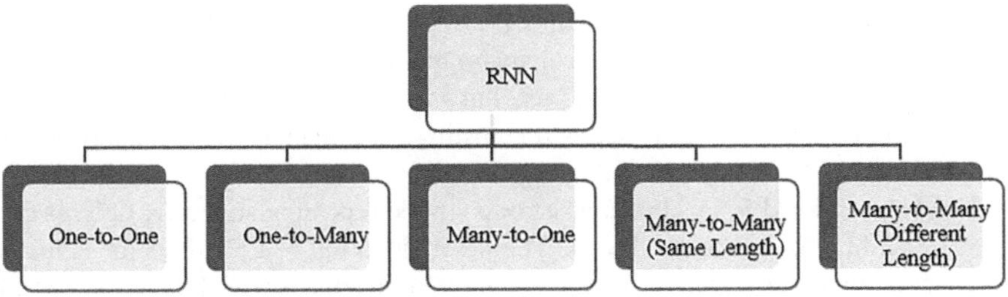

FIGURE 3.2 Types of RNN.

a sequence of inputs to produce a single output, like in sentiment analysis. *Many-to-Many (Same Length)* involves input and output sequences of the same length, often used in tasks like Named Entity Recognition (NER), where each input element corresponds to an output element. *Many-to-Many (Different Length)* handles input and output sequences of varying lengths, as seen in machine translation, where a sentence in one language is translated into another. These different architectures allow RNNs to be adapted to a wide range of sequence-based tasks, making them highly versatile for applications in NLP, speech recognition, and time-series forecasting. The types of RNN is shown in Figure 3.2.

3.2.3 Variants of RNNs

To address the shortcomings of traditional RNNs, several alternatives have been developed:

- **Long Short-Term Memory (LSTM)** [7]**:** LSTMs use gates (input, forget, output) to regulate the flow of information, helping the network to manage long-term dependencies and avoiding the vanishing gradient problem.
- **Gated Recurrent Unit (GRU)** [8]**:** GRUs simplify LSTMs by combining the gates into a single unit, offering a good balance between computation and performance.
- **Bidirectional RNNs** [9]**:** These networks process sequences in both the forward and reverse directions so that the model can understand context from both sides of the sequence and that is especially helpful for applications that involve overall context understanding.

These RNN types enhance the network's ability to understand and store information over time so that they are better suited for complex sequential applications.

3.2.4 Long Short-Term Memory Networks (LSTMs)

LSTM [7] networks are a unique variant of RNNs that are tailored to handle long-term dependencies in sequential data. Traditional RNNs suffer from the vanishing gradient problem, where important information from previous time steps vanishes while longer sequences are processed by the network. LSTMs tackle this problem by using a memory cell and a gating mechanism that selectively retains or rejects information over time. LSTMs are widely used in such domains as NLP, speech recognition, machine translation, time-series forecasting, and financial market analysis. The architecture of LSTM is displayed in Figure 3.3.

Unlike traditional RNNs that consist of a simple repeating structure, LSTMs consist of a number of connected layers. The key innovation of LSTMs is the cell state (C_t), which serves as a memory unit that can hold information for long sequences. In order to manage the information flow, LSTMs have three different kinds of gates: the input gate, the forget gate, and the output gate, which help decide what information is retained.

3.2.4.1 Forget Gate (f_t)

The forget gate controls the degree of previous information that must be forgotten. It takes the previous hidden state and the current input and generates a value between 0 and 1. A value close to 0 erases previous information, while a value close to 1 preserves it. The mathematical formulation of the forget gate is given in the following Equation (3.3).

$$f_t = \sigma(W_f.\left[h_{t-1}, x_t\right] + b_f) \tag{3.3}$$

where f_t is the forget gate, h_{t-1} is the previous hidden state information at time step $t-1$, x_t is the input state at time step t, W_f is the weight matrix, and b_f is the bias.

3.2.4.2 Input Gate (i_t)

The input gate decides how much new information should be stored in the cell state which uses a sigmoid activation function to filter relevant information. A candidate memory update is created, which is scaled and added to the cell state. The mathematical formulation of the input gate is given in the following Equation (3.4).

$$i_t = \sigma(W_i.\left[h_{t-1}, x_t\right] + b_i) \tag{3.4}$$

where i_t is the input gate, W_i is the weight matrix of the input gate and b_i is the bias term of the input gate.

3.2.4.3 Candidate Cell State Update (C_t)

Cell state update combines the forgotten past information and the newly selected information. This ensures that only the most relevant knowledge is carried forward. The mathematical formulation of the candidate cell state is given in the following Equations (3.5) and (3.6).

$$\widetilde{C}_t = tanh(W_c.\left[h_{t-1}, x_t\right] + b_c) \tag{3.5}$$

$$c_t = f_t \odot c_{t-1} + i_t \odot \widetilde{C}_t \tag{3.6}$$

where $\widetilde{C}_t$ is the candidate cell state, and c_t is the cell state.

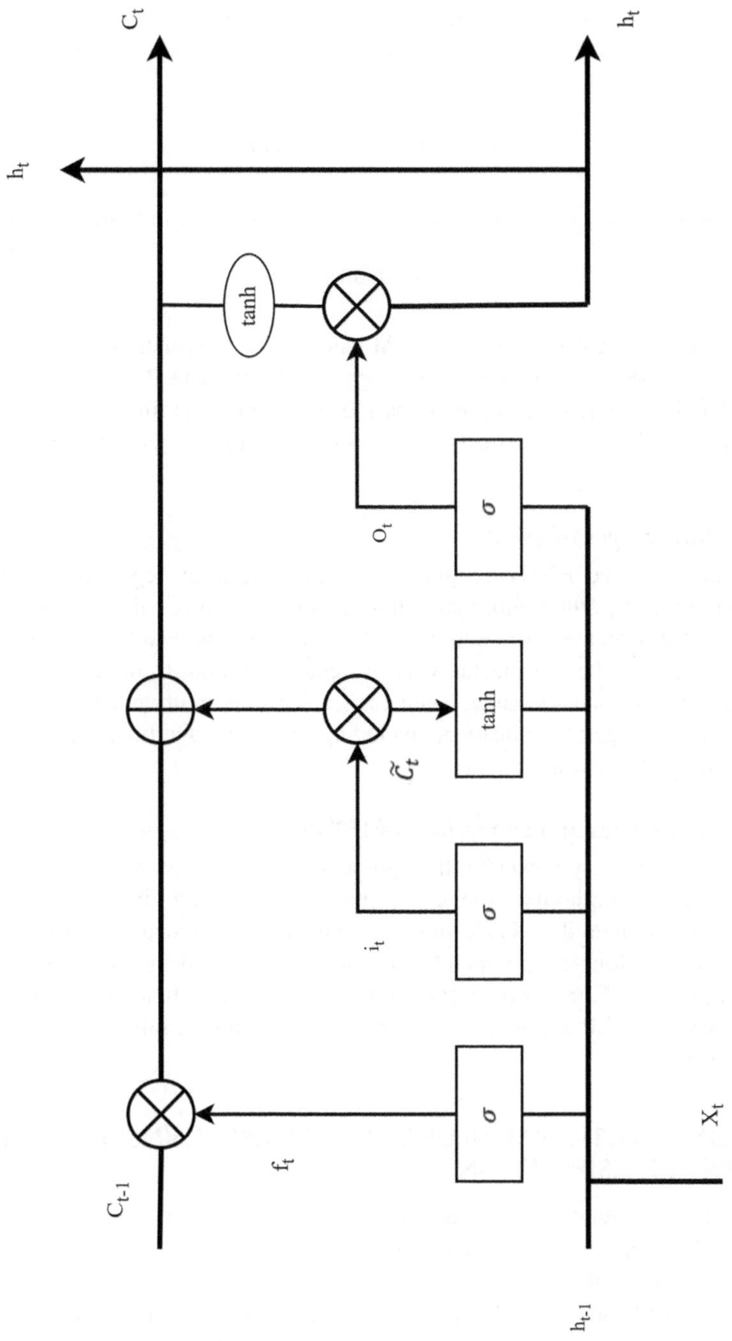

FIGURE 3.3 LSTM.

3.2.4.4 Output Gate (O_t)

Output gate determines what information from the cell state should be passed to the next hidden state. This gate uses the tanh function to scale the updated memory and provide a final output. The mathematical formulation of the output gate is given in the following Equation (3.7).

$$o_t = \sigma(W_o \cdot [\mathrm{h}_{t-1}, x_t] + b_o) \tag{3.7}$$

The hidden state acts as the output at time step t and is shown in Equation (3.8).

$$h_t = o_t \cdot \tanh(C_t) \tag{3.8}$$

These equations ensure that the LSTM can control information flow, remember long-term dependencies, and selectively forget irrelevant data. Together, these gates enable LSTMs to remember important past information while filtering out irrelevant details, making them highly effective for tasks that require understanding sequential patterns.

3.2.4.5 Advantages of LSTMs

LSTMs are advanced RNNs designed to handle long-term dependencies by efficiently retaining important information through long sequences, thereby overcoming the vanishing gradient problem commonly faced by conventional RNNs. Their gated architecture allows them to decide what to retain and what to discard, facilitating more efficient and robust learning against noise. This flexibility makes LSTMs suitable for a wide range of applications, including speech recognition, text generation, and stock market forecasting.

3.2.4.6 Challenges and Limitations of LSTMs

While LSTMs are very powerful, they possess some drawbacks such as increased computational complexity, longer training times, and increased memory requirements compared to basic models. They may also struggle to effectively model extremely long-term dependencies, and with the advent of more complex architectures like Transformers (i.e., GPT, BERT), which tend to outperform LSTMs in many NLP applications, their use is now more limited in state-of-the-art environments.

3.3 CONVOLUTIONAL NEURAL NETWORKS (CNNS) FOR NLP IN TEXT CLASSIFICATION

Traditional NLP models, such as RNNs and LSTMs, are widely used for handling sequential data. However, these models have limitations, such as slow training times and difficulty in parallelization.

On the other hand, CNNs [10]—which have revolutionized computer vision—are now being effectively used in text classification tasks. Instead of treating text as a sequence, CNNs process it as spatial data, extracting meaningful patterns and features from the text. This makes CNNs highly efficient for tasks like:

- Sentiment Analysis (e.g., detecting positive or negative reviews)
- Spam Detection (e.g., classifying emails as spam or not)
- Fake News Classification (e.g., detecting misinformation)
- Topic Categorization (e.g., classifying text into categories such as sports, technology, politics)

CNNs are particularly fast and scalable, making them ideal for large-scale text classification problems.

3.3.1 CNNs Have Several Advantages over Traditional NLP Models

CNNs are well-suited for NLP tasks since they are able to identify local features, like n-gram features, via their convolutional layers and thus spot important phrases such as "not good." CNNs offer parallel processing and efficiency advantages by treating all words together, unlike sequential models such as LSTMs. By taking advantage of word embeddings (e.g., Word2Vec, GloVe, FastText), CNNs build dense feature representations that enhance classification accuracy. Additionally, they consume less memory and are more efficient in processing large datasets, and their invariance to word order variations allows them to perform well even with shuffled inputs.

3.3.2 CNN Architecture for Text Classification

The architecture of CNN for text classification is shown in Figure 3.4. A CNN for text classification consists of the following key components:

3.3.2.1 Input Layer: Word Embeddings

Text is first converted into a numerical form using word embeddings. Each word is represented as a dense vector, capturing semantic meaning.

For example, consider the sentence:

- "The movie was great!"

  This can be represented as a word embedding matrix and is shown in Equation (3.9).

$$X = \begin{bmatrix} w_1 \\ w_2 \\ w_3 \\ w_4 \end{bmatrix} \tag{3.9}$$

  where w_i represents the embedding vector of each word. These embeddings are typically pretrained using models like Word2Vec, GloVe, or FastText.

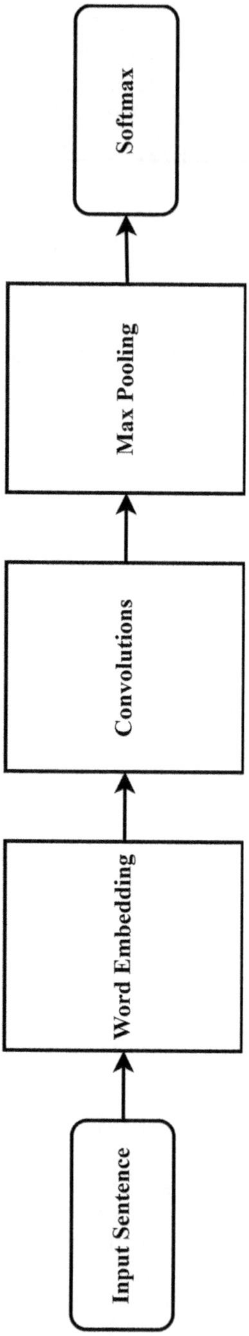

FIGURE 3.4 CNN.

3.3.2.2 Convolutional Layer: Extracting Text Features

CNNs apply convolutional filters (kernels) to extract local patterns in the text, such as bigrams (two-word combinations) and trigrams (three-word combinations). Each filter slides over the word embedding matrix, detecting important phrases in the text.

Example:

- Filter 1 (bigram): Detects "not good" (negative sentiment).
- Filter 2 (trigram): Detects "very bad movie" (strong negative sentiment).

Mathematically, the convolution operation is shown in Equation (3.10).

$$f_i = \tanh(W \cdot X_{i:i+h} + b\ ) \quad (3.10)$$

where W is the filter matrix (learned during training), $X_{i:i+h}$ is the input text segment, b is the bias term, h is the filter size (e.g., 2 for bigrams, 3 for trigrams), tanh or ReLU is the activation function.

3.3.2.3 Pooling Layer: Selecting the Most Important Features

After convolution, pooling is applied to reduce the dimensionality and retain the most important features. Max pooling selects the highest activation from each filter's output, ensuring that important words contribute to classification and is formulated as follows in Equation (3.11).

$$p = \max(f_i) \quad (3.11)$$

where p represents the highest value found among the input features f_i within a specified window.

For Example, Given the feature outputs: [0.3, 0.6, 0.8, 0.4], max pooling selects 0.8, as it represents the most significant feature.

3.3.2.4 Fully Connected Layer and Softmax Output

The pooled feature vector is flattened and passed through a fully connected layer to predict class probabilities. The *softmax* function assigns probabilities to different categories. The output layer is mathematically modelled in Equation (3.12).

$$y = Softmax(W.p\ + b) \quad (3.12)$$

where W is the weight matrix of the fully connected layer, p is the pooled feature vector, b is the bias vector, and y is the output probability vector.

3.4 SEQUENCE-TO-SEQUENCE MODELS

Sequence-to-Sequence (Seq2Seq) models are a class of neural network architectures designed to transform sequences from one domain to sequences in another domain.

They are particularly effective in tasks where the input and output are both sequences, such as machine translation, text summarization, and conversational modeling.

3.4.1 Encoder–Decoder Architecture

The foundational structure of Seq2Seq models is the Encoder–Decoder architecture [11], which comprises two primary components. One is encoder which processes the input sequence and encodes it into a fixed-length context vector and the second is the decoder which takes the context vector and generates the output sequence. The architecture of Encoder–Decoder is shown in Figure 3.5.

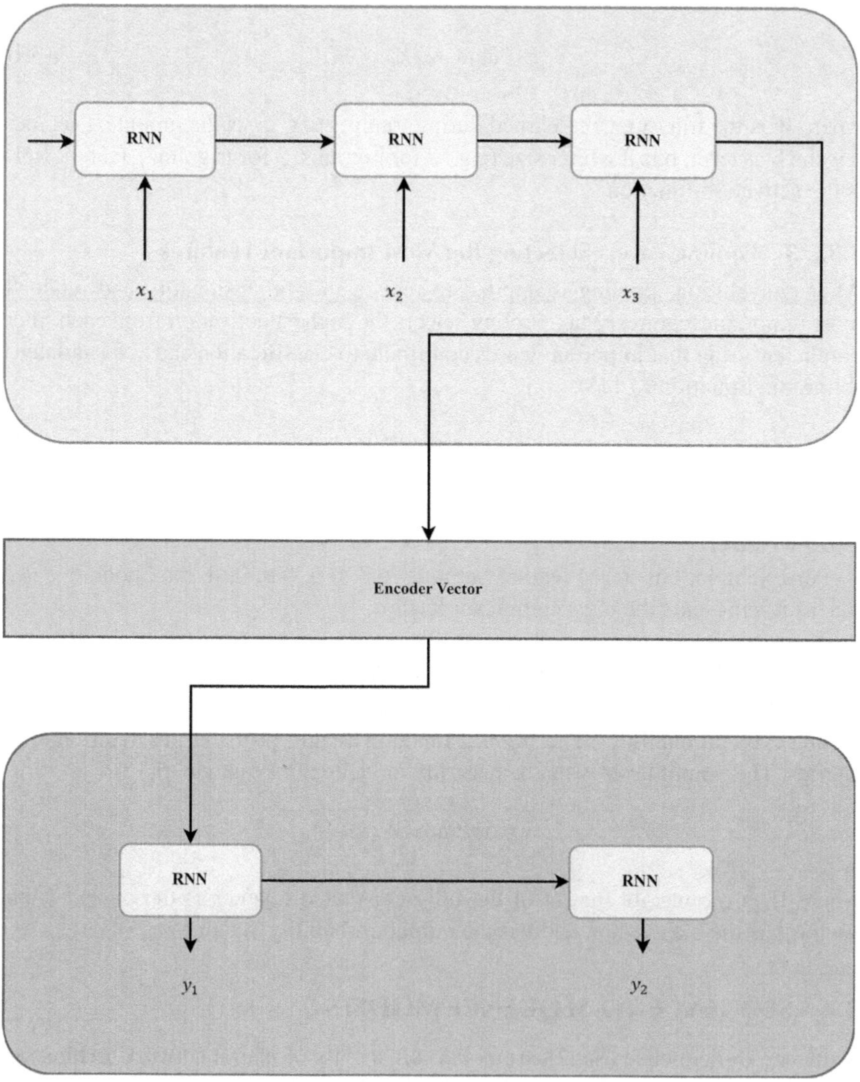

FIGURE 3.5 Encoder–decoder architecture.

3.4.1.1 Encoder

The encoder's role is to compress the input sequence into a context vector that encapsulates its salient features. This is typically achieved using RNNs or their variants like LSTM networks and gated recurrent units (GRUs).

Given an input sequence $X = (x_1, x_2, \ldots, x_n)$, the encoder computes a sequence of hidden states $(h_1, h_2, \ldots, h_n)$ as follows using the following Equation (3.13).

$$h_t = f(h_{t-1}, x_t) \tag{3.13}$$

Here, h_t represents the hidden state at time step t, and f denotes the recurrent function, which could be an LSTM, GRU, or a standard RNN unit.

The final hidden state h_n serves as the context vector c, summarizing the entire input sequence and is calculated using the Equation (3.14).

$$c = h_n \tag{3.14}$$

3.4.1.2 Decoder

The decoder generates the output sequence $Y = (y_1, y_2, \ldots, y_m)$ by predicting one token at a time, conditioned on the context vector and the previously generated tokens. The decoder maintains its own hidden states $(s_1, s_2, \ldots, s_m)$. At each time step t, the decoder computes s_t and $\tilde{y}_t$ using the following Equations (3.15) and (3.16).

$$s_t = f(s_{t-1}, y_{t-1}, c) \tag{3.15}$$

$$\tilde{y}_t = g(s_t) \tag{3.16}$$

Here, s_t is the decoder's hidden state at time step t, y_{t-1} is the previously generated token (with y_0 being a start-of-sequence token), c is the context vector from the encoder, f is the recurrent function, and g is a function (often a softmax layer) that outputs the probability distribution over the target vocabulary for the next token.

3.4.1.3 Attention Mechanism

One limitation of the basic Encoder–Decoder architecture is the fixed-size context vector, which may not effectively capture all necessary information for long input sequences. The attention mechanism addresses this by allowing the decoder to focus on different parts of the input sequence at each decoding step. At each decoding time step t, the context vector c_t is computed as a weighted sum of the encoder's hidden states and is computed using the following Equation (3.17).

$$c_t = \sum_{i=1}^{n} \alpha_{t,i} h_i \tag{3.17}$$

The weights $\alpha_{t,i}$ (attention scores) are calculated using the following Equation (3.18).

$$\alpha_{t,i} = \frac{\exp(e_{t,i})}{\sum_{k=1}^{n} \exp(e_t, k)} \tag{3.18}$$

where, $e_{t,i} = score(s_{t-1}, h_i)$ is an alignment score function that measures the relevance of the encoder hidden state h_i to the decoder's previous hidden state s_{t-1}.

By integrating the attention mechanism, the decoder can dynamically focus on different parts of the input sequence, enhancing performance, especially for longer sequences.

3.4.1.4 Applications

NLP encompasses different uses like machine translation, which alters text into a different language; text summarization, which summarizes lengthy documents into brief informative versions; speech recognition, which turns spoken language into text; and chatbots, which respond as humans in order to allow for interactive dialogue with users.

SUMMARY

Neural network architectures for modeling sequential data in NLP are the main topic of this chapter. It highlights how well these networks can capture textual context, order, and dependencies. It starts by describing the fundamental structure of RNNs, which are appropriate for tasks like language modeling and text synthesis since their output at each time step depends on both the current input and the previously hidden state. LSTM networks overcome the drawbacks of conventional RNNs, such as vanishing and exploding gradients in lengthy sequences, by introducing gating mechanisms (input, forget, and output gates) to selectively retain or discard information, thereby facilitating efficient long-range dependency modeling.

The chapter next delves into CNNs for NLP, demonstrating how they use convolutional filters to capture local n-gram-like characteristics. This makes CNNs useful for text categorization and sentence modeling since they can find significant word patterns at any position.

Sequence-to-Sequence (Seq2Seq) models are then shown for mapping one sequence to another, which is a typical need in dialogue systems, summarization, and machine translation. The main framework is known as the encoder–decoder architecture, in which the input sequence is converted into a fixed-size context vector by the encoder, and the output sequence is produced by the decoder using this representation. Advanced attention-based models and Transformers are made possible by this structure.

The chapter ends by emphasizing how these architectures, which balance the advantages of local pattern detection (CNNs), sequential modeling (RNNs/LSTMs), and flexible input–output mapping (Seq2Seq), constitute the foundation of many contemporary NLP systems.

QUESTIONS

1. Define a RNN. What makes it different from a feedforward neural network?
2. Explain how the gates (input, forget, and output) in an LSTM help in solving the vanishing gradient problem.
3. Describe the role of CNNs in text classification with an example.
4. Draw and explain the Encoder–Decoder architecture used in Seq2Seq models for machine translation.
5. For a simple RNN, if the input $x_t = 1$, previous hidden state $h_{t-1} = 0.5$, weight matrices $W_x = 0.6, W_h = 0.4$, and bias $b = 0.1$, compute the hidden state $h_t = tanh(W_x * x_t + W_h * h_{t-1} + b)$.
6. In an LSTM, if input gate $i_t = 0.7$, forget gate $f_t = 0.5$, output gate $o_t = 0.6$, candidate cell state $\widetilde{C}_t = 0.8$, and previous cell state $C_{t-1} = 0.4$. Compute the new cell state C_t and hidden state h_t.
7. A CNN is applied to a sentence represented as a 5 × 4 matrix (5 words, each with 4 dimensions). A filter of size 2 × 4 is applied. How many convolution operations are possible, and what will be the output feature map size?
8. Compare RNNs, LSTMs, and Seq2Seq models in terms of handling long-term dependencies. Which architecture is most effective and why?
9. Evaluate the effectiveness of CNNs vs RNNs for sentiment analysis tasks. Which would you prefer and justify your choice.
10. Design a Seq2Seq model with attention mechanism for a chatbot. Explain how the encoder and decoder interact during training and inference.
11. **Case Study: Machine Translation with Sequence-to-Sequence Models**
    One of the most impactful applications of sequence modeling in NLP is machine translation, where a sentence in one language is converted into another. Early models using RNNs faced the problem of forgetting long-term dependencies, making them less effective for longer sentences. This limitation was overcome by LSTMs, which use gates to remember or forget information over time, improving translation accuracy. Later, Seq2Seq models with an Encoder-Decoder architecture were introduced. In these models, the encoder reads the input sentence and creates a fixed-length vector representation, while the decoder generates the translated sentence step by step. For example, translating the English sentence "How are you?" into French "Comment ça va?" becomes possible through this framework. CNNs are also used in NLP tasks like sentence classification, but Seq2Seq with LSTMs became a breakthrough in translation systems b efore Transformers took over. Explain how the Encoder–Decoder architecture in Seq2Seq models improves the performance of sequence modeling tasks such as machine translation compared to basic RNNs.

REFERENCES

[1] J. Chung, C. Gulcehre, K. Cho, and Y. Bengio, "Empirical Evaluation of Gated Recurrent Neural Networks on Sequence Modeling," Dec. 2014, [Online]. Available: http://arxiv.org/abs/1412.3555

[2] T. Mikolov, M. Karafiát, L. Burget, J. Černocký, and S. Khudanpur, "Recurrent Neural Network based Language Model," in *Proc. Interspeech,* Makuhari, Japan, ISCA: ISCA, Sep. 2010, pp. 1045–1048, doi: 10.21437/Interspeech.2010-343.

[3] S. Jamshidi, M. Mohammadi, S, Bagheri, H. Esmaeili Najafabadi, A. Rezvanian, M, Gheisari *et al.*, "Effective Text Classification using BERT, MTM-LSTM, and DT," *Data & Knowledge Engineering*, vol. 151, p. 102306, May 2024, doi: 10.1016/j.datak.2024.102306.

[4] K. Han, A. Xiao, E. Wu, J. Guo, C. Xu, and Y. Wang, "Transformer in Transformer," *Proc. Advances in Neural Information Processing Systems (NeurIPS),* vol. 34, pp. 15908–15919, Feb. 2021.

[5] A. Vaswani, N. Shazeer, N. Parmar, J. Uszkoreit, L. Jones, A. N. Gomez *et al.*, "Attention is All You Need," *Advances in Neural Information Processing Systems*, Long Beach, CA, USA, pp. 5998–6008, Jun. 2017.

[6] R. M. Schmidt, "Recurrent Neural Networks (RNNs): A Gentle Introduction and Overview," Nov. 2019, ArXiv abs/1912.05911.

[7] C. B. Vennerød, A. Kjærran, and E. S. Bugge, "Long Short-Term Memory RNN," May 2021, arXiv:2105.06756.

[8] R. Dey, and F. M. Salem, "Gate-Variants of Gated Recurrent Unit (GRU) Neural Networks," in *Proc. IEEE 60th International Midwest Symposium on Circuits and Systems (MWSCAS),* Boston, MA, USA, pp. 1597–1600, Jan. 2017, doi: 10.1109/MWSCAS.2017.8053243.

[9] D. Muthusankar, P. Kaladevi, V. R. Sadasivam, and R. Praveen, "BIDRN: A Method of Bidirectional Recurrent Neural Network for Sentiment Analysis," Nov. 2023, arXiv:2311.07296.

[10] M. Z. Amin, and N. Nadeem, "Convolutional Neural Network: Text Classification Model for Open Domain Question Answering System," 2018, ArXiv abs/1809.02479.

[11] K. Aitken, V. V Ramasesh, Y. Cao, and N. Maheswaranathan, "Understanding How Encoder-Decoder Architectures Attend," Oct. 2021, arXiv:2110.15253.

4 Attention Mechanism and Pretrained Language Models

4.1 TRANSFORMER ARCHITECTURE

Transformer architecture [1] is a neural network designed to process sequential data efficiently. It uses self-attention mechanisms and feed-forward networks to overcome the limitations of RNNs and LSTMs. Transformers consist of an encoder that converts input text into a sequence of vectors and a decoder that generates output tokens using the encoder's output. For example, after generating the first three words of a translation, the decoder predicts the next word using these outputs and the encoder's inputs. The Transformer encoder processes an input sequence through multiple layers, generating contextualized token representations that can be used by the decoder for various tasks such as translation, summarization, or text generation.

4.1.1 Embedding Layer

4.1.1.1 Input Embedding

The tokens in the input sequence (e.g., words) are first converted into embedding vectors using pretrained embedding vectors. These vectors capture the semantic meaning of each token. The mathematical formulation is shown in Equation (4.1).

$$e_i = E.x_i \tag{4.1}$$

where, x_i is integer index of the *i–th* token (e.g., "word1" = 4, "word2" = 7). E represents learnable embedding matrix of shape $(vocab\_size, d)$, and d is an embedding dimension. e_i is token embedding, a vector of size d.

4.1.1.2 Positional Encoding

Transformers process tokens in parallel, so they lack the sequential information inherent in RNNs. To address this, positional encoding is added to the embedding to encode the position of each token in the sequence. The mathematical formulation is shown in Equation (4.2).

DOI: 10.1201/9781003650065-4

$$p_{i,2k} = \sin\left(\frac{i}{10000^{2k/d}}\right)$$

$$p_{i,2k+1} = \cos\left(\frac{i}{10000^{2k/d}}\right) \tag{4.2}$$

where i is position of the token in the sequence (starting from 0), k is dimension index of the embedding vector, and d total embedding dimension.

4.1.1.3 Combined Input

For each token obtained by combining its embedding and positional encoding, the mathematical formulation is shown in Equation (4.3).

$$z_i = e_i + p_{i,2k+j} \tag{4.3}$$

where z_i is the combined representation for the $i-th$ token.

4.1.2 Encoder

The encoder in the Transformer consists of N identical layers (typically 6 in the original implementation). Each layer processes the input sequence to refine token representations by capturing contextual relationships and transforming them for subsequent layers.

(a) **Multi-Head Self-Attention:** This mechanism allows each token in the sequence to attend to every other token. It captures dependencies and relationships between tokens, regardless of their distance in the sequence.

For an input sequence X, each token is transformed into three vectors: *query* (Q) represents what the token is looking for, *key* (K) represents what the token offers as context, and *value* (V) contains the actual information about the token. W_Q, W_K *and* W_V are learnable weight matrices of shape (d, d_k) then $d_k = \frac{d}{num\_heads}$. These are computed as follows using Equation (4.4).

$$Q = X.W_Q,\ K = X.W_K,\ V = X.W_v \tag{4.4}$$

The similarity between each token's query and all tokens' keys is computed using its dot product to compute the attention scores. These are computed as follows using Equation (4.5).

$$\text{Score}(Q, K) = Q.K^T \tag{4.5}$$

The scores are then divided by $\sqrt{d_k}$ to stabilize gradients using the following Equation (4.6).

$$\text{Scaled Score}(Q,K) = \frac{Score(Q,K)}{\sqrt{d_k}} \tag{4.6}$$

The scaled scores are passed through a *softmax* function to compute attention weights α, which determine the importance of each token. These are computed as follows using Equation (4.7).

$$\alpha = softmax\left(\frac{Q.K^T}{\sqrt{d_k}}\right) \tag{4.7}$$

The attention weights α are applied to the value vectors V to compute the weighted sum of values using the following Equation (4.8).

$$Attention(Q,K,V) = \alpha.V \tag{4.8}$$

Instead of a single attention operation, multiple heads are used to capture diverse relationships and are computed using the following Equation (4.9).

$$head_i = Attention(\mathrm{Q}W_i{}^Q\mathrm{Q}, \mathrm{K}W_i{}^K, \mathrm{V}W_i{}^V) \tag{4.9}$$

The outputs of all heads are concatenated and linearly transformed as follows using Equation (4.10).

$$\text{MultiHead}(Q,K,V) = \text{Concat}(head_1, head_2, \ldots .head_h).W^o \tag{4.10}$$

where W^o is the output projection matrix. Multihead self-attention enables the encoder to capture token-to-token relationships effectively, allowing each token in the sequence to focus on other tokens based on their contextual relevance. This mechanism helps the model understand the underlying context, including syntax and semantics, by examining how words or tokens relate to one another. It allows the encoder to model long-range dependencies, ensuring that relationships between distant tokens in the sequence are also considered.

The output of the multihead attention (MHA) is passed through a residual connection and layer normalization using the following Equation (4.11).

$$Y = \text{LayerNorm}(z_i + \text{MultiHead}\ (Q,K,V)) \tag{4.11}$$

Residual connection $(z_i + \text{MultiHead})$ ensures gradient flow and layer normalization stabilizes the learning process by normalizing features.

Then, Y is fed into a fully connected feed forward layer (FFN) which applies nonlinear transformations independently to each token. It enhances the representation by introducing nonlinearity and increasing the model's capacity using the following Equation (4.12).

$$FFN(x) = \max\left(0, xW_1 + b_1\right) W_2 + b_2 \quad (4.12)$$

where the first weight matrix $W_1 \in R^{d_{model}*d_{ff}}$ projects the input x into a higher-dimensional space ($d_{ff} > d_{\text{model}}$), where d_{model} refers to the dimensionality of the input or output token embeddings (e.g., 512), and d_{ff} refers to the dimensionality of the hidden layer in the feed-forward network (e.g., 2048). *ReLU* activation function $max(0,x)$ is applied to introduce nonlinearity. The second weight matrix $W_2 \in R^{d_{model}*d_{ff}}$ reduces the dimensionality back to the original embedding size d_{model}, and bias terms b_1 *and* b_2 are added at each step.

This structure allows the FFN to capture complex patterns in the data by expanding the representation and then reducing it. The increase in dimensionality via W_1 enables the model to capture more complex relationships, while the reduction back to d_{model} preserves the original token representation.

The output of the FFN is also passed through a residual connection and layer normalization using the following Equation (4.13).

$$Z = \text{LayerNorm}(Y + \text{FFN}\ (x)) \quad (4.13)$$

This process is repeated for N identical layers, producing the final contextualized representations for the input sequence. The encoder outputs are passed to the decoder for further processing in sequence-to-sequence tasks.

4.1.3 Decoder

The Decoder follows a similar structure to the encoder but with an additional mechanism for attending to the encoder's output.

The first layer in the decoder is masked multihead self-attention (MMHSA). In this step, the decoder uses the previous tokens to generate the next token in an autoregressive manner. The key idea is that the decoder can only attend to previous tokens (and not future ones), which is controlled using a mask. It ensures that a token x_t can only attend to previous tokens $x_1, x_2, \ldots\ldots, x_t$, preventing information leakage about future tokens. The attention mechanism computes using the following Equation (4.14).

$$\text{Attention}(Q, K, V) = \text{softmax}\left(\frac{Q.K^T}{\sqrt{d_k}}\right).V \quad (4.14)$$

where, $Q = X.W_Q$, $K = X.W_K$, $V = X.W_v$, derived from input, W_Q, W_K *and* W_V are learnable weight matrices and d_k is the dimensionality of the key vectors. To apply masking, a mask matrix is added to the scaled dot product $\left(\frac{Q.K^T}{\sqrt{d_k}}\right)$ setting future token positions to $-\infty$ before applying the *softmax*. This ensures using the following Equation (4.15).

$$\text{Masked Attention}\ (Q, K, V) = softmax\left(\frac{Q.K^T}{\sqrt{d_k}} + Mask\right).V \quad (4.15)$$

Then, the output of the MMHSA is passed through a residual connection and layer normalization using the following Equation (4.16).

$$\text{Output}_1 = \text{LayerNorm}(\text{MaskedAttention}(Q, K, V) + X) \tag{4.16}$$

The decoder then attends to the encoder's output H through MHA. This allows the decoder to align its predictions with relevant encoder information. This ensures using the following Equation (4.17).

$$\text{Attention}\left(Q, K_{\text{encoder}}, V_{\text{encoder}}\right) = \text{softmax}\left(\frac{Q.K_{encoder}^{T}}{\sqrt{d_k}}\right).V_{\text{encoder}} \tag{4.17}$$

where Q is derived from the decoder's intermediate output $Output_1$, K_{encoder} and V_{encoder} come from the encoder's output H.

In the MHA mechanism, multiple attention heads are computed in parallel, allowing the model to attend to different parts of the sequence simultaneously. Each head computes its own attention, and the results are concatenated and passed through a linear transformation. The MHA can be mathematically represented as follows in Equation (4.18).

$$\text{MultiHead}\left(Q, K_{\text{encoder}}, V_{\text{encoder}}\right) = \text{Concat}(\text{head}_1, \text{head}_2, \ldots.\text{head}_\text{h}).W^o \tag{4.18}$$

where each attention head $head_i$ is computed as follows using Equation (4.19).

$$\text{head}_i = \text{Attention}(\text{Q}W_i{}^{Q}, K_{\text{encoder}}W_i{}^{K}, V_{\text{encoder}}W_i{}^{V}) \tag{4.19}$$

where, $W_i{}^{Q}, W_i{}^{K}, W_i{}^{V}$ are learnable weight matrices for the ith attention head, and W^o is the output weight matrix. The attention operation used here is similar to the earlier step, but the key and value matrices come from the encoder's output, and the query matrix comes from the decoder's intermediate output from the previous layer.

Once the MHA operation is complete, a residual connection is applied by adding the input from the previous step to the output of the attention mechanism. After that, layer normalization is applied to stabilize the learning process using Equation (4.20).

$$\text{Output}_2 = \text{LayerNorm}(\text{MultiHeadAttention}(Q, K_{\text{encoder}}, V_{\text{encoder}}) + \text{Output}_1) \tag{4.20}$$

Then, the FFN applies nonlinear transformations independently to each token for the Output_2. This FFN allows the decoder to capture complex patterns in the data by expanding the representation and then reducing it. The increase in dimensionality via W_1 enables the model to capture more complex relationships, while the reduction back to d_{model} preserves the original token representation. The output of the FFN is then passed through another residual connection and layer normalization using Equation (4.21).

$$\text{Output}_3 = \text{LayerNorm}(\text{FFN}(\text{X})) + \text{Output}_2) \tag{4.21}$$

Finally, after passing through the FFN, a final linear layer is applied to map the output back to the size of the vocabulary (for token prediction). A softmax function is applied to convert the logits into probabilities and is represented in Equation (4.22).

$$p = softmax(W_{\text{out}}.\text{Output}_3 + b_{\text{out}}) \quad (4.22)$$

where W_{out} the output is weight matrix and b_{out} is the output bias.

This produces the probability distribution over the vocabulary for the next token, which can then be used for prediction or generating the next token in sequence generation. Figure 4.1 shows the architecture of transformer.

4.2 ATTENTION MECHANISM

The **attention mechanism** [2] is a powerful computational technique that enables neural networks to focus on specific parts of an input sequence when generating an output. Rather than treating all input data equally, it dynamically assigns **weights** to different elements based on their relevance to the task at hand. This prioritization allows models to capture **long-range dependencies** and process complex sequences effectively. In NLP, attention mechanisms replicate human selective focus, increasing a model's capacity to absorb context and make decisions. By computing a **context vector**—a weighted average of the input sequence—attention mechanisms encapsulate the most relevant information, ensuring that the model's output reflects the importance of each input element. This capability is fundamental to **Transformers**, where attention enables tokens to interact and contextualize dynamically, significantly improving model performance and output quality in tasks like translation, summarization, and understanding.

4.2.1 Additive Attention (Bahdanau Attention)

Bahdanau attention [3] is a mechanism designed to improve the alignment of the decoder's focus on specific parts of the encoder's output during sequence-to-sequence tasks. Unlike dot-product attention, which uses a simple dot product to calculate similarity, additive attention uses a feed-forward neural network to compute attention scores, making it more flexible and potentially better at modeling complex relationships.

For an input sequence $X = [x_1, x_2, \ldots\ldots, x_n]$ the encoder generates hidden states $H = [h_1, h_2, \ldots\ldots, h_n]$, where h_i represents the hidden state of the $i-th$ token. At each decoding step t, the decoder computes its hidden state s_t. Additive attention then works as follows:

4.2.1.1 Compatibility Score Calculation

An alignment score e_{ti} is computed to measure the relevance between the decoder hidden states s_t and each encoder hidden state h_i. This is done using a feed-forward neural network with a trainable weight matrix W_a and is shown in Equation (4.23).

$$e_{ti} = v_a^T.\tanh(W_a[s_t; h_i]) \quad (4.23)$$

Here, $[s_t; h_i]$ is the concatenation of s_t and h_i, v_a is a trainable parameter vector.

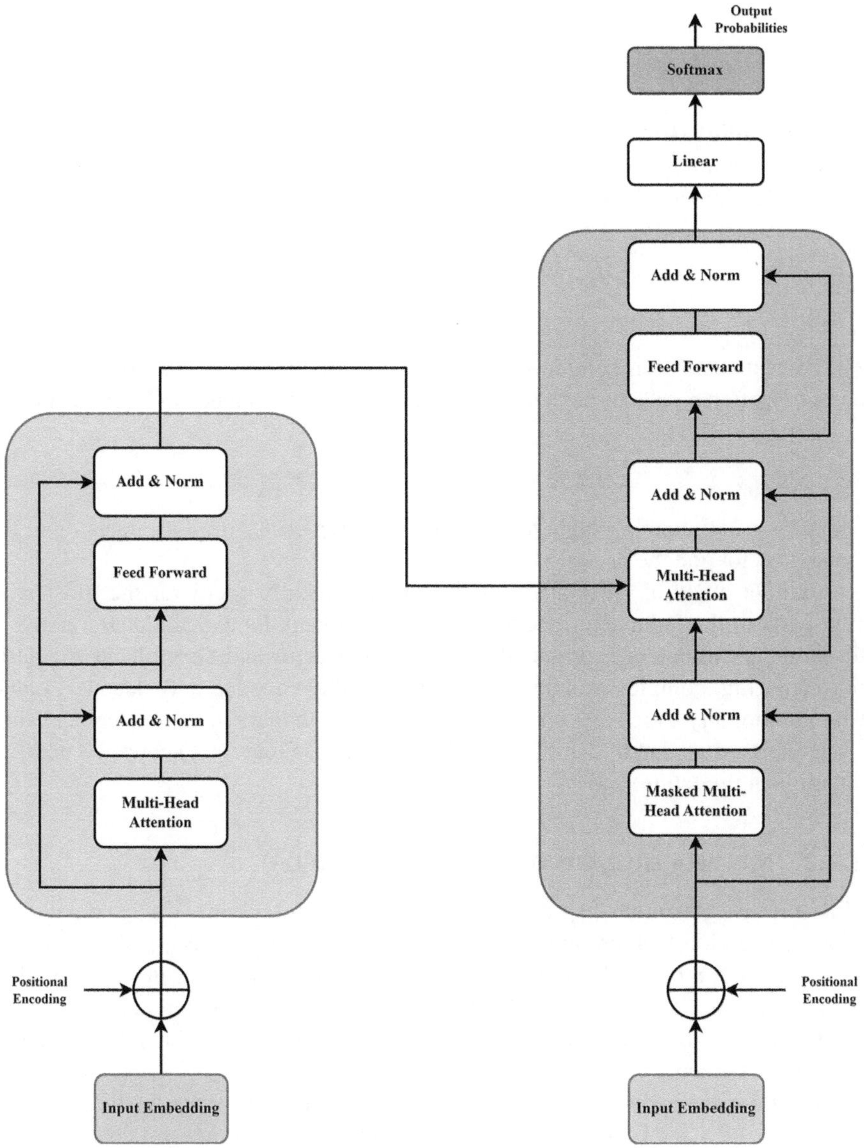

FIGURE 4.1 Transformer architecture.

4.2.1.2 Attention Weights

The alignment scores e_{ti} are passed through a *softmax* function to compute attention weights α_{ti}, which indicates the importance of each encoder hidden state h_i for the current decoding step t. The attention weights are calculated using the following Equation (4.24).

$$\alpha_{ti} = \frac{\exp(e_{ti})}{\sum_{i=1}^{n} \exp(e_{tj})} \quad (4.24)$$

4.2.1.3 Context Vector

Using the attention weights, a context vector c_t is computed as the weighted sum of the encoder hidden states and is shown in Equation (4.25).

$$c_t = \sum_{i=1}^{n} \alpha_{ti}.h_i \quad (4.25)$$

The context vector c_t is combined with the decoder hidden state s_t to produce the final output o_t, often passed through a feed-forward layer is formulated in Equation (4.26).

$$o_t = \tanh(W_c[c_t; s_t]) \quad (4.26)$$

where W_c is a trainable weight matrix, and $[c_t; s_t]$ represents the concatenation of the context vector and the decoder hidden state.

Additive attention allows the model to dynamically focus on the most relevant parts of the input sequence at each decoding step. Its use of a neural network to compute alignment scores makes it more powerful and versatile, particularly for capturing complex relationships between the encoder and decoder states. Computationally expensive for long sequences due to learned parameters and slow for large datasets due to complex matrix operations. Figure 4.2 shows the additive attention architecture.

4.2.2 Multiplicative Attention (Luong Attention)

Multiplicative Attention [4], also known as Luong Attention, is an alternative to additive attention that simplifies computations using dot products, making the process faster and more scalable. It computes the alignment scores using a dot product between the encoder and decoder hidden states, making it computationally more efficient compared to additive attention. This approach is widely used in attention-based models for sequence-to-sequence tasks.

For an input sequence $X = \left[x_1, x_2, \ldots\ldots, x_n\right]$ the encoder generates hidden states $H = [h_1, h_2, \ldots\ldots, h_n]$, where h_i represents the hidden state of the $i-th$ token. At each decoding step t, the decoder computes its hidden state s_t. The Luong attention mechanism works as follows:

4.2.2.1 Compatibility Score Calculation

An alignment score e_{ti} is calculated as a similarity measure between the decoder hidden states s_t and each encoder hidden state h_i. This is computed using the dot product or a variant of it and is calculated using Equation (4.27).

$$e_{ti} = s_t^T.h_i \quad (4.27)$$

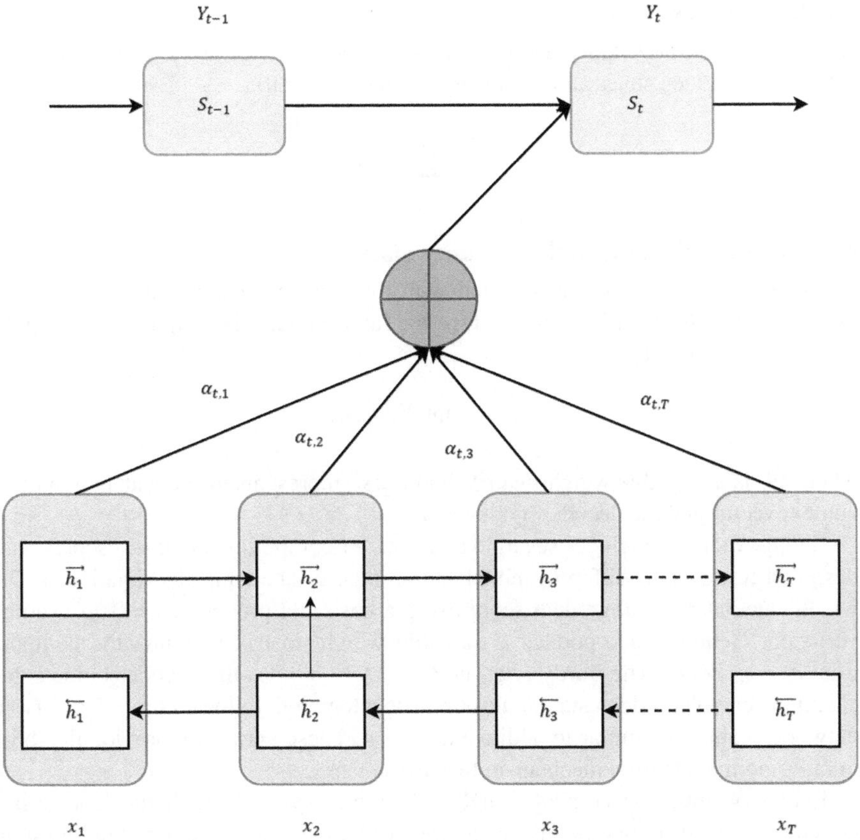

FIGURE 4.2 Additive attention.

Alternatively, a trainable weight matrix W_a can be applied to the encoder hidden state to form a generalized dot product and is shown in Equation (4.28).

$$e_{ti} = s_t^T . W_a . h_i \tag{4.28}$$

4.2.2.2 Attention Weights

The alignment scores e_{ti} are passed through a softmax function to compute attention weights α_{ti}, which indicates the importance of each encoder hidden state for the current decoding step t. The attention weights are calculated using the following Equation (4.29).

$$\alpha_{ti} = \frac{\exp(e_{ti})}{\sum_{j=1}^{n} \exp(e_{tj})} \tag{4.29}$$

4.2.2.3 Context Vector

Using the attention weights, a context vector c_t is computed as the weighted sum of the encoder hidden states and is shown in Equation (4.30).

$$c_t = \sum_{i=1}^{n} \alpha_{ti}.h_i \tag{4.30}$$

4.2.2.4 Combining with the Decoder State

The context vector c_t is concatenated with the decoder hidden state s_t and passed through a feed-forward layer to produce the final output. The output o_t is computed using Equation (4.31).

$$o_t = \tanh(W_c[c_t; s_t]) \tag{4.31}$$

where W_c is a trainable weight matrix, and $[c_t; s_t]$ represents the concatenation of the context vector and the decoder hidden state.

Luong Attention includes several variations for computing alignment scores, each designed to adapt to different model requirements. The simplest variation is Dot, which calculates the alignment score using a basic dot product: $e_{ti} = s_t^T.h_i$. Another variation, General, incorporates a trainable weight matrix to refine the computation: $e_{ti} = s_t^T.W_a.h_i$. The third variation, Concat, combines the decoder hidden state s_t and the encoder hidden state h_i through concatenation, followed by a feed-forward network, making it similar to additive attention. These variations provide flexibility in tailoring the attention mechanism to specific tasks.

Luong Attention is computationally efficient, especially with the Dot variant, which requires fewer operations. Its flexibility in alignment score computations make it adaptable to various models and datasets. It integrates seamlessly with RNNs and LSTMs, making it highly suitable for sequence-to-sequence tasks such as machine translation and summarization. However, while faster, it struggles with very long sequences due to quadratic complexity in input size and is less flexible in capturing complex relationships compared to additive attention. Figure 4.3 shows the multiplicative attention architecture.

4.2.3 Global Attention

The global attention mechanism [5] focuses on the entire sequence rather than limiting attention to specific parts. It allows every decoder hidden state to attend to all the hidden states of the encoder at each decoding step, enabling the model to consider context information and long-range dependencies by accessing the entire input sequence.

The encoders accept the input sequence X and convert it into a hidden state $H = [h_1, h_2, \ldots h_n]$ where h_i is the hidden state at i^{th} input token. The decoder processes the hidden state (H) of the encoder to generate the decoder's hidden state (S) at each time step. This hidden state S acts as a query vector for the attention mechanism.

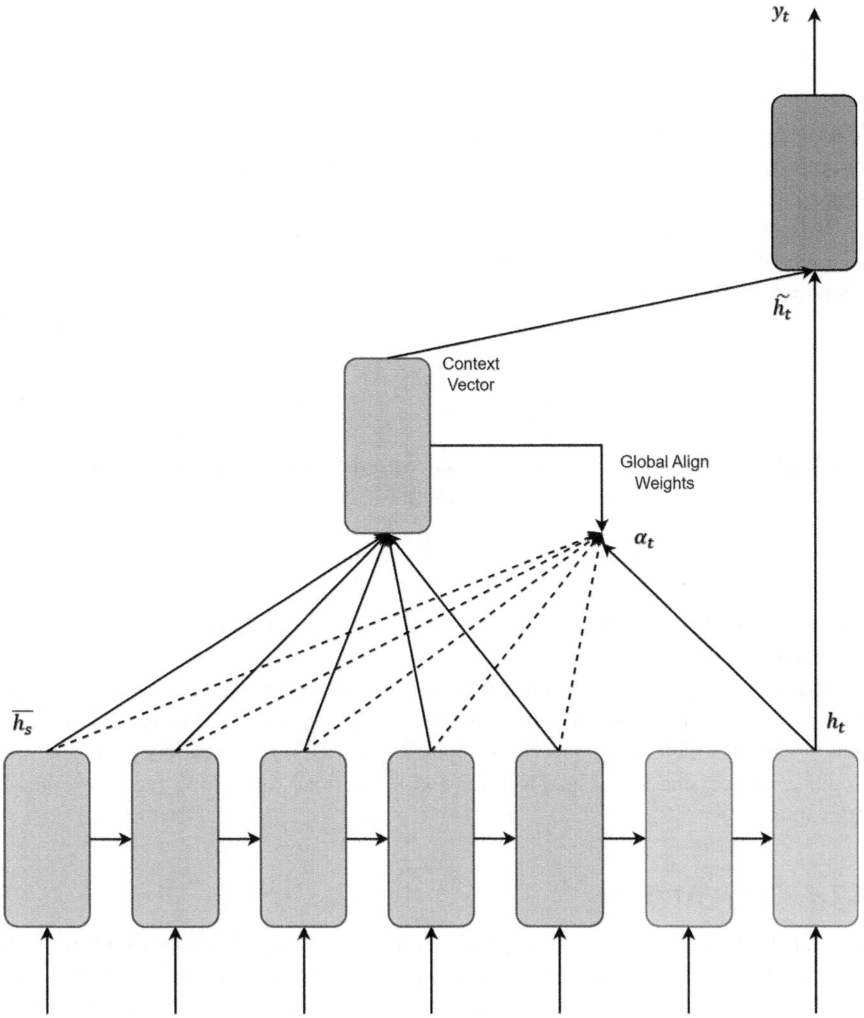

FIGURE 4.3 Multiplicative attention.

The attention mechanism then computes the alignment score to measure the similarity between the encoder hidden state (*H*) and decoder hidden state (*S*) which is formulated as follows in Equation (4.32).

$$as\left(s_t,\ h_i\right) = s_t^{\mathrm{T}}.W_a.h_i \tag{4.32}$$

where W_a is a trainable parameter.

Then, the attention weights are computed by feeding the alignment scores through a *softmax* function and is computed as follows in Equation (4.33).

$$\alpha_i^t = \frac{\exp\left(as\left(s_t, h_i\right)\right)}{\sum_{j=1}^{n} exp(as(s_t,h_j))} \tag{4.33}$$

With the help of the above alignment score α_i^t, the decoder identifies how much importance should be given to each hidden state of the encoder at each decoding step t.

This can be achieved by computing the context vector c_t which is a weighted average of the encoder hidden states to capture the relevant information for each decoding step using the following Equation (4.34).

$$c_t = \sum_{i=1}^{n} \alpha_i^t .\mathrm{h_i} \tag{4.34}$$

Finally, this context vector c_t is combined with the decoder hidden state to generate the final output ($\hat{s}_t$) and is shown in Equation (4.35).

$$\hat{s}_t = \tanh(W_c.[c_t; s_t]) \tag{4.35}$$

where $[c_t; s_t]$ represents the concatenation of context vector and the decoder hidden state at time step t.

The global attention mechanism helps the decoder understand the complete input representation, capturing relationships between distant tokens. However, it is computationally inefficient for very long input sequences, as it considers every element in the sequence, and it can lead to information overload by lacking focus on specific relevant parts.

4.2.4 Local Attention

The local attention mechanism [6] focuses on improving efficiency by limiting the attention to a smaller subset of the encoder's hidden states during each decoding step. Unlike global attention, which considers all hidden states, local attention narrows its focus to a specific window, balancing computational efficiency with contextual relevance.

Local attention processes only a fixed-size window of encoder hidden states, centered around a predicted position and having a size of $2D+1$, where D is a hyperparameter that determines the radius of the windows.

At each decoding step, the model predicts the center of the attention window p_t. This is determined using the previous decoder hidden state s_{t-1} through Equation (4.36).

$$p_t = \text{sigmoid}\left(W_p.s_{t-1}\right).T \tag{4.36}$$

where, W_p is a learnable parameter, s_{t-1} is the decoder's previous hidden state, and T is the total number of encoder hidden states.

To measure the relevance of each encoder hidden state within the window, alignment scores are calculated based on the similarity between the decoder hidden state s_t and the encoder hidden states h_i which is shown in Equation (4.37).

$$as\left(s_t,\ h_i\right) = s_t^{\mathrm{T}}.W_a.h_i \tag{4.37}$$

where W_a is a trainable parameter.

The alignment scores are transformed into attention weights using the *softmax* function, applied only within the restricted window and is formulated in Equation (4.38).

$$\alpha_i^t = \frac{\exp\left(as\left(s_t, h_i\right)\right)}{\sum_{j\in window}^{n} exp(as(s_t,h_j))} \tag{4.38}$$

Using the attention weights, the context vector c_t is computed as a weighted sum of the encoder hidden states within the window and is formulated in Equation (4.39).

$$c_t = \sum_{i\in window}^{n} \alpha_i^t .h_i \tag{4.39}$$

Finally, decoder combines the context vector c_t with its current hidden state s_t to produce the final output and is shown in Equation (4.40).

$$\hat{s}_t = tanh(W_c.[c_t; s_t]) \tag{4.40}$$

where $[c_t; s_t]$ represents the concatenation of context vector and the decoder hidden state at time step t and W_c is a trainable parameter.

Local attention is computationally efficient as it focuses only on a subset of hidden states, making it suitable for handling long input sequences. It ensures the decoder captures the most relevant information at each step, offering an effective balance between efficiency and context sensitivity. This mechanism is particularly useful for tasks where only specific parts of the input sequence are relevant. However, it limits the model's ability to capture global dependencies across the entire input sequence and may miss important context outside the local window.

4.2.5 Self Attention

The self-attention mechanism [1] allows the model to focus on both local and global dependencies dynamically, enabling a token to attend to any other token in the sequence. It enables every token in an input sequence to attend to all other tokens in the same sequence, helping capture contextual relationships and dependencies between tokens, irrespective of their position. Unlike global attention, which operates between the encoder and decoder, self-attention functions within a single input sequence, allowing the model to understand internal relationships effectively.

For an input sequence X, each token is transformed into three vectors: *query* (Q), *key* (K), *and value* (V), through learnable weight matrices W_Q, W_K *and* W_V, respectively. These are computed as follows in Equation (4.41).

$$Q = X.W_Q,\ K = X.W_K,\ V = X.W_v \tag{4.41}$$

where W_Q, W_K and W_v are the learnable weight matrices.

Then, the attention mechanism calculates the attention scores to measure the similarity between the query vector and key vectors, defined by the dot product. To ensure numerical stability, these scores are scaled by the square root of the dimensionality of the key vectors $(\sqrt{d_k})$.

$$Score(Q,K) = \frac{Q.K^T}{\sqrt{d_k}} \tag{4.42}$$

These scores are normalized using the *softmax* function to produce attention weights, which determine the importance of each token relative to others and is shown in Equation (4.43).

$$\alpha_{ij} = \frac{\exp\left(Score\left(Q_i, K_i\right)\right)}{\sum_k exp(Score\left(Q_i, K_k\right))} \tag{4.43}$$

Finally, the attention weights α_{ij} are used to compute a weighted sum of the value vectors V_j for each token and is shown in Equation (4.44).

$$c_i = \sum_j \alpha_{ij}.V_j \tag{4.44}$$

Finally, this context vector c_i is combined with the original input embeddings to produce the model's output for the token. The output representation incorporates both the token's original meaning and its contextual relationships with other tokens in the sequence. Still limited to a single attention mechanism, which may fail to capture diverse patterns or relationships in data. Figure 4.4 shows the architecture of self-attention.

4.2.6 Multihead Self-Attention (MHA)

Even though the self-attention worked well, a single-head attention mechanism may not capture different relationships within the data. MHA [7] solves this by using several attention heads in parallel, allowing the model to focus on different parts of the input simultaneously. Each attention head has its own set of learned weight matrices for queries, keys, and values, enabling each head to focus on different aspects of the input. Attention is computed independently for each head. For each head h, the context vector c_h is computed using scaled dot-product attention using Equation (4.45).

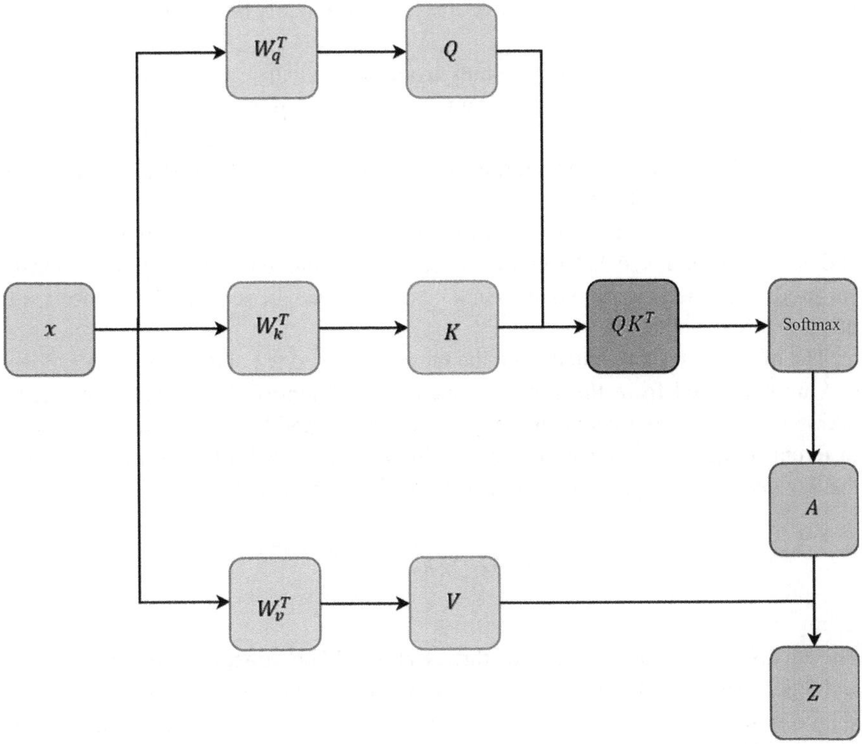

FIGURE 4.4 Self-attention.

$$c_h = \text{Self-Attention}(\mathrm{Q_h}, \mathrm{K_h}, \mathrm{V_h}) \tag{4.45}$$

Once the context vectors from all attention heads are computed, they are concatenated together. The concatenated context vectors are passed through a learned weight matrix W_o to produce the final output and is shown in Equation (4.46).

$$\text{MHA} = \text{Concat}\left(c_1, c_2, \ldots\ldots c_h\right).W_o \tag{4.46}$$

MHA allows the model to focus on various relationships in the data simultaneously, leading to a better understanding and improved performance for complex tasks. It captures different patterns in the input, enhancing overall model performance. However, it is computationally intensive due to multiple parallel attention heads and, while excellent for single-sequence tasks, lacks direct mechanisms for handling intersequence dependencies.

4.2.7 Cross-Attention

Cross-attention [8] is an attention mechanism similar to self-attention but operates between two different sequences rather than within a single sequence. It is commonly used in the encoder–decoder architecture (e.g., in models like Transformer for tasks like machine translation).

In cross-attention, the query comes from one sequence (typically the decoder's input), while the key and value come from a different sequence (typically the encoder's output). This mechanism allows the decoder to focus on different parts of the encoder's output while generating each token, providing the context necessary for producing meaningful outputs.

Input sequences of the cross-attention of source sequence X_s (from the encoder) and the target sequence X_t (from the decoder). The source sequence X_s is responsible for producing the key and value vectors, while the target sequence X_t generates the query vectors.

The query (Q) is generated from the target sequence X_t, and the key (K) and value (V) are generated from the source sequence X_s. Attention scores are calculated by taking the dot product between the query vector Q_t and key vector K_s from the two different sequences, followed by scaling by the square root of the dimensionality of the key vectors $(\sqrt{d_k})$ and is calculated using Equation (4.47).

$$Score(Q_t, K_s) = \frac{Q_t . K_s^T}{\sqrt{d_k}} \tag{4.47}$$

The attention scores are then passed through the *softmax* function to produce attention weights. These weights tell the model how much focus to give to each part of the source sequence while generating a token for the target sequence and is shown in Equation (4.48).

$$\alpha_{ij} = \frac{\exp\left(\text{Score}\left(Q_t, K_s\right)\right)}{\sum_k \exp(\text{Score}\left(Q_t, K_k\right))} \tag{4.48}$$

The context vector for each token in the target sequence is computed as a weighted sum of the value vectors V_s from the source sequence, based on the attention weights.

$$c_t = \sum_j \alpha_{ij} . V_s \tag{4.49}$$

The context vector c_t is then combined with the decoder's current state (usually through a feed-forward neural network) to generate the output token for the target sequence.

Cross-attention is a mechanism that enables one sequence (e.g., the decoder) to attend to another sequence (e.g., the encoder) in tasks involving multiple sequences, such as machine translation and question answering. It enhances context transfer between the sequences, allowing the model to capture dependencies and interrelations between them. While cross-attention improves performance in encoder-decoder models by aligning information across sequences, it inherits the computational complexity of MHA and may face challenges with very large input/output sequences.

4.3 PRETRAINED LANGUAGE MODELS

Pretrained models [9] have been the game changers of language processing, offering a foundation for understanding and generating human language. These models are built using extensive datasets to learn patterns, semantics, syntax, and contextual relationships in text. Leveraging unsupervised learning, these models predict the next word in a sequence based on previous words, capturing the intricate structure of human language. Once trained, these models can be fine-tuned for specific tasks such as sentiment analysis, machine translation, and text summarization. Fine-tuning involves adapting the pretrained model to smaller task-specific datasets, enabling it to specialize while conserving computational resources. The rise of pretrained models has significantly reduced the time, cost, and expertise needed to develop NLP systems from scratch, making them necessary tools in the field.

Transfer learning is the primary mechanism enabling the utility of pretrained models in NLP. It involves applying a model trained on a general dataset to a new, specific task with minimal additional data. This process saves time and resources while improving performance, as the pretrained model has already learned foundational language features. Transfer learning has expanded the potential of NLP applications, including automated text summarization, language translation, and conversational AI.

Pretrained models showed competent performance in the field of NLP by providing efficient and high-performance solutions for diverse applications. Some of the most notable include:

4.3.1 BERT (Bidirectional Encoder Representations from Transformers)

BERT [10], developed by Google, is a revolutionary language model that introduced the concept of bidirectional training. Unlike previous models that processed text from either left-to-right or right-to-left, BERT considers both directions simultaneously, allowing it to fully understand the context of each word in a sentence. This bidirectional approach is particularly effective for tasks that require deep contextual understanding, such as sentiment analysis, named entity recognition (NER), and question answering. By training on vast datasets like Wikipedia, BERT has set a new benchmark for NLP tasks, demonstrating its versatility and power. Variants such as RoBERTa, DistilBERT, and ALBERT further optimize its performance, making it a foundational model in modern NLP.

4.3.2 RoBERTa (Robustly Optimized BERT)

RoBERTa [11] is an enhanced variant of BERT, developed by Facebook AI. By training on larger datasets for extended durations and removing tasks like next-sentence prediction, RoBERTa focuses entirely on masked language modeling. These optimizations improve its ability to process and understand natural language, making it particularly effective for tasks like text classification and sentiment analysis. RoBERTa consistently outperforms its predecessor on multiple benchmarks, showcasing its robustness and adaptability.

4.3.3 DistilBERT

DistilBERT [12], created by Hugging Face, is a lightweight version of BERT designed to maintain high performance with fewer computational resources. By reducing the model size while retaining 97% of BERT's accuracy, DistilBERT is ideal for real-time applications and resource-constrained environments. It excels in tasks like question answering, text classification, and sentiment analysis, making it a practical choice for developers.

4.3.4 ALBERT (A Lite BERT)

ALBERT [13] is a resource-efficient variant of BERT that reduces model size through parameter sharing and factorization techniques. Despite its smaller size, ALBERT achieves similar or even superior performance on many NLP tasks. It is especially suitable for scenarios with limited computational power, offering a balance between efficiency and effectiveness.

4.3.5 XLNet (eXtreme Large-scale Language Model)

XLNet [14], developed collaboratively by Google and Carnegie Mellon University, combines the strengths of autoregressive and autoencoding models to overcome BERT's limitations. Unlike BERT, which uses masked language modeling, XLNet employs permutation-based training, allowing it to process text in a more flexible sequence. This approach captures dependencies between words more effectively, making XLNet excel in tasks like sentiment analysis, question answering, and text completion. By addressing issues such as context fragmentation, XLNet offers superior performance on long-form text and contextual understanding.

4.3.6 GPT (Generative Pre-Trained Transformer)

The GPT series [15], developed by OpenAI, is renowned for its text-generation capabilities. Beginning with GPT and evolving through GPT-2, GPT-3, and GPT-4, these models have grown exponentially in complexity and power. GPT-3, with its 175 billion parameters, is one of the largest language models ever created, capable of generating coherent and contextually accurate text. It is widely used for applications like creative writing, summarization, and conversational AI. GPT-4 extends this legacy by introducing multimodal capabilities, processing both text and images, though its exact technical details remain undisclosed. The GPT series has transformed fields such as customer support, content creation, and virtual assistants, setting new standards in NLP.

4.3.7 T5 (Text-to-Text Transfer Transformer)

T5 [16], developed by Google, reframes all NLP tasks as text-to-text problems. Whether it's translation, summarization, or question answering, T5 takes input text and generates an appropriate textual output. This unifying framework simplifies NLP tasks and enhances model versatility. T5 achieves state-of-the-art performance across a variety of benchmarks, making it one of the most adaptable and powerful models for applications such as machine translation and text summarization.

4.3.8 ELMo (Embeddings from Language Models)

ELMo [17], created by the Allen Institute for Artificial Intelligence, generates contextualized word embeddings by analyzing entire sentence contexts. Unlike static embedding models like GloVe, ELMo adapts word representations based on their usage within a sentence. This dynamic approach makes it highly effective for tasks like text classification, question answering, and sentiment analysis, where word meaning can vary significantly depending on context.

4.3.9 Transformer-XL

Transformer-XL [18] addresses the challenge of long-term dependency in language modeling by introducing a recurrence mechanism that retains information across sequences. Developed by researchers at Carnegie Mellon and Google Brain, it uses relative positional encoding to improve contextual understanding. This innovation makes Transformer-XL particularly effective for tasks requiring long-context comprehension, such as language modeling and text summarization.

4.3.10 Flair

Flair [19], developed by Zalando Research, combines multiple neural architectures to handle a wide range of NLP tasks, including text classification and named entity recognition (NER). It supports domain-specific customizations, making it highly adaptable. Flair's ability to integrate contextual embeddings like BERT and ELMo enhances its performance, offering a powerful toolkit for diverse NLP applications.

4.3.11 ELECTRA (Efficiently Learning an Encoder that Classifies Token Replacements Accurately)

ELECTRA [20] introduces a novel approach to training language models by replacing input tokens with synthetic alternatives generated by a small generator network. This strategy enables the model to learn by distinguishing real tokens from replacements rather than simply predicting masked tokens, as in traditional masked language models like BERT. This training method is computationally efficient and leads to improved performance on tasks such as text classification, sentiment analysis, and question answering, often achieving state-of-the-art results while using fewer resources.

4.3.12 UniLM (Universal Language Model)

UniLM [21] is a versatile pretrained model that combines both unidirectional and bidirectional transformers, making it capable of handling diverse NLP tasks like text generation, summarization, and classification. Its architecture allows it to seamlessly switch between different modes, such as left-to-right generation for tasks like translation and bidirectional understanding for tasks like comprehension. By leveraging this flexibility, UniLM achieves exceptional accuracy across a wide range of benchmarks and is particularly effective for sequence-to-sequence tasks.

4.3.13 MobileBERT

Designed specifically for resource-constrained environments, MobileBERT [22] is an optimized, lightweight version of BERT that achieves high accuracy with significantly reduced computational requirements. It employs techniques like layer-wise distillation and a carefully redesigned architecture to maintain performance levels comparable to BERT while being compact enough for deployment on mobile devices. MobileBERT is ideal for real-time applications such as virtual assistants, chatbots, and mobile-based NLP systems, where computational efficiency is critical.

4.3.14 DeBERTa (Decoding-enhanced BERT with Disentangled Attention)

DeBERTa [23] improves upon the BERT architecture by introducing separated attention mechanisms, which separately encode the content and position of words in a sentence. This separation allows the model to better capture subtle linguistic features, making it highly effective for tasks like sentiment analysis, text classification, and question answering. DeBERTa has achieved state-of-the-art results on several NLP benchmarks, showcasing its ability to handle complex language tasks with greater precision and understanding.

4.3.15 CTRL (Conditional Transformer Language Model)

CTRL [24] is a unique model designed for domain-specific text generation. It enables users to steer the output by providing predefined prompts or control codes, making it particularly useful for creating content tailored to specific needs, such as articles, reports, and dialogues. Its ability to condition text generation on specific topics or styles has made it a valuable tool in fields like content creation, scriptwriting, and customized conversational AI, offering unprecedented control over the generated output.

4.4 PRETRAINING OBJECTIVES

Pretraining objectives [25] guide the model's learning process by defining specific tasks during its initial training phase. This phase is essential for teaching the model to recognize language patterns, contextual relationships, and semantic structures. With these objectives, such as predicting missing words or generating the next token in a sequence, the model captures the underlying language, which enables it to create coherent, contextually relevant text and perform various natural language processing (NLP) tasks. Without pretraining objectives, a model would struggle to understand or produce meaningful language, limiting its usefulness in real-world applications.

This stage is critical in training models with the ability to process and generate language effectively. Depending on the architecture of the model whether Encoder-Only, Decoder-Only, or Encoder-Decoder different pretraining techniques are employed to suit the model's intended applications.

4.4.1 Encoder-Only Models

Encoder-Only models [26], such as BERT, focus on understanding the context and extracting meaningful representations from input data. These models excel in tasks that require detailed comprehension, such as text classification and sentiment analysis.

(a) **Masked Language Modeling (MLM)** [27]**:** One of the most common training techniques for Encoder-Only models is Masked Language Modeling. A portion of the input tokens is randomly masked, and the model is tasked with predicting these masked tokens using the surrounding context. This bidirectional approach enables the model to learn relationships in both forward and backward directions, promoting a deep understanding of input semantics.

(b) **Span Corruption and Reconstruction** [28]**:** In this approach, specific spans or segments of input data are deliberately corrupted, and the model learns to reconstruct the original sequence. This method enhances the model's ability to handle noise and variability in data, fostering robust representations.

(c) **Intra-Sentence and Inter-Sentence Relationships** [29]**:** Encoder-Only models are also trained to capture both intrasentence (within a single sentence) and intersentence (across sentences or documents) dependencies. This capability allows the model to understand contextual relationships at multiple levels, making it versatile for various comprehension tasks.

4.4.2 Decoder-Only Models

Decoder-Only models [30], like GPT-3, focus on generative tasks, where the goal is to predict or generate coherent and contextually appropriate text outputs. These models excel in creative text generation and conversational AI.

(a) **Causal Language Modeling (CLM)** [31]**:** In CLM, the model learns to predict the next token in a sequence based on all preceding tokens. This autoregressive training approach aligns naturally with the sequential nature of text, enabling models to generate grammatically correct and semantically meaningful outputs.

(b) **Autoregressive Training:** This involves predicting tokens one at a time while conditioning on previously generated tokens. This setup ensures the model learns the dependencies and ordering within the sequence, which is crucial for generating fluent text.

(c) **Nucleus Sampling (Top-k Sampling):** During training, nucleus sampling introduces a degree of randomness by selecting the next token from the top-k most likely options. This technique balances creativity with coherence, making the generated text diverse yet controlled.

(d) **Prompt Engineering and Conditioning:** Decoder-Only models can be trained using specific prompts to guide their outputs toward desired topics or styles. This capability enables fine-tuning and task-specific applications, ensuring the model produces tailored results.

4.4.3 Encoder–Decoder Models

Encoder–Decoder models [30] are designed for tasks involving a direct mapping from an input sequence to an output sequence, such as translation and summarization. These models combine the strengths of both Encoder-Only and Decoder-Only architectures.

(a) **Span Corruption and Alignment:** Similar to Encoder-Only models, span corruption in Encoder-Decoder setups involves masking or altering segments of input data. The decoder is trained to reconstruct these spans, ensuring the output aligns meaningfully with the input.
(b) **Sequence-to-Sequence Mapping:** This fundamental training approach involves encoding the input sequence into a contextual representation, which is then used by the decoder to generate a corresponding output sequence. This is a foundational technique for tasks like machine translation.
(c) **Copy Mechanisms and Attention Mechanisms:** Copy mechanisms enhance the ability of Encoder–Decoder models to directly copy tokens from the input sequence to the output, preserving essential information. Attention mechanisms, such as cross-attention, further refine the model's focus, ensuring it prioritizes the most relevant input features.
(d) **Teacher Forcing and Scheduled Sampling:** To address exposure bias during training, techniques like teacher forcing (using true tokens during training) and scheduled sampling (gradual transition to using model predictions) are employed. These methods enhance the consistency and coherence of the model's outputs.

Pretraining objectives play an essential role in shaping the capabilities of language models. By training techniques to the specific architecture like Encoder-Only, Decoder-Only, or Encoder–Decoder, researchers can create models that excel in understanding, generating, or mapping language. The use of objectives like MLM, CLM, span corruption, and attention mechanisms acquires the foundational skills necessary to tackle a wide range of real-world NLP tasks. Understanding these objectives not only provides insights into the working of modern language models but also highlights their transformative potential in applications ranging from creative writing to advanced machine translation.

4.5 FINE-TUNING VS. PROMPT ENGINEERING

Artificial intelligence (AI) has transformed how we handle complex tasks like understanding language, generating text, and creating specialized tools. At the heart of this progress are large language models (LLMs), which can be adapted and optimized to meet specific needs using two key techniques: *Fine-Tuning* and *Prompt Engineering* [32].

Fine-Tuning involves retraining a pretrained model on specialized data to adjust its internal settings, making it ideal for precise and domain-specific applications like medical diagnosis or sentiment analysis. In contrast, *Prompt Engineering* focuses on crafting detailed and effective inputs to guide the model's behavior without altering its underlying structure, making it a quick and flexible option for general-purpose or exploratory tasks. Together, these approaches provide powerful ways to maximize the potential of LLMs, whether through fine-tuning for accuracy or using prompts for rapid, cost-effective solutions

4.5.1 Fine-Tuning

Fine-Tuning is a method of optimizing a pretrained language model by retraining it on task-specific or domain-specific datasets. This process adjusts the model's weights and parameters, allowing it to specialize in particular areas while building on the broad knowledge gained during its initial training. It is particularly valuable for applications that require high accuracy and precision. For example, a chatbot designed for a clothing store needs to understand product-related queries, while a medical chatbot must process patient symptoms and provide relevant guidance. Fine-tuning ensures that the model adapts to such specific needs by learning from curated datasets tailored to the desired task.

Fine-tuning begins with *data preparation*, where a high-quality dataset relevant to the target task or domain is collected and preprocessed. This dataset serves as the foundation for retraining the model. Next, the model undergoes *additional training*, during which its parameters are updated to align with the specific requirements of the task. This process enables the model to adapt and specialize effectively. Finally, the *evaluation and feedback* stage assesses the model's performance, often incorporating human feedback to identify areas for improvement. Iterative adjustments are then made to refine the model's outputs further, ensuring optimal performance for the intended application.

Benefits of Fine-Tuning:

- **High Accuracy:** Fine-tuning allows for detailed customization, producing highly accurate results for specific tasks.
- **Domain Adaptation:** It can train a model to excel in niche domains, such as legal or technical applications.
- **Specialized Outputs:** Fine-tuned models can generate responses tailored to a particular style, tone, or context.

4.5.2 Prompt Engineering

Prompt Engineering takes a different approach by focusing on how the input is structured to guide the model's responses. Instead of modifying the model itself, users craft detailed and specific prompts that leverage the model's existing knowledge. This method is accessible and cost-effective, requiring no additional training or resources. For example, asking a model to "Summarize this article in 50 words" or "Generate a story about a space adventure" are prompts that direct the model's behavior. A well-designed prompt can result in clear, accurate, and contextually relevant outputs without altering the model's parameters.

Crafting effective prompts involves designing precise instructions or questions that clearly specify the desired output. Once the initial prompts are created, different structures are tested through *experimentation* to determine which one yields the most accurate and relevant results. This process is followed by *refinement*, where the prompts are iteratively adjusted to enhance clarity and specificity, ensuring the model consistently produces high-quality responses tailored to the task.

Benefits of Prompt Engineering:

- **Ease of Use:** Does not require technical expertise or retraining the model.
- **Cost-Effective:** Works with pretrained models, eliminating the need for additional computational resources.
- **Flexibility:** Prompts can be adjusted quickly for various tasks.

4.6 TRANSFER LEARNING IN NLP

Transfer Learning [33] is a machine learning approach where a model undergoes initial training on a large, general-purpose dataset and is subsequently refined using a smaller, task-specific dataset. This method allows the model to leverage prelearned knowledge from the initial phase, reducing the time and computational resources required for training on new tasks.

In the context of NLP, transfer learning typically employs large-scale pretrained language models like BERT or GPT, which have been trained on extensive text corpora to grasp language patterns and representations. These models are then fine-tuned for specialized applications, such as sentiment analysis, question answering, or translation tasks.

The key concepts of transfer learning are given as follows.

- **Pre-Training**: The stage where a model is trained on a vast dataset to develop an understanding of universal language patterns, including grammar, syntax, and semantics.
- **Fine-Tuning**: The process of tailoring a pre-trained model to a particular task or domain by training it further on a smaller, relevant dataset.

4.6.1 How Transfer Learning Works in NLP

4.6.1.1 Pretraining

The first step in transfer learning for NLP is the *pretraining* phase. During this phase, a model like *BERT*, *GPT*, or *T5* is trained on a large amount of text data, which could range from books, websites, news articles, and more. The aim here is to learn *language representations* – the syntactic, semantic, and contextual relationships between words, sentences, and even documents. This phase does not focus on any specific NLP task but instead on learning general language patterns that can be transferred to many tasks.

Some popular pretrained models include:

- **BERT** (Bidirectional Encoder Representations from Transformers) — focuses on context from both directions in a sentence.
- **GPT** (Generative Pretrained Transformer) — designed for language generation.
- **T5** (Text-to-Text Transfer Transformer) — treats all NLP tasks as a text generation problem.

4.6.1.2 Fine-tuning

Once pretraining is complete, the model is then adapted to a specific task, such as sentiment analysis, named entity recognition (NER), or text summarization. This is called *fine-tuning*. During fine-tuning, the pretrained model is exposed to a much smaller and domain-specific dataset. The model's parameters are adjusted slightly to adapt to the nuances of the new task while preserving the general knowledge it learned during pretraining.

The process of fine-tuning typically involves:

- Freezing some layers of the model to retain knowledge from pretraining.
- Updating the remaining layers with task-specific data.
- Using techniques like gradient descent to optimize the model's performance on the new task.

(c) Task-Specific Adaptation

After fine-tuning, the model is now ready to perform well on the new task. Its ability to generalize from the pretraining corpus allows it to quickly adjust to tasks even with limited training data. The model can also handle multiple tasks simultaneously, a feature that has been central to the recent rise of multitask learning.

(d) Advantages of Transfer Learning in NLP

- **Efficiency**: Transfer learning significantly reduces the need for large labeled datasets, as pretrained models already possess a robust understanding of language structures.
- **Improved Performance**: Models fine-tuned with transfer learning often achieve state-of-the-art results on various NLP tasks.
- **Reduced Training Time**: Since the pretrained models have already learned foundational features, the fine-tuning phase requires less computational effort compared to training from scratch.
- **Flexibility**: Pretrained models can be adapted to a wide range of downstream tasks across different domains, making them versatile tools for NLP applications.

(e) Applications of Transfer Learning in NLP

1. **Text Classification**: Transfer learning is widely used for sentiment analysis, spam detection, and topic classification tasks. Pretrained models like BERT classify text with high accuracy by understanding contextual relationships in the input data.
2. **Named Entity Recognition (NER)**: Models such as *RoBERTa* and *XLNet* can identify specific entities like names, dates, and locations from text, aiding in tasks such as information extraction and document analysis.
3. **Question Answering**: Fine-tuned models like T5 and BERT excel in tasks where the goal is to extract or generate precise answers from a given context, such as in the *SQuAD* dataset.
4. **Machine Translation**: Pretrained models like *mBERT* and T5 can be fine-tuned to translate text between languages efficiently, offering significant improvements over traditional methods.
5. **Text Summarization**: Transfer learning is employed in models like GPT and T5 to produce coherent and concise summaries of lengthy texts, such as news articles or research papers.

(f) Challenges in Transfer Learning for NLP

- **Domain Mismatch**: A significant difference between the data used for pretraining and fine-tuning can lead to suboptimal performance. Adapting models to specialized domains may require additional data or training.
- **Overfitting**: During fine-tuning, there is a risk of the model overfitting to the small task-specific dataset, reducing its ability to generalize.
- **Computational Requirements**: Pre-trained models are often large and require substantial memory and processing power for fine-tuning and inference.
- **Ethical Concerns**: Biases present in pre-training datasets can carry over to downstream tasks, impacting fairness and reliability.

SUMMARY

This chapter introduces the Transformer architecture and its crucial function in contemporary NLP. It emphasizes how it facilitates effective long-range dependency modeling by substituting parallelizable attention mechanisms for recurrent structures. The attention mechanism, a structure that enables models to concentrate on pertinent segments of the input sequence while generating each output, comes first. There are several types discussed: Scaled Dot-Product Attention (normalizing dot products to improve stability), MHA (capturing multiple types of relationships in parallel), Global Attention (considering all positions in the sequence), Local Attention (limiting focus to a neighborhood), Self-Attention (relating different positions of the same sequence), Multiplicative Attention (dot-product based scoring), Additive Attention (calculating relevance scores using feed-forward networks), and Cross Attention (linking encoder outputs with decoder queries).

Large neural architectures such as BERT, GPT, and T5 are trained on vast corpora to acquire generic linguistic knowledge, which can subsequently be tailored for particular applications, as explained in the section on pretrained language models. It encompasses pretraining goals including Causal Language Modeling, in which models predict the next token in an autoregressive manner, and Masked Language Modeling (MLM), in which certain tokens are hidden and predicted. Additionally, the differences between prompting and fine-tuning are discussed. Prompting uses the frozen model to provide inputs that elicit desirable behavior, typically with no task-specific training, whereas fine-tuning uses labeled data to modify the model's parameters for a target task.

QUESTIONS

1. Define the *Transformer architecture*. How does it differ from RNN-based models?
2. What is *self-attention* and why is it important in NLP?
3. Differentiate between Additive Attention and Multiplicative Attention with examples.
4. Explain what is meant by a *Pretrained Language Model (PLM)*. Give two examples of PLMs.
5. Explain the difference between *Fine-Tuning* and *Prompting* with suitable use cases.
6. If query vector $Q = [1,2]$, key vector $K = [2,1]$, and value vector $V = [3,4]$, compute the scaled dot-product attention score. (*Assume* $d_k = 2$).
7. In *Masked Language Modeling (MLM)*, a sentence "I like to play football" has the word "play" masked. If the model predicts the probabilities as:
   - $P(run) = 0.1$, $P(play) = 0.6$, $P(work) = 0.2$, $P(sleep) = 0.1$. What is the predicted masked word and why?
8. Analyze how MHA improves model performance compared to single-head attention.
9. Differentiate between Self-Attention and Cross Attention in the context of Seq2Seq models (e.g., machine translation).
10. Evaluate the impact of Transfer Learning in NLP. Why is it considered more efficient than training from scratch?
11. Compare causal language modeling (CLM) and masked language modeling (MLM) in terms of advantages, limitations, and typical use cases.
12. Design a Transformer-based pipeline for text summarization. Describe how pretraining, fine-tuning, and attention mechanisms work together in your design.
13. **Case Study: Transformer and Pretrained Language Models**
    Google introduced the Transformer architecture in 2017, which replaced recurrent models with the attention mechanism. The most powerful part is self-attention, which allows the model to capture relationships between all words in a sentence at once. For example, in the sentence "The cat sat on the mat because it was tired", self-attention helps the model understand that

"it" refers to "the cat." Later, pretrained language models like BERT (using Masked Language Modeling) and GPT (using Causal Language Modeling) became popular. These models are first trained on large text data and then fine-tuned for tasks like sentiment analysis, machine translation, or question answering. This shows how attention + pretraining changed NLP, making tasks more accurate and reducing the need for training from scratch. Explain how the attention mechanism in the Transformer helps pretrained models like BERT or GPT perform better in NLP tasks. Give one example to support your answer.

REFERENCES

[1] A. Vaswani, N. Shazeer, N. Parmar, J. Uszkoreit, L. Jones, A. N. Gomez *et al.*, "Attention is All You Need," in *Advances in Neural Information Processing Systems (NeurIPS),* Jun. 2017.

[2] D. Soydaner, "Attention Mechanism in Neural Networks: Where it Comes and Where it Goes," *Neural Computing and Applications*, Apr. 2022, doi: 10.1007/s00521-022-07366-3.

[3] D. Bahdanau, K. Cho, and Y. Bengio, "Neural Machine Translation by Jointly Learning to Align and Translate," in *Proc. of the International Conference on Learning Representations (ICLR)*, May 2016, arXiv:1409.0473.

[4] M.-T. Luong, H. Pham, and C. D. Manning, "Effective Approaches to Attention-based Neural Machine Translation," in *Proc. of the Conference on Empirical Methods in Natural Language Processing (EMNLP)*, Sep. 2015, arXiv:1508.04025.

[5] Y. Liu, Z. Shao, and N. Hoffmann, "Global Attention Mechanism: Retain Information to Enhance Channel-Spatial Interactions," arXiv preprint, Dec. 2021, arXiv:2112.05561.

[6] I. Aguilera-Martos, A. Herrera-Poyatos, J. Luengo, and F. Herrera, "Local Attention Mechanism: Boosting the Transformer Architecture for Long-Sequence Time Series Forecasting," arXiv preprint, Oct. 2024, arXiv:2410.03805.

[7] J.-B. Cordonnier, A. Loukas, and M. Jaggi, "Multi-Head Attention: Collaborate Instead of Concatenate," arXiv preprint, May 2021, arXiv:2006.16362.

[8] H. Liu, W. Zhang, J. Xie, F. Faccio, M. Xu, T. Xiang *et al.*, "Faster Diffusion via Temporal Attention Decomposition," arXiv preprint Feb. 2025, arXiv:2404.02747.

[9] J. Li, T. Tang, W. X. Zhao, J.-Y. Nie, and J.-R. Wen, "Pretrained Language Models for Text Generation: A Survey," *ACM Computing Surveys*, May 2022, arXiv:2201.05273.

[10] J. Devlin, M.-W. Chang, K. Lee, and K. Toutanova, "BERT: Pre-training of Deep Bidirectional Transformers for Language Understanding," ," in *Proc. of the North American Chapter of the Association for Computational Linguistics (NAACL)*, May 2019, arXiv:1810.04805.

[11] Y. Liu, M. Ott, N. Goyal, J. Du, M. Joshi, D. Chen *et al.*, "RoBERTa: A Robustly Optimized BERT Pretraining Approach," arXiv preprint, Jul. 2019, arXiv:1907.11692.

[12] V. Sanh, L. Debut, J. Chaumond, and T. Wolf, "DistilBERT, a Distilled Version of BERT: Smaller, Faster, Cheaper and Lighter," arXiv preprint, Mar. 2020, arXiv:1910.01108.

[13] Z. Lan, M. Chen, S. Goodman, K. Gimpel, P. Sharma, and R. Soricut, "ALBERT: A Lite BERT for Self-Supervised Learning of Language Representations," in *Proc. of the International Conference on Learning Representations (ICLR)*, Feb. 2020, arXiv:1909.11942.

[14] Z. Yang, Z. Dai, Y. Yang, J. Carbonell, R. Salakhutdinov, and Q. V. Le, "XLNet: Generalized Autoregressive Pretraining for Language Understanding," in *Advances in Neural Information Processing Systems (NeurIPS),* Jan. 2020, arXiv:1906.08237.

[15] T. B. Brown, B. Mann, N. Ryder, M. Subbiah, J. Kaplan, P. Dhariwal *et al.*, "Language Models are Few-Shot Learners," in *Advances in Neural Information Processing Systems (NeurIPS)*, Jul. 2020, arXiv:2005.14165.

[16] C. Raffel, N. Shazeer, A. Roberts, K. Lee, S. Narang, M. Matena *et al.*, "Exploring the Limits of Transfer Learning with a Unified Text-to-Text Transformer," *Journal of Machine Learning Research (JMLR)*, Sep. 2023, arXiv:1910.10683.

[17] M. E. Peters, M. Neumann, M. Iyyer, M. Gardner, C. Clark, K. Lee *et al.*, "Deep Contextualized Word Representations," in *Proc. of the North American Chapter of the Association for Computational Linguistics (NAACL)*, Mar. 2018, arXiv:1802.05365.

[18] Z. Dai, Z. Yang, Y. Yang, J. Carbonell, Q. V. Le, and R. Salakhutdinov, "Transformer-XL: Attentive Language Models Beyond a Fixed-Length Context," in *Proc. of the Association for Computational Linguistics (ACL)*, Jun. 2019, arXiv:1901.02860.

[19] R. Xiao, S. Kim, M.-I. Georgescu, Z. Akata, and S. Alaniz, "FLAIR: VLM with Fine-Grained Language-Informed Image Representations," arXiv preprint, Dec. 2024, arXiv:2412.03561.

[20] K. Clark, M.-T. Luong, Q. V. Le, and C. D. Manning, "ELECTRA: Pre-training Text Encoders as Discriminators Rather Than Generators," in *Proc. of the International Conference on Learning Representations (ICLR)*, Mar. 2020, arXiv:2003.10555.

[21] L. Dong, N. Yang, W. Wang, F. Wei, X. Liu, Y. Wang *et al.*, "Unified Language Model Pre-training for Natural Language Understanding and Generation," in *Advances in Neural Information Processing Systems (NeurIPS)*,Oct. 2019, arXiv:1905.03197.

[22] Z. Sun, H. Yu, X. Song, R. Liu, Y. Yang, and D. Zhou, "MobileBERT: A Compact Task-Agnostic BERT for Resource-Limited Devices," in *Proc. of the Association for Computational Linguistics (ACL)*, Apr. 2020, arXiv:2004.02984.

[23] P. He, X. Liu, J. Gao, and W. Chen, "DeBERTa: Decoding-Enhanced BERT with Disentangled Attention," in *Proc. of the International Conference on Learning Representations (ICLR)*, Oct. 2021, arXiv:2006.03654.

[24] N. S. Keskar, B. McCann, L. R. Varshney, C. Xiong, and R. Socher, "CTRL: A Conditional Transformer Language Model for Controllable Generation," arXiv preprint, Sep. 2019, arXiv:1909.05858.

[25] Ç. Yıldız, N. K. Ravichandran, N. Sharma, M. Bethge, and B. Ermis, "Investigating Continual Pretraining in Large Language Models: Insights and Implications," arXiv preprint, Feb. 2025, arXiv:2402.17400.

[26] D. Wu, W. U. Ahmad, and K.-W. Chang, "On Leveraging Encoder-Only Pre-Trained Language Models for Effective Keyphrase Generation," arXiv preprint, Feb. 2024, arXiv:2402.14052.

[27] K. Sinha, R. Jia, D. Hupkes, J. Pineau, A. Williams, and D. Kiela, "Masked Language Modeling and the Distributional Hypothesis: Order Word Matters Pre-training for Little," in *Proc. of the Conference on Empirical Methods in Natural Language Processing (EMNLP)*, Sep. 2021, arXiv:2104.06644.

[28] K. Ye, H. Jiang, A. Rostamizadeh, A. Chakrabarti, G. DeSalvo, J.-F. Kagy *et al.*, "SpacTor-T5: Pre-training T5 Models with Span Corruption and Replaced Token Detection," arXiv preprint, Jan. 2024, arXiv:2401.13160.

[29] P. Gupta, S. Rajaram, H. Schütze, B. Andrassy, and T. Runkler, "Neural Relation Extraction Within and Across Sentence Boundaries," arXiv preprint, Jan. 2019, arXiv:1810.05102.

[30] Z. Fu, W. Lam, Q. Yu, A. M.-C. So, S. Hu, Z. Liu *et al.*, "Decoder-Only or Encoder-Decoder? Interpreting Language Model as a Regularized Encoder-Decoder," arXiv preprint, Apr. 2023, arXiv:2304.04052.

[31] N. Micheletti, S. Belkadi, L. Han, and G. Nenadic, "Exploration of Masked and Causal Language Modelling for Text Generation," arXiv preprint, Aug. 2024, arXiv:2405.12630.

[32] J. Shin, C. Tang, T. Mohati, M. Nayebi, S. Wang, and H. Hemmati, "Prompt Engineering or Fine-Tuning: An Empirical Assessment of LLMs for Code," arXiv preprint, Feb. 2025, arXiv:2310.10508.

[33] Z. Alyafeai, M. S. AlShaibani, and I. Ahmad, "A Survey on Transfer Learning in Natural Language Processing," arXiv preprint, May 2020, arXiv:2007.04239.

5 Fundamentals of Large Language Models

5.1 TOKENIZATION

Tokenization [1] in NLP is the process of breaking down text into smaller units called tokens. These tokens can represent words, subwords, characters, phrases, or numbers, depending on the granularity required for the task. Tokenization serves as the foundational step in the NLP pipeline, transforming unstructured text into a structured format that computers can process and analyze. For example, in the sentence, "Tokenization splits the text into meaningful units", tokenization could segment it into individual words like "Tokenization", "splits", "the", "text", "into", "meaningful", "units".

There are four types of tokenization, one is word tokenization, second is sentence tokenization, third is subword tokenization, and fourth is character tokenization.

(i) **Word Tokenization:** Splits text into individual words, treating each word as a separate token. For example, the input is " Word tokenization is essential for text analysis," and the output is to be "Word," "tokenization," "is," "essential," "for," "text," and "analysis."

(ii) **Sentence Tokenization:** Sentence tokenization breaks text into sentences, making it useful for tasks that require individual sentence analysis or processing. For example, "Tokenization splits the text into meaningful units. Sentence tokenization divides text into individual sentences." and the output of the sentence tokenized is "Tokenization splits the text into meaningful units." "Sentence tokenization divides text into individual sentences."

(iii) **Subword Tokenization:** Words divide into smaller units, such as prefixes, suffixes, or stems. This is especially useful for handling out-of-vocabulary words and morphologically complex languages. For example, "Tokenization" into Token" and "ization"

(iv) **Character Tokenization:** Splits text into individual characters, often used in character-level language models or for analysing types and spellings. For example, "Tokenization" into "T","o","k","e","n","i","z","a","t","i","o","n". **Subword tokenization** methods have been developed, with three widely used techniques being Byte Pair Encoding (BPE), WordPiece Encoding, and

DOI: 10.1201/9781003650065-5

SentencePiece Encoding. These methods break words into smaller subword units, which helps improve model performance, especially when dealing with out-of-vocabulary words or rare terms.

5.2 BYTE PAIR ENCODING (BPE)

BPE [2] is an effective tokenization technique that iteratively merges the most frequent adjacent character pairs to create subword units. This process continues until a predefined vocabulary size is reached, allowing the model to break words into meaningful subcomponents rather than treating them as atomic units. The primary goal of BPE is to reduce vocabulary size while preserving essential linguistic features, making it particularly useful in handling rare or unseen words in NLP tasks. Unlike traditional word-based tokenization, which struggles with out-of-vocabulary words, BPE splits words into subword units, ensuring better generalization and improved model performance.

For example, consider the word "tokenization" in a BPE-based tokenization system. Initially, the word is split into individual character tokens: ['t', 'o', 'k', 'e', 'n', 'i', 'z', 'a', 't', 'i', 'o', 'n']. The algorithm then identifies and merges the most frequently occurring adjacent character pairs. First, "t" and "o" are combined to form "to," resulting in the sequence ['to', 'k', 'e', 'n', 'i', 'z', 'a', 't', 'i', 'o', 'n']. Next, the frequently occurring pair "i" and "z" merge into "iz," and "t" and "i" combine into "ti." After several iterations, the final segmentation might look like ['to', 'ken', 'iz', 'a', 'tion'], reducing the number of tokens while still preserving word structure.

5.2.1 BPE ALGORITHM FORMULA

1. Start with a vocabulary containing all unique characters in the corpus.
2. Compute the frequency of adjacent character pairs.
3. Merge the most frequent pair (A, B) → AB.
4. Repeat until the desired vocabulary size is reached.

Mathematically, the merge process can be represented as follows using Equation (5.1).

$$V_t = V_{t-1} \cup \{AB\} \tag{5.1}$$

where V_t is the vocabulary at step t, V_{t-1} is the vocabulary from the previous step, and AB is the merged pair.

For example, Consider the word *"tokenization"* in a BPE-based tokenization system. Initially, the word is split into individual character tokens.

$$['t','o','k','e','n','i','z','a','t','i','o','n']$$

The algorithm identifies and merges the most frequently occurring adjacent character pairs. First, "*t*" and "*o*" are combined to form to.

$$['to','k','e','n','i','z','a','t','i','o','n']$$

Next, "*i*" and "*z*" merge into "*iz*" and "*t*" and "*i*" combine into "*ti*." After several iterations, the final segmentation might look like the following

$$['to','ken','iz','a','tion']$$

reducing the number of tokens while still preserving word structure.

The advantage of BPE lies in its ability to efficiently reduce vocabulary size while maintaining flexibility in representing various words. It is particularly beneficial for languages with complex morphology, where traditional tokenization methods might fail. BPE also enhances text compression and speeds up model training by limiting the number of unique tokens. In NLP applications, it is widely used in models such as BERT, GPT, and T5, where tokenization plays a crucial role in processing vast amounts of text data.

5.2.2 Word Piece Encoding

Word piece encoding [3] is another subword tokenization technique widely used in modern NLP models like BERT and ALBERT. Unlike BPE, which merges the most frequent adjacent character pairs, Word Piece builds its vocabulary based on the probability of word sequences, optimizing how words are segmented. It helps improve the handling of rare and out-of-vocabulary words by breaking them into meaningful subword components, making it particularly effective for morphologically rich languages. Word piece starts with an initial vocabulary containing all individual characters and iteratively adds new subwords based on their likelihood in the training corpus. The model learns to segment words efficiently by maximizing the likelihood of the training data. Instead of merging based on frequency alone (like BPE), Word Piece uses a probabilistic approach, selecting merges that contribute most to overall data representation.

For example, the word "tokenization" is first split into individual characters: ['t', 'o', 'k', 'e', 'n', 'i', 'z', 'a', 't', 'i', 'o', 'n']. The algorithm then merges the most frequently occurring subword pairs. First, "to" and "ken" are combined to form ['to', 'ken', 'ization']. After further merging, the final tokenization becomes ['token', '##ization'], where "##" indicates that "ization" is a continuation of a previous token rather than a standalone word. This method ensures that common prefixes and suffixes remain intact, helping the model understand different word variations.

5.2.2.1 Word-Piece Algorithm

The WordPiece algorithm follows a probabilistic approach using the following Equation (5.2).

$$P(w) = P(w_1) \times P(w_2 \mid w_1) \times \ldots \times P(w_n \mid w_{n-1}) \tag{5.2}$$

where $P(w)$ represents the probability of the entire word sequence, and each subword token is chosen based on maximizing likelihood over the training corpus.

For example, the word "***tokenization***" is first split into individual characters.

$$['t','o','k','e','n','i','z','a','t','i','o','n']$$

The algorithm merges the most frequent subword pairs. First, "*to*" and "*ken*" are combined to form the $['to','ken','ization']$.

After further merging, the final tokenization becomes ['*token*', '##*ization*'].

where "##" indicates that "*ization*" is a continuation of a previous token rather than a standalone word.

It reduces vocabulary size while preserving meaningful subword components, making it efficient for memory and computation. It helps handle rare or unseen words by breaking them into familiar subunits instead of using an unknown token. By maintaining common prefixes and suffixes, it allows models to recognize patterns across similar words, improving understanding. This is especially useful for morphologically complex languages and low-resource languages. Word Piece also enhances contextual representation, making models like BERT more effective for tasks like translation and sentiment analysis. Its efficient structure speeds up training and improves accuracy in deep learning applications.

5.2.3 Sentence Piece Encoding

Sentence Piece [4] is another powerful subword tokenization technique widely used in NLP. Unlike BPE and Word Piece, which require whitespace-based text segmentation before tokenization, Sentence Piece processes raw text without requiring predefined token boundaries. This makes it highly effective for languages that do not use spaces (e.g., Chinese, Japanese) and for handling multilingual data efficiently. Sentence Piece treats text as a continuous sequence of characters rather than predefined words or spaces. It learns subword units using techniques like Unigram Language Model (ULM) or BPE to create a flexible vocabulary. This allows it to tokenize text efficiently, handling out-of-vocabulary words and maintaining language structure across different writing systems.

For example, consider the word "tokenization" being processed using Sentence Piece. Given the input text "Tokenization is important," the tokenization output produced by Sentence Piece would be ['_token', 'ization', '_is', '_important', '.']. In this output, the underscore (_) denotes a space, indicating the beginning of a new word. The word "tokenization" is split into two subword tokens: "token" and "ization." This allows the model to efficiently handle variations of the word, such as "organization." In this case, the word "organization" would be tokenized as ["organ", "ization"]. Thus, Sentence Piece enables the model to recognize and process similar words more effectively by breaking them down into smaller, meaningful subword units.

5.2.3.1 Sentence Piece Algorithm

Sentence piece follows a probabilistic approach using either ULM or BPE to learn subword units and is formulated using the following Equation (5.3).

$$P(w) = \prod_{i=1}^{n} P\left(s_i\right) \tag{5.3}$$

where w is a sequence of subwords s_i, and the algorithm maximizes the probability of segmenting text optimally.

For example, Consider the word *"tokenization"*being processed using SentencePiece. Given the input text *"Tokenization is important,"* the tokenization output produced by SentencePiece would be

$$['\_token','ization','\_is','\_important','.']$$

In this output, the underscore (_) denotes a space, indicating the beginning of a new word. The word *"tokenization"* is split into two subword tokens:*"token"* and *"ization."* This allows the model to efficiently handle variations of the word, such as *"organization,"* which would be tokenized as [*"organ"*, *"ization"*].

Thus, Sentence piece enables the model to recognize and process similar words more effectively by breaking them down into smaller, meaningful subword units.

Sentence piece encoding handles whitespace-free languages like Chinese and Japanese, which do not use spaces for word separation. It learns subword units dynamically, making it flexible and adaptable for various NLP tasks. Like BPE and word piece, sentence piece breaks down rare or unknown words into meaningful sub-words, improving the model's handling of these words. It also provides better multilingual support by working efficiently across different languages without requiring separate tokenization rules. Sentence piece is used in popular NLP models like T5, mT5, and ALBERT, offering a robust approach to text tokenization and enhancing the performance of deep learning models across multiple languages and domains.

5.3 ENCODING POSITIONS

The transformer model, which has revolutionized natural language processing (NLP) and other sequence-based tasks, relies on positional encoding to incorporate sequential information. Positional encoding is essential for the model to distinguish the relative positions of tokens in the input sequence, as transformers themselves do not inherently model sequence order. Various methods of positional encoding have been proposed to address this challenge, each with its unique approach to capturing positional information.

5.3.1 ABSOLUTE POSITIONAL ENCODING

This method [5] assigns a unique positional embedding to each token in the sequence, which is added to the token embeddings. The positional embeddings can be either fixed (e.g., sinusoidal functions) or learned. The formula for the positional encoding PE at position i and dimension d is formulated as follows in Equations (5.4) and (5.5).

$$PE_{i,2d} = \sin\left(\frac{i}{10000^{2d/d_{model}}}\right) \tag{5.4}$$

$$PE_{i,2d+1} = \cos\left(\frac{i}{10000^{2d/d_{model}}}\right) \tag{5.5}$$

where d_{model} is the dimensionality of the model.

5.3.2 Relative Positional Encoding (RPE)

Absolute position encoding adds position information of each token in the sequence. But it failed to map the relative distance between tokens. This leads to incorrect modeling of tasks where relative order is needed [6]. To handle this issue, Shaw et al. [7] proposed a self-attention mechanism to consider the pairwise relationship between input tokens. Here, relative positional information is supplied to input tokens at two levels. One is at the key and the other is at the value.

In the first level, positional information is added to the key level and is formulated as follows in Equation (5.6).

$$e_{ij} = \frac{x_i W^Q (x_j.W^K + a_{ij}^K)}{\sqrt{d_z}} \tag{5.6}$$

where, x_i and x_j are two input tokens, W^Q is the weight matrix of query, W^K is the weight matrix of key a_{ij}^k is the relative positional information of key, and d_Z is the dimension.

Then, a softmax operation is applied, which is formulated as follows in the Equation (5.7).

$$\alpha_{ij} = softmax(e_{ij}) \tag{5.7}$$

Then relative position information is added at the value level and is formulated as follows using Equation (5.8).

$$z_i = \sum_{j=1}^{n} \alpha_{ij}.(x_j W^v + a_{ij}^v) \tag{5.8}$$

Instead of simply combining semantic embedding with absolute positional and relative positional information, it is added at two different levels: keys and values.

To achieve relative positions, a clipping method is introduced and is formulated as follows using the Equation (5.9).

$$clip\left(d(i,j)\right) = \min(\max\left(d(i,j), r_{min}\right), r_{max}) \tag{5.9}$$

where $d(i,j)$ is the relative distance between the positions of two tokens i and j, r_{min} is the minimum allowable distance, r_{max} is the maximum allowable distance.

After clipping, the RPE $r(i,j)$ is calculated as follows using Equation (5.10).

$$r(i,j) = W.(clip(d(i,j))) \tag{5.10}$$

where, w(.) is the learned embedding function.

5.3.3 Rotary Positional Encoding (RoPE)

Rotary positional encoding (RoPE) [8] was introduced as an enhancement to traditional positional encoding methods. Unlike absolute or RPE, RoPE directly encodes positional information into the attention mechanism by applying rotations to the query and key vectors. Instead of adding or concatenating position embeddings, RoPE multiplies the query and key vectors with a position-dependent rotation matrix. This allows the attention mechanism to inherently capture relative position information while maintaining the original structure of the Transformer.

For a given token at position t, the query and key vectors are represented using Equation (5.11).

$$Q_t, K_t \in R^d \tag{5.11}$$

where d is the model's hidden dimension. Each position t has an associated rotation matrix $R_\theta^{(t)}$, which is defined as follows in Equation (5.12).

$$R_\theta^{(t)} = \begin{pmatrix} \cos(t\theta) & -\sin(t\theta) \\ \sin(t\theta) & \cos(t\theta) \end{pmatrix} \tag{5.12}$$

This matrix performs a rotation by an angle $t\theta$, where θ is a predefined frequency. Each query Q_t and key K_t undergoes a transformation using the rotation matrix and is formulated as follows using Equation (5.13).

$$Q_t' = R_\theta^{(t)} Q_t,\ K_t' = R_\theta^{(t)} K_t \tag{5.13}$$

This transformation encodes positional information directly into the query and key vectors without needing separate position embeddings. Since attention scores are computed as a dot product between queries and keys which is shown in the following Equation (5.14).

$$A_{ts} = Q_t'.K_s' \tag{5.14}$$

The rotation ensures that the attention score inherently captures relative positional information, meaning the model learns the relative distance between tokens naturally.

5.3.4 Relative Bias Positional Encoding

Relative bias positional encoding [9] is an extension of RPE that introduces learnable bias terms to enhance attention mechanisms. Instead of encoding positional information through embeddings alone, it modifies attention scores by incorporating trainable position-dependent biases. This method improves Transformer performance by allowing models to learn finer-grained positional interactions, which is useful for tasks like machine translation, NLP, and long-sequence processing.

The standard self-attention computation in Transformers is formulated as follows in Equation (5.15).

$$A_{ts} = \frac{Q_t.K_s{}^T}{\sqrt{d}} \tag{5.15}$$

where, Q_t *and* K_s are the query and key vectors for tokens at positions t and s. d is the model dimension. A_{ts} is the raw attention score. A trainable relative bias term B_{ts} is introduced and is given in Equation (5.16).

$$A_{ts} = \frac{Q_t.K_s{}^T}{\sqrt{d}} + B_{ts} \tag{5.16}$$

where, B_{ts} is learned based on the relative position $(t-s)$, helping the model distinguish token interactions based on distance. The relative bias is typically parameterized as follows in Equation (5.17).

$$B_{ts} = W_b.f(t-s) \tag{5.17}$$

where, W_b is a learnable weight matrix and $f(t-s)$ is a function of the relative distance. A common choice for $f(t-s)$ is clipping, which restricts the range of relative positions and is formulated as follows in Equation (5.18).

$$f(t-s) = w_k(clip(t-s,r)) \tag{5.18}$$

where, w_k is a learnable embedding for relative distance $(t-s)$ and $clip(t-s,r) = max(-\mathrm{r}, \min(\mathbf{r}, \mathbf{t}-\mathbf{s}))$ limits the range to $[-r,r]$.
The final attention score with relative bias is calculated using the following Equation (5.19).

$$M_t = \sum_{s=1}^{t_{max}} Softmax(A_{ts})\, W(v) U_s + B_{ts} \tag{5.19}$$

where, the bias term shifts attention weights, influencing token relationships based on distance. Clipping prevents extremely large biases for distant tokens, stabilizing training.

5.4 ACTIVATION FUNCTIONS

Activation functions are a fundamental component of deep learning models. They introduce nonlinearity into neural networks, enabling them to learn complex patterns beyond simple linear transformations. Without activation functions, deep networks would behave like a linear regression model, limiting their ability to capture intricate relationships in data. The choice of activation function significantly impacts the efficiency, accuracy, and training stability of deep neural networks. Over the years, numerous activation functions have been developed, each with its strengths and weaknesses. This section explores the most widely used activation functions in deep learning, categorizing them based on their mathematical properties and practical applications.

5.4.1 Rectified Linear Unit (ReLU)

Rectified linear unit (ReLU) [10] is one of the most popular activation functions in deep learning. It is defined as follows in the Equation (5.20).

$$f(x) = \max(0, max) \tag{5.20}$$

It means outputs zero for negative inputs and retains positive values as they are. ReLU is computationally efficient and helps mitigate the vanishing gradient problem, making it ideal for deep networks. However, it suffers from dead neurons, where neurons can become inactive if they consistently receive negative inputs.

5.4.2 Gaussian Error Linear Unit

Gaussian error linear unit (GELU) [11] is a smooth activation function used in modern transformer-based architectures like BERT and GPT. The GELU is calculated using the following Equation (5.21).

$$f(x) = x.\Phi(\mathrm{x}),\quad \Phi(\mathrm{x}) = \frac{1}{2}\left(1 + \tanh\left(\sqrt{\frac{2}{\pi}}\left(x + 0.044715x^3\right)\right)\right) \tag{5.21}$$

where, the GELU activation function is $x.\Phi(\mathrm{x})$ *and* $\Phi(\mathrm{x})$ *is* the standard Gaussian cumulative distribution function. Unlike ReLU, GELU applies a probabilistic approach by weighting inputs based on a Gaussian distribution. This results in a smoother gradient flow, improving training stability and accuracy in NLP and vision tasks.

5.4.3 Sigmoid Activation Function

The sigmoid function [12] maps any input to a range between 0 and 1, making it useful for binary classification tasks. The mathematical formulation of sigmoid activation function is given in Equation (5.22).

$$f(x) = \frac{1}{1 + e^{-x}} \tag{5.22}$$

However, it suffers from the vanishing gradient problem, where gradients become too small during backpropagation, slowing down training. Due to this limitation, sigmoid is rarely used in deep networks but remains relevant for logistic regression and certain probabilistic models.

5.4.4 Hyperbolic Tangent (Tanh) Activation

Tanh is similar to the sigmoid function but centers outputs around zero, mapping inputs to a range between −1 and 1. The mathematical formulation of *tanh* activation function is given in Equation (5.23).

$$f(x) = \frac{e^x - e^{-x}}{e^x + e^{-x}} \tag{5.23}$$

This property makes it more effective than sigmoid in some cases, as it allows for stronger gradients. However, it still suffers from vanishing gradients, making it less preferable for very deep networks.

5.4.5 Leaky ReLU

Leaky ReLU [13] is an extension of ReLU that allows small negative values instead of completely zeroing them out. This prevents dead neurons, ensuring that all units can contribute to learning. The function is defined as follows using Equation (5.24).

$$f(x) = \begin{cases} x, & x \geq 0 \\ \alpha x, & x < 0 \end{cases} \tag{5.24}$$

where, α is a small constant(e.g., 0.01).It is used in GANs, deep CNNs.

5.4.6 Swish (Self-Gated Activation)

The Swish activation function is a continuous, non-monotonic function that was developed by researchers at Google. It is defined as follows in Equation (5.25).

$$f(x) = x.\sigma(x) \tag{5.25}$$

where $\sigma(x) = \frac{1}{1+e^x}$ is the sigmoid function.

Unlike ReLU, Swish is smooth and nonmonotonic, leading to better gradient flow and improved accuracy in deep models like EfficientNet.

5.4.7 Softplus Activation

The *Softplus* activation function serves as a gentle approximation of the ReLU (ReLU) function. It can be expressed through the definition provided in Equation (5.26).

$$f(x) = \ln(1 + e^x) \tag{5.26}$$

Unlike ReLU, it allows for small positive values even for negative inputs, preventing dead neurons. However, it is computationally more expensive than ReLU.

5.4.8 Exponential Linear Unit

Exponential linear unit (ELU) improves on ReLU by allowing negative values, preventing neuron death while maintaining strong positive activations. It is defined as follows in Equation (5.27).

$$f(x) = \begin{cases} x, & x \geq 0 \\ \alpha(e^x - 1), & x < 0 \end{cases} \tag{5.27}$$

where α is a hyperparameter.

5.4.9 Mish Activation Function

Mish is a newer activation function that smoothly approximates ReLU and Swish. It improves gradient flow and generalization, making it useful for computer vision and NLP models. The function is defined as follows in Equation (5.28).

$$f(x) = x\tanh(\ln(1 + e^x)) \tag{5.28}$$

where *tanh* is the hyperbolic tangent, introducing smoothness and bounded output.

5.4.10 Parametric ReLU

Parametric ReLU (PReLU) is a variation of Leaky ReLU where the negative slope is a learnable parameter rather than a fixed value. This allows the network to adaptively learn optimal slopes for different neurons, improving performance in deep networks. The function is defined as follows in Equation (5.29).

$$f(x) = \begin{cases} x, & x \geq 0 \\ \alpha x, & x < 0 \end{cases} \tag{5.29}$$

where, α is learnable parameter.

5.4.11 Maxout Activation Function

Maxout does not follow a fixed function but learns the best activation dynamically. It is used in adversarial learning and GANs to prevent vanishing gradients while maintaining flexibility. It is defined as follows in Equation (5.30).

$$f(x) = \max(w_1^T x + w_2^T x + b) \tag{5.30}$$

where w_1 and w_2 are the learnable parameters, and b is the bias.

5.4.12 Siren (Periodic Activation Function)

Siren is a periodic activation function used in implicit neural representations (INR) for modeling continuous signals. Provides periodicity useful for wave-based and physics-informed models. It is defined as follows in Equation (5.31).

$$f(x) = \sin(Wx) \tag{5.31}$$

where W is the learnable parameter.

5.4.13 Sigmoid-Weighted Linear Unit (SiLU) – Swish Activation

The sigmoid-weighted linear unit (SiLU), also known as Swish, is an activation function designed to improve gradient flow in deep neural networks. Unlike traditional activation functions like ReLU, which zero out negative values, SiLU smoothly scales negative inputs instead of suppressing them completely. This property helps improve gradient-based optimization and prevents issues like dying neurons in deep networks.

$$f(x) = x.\sigma(x) \tag{5.32}$$

where $\sigma(x) = \frac{1}{1+e^x}$ is the sigmoid function.

This means that each input value is scaled by its sigmoid activation, allowing smooth transitions for both negative and positive values.

Activation functions are an essential component of deep learning models, impacting convergence speed, accuracy, and training stability. While ReLU and GELU are widely used due to their efficiency, newer functions like Swish, Mish, and SiLU are gaining popularity for their improved gradient flow. The choice of activation function depends on the model architecture, computational constraints, and task requirements.

5.5 LAYER NORMALIZATION

Layer Normalization (LayerNorm) [14] is a crucial component in Transformers, ensuring stable training and efficient learning. Unlike Batch Normalization, which operates across batches, LayerNorm normalizes features within each input independently. This makes it highly effective for sequence-based models like Transformers.

Mathematically, LayerNorm for an input vector v with d features is calculated using Equation (5.33).

$$\text{LayerNorm}(v) = \gamma \frac{v-\mu}{\sqrt{\sigma^2+\varepsilon}} + \beta \tag{5.33}$$

where μ *is the* mean of the elements in v and is formulated in Equation (5.34).

$$\mu = \frac{1}{d} \sum_{k=1}^{d} v_k \tag{5.34}$$

σ^2 is the variance of $\mathbf{v}$ and is formulated in Equation (5.35).

$$\sigma^2 = \frac{1}{d}\sum_{k=1}^{d}(v_k - \mu)^2 \tag{5.35}$$

where γ is the trainable scaling parameter, β is the trainable bias parameter, and ε is a small constant added for numerical stability.

In the context of Transformers, LayerNorm is applied to the input of sub-layers, such as the multihead self-attention mechanism and the position-wise feed-forward network. This normalization helps stabilize and accelerate the training by ensuring that the inputs to each sublayer have a consistent distribution, thereby mitigating issues related to internal covariate shift. By normalizing the activations within each layer, LayerNorm enables more stable and efficient training of deep neural networks, particularly in architectures where batch-dependent normalization is less effective or feasible.

Layer normalization adjusts the inputs to a neural network layer to have a mean of 0 and a standard deviation of 1. Here's a simple example: Imagine we have three inputs: 3, 4, and 5. First, we find the average (mean) of these values, which is 4. Then, we calculate the standard deviation, which measures how spread out the values are (in this case, it's about 0.82). Finally, we subtract the mean from each input and divide by the standard deviation to normalize the values. The result would be normalized values like −1.22, 0, and 1.22. This makes sure the network learns in a more stable and efficient way.

5.6 DISTRIBUTED LLM TRAINING

Large language models (LLMs) have revolutionized NLP by achieving state-of-the-art results in a wide range of tasks. However, training these models requires extensive computational resources due to their massive number of parameters and dataset size. Distributed training techniques [15] have emerged as a solution to efficiently scale LLM training across multiple GPUs or TPUs. This chapter explores different distributed training strategies used in transformer-based LLMs, their advantages, challenges, implementation frameworks, and mathematical formulations.

5.6.1 Challenges in Training Large Language Models

- **Memory Constraints**: LLMs contain billions of parameters, often exceeding the memory capacity of a single GPU.
- **Compute Requirements**: The high number of matrix multiplications in transformers demands extensive parallel computation.
- **Communication Overhead**: Synchronizing parameters across multiple devices introduces latency.
- **Efficient Utilization**: Optimally distributing workloads across multiple GPUs or nodes to minimize bottlenecks is complex.

5.6.2 Distributed Training Paradigms

To address these challenges, different parallelism strategies are used and is explained as follows.

5.6.2.1 Data Parallelism (DP)

The dataset is split into smaller batches and distributed across multiple GPUs. Each GPU holds a copy of the full model and processes different mini-batches simultaneously. Model parameters are synchronized after every gradient update [16].

Mathematical Formulation: If W represents model parameters and X_i represents input data for GPU i, then gradient update is calculated using the Equation (5.36).

$$W^{(t+1)} = W^{(t)} - \eta . \frac{1}{N} \sum_{i=1}^{N} \nabla \mathrm{L_i}(W^{(t)}) \tag{5.36}$$

where η is the learning rate, N is the number of GPUs, and L_i is the loss function for GPU i.

Example: Suppose you have a dataset of 1,000 images and 4 GPUs. Each GPU processes 250 images and computes gradients. The gradients are then averaged across all GPUs to update the model parameters.

5.6.2.2 Model Parallelism (MP)

The model itself is split across multiple GPUs, with each GPU handling different layers or partitions of the model. Used when a single model is too large to fit in one GPU [17].

Mathematical Formulation: Given a model function $f(W,X)$ split across N GPUs, the subfunctions f_i is defined using the following Equation (5.37).

$$f(X) = f_N\left(f_{N-1}\left(\ldots f_1(X)\right)\right) \tag{5.37}$$

Each GPU i computes its respective subfunction f_i and passes intermediate outputs to the next GPU.

In a framework consisting of 12 transformer layers and utilizing 3 GPUs, each GPU manages four layers, with data progressing sequentially across the GPUs. The ultimate output is generated by the final GPU. This strategy enables the training of exceptionally large models that surpass the memory limits of a single device. Nevertheless, it entails significant inter-GPU communication overhead and a complicated implementation.

5.6.2.3 Pipeline Parallelism (PP)

The model is divided into multiple stages, where different minibatches are processed in different stages concurrently. Enables efficient GPU utilization by overlapping computation and communication [18].

Mathematical Formulation: If the model is divided into S stages, then for a batch B the total is calculated using the following Equation (5.38).

$$Total \approx \frac{S+B-1}{S} T_{Single} \tag{5.38}$$

where T_{Single} is the time required to process a batch on a single device.

In a setup distributed over three GPUs, each GPU concurrently processes its own batch—GPU 1 works on batch 1, GPU 2 manages batch 2, and GPU 3 takes care of batch 3—maximizing GPU usage. This method lowers the memory requirements in comparison to complete model parallelism. Nonetheless, it leads to higher latency because of the sequential dependencies present between the stages of the pipeline.

5.6.2.4 Tensor Parallelism (TP)

Individual weight matrices of a model are split across multiple devices, enabling parallel computation of matrix multiplications. Useful for transformer models where self-attention and feedforward layers contain large parameter matrices [19].

Mathematical Formulation: Given a matrix multiplication $Y = XW$, tensor parallelism splits W into W_i across N GPUs and is formulated as follows in Equation (5.39).

$$Y = \sum_{i=1}^{N} XW_i \tag{5.39}$$

To manage a substantial weight matrix (10,000 × 10,000) that surpasses the memory capacity of a single GPU, it can be divided into four smaller matrices of dimensions 10,000 × 2,500, with each matrix designated to a separate GPU. This approach lowers the memory requirements without necessitating complete model duplication. Nevertheless, fast interconnects are crucial to reduce the communication overhead among GPUs.

5.6.2.5 Zero Redundancy Optimizer (ZeRO)

A memory-efficient optimizer that eliminates redundant copies of model states across devices [20].

ZeRO has three stages:

- **ZeRO-1:** Optimizer states are partitioned.
- **ZeRO-2:** Gradients are also partitioned.
- **ZeRO-3:** Model parameters are fully sharded.

Mathematical Formulation: If G represents gradients, S represents optimizer states, and P represents parameters then ZeRO is formulated using the Equation (5.40).

$$G = \sum_{i=1}^{N} G_i,\ S = \sum_{i=1}^{N} S_i,\ P = \sum_{i=1}^{N} P_i \tag{5.40}$$

ZeRO minimizes memory consumption by dividing the optimizer state among multiple GPUs, so that each GPU retains only a portion of the necessary memory instead of the complete state. This method removes redundancy and enables the use of larger batch sizes. Nonetheless, it introduces a more intricate implementation and greater synchronization overhead.

5.7 DISTRIBUTED LLM TRAINING

Numerous advanced frameworks have been created to facilitate the distributed training of transformer-based LLMs, tackling the significant computational and memory requirements of these models by employing data, model, and pipeline parallelism techniques. Notable frameworks include:

5.7.1 PyTorch Distributed (torch.distributed)

PyTorch's built-in distributed package offers a versatile set of communication primitives aimed at enabling distributed training across multiple GPUs and nodes. It supports:

- **Data Parallelism:** The most widely used method where several replicas of the full model are trained on separate subsets of the input data, efficiently synchronizing gradients across GPUs via Distributed Data Parallel (DDP). DDP enhances GPU usage by overlapping computation with communication.
- **Model Parallelism:** This method allows for the division of a large model's layers or parameters across multiple GPUs, which is beneficial when the model size surpasses the memory capacity of a single device.
- **Pipeline Parallelism:** This approach permits the segmentation of the model into sequential stages across devices, where microbatches progress through the pipeline, thereby enhancing throughput through the concurrent execution of different model components.

PyTorch Distributed is highly adaptable and serves as the foundation for various higher-level frameworks.

5.7.2 DeepSpeed

Created by Microsoft, DeepSpeed [21] is a comprehensive library for optimizing deep learning designed to facilitate the efficient training of extremely large transformer models, including those containing trillions of parameters. Its primary features include:

- **ZeRO (Zero Redundancy Optimizer):** A collection of memory optimization strategies that distribute model states (optimizer states, gradients, and parameters) across GPUs to significantly lower memory usage and allow for the training of larger models.
- **Mixed Precision Training:** Facilitates FP16 and BF16 to hasten training while preserving accuracy through dynamic loss scaling.
- **Sparse Attention and Communication Optimizations:** Enhances training speed and efficiency by minimizing unnecessary computations and communication load.

DeepSpeed integrates seamlessly with PyTorch and accommodates a variety of parallelism strategies, including data, model, and pipeline parallelism.

5.7.3 FairScale

Developed by Meta (previously known as Facebook), FairScale is a PyTorch extension library that offers modular and reusable components for training large-scale models. It features:

- **ZeRO Implementations**: Includes various versions of ZeRO optimizations that enable scalable training by distributing model states.
- **Pipeline Parallelism:** Allows the division of models into pipeline stages, featuring built-in support for checkpointing and activation recomputation to conserve memory.
- **Sharded Data Parallel:** A variation of DDP that distributes optimizer states and gradients across GPUs to optimize memory usage.

FairScale is designed to be lightweight and versatile, enabling researchers to effectively combine different parallelism techniques.

5.7.4 TensorFlow Distributed Strategy

TensorFlow offers a high-level API for distributed training known as tf.distribute. Strategy, which simplifies many complexities associated with multidevice and multinode training. Its primary strategies consist of:

- **Mirrored Strategy:** Facilitates synchronous data parallel training on several GPUs within a single machine by creating model replicas (mirrors) on each device and aggregating gradients.
- **MultiWorkerMirrored Strategy:** Extends the Mirrored Strategy to multi-node clusters, coordinating gradient updates through all-reduce communication.
- **TPU Strategy:** Tailored for Google Cloud TPUs, this strategy harnesses TPU hardware architecture for high-throughput training employing model and data parallelism.

TensorFlow's distributed strategies offer smooth scaling and easy integration with TensorFlow's ecosystem, including Keras.

5.7.5 NVIDIA Megatron-LM

Megatron-LM is an open-source framework developed by NVIDIA that is specifically designed to train extremely large transformer models efficiently. It implements:

- **Tensor Model Parallelism:** This technique divides individual tensor operations (such as matrix multiplications within transformer layers) across multiple GPUs to manage exceptionally large parameter matrices.
- **Pipeline Parallelism:** This method segments the model into stages and executes them in a pipelined manner to enhance throughput.
- **Optimized CUDA Kernels and Communication:** It utilizes highly optimized kernels and communication libraries (such as NCCL) to reduce overhead and maximize GPU efficiency.

Megatron-LM supports mixed precision training and integrates with PyTorch, allowing the training of models with hundreds of billions or even trillions of parameters.

5.8 LIBRARIES IN LARGE LANGUAGE MODELS (LLMS)

LLMs have revolutionized NLP, enabling machines to perform tasks such as text generation, translation, sentiment analysis, and more with remarkable accuracy. Behind these advancements, a variety of powerful libraries and frameworks have been developed to train, fine-tune, and deploy LLMs. This chapter explores the most widely-used libraries in the field of LLMs, including their features, strengths, and how they contribute to the development of cutting-edge AI applications.

5.8.1 Hugging Face Transformers

Hugging face transformers is arguably the most popular library in the world of LLMs. It provides a simple, unified interface to a wide array of pre-trained transformer models like BERT, GPT, and T5, which can be fine-tuned for specific tasks. The library's user-friendly design and support for PyTorch and TensorFlow make it highly versatile for both research and production. Hugging Face also provides tools for tokenization, which is essential for preparing text data before feeding it into an LLM.

Hugging face transformers is a flexible library that provides a wide array of pre-trained models for various NLP tasks, compatible with both PyTorch and TensorFlow frameworks. It includes a built-in model hub that enables users to effortlessly share, retrieve, and deploy models. Moreover, its intuitive pipelines make it easier to utilize sophisticated models, facilitating rapid and effective integration into diverse applications.

5.8.2 TensorFlow

TensorFlow, an open-source deep learning framework developed by Google, is one of the most widely adopted platforms for developing machine learning models, including LLMs. TensorFlow provides extensive support for neural networks, including those based on the transformer architecture. It offers tools like *TensorFlow Hub*, which allows for the easy sharing and reuse of pretrained models. Additionally, TensorFlow supports deployment across different platforms including cloud, mobile, and edge devices, making it a flexible choice for LLMs.

TensorFlow is a powerful framework for machine learning, recognized for its strong capabilities in distributed training and scalable model creation. It features TensorFlow Hub, a platform that enables the sharing and reuse of pretrained models, and accommodates cross-platform deployment, even on mobile devices. Furthermore, TensorFlow offers a wide range of libraries dedicated to model optimization and fine-tuning, making it an all-in-one solution for developing and deploying machine learning applications.

5.8.3 PyTorch

PyTorch, a deep learning framework developed by Facebook's AI Research, has gained immense popularity among researchers due to its dynamic computation graph and intuitive API. PyTorch is ideal for LLMs, as it allows for easy experimentation with custom architectures while still providing robust tools for training and deploying large models. Libraries like *torchtext* extend PyTorch's capabilities for NLP tasks, and its integration with *Hugging Face* makes it a favorite for those working with transformer-based models.

PyTorch boasts a dynamic computation graph that allows for adaptable model development, in addition to robust GPU acceleration to improve performance. It integrates smoothly with NLP-centric libraries like Hugging Face, making it especially beneficial for tasks in NLP. With a focus on research, PyTorch is ideal for quick prototyping and experimentation.

5.8.4 OpenAI's GPT via API

OpenAI's GPT (Generative Pretrained Transformer) models, including GPT-3 and GPT-4, are at the forefront of the LLM revolution. Though users do not directly manipulate the model's underlying code, OpenAI provides an API that allows seamless integration into applications. GPT models are capable of a wide variety of tasks, including text generation, summarization, and even code generation. OpenAI's platform enables access to some of the most advanced language models without requiring significant computational resources from the user.

OpenAI's GPT, available through an API, delivers robust language models that can adapt to various NLP tasks. It allows developers to utilize sophisticated AI without relying on local hardware, presenting a scalable and handy option. Furthermore, the API facilitates fine-tuning, enabling personalization for particular applications and scenarios.

5.8.5 spaCy

spaCy is another widely-used NLP library, known for its high-performance capabilities. While it is not specifically designed for LLMs, it is an essential tool in the NLP pipeline, handling tasks like tokenization, named entity recognition (NER), and dependency parsing. When combined with LLMs, spaCy can be used to preprocess and enhance text data before feeding it into transformer-based models, thus improving the overall performance of NLP systems.

spaCy is a fast and efficient NLP library that offers built-in support for essential tasks such as tokenization, NER, and dependency parsing. It is designed for high-speed processing and integrates easily with deep learning frameworks like PyTorch and TensorFlow, making it suitable for both production use and advanced NLP applications.

5.8.6 AllenNLP

AllenNLP, built on PyTorch, is an open-source NLP research library designed to make it easy to design and evaluate complex deep learning models. It provides tools for building custom LLMs and other NLP systems, while also offering several pretrained models for tasks such as text classification and question answering. AllenNLP's focus on research makes it a great tool for experimenting with new architectures in the LLM space.

AllenNLP is a highly extensible framework designed for building custom NLP models, offering flexibility for researchers and developers. It includes a range of pretrained models for various NLP tasks and provides tools for model interpretability and visualization, making it easier to understand and analyze model behavior.

5.8.7 DeepSpeed

DeepSpeed, developed by Microsoft, is an optimization library specifically designed for training extremely large models, such as LLMs. It focuses on enhancing the efficiency and scalability of deep learning models. By supporting distributed training, mixed-precision training, and memory optimization, DeepSpeed allows researchers and organizations to train large transformer models like GPT-3 with more manageable resource requirements.

DeepSpeed is an optimization library for deep learning that facilitates distributed and parallel training, which is perfect for developing large-scale models. It provides mixed-precision training and memory optimization methods to enhance efficiency and minimize resource usage. Working in conjunction with PyTorch, DeepSpeed ensures smooth integration with current models and workflows.

5.8.8 Fairseq

Fairseq, developed by Facebook AI Research, is another powerful framework for sequence-to-sequence models like transformers. It is particularly well-suited for tasks such as machine translation and text summarization. Fairseq allows for easy training and experimentation with state-of-the-art models, making it an excellent choice for researchers and practitioners working with LLMs in production environments.

Fairseq is a versatile sequence modeling toolkit that provides a range of pretrained models for various NLP applications. It supports multi-GPU setups, enabling efficient large-scale training, and offers a highly configurable framework that allows users to build and experiment with custom model architectures tailored to their specific needs.

The development and deployment of LLMs have been greatly facilitated by the availability of these libraries, each offering unique strengths suited to different stages of the machine learning pipeline. From pretrained models in Hugging Face Transformers to highly scalable training with DeepSpeed, these tools make working with LLMs more accessible and efficient. Whether you're conducting research or deploying production systems, understanding these libraries and their capabilities is essential for leveraging the power of LLMs in real-world applications.

SUMMARY

The fundamental elements and methods of LLMs are described in this chapter. Tokenization, the process of breaking up unprocessed text into smaller chunks (tokens) that models can understand, is the first step. The following schemes are discussed: SentencePiece Encoding, which is language-independent and treats text as a sequence of Unicode characters, allowing for the efficient handling of diverse scripts; WordPiece Encoding, which uses subword units optimized for probability-based segmentation; and BPE, which combines frequent character pairs.

In order to supply sequence order information that is missing from conventional Transformer topologies, positional encoding techniques are then presented. Rotating position embeddings (RoPE) rotate token embeddings in multidimensional space to maintain relative positioning, absolute positional embeddings assign fixed positional vectors, relative positional embeddings represent distances between tokens, and relative positional bias introduces position-aware bias terms in attention calculations.

The chapter also discusses layer normalization, which stabilizes and speeds up training by normalizing activations inside layers, and activation functions like ReLU, GELU, and SwiGLU, which add nonlinearity to neural networks.

In order to manage the enormous computational demands of training big models, it concludes by examining distributed LLM training and outlining techniques like data parallelism, model parallelism, and pipeline parallelism. It ends with a summary of well-known libraries that offer resources for effective LLM development, training, and deployment, such as Hugging Face Transformers, DeepSpeed, and Megatron-LM.

QUESTIONS

1. Define *tokenization* in NLP. Why is it important for LLMs?
2. List any four commonly used *activation functions* in deep learning.
3. Differentiate between *Byte Pair Encoding (BPE), WordPiece, and SentencePiece* tokenization methods.

4. Explain the difference between absolute and relative positional embeddings with examples.
5. Describe the purpose of *layer normalization* in transformer architectures.
6. For the input value x = -2, compute the output of:
   - Sigmoid
   - ReLU
   - Tanh
7. In Rotary Position Embeddings (RoPE), if query vector $q = [1, 0]$ and key vector $k = [0, 1]$ are rotated by angle $\theta = 90°$, compute the transformed vectors.
8. Analyze how relative positional bias helps transformer models capture dependencies in long sequences.
9. Break down the challenges of distributed LLM training in terms of memory, communication overhead, and model parallelism.
10. Evaluate the effectiveness of subword tokenization compared to word-level and character-level tokenization.
11. Compare the performance of ReLU vs GELU activation functions in transformer models. Which one is generally preferred and why?
12. Design a workflow for training a Transformer-based LLM using popular libraries (e.g., Hugging Face Transformers, DeepSpeed, PyTorch). Explain how tokenization, positional embeddings, normalization, and distributed training fit into your design.
13. **Case Study: Tokenization and Positional Embeddings in Large Language Models**
    When building a LLM, one important step is tokenization, which breaks text into smaller units. For example, the word "unbelievable" may be split using BPE into "un" + "believ" + "able." This helps the model handle rare or unknown words. Another key part is positional encoding, which tells the model the order of words in a sentence. For instance, in the sentence "I love NLP," the word "I" comes before "love." Without positional information, the model would treat sentences like "I love NLP" and "NLP love I" the same. By combining tokenization and positional embeddings, LLMs can understand both the meaning of words and their order in a sequence, which improves tasks like translation and question answering. Explain why both tokenization and positional embeddings are important in training LLMs. Give one example of how a sentence meaning can change without positional information.

REFERENCES

[1] C. W. Schmidt, V. Reddy, H. Zhang, A. Alameddine, O. Uzan, Y. Pinter *et al.*, "Tokenization is More Than Compression," arxiv preprint, Oct. 2024, arXiv:2402.18376.

[2] K. Bostrom, and G. Durrett, "Byte Pair Encoding is Suboptimal for Language Model Pretraining," in *Findings of the Association for Computational Linguistics: EMNLP 2020*, pp. 4617–4624, Online, Oct. 2020.

[3] X. Song, A. Salcianu, Y. Song, D. Dopson, and D. Zhou, "Fast WordPiece Tokenization," in *Proceedings of the 2021 Conference on Empirical Methods in Natural Language Processing*, pp. 2089–2103, Online and Punta Cana, Dominican Republic, Oct. 2021.

[4] T. Kudo, and J. Richardson, "SentencePiece: A Simple and Language Independent Subword Tokenizer and Detokenizer for Neural Text Processing," in *Proceedings of the 2018 Conference on Empirical Methods in Natural Language Processing: System Demonstrations*, pp. 66–71, Brussels, Belgium, Aug. 2018.

[5] K. Sinha, A. Kazemnejad, S. Reddy, J. Pineau, D. Hupkes, and A. Williams, "The Curious Case of Absolute Position Embeddings," in *Findings of the Association for Computational Linguistics: EMNLP 2022*, pp. 4449–4472, Abu Dhabi, United Arab Emirates. Association for Computational Linguistics, Oct. 2022.

[6] A. Liutkus, O. Cífka, S.-L. Wu, U. Şimşekli, Y.-H. Yang, and G. Richard, "Relative Positional Encoding for Transformers with Linear Complexity," Jun. 2021, ArXiv abs/2105.08399.

[7] P. Shaw, J. Uszkoreit, and A. Vaswani, "Self-Attention with Relative Position Representations," in *Proceedings of the 2018 Conference of the North American Chapter of the Association for Computational Linguistics: Human Language Technologies*, vol 2 (Short Papers), pp. 464–468, New Orleans, Louisiana, Apr. 2018.

[8] J. Su, Y. Lu, S. Pan, A. Murtadha, B. Wen, and Y. Liu, "RoFormer: Enhanced Transformer with Rotary Position Embedding," *Neurocomputing*, vol. 568, p. 127063, Nov. 2023, https://doi.org/10.1016/j.neucom.2023.127063.

[9] G. Angelotti, "HyPE: Attention with Hyperbolic Biases for Relative Positional Encoding," Oct. 2023, arXiv:2310.19676.

[10] A. F. Agarap, "Deep Learning using Rectified Linear Units (ReLU)," 2018, arXiv:1803.08375.

[11] D. Hendrycks, and K. Gimpel, "Gaussian Error Linear Units (GELUs)," 2016, arXiv:1606.08415.

[12] S. R. Dubey, S. K. Singh, and B. B. Chaudhuri, "Activation Functions in Deep Learning: A Comprehensive Survey and Benchmark," *Neurocomputing*, vol. 503, pp. 92–108, Jun. 2022, https://doi.org/10.1016/j.neucom.2022.06.111.

[13] J. Ackermann, A. Jentzen, T. Kruse, B. Kuckuck, and J. L. Padgett, "Deep Neural Networks with ReLU, Leaky ReLU, and Softplus Activation Provably Overcome the Curse of Dimensionality for Kolmogorov Partial Differential Equations with Lipschitz Nonlinearities in the L^p-sense," Jun. 2025, arXiv:2309.13722.

[14] J. L. Ba, J. R. Kiros, and G. E. Hinton, "Layer Normalization," Jul. 2016, arXiv:1607.06450.

[15] J. Duan, S. Zhang, Z. Wang, L. Jiang, W. Qu, Q. Hu *et al.*, "Efficient Training of Large Language Models on Distributed Infrastructures: A Survey," *Vicinagearth* vol. 3, p. 9, 2026, https://doi.org/10.1007/s44336-026-00038-z.

[16] S. Li, Y. Zhao, R. Varma, O. Salpekar, P. Noordhuis, T. Li *et al.*, "PyTorch Distributed: Experiences on Accelerating Data Parallel Training," in *Proc. VLDB Endowment*, vol. 13, no. 12, pp. 3005–3018, Aug. 2020, https://doi.org/10.14778/3415478.3415530.

[17] A. Klawonn, M. Lanser, and J. Weber, "Model Parallel Training and Transfer Learning for Convolutional Neural Networks by Domain Decomposition," Aug. 2024, arXiv:2408.14442.

[18] A. Xhebraj, S. Lee, H. Chen, and V. Grover, "Scaling Deep Learning Training with MPMD Pipeline Parallelism," Dec. 2024, arXiv:2412.14374.

[19] I. Lamprecht, A. Karnieli, Y. Hanani, N. Giladi, and D. Soudry, "Tensor-Parallelism with Partially Synchronized Activations," Jun. 2025, arXiv:2506.19645.

[20] S. Rajbhandari, J. Rasley, O. Ruwase, and Y. He, "ZeRO: Memory Optimizations Toward Training Trillion Parameter Models," *SC20: International Conference for High Performance Computing, Networking, Storage and Analysis*, Atlanta, GA, USA, pp. 1–16, May 2020, doi: 10.1109/SC41405.2020.00024.

[21] R. Y. Aminabadi. S.Rajbhandari, A. A. Awan, C. Li, D. Li, E. Zheng, *et al.*, "DeepSpeed Inference: Enabling Efficient Inference of Transformer Models at Unprecedented Scale," *SC22: International Conference for High Performance Computing, Networking, Storage and Analysis*, Dallas, TX, USA, pp. 1–15, Jun. 2022, doi: 10.1109/SC41404.2022.00051.

6 Variants of LLM Architecture

6.1 INTRODUCTION

Deep learning models' handling of sequential input, particularly in natural language processing (NLP), has been drastically altered by the Transformer architecture. Various Transformer variations have been created to maximize performance for particular applications. These designs, which are each made for a distinct NLP difficulty, can be roughly divided into encoder-based models, decoder-based models, and encoder–decoder models.

6.2 ENCODER-ONLY TRANSFORMERS

Encoder-only Transformer models are designed to process input text efficiently by capturing contextual relationships between words. These models use self-attention mechanisms to understand long-range dependencies, making them highly effective for tasks like text classification, named entity recognition (NER), and search engines. Below are some of the most notable encoder-only Transformer variants.

6.2.1 Bidirectional Encoder Representations from Transformers (BERT)

Bidirectional Encoder Representations from Transformers (BERT) [1] is a deep learning model designed for NLU. Developed by Google AI in 2018, BERT introduced bidirectional pretraining, enabling models to grasp both left and right contexts in a sentence. Unlike previous unidirectional models like GPT (which read left to right), BERT processes an entire sentence simultaneously, making it highly effective for tasks like text classification, NER, and question answering (QA).

BERT is based on the Transformer model, first introduced by Vaswani et al. [2] in their 2017 paper, **"Attention is All You Need."** Unlike RNNs and LSTMs, which process text sequentially, Transformers use self-attention and parallel computation, making them highly efficient for large-scale NLP tasks.

6.2.1.1 Architecture of BERT

BERT consists of stacked encoder layers and does not include decoders like GPT. It processes input text through multiple layers of self-attention and feed-forward

DOI: 10.1201/9781003650065-6

networks, making it highly effective for contextual understanding. The core components of BERT include Token embeddings, which convert words into numerical vectors; segment embeddings, which differentiate between sentence pairs in tasks like question-answering; and positional embeddings, which help retain the order of words in a sentence since transformers do not have built-in sequence awareness. These embeddings are crucial for BERT's ability to understand syntax and semantics effectively.

6.2.1.2 Variants of BERT

BERT comes in two primary versions based on the model size and computational complexity. BERT-Base consists of 12 encoder layers, 768 hidden units, and 110 million parameters, making it a balanced choice for various NLP applications. BERT-Large, on the other hand, has 24 encoder layers, 1024 hidden units, and 340 million parameters, offering superior performance at the cost of increased computational requirements. The choice between BERT-Base and BERT-Large depends on the specific NLP task and available computational resources. Figure 6.1 shows the BERT base and BERT large.

BERT has a unique way of processing and understanding context in natural language. Unlike earlier models that process text from left to right or right to left, BERT

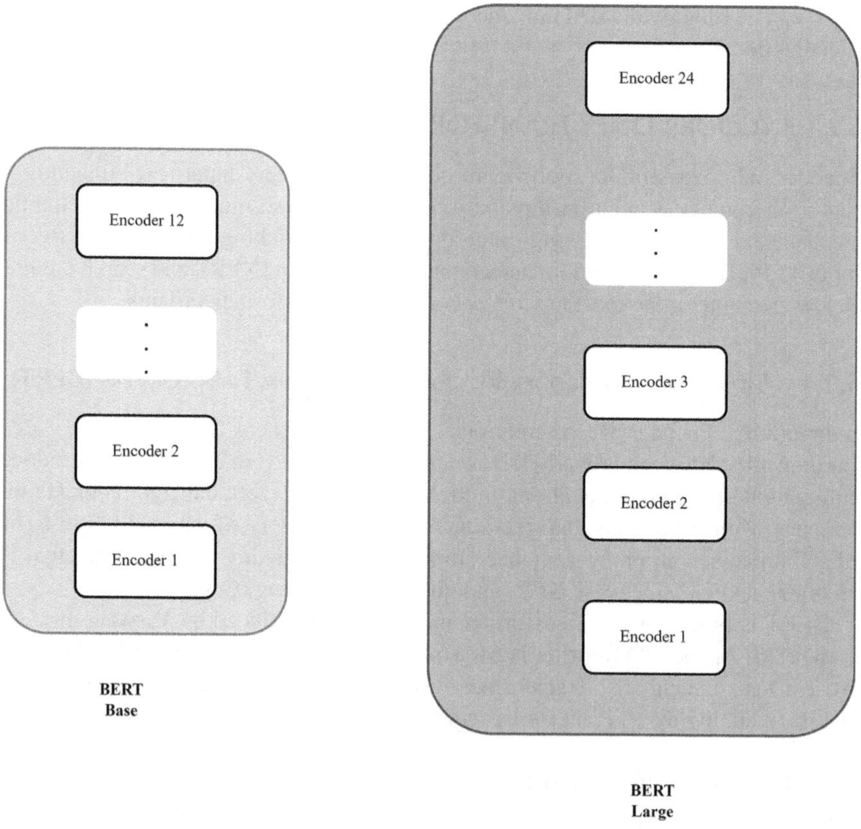

FIGURE 6.1 BERT base and BERT large.

looks at both directions simultaneously, making it more effective in understanding important meanings, especially when context plays a significant role.

For example, consider the word "bank." In one sentence, it might refer to a financial institution:

- "I need to go to the bank to withdraw money."

In another sentence, it might refer to the side of a river:

- "The boat was anchored at the bank of the river."

BERT is able to understand the correct meaning of "bank" in each case by considering the surrounding words, giving it a strong advantage over models that rely on simpler embeddings.
Let's look at another case:

- "I bought a bat from the store."
- "He swung the bat at the ball."

In the first sentence, "bat" refers to an object used in sports, while in the second, it refers to a flying mammal. BERT's bidirectional processing allows it to determine which "bat" is meant by looking at the context in both directions.

By predicting missing words in a sentence (masked language modeling) and analyzing sequences with no predetermined direction, BERT can grasp these subtle differences in meaning, enhancing its ability to understand complex language structures and improve tasks like classification, translation, and QA. Figure 6.2 displays the architecture of BERT.

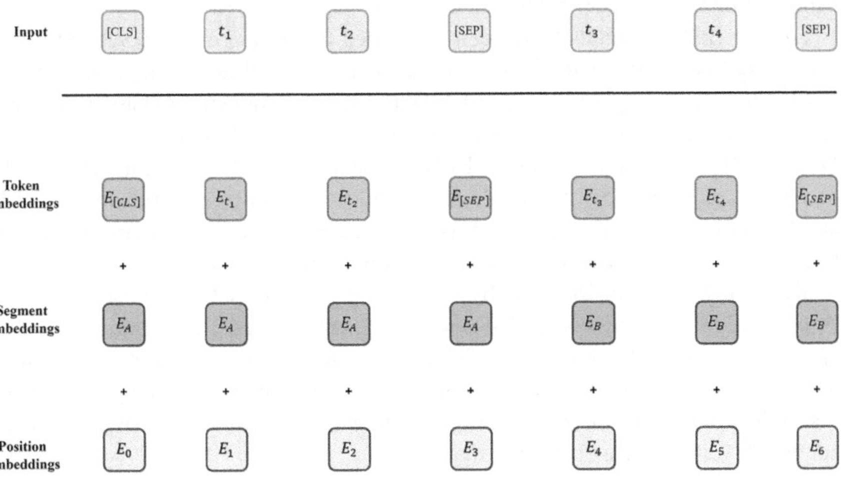

FIGURE 6.2 BERT.

To overcome this challenge, BERT is pretrained on two different NLP tasks.

- Masked Language Modeling (MLM)
- Next Sentence Prediction (NSP)

6.2.1.3 Pretraining of BERT

BERT undergoes pretraining on massive text datasets, including Wikipedia and Book Corpus, using two primary objectives: masked language modeling (MLM) and next sentence prediction (NSP).

MLM involves randomly masking 15% of words in a sentence and training the model to predict them based on surrounding words. This allows BERT to learn contextual dependencies bidirectionally. For example, given the sentence "The cat sat on the [MASK]," BERT predicts the missing word as "mat."

Next sentence prediction (NSP) trains BERT to determine if one sentence logically follows another. Given Sentence A: "She went to the market." and Sentence B: "She bought vegetables.", BERT predicts whether Sentence B is a logical continuation of Sentence A. If the next sentence is unrelated ("The sky is blue."), BERT correctly classifies it as incorrect. This task enhances BERT's understanding of sentence relationships, making it effective for QA and text coherence tasks.

6.2.1.4 Fine-Tuning BERT for NLP Tasks

After pretraining, BERT is fine-tuned on specific NLP tasks by training on labeled datasets. Fine-tuning adapts the pretrained model to specialized domains like healthcare, finance, and legal NLP. Common fine-tuning applications include Text Classification, where BERT is used for sentiment analysis and spam detection; NER, which helps identify proper names like locations and organizations in text; QA, where BERT is trained on datasets like SQuAD to generate precise answers to queries; and Text Summarization, which extracts key information from large documents. Fine-tuning typically involves adding a task-specific output layer and training the model using gradient-based optimization techniques.

Several BERT variants have been developed to address efficiency, accuracy, and scalability issues. RoBERTa removes the NSP task and adopts dynamic masking, improving pretraining robustness. ALBERT reduces model size by parameter-sharing techniques, making it computationally efficient while maintaining high performance. DistilBERT is a lighter version of BERT, reducing model size while retaining 97% of its accuracy, making it suitable for mobile and real-time applications. XLNet, an alternative to BERT, overcomes its NSP limitations by using permutation-based training, allowing for a more flexible contextual representation.

BERT has revolutionized NLP by introducing bidirectional contextual embeddings, significantly enhancing text understanding in search engines, chatbots, and AI-driven applications. Its ability to capture rich contextual meaning has set new benchmarks in NLP, making it a go-to model for modern deep learning-based language tasks. As research progresses, optimized BERT variants will continue improving efficiency, adaptability, and real-world performance.

6.2.2 RoBERTa (Robustly Optimized BERT Approach)

RoBERTa (Robustly Optimized BERT Approach) [3] is an advanced version of BERT designed to enhance performance on NLP tasks through improved training strategies. While RoBERTa retains BERT's Transformer-based architecture, it introduces key modifications that significantly boost its effectiveness.

6.2.2.1 Architecture of RoBERTa

RoBERTa follows the same base architecture as BERT, which is built on a multilayer bidirectional Transformer encoder. However, it differs in the way it is trained and optimized.

6.2.2.1.1 Transformer Encoder

RoBERTa, like BERT, consists of multiple self-attention layers to process input text bidirectionally. It uses WordPiece embeddings with a Byte-Pair Encoding (BPE) tokenizer, enhancing efficiency in handling unseen words. Figure 6.3 shows the architecture of RoBERTa.

Each input sequence starts with the special [CLS] token for classification tasks. Sentences are separated by [SEP] tokens, but unlike BERT, RoBERTa removes the

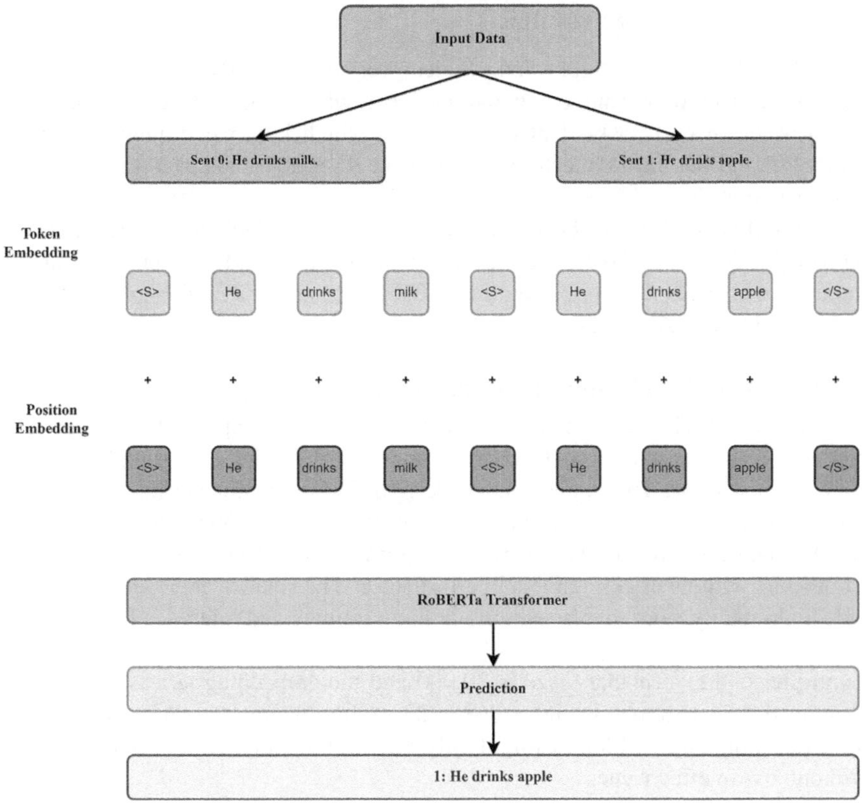

FIGURE 6.3 RoBERTa.

NSP objective. Unlike BERT, which was trained on both MLM and NSP, RoBERTa removes NSP entirely. Instead, it trains on a much larger dataset with dynamic masking, leading to better generalization. BERT used static masking, meaning the same masked words were used in each training epoch. RoBERTa applies dynamic masking, meaning different words are masked in each training epoch, improving contextual learning. RoBERTa is trained on ten times more data than BERT, leading to better model robustness. It uses larger batch sizes and longer training times to achieve superior language understanding. Like BERT, RoBERTa adds learned positional embeddings to tokens, allowing it to capture word order dependencies effectively.

For example, consider the ambiguous word "lead" in two sentences:

"He will lead the team." (Verb: to guide)
"The pipe is made of lead." (Noun: a metal)

RoBERTa's improved training techniques allow it to better distinguish meanings by leveraging contextual embeddings more effectively than BERT. RoBERTa maintains the same Transformer-based architecture as BERT but optimizes training methods, leading to better language understanding and improved performance on NLP tasks.

6.2.3 A Lite BERT for Self-Supervised Learning of Language Representations (ALBERT)

ALBERT [4] is a lightweight and efficient version of BERT designed to reduce memory consumption and computational cost while maintaining state-of-the-art performance in NLP tasks. Unlike RoBERTa, which improves training strategies, ALBERT modifies the architecture itself to make it scalable and faster while requiring fewer parameters.

The backbone of ALBERT architecture is similar to BERT that is encoder layers with GELU (Gaussian Error Linear Unit) activation function. However, below are the three main changes that are present in ALBERT but not in BERT. Figure 6.4 shows the architecture of ALBERT.

6.2.3.1 Factorized Embedding Parameterization

In standard BERT, the embedding size (used for word representations) and the hidden layer size (used for model computations) are the same. For example, in BERT Base, both sizes are 768 dimensions, making the model parameter heavy. ALBERT decouples these two sizes, meaning that the vocabulary embedding size is much smaller than the hidden layer size. This significantly reduces the total number of parameters without affecting model performance. The smaller embeddings still provide high-quality word representations, making training and inference faster.

Example: If the vocabulary size is 30,000 and the embedding size is 768, storing all embeddings requires 30,000 × 768 = 23 million parameters. ALBERT reduces the embedding size to 128, making it only 3.8 million parameters—saving memory without loss in effectiveness.

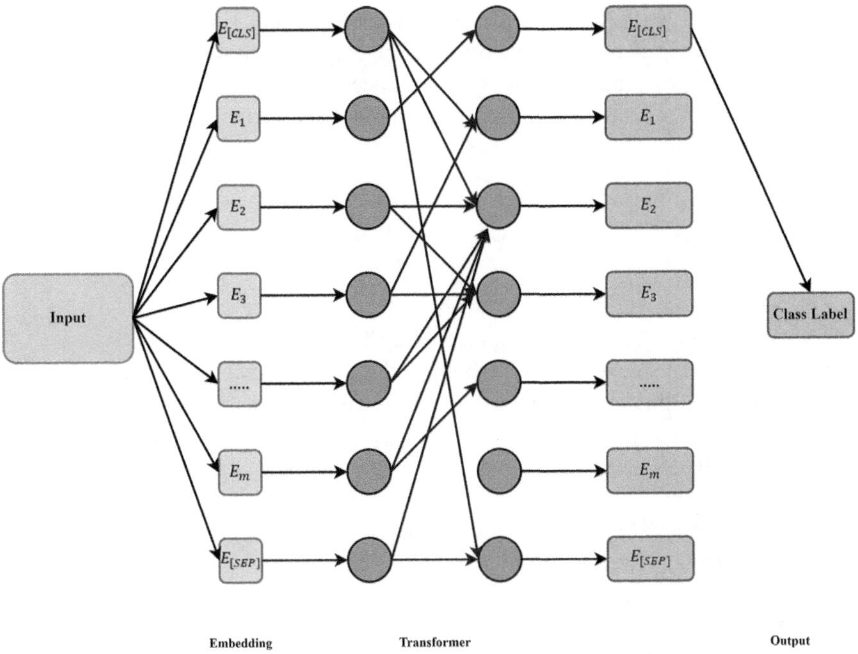

FIGURE 6.4 AlBERT.

6.2.3.2 Cross-Layer Parameter Sharing

In traditional BERT, each Transformer layer has separate parameters, meaning that the deeper the network, the more parameters are needed. Techniques used by ALBERT for Optimization are given as follows.

- Instead of learning unique parameters for every layer, ALBERT shares parameters across all Transformer layers.
- This significantly reduces the total number of parameters while maintaining model depth.
- The model effectively learns richer representations with less memory overhead.

For Example, BERT Base (12 layers) → 110M parameters while ALBERT Base (12 layers with shared weights) → 12M parameters.

By sharing parameters, ALBERT achieves similar performance with far fewer parameters, making it more efficient for large-scale NLP applications.

6.2.3.3 Sentence Order Prediction (SOP) instead of NSP

BERT introduced NSP to help with sentence relationships. However, research found that NSP did not improve model accuracy significantly and was often misleading. Techniques used by ALBERT for optimization are given as follows.

- Instead of NSP, ALBERT uses sentence order prediction (SOP).
- SOP checks if two consecutive sentences appear in the correct order rather than just predicting whether two sentences are related.
- This improves the model's ability to understand textual coherence and logical relationships.

For Example,
NSP Task (BERT)

- Sentence 1: "He bought a new phone."
- Sentence 2: "The weather is nice today."
- The model must predict whether these two sentences belong together. (However, this may not be useful for downstream tasks.)

SOP Task (ALBERT)

- Sentence 1: "He bought a new phone."
- Sentence 2: "Then he installed his favorite apps."
- In another case, the order is reversed:
  - Sentence 2: "Then he installed his favorite apps."
  - Sentence 1: "He bought a new phone."
- The model must determine whether the order is correct or incorrect, leading to better sentence understanding.

6.2.4 XLNet: Generalized Autoregressive Pretraining for Language Understanding

XLNet [5] builds upon the Transformer architecture and consists of the following main components.

6.2.4.1 Input Embeddings

XLNet uses the same input representation as other transformer-based models and are given below.

- **Token Embeddings:** These represent the word or subword units in the input text.
- **Position Embeddings:** These represent the position of each token in the sequence, which helps the model understand the order of tokens.
- **Segment Embeddings:** These are used for distinguishing between different segments (e.g., sentences) in tasks like QA.

6.2.4.2 Permutation-Based Pretraining Objective

Unlike traditional transformers like BERT, which use a masked language model (MLM) for training, XLNet introduces a permutation-based objective. This approach allows XLNet to capture bidirectional context while also maintaining an autoregressive model structure.

Given an input sequence, XLNet is trained to predict each token in the sequence conditioned on the previous tokens, but in a random permutation order rather than left-to-right or right-to-left sequences.

The formula for the training objective is given in the following Equation (6.1).

$$\max_{\theta} \mathbb{E}_{z \sim \mathcal{Z}_T} \left[\sum_{t=1}^{T} log p_{\theta}(x_{z_t} | X_{Z<t}) \right] \tag{6.1}$$

where θ is the model parameters to be optimized, $\mathbb{E}_{z \sim \mathcal{Z}_T}$ is the expectation over all possible permutations of the input tokens, and $\sum_{t=1}^{T} log p_{\theta}(x_{z_t} \mid X_{Z<t})$ is the sum of log-like hoods of predicting each token x_{z_t} based on the preceding tokens $X_{Z<t}$.

This training objective considers the input sequence in all possible permutations of token order, allowing XLNet to capture long-range dependencies and bidirectional relationships in the data.

6.2.4.3 XLNet Encoder Architecture

The architecture of XLNet's encoder is largely based on the Transformer encoder, with a few key differences and is given as follows.

Self-Attention Mechanism

As with standard transformers, XLNet uses self-attention to compute contextual embeddings for each token in the sequence. However, the key difference lies in how it processes the sequence: rather than using a fixed left-to-right or right-to-left order, XLNet uses permutation-based input sequences.

Feed-Forward Layers

After the attention mechanism, the output is passed through a feed-forward neural network, which is similar to other transformer models.

Layer Normalization

XLNet uses layer normalization after each layer in the encoder, improving training stability.

6.2.4.4 Permutation Language Modeling

Instead of masking a subset of tokens like BERT does (for example, using the MLM objective), XLNet applies a permutation language modeling approach. During training, for each input sequence, it generates multiple permutations of the token positions. For each permutation, the model predicts each token based on the tokens that appear before it, in a causal (autoregressive) manner. This method is different from the masked token approach because it retains the full sequence and learns contextual dependencies from all positions.

6.2.4.5 Final Prediction Layer

At the end of the encoder, XLNet uses a final output layer to predict the probability of each token in the vocabulary at each position and is given in Equation (6.2).

$$P\left(w_t \mid w_1, w_2, \ldots, w_{t-1}\right) = \frac{\exp(h_t W_o)}{\sum_{j-1}^{V} \exp(h_j W_o)} \tag{6.2}$$

where h_t is the hidden representation for token t, W_o is the output weight matrix, and V is the size of the vocabulary.

The probability is computed for each token in the sequence at each position, conditioned on the previous tokens, following the autoregressive style of prediction.

XLNet is a powerful transformer model that improves upon traditional models like BERT by leveraging permutation-based training. By using a permutation objective, XLNet captures bidirectional dependencies in a more flexible way than BERT, making it more suitable for tasks requiring nuanced context understanding and long-range dependencies.

6.2.5 DistilBERT: A Smaller and Faster Version of BERT

DistilBERT [6] is a distilled version of the BERT model that aims to provide similar performance while being smaller, faster, and more efficient. It is built using the knowledge distillation technique, which transfers knowledge from a larger, more complex model (like BERT) into a smaller one without sacrificing too much accuracy.

6.2.5.1 Distillation Process

The primary idea behind distillation is to train a smaller model (the student) to replicate the behavior of a larger, pre-trained model (the teacher). DistilBERT follows this approach by learning from BERT's outputs.

- **Teacher Model (BERT):** The original, larger model that has been pretrained on large corpora (like Wikipedia and BookCorpus).
- **Student Model (DistilBERT):** A smaller model that is trained to mimic the behavior of the teacher model. The student model is initialized with random weights and then learns by minimizing a loss function that includes both the traditional task loss and a loss term that encourages it to match the output of the teacher.

The knowledge distillation process uses the following Equation (6.3) for the loss.

$$\mathcal{L}_{distill} = \mathcal{L}_{task} + \lambda \cdot \mathcal{L}_{KD} \tag{6.3}$$

where $\mathcal{L}_{task}$ is the regular task-specific loss (e.g., cross-entropy loss for classification), $\mathcal{L}_{KD}$ the knowledge distillation loss, which measures the difference between the soft targets (logits) of the teacher and the student models, and λ is a hyperparameter that controls the weight of the knowledge distillation loss compared to the task loss.

6.2.5.2 Training DistilBERT

DistilBERT is trained using the following strategy:

Pretraining: Just like BERT, DistilBERT is first pretrained on large amounts of text using unsupervised learning. It uses the MLM objective to predict masked tokens within a sequence.

Distillation: During pretraining, DistilBERT also learns from the outputs of the BERT model. The teacher model (BERT) generates logits (the unnormalized predictions) for each token in the sequence. DistilBERT minimizes the difference between its own logits and those of the teacher using a soft target loss.

The soft target loss for distillation is defined as follows in Equation (6.4).

$$\mathcal{L}_{KD} = -\sum_{i=1}^{N} p_{teacher,i} \log(p_{student,i}) \tag{6.4}$$

where $p_{teacher,i}$ is the probability distribution over the classes for token i from the teacher model, $p_{student,i}$ is the probability distribution over the classes for token i from the student model, and N is the number of tokens in the sequence.

Task-Specific Fine-tuning: After pretraining and distillation, DistilBERT is fine-tuned for downstream tasks like text classification, NER, or QA. This fine-tuning is similar to how BERT is fine-tuned for specific tasks.

6.2.5.3 DistilBERT Architecture Details

- Layer-wise Reduction: DistilBERT reduces the number of layers, but it still maintains the core components of the transformer architecture, such as self-attention and feed-forward networks.
- Transformer Layers: Each transformer layer in DistilBERT consists of multi-head attention and a feed-forward network, just like in BERT.
- Output: After processing through the transformer layers, the final hidden states are passed to the task-specific layers for downstream tasks like classification, regression, or token prediction.

6.2.5.4 Fine-tuning DistilBERT

Fine-tuning DistilBERT is the same as fine-tuning BERT. After pretraining, you simply add a task-specific head on top of the model and fine-tune it on a labeled dataset. The common fine-tuning tasks include:

- **Text Classification:** Adding a fully connected layer on top to classify text into categories.
- **Sequence Labeling:** Adding a sequence labeling head for token classification tasks (e.g., NER).

- **Question Answering:** Adding a start and end span head for answering questions from a context.

For text classification, the fine-tuning loss is typically calculated using cross-entropy and is given in Equation (6.5).

$$\mathcal{L}_{classification} = -\sum_{i=1}^{N} y_i \log(p_{student,i}) \tag{6.5}$$

where y_i is the true label for token i, and $p_{student,i}$ is the predicted probability for token i.

DistilBERT offers an excellent balance of speed, size, and accuracy. By leveraging knowledge distillation, it provides a more efficient version of BERT without significant losses in performance. This makes it an ideal choice for NLP tasks in real-time or resource-constrained environments. Whether you're building chatbots, search engines, or real-time recommendation systems, DistilBERT is a practical choice for deploying state-of-the-art language models with improved computational efficiency.

6.2.6 Efficiently Learning an Encoder that Classifies Token Replacements Accurately (ELECTRA)

ELECTRA [7] is an innovative pretraining method for transformer models, designed to be more computationally efficient while maintaining high performance. It was proposed by Clark et al. [7] as an alternative to traditional pretraining techniques like BERT (Bidirectional Encoder Representations from Transformers). The primary goal of ELECTRA is to reduce the computational cost of pretraining without sacrificing performance on downstream NLP tasks. Figure 6.5 shows the architecture of ELECTRA.

6.2.6.1 ELECTRA Consists of Two Main Models

Generator *G* – A small masked language model (MLM) that replaces some tokens with plausible alternatives. The generator is a smaller, MLM (similar to BERT) that creates fake tokens (replacements) for a portion of the input. During pretraining, a certain percentage (usually around 50%) of the tokens in a given input sequence are replaced with plausible substitutes by the generator. These substitutions are not necessarily the original tokens but are generated in such a way that they resemble the original tokens in meaning or context. The generator's task is to generate reasonable replacements for the masked tokens, which are then used by the discriminator. The generator's output is not used directly for downstream tasks but rather serves as input for the next stage.

Discriminator *D* – A larger model trained to classify whether each token in the input sequence is real (original) or fake (replaced by the generator). The discriminator is a larger model that performs the primary task of distinguishing between the original (real) tokens and the fake (replaced) tokens generated by the generator. For every token in the sequence, the discriminator decides whether the token is real (i.e., it was

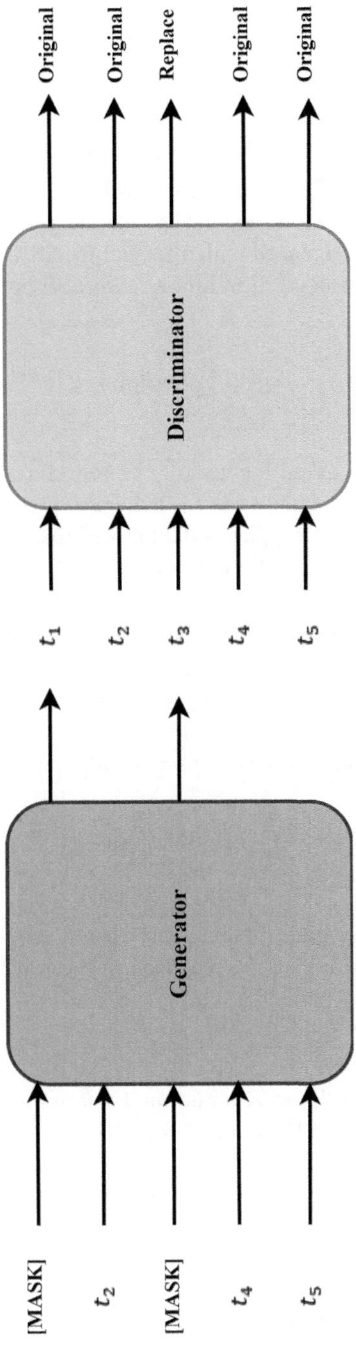

FIGURE 6.5 ELECTRA.

not replaced) or fake (i.e., it was replaced by the generator). Instead of only predicting masked tokens as in BERT, the discriminator in ELECTRA makes predictions for all tokens in the input sequence. It is trained to classify each token, whether it is the original token or one of the replacements, and its task is to learn to distinguish between real and replaced tokens effectively.

6.2.6.2 Generator Loss ($\mathcal{L}_G$): Masked Language Modeling (MLM)

The generator G is trained like a traditional MLM, predicting the masked tokens based on context. Given an input sequence $x = (x_1, x_2, \ldots\ldots, x_n)$, a subset of tokens x_m are randomly selected and replaced with a special [MASK] token.

The generator is then trained to minimize the cross-entropy loss and is given in Equation (6.6).

$$\mathcal{L}_G = -\mathbb{E}_{(x_m, x)} \sum_{t \varepsilon m} \log P_G(x_t \mid x^{masked}) \tag{6.6}$$

where x_m represents the masked tokens, x^{masked} represents the context excluding x_t and $P_G(x_t \mid x^{masked})$ is the probability of the generator predicting the correct token x_t.

After training, the generator replaces the masked tokens with its predicted tokens $\widetilde{x}_t$, which are used as input to the discriminator.

6.2.6.3 Discriminator Loss ($\mathcal{L}_D$)- Token Classification

The discriminator D is trained to distinguish between original tokens and tokens replaced by the generator. For each token x_t in the sequence, the discriminator predicts a probability $D(x_t)$ that the token is real.

The binary classification loss for the discriminator and is given in Equation (6.7).

$$\mathcal{L}_D = -\mathbb{E}_{(x_m, \widetilde{x})} = -\sum_{t=1}^{n} [y_t log D(x_t) + (1 - y_t) log(1 - D(x_t))] \tag{6.7}$$

where $y_t = 1$ if x_t is an original token, otherwise $y_t = 0$, $D(x_t)$ is the probability assigned by the discriminator that x_t is real and $\widetilde{x}$ is the corrupted sequences produced by the generator.

6.2.6.4 Joint Training Loss

ELECTRA jointly trains both the generator and discriminator using a weighted sum of their losses and is shown in Equation (6.8).

$$\mathcal{L} = \mathcal{L}_D + \lambda \mathcal{L}_G \tag{6.8}$$

where λ is a hyperparameter that controls the weight of the generator's loss relative to the discriminator's loss.

Since the generator is typically much smaller than the discriminator, λ is usually set to a small value (e.g., 0.1) to prevent the generator from dominating the training.

The key difference in ELECTRA compared to traditional MLMs is that the discriminator is trained to detect fake tokens (those replaced by the generator) throughout the entire input sequence. This provides a denser signal for training, meaning that the model can use more information to learn at each step, and thus it learns faster and more efficiently.

ELECTRA presents a novel and efficient pretraining strategy that significantly reduces the computational cost of training large language models (LLMs) while maintaining high performance. By leveraging a discriminator to classify token replacements, ELECTRA can achieve superior sample efficiency and faster convergence compared to traditional methods like BERT. This makes it a powerful alternative for deploying transformer-based models in real-world NLP applications.

6.3 DECODER-ONLY TRANSFORMERS

Decoder-only transformer models are designed primarily for text generation rather than comprehension. Unlike encoder-based models, which process the entire input sequence simultaneously with bidirectional attention, decoders employ causal (unidirectional) attention. This means they generate text sequentially, predicting each word based on the previous words, without access to future tokens. This autoregressive nature makes decoder-based models highly effective for applications such as language modeling, conversational AI, and creative text generation.

A decoder consists of multiple layers of self-attention and feedforward neural networks, but unlike encoders, it is designed to generate text one token at a time. During training, each token only attends to previous tokens, preventing the model from "looking ahead" and ensuring logical text generation. This approach allows for smooth, fluent, and contextually accurate text output, making decoders ideal for applications that require dynamic text creation. Many modern AI-based writing tools, chatbots, and programming assistants rely on decoder-based Transformers to generate meaningful responses in real time. Below are some of the most notable decoder-based Transformer variants:

6.3.1 GENERATIVE PRETRAINED TRANSFORMER (GPT)

The generative pretrained transformer (GPT) [8], developed by OpenAI, is a groundbreaking model that enables machines to understand and generate human-like text. By transforming human–computer interactions, GPT has significantly improved the way AI assists with various NLP tasks. This article delves into the evolution, architecture, training, applications, and ethical implications of GPT models.

GPT is built upon the transformer architecture, introduced in the influential paper "Attention is All You Need" by Vaswani et al. (2017). Unlike traditional models that process text sequentially, transformers leverage self-attention mechanisms to analyze the relationship between words irrespective of their position in a sentence. This allows for a deeper contextual understanding, enabling GPT to generate coherent and contextually relevant responses.

6.3.1.1 GPT Works as a Generative Model

As a generative model, GPT excels at producing text by predicting the next word based on previous words in a given prompt. This ability makes it highly effective in applications like content generation, creative writing, and conversational AI. By fine-tuning its training data, GPT can generate meaningful and human-like responses across diverse contexts.

6.3.1.1.1 Evolution of GPT Models

OpenAI has continually advanced GPT models, significantly enhancing their performance over time:

1. GPT-1 (June 2018)
    - First pretrained transformer introduced by OpenAI.
    - Featured 12 layers, 768 hidden units, and 12 attention heads with 117 million parameters.
    - Achieved state-of-the-art performance on multiple NLP benchmarks.
2. GPT-2 (February 2019)
    - Expanded to 48 layers, 1,600 hidden units, and 1.5 billion parameters in its largest version.
    - Showcased remarkable text generation capabilities, leading to concerns about potential misuse, which delayed its full release.
3. GPT-3 (June 2020)
    - A major leap in model scale with 175 billion parameters.
    - Demonstrated impressive zero-shot and few-shot learning abilities, reducing the need for task-specific fine-tuning.
    - Enabled more advanced NLU and reasoning.
4. GPT-4 (March 2023)
    - Further improved accuracy, contextual understanding, and reasoning abilities.
    - While the exact parameter count remains undisclosed, it surpasses GPT-3 in performance across technical, creative, and general NLP tasks.

6.3.1.1.2 GPT's Transformer Architecture

GPT's decoder-based transformer consists of multiple layers that process and generate text efficiently. Its key elements are given as follows.

Self-Attention Mechanism: Determines the relevance of each word within a sentence by evaluating relationships between all tokens. Enables better contextual understanding and fluent text generation.

Positional Encoding: Since transformers do not process text sequentially, positional encodings are added to preserve word order.

Layer Normalization and Residual Connections: Helps stabilize training by addressing vanishing and exploding gradient problems.

Feedforward Neural Networks: Adds abstraction and enhances pattern recognition, sitting between self-attention layers.

6.3.1.1.3 Architecture of GPT

The original text is tokenized to break it down into sub-word tokens, which are subsequently converted into high-dimensional vectors via an embedding layer. Positional encoding is incorporated to maintain the sequence of words. The data then flows through transformer blocks that include multihead self-attention for understanding contextual connections, as well as residual connections and normalization to ensure stable training, and a feedforward network for enhanced processing. In the end, the output is normalized using layer normalization and modified through a linear transformation followed by a *softmax* function to yield probability scores for the subsequent possible token. Figure 6.6 shows the architecture of GPT.

6.3.1.1.4 Training Process of GPT Models

GPT is trained using large-scale textual data in two main stages and is given as follows.

Pretraining (Unsupervised Learning)

GPT is exposed to a vast amount of internet text, learning to predict the next word in a sequence. The maximum likelihood estimation (MLE) is used as the training objective and is given in Equation (6.9).

$$\mathcal{L} = -\sum_{t=1}^{n} \log P(x_t \mid x_{<t}) \tag{6.9}$$

where x_t is the predicted token based on preceding tokens $x_{<t}$.

Fine-tuning (Supervised Learning)

The model is fine-tuned for specific applications using domain-specific datasets. Enhances performance on targeted tasks like customer support, legal document analysis, and medical text generation.

(v) Applications of GPT Models

GPT models power a diverse range of real-world applications, including:

- Content Creation: Assists writers by generating articles, blogs, poetry, and scripts.
- Chatbots and Virtual Assistants: Provides human-like conversational AI for customer service.
- Education and Learning: Generates summaries, explanations, and tutoring materials.
- Programming Assistance: Converts natural language instructions into code snippets and debugging solutions.
- Healthcare and Medical Analysis: Helps generate medical reports and research summaries.

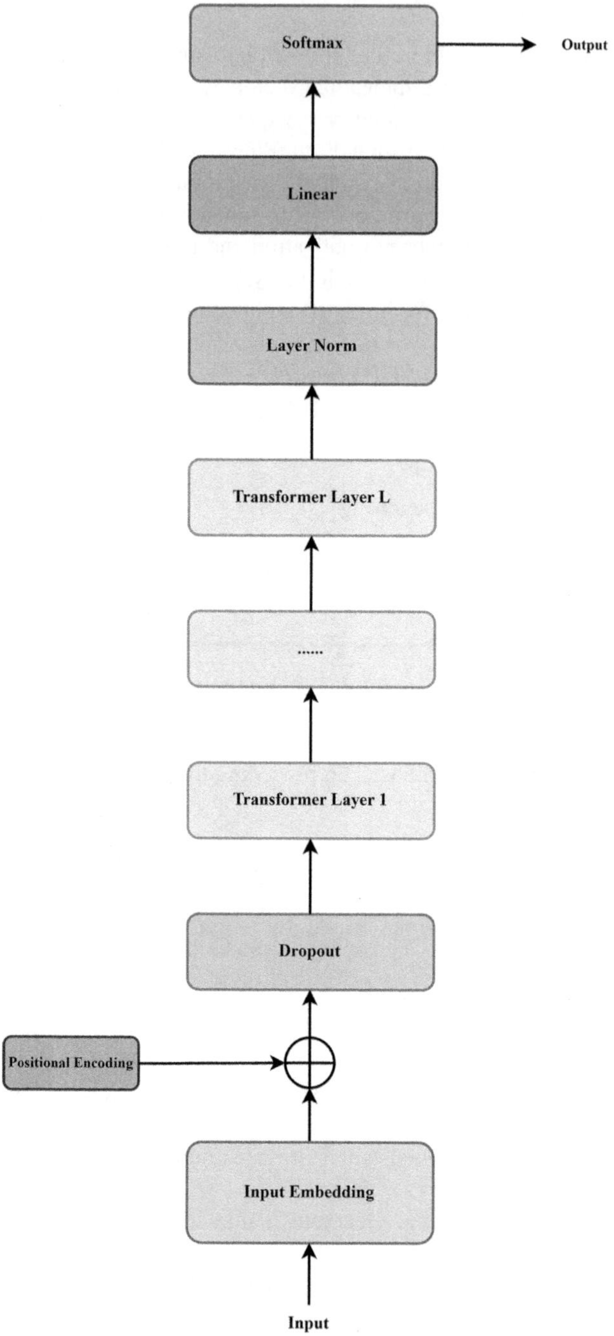

FIGURE 6.6 GPT.

6.3.2 Conditional Transformer for Long-Form Generation (CTRL)

CTRL (Conditional Transformer for Long-Form Generation) [9] is a decoder-only transformer model developed by Salesforce AI Research. It is specifically designed to generate coherent and controllable text based on user-specified control codes. Unlike standard generative models like GPT, which generate text based on general context, CTRL allows users to direct the generation process by providing specific control signals that influence the style, topic, or domain of the generated content.

6.3.2.1 Control Codes for Guided Generation

CTRL uses predefined control codes to influence the text output. Some examples are given as follows:

- News → Generates factual, news-like content.
- Opinion → Produces subjective and opinionated text.
- Horror → Creates eerie, suspenseful stories.
- Wikipedia → Outputs encyclopedia-style information.
- Jokes → Generates humorous content.

6.3.2.2 Large-Scale Pretraining

CTRL is trained on a massive dataset with structured text, associating different text types with specific control codes. This allows the model to generate text with domain-specific accuracy.

6.3.2.3 Autoregressive Text Generation

Like GPT, CTRL generates text token by token, predicting the next word while maintaining coherence. This ensures smooth and logical sentence construction.

6.3.2.4 Enhanced User Control

Unlike free-form generative models, CTRL follows user instructions through control tokens, improving consistency and relevance of generated content.

6.3.2.5 Model Architecture

CTRL is based on the GPT-2 transformer architecture but modified for conditional text generation. The key components are given as follows.

Input Processing

Control code injection begins with a control token (like "News:") to direct the model's actions, followed by text provided by the user. This unified input is then tokenized utilizing Byte-Pair Encoding (BPE), which segments it into subword tokens that are converted to high-dimensional vectors via an embedding layer for subsequent processing.

Transformer Decoder Blocks

The model uses multi-head self-attention to focus on relevant words within a sequence, while residual connections combined with layer normalization help stabilize training and boost performance. A feedforward neural network then refines the output, enhancing the model's overall language understanding.

Output Generation

After processing, a linear layer converts the model's output into logits that reflect the raw scores for each token within the vocabulary, which are subsequently fed into a softmax function to transform them into probability distributions. During the text generation phase, methods like top-k sampling (which limits options to the top-k most likely tokens) and temperature scaling (which modifies the confidence of the distribution by either sharpening or softening it) are utilized to manage the level of randomness and creativity in the generated text.

6.3.2.6 Training Process

CTRL is trained using a large-scale dataset that links control codes with text types. The training objective follows MLE and is given in Equation (6.10).

$$\mathcal{L} = -\sum_{t=1}^{n} \log P(x_t \mid x_{<t}, c) \tag{6.10}$$

where x_t is the next predicted token, $x_{<t}$ represents previous tokens, and c is the control code that guides text generation.

By associating text with specific control tokens, CTRL ensures that its outputs are structured, relevant, and domain appropriate.

CTRL introduces a new paradigm in text generation by allowing users to guide AI-generated content using control codes. This improves coherence, relevance, and adaptability, making it a powerful tool for journalism, creative writing, and AI-driven content creation. While it enhances controllability, further research is needed to address biases and improve content generalization.

6.3.3 Transformer-XL

Transformer-XL (Extended Transformer) [10] is an advanced decoder-based transformer model designed to handle long-term dependencies in text. Developed by Google AI, it overcomes the limitations of standard transformers by introducing a segment-level recurrence mechanism and relative positional encodings.

Traditional transformers struggle with fixed-length context windows, limiting their ability to retain long-range dependencies. Transformer-XL extends context length by reusing hidden states from previous segments, making it highly efficient for tasks requiring deep contextual understanding.

The key features of Transformer-XL are given as follows.

1. **Segment-Level Recurrence:** Instead of processing text in isolated chunks, Transformer-XL allows hidden states from previous segments to be carried

forward. This reduces the loss of contextual information and improves coherence.

2. **Relative Positional Encoding:** Standard transformers use absolute positional encoding, which limits their flexibility. Transformer-XL uses relative positional encodings, enabling better long-distance dependency modeling.
3. **Autoregressive Generation:** Like GPT models, Transformer-XL generates text sequentially (left-to-right), making it ideal for text completion and generation.
4. **Memory Mechanism for Efficient Computation:** Maintains a memory of past activations, reducing the need to recompute hidden states. Leads to faster training and inference.

6.3.3.1 Architecture of Transformer-XL

Transformer-XL improves upon the standard transformer architecture by incorporating a recurrence mechanism and relative positional embeddings.

6.3.3.1.1 Input Processing

The tokenization process breaks input text into subword tokens, enabling the model to handle rare or unknown words more effectively. These tokens are then passed through an embedding layer, which maps each one to a high-dimensional vector representation that captures semantic and contextual information for further processing by the model.

6.3.3.1.2 Segment-Level Recurrence Mechanism

Instead of processing fixed-length segments independently, Transformer-XL retains hidden states across segments. The recurrence formula is given as follows in Equation (6.11).

$$h_t^n = f(h_t^{n-1}, h_{t-1}^{n-1}, x_t) \tag{6.11}$$

where h_t^n is the hidden state at layer n for time step t, and h_{t-1}^{n-1} is the hidden state from the pervious segment.

6.3.3.1.3 Relative Positional Encoding

In contrast to traditional transformers that rely on fixed position embeddings, Transformer-XL utilizes relative positional encodings tied to the position of the query, which improves its capacity to understand long-range dependencies.

6.3.3.1.4 Multi-Head Self-Attention and Feedforward Layers

Transformer-XL retains the standard multihead attention mechanism while incorporating residual connections and layer normalization to enhance training stability.

6.3.3.1.5 raining Process

Transformer-XL utilizes an autoregressive language modeling method, which involves predicting the next token based on a series of previous tokens.

6.3.3.2 Memory-Augmented Training

During training, Transformer-XL maintains memory states across sequences, leading to improved learning of long-range dependencies. The training objective follows MLE and is given in Equation (6.12).

$$\mathcal{L} = -\sum_{t=1}^{n} \log P\left(x_t \middle| x_{<t}\right) \tag{6.12}$$

where x_t is the predicted token based on preceding tokens $x_{<t}$.

Transformer-XL represents a major leap forward in transformer architectures by addressing long-range dependency limitations. Its segment-level recurrence mechanism and relative positional embeddings allow it to model much longer contexts efficiently. This makes it an excellent choice for applications requiring coherent text generation, machine translation, and speech recognition. As AI continues to evolve, Transformer-XL remains a key innovation in language modeling and sequence processing.

6.3.4 BigScience Large Open-Science Open-Access Multilingual Language Model (BLOOM)

BLOOM [11] is a 176-billion-parameter multilingual language model developed by the BigScience initiative. Designed as an open-access model, BLOOM is capable of generating text in 46 natural languages and 13 programming languages. It represents a significant step toward democratizing AI research by providing a powerful tool accessible to the global research community.

The key features of BLOOM are given as follows.

- **Multilingual Proficiency:** BLOOM can generate text in 46 natural languages, including Spanish, French, and Arabic, making it one of the most versatile language models available.
- **Programming Language Support:** In addition to natural languages, BLOOM supports 13 programming languages, enhancing its utility for code generation and related tasks.
- **Open-Access Model:** Unlike many LLMs developed by resource-rich organizations and kept proprietary, BLOOM is publicly released under the Responsible AI License, promoting transparency and collaboration in AI research.

6.3.4.1 Architecture of BLOOM

BLOOM is a decoder-only Transformer language model, trained to continue text from a prompt using an autoregressive approach. This design enables it to generate coherent and contextually relevant text across various languages and domains.

Training Data: The model was trained on the ROOTS corpus, a dataset comprising hundreds of sources in 46 natural and 13 programming languages. This diverse training data enables BLOOM to perform competitively across a wide variety of benchmarks. Figure 6.7 displays the architecture of BLOOM.

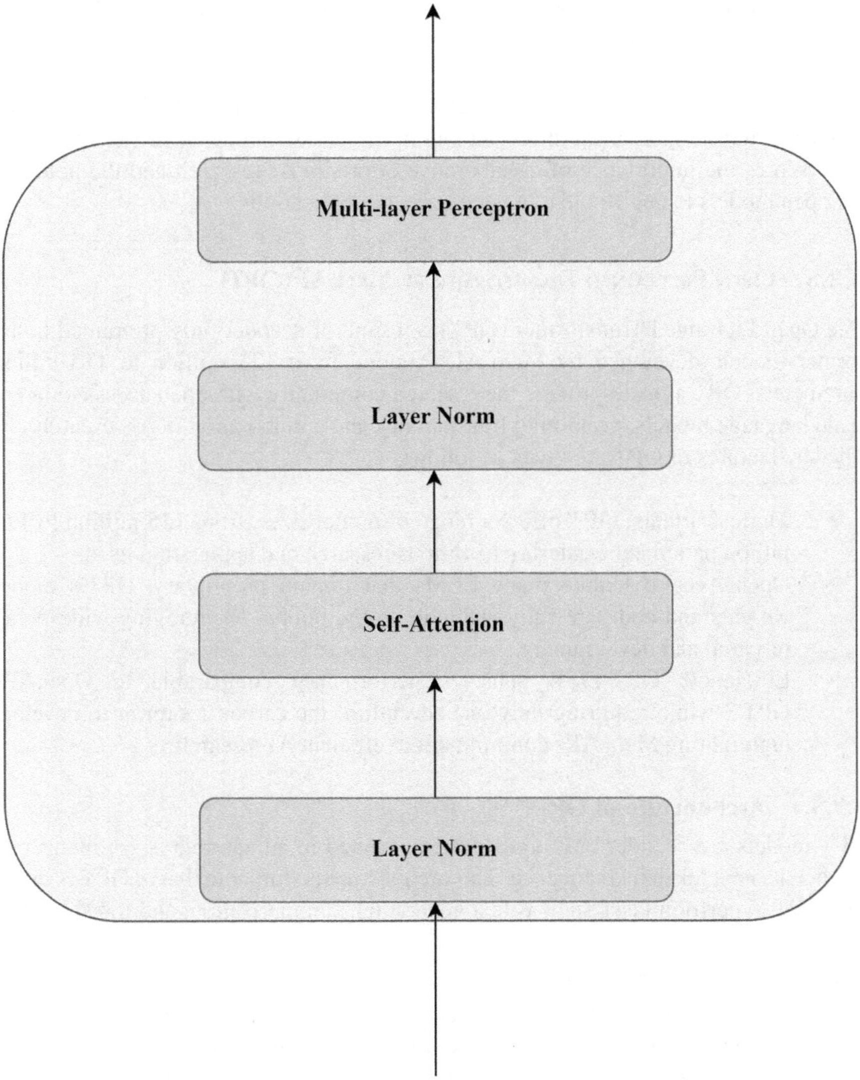

FIGURE 6.7 BLOOM.

6.3.4.2 Applications

BLOOM's multilingual and programming language capabilities make it suitable for a range of applications, including:

- **Text Generation:** Creating coherent and contextually relevant text in multiple languages.
- **Code Generation:** Assisting in writing code across various programming languages.

- **Research:** Serving as a tool for studying LLMs and their applications in different linguistic contexts.

BLOOM represents a significant advancement in the field of LLMs, combining extensive multilingual capabilities with an open-access framework. Its development underscores the importance of collaborative efforts in AI research and the potential for open models to contribute to a wide array of applications.

6.3.5 Open Pretrained Transformer by Meta AI (OPT)

The Open Pretrained Transformer (OPT) is a suite of decoder-only pretrained transformer models developed by Meta AI. Ranging from 125 million to 175 billion parameters, OPT aims to provide the research community with open access to large-scale language models, promoting transparency and collaboration in AI research. The key features of OPT are given as follows.

- Model Variants: OPT offers a range of model sizes, from 125 million to 175 billion parameters, catering to various research and application needs.
- Open Access: Unlike many LLMs that remain proprietary, OPT's model weights and code are fully available to the public, encouraging widespread research and development.
- Efficiency: OPT-175B achieves performance comparable to OpenAI's GPT-3 while requiring only one-seventh of the carbon footprint to develop, highlighting Meta AI's commitment to efficient AI research.

6.3.5.1 Architecture of OPT

OPT models are decoder-only transformers, trained in an autoregressive manner to predict the next token in a sequence. This architecture is similar to that of GPT-3, enabling OPT to perform tasks such as text generation, summarization, and translation.

6.3.5.1.1 Training Process

The training of OPT models involved meticulous documentation of the infrastructure challenges and solutions encountered. Meta AI has released a detailed logbook outlining these aspects, providing valuable insights for future large-scale model training endeavors.

OPT represents a significant advancement in the democratization of AI research, providing the community with access to large-scale language models. Its development underscores the importance of transparency, efficiency, and ethical considerations in the evolution of AI technologies.

6.4 ENCODER–DECODER TRANSFORMERS (SEQ2SEQ MODELS)

Encoder–Decoder architectures are designed for sequence-to-sequence tasks, where an input sequence is transformed into a meaningful output sequence. These models are highly effective for translation, summarization, and text transformation tasks.

- The Encoder processes the input sequence and generates a contextual representation of the text.
- The Decoder then takes this representation and generates the output sequence, attending to the encoder's hidden states while predicting words one at a time.
- These models combine bidirectional attention in the encoder with unidirectional attention in the decoder, allowing them to both understand and generate text efficiently.

6.4.1 Bidirectional and Auto-Regressive Transformer (BART)

In the ever-evolving field of NLP, pretrained language models have significantly improved performance across a variety of tasks. Among these models, BART stands out as a powerful sequence-to-sequence autoencoder designed to handle denoising tasks and enhance text generation, summarization, and translation.

BART [12] combines the strengths of two leading models—BERT and GPT. By incorporating a bidirectional encoder and an autoregressive decoder, BART creates a robust system capable of reconstructing corrupted text sequences and generating coherent outputs. Figure 6.8 shows the architecture of BART.

6.4.1.1 Architecture of BART

BART's architecture consists of two main components and is given as follows.

- Bidirectional Encoder: Processes the input sequence in both directions to capture a complete contextual representation of the text.
- Autoregressive Decoder: Generates text sequentially, using past predictions to refine future outputs.

The architecture follows the Transformer framework, incorporating multiple layers of self-attention mechanisms, add-and-norm layers, and feed-forward networks to enhance learning efficiency.

Multihead Attention Mechanism: Attention mechanisms enable BART to focus on relevant parts of the text while processing sequences. Multihead attention allows the model to compute multiple attention distributions in parallel, improving its ability to capture intricate patterns in language.

The attention score between a query Q and a key K is computed using the following Equation (6.13).

$$\text{Attention}(Q,K,V) = \text{softmax}\left(\frac{QK^T}{\sqrt{d_k}}\right) V \tag{6.13}$$

where, $Q, K, \textit{and } V$ are the query, key, and value matrices. d_k is the dimension of the key.

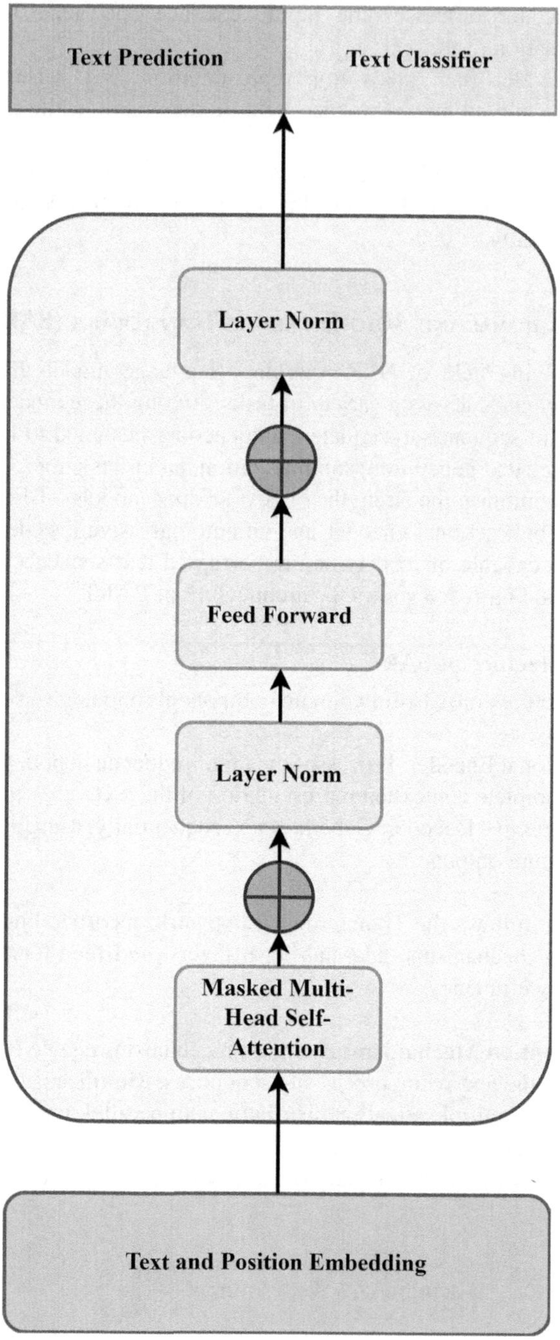

FIGURE 6.8 BART.

Addition and Normalization Layers: Each layer of the encoder and decoder contains an add-and-norm mechanism. This ensures that information is efficiently propagated while maintaining numerical stability across multiple training iterations. The normalization is computed as follows using Equation (6.14).

$$\text{LayerNorm}(x) = \frac{x-\mu}{\sigma+\varepsilon} + \beta \tag{6.14}$$

where, μ and σ are the mean and standard deviation of the input.γ and β are learnable parameters.

6.4.1.2 Feed-Forward Networks

These layers serve as the fundamental building blocks of the model, transforming input representations into meaningful embeddings. Information flows unidirectionally through these layers, ensuring structured learning across different sequences. The transformation is defined as follows using Equation (6.15).

$$\text{FFN}(x) = \max\left(0, xW_1 + b_1\right) W_2 + b_2 \tag{6.15}$$

where W_1, W_2, b_1, b_2 are learnable weights and biases.

6.4.1.3 Training BART

BART is trained using a denoising autoencoding approach, which involves two primary steps:

- Corrupting the input text using various techniques, including token masking, token deletion, text infilling, sentence permutation, and document rotation.
- Reconstructing the original sequence by training the model to recover the corrupted text.

The loss function used is the standard cross-entropy loss and is shown in Equation (6.16).

$$\mathcal{L} = -\sum y \log(\hat{y}) \tag{6.16}$$

where y is the true label and $\hat{y}$ is the predicted probability.

These training strategies enable BART to develop a deeper understanding of language structure, making it highly effective for text generation tasks.

6.4.1.4 The Power of Pretraining

Pretraining plays a crucial role in the success of BART. Unlike traditional MLMs, BART applies diverse corruption strategies that allow it to generalize well across multiple NLP tasks. BART's ability to learn from incomplete, shuffled, or masked inputs makes it especially useful for tasks that require sentence restructuring or paraphrasing.

6.4.1.5 Applications of BART

BART has been fine-tuned and applied to a variety of NLP challenges. Some of its key applications include:

- **Text Summarization:** BART achieves state-of-the-art performance on datasets like CNN/DailyMail and XSum, producing concise and informative summaries that preserve essential content.
- **Machine Translation:** By leveraging its pretrained decoder, BART improves translation accuracy, particularly when only monolingual target-language data is available.
- **Question Answering:** BART performs well on benchmark datasets like SQuAD, enabling more accurate comprehension-based answer retrieval.
- **Dialogue Generation:** Conversational AI benefits greatly from BART's ability to generate coherent and context-aware responses.

6.4.2 Text-to-Text Transfer Transformer (T5)

Text-to-Text Transfer Transformer (T5) [13] was introduced by Google Research and builds upon the standard Transformer architecture. Unlike traditional models that treat different NLP tasks with separate mechanisms (e.g., classification, question-answering, translation), T5 reframes all problems into a text-to-text format, making it a versatile and unified model for a variety of NLP tasks.

6.4.2.1 Encoder–Decoder Architecture

At the core of T5 lies the Transformer-based encoder-decoder architecture, which allows the model to handle a wide range of NLP tasks in a consistent and efficient manner. The encoder–decoder structure, originally introduced in Transformer models, is central to T5's design.

6.4.2.1.1 Encoder

The encoder processes the input text and converts it into an embedding representation, which is a dense vector capturing the semantic information of the text. It works by first tokenizing the input, converting the tokens into embeddings, and then passing these through multiple layers of self-attention and feed-forward networks.

6.4.2.1.2 Decoder

The decoder takes the encoded representation from the encoder and generates the target text sequence autoregressively. It does this by attending to the encoder's output as well as its own previously generated tokens, ensuring the generation of coherent and contextually relevant text. This autoregressive generation process makes T5 highly effective in tasks like summarization, translation, and text generation.

This architecture, similar to BART, enables T5 to reconstruct corrupted sequences and generate meaningful outputs across a wide range of tasks. Figure 6.9 shows the architecture of T5.

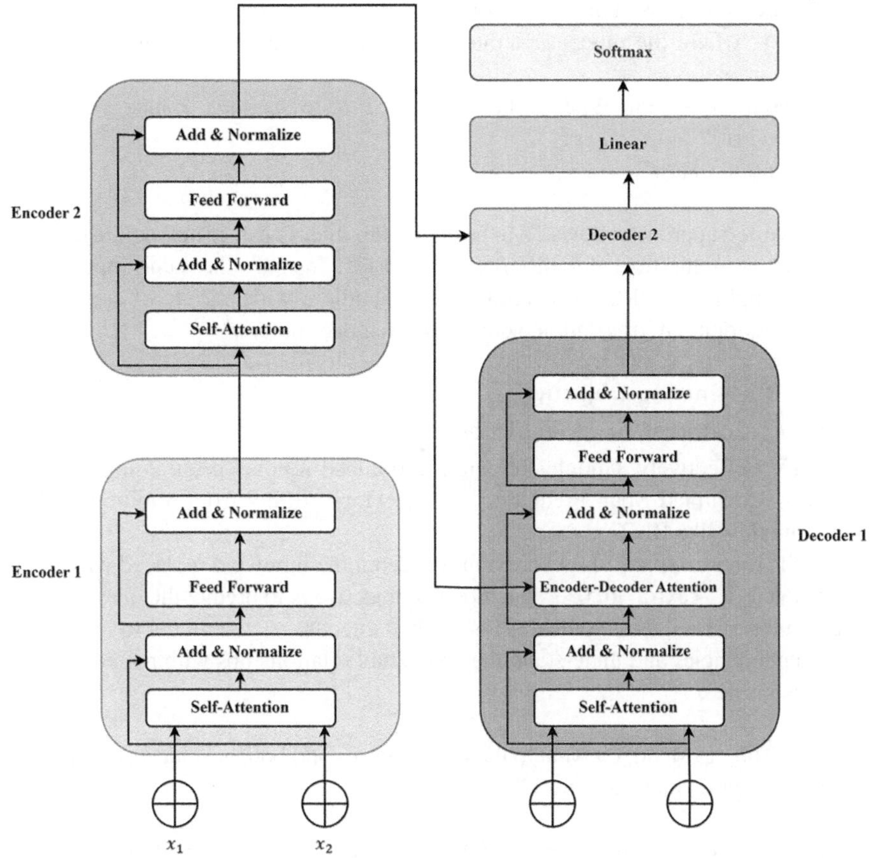

FIGURE 6.9 T5.

6.4.2.2 Unified Text-to-Text Framework

One of the most distinctive features of T5 is its unified text-to-text framework, which converts every NLP problem into a text generation task. This simplifies the task-specific nuances found in traditional models, where different tasks may require different processing mechanisms.

For example:

- **Summarization:** In T5, summarization is treated as a text generation problem where the input text is "summarized" to produce a shorter version. Example:
  Input: "summarize: The man went to the store and bought some milk."
  Output: "The man bought milk."
- **Translation:** Translation is framed as a text-to-text task where the model translates text from one language to another. Example:
  Input: "translate English to French: How are you?"
  Output: "Comment ça va?"

- **Question Answering:** Question answering is also treated as a text generation task, where the model generates an answer based on the context provided. Example:
  Input: "question: What is the capital of France? context: France's capital is Paris."
  Output: "Paris"

This unified approach allows T5 to be highly flexible, as it does not require different models or configurations for different NLP tasks. Instead, the same input-output format is applied to all tasks, enabling T5 to handle a wide variety of applications such as classification, translation, summarization, and more.

6.4.2.3 Pre-training Objective

6.4.2.3.1 Corrupted Span Prediction (CSP)

To train T5 effectively, Google Research introduced a novel pre-training objective known as Corrupted Span Prediction (CSP), which differs from traditional MLM used in models like BERT.

In CSP, random spans of text are removed from the input and replaced with a sentinel token (e.g., <extra_id_0>). The model's objective is to predict the missing spans based on the surrounding context. This method encourages the model to learn long-range dependencies and understand the contextual relationships within text.

For example,

Input: "The <extra_id_0> went to the <extra_id_1> and bought some <extra_id_2>."
Target Output: "man store milk"

This technique helps improve the model's ability to generate coherent text and better capture context over long distances, which is especially useful for tasks like text generation and summarization.

Scaling Up: T5 Variants

T5 is available in multiple variants, ranging from smaller models suitable for general use to larger models designed for more complex tasks. These variants offer different parameter sizes, allowing the user to choose the best model depending on their computational resources and the complexity of the tasks at hand.

Larger versions of T5, such as T5-3B and T5-11B, perform significantly better on complex NLP tasks but require more computational resources, including increased memory and processing power. Choosing the right variant depends on the task complexity and available resources.

6.4.3 Masked Sequence to Sequence (MASS)

Masked Sequence to Sequence (MASS) [14] is a powerful sequence-to-sequence pretraining model introduced by Microsoft Research. It is designed specifically for

FIGURE 6.10 MASS.

tasks like machine translation, text summarization, and text generation. Unlike other transformer-based models such as BERT (which focuses on token-level masking) or GPT (which follows an autoregressive approach), MASS applies masking to both the encoder and decoder during training, making it particularly effective for sequence generation tasks. Figure 6.10 shows the workflow of MASS.

6.4.3.1 Architecture of MASS

MASS follows a Transformer-based sequence-to-sequence (seq2seq) structure, consisting of the following.

- Encoder: Processes partially masked input sequences and learns contextual representations.
- Decoder: Reconstructs the missing spans in the target sequence by attending to the encoder's representations.

This bidirectional and autoregressive setup enables MASS to be highly effective in sequence generation tasks such as machine translation, text summarization, and QA.

6.4.3.2 Pretraining Objective

6.4.3.2.1 Masked Span Prediction (MSP)

The key idea of MASS is to randomly mask continuous spans of tokens in the input and train the model to predict those missing tokens. This approach is different from BERT's token-wise masking and is more aligned with models like T5, which also use span prediction.

The MASS objective function is defined as follows in Equation (6.17).

$$L(\theta) = -\mathbb{E}_{x \sim D} \sum_{t \in M} \log P(x_t \mid x_{\setminus M}, \theta) \tag{6.17}$$

where, x is the input sequence, M represents the masked tokens, $x_{\setminus M}$ denotes the unmasked tokens, $P\left(x_t \mid x_{\setminus M}, \theta\right)$ is the probability of predicting the masked tokens given the unmasked sequence.

For example,

- Input: "The ** went to the ** and bought some milk."
- Target Output: "man store"

The MASS pretraining strategy forces the decoder to generate only the masked tokens, making it better suited for seq2seq tasks compared to standard language models.

MASS has been fine-tuned for various NLP applications, particularly neural machine translation (NMT) and abstractive text summarization, achieving state-of-the-art performance in these areas.

6.4.3.3 Applications of MASS

Neural Machine Translation (NMT): MASS significantly improves translation performance by training on parallel text corpora. By masking parts of a sentence and forcing the decoder to reconstruct missing content, MASS achieves state-of-the-art accuracy in low-resource translation scenarios.

Text Summarization: While MASS is primarily designed for translation, it also performs well in abstractive text summarization by learning to predict missing spans in long-form content.

Question Answering: MASS can be fine-tuned for question-answering tasks by masking relevant portions of context passages and training the model to generate correct responses.

Dialogue Generation: By leveraging span-based prediction, MASS can be used in chatbots and dialogue systems to generate more natural and context-aware responses.

MASS introduces a novel approach to sequence-to-sequence pretraining by leveraging masked span prediction. It is highly optimized for NMT and performs well in text generation tasks. As Transformer-based models continue to evolve, future improvements in MASS could focus on the following.

- **Expanding beyond translation:** Enhancing its adaptability to more general NLP tasks.
- **More efficient training:** Reducing computation costs while maintaining high performance.
- **Multilingual support:** Further optimizing MASS for cross-lingual understanding and translation.

With its powerful span-based pretraining, MASS is a crucial advancement in sequence generation and will continue influencing future research in NLP.

6.5 OTHER VARIANTS

6.5.1 Longformer: Efficient Transformer for Long Documents

Traditional Transformer models, such as BERT and GPT, have revolutionized NLP but struggle with long documents due to their quadratic self-attention complexity. The Longformer model, introduced by Beltagy et al. (2020), addresses this limitation by using an efficient attention mechanism that allows it to process long sequences while maintaining performance.

Longformer [15] extends the Transformer architecture to handle documents with thousands of tokens, making it suitable for text classification, summarization, and QA over long-form text.

This model features a scalable attention mechanism that significantly reduces computational costs while preserving high accuracy. It efficiently handles long documents by supporting much longer inputs than traditional Transformer models, all while maintaining effective memory usage that prevents GPU overload. These capabilities enable it to achieve strong, competitive performance on a variety of NLP tasks that demand long-context comprehension.

Standard transformers rely on self-attention, where each token attends to every other token in the sequence. This results in a quadratic complexity of $O(n^2)$, making it computationally expensive and impractical for long documents.

For example, BERT can only process sequences up to 512 tokens, limiting its application to short texts. While some approaches like GPT-3 and T5 use larger models to extend sequence length, they still face efficiency challenges due to self-attention's high memory requirements.

Standard transformers face key challenges, including high computational cost due to their $O(n^2)$ attention complexity, fixed-length sequence limitations (such as BERT's 512-token cap), and inefficiency in processing long documents like research papers or legal texts. Longformer addresses these issues by replacing full self-attention with a combination of local and global attention mechanisms, enabling efficient and scalable processing of extended sequences.

6.5.1.1 Longformer's Attention Mechanism

To address the inefficiencies of standard Transformers, Longformer introduces a new sparse attention mechanism that scales linearly ($O(n)$) instead of quadratically ($O(n^2)$).

6.5.1.1.1 Local Windowed Attention

Instead of attending to all tokens, Longformer restricts attention to a fixed-size window around each token. This significantly reduces computational complexity while retaining context within a local neighborhood.

The attention complexity of traditional self-attention is given by Equation (6.18).

$$\text{Attention compexity}_{\text{full}} = O(n^2) \tag{6.18}$$

For Longformer, the attention complexity is reduced by attending only to local windows and is given in Equation (6.19).

$$\text{Attention compexity}_{\text{local}} = O(k.n) \tag{6.19}$$

where, n is the number of tokens in the sequence and k is the size of the local window. This modification allows the model to handle much larger sequences efficiently.

- Each token attends to only nearby tokens within a fixed window (e.g., 256 tokens).
- Local attention helps capture short-range dependencies, similar to convolutional neural networks (CNNs).
- Reduces memory usage and allows efficient processing of long sequences.

Example: If a document has 4000 tokens, instead of attending to all 4000 tokens, each token only attends to its surrounding 256 tokens.

6.5.1.2 Global Attention for Key Tokens

While local attention captures short-range dependencies, some tasks require long-range dependencies (e.g., summarization, QA).

Longformer introduces global attention for important tokens (e.g., question words, key entities) that require a broader context.

- Some tokens get full attention access, attending to all tokens in the document.
- Helps retain long-range dependencies and improve model accuracy.
- Global attention tokens are task-specific (e.g., [CLS] for classification, question words for QA).

For example,

In a question-answering task, question words like "What," "Where," and "When" are assigned global attention to ensure they access the entire passage.

6.5.1.3 Dilated Sliding Window Attention

Longformer improves efficiency further by using dilated attention patterns, where attention skips every few tokens instead of attending to consecutive ones. This helps the model scale without losing long-range information.

- **Standard Windowed Attention:** Each token attends to a continuous local window.
- **Dilated Attention:** Some tokens in the window are skipped, improving efficiency.
- **Hybrid Approach:** Combines dense local attention with sparse long-range attention.

This hybrid mechanism allows Longformer to efficiently process long texts while maintaining Transformer-level performance.

6.5.1.4 Training and Fine-Tuning Longformer

Longformer is pretrained in a similar fashion to BERT, using MLM and NSP. However, it incorporates sparse attention mechanisms from the beginning, making it more efficient for long-text training.

6.5.1.5 Fine-Tuning for Specific Tasks

Longformer can be fine-tuned on domain-specific tasks using datasets with long documents. Some examples include:

- Document Classification (e.g., classifying legal documents, research papers).
- Summarization (e.g., generating concise summaries for news articles, books).
- Question Answering (QA) (e.g., answering questions from long-form text).
- Biomedical NLP (e.g., analyzing patient records, medical research papers).

6.5.1.6 Advantages of Longformer

- Handles sequences up to 16,000 tokens, far exceeding BERT's 512-token limit.
- Linear complexity (O(n)), making it more efficient than standard Transformers.
- Maintains accuracy while reducing memory usage, making it practical for real-world applications.

6.5.1.7 Applications of Longformer

Longformer is highly effective in long-document NLP tasks where traditional Transformers struggle.

- **Legal Document Analysis:** Automatically classifying contracts, laws, and regulations. Extracting key information from lengthy legal texts.
- **Scientific Literature Summarization:** Summarizing research papers efficiently. Extracting insights from large academic databases.
- **Biomedical NLP:** Analyzing medical records and patient history. Assisting in medical research by processing large datasets.
- **Question Answering for Long Texts:** Answering questions from books, Wikipedia, or research papers. Enhancing AI assistants by improving context comprehension.

Longformer overcomes the limitations of traditional transformers by introducing efficient sparse attention mechanisms that scale linearly (O(n)), enabling the processing of thousands of tokens in a single pass.

With its local + global attention strategy, Longformer excels at long-text NLP tasks, including summarization, document classification, and QA. Future research may focus on further optimizing attention mechanisms to enhance efficiency in large-scale AI applications.

6.5.2 BigBird: Efficient Transformers for Ultra-Long Sequences

While Longformer provides a significant improvement in processing long documents, BigBird [16] extends the idea further by enabling even larger sequences to be processed efficiently. Developed by researchers at Google Research and Carnegie Mellon University, BigBird is another sparse attention-based model that can handle ultra-long sequences of up to 8,000 to 16,000 tokens (or more). It is designed to process extremely long documents, such as those found in research papers, books, or legal documents while maintaining the effectiveness of Transformer models.

The primary goal of BigBird is to scale transformer models to sequences that were previously impractical due to their quadratic attention complexity. By leveraging sparse attention, BigBird improves both training efficiency and memory usage while preserving the model's ability to capture long-range dependencies in the data.

This model excels at handling ultra-long sequences of up to 16,000 tokens or more by employing a sparse attention mechanism that reduces computational complexity from quadratic to linear. It integrates global, local, and random attention patterns to effectively capture long-range dependencies, enabling state-of-the-art performance across various NLP benchmarks, even with extended inputs.

The Limitations of Traditional Transformers for Ultra-Long Sequences: Like BERT and GPT, traditional transformer models use self-attention to compute representations of each token in relation to all other tokens in the sequence. However, as discussed earlier, this method has quadratic complexity ($O(n^2)$), which becomes computationally infeasible for sequences of large length. For instance, BERT's maximum input size is limited to 512 tokens, and even newer models like T5 and GPT-3 still face difficulties when processing sequences of several thousand tokens.

Traditional transformer models face high computational costs due to their $O(n^2)$ attention complexity, significant memory constraints from full self-attention, and inefficient handling of long-range dependencies, which limits their ability to effectively process and understand long documents.

6.5.2.1 BigBird's Attention Mechanism

BigBird introduces a novel sparse attention mechanism that significantly reduces the computational complexity from quadratic to linear ($O(n)$), making it feasible to process ultra-long sequences. BigBird achieves this by combining three types of attention patterns: local attention, global attention, and random attention.

6.5.2.2 Local Attention

Local attention is similar to Longformer's approach, where each token attends only to its neighbors within a fixed-size window. This captures short-range dependencies within a document while reducing computational cost and is displayed in Equation (6.20).

$$\text{Attention compexity}_{\text{local}} = O(k.n) \tag{6.20}$$

where, n is the number of tokens in the sequence and k is the size of the local window.

This reduces the quadratic complexity of the traditional full attention to linear complexity with respect to the length of the sequence.

6.5.2.3 Global Attention

Global attention is used to ensure that important tokens, such as special tokens (e.g., [CLS] or [SEP] in BERT), or key words (e.g., question words in a question-answering task), attend to all other tokens in the sequence. This preserves the model's ability to capture long-range dependencies.

For example, in QA, global attention would be given to question words, enabling them to access all relevant information across the document.

6.5.2.4 Random Attention

BigBird also incorporates a random attention pattern, where each token attends to a random subset of tokens in the sequence. This randomness ensures that the model captures diverse dependencies across the document without requiring the quadratic computation of full attention and is displayed in Equation (6.21).

$$\text{Attention compexity}_{\text{random}} = O(n) \tag{6.21}$$

This random attention mechanism helps the model to discover global context while maintaining the efficiency of sparse attention.

6.5.2.5 Combining the Attention Patterns

BigBird's hybrid attention mechanism uses a combination of local, global, and random attention patterns to achieve both efficiency and performance. The attention mechanism of BigBird can be summarized as follows in Equation (6.22).

$$\text{Attention compexity}_{\text{total}} = O(n) \tag{6.22}$$

This allows BigBird to handle sequences that are orders of magnitude longer than what traditional models can process.

Training and Fine-Tuning BigBird: BigBird can be pre-trained similarly to BERT, using MLM. However, due to the sparse attention mechanism, training BigBird on long sequences is more memory-efficient and computationally feasible.

6.5.2.6 Fine-Tuning for Specific Tasks

BigBird can be fine-tuned on tasks that involve long documents, such as document classification, summarization, and QA. Some examples are given as follows.

- **Document Classification:** Categorizing legal documents, research papers, or news articles based on their content.
- **Summarization:** Generating summaries of lengthy articles, books, or scientific papers.
- **Question Answering (QA):** Answering questions from extended passages or research papers, where context from the entire document is needed.

BigBird's ability to process long sequences allows it to outperform models like BERT and GPT in these tasks, especially when the document length exceeds traditional sequence limits.

6.5.2.7 Advantages of BigBird

- Handles sequences up to 16,000 tokens and beyond, far exceeding BERT's 512-token limit.
- Linear complexity (O(n)), making it efficient for processing large documents.
- Uses a hybrid attention mechanism to balance computational efficiency and long-range context understanding.

BigBird represents a significant advancement in the efficient processing of ultra-long sequences by utilizing a hybrid sparse attention mechanism. It combines local, global, and random attention to handle sequences of up to 16,000 tokens, making it highly efficient for long-document NLP tasks such as summarization, document classification, and QA.

6.5.3 Reformer: Efficient Transformers with Reversible Layers and Hashing

Reformer [17] introduces key innovations to address the memory and computational efficiency problems encountered in standard Transformers. Developed by Google Research, Reformer utilizes two main techniques—locality-sensitive hashing (LSH) for attention and reversible layers—to reduce the memory and time complexity of processing long sequences. These innovations allow Reformer to scale efficiently while maintaining Transformer-level performance.

Reformer is designed to process sequences of arbitrary length without the quadratic complexity that plagues traditional self-attention mechanisms. This makes it an excellent solution for tasks involving long documents, such as document classification, sequence generation, and large-scale text understanding.

This model leverages LSH to reduce attention complexity by grouping tokens and employs reversible layers to improve gradient computation efficiency and save memory during training. These innovations enable it to process much longer sequences than traditional Transformers while achieving state-of-the-art performance on NLP benchmarks.

6.5.3.1 Reformer's Attention Mechanism: Locality-Sensitive Hashing (LSH)

Reformer uses LSH to reduce the time complexity of the attention mechanism from $O(n^2)$ to $O(n \log n)$. This is achieved by mapping the input tokens to hash bins, such that tokens with similar representations are grouped together and attend to each other more efficiently.

In traditional attention, each token attends to all other tokens, leading to quadratic complexity. Reformer uses LSH to map tokens into hash bins, significantly reducing the number of tokens each one attends to.

- Hashing Process: Each token is hashed into a bin based on its token embedding. Tokens with similar embeddings are assigned to the same bin.
- Attention within Bins: Tokens only attend to other tokens within their assigned hash bin, greatly reducing the number of comparisons.
- Reduced Complexity: Instead of attending to all n tokens, a token only attends to the tokens in its hash bin, which brings the attention complexity closer to $O(nlogn)$

This hashing mechanism reduces computational cost without sacrificing the ability to capture important contextual relationships, especially for long-range dependencies.

Hashing Function: The hashing function used in LSH is designed to group tokens with similar representations together. This allows the attention mechanism to focus

on important tokens while ignoring less relevant ones, enabling efficient processing of long documents.
The formula for LSH-based attention complexity is given in Equation (6.23).

$$\text{Attention compexity}_{\text{LSH}} = O(nlogn) \tag{6.23}$$

where, n is the sequence length. The log term represents the logarithmic time complexity due to the binning process.

This is a significant improvement over the traditional quadratic complexity ($O(n^2)$) of standard self-attention.

6.5.3.2 Reversible Layers: Saving Memory During Training

One of the key innovations in Reformer is the use of reversible layers. In traditional transformers, each layer produces an output that needs to be stored during the forward pass in order to compute the gradient during backpropagation. This can lead to high memory consumption.

6.5.3.3 How Reversible Layers Work?

In Reformer, each layer is made reversible, meaning that the output of each layer can be recomputed from the input when needed. This eliminates the need to store intermediate activations during the forward pass.

- **Reversibility:** For each layer, the output is computed by applying a transformation to the input. The model only needs to store the input of the current layer, not the output.
- **Backward Pass:** During backpropagation, the input to the layer is used to recompute the output, allowing gradients to be computed without storing the intermediate activations.
- **Memory Efficiency:** This approach allows Reformer to reduce the memory footprint by half compared to traditional Transformer models.

6.5.3.4 Formula for Memory Complexity

The memory complexity of a typical Transformer is $O(n.d)$, where n is the sequence length and d is the hidden dimension. However, using reversible layers, Reformer reduces the memory usage and is displayed in Equation (6.24).

$$\text{Memory compexity}_{\text{Reformer}} = O(n.d)/2 \tag{6.24}$$

This makes Reformer highly memory-efficient, particularly for long sequences.

Training and Fine-Tuning Reformer: Reformer can be pretrained in a similar way to BERT using MLM. During pretraining, Reformer learns to predict missing tokens in a sequence while using its efficient attention and reversible layer techniques to handle longer sequences without exhausting memory.

6.5.3.5 Fine-Tuning for Specific Tasks

Once pretrained, Reformer can be fine-tuned for a wide range of NLP tasks, including:

- **Document Classification:** Categorizing large text documents, such as news articles, legal documents, or research papers.
- **Text Summarization:** Summarizing long-form content such as books or academic papers.
- **Question Answering:** Answering questions based on long passages, which require understanding from the entire document.
- **Sequence Generation:** Generating long sequences, such as text completion or code generation.

Reformer can also be fine-tuned using the Hugging Face Transformers library, which provides pretrained Reformer models for different NLP applications.

Reformer outperforms traditional transformers in tasks requiring long-context understanding, particularly for ultra-long sequences.

Reformer introduces two key innovations—LSH for attention and reversible layers—that make it memory-efficient and computationally efficient for long-sequence tasks. Reformer's ability to handle long sequences with logarithmic complexity (O(n log n)) for attention, combined with reversible layers to reduce memory usage, makes it an excellent solution for ultra-long document processing.

With state-of-the-art performance across multiple NLP benchmarks, Reformer is well-suited for tasks involving document classification, summarization, and QA. Future work may explore further optimizations to enhance scalability and adapt Reformer for specialized tasks in scientific research, legal analysis, and biomedical applications.

SUMMARY

This chapter surveys the major *architectural variants of LLMs*, categorized by their core Transformer configuration. *Encoder-only architectures* process the entire input bidirectionally, excelling at understanding tasks such as classification, sentiment analysis, and question answering. Examples include *BERT*, which uses MLM; *RoBERTa*, which optimizes BERT's training with more data and dynamic masking; *ALBERT*, which reduces parameters through weight sharing; *XLNet*, which combines autoregressive and permutation-based training; *DistilBERT*, a lightweight distilled version of BERT; and *ELECTRA,* which replaces masked token prediction with a more sample-efficient replaced token detection task.

Decoder-only architectures work well for open-ended text creation and language modeling since they produce text autoregressively. This group comprises the following models: Transformer-XL, which extends context length using segment-level recurrence; BLOOM, an open multilingual LLM; OPT, a parameter-efficient alternative to GPT-style models; CTRL, which enables controllable text generation via control codes; and GPT series, which only concentrate on next-token prediction.

Encoder–decoder architectures are perfect for sequence-to-sequence tasks like summarization and translation because they combine autoregressive decoding with bidirectional encoding. Important models include MASS, which use masked sequence-to-sequence pretraining; BART, which combines generative decoding and bidirectional encoding for denoising tasks; and T5, which reformulates tasks into text-to-text format.

The chapter also covers other variations that are intended to manage longer contexts and enhance efficiency: Reformer, which uses reversible layers and LSH to lower memory and computational costs, and Longformer and BigBird, which scale to longer sequences using sparse attention patterns.

QUESTIONS

1. Define encoder-only architecture in transformers. Give two examples.
2. List any three models that use decoder-only architecture.
3. Differentiate between BERT, RoBERTa, and ALBERT in terms of training strategy and efficiency.
4. Explain how GPT and CTRL differ in their pretraining objectives.
5. Describe the encoder–decoder architecture with examples from T5, MASS, and BART.
6. DistilBERT reduces parameters compared to BERT. If BERT has 110M parameters and DistilBERT uses 40% fewer parameters, calculate the approximate parameter count of DistilBERT.
7. OPT model scaling: If OPT-175B requires 350 GB of GPU memory and OPT-13B requires 27 GB, estimate the GPU memory required for OPT-30B assuming near-linear scaling.
8. Analyze how XLNet and ELECTRA improve upon BERT's limitations.
9. Compare encoder-only, decoder-only, and encoder–decoder architectures in terms of suitability for classification, generation, and translation tasks.
10. Evaluate the effectiveness of Transformer-XL and BLOOM for handling long-context tasks.
11. Assess how LongFormer, BigBird, and ReFormer address the quadratic complexity of standard transformers. Which do you find most effective and why?
12. Propose a hybrid model that combines strengths of encoder-only (BERT), decoder-only (GPT), and encoder–decoder (T5) architectures for a question-answering system.
13. Design an experiment to test ReFormer vs BigBird for document summarization. Outline the evaluation metrics you would use.
14. **Case Study: Variants of LLM Architecture**

A research team is working on *different types of LLMs* to handle tasks like *text classification, translation, and story generation.*

- For *text classification*, they choose *BERT*, which uses an *encoder-only* architecture to understand sentence meaning.

- For *story generation*, they apply *GPT*, a *decoder-only* model designed to predict the next word in a sequence.
- For *translation*, they use *BART*, an *encoder–decoder* model that learns to convert one sequence (English) into another (French).

This case shows how each *variant of LLM architecture* is suitable for different tasks:

- Encoder-only → understanding text
- Decoder-only → generating text
- Encoder–Decoder → transforming text

If you are building a system for summarizing long articles, which type of LLM architecture (Encoder-only, Decoder-only, or Encoder–Decoder) would you choose and why?

REFERENCES

[1] J. Devlin, M.-W. Chang, K. Lee, and K. Toutanova, "BERT: Pre-Training of Deep Bidirectional Transformers for Language Understanding," in *Proc. NAACL-HLT, Minneapolis*, MN, USA, pp. 4171–4186, May 2019.

[2] A. Vaswani, N. Shazeer, N. Parmar, J. Uszkoreit, L. Jones, A. N. Gomez *et al.*, "Attention is All You Need," in *Proc. Advances in Neural Information Processing Systems (NeurIPS)*, Long Beach, CA, USA, pp. 5998–6008, Jun. 2017.

[3] Y. Liu, M. Ott, N. Goyal, J. Du, M. Joshi, D. Chen *et al.*, "RoBERTa: A Robustly Optimized BERT Pretraining Approach," arxiv preprint, Jul. 2019, arXiv:1907.11692.

[4] Z. Lan, M. Chen, S. Goodman, K. Gimpel, P. Sharma, and R. Soricut, "ALBERT: A Lite BERT for Self-supervised Learning of Language Representations," in *Proc. International Conference on Learning Representations (ICLR)*, Feb. 2020.

[5] Z. Yang, Z. Dai, Y. Yang, J. Carbonell, R. Salakhutdinov, and Q. V. Le, "XLNet: Generalized Autoregressive Pretraining for Language Understanding," in *Proc. Advances in Neural Information Processing Systems (NeurIPS)*, pp. 5754–5764, 2019.

[6] V. Sanh, L. Debut, J. Chaumond, and T. Wolf, "DistilBERT, a Distilled Version of BERT: Smaller, Faster, Cheaper and Lighter," 2019, arXiv:1910.01108.

[7] K. Clark, M.-T. Luong, Q. V. Le, and C. D. Manning, "ELECTRA: Pre-training Text Encoders as Discriminators Rather Than Generators," in *Proc. International Conference on Learning Representations (ICLR)*, Mar. 2020.

[8] K. S. Kalyan, "A Survey of GPT-3 Family Large Language Models Including ChatGPT and GPT-4," *Natural Language Processing Journal*, vol. 6, Art. no. 100048, Oct. 2023.

[9] N. S. Keskar, B. McCann, L. R. Varshney, C. Xiong, and R. Socher, "CTRL: A Conditional Transformer Language Model for Controllable Generation," Sep. 2019, arXiv:1909.05858.

[10] Z. Dai, Z. Yang, Y. Yang, J. Carbonell, Q. V. Le, and R. Salakhutdinov, "Transformer-XL: Attentive Language Models Beyond a Fixed-Length Context," in *Proc. Annual Meeting of the Association for Computational Linguistics (ACL)*, Florence, Italy, pp. 2978–2988, Jun. 2019.

[11] B. Workshop *et al.*, "BLOOM: A 176B-Parameter Open-Access Multilingual Language Model," Jun. 2022, arXiv:2211.05100.

[12] M. Lewis *et al.*, "BART: Denoising Sequence-to-Sequence Pre-training for Natural Language Generation, Translation, and Comprehension," in *Proc. Annual Meeting of the Association for Computational Linguistics (ACL)*, pp. 7871–7880, 2020.

[13] C. Raffel, N. Shazeer, A. Roberts, K. Lee, S. Narang, M. Matena *et al.*, "Exploring the Limits of Transfer Learning with a Unified Text-to-Text Transformer," *Journal of Machine Learning Research*, vol. 21, no. 140, pp. 1–67, 2020.

[14] K. Song, X. Tan, T. Qin, J. Lu, and T.-Y. Liu, "MASS: Masked Sequence to Sequence Pre-training for Language Generation," in *Proc. International Conference on Machine Learning (ICML)*, pp. 5926–5936, Jun. 2019.

[15] I. Beltagy, M. E. Peters, and A. Cohan, "Longformer: The Long-Document Transformer," Dec. 2020, arXiv:2004.05150.

[16] M. Zaheer *et al.*, "Big Bird: Transformers for Longer Sequences," in Proc. Advances in Neural Information Processing Systems (NeurIPS), vol. 33, pp. 17283–17297, 2020.

[17] N. Kitaev, Ł. Kaiser, and A. Levskaya, "Reformer: The Efficient Transformer," in *Proc. International Conference on Learning Representations (ICLR)*, Feb. 2020.

7 Pretrained LLMs

7.1 SINGLE-MODAL PRETRAINED LARGE LANGUAGE MODELS (LLMS)

7.1.1 INTRODUCTION

Large language models (LLMs) [1] have significantly transformed the field of artificial intelligence, enabling advancements in natural language processing (NLP), computer vision, and speech recognition. While many models are designed to handle multiple modalities, such as text and images together, a significant number of powerful models specialize in processing only a single modality. These are referred to as single-modal pretrained LLMs.

Single-modal LLMs are trained exclusively on one type of data, such as text, images, or speech. They excel in domain-specific tasks, such as text generation, image recognition, and speech-to-text conversion. By focusing on a single modality, these models achieve greater efficiency and accuracy in specialized tasks compared to their multimodal counterparts.

Three primary types of single-modal LLMs are given as follows.

- Text-Only LLMs – Trained on textual data for NLP tasks.
- Vision-Only LLMs – Designed for image understanding.
- Speech-Only LLMs – Optimized for audio and speech recognition.

7.1.2 TEXT-ONLY PRETRAINED LARGE LANGUAGE MODELS

Text-only LLMs [2] are pretrained on vast textual corpora, such as books, research articles, web pages, and code repositories. These models use transformer architectures, which enable efficient context-based understanding and text generation.

The main goals for training language models consist of masked language modeling (MLM), where specific words in a sentence are concealed and the model learns to forecast them (as implemented in BERT); causal language modeling (CLM), which entails predicting the next word based on the words that come before it (as observed in GPT); and next sentence prediction (NSP), employed to assist models in

DOI: 10.1201/9781003650065-7

comprehending relationships between sentences for tasks such as question answering and summarization.

1. **BERT (Bidirectional Encoder Representations from Transformers)** [2]**:** BERT, developed by Google, introduced bidirectional training, allowing it to understand the full context of words in a sentence. It is widely used in sentiment analysis, text classification, and question answering.
   Example: A search engine using BERT can understand user queries better. If a user searches "bank account open online," BERT recognizes that "bank" refers to a financial institution, not a riverbank.
2. **RoBERTa (Robustly Optimized BERT Pretraining Approach)** [3]**:** RoBERTa, developed by Facebook AI, improves upon BERT by removing NSP and training on larger datasets for longer durations, leading to better performance.
   Example: A chatbot using RoBERTa can analyze customer complaints and categorize them for efficient resolution.
3. **GPT Series (Generative Pre-Trained Transformer)** [4]**:** GPT models, introduced by OpenAI, use CLM for text generation, chatbots, and creative writing. The GPT-4 model is one of the most powerful LLMs for natural language understanding.
   Example: GPT-4 can generate human-like responses in chatbots, such as writing emails or summarizing documents.
4. **XLNet** [5]**:** XLNet, developed by Google and Carnegie Mellon University, improves upon BERT by using permutation-based training, allowing it to learn bidirectional dependencies while preserving autoregressive properties.
   Example: XLNet improves upon BERT and is used in AI-powered legal document analysis, understanding complex legal terms.
5. **T5 (Text-to-Text Transfer Transformer)** [6]**:** T5, introduced by Google, reframes NLP tasks as text-to-text problems, making it highly flexible for translation, summarization, and question answering.
   Example: T5 can rephrase sentences while retaining their original meaning, useful for paraphrasing in content creation.

Text-only LLMs have a wide range of applications, including powering chatbots and virtual assistants like ChatGPT and Google Assistant, generating concise summaries from lengthy texts, assisting with code generation through tools like GitHub Copilot, enabling machine translation services such as DeepL and Google Translate, and performing sentiment analysis to interpret public opinion on platforms like social media.

7.1.3 Vision-Only Pre-Trained Large Language Models

Vision-only LLMs process and interpret image data, focusing on object detection, image segmentation, and facial recognition. These models are trained using large-scale image datasets like ImageNet and COCO.

Vision Transformer (ViT) [7]**:** ViT, developed by Google, applies transformer-based architectures to images, breaking them into patches and processing them similarly to word tokens in NLP.

Example: A medical imaging system using ViT can detect cancerous tumors in X-ray scans.

Swin Transformer [8]**:** Swin Transformer, introduced by Microsoft, improves upon ViT by using hierarchical feature maps, making it more efficient for high-resolution image tasks.

Example: Swin Transformer is used in video surveillance to track moving objects efficiently.

DETR (Detection Transformer) [9]**:** DETR, by Facebook AI, applies transformers to object detection, removing the need for traditional anchor boxes used in convolutional networks.

Example: DETR enables autonomous drones to detect and classify objects in real-time.

Vision-only LLMs are applied in various fields, including facial recognition systems for security authentication, medical imaging analysis for tasks such as tumor detection in radiology, autonomous vehicles for identifying road signs and pedestrians, and retail or surveillance settings for object tracking and monitoring in stores.

7.1.4 Speech-Only Pretrained Large Language Models

Speech-only LLMs process and analyze voice data, handling tasks like speech recognition, speaker identification, and voice synthesis.

Whisper [10]**:** Developed by OpenAI, Whisper is a powerful automatic speech recognition (ASR) model trained on multilingual datasets.

Example: A podcast transcription service uses Whisper to convert spoken content into text accurately.

wav2vec 2.0 [11]**:** Created by Facebook AI, wav2vec 2.0 uses self-supervised learning to recognize speech without relying on labeled data.

Example: wav2vec 2.0 enables AI assistants to recognize speech commands even in noisy environments.

DeepSpeech [12]**:** Developed by Mozilla, DeepSpeech is an open-source speech recognition system optimized for real-time transcription.

Example: DeepSpeech powers automatic captioning for online lecture videos.

Speech-only LLMs are used in a variety of applications, including voice assistants like Siri and Alexa, speech-to-text transcription services such as Google Speech-to-Text, voice biometrics for authentication based on unique vocal patterns, and call center automation to enhance customer support through AI-driven voice interactions.

Single-modal pretrained LLMs have revolutionized their respective fields, whether in text processing, image recognition, or speech analysis. These models continue to evolve, offering improved efficiency, accuracy, and real-world applicability. With ongoing research in efficient architectures and multimodal learning, the future holds promising advancements that will further integrate AI into everyday tasks.

7.2 MULTIMODAL TRANSFORMERS: BRIDGING MULTIPLE MODALITIES FOR INTELLIGENT SYSTEMS

Multimodal models [13] are deep learning models designed to process and integrate different types of data—such as text, images, video, and audio—simultaneously. These models are engineered to generate more context-specific, comprehensive outputs by understanding and synthesizing information from diverse sources. In comparison, unimodal models are limited to processing only one type of data at a time. For instance, YOLO (You Only Look Once) is a popular object detection model that operates solely on visual data.

While unimodal models are simpler and computationally less demanding, multimodal frameworks provide enhanced accuracy and a more robust user experience, making them ideal for tasks involving multiple data inputs. This ability to handle various forms of data simultaneously has made multimodal models indispensable in fields like healthcare, autonomous driving, and robotics. For example, in healthcare, multimodal AI systems can analyze both medical images and text-based patient history to offer more accurate diagnostic support.

A multimodal large language model (MLLM) is an advanced form of artificial intelligence that integrates the reasoning capabilities of LLMs such as GPT-3 and LLaMA-3 with the ability to process multiple forms of data—text, images, audio, and video. The core idea behind MLLMs is to enhance the model's understanding by combining different modalities, allowing for richer and more context-aware outputs.

For example, imagine a healthcare AI system that is presented with two inputs: a medical image and a text query asking, "Is pleural effusion present in this image?" The MLLM can analyze the image, understand the content, and provide a text-based prediction, bridging the gap between visual data and linguistic information. This is what makes MLLMs particularly powerful in fields like healthcare, autonomous driving, and robotics.

7.2.1 The Rise of Multimodal AI

Over the last few years, there has been a significant transformation in the field of artificial intelligence (AI) [14], largely driven by the rise of the transformer architecture. Introduced by Google in 2017, transformers revolutionized NLP tasks and sparked the development of large-scale language models. These advancements eventually influenced the domain of computer vision, where transformers were applied to image data.

One notable example of this application is vision transformers (ViT). Vision Transformers use the transformer architecture to segment an image into multiple patches and treat these patches as individual tokens, much like how words or subwords are processed in NLP. This approach was a breakthrough for image classification and other visual tasks, as it allowed the transformer model to understand spatial relationships and patterns in images.

The development of LLMs such as GPT-3 [15] and BERT led to a natural progression toward MLLMs. These models evolved from the growing need to process multimodal data (e.g., combining text and images), leading to the creation of models that could reason with both language and visual content. Figure 7.1 shows the schematic view of unimodal versus multimodal models.

7.2.2 How Multimodal Transformers Work?

Multimodal transformers [13] generally share a similar architecture, consisting of several components designed to handle and process diverse data inputs. These components include encoders, a fusion mechanism, and decoders, each playing a

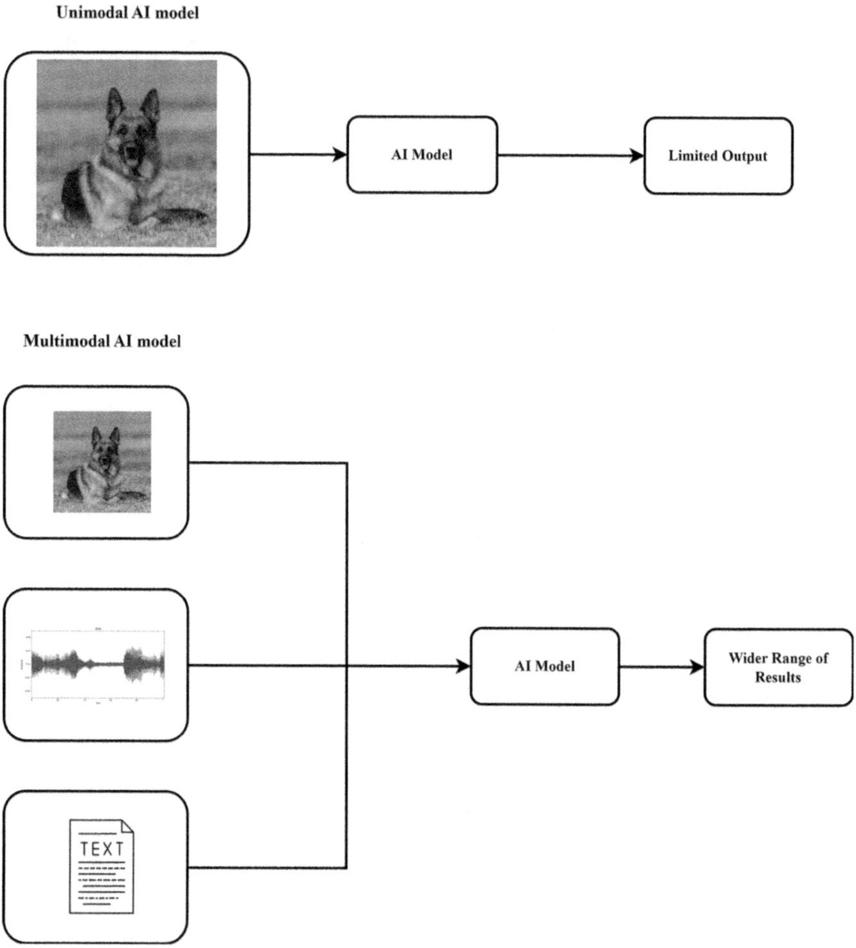

FIGURE 7.1 Unimodal vs multimodal models.

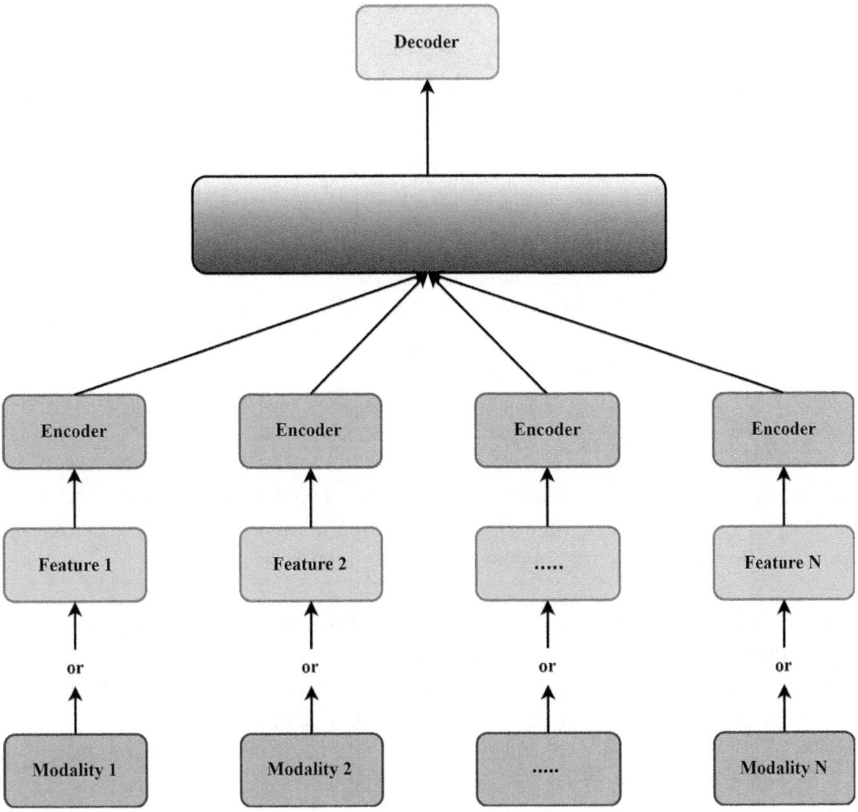

FIGURE 7.2 Multimodal transformers.

crucial role in the model's ability to interpret complex, multimodal data. Figure 7.2 shows the architecture of multimodal transformers.

7.2.3 Encoders

The encoders in a multimodal model are responsible for transforming raw data (e.g., images, text, audio) into machine-readable representations, often referred to as embeddings. These embeddings capture the essential features of each modality, enabling the model to understand the data's content. Figure 7.3 shows the schematic view of the Embedding model.

- **Image Encoders:** Convolutional neural networks (CNNs) are commonly used for image encoding. They convert the pixel data from images into feature vectors, which help the model interpret key visual features.
- **Text Encoders:** For text data, models often use transformer-based architectures, such as GPT (generative pretrained transformer), to convert text into embeddings that are used for further processing.

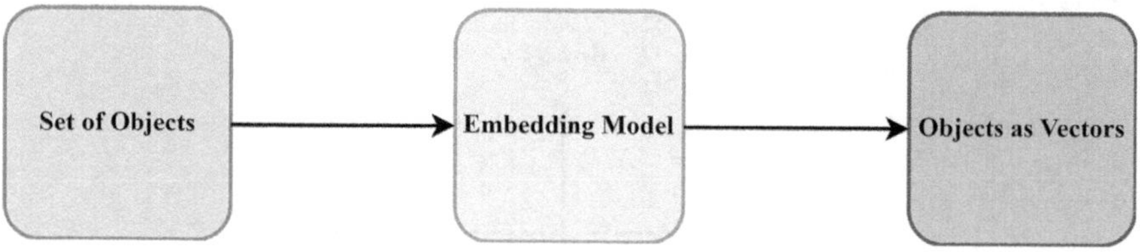

FIGURE 7.3 Embedding.

- **Audio Encoders:** Audio data is processed using encoders like Wav2Vec2, which convert raw audio into feature vectors that capture tonal, rhythmic, and contextual elements of sound.

7.2.4 Fusion Mechanism

Once each modality is encoded into its respective feature representation, the fusion mechanism combines these embeddings to form a comprehensive view of the data. Various fusion strategies are employed depending on the task:

- Early Fusion: In this strategy, all modalities are combined before passing them to the model for further processing.
- Intermediate Fusion: Here, each modality is projected into a latent space, and the representations are fused for more effective processing.
- Late Fusion: In this approach, each modality is processed separately, and the output from each modality is combined later.
- Hybrid Fusion: Combines different fusion strategies during different stages of model processing.

7.2.5 Fusion Methods

The fusion process can be performed using several techniques and can be explained as follows.

- **Attention-Based Methods:** These methods, based on the Transformer architecture, use a query-key-value structure to align the features from different modalities. The attention mechanism helps models focus on the most relevant parts of each modality, improving integration.
- **Concatenation:** This method combines embeddings from various modalities into a single vector. For instance, the text embedding might be concatenated with the image embedding, allowing the model to process them together in an integrated form.
- **Dot Product:** This method calculates the element-wise multiplication of embeddings from different modalities to capture correlations and interactions between them.

7.2.6 Decoders

The decoders in multimodal models are tasked with processing the fused feature representations to generate outputs. Depending on the task, decoders may be built using different architectures and can be listed as follows.

- RNNs (Recurrent Neural Networks): Often used for sequential tasks such as language translation.
- CNNs (Convolutional Neural Networks): Applied when the output involves images or visual tasks.
- GANs (Generative Adversarial Networks): Useful for generative tasks like creating new images or video frames.

In multimodal transformers, decoders often utilize cross-attention techniques, enabling the model to attend to the most relevant parts of the input from each modality and generate the required output.

7.2.7 Architecture of MLLMs

The architecture of a MLLM is divided into three key components and is given as follows.

- **Modality Encoder** [16]**:** This component processes different data formats (such as images, audio, or video) and condenses them into a form that can be interpreted by the model. Pretrained encoders, like Contrastive Language Image Pretraining (CLIP), are often used to process nontext data and convert them into feature representations that the MLLM can understand. These encoders allow the model to recognize objects in images, interpret audio signals, and more.
- **LLM Backbone** [17]**:** The backbone of the MLLM is a LLM, such as GPT or LLaMA, that processes the features generated by the encoder. The LLM acts as the "brain" of the MLLM, generating textual outputs based on the encoded input features. This is the part of the model that is responsible for generating meaningful responses or predictions, whether in the form of text, image captions, or even audio responses.
- **Modality Interface** [18]**:** The modality interface acts as a connector between the encoder and the LLM backbone. Since LLMs are primarily designed to handle text, this interface ensures that the different types of data—such as images or audio—can be effectively integrated and interpreted. The modality interface thus serves as a crucial bridge, enabling the MLLM to reason across multiple data modalities.

7.2.8 Applications of Multimodal Transformers

Multimodal models are increasingly being used in complex, real-world tasks that require the integration of multiple data sources. Some of the key applications include the following.

- **Visual Question Answering (VQA)** [19]: VQA tasks involve answering questions based on visual content. For example, a healthcare professional might ask a model to identify signs of disease in a medical image. Multimodal models combine both text and image inputs to generate accurate answers.
- **Image-to-Text and Text-to-Image Search** [20]: In these systems, multimodal models enable users to search for images using text descriptions or retrieve documents based on image inputs.
- **Generative AI:** Multimodal generative models can produce both images and text. For instance, a user might provide an image and ask the model to generate a caption or, conversely, provide a text prompt to generate a relevant image.
- **Image Segmentation:** Multimodal models can assist in segmenting parts of an image based on textual descriptions. This is particularly useful in medical imaging, where different regions of an image may need to be labeled or isolated.

7.2.9 Leading Multimodal Models

Several state-of-the-art multimodal models have emerged, each contributing unique features to the field. Some of the most notable models includes the following.

7.2.9.1 CLIP (Contrastive Language Image Pretraining): OpenAI's Vision-Language Model

CLIP [21] is a vision-language model designed to understand images and text together, enabling zero-shot learning for various AI applications. Unlike traditional image classification models, CLIP can recognize unseen objects by associating images with text descriptions.

CLIP is capable of identifying unfamiliar objects by connecting images to their textual descriptions, facilitating a robust understanding across different modalities. Its primary characteristics involve contrastive learning applied to image-text pairs to align visual and linguistic representations, incorporating Transformer-based models (Vision Transformer for visual data and a text encoder for textual data), the ability to perform zero-shot classification of images without the need for task-specific fine-tuning, and effective searching and retrieval of information by correlating images with appropriate text descriptions. Applications of CLIP and similar models include improving AI-driven search engines with enhanced image-to-text and text-to-image searching functions, assisting in content moderation by detecting inappropriate or copyrighted images on social media platforms, and supporting medical imaging and diagnostics by enabling physicians to analyze X-rays, CT scans, and MRIs through text-guided interpretations.

By employing contrastive learning to train a dual-encoder architecture—an image encoder and a text encoder—on 400 million image-text pairs, the CLIP (Contrastive Language–Image Pretraining) model is able to learn transferable visual representations. Cosine similarity is used to measure alignment in the shared embedding space that each encoder maps inputs into. A symmetric contrastive loss, scaled by a temperature parameter, is used to optimize the model, pushing mismatched image-text pairings apart and matching image-text pairs closer. By comparing a picture's embedding to embeddings of class-descriptive text prompts, CLIP allows zero-shot image classification during testing, choosing the class that is most similar. This approach's large-scale, language-supervised training and promptable classification mechanism allow it to attain competitive accuracy on benchmarks such as ImageNet without the need for labeled training data. It also generalizes well across a variety of tasks.

CLIP consists of Image encoder $f_I(x) \in R^d$, Text encoder $f_T(y) \in R^d$ where x is an image and y a text (caption or prompt). Outputs are projected into a common d-dimensional multimodal embedding space.

Given a batch of N image-text pairs $\{(x_i, y_i)\}_{i=1}^{N}$, compute cosine similarities are given in Equation (7.1).

$$s_{ij} = \frac{f_I(x_i) . f_T(y_j)}{\|f_I(x_i)\| . \|f_T(y_j)\|} \tag{7.1}$$

Define a temperature parameter τ (often trainable). Then, the *symmetric contrastive loss* can be given in Equation (7.2).

$$L = \frac{1}{2N} \sum_{i=1}^{N} \left(-\log \frac{exp\left(\frac{s_{ii}}{\tau}\right)}{\sum_{j=1}^{N} exp\left(\frac{s_{ij}}{\tau}\right)} - \log \frac{exp\left(\frac{s_{ii}}{\tau}\right)}{\sum_{j=1}^{N} exp\left(\frac{s_{ji}}{\tau}\right)} \right) \tag{7.2}$$

This encourages matching pairs (i, i) to have high similarity, and mismatched pairs (i,j), $i \neq j$ to be dissimilar.

At test time, CLIP performs zero-shot classification by generating a textual prompt y_c for each candidate class c, then computing its corresponding text embedding $t_c = f_T(y_c)$. For a given image x, the image embedding $f_I(x)$ is computed, and the class prediction is made by selecting the class whose text embedding t_c has the highest cosine similarity with $f_I(x)$. This is formulated as follows as in Equation (7.3).

$$\hat{c} = \underset{c}{argmax} \frac{f_I(x).t_c}{\|f_I(x)\| . \|t_c\|} \tag{7.3}$$

7.2.9.2 DALL-E: AI-Powered Text-to-Image Generation Model

DALL-E [22] is OpenAI's generative model that creates images from text prompts using a combination of Transformer-based architecture and diffusion models. It can generate realistic, artistic, and abstract images based on user input.

DALL·E is an advanced model for generating images, featuring a CLIP-based structure that aligns textual descriptions with visual ideas, a diffusion decoder that produces and refines images based on text prompts, a sizable context window of up to 1,280 tokens for crafting intricate and detailed scenes, and enhanced inpainting and editing features that allow users to alter specific areas of an image using straightforward language instructions. DALL·E caters to a wide range of applications, including the creation of content and marketing by producing distinctive digital artwork, supporting e-commerce and product design through the visualization of innovative

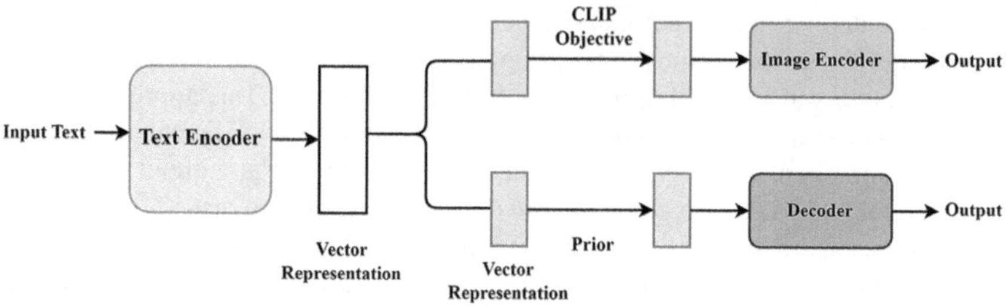

FIGURE 7.4 DALL-E.

product ideas, and improving education and research by depicting historical events, scientific phenomena, and abstract concepts. Figure 7.4 displays the architecture of DALL-E.

DALL·E, a model that generates images from text prompts using a discrete variational autoencoder (dVAE) and an autoregressive transformer. Images are first compressed into sequences of discrete tokens $\{x_1, x_2, \ldots, x_{1024}\}$ using dVAE, while text prompts are tokenized as $\{y_1, y_2, \ldots, y_T\}$. These are concatenated into a joint sequence $z = [y_1, \ldots, y_T, x_1, \ldots, x_{1024}]$, and the model learns the joint distribution using the following Equation (7.4).

$$P(z) = \prod_{t=1}^{T+1024} P(z_t \mid z_{<t}) \tag{7.4}$$

It is trained to maximize the log-likelihood of this sequence, minimizing the following loss function shown in Equation (7.5).

$$L = -\sum_{t=1}^{T+1024} logP_\theta \left(z_t|z_{<t}\right) \tag{7.5}$$

During inference, DALL·E samples image tokens conditioned on a given text prompt and decodes them via the dVAE, enabling zero-shot image generation for novel textual descriptions.

7.2.9.3 LLaVA (Large Language and Vision Assistant): Open-Source Multimodal AI

LLaVA [23] is an open-source multimodal AI model that integrates vision-language processing for chat-based interactions. It is a fine-tuned combination of Vicuna (text model) and CLIP (vision encoder), making it an efficient visual assistant.

LLaVA is a multimodal artificial intelligence model developed for sophisticated visual reasoning, incorporating instruction tuning with data generated by GPT-4, and using a Vicuna-based language decoder to provide accurate text responses related to images. With impressive performance on benchmarks such as Science QA, achieving an accuracy of 92.53%, LLaVA is both open-source and customizable. This model can be adapted for particular fields. Its primary applications include enabling intelligent chatbots to understand and answer queries related to images, aiding online learning platforms by clarifying visual information, and improving retail experiences through image-driven product discovery and AI shopping assistance.

LLaVA is a vision-language model that combines a big language model with a vision encoder to enable natural language education based on visual inputs. LLaVA uses an input image, X_v, to calculate visual features, $v = E_v\,(X_v)$, then projects them into the language model's embedding space via a linear transformation, $v = Wv$.

It then conditions language generation on both the instruction i and the projected visual features v', producing a response $r = [r_1, \ldots, r_T]$ with the following probability given in Equation (7.6).

$$P\left(r|i, v'\right) = \prod_{t=1}^{T} P\left(r_t|r_{<t}, i, v'\right) \tag{7.6}$$

The model is fine-tuned to minimize the negative log-likelihood loss given in the following Equation (7.7).

$$L = -\sum_{t=1}^{T} \log P_\theta\left(r_t|r_{<t}, i, v\right) \tag{7.7}$$

This function allowing it to generate coherent and contextually grounded responses for a wide range of visual instruction tasks.

7.2.9.4 CogVLM (Cognitive Visual Language Model): Alibaba's Multimodal AI

CogVLM [24] is a vision-language foundation model developed by Alibaba Cloud. It uses deep fusion techniques to achieve superior image-text understanding, making it a powerful tool for VQA and image captioning.

CogVLM is a multimodal model that merges visual and textual comprehension through attention-driven integration, employing a visual expert module and the EVA2-CLIP-E Vision Transformer for processing high-resolution images. It incorporates the Vicuna 1.5-7B language model to produce intelligent, context-sensitive responses and facilitates cross-modal learning to comprehend spatial relationships in images. Notable applications include AI-assisted image captioning for content generation, aiding healthcare providers in evaluating medical images through text-based inquiries, and boosting retail and e-commerce with visual search and product recommendation systems. Figure 7.5 shows the architecture of cogVLM.

CogVLM presents a visual expert module that can be immediately integrated into a frozen pretrained language model's (LM) transformer blocks. In contrast to conventional shallow alignment, which projects picture features into the input space of the LM, CogVLM uses feed-forward networks and attention to inject visual signals deeply within each layer, allowing for richer multimodal fusion without changing the underlying LM.

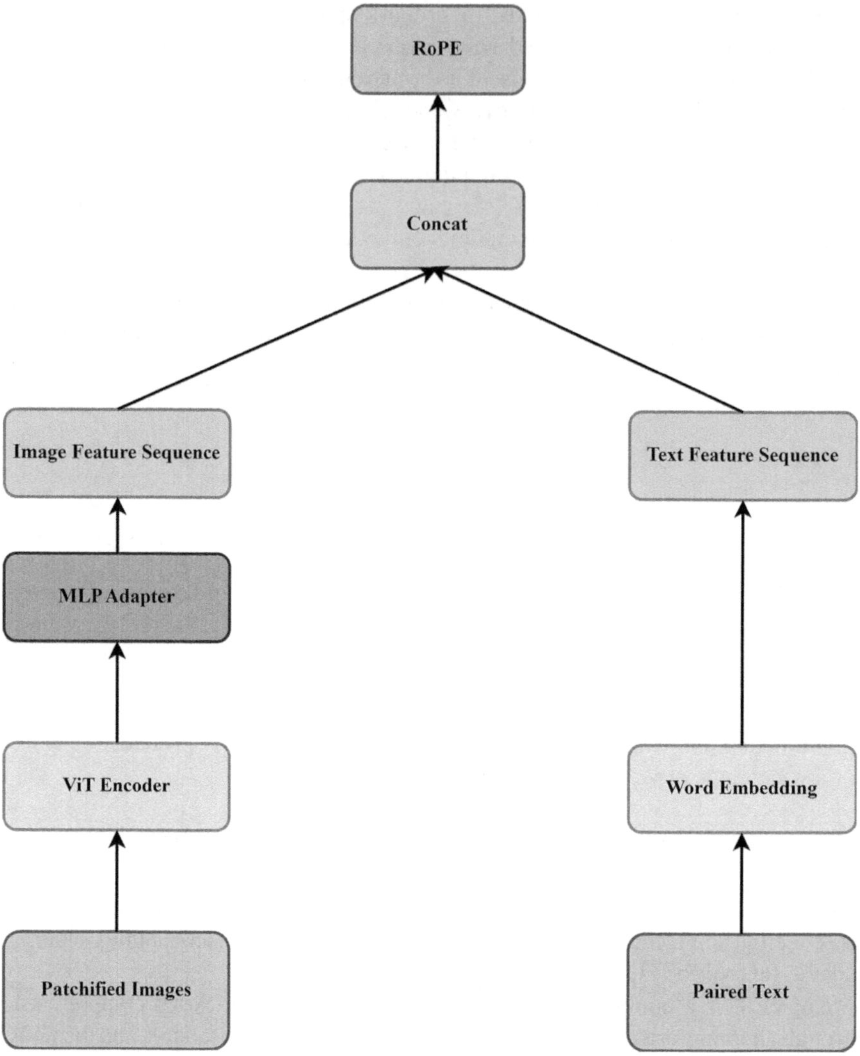

FIGURE 7.5 CogVLM.

Given an image X, images features are extracted via a frozen image encoder and is shown in Equation (7.8).

$$v = E_v(X) \tag{7.8}$$

A positional encoder and projection adapt v for multimodal layers. By adding trainable visual experts that facilitate deep multimodal integration, CogVLM improves each transformer block. In particular, the visual expert adds extra attention heads to each layer that focus on the visual features v directly, enabling the model to use multimodal attention to include visual context. Furthermore, by injecting linearly projected representations of v into the feed-forward sub-layer, the visual expert helps the network integrate visual information with the text stream at both the feed-forward and attention levels. Effectively, at layer l, the model processes tokens z_l (text tokens) as follows in Equation (7.9).

$$\widetilde{L} = FFN_l\left(z_l + Attn_l\left(z_l, z_l, z_l\right) + VE_l^{att}(v)\right) + VE_l^{aff}(v) \quad (7.9)$$

where VE_l^{att} and $VE_l^{aff}(v)$ are visual expert contributions learned during fine-tuning.

In order to train CogVLM for multimodal tasks (such as picture captioning, VQA, and grounding), the additional modules are fine-tuned while the image encoder and basic LM remain fixed. When given a dataset of image–text pairs (X_i, y_i) with responses r, the model maximizes the conditional likelihood and is shown in Equation (7.10).

$$P_\theta\left(r|X, i\right) = \prod_{t=1}^{T_r} P_\theta\left(r_t|r_{<t}, i, v\right) \quad (7.10)$$

The training objective is to minimize the following Equation (7.11).

$$L(\theta) = -\sum_{i,t} \log P_\theta\left(r_t|r_{<t}, i, v\right) \quad (7.11)$$

7.2.9.5 GPT-4o: OpenAI's Most Advanced Multimodal Model

GPT-4o (Omni) [4] is OpenAI's most powerful multimodal AI model, capable of handling text, images, audio, and video inputs and generating outputs in real time. It surpasses previous models in terms of speed, efficiency, and reasoning capabilities.

GPT-4o is a flexible multimodal model that uses a chain-of-thought reasoning method for logical decision-making involving text, images, and audio, processing inputs in real-time. It accommodates more than 50 languages for effective cross-language understanding and translation, and is tailored for smooth integration through OpenAI's API. Notable applications include AI tutors offering immediate academic support, sophisticated customer support chatbots managing text, image, and voice interactions, and creative uses such as crafting stories, poetry, and precise image descriptions.

Fundamentally, GPT-4 is a large-scale Transformer model that has been trained to anticipate the subsequent token in a series of embeddings that are produced from images and interleaved text. If the sequence of input is $z = \left[z_1, z_2, \ldots, z_T\right]$ where each z_t may be a text token or an image feature token, the generative probability is modelled as follows in Equation (7.12).

$$P_\theta(z) = \prod_{t=1}^{T} P_\theta\left(z_t|z_{<t}\right) \quad (7.12)$$

The training objective is to minimize the negative log likelihood of the following Equation (7.13).

$$l_{\text{pretrain}} = -\sum_{t=1}^{T} \log P_\theta \left(z_t | z_{<t}\right) \tag{7.13}$$

The developers fitted a power-law scaling law connecting training compute C to predicted loss L in order to predict its final training performance and is given in Equation (7.14).

$$L = a.C^b + c \tag{7.14}$$

where smaller-scale models were used to approximate the constants a, b, and c. Even at full scale, this enabled precise pre-training predictions.

Following pre-training, Reinforcement Learning from Human Feedback (RLHF) is used to align GPT-4 and is formulated as follows in Equation (7.15).

$$\max_\theta \mathbb{E}_{r \sim \pi_\theta(.|\text{prompt})} \left[R_{\text{human}} \left(r | \text{prompt}, \text{context}\right)\right] \tag{7.15}$$

where r is a generated response, π_θ is the policy (model), and R_{human} is a reward function derived from human feedback.

7.2.9.6 Gemini: Google's Multimodal AI Model

Gemini [25] is Google's family of multimodal AI models designed to process and generate text, images, audio, and video. It is built to handle complex reasoning and large-scale AI tasks, making it one of the most advanced AI models today. Gemini 1.5, released in 2024, introduced improved long-context understanding and real-time multimodal processing.

Gemini presents three versions—Ultra for intricate tasks, Pro for scalable applications, and Nano for AI on mobile devices—utilizing a transformer-based design that amalgamates text, images, video, and audio for multimodal learning. With an impressive context window of up to 2 million tokens in Gemini 1.5 Pro, it is adept at handling large volumes of content such as books and research papers. Improved through supervised fine-tuning and reinforcement learning informed by human feedback, Gemini provides safer and higher-quality responses. Its uses range from educational AI assistants that interpret handwritten notes and graphs, to medical AI for summarizing reports and diagnostics that integrate text and images, as well as Gemini Ultra's superior abilities in code generation and debugging for software development. Figure 7.6 shows the schematic view of Gemini.

7.2.9.7 Gen2: Text-to-Video and Image-to-Video Generation Model

Gen2 [26] is an advanced text-to-video and image-to-video AI model that enables users to create high-quality videos from textual descriptions or static images. Developed by Runway, Gen2 employs diffusion-based techniques to generate realistic and contextually accurate videos.

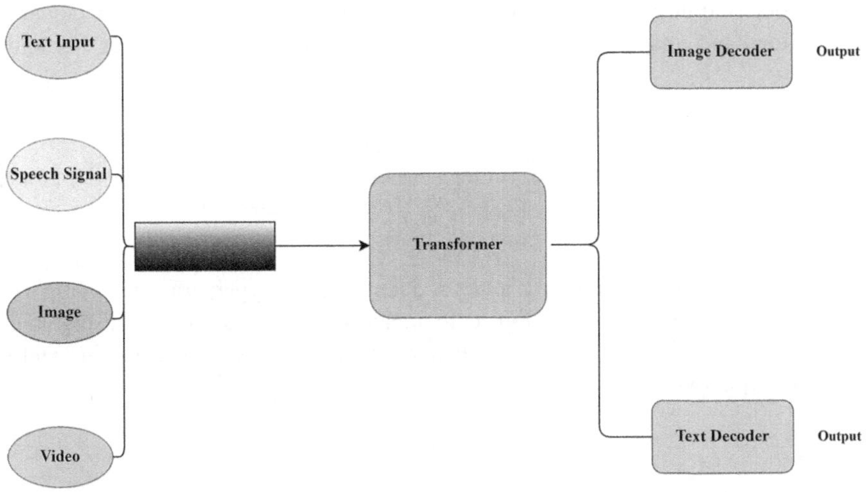

FIGURE 7.6 Gemini.

Gen2 is an advanced video generation model that creates short videos from text prompts and synthesizes dynamic videos from single images by adding motion based on scene understanding. Leveraging MiDaS for depth estimation and a cross-attention mechanism, it produces realistic and smooth video transitions by integrating structural and content features. Key use cases include empowering filmmakers, designers, and marketers to generate concept videos efficiently, as well as assisting game developers and animators in creating AI-driven animations from simple sketches or text descriptions.

7.2.9.8 ImageBind: A Multimodal AI Model from Meta

ImageBind [27] is a cutting-edge multimodal learning model developed by Meta AI. It is capable of binding multiple data types—including text, images, audio, video, depth, thermal, and motion data (IMU)—into a single embedding space.

ImageBind is a versatile multimodal model that supports six data types—text, video, audio, depth, thermal, and IMU sensor data—enabling seamless cross-modal retrieval, such as generating audio from images or finding images from sound clips. It uses InfoNCE loss and contrastive learning to effectively align diverse modalities, enhancing retrieval accuracy. Key applications include AI-powered search engines that allow audio-based queries for images or videos, advanced medical imaging combining thermal and depth data for improved diagnosis, and AI-generated music and sound effects from images or text prompts, benefiting content creators.

ImageBind learns a shared embedding space across six modalities—image, text, audio, depth, thermal, and IMU—by aligning all nonimage modalities indirectly through images. Concretely, each modality m has its own encoder $E_m(\cdot)$, producing an embedding vector and is given in the following Equation (7.16).

$$u_m = E_m\left(x_m\right) \tag{7.16}$$

The model is trained to minimize a contrastive alignment loss between modality embeddings and image embeddings. This is formulated as follows using Equation (7.17).

$$L_{align} = -\sum_{(m, x_m, x_{img})} \log \frac{exp\left(\frac{sim(u_m, u_{img})}{\tau}\right)}{\sum_{m', j} exp\left(\frac{sim(u_{m'}, u_{img,j})}{\tau}\right)} \tag{7.17}$$

where $sim(\cdot,\cdot)$ is cosine similarity, and τ is a temperature hyperparameter.

Because all modalities are aligned to image embeddings, emergent alignment arises between modalities m_a and m_b that were never paired during training and is shown in Equation (7.18).

$$u_{m_a} \approx u_{img} \approx u_{m_b} \tag{7.18}$$

This enables zero-shot tasks (e.g., audio or depth classification via text prompts) without direct supervision.

Given an input x_m in modality m, compute u_m, and compare it to text embeddings, the predictions are made by the following Equation (7.19).

$$\hat{c} = \underset{c}{\operatorname{argmax}} \frac{u_m . u_{text,c}}{\|u_m\| . \|u_{text,c}\|} \tag{7.19}$$

Even for modalities like audio or thermal, the alignment enables the mapping $u_{audio} \leftrightarrow u_{text}$.

7.2.9.9 Flamingo: DeepMind's Vision-Language Model for Multimodal Understanding

Flamingo [28] is a vision-language model developed by DeepMind, designed to process images, videos, and text and provide text-based responses. It bridges the gap between LLMs and computer vision.

Flamingo features a Perceiver Resampler that efficiently condenses high-dimensional visual inputs into manageable tokens, combined with cross-attention layers that seamlessly integrate visual and textual information. Its few-shot learning capability enables it to understand and respond to images or videos with minimal examples, eliminating the need for extensive fine-tuning. Key applications include automatic image captioning, VQA, and document processing, such as extracting and structuring text from handwritten notes and other images.

Flamingo combines a frozen pretrained language model (LLM) with a vision encoder via perceiver resamplers to process interleaved sequences of images and text. Let the input sequence be $z = [y_1, \ldots, y_{t_1}, img_1, y_{t_1+1}, \ldots, img_k, \ldots]$, where y_i are text tokens and img_j are image token sets reduced by the perceiver module. The language model attends to visual contexts using specialized cross-attention layers (XATTN). For each transformer layer l, the cross-attention is formulated as follows in Equation (7.20).

$$h_l = \text{LayerNorm}\left(x_l + \alpha_l.XATTN_l\left(x_l, I\right)\right) \tag{7.20}$$

where x_l are the text token embeddings at layer l, I are the image tokens, and α_l is a learnable gating scalar (initialized to zero and passed through *tanh* for stability).

During training and inference, Flamingo generates text autoregressively conditioned on preceding text and image context, optimizing using the following Equation (7.21).

$$P\left(y_t \middle| \text{context, images}\right) = \text{softmax}\left(W.h_{L,t}\right) \tag{7.21}$$

for each next token y_t. The training loss is given in Equation (7.22).

$$L = -\sum_t \log P\left(y_t \middle| \text{context, images}\right) \tag{7.22}$$

over large multimodal corpora with interleaved text-image pairs.

7.2.9.10 Claude 3: Anthropic's Multimodal AI Model

Claude 3 is Anthropic's latest vision-language model, designed to understand text and images with enhanced reasoning and processing capabilities. It includes three versions:

- Claude 3 Haiku (fastest, lightweight)
- Claude 3 Sonnet (balanced performance)
- Claude 3 Opus (most powerful and advanced)

Claude 3 is a powerful multimodal model with a long context window capable of processing over one million tokens, making it well-suited for analyzing lengthy documents. It excels in understanding images, text, and documents, including graphs, charts, and scanned materials, which is valuable for academic and research tasks. Designed with enhanced safety and accuracy, Claude 3 minimizes hallucinations and bias. Its key applications include aiding researchers in analyzing complex documents, automating business report generation from large datasets, and supporting legal and financial professionals in reviewing intricate contracts and financial reports.

7.2.9.11 Qwen-VL: Alibaba Cloud's Vision-Language Model

Qwen-VL [29] is a powerful multimodal AI model developed by Alibaba Cloud, designed for vision-language understanding. It extends the Qwen language model to support both text and image-based tasks, making it highly effective for applications like image captioning, visual reasoning, and multimodal search.

The model has two enhanced versions:

- Qwen-VL-Plus: Improved image reasoning and detailed analysis.
- Qwen-VL-Max: Supports high-resolution images with varied aspect ratios, making it ideal for advanced computer vision applications.

Qwen-VL is a sophisticated multimodal model that excels in merging images and text for activities such as visual question answering and reasoning based on images. It delivers high-resolution image processing that is perfect for tasks like document analysis, scientific exploration, and medical imaging, while also providing efficient cross-modal retrieval to improve search engines and recommendation systems. Being open-source and customizable, it presents a budget-friendly option for developers. Major applications include visual product searches and recommendations in e-commerce, aiding medical professionals by integrating radiology images with patient records, supporting education and research through comprehensive explanations of intricate visuals, and facilitating fashion discovery by correlating uploaded images with clothing options.

Multimodal transformers are at the forefront of AI innovation, enabling models to process and integrate multiple types of data for enhanced understanding and output generation. From healthcare to autonomous vehicles, these models are pushing the boundaries of what AI can accomplish, offering more accurate and context-aware solutions. As multimodal transformers continue to evolve, their applications in real-world problems will only grow, unlocking new opportunities across industries.

SUMMARY

The landscape of pre-trained LLMs is examined in this chapter, with a distinction made between single-modal and multi-modal variations. Pre-trained LLMs that are single-modal only use one type of data. For tasks like text generation, categorization, and question answering, text-only LLMs—including GPT, BERT, and LLaMA—are trained solely on text corpora. Vision Transformers (ViT) and Swin Transformers are examples of vision-only LLMs that are tailored for computer vision and picture comprehension applications. Speech-only LLMs, like Whisper and wav2vec 2.0, concentrate on audio-based processing, such as speaker identification and speech recognition. Modern single-modal models are presented in the section's conclusion, along with their best benchmarks and specific skills in their fields.

After that, the chapter looks about multimodal pretrained LLMs, which combine data from several modalities—like text, photos, audio, and video—into a single architecture. The need for models that can reason across several data kinds to produce richer and more context-aware outputs is linked to the growth of multimodal LLMs. The operation of multimodal LLMs is explained in the section on how various data streams are aligned for collaborative reasoning using common latent spaces and modality-specific encoders. Applications include multisensory human–computer interaction, video summary, audio-visual scene interpretation, visual question answering, and image captioning. Lastly, cutting-edge multimodal models such as CLIP, Flamingo, GPT-4V, and ImageBind are examined, demonstrating their great accuracy and versatility in handling challenging cross-modal tasks.

QUESTIONS

1. Define Text-only, Vision-only, and Speech-only LLMs with one example each.
2. Explain the key differences between single-modal and multimodal pretrained LLMs.

3. Describe the reasons behind the rise of multimodal LLMs in recent AI research.
4. Explain how multimodal LLMs integrate text and vision information during training.
5. Give two real-world applications of multimodal LLMs in healthcare and education.
6. A text-only LLM has a vocabulary size of 50,000 tokens and uses embeddings of dimension 1024. Calculate the total number of parameters in the embedding layer.
7. Compare state-of-the-art models like CLIP (multimodal) and GPT-4 (text-only part) in terms of their ability to handle cross-domain tasks.
8. Analyze the advantages and limitations of single-modal vs multi-modal LLMs for real-time decision-making tasks.
9. Evaluate the ethical and privacy concerns that arise when using multimodal LLMs in surveillance and medical applications.
10. Design a multimodal LLM pipeline that can process text, images, and speech together for a smart classroom assistant. Outline how the modalities would be integrated.
11. **Case Study: Pretrained LLMs in Action**

A hospital wants to build a smart assistant for **patient care**.

- For *medical report analysis*, they use *BERT* (a text-only pre-trained LLM) to extract key information from patient records.
- For *X-ray image analysis*, they use *Vision Transformers (ViT)*, a vision-only pretrained model.
- For *doctor–patient conversations*, they use *Whisper*, a speech-only LLM, to convert speech into text.
- Later, they upgrade the system with *GPT-4V, a multimodal LLM*, so the assistant can read X-rays, understand medical notes, and also answer questions from doctors in natural language.

  This case highlights the progression from single-modal to multimodal LLMs for real-world healthcare applications. If the hospital wants the assistant to summarize both a patient's medical history (text) and their X-ray findings (images) together, which type of LLM should they use—single-modal or multimodal? Explain your choice.

REFERENCES

[1] H. Naveed, A. U. Hassan, S. Aslan, C. Rubio-Campillo, A. M. Qamar, A. K. Al-Makhadmeh *et al.*, "A Comprehensive Overview of Large Language Models," Oct. 2024, arXiv:2307.06435.

[2] J. Devlin, M.-W. Chang, K. Lee, and K. Toutanova, "BERT: Pre-training of Deep Bidirectional Transformers for Language Understanding," in *Proc. of the North American Chapter of the Association for Computational Linguistics (NAACL)*, May 2019, arXiv:1810.04805.

[3] Y. Liu, M. Ott, N. Goyal, J. Du, M. Joshi, D. Chen *et al.*, "RoBERTa: A Robustly Optimized BERT Pretraining Approach," arXiv preprint, Jul. 2019, arXiv:1907.11692.
[4] OpenAI, "GPT-4 Technical Report," arXiv preprint, Mar. 2024, arXiv:2303.08774.
[5] Z. Yang, Z. Dai, Y. Yang, J. Carbonell, R. Salakhutdinov, and Q. V. Le, "XLNet: Generalized Autoregressive Pretraining for Language Understanding," in *Advances in Neural Information Processing Systems (NeurIPS)*, Jan. 2020, arXiv:1906.08237.
[6] C. Raffel, N. Shazeer, A. Roberts, K. Lee, S. Narang, M. Matena *et al.*, "Exploring the Limits of Transfer Learning with a Unified Text-to-Text Transformer," *Journal of Machine Learning Research (JMLR)*, Sep. 2023, arXiv:1910.10683.
[7] A. Dosovitskiy, L. Beyer, A. Kolesnikov, D. Weissenborn, X. Zhai, T. Unterthiner *et al.*, "An Image is Worth 16x16 Words: Transformers for Image Recognition at Scale," in *Proc. of the International Conference on Learning Representations (ICLR)*, Jun. 2021, arXiv:2010.11929.
[8] Z. Liu, Y. Lin, Y. Cao, H. Hu, Y. Wei, Z. Zhang *et al.*, "Swin Transformer: Hierarchical Vision Transformer using Shifted Windows," ," in *Proc. of the IEEE/CVF International Conference on Computer Vision (ICCV)*, Mar. 2021, arXiv:2103.14030.
[9] N. Carion, F. Massa, G. Synnaeve, N. Usunier, A. Kirillov, and S. Zagoruyko, "End-to-End Object Detection with Transformers," in *Proc. of the European Conference on Computer Vision (ECCV)*, May 2020, arXiv:2005.12872.
[10] X. de Zuazo, E. Navas, I. Saratxaga, and I. H. Rioja, "Whisper-LM: Improving ASR Models with Language Models for Low-Resource Languages," arXiv preprint, Mar. 2025, arXiv:2503.23542.
[11] A. Baevski, H. Zhou, A. Mohamed, and M. Auli, "wav2vec 2.0: A Framework for Self-Supervised Learning of Speech Representations," in *Advances in Neural Information Processing Systems (NeurIPS)*, Oct. 2020, arXiv:2006.11477.
[12] A. Hannun, C. Case, J. Casper, B. Catanzaro, G. Diamos, E. Elsen *et al.*, "Deep Speech: Scaling up end-to-end Speech Recognition," arXiv preprint, Dec. 2014, arXiv:1412.5567.
[13] P. Xu, X. Zhu, and D. A. Clifton, "Multimodal Learning with Transformers: A Survey," *IEEE Transactions on Pattern Analysis and Machine Intelligence (TPAMI)*, May 2023, arXiv:2206.06488.
[14] S. Munikoti, V. K. T. Dasu, M. S. Munir, M. A. Hasan, and P. Kulkarni, "Generalist Multimodal AI: A Review of Architectures, Challenges and Opportunities," arXiv preprint, Jun. 2024, arXiv:2406.05496.
[15] K. S. Kalyan, "A Survey of GPT-3 Family Large Language Models Including ChatGPT and GPT-4," *Natural Language Processing Journal*, Oct. 2023, arXiv:2302.11382.
[16] T. Parag, and A. Elgammal, "Modality Agnostic Efficient Long Range Encoder," arXiv preprint, Jul. 2025, arXiv:2507.19409.
[17] B. Jiang, X. Wei, L. Li, Z. Wang, Y. Zhang, and X. Xue, "Understanding the Role of LLMs in Multimodal Evaluation Benchmarks," arXiv preprint, Oct. 2024, arXiv:2410.12329.
[18] R. Cai, B. Li, X. Wen, M. Chen, and Z. Zhao, "Diagnosing and Mitigating Modality Interference in Multimodal Large Language Models," arXiv preprint, May 2025, arXiv:2505.19616.
[19] A. Agrawal, J. Lu, S. Antol, M. Mitchell, D. Batra, C. L. Zitnick *et al.*, "VQA: Visual Question Answering," in *Proc. of the IEEE International Conference on Computer Vision (ICCV)*, Oct. 2016, arXiv:1505.00468.

[20] A. S. Das, and S. Saha, "Self-Supervised Image-to-Text and Text-to-Image Synthesis," *SN Computer Science*, Dec. 2021, doi: 10.1007/978-3-030-92273-3_34, arXiv:2112.04928.

[21] H.-Y. Chen, J. Liang, L. Li, H. Li, and L. Lin, "Contrastive Localized Language-Image Pre-Training," arXiv preprint, Feb. 2025, arXiv:2410.02746.

[22] A. Ramesh, M. Pavlov, G. Goh, S. Gray, C. Voss, A. Radford *et al.*, "Zero-Shot Text-to-Image Generation," ," in *Proc. of the International Conference on Machine Learning (ICML)*, Feb. 2021, arXiv:2102.12092.

[23] H. Liu, C. Li, Q. Wu, and Y. J. Lee, "Visual Instruction Tuning," in *Advances in Neural Information Processing Systems (NeurIPS)*, Dec. 2023, arXiv:2304.08485.

[24] W. Wang, Q. Lv, W. Yu, W. Hong, J. Qi, Y. Wang *et al.*, "CogVLM: Visual Expert for Pretrained Language Models," arXiv preprint, Feb. 2024, arXiv:2311.03079.

[25] Gemini Team, Google, "Gemini: A Family of Highly Capable Multimodal Models," arXiv preprint, May 2025, arXiv:2312.11805.

[26] S. Jennings, "Scale, Speed and Stepping Stones: The Path to Gen-2," *RunwayML Research Blog,* 2023.

[27] R. Girdhar, A. El-Nouby, Z. Liu, M. Singh, K. V. Alwala, A. Joulin *et al.*, "ImageBind: One Embedding Space To Bind Them All," in *Proc. of the IEEE/CVF Conference on Computer Vision and Pattern Recognition (CVPR)*, May 2023, arXiv:2305.05665.

[28] J.-B. Alayrac, J. Donahue, P. Luc, A. Miech, I. Barr, Y. Hasson *et al.*, "Flamingo: a Visual Language Model for Few-Shot Learning," in *Advances in Neural Information Processing Systems (NeurIPS)*, Nov. 2022, arXiv:2204.14198.

[29] J. Bai, S. Bai, S. Yang, S. Wang, S. Tan, P. Wang *et al.*, "Qwen-VL: A Versatile Vision-Language Model for Understanding, Localization, Text Reading, and Beyond," arXiv preprint, Oct. 2023, arXiv:2308.12966.

8 Fine-tuning of LLMs

8.1 INTRODUCTION TO FINE-TUNING OF LARGE LANGUAGE MODELS (LLMS)

Fine-tuning [1, 2] is the process of taking a pretrained large language model (LLM) and adapting it to a specific task or domain by training it on additional data. This method improves the model's performance, ensuring it aligns with the requirements of a particular industry, dataset, or application.

For example, GPT-4 is a general-purpose model trained on a vast corpus of text. However, if we want it to specialize in legal document analysis, fine-tuning it with a dataset containing legal cases, contracts, and regulatory texts will enhance its expertise in that domain. Figure 8.1 displays the schematic view of Fine-tuning.

Why Fine-Tune LLMs?

Pretrained LLMs are designed to handle a broad range of tasks but may not perform optimally in domain-specific applications. Fine-tuning provides several advantages:

- **Improves Task-Specific Performance:** A fine-tuned LLM can deliver better accuracy in specialized fields like medicine, law, or coding.
- **Reduces Hallucinations:** The model becomes less likely to generate misleading or incorrect information.
- **Enhances Efficiency:** The model can produce more contextually relevant responses, improving user interaction.
- **Optimizes Cost and Resources:** Reducing the need for complex prompt engineering.

8.2 PROCESS OF LLM FINE-TUNING

The process of LLM Fine-tuning involves the following key steps.

- **Choosing a Pretrained Model:** The first step is to carefully select a pretrained base model that suits the desired architecture and functionality. These models are general purpose, having been trained on a vast amount of unlabeled data.

DOI: 10.1201/9781003650065-8

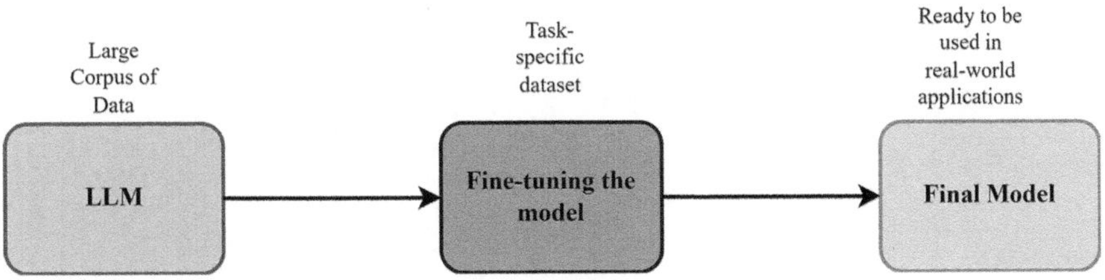

FIGURE 8.1 Fine-tuning.

- **Collecting a Relevant Dataset:** Next, a dataset that is closely related to the target task needs to be gathered. This dataset should be structured or labeled in a way that facilitates learning for the model.
- **Preparing the Dataset:** After the dataset is collected, it requires preprocessing. This involves cleaning the data, dividing it into training, validation, and test sets, and ensuring its compatibility with the pretrained model for fine-tuning.
- **Fine-tuning the Model:** Once the model is selected and the dataset is preprocessed, fine-tuning can begin. This step involves adapting the pretrained model to the specific dataset, which could be tailored to a certain domain or application, enabling the model to specialize in that area.
- **Adapting for the Specific Task:** During fine-tuning, the model's parameters are adjusted to align with the new dataset, helping it to better understand and generate relevant content for the task. This retains the general language knowledge from the pretraining phase while customizing the model for the target domain's specifics.

Fine-tuning LLMs is widely used in natural language processing tasks such as sentiment analysis, named entity recognition, summarization, translation, or any application that requires context understanding and coherent language generation. This approach enables the model to leverage its pretrained knowledge for more specialized and domain-specific applications.

8.3 TYPES OF FINE-TUNING METHODS

There are several approaches to fine-tuning an LLM, each suited to different computational resources and objectives [3].

8.3.1 Supervised Fine-tuning (Transfer Learning)

Transfer learning is a technique that allows a model to integrate domain-specific expertise without requiring training from scratch. It involves adapting a pretrained model to a specific task or domain using labeled datasets. For example, a general-purpose LLM trained on diverse internet text can be fine-tuned on a legal dataset containing contracts, case laws, and regulatory documents. This adaptation ensures that the model generates legally precise and contextually relevant responses, making

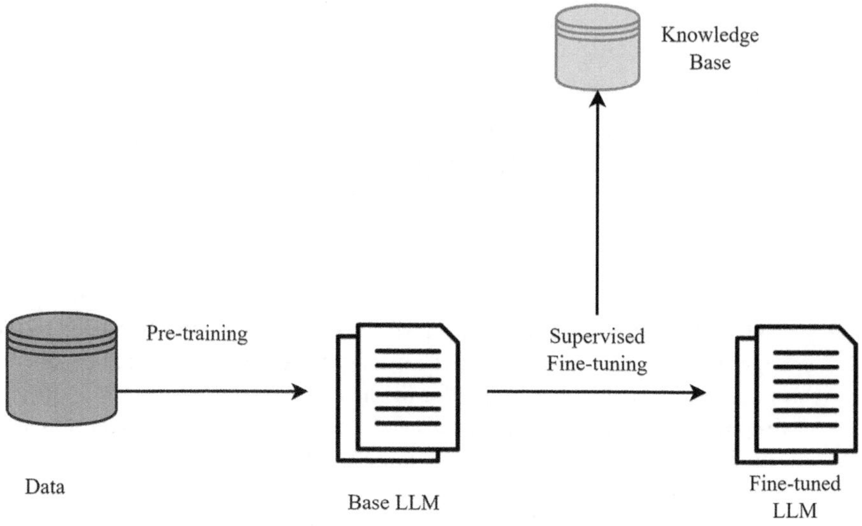

FIGURE 8.2 Transfer learning.

it useful for applications such as contract analysis and legal document drafting. Figure 8.2 displays the workflow architecture of transfer learning.

In transfer learning, the knowledge gained from the initial pretraining on large, general datasets is transferred to the target domain, where it is further refined using a smaller, task-specific dataset. This allows the model to retain its general knowledge while becoming more proficient in understanding domain-specific terminology and nuances.

By using transfer learning with supervised fine-tuning (SFT), the model's performance is significantly enhanced for specialized tasks within the legal domain. The process involves training the model on labeled data, where the correct output is provided alongside the input. As a result, the model learns to understand the specific language, terminology, and context of the legal field, improving its ability to address complex queries or generate content that adheres to legal standards.

This technique can also be applied to other domains, such as healthcare, finance, or customer service, allowing models to be adapted for industry-specific needs without the need to train from scratch. Transfer learning thus saves both time and computational resources while improving task-specific performance.

8.3.2 Full Fine-tuning

Full fine-tuning involves updating all parameters of a pretrained model using a domain-specific dataset. This approach requires significant computational resources and large datasets but results in highly specialized models with deep adaptation to the target domain. For instance, fine-tuning GPT-4 on a legal dataset containing contracts, court rulings, and case law enables it to provide precise legal analysis and contract drafting support. Example: Fine-tuning GPT-4 on a dataset of legal documents to create an AI-powered contract reviewer.

8.3.3 Parameter-Efficient Fine-tuning (PEFT)

Parameter-efficient fine-tuning (PEFT) optimizes model training by adjusting only a small subset of parameters while keeping the majority of the model frozen. This reduces computational costs and storage requirements while maintaining performance. Techniques like LoRA (Low-Rank Adaptation), Adapters, and Prefix Tuning are commonly used. For example, applying LoRA to a chatbot model helps refine its responses for technical customer support without requiring full retraining.

8.3.4 Instruction Tuning

Instruction tuning involves training models with explicit human instructions to enhance performance on specific tasks. This process improves the model's ability to generalize across new, unseen prompts. For example, an AI assistant fine-tuned with structured instructions can better summarize emails, draft professional responses, and follow detailed user commands accurately.

8.3.5 Reinforcement Learning with Human Feedback (RLHF)

Reinforcement learning with human feedback (RLHF) fine-tunes a model using human-labeled feedback, guiding it towards more useful and ethical responses. This technique aligns model behavior with human values and preferences. For example, OpenAI's ChatGPT was fine-tuned using RLHF to ensure safer, contextually appropriate, and user-friendly interactions, reducing harmful or misleading outputs.

This paper presents a two-stage fine-tuning approach to align LLMs with user intent by incorporating human feedback, resulting in models called InstructGPT. First, SFT is performed on a base GPT-3 model using a dataset of human-written demonstrations of ideal responses, where the model parameters θ are optimized to minimize the cross-entropy loss as follows in Equation (8.1).

$$L_{\text{SFT}}(\theta) = -\sum_i y_i.\log\left(p_\theta(x)\right) \tag{8.1}$$

with x_i as the input tokens and y_i the human demonstration tokens. Next, reinforcement learning from human feedback (RLHF) further refines the model by collecting human rankings of model-generated outputs and training a reward model r_ϕ to predict these rankings. Using proximal policy optimization (PPO), the policy (the language model) is updated to maximize expected reward as follows in Equation (8.2).

$$\text{objective} = \max_\theta \text{E}_{x\text{~}D}\left[r_\phi\left(\text{model output}\middle|x\right)\right] \tag{8.2}$$

while keeping the policy close to the supervised fine-tuned model to ensure stable training. This process yields models that, despite being smaller (e.g., 1.3B parameters), outperform much larger models (175B GPT-3) in human evaluations, producing outputs that are more truthful, less toxic, and better aligned with user instructions. The paper demonstrates that incorporating human preferences via RLHF effectively guides model behavior beyond what standard supervised learning can achieve, significantly improving the quality and safety of LLM outputs without sacrificing performance on standard NLP benchmarks.

8.3.6 Multimodal Fine-tuning

Multimodal fine-tuning enables LLMs to process and integrate multiple data types, including text, images, and audio. This approach improves model versatility and real-world application. For instance, fine-tuning a model like CLIP to analyze images and generate contextual descriptions enhances its capabilities in applications like medical diagnostics, image captioning, and autonomous systems.

8.4 INSTRUCTION TUNING

Instruction tuning is a crucial process in refining LLMs to enhance their ability to follow human instructions more effectively. The goal is to train these models on datasets that contain explicit instructions and commands, which improves their adaptability and performance in executing user queries. Figure 8.3 shows the architecture of instruction tuning [4, 5].

8.4.1 Instruction-Tuning with Manually Created Datasets

This method involves human experts curating datasets specifically designed to teach the model how to behave in various scenarios. These datasets consist of carefully constructed question-answer pairs or instructional prompts that guide the LLM to respond appropriately. For example, in a customer support scenario, a chatbot might be fine-tuned with human-annotated dialogues that address common complaints. By learning from these interactions, the chatbot is able to adopt a more polite, structured, and effective approach when responding to users. The fine-tuned model becomes better at understanding customer queries and providing accurate solutions in a helpful tone.

8.4.2 Instruction-Tuning with LLM-Generated Datasets

In this approach, an LLM generates its own synthetic instructional data, which serves as a cost-effective and scalable alternative to manually creating datasets. This allows

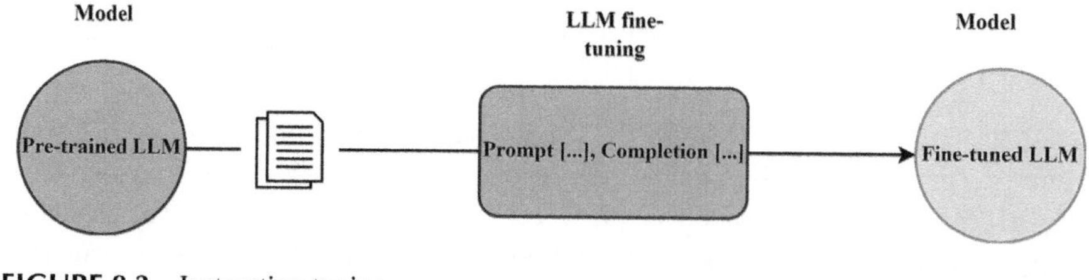

FIGURE 8.3 Instruction tuning.

the training process to be more automated, reducing the time and effort required from human experts. For example: GPT-4, a powerful LLM, can be used to generate training data for a smaller model, like LLaMA. It can create diverse sets of question-answer pairs that cover a range of topics and queries. These synthetic datasets help the smaller model improve its performance and ability to understand and respond to instructions, all without requiring direct human involvement. This method allows for rapid expansion of the model's capabilities in an efficient manner.

This approach builds instruction-tuning datasets by combining human-written instructions with responses generated by open-weight LLMs, such as Llama-3.1 and Gemma-2. The core idea is to use real human instructions extracted from a large conversational dataset (LMSYS-Chat-1M) and generate high-quality responses automatically from these open models, creating large-scale (instruction, response) pairs without relying on proprietary data. These pairs are then used to fine-tune base LLMs through supervised learning, where the model parameters are updated to minimize a loss function—typically cross-entropy—defined as follows in Equation (8.3).

$$L = -\sum_{i} y_i log\left(p_i\right) \tag{8.3}$$

where y_i are the true tokens in the response and p_i are the predicted probabilities by the model.

The fine-tuned models demonstrate superior performance on standard instruction-following benchmarks compared to models trained on previously available instruction-tuning datasets. Furthermore, this method extends well to other languages, such as Japanese, where models trained on synthesized instruction-response pairs show state-of-the-art instruction-following abilities, despite lacking some culture-specific knowledge. This work highlights a scalable and open alternative to traditional dataset creation, leveraging the capabilities of open-weight LLMs to generate training data that effectively improves the instruction-following behavior of language models.

8.5 ALIGNMENT TECHNIQUES

Alignment refers to ensuring that LLMs generate responses that align with human values, ethics, and user expectations. These techniques help ensure that the behavior of AI models matches what humans deem appropriate or beneficial [6, 7].

8.5.1 Direct Preference Optimization (DPO)

Direct preference optimization (DPO) [8] is a simpler alternative to Reinforcement Learning with Human Feedback (RLHF). Instead of using complex reward models to evaluate responses, DPO directly incorporates human-approved outputs to train the model. This means that the model learns from examples of responses that humans have explicitly deemed preferable. For example, in a scenario where a language model needs to learn how to provide useful and polite responses, the model can be fine-tuned using a set of answers that human evaluators have already approved. These

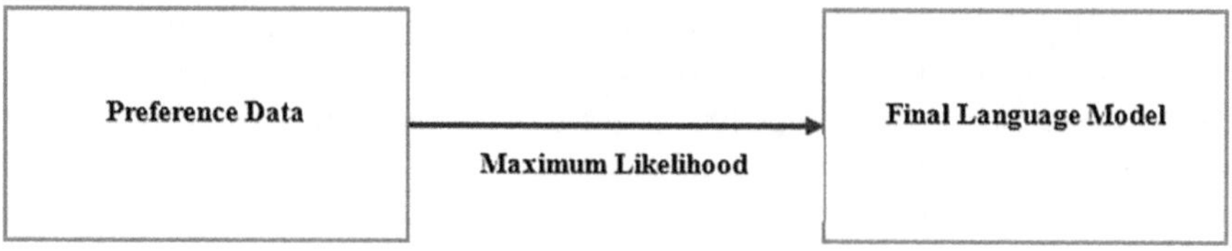

FIGURE 8.4 Direct preference optimization.

selected answers act as a guide for the model to learn the preferred tone, structure, and content of responses, without the need for large, manually ranked datasets.

DPO redefines the task of learning human preferences as a straightforward classification problem, whereby the language model is adjusted to give higher probabilities to preferred responses rather than those that are not preferred, by maximizing the likelihood of preference pairs through a logistic loss applied to the difference in their log-probabilities. This method eliminates the necessity for a separately trained reward model and the use of reinforcement learning by directly refining the model's parameters to enhance the relative probability of favored responses while also constraining the fine-tuned model to remain close to the distribution of the original pretrained model, thereby ensuring alignment with human preferences in a stable and efficient manner.

The objective is to maximize the likelihood of the preferred outputs over the nonpreferred ones and is formulated in Equation (8.4).

$$L_{DPO}(\theta) = \sum_i log\left(\frac{p_\theta\left(y_i^+ \middle| x_i\right)}{p_\theta\left(y_i^+ \middle| x_i\right) + p_\theta\left(y_i^- \middle| x_i\right)}\right) \quad (8.4)$$

where $p_\theta\left(y_i \middle| x_i\right)$ be the probability distribution of the model's output y given input x, parameterized by θ, $D = \{(x_i, y_i^+, y_i^-)\}$ be the dataset of preference pairs, where y_i^+ is a preferred output and y_i^- is a non-preferred output for input x_i. Figure 8.4 shows the workflow of DPO.

8.5.2 Reinforcement Learning with AI Feedback (RLAIF)

RLAIF [9] leverages AI-generated feedback rather than human evaluators to help the model learn. This reduces the cost and time associated with aligning models, making it a more scalable approach. The feedback provided by AI systems is used to optimize the model's behavior and decision-making. For example, for an essay grading system powered by AI, RLAIF can be used to teach the model to score essays based on predefined grading rubrics. Instead of relying on human graders to evaluate every essay, the system uses AI-generated feedback to adjust and improve its grading process, ensuring consistency and alignment with the rubric.

Let $p_\theta(y \mid x)$ denotes the probability distribution of the model's output y given input x, parameterized by θ. In RLHF, a reward model $r_\phi(x, y)$ is trained to predict human preferences, and reinforcement learning algorithms like PPO are used to fine-tune the policy.

In contrast, RLAIF directly uses an off-the-shelf LLM to generate preference labels, which are then used to train the policy. The reward model $r_\phi(x,y)$ is replaced by the AI-generated preferences, reducing the complexity and cost associated with human annotations. The objective in both RLHF and RLAIF is to maximize the expected reward and is formulated as follows in Equation (8.5).

$$E_{x\sim p_{data}}[E_{y\sim p_\theta(y|x)}[r_\phi(x,y)]] \tag{8.5}$$

where p_{data} is the distribution of inputs, and $r_\phi(x,y)$ represents the reward function.

In d-RLAIF, the reward function is directly obtained from the LLM, eliminating the need for a separate reward model and is formulated as follows in Equation (8.6).

$$E_{x\sim p_{data}}[E_{y\sim p_\theta(y|x)}[r_{AI}(x,y)]] \tag{8.6}$$

where $r_{AI}(x,y)$ is the reward function generated by the off-the-shelf LLM.

8.5.3 Reward Augmented Fine-tuning (RAFT)

RAFT [10] combines reinforcement learning techniques with reward-based fine-tuning to adjust the model's behavior for specific tasks or use cases. This method emphasizes learning from rewards associated with correct actions and adjusting based on feedback. For example, in a social media moderation system, RAFT can be used to fine-tune the AI so that it learns to prioritize the removal of harmful content, such as hate speech or explicit material, while still respecting free speech. By incorporating reward-based learning, the AI can adjust its moderation decisions to balance safety and expression, ensuring that the system behaves according to the desired ethical standards.

RAFT's training methodology entails retrieving a collection of documents related to each query from a specialized corpus, followed by the selection of one pertinent document from a set of distractors. The model undergoes fine-tuning to enhance the likelihood of producing the correct answer based on the relevant document while reducing the influence of the distractors. Furthermore, chain-of-thought prompting is utilized to train the model to produce intermediate reasoning steps, which bolsters its capability to synthesize information from various documents. This integrated approach enables the model to effectively utilize external knowledge, thereby enhancing its performance in domain-specific question-answering scenarios.

Given a question q and a set of retrieved documents $D = \{d_1, d_2, \ldots, d_k\}$, RAFT aims to fine-tune the LLM parameters θ to maximize the likelihood of generating the correct answer a conditioned on the question and the relevant documents. The objective function can be expressed as follows in Equation (8.7).

$$L_{RAFT}(\theta) = -E_{q,D,a}\left[\log p_\theta\left(a \middle| q, D\right)\right] \tag{8.7}$$

where $p_\theta(a \mid q, D)$ is the probability of generating the answer a given the question q and the set of documents D, the expectation is taken over the distribution of questions, documents, and answers in the training dataset.

RAFT employs a chain-of-thought prompting strategy, encouraging the model to reason step-by-step through the retrieved documents to arrive at the correct answer.

8.6 ADVANCED FINE-TUNING TECHNIQUES

8.6.1 Low-Rank Adaptation (LoRA)

LoRA [11] is an efficient fine-tuning technique that adds low-rank matrices to the pretrained model's weights rather than updating the full model. This reduces the computational load and memory usage, making it ideal for fine-tuning large models on domain-specific datasets with fewer resources. LoRA enables faster and more memory-efficient adaptation while retaining the pretrained model's knowledge.

Consider a weight matrix $W_0 \in \mathbb{R}^{d \times k}$ in a Transformer layer, where d is the input dimension and k is the output dimension. Instead of updating W_0 directly, LoRA introduces two trainable matrices $A \in \mathbb{R}^{r \times k}$ and $B \in \mathbb{R}^{d \times r}$. Here, r is a hyperparameter representing the rank of the adaptation, and $r \ll min(d,k)$. The weight update is then expressed as follows in Equation (8.8).

$$W = W_O + \Delta W = W_O + \mathrm{BA} \tag{8.8}$$

Initially, A is randomly initialized, and B is set to zero. This ensures that the initial adaptation ΔW is zero, preserving the original model's behavior. During training, only A and B are updated, significantly reducing the number of trainable parameters.

The fundamental concept of LoRA stems from the realization that updates to weights in large pretrained models typically exhibit a low intrinsic rank. By representing these updates using low-rank matrices, LoRA effectively captures the key modifications without requiring extensive retraining. This method utilizes the observation that numerous downstream tasks can be successfully addressed by altering only a limited number of parameters, resulting in considerable reductions in computational resource usage.

For example, suppose you have a large pretrained language model, like GPT-3, and you need to adapt it to a financial task, such as detecting fraudulent transactions in textual data. Instead of fine-tuning all the parameters of the model, you can use LoRA to add low-rank matrices to specific layers of the model. This enables efficient adaptation with fewer computational resources while maintaining the performance of the original model. LoRA could help fine-tune the model with a small financial dataset, keeping the large model's general language understanding intact. Figure 8.5 shows the architecture of LoRA.

8.6.2 Adapter Layers

Adapter layers [12] involve inserting small, trainable layers between the existing layers of the pretrained model. These layers are fine-tuned for specific tasks while keeping the original model parameters frozen. This approach is highly efficient because it

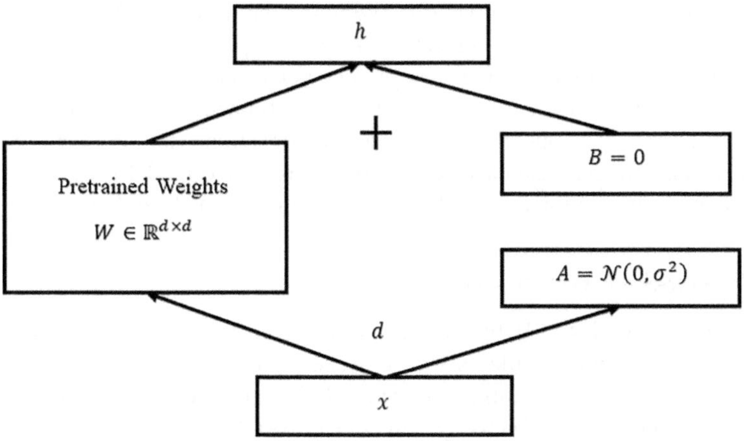

FIGURE 8.5 LoRA.

minimizes the number of parameters that need to be updated, reducing the risk of overfitting on smaller datasets and maintaining the original model's capabilities.

The *LLM-Adapters* proposes a PEFT method for LLMs by inserting small adapter modules—bottleneck neural networks with trainable parameters—into the frozen pretrained model layers. Instead of updating all model parameters θ, only the adapter parameters ϕ are fine-tuned, enabling efficient adaptation through a residual function $h' = h + W_2\sigma(W_1 h)$, where h is the original activation and W_1, W_2 are low-rank matrices. This approach significantly reduces computation and memory costs while maintaining or improving performance on reasoning tasks compared to full fine-tuning of much larger models, making it a scalable and flexible solution for adapting large-scale LLMs to diverse downstream tasks.

In traditional fine-tuning, all parameters of a pretrained model are updated. In contrast, adapter-based fine-tuning involves inserting small, trainable modules (adapters) into the model, allowing for task-specific adjustments without modifying the entire model. Mathematically, this can be represented as follows in Equation (8.9).

$$\text{output}_{\text{adapter}} = \text{Activation}_{\text{input}} + \text{Adapter}\left(\text{Activation}_{\text{input}}\right) \tag{8.9}$$

Here, the adapter learns the residual mapping between the input and output activations, enabling efficient task adaptation. Adapters are inserted within each transformer layer, e.g., after the feed-forward network (FFN) or self-attention blocks. This modifies activations gradually without retraining the entire model.

The training objective for adapter fine-tuning minimizes task loss with respect to ϕ only as follows in Equation (8.10).

$$L = \min_{\phi} E_{(x,y)\sim D}\left[L\left(y, f_\theta(x) + g_\phi\left(f_\theta(x)\right)\right)\right] \tag{8.10}$$

where θ remains fixed, greatly reducing computational cost.

For example, imagine you want to fine-tune a pretrained LLM for medical text classification, specifically for detecting different types of cancer from pathology reports. Instead of modifying the entire model, you can insert adapter layers between the model's original layers. These small layers are trained with labeled medical data, allowing the model to specialize in cancer classification without losing its general language capabilities. Adapter layers keep the pretrained model parameters frozen, reducing the computational cost while tailoring it to the medical domain.

8.6.3 Few-Shot Fine-tuning

In few-shot fine-tuning [13], the model is trained with a very small amount of labeled data. By using techniques like prompt engineering or few-shot learning, LLMs can adapt to specific tasks with minimal data, relying on their pretrained knowledge to generalize to new tasks effectively. This is particularly useful when labeled data is scarce or costly to obtain.

For example, you have a general-purpose pretrained model and a small dataset of customer feedback for a specific brand. Instead of training the model from scratch, you can apply few-shot fine-tuning by providing just a few labeled examples of customer sentiment (positive/negative) to adjust the model for the task. The model uses its pretrained knowledge and adapts to the specific sentiment analysis task even with minimal data.

8.6.4 Prompt-based Fine-tuning

In this technique, rather than updating the model's weights, the focus is on designing task-specific prompts [14]. By carefully crafting the input prompts, the model can be guided to perform a desired task. For example, adding instructions in the form of natural language prompts can encourage the model to generate contextually appropriate responses. This method often requires less computational overhead and can be combined with other fine-tuning approaches.

For example, you're working with a general-purpose pretrained model and want to specialize it for creative writing tasks, like generating marketing copy for a new product. Instead of fine-tuning the model's weights, you craft specific prompts such as, "Generate a catchy slogan for a new energy drink targeting young adults." The model, using its pretrained knowledge, can generate content that matches the task requirements based on the prompts, saving the need for computationally expensive fine-tuning.

8.6.5 Continual Fine-tuning (Incremental Learning)

Continual fine-tuning [15] involves adapting the model progressively as new data becomes available, without forgetting previous knowledge. This is often done using elastic weight consolidation (EWC) to prevent catastrophic forgetting, ensuring that the model maintains performance across a series of related tasks over time. It's especially useful for applications requiring long-term model updates or adjustments to evolving datasets.

For example, Let's say you have a chatbot model trained on general conversations, and you want to continually adapt it to a customer service role for a specific company. Over time, as new types of customer queries arise, you can apply continual fine-tuning. By adding new data regularly and using techniques like EWC, the model will learn from fresh data without forgetting previous customer service knowledge.

8.6.6 Task-Specific Data Augmentation

Using techniques such as backtranslation (translating text to another language and back to the original) or paraphrasing, you can generate additional synthetic training data that helps the model generalize better to the target task. This is especially useful when there is limited labeled data available for fine-tuning [16].

For example, you have a small dataset of movie reviews for training a sentiment analysis model. To augment this dataset, you can use *backtranslation*—translating the reviews into a different language and then back to the original. This process generates additional varied training samples, improving the model's ability to generalize sentiment across different styles of text, without needing more labeled data.

8.6.7 Meta-Learning (Learning to Fine-tune)

Meta-learning [17], or "learning to learn," focuses on training a model to adapt quickly to new tasks with minimal data. By using meta-learning, LLMs can be optimized for fast adaptation in various contexts, allowing them to fine-tune on a new task with fewer examples and more efficient learning processes.

For example, suppose you are working on a natural language processing model that needs to adapt quickly to new legal tasks. Using meta-learning, you train the model on various legal domains (e.g., contract law, intellectual property law, criminal law) so it can rapidly adapt to a completely new area, like environmental law, with minimal task-specific data. The model learns to fine-tune itself efficiently in different domains, using fewer examples from the new domain.

8.6.8 Cross-Domain Fine-tuning

When the task-specific dataset is from a different domain than the pretrained model's data, cross-domain fine-tuning adapts the model to new domains by minimizing the domain gap. Techniques like domain-adversarial training or regularization strategies (e.g., domain alignment) help the model generalize better to out-of-distribution data, improving performance across various fields.

For example, you have a model trained on news articles and want to fine-tune it for a healthcare application, such as generating medical summaries from clinical trial reports. To achieve this, you apply *cross-domain fine-tuning* [18] techniques, where domain-specific techniques like domain-adversarial training help align the model's knowledge between general news content and medical text, ensuring it generates accurate and domain-relevant summaries.

8.6.9 Semi-supervised Fine-tuning

In semi-SFT [19], both labeled and unlabeled data are used to improve the model. Unlabeled data can be leveraged using techniques like self-training or pseudo-labeling, where the model generates labels for the unlabeled data and then fine-tunes itself on both the labeled and newly labeled data. This can significantly boost performance when labeled data is limited.

For example, you have a large unlabeled dataset of product descriptions but only a small set of labeled data (few hundred labeled examples indicating product categories). Using semi-SFT, you can leverage both the labeled and unlabeled data, where the model generates pseudo-labels for the unlabeled data. These pseudo-labeled examples are then used to further fine-tune the model, improving its ability to classify products with minimal labeled data.

8.6.10 Knowledge Distillation

Knowledge distillation [20] involves transferring knowledge from a larger, more powerful model (teacher) to a smaller, more efficient model (student). In fine-tuning, the teacher model is fine-tuned on a specific task, and then, its knowledge is transferred to the student model through techniques such as soft-target supervision, enabling the student model to learn effectively from the teacher.

Knowledge distillation (KD) has emerged as a crucial method for improving the efficiency, availability, and versatility of LLMs. This methodology is built upon a framework consisting of three core elements: algorithms, skills, and verticalization. These components differentiate the fundamental techniques used for knowledge transfer, the specific skills being distilled—such as reasoning or alignment—and the practical uses in specialized domains. Initially, KD was largely concerned with compressing substantial models into smaller, deployable formats. However, its application has broadened considerably to include the transfer of behaviors, instruction-following capabilities, and safety features from powerful teacher models like GPT-3.5 or GPT-4 to lighter or open-source student models.

At the heart of the distillation process are mechanisms for knowledge elicitation and injection. Knowledge elicitation encompasses extracting information from teacher models using various strategies: direct labeling by the teacher offers output supervision; data expansion creates new training examples in the form of prompts and responses; feature distillation allows students to replicate internal representations such as hidden states or logits of the teacher; and feedback-based distillation involves the iterative assessment and critique of student outputs by the teacher. This knowledge is then integrated into student models through methods like SFT, reinforcement learning, or contrastive alignment. Contemporary KD processes often utilize data augmentation techniques generated by the teacher model, producing rich synthetic datasets that enable student models to grasp complex behaviors with little human oversight.

In addition to these technical components, knowledge distillation also emphasizes skill-oriented and domain-specific adaptations. Skill distillation focuses on imparting cognitive or behavioral qualities—such as chain-of-thought reasoning, coherence in multi-turn dialogue, safety alignment, and tool utilization—to student models. These qualities are typically conveyed through examples that clearly illustrate the intended behavior, produced by the teacher. Verticalization refers to the modification of student models for particular fields like medicine, law, finance, or code generation, employing teacher-generated data that is customized for those areas. Ethical and legal factors significantly influence this process, particularly when distilling from proprietary or restricted-access models, raising crucial considerations regarding licensing, usage rights, and data provenance. This comprehensive approach to knowledge distillation provides a strong basis for creating smaller, specialized, and more accessible AI systems capable of sophisticated language understanding and generation.

For example, suppose you want to deploy a lightweight version of a large pretrained model, like BERT, on mobile devices for text classification tasks, but the full model is too large to run efficiently. You could use *knowledge distillation*, where a smaller "student" model is trained to mimic the behavior of a larger "teacher" model. The student model learns from the teacher by using its soft predictions (probabilities over classes), which allows it to perform well on the task while being more efficient.

8.6.11 Multitask Learning

In multitask learning [21], a model is fine-tuned on several tasks simultaneously, allowing it to learn shared representations across tasks. This approach can improve generalization, especially when the tasks are related, as it allows the model to transfer knowledge between tasks and avoid overfitting to any single task.

LLMs exhibit extraordinary abilities across various tasks, often accomplished through multi-task learning, in which a single model is simultaneously trained on multiple objectives. Understanding how LLMs successfully navigate such a range of skills hinges on identifying specialized neurons—neurons that are selectively activated by specific tasks. By utilizing gradient-based attribution techniques to assess the significance of neurons on task-specific data, it becomes feasible to identify these specialized neurons. This finding uncovers an internal modularity within LLMs, where distinct collections of neurons encode information relevant to individual tasks, shedding light on the organization of knowledge within a single framework.

Multitask learning in LLMs confronts two major challenges: generalization—the model's capacity to perform effectively on unseen examples across different tasks—and catastrophic forgetting—the tendency to lose previously acquired knowledge when adjusting to new tasks. Research indicates that the degree of overlap among task-specific neurons across various tasks significantly influences these issues. Tasks with minimal neuron overlap generally exhibit better generalization, as interference is reduced. Additionally, the similarity in parameters of these neurons within certain layers correlates positively with generalization performance. These findings underscore the significance of managing neuron specialization and overlap to strike a balance between preserving existing knowledge and developing new capabilities.

Leveraging these insights, a new method of neuron-level continuous fine-tuning is proposed. Rather than fine-tuning the entire model when adapting to new tasks, this technique selectively updates only the neurons determined to be relevant for the current task. This focused adaptation safeguards the parameters of neurons that are essential for prior tasks, thereby effectively reducing catastrophic forgetting. Empirical tests across various benchmarks show that neuron-level fine-tuning improves both the consistency of continual learning and overall generalization compared to conventional fine-tuning methods. This study offers both theoretical insights and practical strategies for enhancing multitask learning and ongoing adaptation in LLMs through neuron-level understanding and optimization.

For example, you're working on a model for a virtual assistant that needs to handle a variety of tasks like scheduling appointments, answering questions, and setting reminders. Instead of training separate models for each task, you use *multi-task learning* to fine-tune a single model on all tasks simultaneously. The model learns shared representations, improving its performance across tasks by transferring knowledge between related tasks (e.g., scheduling and answering questions).

8.6.12 Regularization Techniques (e.g., Dropout, Weight Decay)

Advanced fine-tuning can involve incorporating various regularization methods [22] like dropout (randomly setting some model weights to zero) or weight decay (penalizing large weights) to prevent overfitting during fine-tuning, especially when the dataset is small or noisy. These techniques help maintain the generalization ability of the model while adapting it to the new task.

Training LLMs frequently faces issues of instability, especially when utilizing high learning rates. A major contributor to this instability is the increase in logits within the attention components of transformer-based architectures, which can ultimately result in model divergence. Besides concentrating on the size of these logits, it is essential to investigate the outputs of all linear layers within the Transformer block, encompassing the Query-Key-Value (QKV), projection (Proj), and fully connected (FC2) layers. Observations from empirical studies indicate that at higher learning rates, the L2 norms of outputs from these layers progressively increase during training, which further intensifies instability.

To tackle these issues, various architectural and normalization methods can be utilized. Implementing layer normalization not only after the QK layers but also after the Proj and FC2 layers aids in controlling the growth of intermediate representations. Another useful approach is to perform layer normalization right after the QKV layer while omitting the standard prenormalization step. Merging QK layer normalization with softmax capping also shows positive effects. Together, these strategies enable a substantial increase—up to 1.5 times—in the learning rate without causing divergence, outperforming methods that only normalize the QK layers. Additionally, these techniques lead to significant enhancements in model performance, as evidenced by lower perplexity scores.

This set of findings highlights the necessity of thoroughly examining the sources of instability in Transformer architectures and applying precise normalization methods to ensure stable training. By alleviating the explosive growth of intermediate representations through careful normalization placements, training large-scale language models becomes both more effective and reliable. These observations offer valuable insights for researchers and practitioners aiming to scale up LLMs while achieving consistent convergence and improved performance.

For example, during fine-tuning of a sentiment analysis model, you notice that it overfits on the small dataset you have for fine-tuning. To address this, you apply *dropout* during training, randomly "dropping" units in the network to prevent the model from becoming too dependent on any single unit. Additionally, you can use *weight decay* to penalize large weights, which further helps in avoiding overfitting and improving generalization.

8.7 CHALLENGES IN FINE-TUNING

The research encountered various obstacles, particularly regarding high computational expenses, which were alleviated by utilizing strategies like LoRA (Low-Rank Adaptation) and PEFT to minimize resource demands. Issues related to data quality were resolved through the careful selection of high-quality, domain-specific datasets to guarantee relevance and precision. To avoid model overfitting, regularization techniques were employed along with the use of varied datasets. Ethical issues were addressed by incorporating bias detection methods and utilizing reinforcement learning-based safety measures to ensure responsible model performance.

Fine-tuning LLMs unlocks their full potential, making them more task-specific, efficient, and ethical. Whether in healthcare, law, finance, or customer service, fine-tuning ensures that LLMs perform optimally while addressing alignment challenges and computational efficiency. As the field evolves, advanced fine-tuning techniques like LoRA, RLHF, and instruction tuning will continue shaping the future of AI applications.

SUMMARY

The goal and function of fine-tuning LLMs in modifying previously trained models for particular tasks are covered in detail in this chapter. It describes the method of LLM fine-tuning, which includes evaluation, model modification, and dataset preparation. Various techniques for fine-tuning are discussed—full fine-tuning to modify only a subset of parameters, transfer learning to leverage pretrained knowledge, reinforcement learning with human feedback (RLHF) to improve response quality, instruction tuning to align models with task-specific prompts, multimodal fine-tuning to handle multiple data types, and transfer learning to leverage pretrained knowledge. In order to better align with human or AI preferences, the chapter explores instruction tuning in greater detail, comparing manually curated datasets with those produced by LLMs and outlining alignment techniques like direct preference optimization (DPO), reinforcement learning with AI feedback (RLAIF), and reward augmented fine-tuning (RAFT). In addition to discussing key challenges such as data scarcity, computational costs, overfitting risk, and preserving generalization while enhancing domain-specific performance, it ends with advanced fine-tuning techniques.

QUESTIONS

1. Define fine-tuning in the context of LLMs.
2. List three differences between transfer learning, full fine-tuning, and PEFT.
3. Explain the general process of fine-tuning an LLM.
4. Describe the difference between instruction tuning and RLHF (Reinforcement Learning with Human Feedback).
5. Explain how manually created datasets differ from LLM-generated datasets in instruction tuning.
6. Give two real-world applications of multimodal fine-tuning in healthcare and education.
7. A base LLM has 6 billion parameters. If we perform full fine-tuning that updates all parameters, and each parameter requires 2 bytes, calculate the memory required to store the fine-tuned model.
8. A PEFT method updates only 2% of parameters in the same 6B parameter model. Calculate the memory required. Compare with Q7.
9. Analyze the tradeoffs between transfer learning, full fine-tuning, and PEFT in terms of computational efficiency and performance.
10. Compare transfer learning and instruction tuning in terms of dataset requirements and adaptability.
11. Evaluate the benefits and risks of using RLHF vs multimodal fine-tuning for alignment.
12. Discuss the major challenges in fine-tuning LLMs (e.g., catastrophic forgetting, bias, compute cost).
13. Propose a hybrid fine-tuning strategy combining PEFT + Instruction Tuning + RLHF for a legal AI assistant.
14. Design an experiment comparing PEFT vs full fine-tuning vs multimodal fine-tuning for a medical chatbot. Define evaluation metrics you would use.
15. Case Study: Fine-tuning GPT-3 with reinforcement learning from human feedback (RLHF)

    OpenAI used *Reinforcement Learning with Human Feedback (RLHF)* to fine-tune GPT-3 into ChatGPT. Initially, GPT-3 could generate fluent text but often produced irrelevant, unsafe, or biased responses. To improve alignment with user needs, researchers applied a three-step process:

    1. **Supervised Fine-Tuning** – Human trainers provided example inputs and ideal outputs to guide the model.
    2. **Reward Model Training** – Human evaluators ranked multiple responses, and the rankings trained a reward model.
    3. **Policy Optimization (RLHF)** – The model was further trained using reinforcement learning, where it learned to maximize rewards based on the human-preference feedback.

       This approach significantly improved the *helpfulness, safety, and factual accuracy* of the model. RLHF has since become a standard fine-tuning method for many LLMs, ensuring better alignment with ethical and practical user requirements. Explain how RLHF improves the alignment of LLMs compared to full fine-tuning. Give one advantage and one limitation of RLHF.

REFERENCES

[1] J. Zheng, H. Hong, X. Wang, J. Su, Y. Liang, and S. Wu , "Fine-tuning Large Language Models for Domain-Specific Machine Translation," arXiv preprint, Dec. 2024, arXiv:2402.15061.

[2] V. B. Parthasarathy, A. Zafar, A. Khan, and A. Shahid, "The Ultimate Guide to Fine-Tuning LLMs from Basics to Breakthroughs: An Exhaustive Review of Technologies, Research, Best Practices, Applied Research Challenges and Opportunities," arXiv preprint, Oct. 2024, arXiv:2408.13296.

[3] K. P. V. Srinivasan, P. Gumpena, M. Yattapu, and V. H. Brahmbhatt, "Comparative Analysis of Different Efficient Fine Tuning Methods of Large Language Models (LLMs) in Low-Resource Setting," arXiv preprint, May 2024, arXiv:2405.13181.

[4] Z. Ma, H. Guo, J. Shi, J. Wu, Y.-S. Ong, and Y.-J. Gong, "LLaMoCo: Instruction Tuning of Large Language Models for Optimization Code Generation," arXiv preprint, Mar. 2024, arXiv:2403.01131.

[5] S. Zhang, L. Dong, X. Li, S. Zhang, X. Sun, S. Wang *et al.*, "Instruction Tuning for Large Language Models: A Survey," *ACM Computing Surveys,* Dec. 2024, arXiv:2308.10792.

[6] T. Shen, R. Jin, Y. Huang, C. Liu, W. Dong, Z. Peng *et al.*, "Large Language Model Alignment: A Survey," arXiv preprint, Sep. 2023, arXiv:2309.15025.

[7] L. Kong, H. Wang, W. Mu, Y. Du, Y. Zhuang, Y. Zhou *et al.*, "Aligning Large Language Models with Representation Editing: A Control Perspective," in *Advances in Neural Information Processing Systems (NeurIPS)*, Nov. 2024, arXiv:2406.05954.

[8] R. Rafailov, A. Sharma, E. Mitchell, S. Ermon, C. D. Manning, and C. Finn, "Direct Preference Optimization: Your Language Model is Secretly a Reward Model," in *Advances in Neural Information Processing Systems (NeurIPS)*, Jul. 2024, arXiv:2305.18290.

[9] H. Lee, S. Phatale, H. Mansoor, T. Mesnard, J. Ferret, K. R. Lu *et al.*, "RLAIF vs. RLHF: Scaling Reinforcement Learning from Human Feedback with AI Feedback," in *Proc. of the International Conference on Machine Learning (ICML)*, Sep. 2024, arXiv:2309.00267.

[10] T. Zhang, S. G. Patil, N. Jain, S. Shen, M. Zaharia, I. Stoica *et al.*, "RAFT: Adapting Language Model to Domain Specific RAG," arXiv preprint, Jun. 2024, arXiv:2403.10131.

[11] E. J. Hu, Y. Shen, P. Wallis, Z. Allen-Zhu, Y. Li, S. Wang *et al.*, "LoRA: Low-Rank Adaptation of Large Language Models," in *Proc. of the International Conference on Learning Representations (ICLR)*, Oct. 2021, arXiv:2106.09685.

[12] Z. Hu, Y. Lan, L. Wang, W. Xu, E. Lim, R. K.-W. Lee *et al.*, "LLM-Adapters: An Adapter Family for Parameter-Efficient Fine-Tuning of Large Language Models," in *Proc. of the Conference on Empirical Methods in Natural Language Processing (EMNLP)*, Oct. 2023, arXiv:2304.01933.

[13] S. Fatemi, and Y. Hu, "A Comparative Analysis of Fine-Tuned LLMs and Few-Shot Learning of LLMs for Financial Sentiment Analysis," arXiv preprint, Dec. 2023, arXiv:2312.08725.

[14] A. G. Møller, and L. M. Aiello, "Prompt Refinement or Fine-tuning? Best Practices for using LLMs in Computational Social Science Tasks," ," in *Proc. of the Third Workshop on Social Influence in Conversations (SICon)*, Aug. 2024, arXiv:2408.01346.

[15] H. Shi, Z. Xu, G. Tao, Y. Zhai, B. Yang, and H. Wang, "Continual Learning of Large Language Models: A Comprehensive Survey," *ACM Computing Surveys*, Nov. 2024, arXiv:2404.16789.

[16] X. Liang, X. Hu, S. Zuo, Y. Gong, Q. Lou, Y. Liu *et al.*, "Task Oriented In-Domain Data Augmentation," in *Proc. of the Conference on Empirical Methods in Natural Language Processing (EMNLP)*, Jun. 2024.

[17] S. Sinha, Y. Yue, V. Soto, M. Kulkarni, J. Lu, and A. Zhang, "MAML-en-LLM: Model Agnostic Meta-Training of LLMs for Improved In-Context Learning," in *Proc. of the ACM SIGKDD International Conference on Knowledge Discovery and Data Mining (KDD)*, May 2024, arXiv:2405.11446.

[18] Y. Gao, M. R. Scamarcia, J. Fernandez-Marques, M. Naseri, C. S. Ng, D. Stripelis *et al.*, "FlowerTune: A Cross-Domain Benchmark for Federated Fine-Tuning of Large Language Models," in *Advances in Neural Information Processing Systems (NeurIPS)*, Jun. 2025, arXiv:2506.02961.

[19] J. Luo, X. Luo, X. Chen, Z. Xiao, W. Ju, and M. Zhang, "Semi-supervised Fine-tuning for Large Language Models," in *Proc. of the Annual Conference of the North American Chapter of the Association for Computational Linguistics (NAACL)*, Feb. 2025, arXiv:2410.14745.

[20] X. Xu, M. Li, C. Tao, T. Shen, R. Cheng, J. Li *et al.*, "A Survey on Knowledge Distillation of Large Language Models," arXiv preprint, Oct. 2024, arXiv:2402.13116.

[21] Y. Leng, and D. Xiong, "Towards Understanding Multi-Task Learning (Generalization) of LLMs via Detecting and Exploring Task-Specific Neurons," arXiv preprint, Jan. 2025, arXiv:2407.06488.

[22] O. Rybakov, M. Chrzanowski, P. Dykas, J. Xue, and B. Lanir, "Methods of Improving LLM Training Stability," arXiv preprint, Oct. 2024, arXiv:2410.16682.

9 Efficient Large Language Models

9.1 INTRODUCTION TO EFFICIENT LARGE LANGUAGE MODELS (LLMS)

In recent years, LLMs have revolutionized the realm of artificial intelligence by allowing machines to comprehend, produce, and engage with human language in an impressively human-like manner. These sophisticated AI systems, trained on extensive and varied datasets, drive a multitude of applications—from virtual assistants and automatic translation to content generation and chatbots. Their capacity to execute tasks including text completion, summarization, and question-answering has rendered them essential across various sectors [1].

Nevertheless, as LLMs continue to evolve in both complexity and scale, they introduce significant challenges. Considerable computational expenses, vast data requirements, and urgent ethical issues have arisen alongside their swift progress. This chapter investigates the significance of LLMs, analyzes the scalability challenges they encounter, and reviews effective strategies aimed at enhancing their performance while tackling these issues [2].

9.1.1 Challenges in Scaling LLMs

Increasing the size of LLMs to improve their capabilities and performance presents a number of significant challenges, which are detailed below [2].

Computational Demands: Training LLMs requires substantial computational resources, including powerful hardware accelerators and extensive energy consumption. This demand increases with model size, leading to higher operational costs and environmental concerns.

Data Requirements: LLMs necessitate large and diverse datasets to achieve high performance. Acquiring and curating such datasets can be resource-intensive, and ensuring data quality is crucial to prevent the propagation of biases and inaccuracies.

Latency and Efficiency: As models grow in size, inference times can increase, leading to latency issues in real-time applications. Optimizing LLMs for efficiency without compromising performance is a significant challenge.

DOI: 10.1201/9781003650065-9

Specialized Talent Scarcity: Developing and maintaining LLMs require expertise in machine learning and natural language processing (NLP). There is a limited pool of professionals with the necessary skills, making it challenging for organizations to build and manage teams capable of handling LLM projects.

Ethical and Safety Considerations: Ensuring that LLMs generate safe and ethical outputs is paramount. Addressing issues related to bias, misinformation, and alignment with human values requires ongoing research and robust evaluation frameworks.

9.2 PARAMETER-EFFICIENT FINE-TUNING TECHNIQUES

(PEFT) Fine-tuning LLMs [3–5] for specific tasks traditionally involves updating all model parameters, which is computationally intensive and resource demanding. Parameter-efficient fine-tuning (PEFT) methods address this challenge by adjusting only a subset of parameters, reducing computational costs and storage requirements while maintaining performance. These methods have gained prominence due to their efficiency and effectiveness in adapting LLMs to various downstream tasks.

By utilizing low-rank updates, adapter layers, and prompt-based approaches, PEFT methods make it possible to fine-tune LLMs efficiently without compromising their ability to generalize across different tasks. This section explores various PEFT techniques, their underlying mechanisms, and practical applications.

9.2.1 Low-Rank Adaptation (LoRA)

LoRA [6] introduces low-rank matrices to approximate the weight updates during fine-tuning. Instead of updating the full weight matrix W, LoRA decomposes the update into two low-rank matrices A *and* B. The decomposition of weight matrix is given in Equation (9.1).

$$W' = W + \Delta W \tag{9.1}$$

where $\Delta W = A + B$. Here, A *and* B have ranks much lower than W, significantly reducing the number of trainable parameters. This approach allows the model to adapt to new tasks efficiently without extensive computational resources.

For example, suppose a pretrained LLM is fine-tuned for sentiment analysis. Instead of modifying the full model, LoRA introduces low-rank matrices to adjust only a fraction of the parameters, capturing sentiment-specific nuances with minimal computational overhead.

LoRA provides considerable benefits by decreasing the memory requirements necessary for fine-tuning, making it more feasible to adjust large pretrained models without demanding substantial computational power. It accomplishes this by incorporating low-rank updates that maintain the fundamental knowledge of the original model while allowing for efficient customization tailored to specific tasks. This method is especially beneficial for large-scale applications, where hardware constraints frequently limit the capability to fully fine-tune extensive models, enabling quicker and

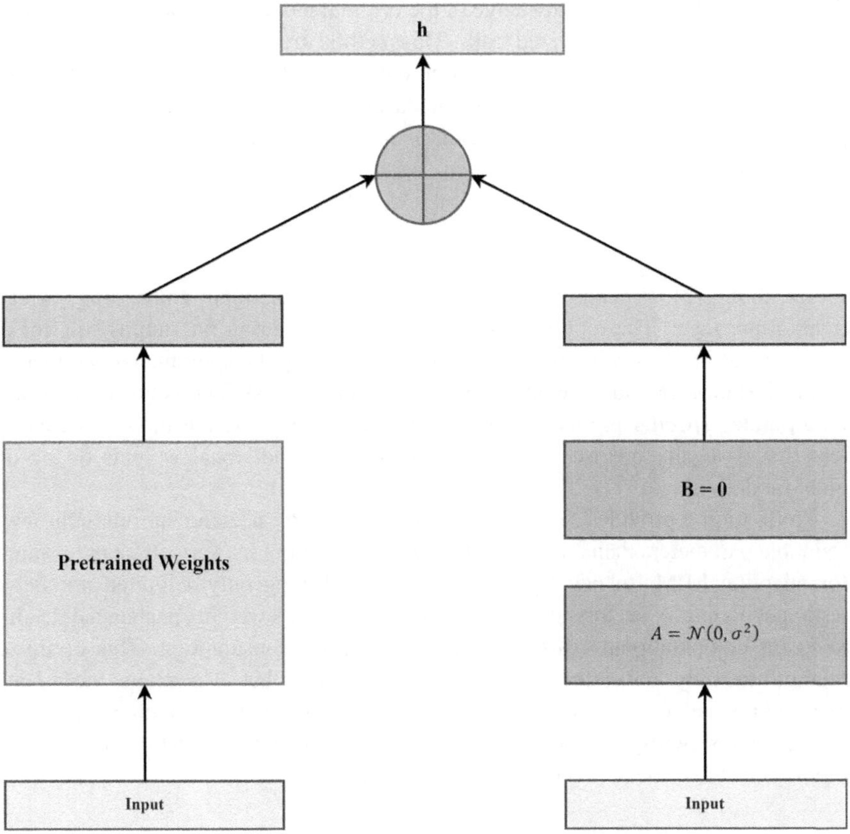

FIGURE 9.1 LoRA.

more resource-efficient adjustments without compromising performance. Figure 9.1 shows the architecture of LoRA.

9.2.2 Adapter Layers

Adapter layers [7] introduce small neural network modules between the existing layers of a pretrained model. During fine-tuning, only these adapter modules are trained, while the original model parameters remain unchanged. This ensures that the pretrained knowledge is preserved while allowing efficient domain-specific adaptation.

For example, in machine translation, adapter layers can be added to specialize the model for translating between specific language pairs, ensuring efficient adaptation without modifying the core model.

Adapter layers offer a significant advantage for fine-tuning large models by enabling the simultaneous learning of multiple tasks without the necessity to retrain the entire model. By incorporating small, trainable components into the pretrained framework, they maintain the general knowledge of the original model while facilitating effective adaptation to various specialized tasks. This method greatly lowers the computational and memory requirements in comparison to complete fine-tuning, making it particularly effective for handling several distinct tasks at once. Consequently, adapter layers provide a scalable and resource-efficient means of tailoring LLMs for a wide range of applications.

9.2.3 Prefix Tuning

Prefix tuning [8] prepends trainable prefix tokens to the input embeddings of each transformer layer. These prefix tokens are optimized during fine-tuning to steer the model toward task-specific behavior without modifying the main model parameters.

For instance, in a task involving the generation of legal documents, prefix tuning incorporates specific prefixes related to the task that guide the model to generate text that is legally precise, without changing the foundational weights of the original model.

Prefix tuning provides several significant benefits by needing substantially fewer trainable parameters than complete fine-tuning, rendering it a very efficient technique for adapting LLMs to new applications. By modifying only a limited number of task-specific prefix vectors, it keeps the original model's weights unchanged, leading to lower computational costs and reduced memory consumption. This optimized method not only makes the fine-tuning process easier but also retains the model's overall knowledge while enhancing precision on focused tasks, which is particularly beneficial for swiftly personalizing LLMs in environments with limited resources. Figure 9.2 shows the architecture of prefix tuning.

9.2.4 Prompt Tuning

Prompt tuning [9] involves optimizing continuous prompt vectors that are concatenated with the input embeddings. These prompt vectors are the only parameters updated

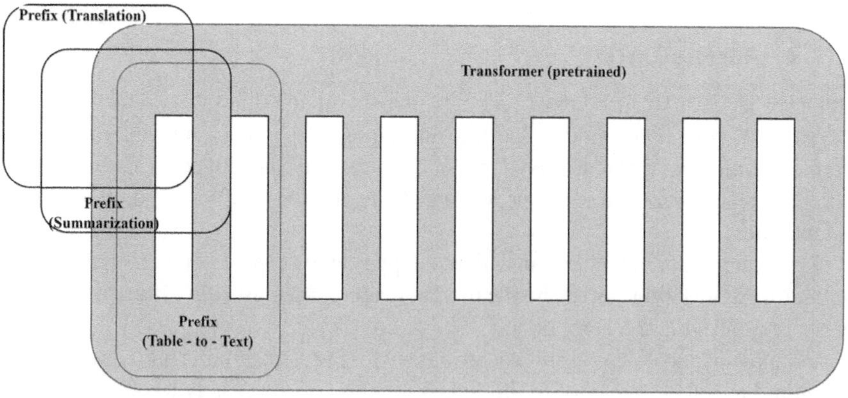

FIGURE 9.2 Prefix tuning.

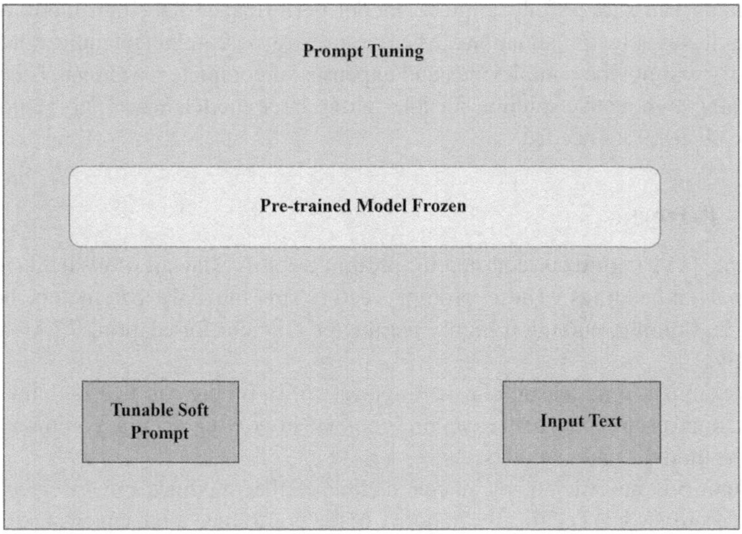

FIGURE 9.3 Prompt tuning.

during fine-tuning, making it highly parameter-efficient for adapting LLMs to specific tasks.

For example, in a question-answering system, prompt tuning can fine-tune the model by adjusting prompts to better capture context, improving accuracy without modifying the model's main weights.

Prompt tuning provides a highly effective method for customizing LLMs by focusing on optimizing just a small number of input prompts instead of modifying the whole model, requiring fewer computational resources. This technique facilitates quick adjustments to new tasks, making it especially beneficial in situations where time or resources are constrained. Furthermore, prompt tuning performs exceptionally well in scenarios with limited data, where comprehensive fine-tuning is not feasible, enabling models to achieve good performance with few examples by using thoughtfully crafted prompts to steer their behavior without the need for extensive retraining. Figure 9.3 displays the architecture of prompt tuning.

9.2.5 Bias Tuning

Bias tuning [10] adjusts only the bias terms of the model's neurons during fine-tuning, keeping the weight matrices fixed. This reduces the number of trainable parameters while still allowing the model to adapt to new tasks.

For example, when adapting an LLM to regional dialects, bias tuning can adjust the model's bias terms to account for linguistic variations, improving accuracy with minimal parameter updates.

Bias tuning is a highly efficient fine-tuning technique that targets just the bias terms in a model's layers, greatly minimizing the computational demands compared to more comprehensive fine-tuning methods. Even with limited parameter changes, bias tuning can successfully improve model performance for slight modifications, making it suitable for situations where rapid, resource-efficient adjustments are necessary without the complexities and expenses of complete retraining. This makes bias tuning an effective solution for fine-tuning large models when only minor task-specific changes are needed.

9.2.6 P-Tuning

P-Tuning [11] optimizes continuous prompt vectors that are concatenated with the input embeddings. These prompt vectors are the only parameters updated during fine-tuning, making it highly parameter-efficient for adapting LLMs to specific tasks.

For example, in a question-answering system, P-Tuning can fine-tune the model by adjusting prompts to better capture context, improving accuracy without modifying the model's main weights.

P-Tuning is an efficient parameter technique that modifies only a selection of prompt vectors while keeping the majority of the pre-trained model unchanged, which significantly decreases the number of parameters that need training. This method is advantageous in terms of memory usage, requiring less storage and computational resources than full fine-tuning, making it ideal for situations with limited capacity. P-Tuning allows for the rapid adaptation of LLMs to new tasks with minor alterations, simplifying the fine-tuning procedure. Furthermore, it demonstrates strong performance in scenarios with few labeled training examples by utilizing prompt optimization to steer the model's performance without extensive retraining. Figure 9.4 shows the architecture of P-tuning.

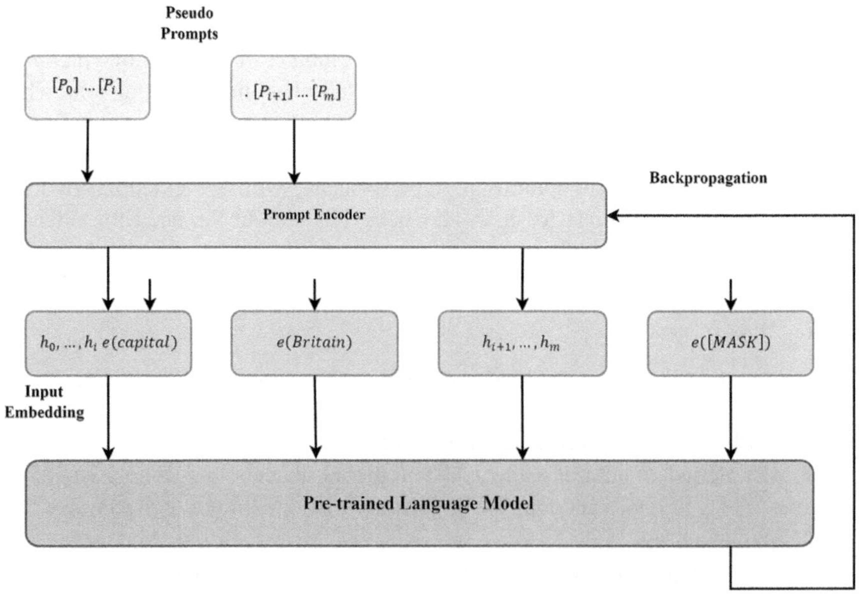

FIGURE 9.4 P-tuning.

9.2.7 (IA)³

(IA)³, or "Intrinsic Attention Augmentation," [12] is a technique that enhances the model's attention mechanisms by introducing additional trainable parameters within the attention layers. This method allows for more focused and efficient learning of task-specific patterns without altering the entire model architecture.

For example, when adapting a language model for legal document analysis, (IA)³ can adjust the attention mechanisms to prioritize legal terminology and context, improving comprehension and relevance.

(IA)³ provides multiple benefits by improving the efficiency of the model's attention mechanism, allowing for better focus on pertinent information and enhancing performance in specialized tasks. This approach facilitates task-specific adjustments with minimal modifications to the foundational model weights, maintaining the original model's knowledge while fine-tuning its attention structures. Moreover, (IA)³ enhances interpretability by offering clearer insights into which segments of the input the model prioritizes during processing. This blend of efficient attention improvement, targeted customization, and enhanced transparency renders (IA)³ a powerful resource for optimizing LLMs in specialized contexts. Figure 9.5 displays the architecture of IA³.

9.2.8 Quantized Low-Rank Adaptation (QLoRA)

QLoRA [13] combines quantization and low-rank adaptation to fine-tune LLMs efficiently. By quantizing the pre-trained model weights to lower precision (e.g., 4-bit) and applying low-rank adaptations, QLoRA significantly reduces memory usage without compromising performance.

For example, fine-tuning a 65-billion parameter model on a single 48GB GPU becomes feasible with QLoRA, enabling high-performance adaptation for specific tasks with limited hardware resources.

QLoRA provides an effective strategy for fine-tuning LLMs by utilizing quantization methods to significantly decrease memory requirements, allowing for substantial memory savings while preserving model accuracy. Even when functioning at lower numerical precision, QLoRA delivers performance that is nearly equivalent to that of full-precision models, making it particularly effective in environments with limited resources. This efficient memory usage enables users to fine-tune very large models on standard consumer-grade GPUs, significantly enhancing accessibility. By integrating low-rank adaptation with quantization, QLoRA strikes a favorable balance between efficiency and flexibility, positioning it as an ideal choice for scalable and high-performance model fine-tuning. Figure 9.6 shows the architecture of QLoRA.

9.2.9 Alternative PEFT Approaches

Some PEFT [14] strategies are categorized as *Additive Methods*, which introduce additional trainable parameters while keeping most of the pretrained model intact. Examples of this include adapters, which insert small fully connected layers between transformer layers to assist the model in adjusting to new tasks, and soft prompts,

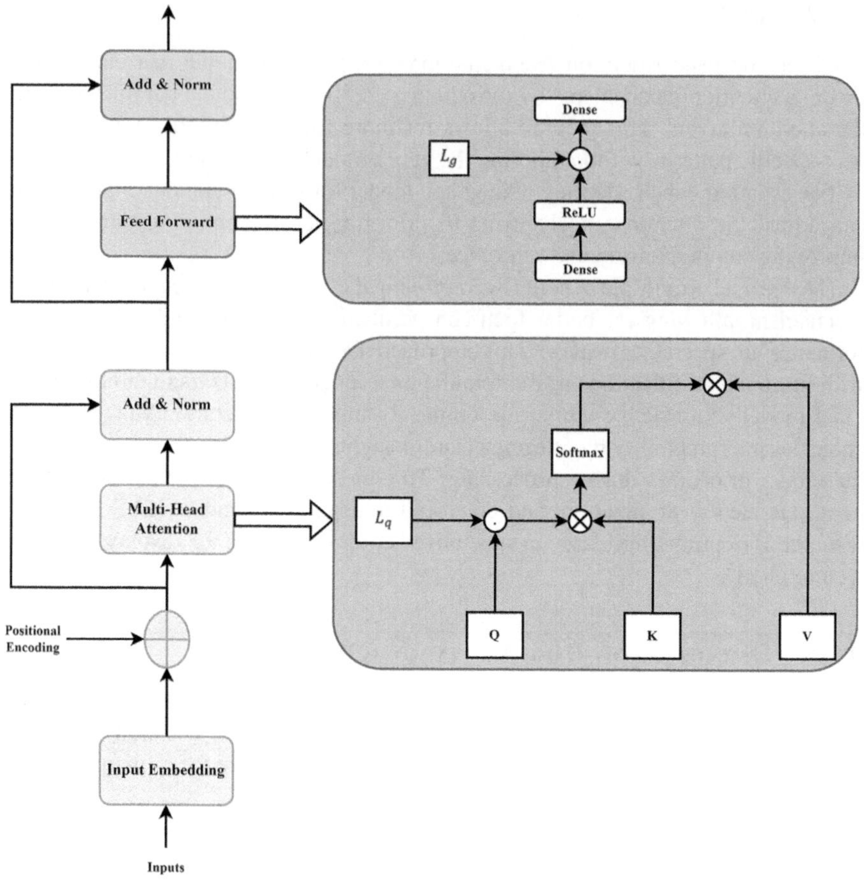

FIGURE 9.5 IA^3.

which alter input embeddings instead of changing internal weights. For example, in low-resource language processing, soft prompts facilitate quick domain adaptation by fine-tuning a model without altering its pretrained parameters, making it a practical approach when data or resources are scarce.

Another category is *Selective Methods*, where only certain parts of the model are trained rather than fine-tuning the entire network. This includes techniques like top layer fine-tuning, which updates only the upper layers of the model while keeping the lower layers fixed, and sparse updates, which selectively adjust a subset of parameters based on their significance. For instance, in image-captioning models, adapting only the top layers allows the model to adjust to new image datasets efficiently without the necessity of retraining the foundational layers that capture general features.

Lastly, *Reparameterization-Based Methods* focus on lowering the number of trainable parameters by utilizing low-rank approximations. Techniques such as LoRA use

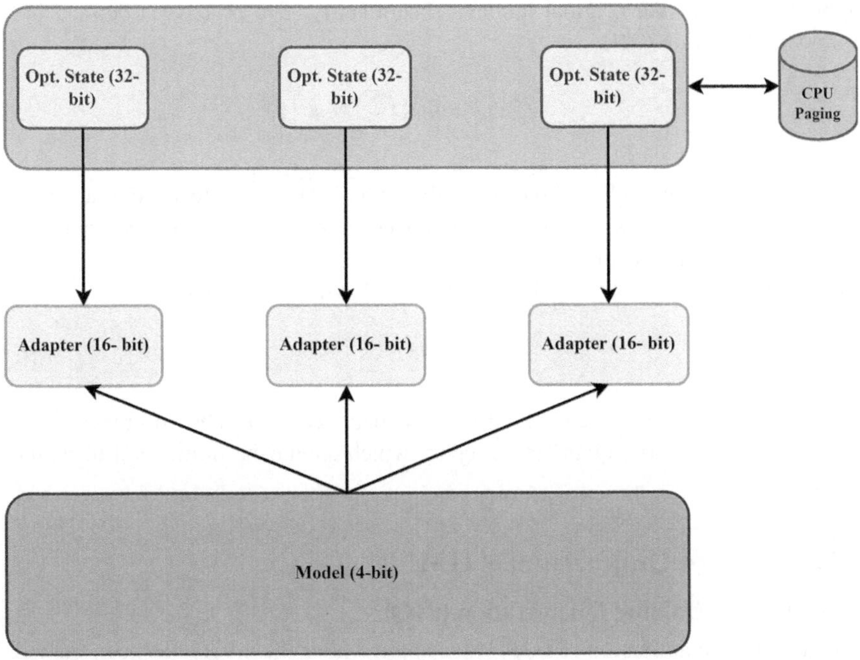

FIGURE 9.6 QLoRA.

low-rank matrices to provide an efficient approximation of weight updates, whereas methods like Intrinsic SAID employ Fastfood transforms for a compact representation of these updates. For example, LoRA has been applied in financial fraud detection to fine-tune a LLM for analyzing transaction data, effectively adapting the model without needing to change all of its original weights.

9.3 QUANTIZATION TECHNIQUES IN EFFICIENT LARGE LANGUAGE MODELS (LLMS)

As LLMs continue to grow in size and complexity, the need for efficient model compression techniques has become critical. Quantization [15] is one such optimization technique that reduces the memory footprint and computational cost of LLMs by lowering the precision of numerical representations in model weights and activations.

By converting high-precision floating-point values (e.g., 32-bit FP32) into lower-bit representations (e.g., INT8, INT4, or even binary values), quantization enables faster inference, lower energy consumption, and efficient deployment on edge devices while maintaining acceptable accuracy levels.

Quantization is the process of mapping real-valued weights (or activations) to discrete values from a smaller set. The general idea behind quantization is to replace each parameter with a lower-precision integer value while maintaining a close approximation of the original model's functionality. The process is defined in the following Equation (9.2).

$$Q(x) = \text{round}\left(\frac{x}{s}\right) \times \text{s} \tag{9.2}$$

where, x is the original high-precision value (e.g., FP32), s is the scaling factor (used to normalize the values), $Q(x)$ is the quantized output, and $round(\cdot)$ = function that rounds values to the nearest discrete level.

The dequantization process is defined in the following Equation (9.3).

$$x' = Q(x) \times \text{s} \tag{9.3}$$

where x' is the reconstructed value from the quantized form. The difference between x *and* x' represents the quantization error, which should be minimized to maintain accuracy.

9.3.1 Types of Quantization in LLMs

9.3.1.1 Post-training Quantization (PTQ)

Post-training Quantization (PTQ) [16] is applied after the model has been trained. It converts pretrained floating-point weights into lower-bit representations (e.g., FP32 → INT8), reducing memory requirements without modifying the model's training process.

PTQ is a simple and efficient method applied after a model is fully trained. It quantizes the weights and activations to lower-bit precision (such as INT8 or INT4) without retraining the model. PTQ is quick to implement and does not require additional training, making it a popular choice for large-scale deployment. However, PTQ may cause slight accuracy loss due to the reduction in precision. The PTQ process is computed using the following Equation (9.4).

$$W_q = \text{round}\left(\frac{W}{s}\right) \times \text{s} \tag{9.4}$$

where, W is the original model weights, W_q is the quantized weights, and s is the scaling factor for normalization.

For example, converting a BERT-based chatbot from FP32 to INT8 to optimize memory and run on mobile devices.

PTQ provides multiple benefits, particularly in situations that demand rapid and efficient deployment. It eliminates the need for model retraining, resulting in a quick and uncomplicated process that suits resource-limited devices like mobile phones and embedded systems. PTQ is also economical, as it requires minimal computational power. However, there are certain drawbacks. A significant limitation is the risk of accuracy loss, particularly if the quantization settings are not optimized. Since the model does not undergo retraining to adjust for quantized weights and activations, PTQ offers reduced flexibility and resilience to quantization errors compared to quantization-aware training (QAT). This lack of adaptability can pose challenges in applications where high accuracy is essential, as the model may find it difficult to sustain performance following conversion.

9.3.2 Quantization-Aware Training

QAT [17] is a more sophisticated approach where quantization is simulated during the model's training phase. This allows the model to adjust its parameters to minimize the negative effects of reduced precision. By simulating quantization effects during training, QAT helps the model maintain higher accuracy even with lower-precision weights. The QAT process can be computed using the following Equation (9.5).

$$\hat{W} = argmin_W \sum (L(Q(W), Y)) \tag{9.5}$$

where, $\hat{W}$ is the optimized weight values after QAT, $Q(W)$ is the quantized version of weights, L is the loss function, and Y is the ground truth.

For example, training a fraud detection model while simulating INT8 quantization to ensure high accuracy in low-bit formats.

QAT offers higher accuracy than PTQ because the model actively adapts to reduced precision during training, making it especially suitable for critical applications like healthcare and finance where minimizing performance loss is essential. Additionally, QAT provides greater flexibility in handling complex models. However, these benefits come at the cost of increased computational resources and longer training times, presenting challenges related to higher training expenses and complexity.

9.3.3 Dynamic Quantization

Dynamic quantization [18] is applied during inference, where activations are quantized to lower precision, but the weights remain in their full precision (FP32). Dynamic quantization helps speed up inference by reducing the precision of intermediate values without affecting the model's overall architecture. The dynamic quantization is computed using the following Equations (9.6).

$$A_q = \text{quantize}(A) \tag{9.6}$$

where, A_q is the dynamically quantized activation values, $Quantize\ (\cdot)$ is the function that applies low-bit conversion.

For example, in speech recognition models, real-time activation quantization (INT8) speeds up response time without retraining.

Dynamic quantization presents the benefit of not needing retraining, as it makes precision adjustments solely during inference, allowing for quick and simple implementation. This method considerably decreases inference latency and is ideal for hardware optimized for low-precision calculations, facilitating efficient deployment without significant overhead. However, dynamic quantization may result in a reduction of precision during inference, which could adversely impact the accuracy of intricate models or those with broad dynamic ranges. As a result, the accuracy might fluctuate based on the complexity of the input data, creating challenges for applications that require consistently high precision.

9.3.4 Static Quantization

Static quantization [19] is a method where both the weights and activations of a trained model are converted into lower-precision representations before inference. This technique is applied after the model has been trained and requires a calibration phase to determine the range of values for both weights and activations. During this phase, the minimum and maximum values of the parameters are observed, and a scaling factor is computed to map these values to a reduced bit-width range (e.g., 8-bit integers).

$$X_q = \frac{X - X_{min}}{X_{max} - X_{min}} \times (2^b - 1) \tag{9.7}$$

$$b = \text{bit} - \text{width (e.g., } 8 - \text{bit)} \tag{9.8}$$

where X_q is the statically quantized value, X is the original high-precision value (e.g., FP32), X_{min}, X_{max} is the minimum and maximum observed values, $2^b - 1$ is the number of distinct values that can be represents with b-bit precision.

This formula ensures that the range of values is compressed into the available quantized range while minimizing distortion. The scaling factor s ensures that the quantized values X_q are mapped proportionally to the available range, preserving the relationships between values.

Once the model is quantized, the dequantization process reconstructs the quantized values back to their original range. This is done using the following Equation (9.9).

$$X' = X_q \times \frac{X_{max} - X_{min}}{2^b - 1} \times X_{min} \tag{9.9}$$

where, X' is the reconstructed original value after dequantization, X_q is the quantized value, and X_{min}, X_{max} is the minimum and maximum used for scaling.

This ensures that after the model operates on the quantized values, the approximate original values are maintained when needed for downstream tasks.

For example, compressing a legal document AI model to run on IoT devices with fixed storage capacity.

Static quantization provides notable advantages by decreasing model size and memory consumption, making it feasible for use on devices with limited resources such as smartphones and IoT devices. This reduction in precision enhances computational speed, leading to quicker model predictions and reduced latency, which is essential for real-time applications like voice assistants. Furthermore, static quantization is more efficient in terms of energy use, making it ideal for devices that rely on battery power. However, it necessitates a calibration phase that utilizes representative sample data to adjust the quantization parameters, which can prove difficult if relevant domain-specific data is limited. In addition, the fixed low-precision format (typically

INT8) can result in a loss of accuracy, particularly for intricate models or tasks that demand higher precision. Compatibility with devices may also be restricted, as not all hardware is capable of supporting low-precision arithmetic, potentially limiting its use.

9.3.5 Quantized Low-Rank Adaptation (QLoRA)

Quantized Low-Rank Adaptation (QLoRA) [13] combines the principles of low-rank adaptation (LoRA) and quantization to fine-tune large models efficiently. By applying 4-bit quantization to the weights and using low-rank matrices for adaptation, QLoRA allows for fine-tuning large-scale models even with limited memory.

The weight update is defined as follows in Equation (9.10).

$$W' = Q(W) + A \times \mathrm{B} \tag{9.10}$$

where, $Q(W)$ is the 4-bit quantized weights, and A, B is the low-rank adaptation matrices.

For example, QLoRA makes it possible to fine-tune a 65B-parameter LLaMA model on a single 48 GB GPU by training low-rank adapters while keeping the quantized base model frozen.

QLoRA significantly reduces memory usage while maintaining model effectiveness, making it feasible to fine-tune LLMs on consumer-level hardware, such as GPUs with approximately 48GB of memory. This makes it particularly valuable for environments with limited resources where standard fine-tuning would be unfeasible due to hardware constraints. However, QLoRA is dependent on its integration with low-rank adaptation (LoRA) techniques for efficient modification, which can introduce complexity and may pose challenges for individuals lacking specialized expertise in model optimization. Furthermore, to utilize QLoRA effectively, hardware that is compatible with advanced quantization operations may be necessary, leading to additional implementation difficulties.

9.4 PRUNING STRATEGIES

As LLMs grow in size, their computational and memory demands increase significantly. Pruning [20] is a technique used to reduce these demands by removing less important components of the model, thereby making it more efficient without substantially compromising performance.

Pruning involves eliminating certain weights, neurons, or even entire layers from a neural network. The goal is to create a sparser model that maintains accuracy while being more resource efficient. In the context of LLMs, pruning helps in the following.

- Reducing Model Size: Decreasing the number of parameters to save storage space.
- Enhancing Inference Speed: Speeding up the model's predictions by simplifying computations.

- Lowering Energy Consumption: Reducing the computational load leads to less power usage, which is crucial for deployment on devices with limited resources.

9.4.1 Types of Pruning

Pruning methods can be broadly categorized into the following.

- **Unstructured Pruning:** Removes individual weights based on certain criteria, leading to sparse weight matrices. While it can achieve high sparsity levels, it may not always result in practical speedups due to irregular memory access patterns.
- **Structured Pruning:** Eliminates entire neurons, attention heads, or layers, resulting in a model with a regular structure that is more amenable to optimization and acceleration on hardware.

9.4.2 Unstructured Pruning

Unstructured pruning is a technique in neural network optimization that involves removing individual weights from the model's parameters without considering any specific structure or pattern. This method aims to create a sparser network by setting certain weights to zero, effectively eliminating less significant connections between neurons. The primary goal is to reduce the model's complexity and computational requirements while maintaining its performance.

The key characteristic of unstructured pruning is given as follows.

- **Granularity:** Targets individual weights within the neural network, allowing for fine-grained adjustments.
- **Flexibility:** Does not adhere to any specific pattern or structure when removing weights, providing flexibility in the pruning process.
- **Sparsity:** Results in sparse weight matrices, which can lead to reduced memory usage and potentially faster computations, depending on hardware support.

9.4.2.1 Approaches in Unstructured Pruning

9.4.2.1.1 Magnitude-Based Pruning

This approach involves removing weights with the smallest absolute values, under the assumption that these weights contribute the least to the model's output [20, 21]. The process can be summarized as follows.

- **Compute Weight Magnitudes:** Calculate the absolute value of each weight in the network.
- **Determine Pruning Threshold:** Set a threshold value, below which weights will be pruned. This can be a fixed value or determined based on a desired sparsity level.
- **Prune Weights:** Set weights with magnitudes below the threshold to zero.

Mathematically, if w represents a weight and θ is the pruning threshold, the pruning operation $P(w)$ can be defined as follows in Equation (9.11).

$$P(w) = \begin{cases} 0 & if\,|w| < \theta \\ w & otherwise \end{cases} \tag{9.11}$$

This method is straightforward and has been widely used in various neural network pruning studies.

9.4.2.1.2 Activation-Based Pruning

Recent methods, such as the Wanda approach, consider both weight magnitudes and activation values to determine which weights to prune. The intuition is that weights connected to neurons with low activation values have a minimal impact on the network's output and can be pruned. The pruning criterion in this case involves the product of the weight magnitude and the corresponding activation norm. This approach has been shown to be effective in pruning LLMs without the need for retraining [22].

While unstructured pruning can lead to significant reductions in the number of parameters, the resulting irregular sparsity patterns may not always translate to computational speedups on standard hardware. Specialized hardware or software optimizations are often required to fully leverage the benefits of unstructured pruning.

Care must be taken to ensure that pruning does not degrade the model's performance. It's common to fine-tune the pruned model to recover any potential loss in accuracy.

unstructured pruning is a valuable technique for reducing the complexity of neural networks by removing individual weights based on specific criteria. When applied carefully, it can lead to more efficient models with minimal impact on performance.

9.4.3 Structured Pruning

Structured pruning is a neural network optimization technique that involves removing entire components—such as neurons, filters, channels, or layers—based on specific criteria. Unlike unstructured pruning, which eliminates individual weights, structured pruning maintains the network's architecture, resulting in models that are more efficient and better suited for hardware acceleration.

The key characteristic of structured pruning is given as follows.

- **Granularity:** Targets larger structures within the network, such as entire neurons in fully connected layers or filters in convolutional layers.
- **Hardware Efficiency:** By maintaining a regular structure, the pruned model can leverage optimized hardware and software for dense computations, leading to actual speedups in deployment.
- **Interpretability:** Removing entire components can make the network's behavior more interpretable, as it simplifies the architecture.

9.4.3.1 Approaches in Structured Pruning

- Filter Pruning in Convolutional Neural Networks (CNNs): This method involves removing entire filters (kernels) from convolutional layers. Filters with minimal contribution to the output are identified and pruned, resulting in reduced computational load and model size.
- Channel Pruning: Channels (feature maps) in CNNs that contribute least to the model's performance are pruned. This approach reduces the width of layers, leading to decreased computational complexity.
- Neuron Pruning in Fully Connected Layers: Entire neurons in fully connected layers are removed based on their importance, which is often determined by the magnitude of their weights or their activation levels.

9.4.3.2 Pruning Criterion

A common criterion for structured pruning is based on the magnitude of the parameters associated with the structures to be pruned. For example, in filter pruning, the norm of a filter's weights can be used to assess its importance. Filters with smaller norms are considered less important and are candidates for pruning. Mathematically, if W_i represents the weights of the $i-th$ filter, its importance can be evaluated using the l_2-norm and is given in Equation (9.12).

$$\|W_i\|_2 = \sqrt{\sum_j w_{i,j}^2} \tag{9.12}$$

Filters with l_2-norm below a certain threshold are pruned.

It is crucial to ensure that pruning does not significantly degrade the model's accuracy. Often, a fine-tuning process is employed after pruning to recover any lost performance. Different layers may have varying levels of redundancy. Applying uniform pruning rates across all layers might not be optimal. Adaptive methods that determine layer-specific pruning rates can lead to better results. Incorporating regularization methods during training can encourage sparsity, making the model more amenable to pruning. For instance, adding a sparsity-inducing penalty to the loss function can promote the development of unimportant structures that can be pruned later.

Structured pruning is a powerful technique for optimizing neural networks that eliminates complete components—such as neurons, filters, or layers—resulting in a more streamlined and organized model architecture. This optimized design improves compatibility with conventional hardware enhancements, yielding significant gains in inference speed and efficiency. By preserving a consistent and simplified model structure, structured pruning not only minimizes computational demands but also facilitates implementation and upkeep. This makes it especially useful for deploying high-performance models in environments with limited resources, where both speed and efficiency are crucial.

9.5 EFFICIENT ATTENTION MECHANISMS

Efficient attention mechanisms are crucial in processing long sequences in NLP and other domains. Traditional attention mechanisms, like those in standard transformers, have quadratic time and memory complexity concerning the input sequence length, making them less suitable for long sequences. To address this, researchers have developed methods such as sparse attention mechanisms and linear attention models to enhance efficiency.

9.5.1 Sparse Attention Mechanisms

Sparse attention mechanisms [23] aim to reduce the computational burden by limiting the number of elements each token attends to, rather than considering all possible pairs. This sparsity reduces the complexity from quadratic to linear or near linear, depending on the specific approach.

The key approach of sparse attention is given us follows.

- **Fixed Patterns:** Some models define fixed sparse patterns where each token attends to a predefined subset of tokens. For example, the *BigBird* model combines local attention, random attention, and global attention to capture various dependencies efficiently.
- **Learned Patterns:** Other approaches allow the model to learn which tokens to attend to during training, enabling dynamic sparsity that adapts to the data. The Rectified Linear Attention (*ReLA*) model replaces the *softmax* function with a ReLU activation to induce sparsity naturally.

For example, Rectified Linear Attention (*ReLA*) modifies the attention mechanism by replacing the softmax activation with a ReLU function, promoting sparsity. This change leads to more efficient computations and has been shown to maintain performance across various tasks.

9.5.2 Linear Attention Models

Linear attention models [24] aim to reduce the quadratic complexity of traditional attention mechanisms by approximating the attention function in a way that scales linearly with the sequence length.

The key approach of linear attention is given us follows.

- **Kernel-Based Methods:** These methods approximate the *softmax* function using kernel functions, allowing the attention computation to be reformulated into a series of matrix multiplications that scale linearly. For instance, the Performer model uses positive orthogonal random features to achieve this.
- **Low-Rank Approximations:** By assuming that the attention matrix is low-rank, these methods approximate it with matrices that require less computation. This approach reduces the complexity while aiming to retain essential information.

For example, this model introduces a linear dispatcher attention mechanism that significantly reduces the quadratic complexity, making the model feasible for modelling extremely long sequences. It achieves up to 90% GPU memory usage reduction and 2.7 times inference speedup.

Efficient attention mechanisms like sparse attention and linear attention models are pivotal in handling long sequences in NLP and other fields. By reducing computational complexity and memory usage, these methods enable the processing of longer contexts, enhancing the performance and applicability of models in various tasks.

9.6 DISTRIBUTED AND PARALLEL COMPUTING FOR LLMS

Training LLMs efficiently necessitates the use of distributed and parallel computing strategies to manage their substantial computational demands. Two primary approaches in this context are data parallelism and model parallelism, each with distinct methodologies and applications [25, 26].

9.6.1 Data Parallelism

In data parallelism, the entire model is replicated across multiple devices, and the dataset is divided into smaller batches, each assigned to a different device. Each device processes its batch independently, performing forward and backward passes to compute gradients. Afterward, the gradients are aggregated (typically through an all-reduce operation), and the model parameters are updated synchronously to ensure consistency across all devices.

Data parallelism makes implementation easier by duplicating the entire model across multiple devices, facilitating straightforward scaling as additional devices are incorporated. This method allows for effective distribution of training workloads and can greatly speed up the training process. However, each device needs to possess sufficient memory to hold a complete copy of the model, which can pose a significant challenge for extremely large models. Furthermore, the communication overhead associated with gradient aggregation among devices can serve as a bottleneck, especially when scaling up to a substantial number of devices, potentially hindering overall efficiency and acceleration.

9.6.2 Model Parallelism

Model parallelism involves partitioning the model itself across multiple devices, with each device responsible for computing a portion of the model. This approach is beneficial when the model is too large to fit into the memory of a single device. There are various strategies for model parallelism, including the following.

- **Tensor Parallelism:** Splits individual layers or tensors across devices.
- **Pipeline Parallelism:** Divides the model into sequential stages, with each stage assigned to a different device.

Model parallelism enables the training of models that exceed the memory limits of a single device by distributing the model parameters across multiple devices, which minimizes memory redundancy and facilitates larger models. Nevertheless, this method adds a layer of implementation complexity, necessitating careful division of the model and accurate synchronization between devices for efficient operation. Furthermore, uneven distribution can result in load imbalance, with some devices becoming bottlenecks and diminishing overall performance. To tackle these issues and enhance efficiency, a hybrid parallelism approach that integrates both data and model parallelism is frequently utilized, capitalizing on the advantages of each technique to improve memory efficiency and processing speed.

9.6.3 Distributed Training Strategies

Efficiently training LLMs requires sophisticated distributed training strategies that balance computational load and minimize communication overhead. The key strategies includes the following.

- **ZeRO (Zero Redundancy Optimizer):** ZeRO is a memory optimization technique that partitions the model states (optimizer states, gradients, and parameters) across devices to reduce memory redundancy. This allows for training larger models by effectively utilizing available memory resources.
- **Gradient Accumulation:** This technique accumulates gradients over multiple mini-batches before performing a parameter update. It effectively increases the batch size without requiring additional memory, facilitating stable training and efficient utilization of hardware resources.
- **Asynchronous Training:** In asynchronous training, devices perform computations and update parameters independently, without waiting for synchronization with other devices. This approach can lead to faster training times but may introduce challenges related to model convergence and consistency.
- **Federated Learning:** Federated learning involves training models across decentralized devices or servers, where each device trains on its local data and periodically aggregates model updates. This strategy is particularly useful for privacy-preserving training and scenarios with distributed data sources.

Implementing these strategies requires careful consideration of factors such as hardware capabilities, network bandwidth, and the specific characteristics of the model and dataset. Frameworks like DeepSpeed and Megatron-LM provide tools to facilitate efficient distributed training of LLMs.

9.7 ENERGY EFFICIENCY IN LLM INFERENCE

9.7.1 Hardware Accelerators

Hardware accelerators are specialized processors designed to perform specific computational tasks more efficiently than general-purpose CPUs. In the context of LLM inference, accelerators such as graphics processing units (GPUs), tensor processing units (TPUs), and application-specific integrated circuits (ASICs) are utilized to enhance performance and reduce energy consumption [27, 28].

- GPUs are widely used due to their high parallel processing capabilities, making them suitable for the matrix operations prevalent in LLMs.
- TPUs, developed by Google, are tailored for machine learning tasks, offering optimized performance for both training and inference phases.
- ASICs are custom-designed chips that provide high efficiency for specific applications, including LLM inference, by minimizing unnecessary functionalities present in general-purpose processors.

These hardware accelerators contribute to significant reductions in energy consumption during LLM inference by streamlining computational processes and enhancing throughput.

9.7.2 Energy-Efficient Model Design

Designing energy-efficient models involves optimizing architectures to reduce computational complexity without compromising performance. Techniques such as model pruning, quantization, and knowledge distillation are pivotal in this endeavor.

- Model pruning removes redundant parameters from the model, decreasing its size and computational requirements.
- Quantization reduces the precision of the model's parameters, leading to lower memory usage and faster computations.
- Knowledge distillation involves training a smaller model (student) to replicate the behavior of a larger model (teacher), resulting in a more compact and efficient model suitable for inference tasks.

Implementing these techniques leads to models that are not only faster but also more energy-efficient, facilitating deployment in resource-constrained environments.

9.8 OPTIMIZING LLMS FOR EDGE DEVICES

9.8.1 Model Compression Techniques

Deploying LLMs on edge devices necessitates reducing model size to fit within limited hardware resources. Model compression techniques such as pruning, quantization, and knowledge distillation are employed to achieve this goal [29].

- Pruning eliminates unnecessary neurons or connections, resulting in a sparser and smaller model.
- Quantization involves converting model weights to lower precision formats, reducing memory footprint and computational load.
- Knowledge distillation transfers knowledge from a large model to a smaller one, maintaining performance while reducing size.

These methods enable the deployment of LLMs on edge devices by ensuring models are compact and efficient.

9.8.2 Real-Time Inference Strategies

Achieving real-time inference on edge devices requires strategies that minimize latency and optimize resource utilization. Techniques such as model quantization, efficient model architectures, and hardware acceleration are crucial [30].

- Model quantization reduces computation time by lowering numerical precision.
- Efficient model architectures are designed to require fewer computations, facilitating faster inference.
- Hardware acceleration leverages specialized processors to expedite inference processes.

Implementing these strategies ensures that LLMs can operate effectively on edge devices, providing timely responses in applications such as real-time language translation and voice assistants.

9.9 PRACTICAL APPLICATIONS OF EFFICIENT LLMS

Efficient LLMs have diverse real-world uses in multiple fields, particularly in situations where limitations in computing power, response time, or energy usage are significant factors. These uses encompass the following.

1. **Chatbots and Virtual Assistants:** Efficient LLMs power chatbots and virtual assistants by enabling natural language understanding and generation with reduced computational resources. This efficiency allows for deployment on devices with limited processing power, providing users with responsive and intelligent interactions.
2. **Healthcare and Finance:** In sectors like healthcare and finance, efficient LLMs facilitate tasks such as data analysis, report generation, and customer support. The reduced energy consumption and faster processing times are critical in environments where timely and accurate information is essential.
3. **Mobile Applications:** Deploying efficient LLMs in mobile applications enables features like real-time language translation, voice recognition, and personalized content delivery. The optimized models ensure that these applications run smoothly on mobile devices without excessive battery drain.

SUMMARY

The methods for creating and implementing efficient LLMs that preserve performance while lowering computing costs are the main topic of this chapter. Parameter-efficient fine-tuning techniques, which adapt models with minimal parameter changes, such as LoRA, adapter layers, prefix tuning, prompt tuning, and bias tuning, come after an introduction to the necessity of efficiency in LLMs. After that, quantization techniques are examined, including QAT to maintain accuracy during compression and PTQ to compress models after training. Pruning techniques are covered, such as unstructured pruning (removing individual weights) and structured pruning (removing entire neurons or layers). Additionally, the chapter discusses efficient attention mechanisms, such as linear attention to scale well with sequence length and sparse attention to restrict computation to critical tokens. To speed up large-scale training, distributed and parallel computing methods are described, as well as energy-efficient inference and optimizing LLMs for edge devices. Practical applications are included at the end to demonstrate how efficiency allows for real-world deployment in low-resource contexts without requiring significant performance tradeoffs.

QUESTIONS

1. Define parameter-efficient fine-tuning and explain its importance in the context of LLMs.
2. Differentiate between LoRA, adapter layers, and prefix tuning with suitable examples.
3. Explain the concept of quantization and its role in reducing LLM computational cost.
4. Describe structured pruning and unstructured pruning. Provide real-world use cases for each.
5. Summarize how distributed and parallel computing improves the scalability of LLMs.
6. Apply LoRA fine-tuning to a sample model with 1 billion parameters. If LoRA reduces trainable parameters by 90%, calculate the number of parameters updated during training.
7. Analyze the tradeoffs between PTQ and QAT.
8. Suppose a model with 200 million parameters undergoes structured pruning with a 30% reduction. Calculate the remaining parameters.
9. Compare sparse attention mechanisms and linear attention models in terms of time complexity and scalability.
10. Examine how bias tuning can be applied to multilingual models for domain adaptation.
11. Evaluate the energy efficiency of LLM inference by comparing GPU-based deployment vs. edge-device deployment.
12. Propose an efficient fine-tuning pipeline that combines LoRA + Quantization + Sparse Attention for medical NLP applications.
13. Critically assess the limitations of pruning strategies when applied to real-time edge devices.
14. Design an experiment where an LLM is optimized for edge devices. Include choices of fine-tuning, quantization, and pruning methods.
15. If a model has 6 billion parameters, and LoRA reduces trainable parameters to 0.5%, calculate how many parameters are trained during fine-tuning.
16. Consider an LLM with 4 layers, each having 200M parameters. After applying structured pruning that removes 30% of weights per layer, compute:
    - The remaining parameters per layer.
    - The total parameter count after pruning.

17. **Case Study: Optimizing LLMs for Edge Devices**
A healthcare startup wanted to deploy a LLM on *portable diagnostic devices* used in rural areas. Running a full-sized LLM on these small devices was not possible due to *limited memory, power, and processing capacity*. To solve this, the company used *LoRA (Low-Rank Adaptation)* for parameter-efficient fine-tuning, combined with *quantization techniques* to reduce model size and speed up inference. They also applied *structured pruning* to remove less important parameters and optimized the model using *sparse attention mechanisms*. As a result, the LLM could run on *edge devices with lower energy consumption*, while still providing accurate medical recommendations to doctors in the field. How did parameter-efficient fine-tuning, quantization, and pruning help the healthcare startup successfully deploy LLMs on edge devices?

REFERENCES

[1] Z. Yuan, W. Sun, Y. Liu, H. Zhou, R. Zhou, Y. Li *et al.*, "EfficientLLM: Efficiency in Large Language Models," arXiv preprint, May 2025, arXiv:2505.13840.
[2] Z. Wan, X. Wang, C. Liu, S. Alam, Y. Zheng, J. Liu *et al.*, "Efficient Large Language Models: A Survey," *Transactions on Machine Learning Research (TMLR)*, May 2024, arXiv:2312.03863.
[3] C. C. S. Balne, S. Bhaduri, T. Roy, V. Jain, and A. Chadha, "Parameter Efficient Fine Tuning: A Comprehensive Analysis Across Applications," arXiv preprint, Apr. 2024, arXiv:2404.13506.
[4] Z. Han, C. Gao, J. Liu, J. Zhang, and S. Q. Zhang, "Parameter-Efficient Fine-Tuning for Large Models: A Comprehensive Survey," arXiv preprint, Sep. 2024, arXiv:2403.14608.
[5] L. Xu, H. Xie, S.-Z. J. Qin, X. Tao, and F. L. Wang, "Parameter-Efficient Fine-Tuning Methods for Pretrained Language Models: A Critical Review and Assessment," arXiv preprint, Dec. 2023, arXiv:2312.12148.
[6] E. J. Hu, Y. Shen, P. Wallis, Z. Allen-Zhu, Y. Li, S. Wang *et al.*, "LoRA: Low-Rank Adaptation of Large Language Models," in *Proc. of the International Conference on Learning Representations (ICLR)*, Oct. 2021, arXiv:2106.09685.
[7] Z. Hu, Y. Lan, L. Wang, W. Xu, E. Lim, R. K.-W. Lee *et al.*, "LLM-Adapters: An Adapter Family for Parameter-Efficient Fine-Tuning of Large Language Models," in *Proc. of the Conference on Empirical Methods in Natural Language Processing (EMNLP)*, Oct. 2023, arXiv:2304.01933.
[8] X. L. Li, and P. Liang, "Prefix-Tuning: Optimizing Continuous Prompts for Generation," in *Proc. of the Association for Computational Linguistics (ACL)*, Jan. 2021, arXiv:2101.00190.
[9] C. Peng, X. Dong, M. Lyu, D. Paredes, Y. Zhang, and Y. Wu, "Model Tuning or Prompt Tuning? A Study of Large Language Models for Clinical Concept and Relation Extraction," *Journal of Biomedical Informatics*, Oct. 2023, doi: 10.1016/j.jbi.2024.104630.
[10] S. Raza, A. Raval, and V. Chatrath, "MBIAS: Mitigating Bias in Large Language Models While Retaining Context," arXiv preprint, Jun. 2024, arXiv:2405.11290.
[11] X. Liu, K. Ji, Y. Fu, W. L. Tam, Z. Du, Z. Yang *et al.*, "P-Tuning v2: Prompt Tuning Can Be Comparable to Fine-tuning Universally Across Scales and Tasks," in *Proc. of the Association for Computational Linguistics (ACL)*, Mar. 2022, arXiv:2110.07602.

[12] H. Liu, D. Tam, M. Muqeeth, J. Mohta, T. Huang, M. Bansal *et al.*, "Few-Shot Parameter-Efficient Fine-Tuning is Better and Cheaper than In-Context Learning," in *Advances in Neural Information Processing Systems (NeurIPS)*, Aug. 2022, arXiv:2205.05638.

[13] T. Dettmers, A. Pagnoni, A. Holtzman, and L. Zettlemoyer, "QLoRA: Efficient Finetuning of Quantized LLMs," in *Advances in Neural Information Processing Systems (NeurIPS)*, May 2023, arXiv:2305.14314.

[14] Z. Han, C. Gao, J. Liu, J. Zhang, and S. Q. Zhang, "Parameter-Efficient Fine-Tuning for Large Models: A Comprehensive Survey," arXiv preprint, Sep. 2024, arXiv:2403.14608.

[15] J. Lang, Z. Guo, and S. Huang, "A Comprehensive Study on Quantization Techniques for Large Language Models," arXiv preprint, Oct. 2024, arXiv:2411.02530.

[16] S. Sharify, U. Saxena, Z. Xu, W. Yazar, I. Soloveychik, and X. Wang, "Post Training Quantization of Large Language Models with Microscaling Formats," arXiv preprint, Oct. 2024, arXiv:2405.07135.

[17] Y. Bondarenko, R. Del Chiaro, and M. Nagel, "Low-Rank Quantization-Aware Training for LLMs," arXiv preprint, Sep. 2024, arXiv:2406.06385.

[18] G. Yang, D. Lo, R. Mullins, and Y. Zhao, "Dynamic Stashing Quantization for Efficient Transformer Training," in *Proc. of the Conference on Empirical Methods in Natural Language Processing (EMNLP)*, Mar. 2023.

[19] M. Chen, Y. Liu, J. Wang, Y. Bin, W. Shao, and P. Luo, "PrefixQuant: Eliminating Outliers by Prefixed Tokens for Large Language Models Quantization," arXiv preprint, Jan. 2025, arXiv:2410.05265.

[20] H. Huang, H.-J. Song, and H.-K. Pao, "Large Language Model Pruning," arXiv preprint, May 2024, arXiv:2406.00030.

[21] M. Sun, Z. Liu, A. Bair, and J. Z. Kolter, "A Simple and Effective Pruning Approach for Large Language Models," in *Proc. of the International Conference on Learning Representations (ICLR)*, May 2024, arXiv:2306.11695.

[22] Y. Wang, M. Ma, Z. Wang, J. Chen, H. Fan, L. Shan *et al.*, "CFSP: An Efficient Structured Pruning Framework for LLMs with Coarse-to-Fine Activation Information," in *Proc. of the International Conference on Computational Linguistics (COLING)*, Dec. 2024, arXiv:2409.13199.

[23] C. Lou, Z. Jia, Z. Zheng, and K. Tu, "Sparser is Faster and Less is More: Efficient Sparse Attention for Long-Range Transformers," arXiv preprint, Jun. 2024, arXiv:2406.16747.

[24] H. You, Y. Fu, Z. Wang, A. Yazdanbakhsh, and Y. C. Lin, "When Linear Attention Meets Autoregressive Decoding: Towards More Effective and Efficient Linearized Large Language Models," in *Proc. of the International Conference on Machine Learning (ICML)*, Jul. 2024.

[25] H. Amini, M. J. Mia, Y. Saadati, A. Imteaj, S. Nabavirazavi, U. Thakker *et al.*, "Distributed LLMs and Multimodal Large Language Models: A Survey on Advances, Challenges, and Future Directions," arXiv preprint, Mar. 2025, arXiv:2503.16585.

[26] F. Brakel, U. Odyurt, and A.-L. Varbanescu, "Model Parallelism on Distributed Infrastructure: A Literature Review from Theory to LLM Case-Studies," arXiv preprint, Mar. 2024, arXiv:2403.03699.

[27] N. Koilia, and C. Kachris, "Hardware Acceleration of LLMs: A Comprehensive Survey and Comparison," arXiv preprint, Sep. 2024, arXiv:2409.03384.

[28] C. Kachris, "A Survey on Hardware Accelerators for Large Language Models," *Applied Sciences*, Jan. 2024, doi: 10.3390/app15020586.

[29] X. Zhu, J. Li, Y. Liu, C. Ma, and W. Wang, "A Survey on Model Compression for Large Language Models," arXiv preprint, Jul. 2024, arXiv:2308.07633.

[30] D. Liu, Y. Yu, Y. Wang, J. Wu, Z. Wan, S. Alinejad *et al.*, "Designing Large Foundation Models for Efficient Training and Inference: A Survey," arXiv preprint, Apr. 2025, arXiv:2409.01990.

10 Increasing Context Window in Large Language Models

10.1 POSITION INTERPOLATION

Large language models (LLMs) like GPT, LLaMA, and PaLM have revolutionized natural language processing (NLP). These models leverage self-attention mechanisms to process large sequences of text, but they often face limitations due to fixed context windows. The context window refers to the maximum number of tokens the model can process at once.

Many LLMs use Rotary Position Embeddings (RoPE) [1], a technique that encodes relative positional information efficiently. However, RoPE-based models have a fixed context length, typically 2048 tokens, beyond which they fail to generalize due to extrapolation errors in attention scores.

A critical challenge is to increase the context window without retraining the entire model from scratch. One effective approach is position interpolation (PI), which rescales position indices instead of extrapolating them.

RoPE-based models encode token positions using a rotational function, defined as follows in Equation (10.1).

$$f(x, m) = e^{im\theta_j}\, x \tag{10.1}$$

where, m is positional index, $\theta_j = c^{-2j/d}$ is a frequency scaling factor, and x represents the input token embeddings. The issue arises when the model encounters positions beyond its trained context window. The self-attention mechanism struggles to handle these unseen positions, leading to degraded performance. This is due to the exponential nature of RoPE, where the attention score becomes unstable for out-of-bound positions $s > L$.

Instead of extrapolating positions beyond, PI rescales the position indices to fit within the original range. This transformation is defined as follows in Equation (10.2).

$$f'(x, m) = f\left(x, \frac{mL}{L'}\right) \tag{10.2}$$

where, $f(x,m)$ is the feature mapping, m is the positional index L is the original context window, and L' is the extend context window. This method ensures that all

DOI: 10.1201/9781003650065-10

position indices remain within a stable range, avoiding extrapolation errors in self-attention calculations.

To analyze the mathematical stability of the interpolated attention scores, the error bound between interpolated and linearly estimated attention scores is calculated. The interpolation error is given by Equation (10.3).

$$\left|a(s)-a_{linear}(s)\right| \leq \frac{d}{8\ \mathrm{lnc}} \max_j \left|h_j\right| (s-s_1)(s_2-s) \tag{10.3}$$

where, $a(s)$ is the true attention score, $a_{linear}(s)$ is the linear interpolation of two known grid points s_1, s_2, d is the embedding dimension, and c is the RoPE scaling factor (typically 10,000).

Since $\left(s-s_1\right)\left(s_2-s\right) \leq \frac{1}{4}$, the bound simplifies to the following Equation (10.4).

$$\left|a(s)-a_{linear}(s)\right| \leq \frac{d}{8\ lnc} \max_j \left|h_j\right| \tag{10.4}$$

This bound is significantly lower than the extrapolation error, proving that interpolation ensures smoother attention scores and preventing model instability when extending the context window.

Fine-Tuning to Adapt to Extended Context: After applying PI, the model undergoes a fine-tuning phase to adapt to the extended context. The fine-tuning objective uses next-token prediction with the following loss function shown in Equation (10.5).

$$\mathrm{Loss} = -\sum P_{model}(y \mid x) \log P_{true}(y \mid x) \tag{10.5}$$

where, $P_{model}\left(y\middle|x\right)$ is the predicted token probability and $P_{true}\left(y\middle|x\right)$ is the actual token probability.

Fine-tuning requires only tens to hundreds of thousands of training examples, making it computationally efficient. The model does not need to learn new knowledge, but rather adapt to longer sequence processing.

- PI enables extending the context window without altering the model's architecture.
- It provides a 600× smaller error bound compared to extrapolation, ensuring stable self-attention computations.
- The model smoothly adapts to the extended context after a short fine-tuning phase.

10.1.1 YaRN: Efficient Context Window Extension of Large Language Models

Due to the limitations of PI, an alternative approach is necessary to extend context windows efficiently without significant fine-tuning. YaRN (Yet another RoPE extensioN method) [2] addresses this by introducing a dynamic scaling mechanism that minimizes the need for additional training.

YaRN significantly reduces the number of training steps required for adaptation, allowing LLaMA models to process up to 128k tokens with minimal computational cost. This method extends context without requiring heavy modifications to the existing model architecture.

Yet another RoPE extensioN method (YaRN) is an advanced technique for efficiently extending the context window of RoPE-based LLMs. Unlike traditional methods, which require extensive fine-tuning, YaRN significantly reduces the number of training steps required for adaptation. It enables LLaMA models to process up to 128k tokens with minimal computational cost.

YaRN introduces dynamic scaling, which adjusts positional embeddings at inference time. The transformation is defined as follows in Equation (10.6).

$$f'(x,m) = f\left(x, \frac{mL}{L'}\right) \cdot g\left(m, L, L'\right) \tag{10.6}$$

where, $g\left(m, L, L'\right)$ is a scaling function that adapts positional encodings dynamically. Additionally, the model ensures numerical stability by enforcing in Equation (10.7).

$$\sum_{m=1}^{L'} A(m,n) \le C \tag{10.7}$$

where C is a context-dependent constant that prevents the amplification of attention scores.

YaRN requires 10× fewer tokens and 2.5× fewer steps than previous methods.

It achieves state-of-the-art performance by efficiently adapting LLMs to longer contexts. Dynamic scaling ensures robust performance with minimal architectural changes.

Despite the advantages of YaRN, certain challenges remain, such as degradation in performance for very large context windows and the need for extensive benchmarking on long-context tasks. To address these issues, researchers introduced Giraffe, a method focused on zero-shot extrapolation rather than heavy fine-tuning. Figure 10.1 shows the schematic view of YARN.

10.1.2 Giraffe: Expanding Context Lengths in LLMs

GIRAFFE [3] stands for Generative Image Representations with Attribute and Feature Factorization. It combines compositional 3D scene representation with neural rendering, enabling photorealistic image synthesis. A key challenge arises when extending the context window to manage more complex scenes. PI (PI) provides a solution, ensuring smooth integration of additional context without destabilizing the model.

Giraffe is a new approach for extending LLMs' context lengths efficiently. It introduces a truncated basis for position encodings and evaluates different

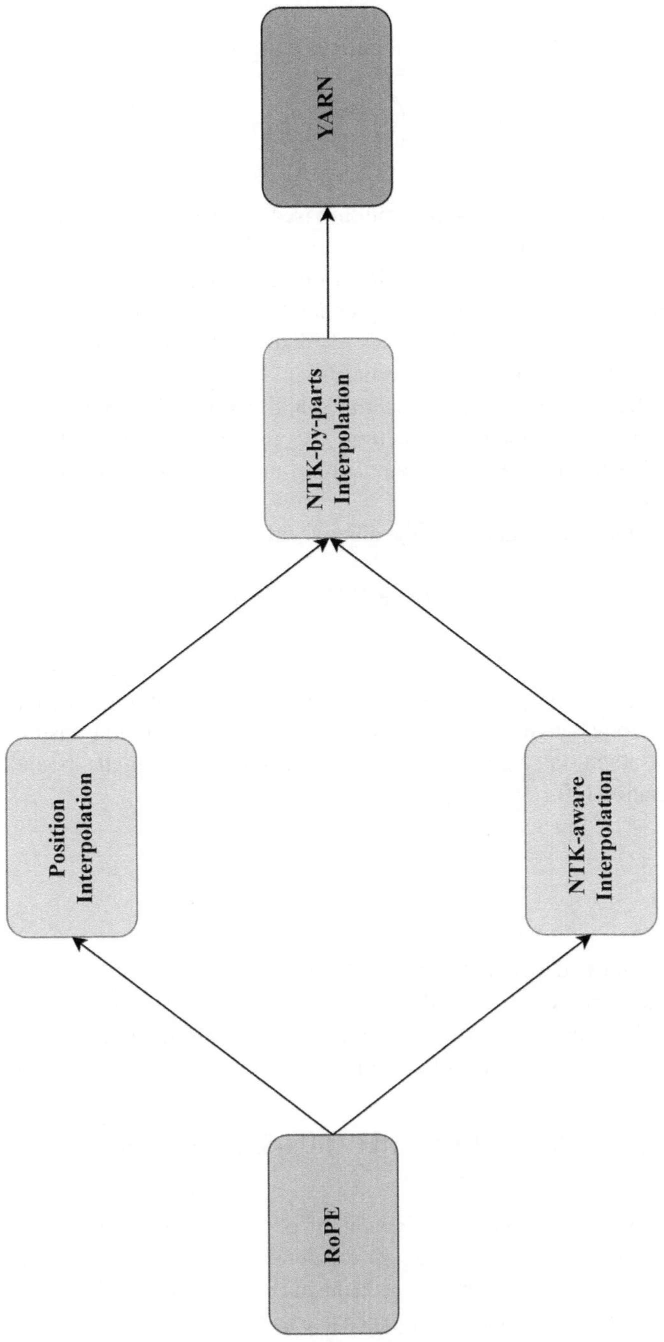

FIGURE 10.1 YARN.

extrapolation techniques. Instead of relying solely on interpolation or scaling, it employs linear scaling, which has been found to be the most effective method for extending context length.

The transformation introduced by Giraffe is defined as follows in Equation (10.8).

$$f'(x,m) = f\left(x, \frac{mL}{L'}\right) \,.\, h\left(m, L, L'\right) \tag{10.8}$$

where, $h(m,L,L')$ represents a truncation-based adjustment that enhances long-context processing stability.

Giraffe achieves up to 32k context length in LLaMA-based architectures. It significantly improves performance on long-context benchmarks such as FreeFormQA, lteredNumericQA, and LongChat-Lines. Unlike YaRN, it focuses on zero-shot extrapolation, reducing fine-tuning overhead.

In the Giraffe method, the model learns a modified position embedding function by incorporating a truncated basis function. This function is optimized to retain relative positional dependencies while maintaining numerical stability across different context lengths.

Equation (10.9) is used to calculate the adjustments for attention weights in Giraffe.

$$A(m,n) = e^{i(m-n)\theta_k} \,.\, g(m,n) \tag{10.9}$$

where, $A(m,n)$ represents the modified attention weight between positions m and n, θ_k is the rotation factor from RoPE, and $g(m,n)$ is an adaptive scaling function that stabilizes long range dependencies. Additionally, the method ensures that the summation of attention scores over long-context sequences remains bounded and is shown in Equation (10.10).

$$\sum_{m=1}^{L'} A(m,n) \leq C \tag{10.10}$$

where C is a context-dependent constant that prevents the amplification of attention scores beyond numerical limits. By leveraging this formulation, Giraffe successfully extends the context window while mitigating instability, making it a practical approach for real-world applications requiring extended sequence processing.

10.2 EFFICIENT ATTENTION MECHANISMS FOR INCREASING CONTEXT WINDOW

As transformers have become the foundation of modern NLP and deep learning, their ability to handle longer sequences efficiently has become a crucial research challenge. Traditional self-attention mechanisms scale quadratically with sequence length, making them computationally expensive and impractical for large documents, scientific texts, or long-form conversations.

To address this, efficient attention mechanisms have been introduced to reduce complexity while preserving model performance. One such method is sliding window attention (SWA), which limits attention to a local window of neighboring tokens rather than attending to all tokens in a sequence. While SWA significantly improves efficiency, it introduces challenges in handling long-range dependencies. To overcome this, Longformer and BigBird extend SWA by incorporating global attention tokens and sparse attention mechanisms, making them more suitable for long-context applications.

10.2.1 Sliding Window Attention

Traditional self-attention in transformers has a quadratic complexity of $O(n^2)$, making it inefficient for handling long sequences. When increasing the context window (i.e., processing longer sequences), memory and computation costs grow exponentially. SWA helps mitigate this by limiting the number of tokens each token attends to, significantly improving efficiency while maintaining model performance.

In standard transformers, each token in a sequence attends to every other token, resulting in a computational complexity of $O\left(n^2d\right)$. Here, n is the sequence length and d is the model dimension. This quadratic growth limits the feasibility of processing long sequences.

SWA [4] optimizes this by enforcing local attention—each token attends to only a fixed number of nearby tokens, reducing complexity to $O(nwd)$. Here, w is the window size, and $w \ll n$ ensures significant efficiency gains. Figure 10.2 shows the schematic view of sliding window.

10.2.1.1 Steps in Sliding Window Attention

1. **Define a Fixed Window Size** (w)
   - Instead of computing attention over the entire sequence, each token attends to only w tokens before and after it.
   - For instance, if $w = 5$, each token considers 5 preceding and 5 succeeding tokens.
2. **Localized Attention Computation**
   - The model computes attention weights only within this fixed window, reducing computational cost.
3. **Overlapping Windows for Information Flow**
   - Overlapping windows allow gradual propagation of information across distant tokens, mitigating some loss of global context.

SWA provides significant benefits by reducing memory and computational costs, lowering the complexity from quadratic $O(n^2)$ to linear $O(nw)$. This makes SWA particularly well-suited for efficiently processing long sequences. It effectively maintains local context, which is advantageous for tasks such as speech recognition and biomedical text analysis, and it can handle much longer input lengths than standard self-attention models.

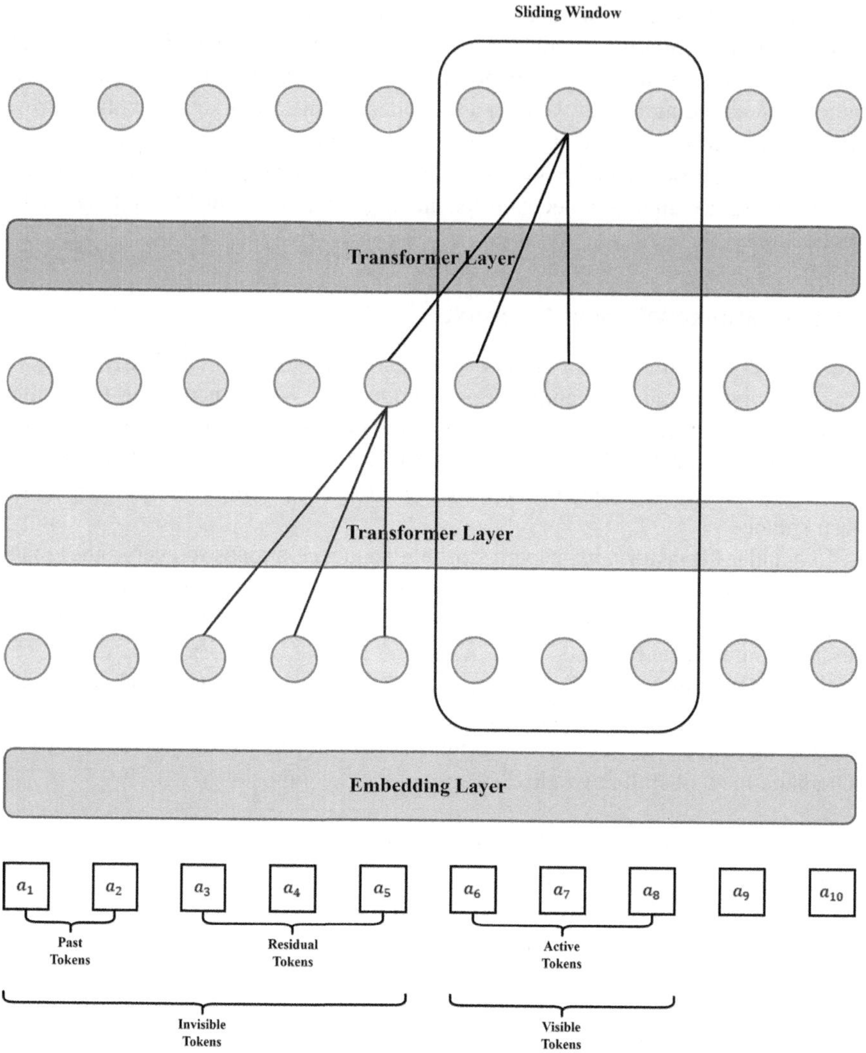

FIGURE 10.2 Sliding window.

However, SWA also has limitations. It struggles to capture global context, which can negatively affect performance on tasks that require understanding long-range dependencies, such as summarization and reasoning. To address this issue, these tasks often need additional mechanisms, like global tokens, to supplement SWA's focus on localized information.

10.2.2 Longformer: Enhancing Sliding Window Attention

Longformer [5] extends SWA by introducing global attention tokens that help the model capture long-range dependencies efficiently. SWA improves efficiency

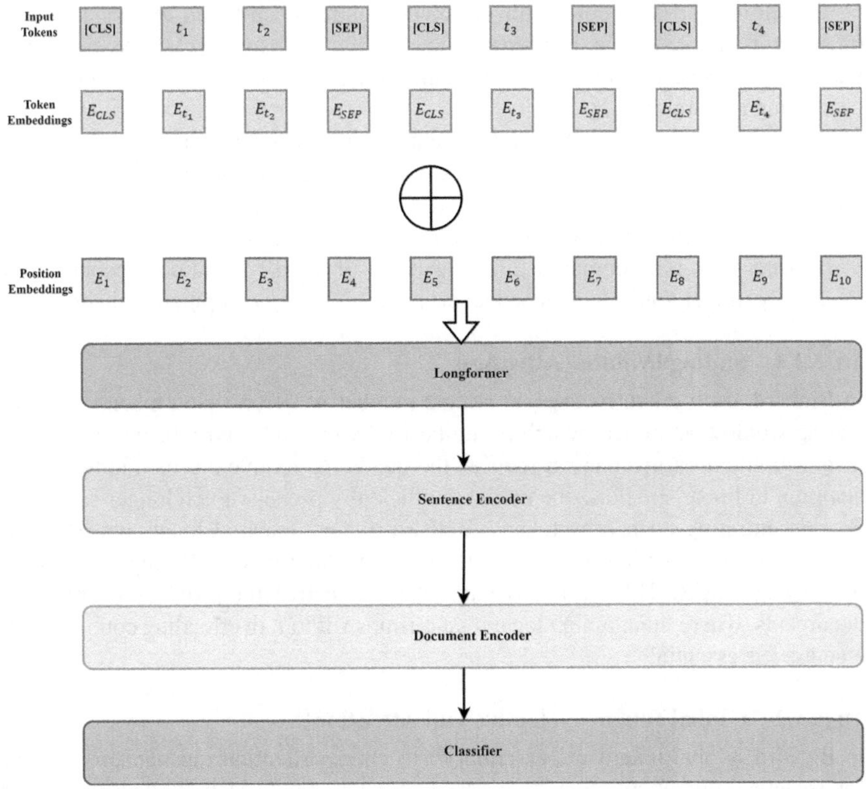

FIGURE 10.3 Longformer.

by concentrating on local context, while global attention tokens enable important tokens—such as CLS tokens used in classification tasks—to attend to the entire sequence. This combination allows the model to capture a broader context. Together, these mechanisms create a hybrid attention system that merges local and global attention, significantly enhancing the model's ability to understand and process long texts.

Longformer achieves an optimized hybrid attention mechanism with complexity $O(nwd)+O(gnd)$. Here, g is the number of global tokens. Since $g \ll n$, this remains significantly more efficient than standard self-attention.

The model provides significant performance advantages, managing documents up to 16 times longer than BERT and excelling in tasks such as question answering, summarization, and document classification. Figure 10.3 shows the architecture of Longformer.

10.2.3 BigBird: Further Optimizing Longformer

BigBird [6] further extends Longformer by introducing sparse attention mechanisms, making it even more efficient for long sequences.

Traditional self-attention in transformers requires each token to attend to every other token in a sequence, resulting in quadratic complexity $O(n^2d)$. As the context window increases, this computation becomes infeasible due to excessive memory and processing requirements.

Sparse Attention is an optimization technique that selectively reduces the number of attention connections between tokens, lowering computational complexity while preserving model expressiveness. Instead of attending to all tokens, a token attends only to a subset, making attention calculations more efficient.

BigBird uses a combination of three types of sparse attention mechanisms to effectively model long-range dependencies while keeping computational costs low.

10.2.3.1 Sliding Window Attention

In BigBird, each token focuses on a fixed number of neighboring tokens through a sliding window approach, which is similar to the method used in Longformer. This localized attention mechanism reduces the quadratic complexity of traditional self-attention to linear, enabling the model to efficiently process much longer sequences. By concentrating on nearby tokens, BigBird retains essential local context, which is vital for understanding syntax, short-range dependencies, and immediate context in language tasks. This design is particularly effective for processing large-scale documents, where maintaining local relationships without overloading computational resources is essential.

10.2.3.2 Global Tokens (Selective Full Attention)

In BigBird, global tokens are essential to its sparse attention mechanism, allowing for selective full attention without the computational burden of dense attention. These global tokens—often special-purpose tokens like classification ([CLS]) tokens, segment identifiers, or other task-specific markers—are designed to attend to all tokens in the input sequence and, in turn, be attended to by all tokens. This mutual connectivity enables the model to maintain access to global context and share information across distant parts of the sequence. By incorporating these strategically positioned global tokens, BigBird addresses a key limitation of local attention: the loss of long-range dependency information. This is achieved while also ensuring sub-quadratic computational efficiency. As a result, BigBird is particularly effective for tasks that require a comprehensive understanding, such as document classification, summarization, and question answering over lengthy texts.

10.2.3.3 Random Sparse Attention

BigBird enhances its sparse attention mechanism by incorporating random attention. In this approach, a subset of tokens attends to a randomly selected group of distant tokens, in addition to their fixed local neighbors. This design choice enables the model to establish long-range connections throughout the sequence without relying on full self-attention, which would be computationally expensive.

The introduction of randomness creates diversity in the attention patterns, allowing tokens to indirectly exchange information with distant parts of the input, even when they are not directly connected. Across multiple layers, these random links facilitate global information propagation, enabling the model to effectively learn long-range dependencies.

By combining local and global attention patterns, BigBird approximates the performance of full attention while maintaining linear scalability. BigBird achieves efficient and scalable attention by combining three distinct attention mechanisms: sliding window, global, and random sparse attention. The sliding window component ensures that each token only attends to a fixed number of nearby tokens, effectively capturing local dependencies that are crucial for tasks like syntax parsing and understanding phrases. Global attention allows a small, carefully selected set of tokens—such as classification tokens or question markers—to interact with all other tokens in the sequence. This enhances the model's ability to maintain a strong understanding of the overall context. Meanwhile, random sparse attention introduces stochastic connections between tokens and randomly selected distant tokens, ensuring that long-range dependencies are preserved and that information can flow throughout the entire sequence.

Together, these mechanisms enable BigBird to scale linearly with the length of the sequence while maintaining performance comparable to full self-attention. This makes it especially suitable for tasks involving long documents, such as summarization, question answering, and document classification.

Instead of the standard $O\left(n^2d\right)$ complexity of transformers, BigBird's sparse attention mechanism achieves $O(nwd)+O(rd)$. Here, w is the sliding window size (local attention) and r is the number of random sparse attention tokens (distant attention).

Since $w,r \ll n$ BigBird achieves near-linear scaling, making it more memory-efficient than Longformer and enabling the processing of even longer contexts.

BigBird outperforms models like Longformer by handling much longer contexts—over four times the length—while maintaining computational efficiency and memory savings. It combines SWA with global tokens and random sparse attention to effectively capture both local and long-range dependencies, achieving expressiveness comparable to full self-attention. These advances enable state-of-the-art performance on NLP tasks requiring understanding of long documents. As transformer architectures evolve, efficient attention mechanisms like those in BigBird are critical for scaling to large context windows without prohibitive computational costs, building on foundational techniques like SWA and extending them with sparse and global attention strategies.

10.2.4 LongT5: Efficient Attention for Increasing Context Window

Efficient attention mechanisms are crucial for handling long-sequence processing in transformers. While BigBird introduced sparse attention to reduce computational overhead, further advancements have been made to improve scalability and efficiency. LongT5 extends these efforts by integrating Transient Global (TGlobal) Attention, allowing transformers to handle longer context windows efficiently. g_m

LongT5 [7] is an optimized version of T5 (Text-to-Text Transfer Transformer), designed to address the inefficiencies of full self-attention while scaling up the context window. Unlike BigBird, which primarily relies on sparse attention patterns,

LongT5 introduces a more structured hybrid attention approach that balances local and global dependencies.

LongT5 introduces several key innovations for efficiently managing attention over long sequences, making it particularly well-suited for tasks that require an understanding of extended contexts. One major feature is Transient Global (TGlobal) Attention, which is a selective attention mechanism inspired by extended transformer construction (ETC). TGlobal allows the model to dynamically combine local and global attention, enabling important tokens to interact across distant parts of the sequence without the heavy memory overhead associated with full global attention.

In addition, LongT5 employs Windowed Local Attention, which is similar to the sliding window mechanisms found in Longformer and BigBird, but it has been optimized for greater computational efficiency. This mechanism ensures that each token focuses on a limited neighborhood, preserving vital local context while still contributing to global comprehension through TGlobal attention.

Together, these mechanisms enable LongT5 to efficiently handle input lengths that exceed the typical 4,000-token limit of standard transformers. As a result, LongT5 is particularly effective for document-level NLP tasks, such as summarization and retrieval, as well as other applications that require long-range dependencies and a comprehensive understanding of the text.

Computational Complexity of LongT5's Efficient Attention: The primary limitation of standard self-attention is its quadratic complexity, expressed as $O(n^2d)$. Here, n is sequence length, and d is model dimension.

LongT5 reduces complexity by implementing TGlobal Attention, leading to the following optimized $O(nwd)+O(gnd)$. Here, w is the window size for localized attention ($w \ll n$), and g is the number of global tokens $g \ll n$. Since $w, g \ll n$, LongT5 achieves a near-linear computational scaling, making it a highly efficient model for long-sequence tasks.

LongT5 represents a significant advancement in efficient attention mechanisms, specifically aimed at extending the context window for transformer models. By employing a hybrid attention approach that combines both local and global attention, LongT5 notably reduces memory consumption without sacrificing accuracy. This innovative design outperforms previous sparse attention models by enabling more effective information flow across long sequences. Moreover, LongT5 can process sequences longer than 16,000 tokens, making it highly practical for real-world NLP applications that involve extensive documents. Figure 10.4(a) shows the architecture of LongT5 with local attention, and Figure 10.4(b) shows the architecture of LongT5 with transient global attention.

In terms of applications, LongT5 excels in long-document summarization, achieving state-of-the-art performance on challenging datasets such as arXiv, PubMed, and BigPatent, where document lengths often exceed 10,000 tokens. It also demonstrates superior results in long-document question answering, especially in retrieval-based open-domain question answering tasks that require understanding and reasoning over entire articles. Additionally, LongT5 is well-suited for specialized domains, including legal, financial, and scientific document understanding, where the ability to process and reason over large-scale textual information is essential. This

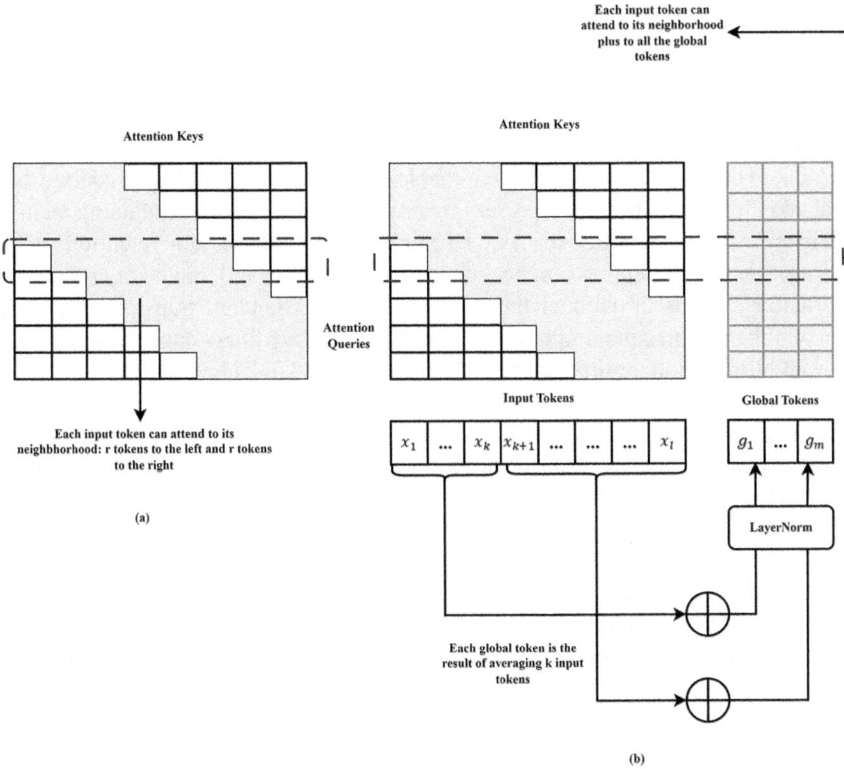

FIGURE 10.4 (a) LongT5 local attention and (b) LongT5 transient global attention.

versatility underscores LongT5's significance as a powerful model for a wide range of long-context NLP challenges.

10.2.5 COLT5: Compressive Long-Text T5 for Efficient Attention

Building upon LongT5, COLT5 (Compressive Long-Text T5) [8] introduces compressed memory representations to further enhance efficiency in long-context processing. While LongT5 extends the context window using TGlobal Attention, COLT5 improves memory efficiency by reducing redundant information and selectively retaining important tokens.

COLT5 is particularly optimized for long-text tasks, where transformers struggle due to exponential memory growth as sequence length increases. By implementing compressive memory mechanisms, COLT5 allows transformers to handle even longer sequences without excessive resource consumption.

COLT5 introduces several advanced mechanisms designed to efficiently handle extremely long sequences, surpassing the limitations of traditional transformer architectures. One of its key innovations is the compressive memory mechanism, which stores essential past information in a compressed format rather than retaining all token-level details. This method significantly reduces memory overhead, allowing the model to effectively manage and recall critical context even in documents that exceed 32,000 tokens in length, all without overwhelming computational resources.

In addition, COLT5 employs hierarchical attention, a multilevel attention strategy that dynamically identifies and focuses on the most relevant tokens at different levels of detail. This hierarchical approach enables the model to efficiently capture both local and global dependencies, preserving crucial context while maintaining memory efficiency. Complementing this, COLT5 utilizes selective token retention, which leverages learned compression techniques to prioritize and retain only the most informative tokens throughout the sequence. Unlike standard transformers, which treat all tokens with equal importance, COLT5 selectively filters out redundant or less relevant information, optimizing both performance and resource usage.

Together, these mechanisms empower COLT5 to excel at processing ultra-long documents with a rich contextual understanding, while keeping memory and computational demands manageable. This makes it ideal for complex tasks in fields that require extensive context modeling.

The quadratic complexity of self-attention in standard transformers is $O\left(n^2 d\right)$. Here, n is sequence length, and d is model dimension. COLT5 optimizes this using compressive memory attention, reducing complexity to $O(nwd) + O(cd)$. Here, w is the window size for localized attention ($w \ll n$) and c compressed memory representation, storing past context efficiently. Since $w, c \ll n$, COLT5 significantly improves long-sequence efficiency, making it faster and more scalable than standard attention-based models.

COLT5 represents a significant advancement in efficient attention mechanisms designed for handling ultra-long sequences. It effectively reduces memory consumption while maintaining strong performance on tasks that involve long contexts, addressing one of the main challenges in scaling transformers for extremely long inputs. Unlike models that require exponentially increasing computational resources as sequence length increases, COLT5 ensures smooth and effective context retention through its innovative compressive memory and hierarchical attention techniques. This enables scalable and practical processing of sequences that exceed 50,000 tokens.

Notably, COLT5 consistently outperforms models like LongT5 on super-long document tasks, demonstrating its superior efficiency and accuracy. In practical applications, COLT5 excels in ultra-long document summarization, achieving state-of-the-art results on benchmarks where documents exceed 100,000 tokens—far surpassing the capabilities of most existing models.

Its ability to retain and compress historical context also makes it highly effective in conversational AI, where maintaining a long-term memory of past interactions is crucial without incurring excessive memory costs. Furthermore, COLT5 is well-suited for analyzing scientific and legal documents, facilitating efficient retrieval and understanding of vast, complex datasets such as legal case files, financial records, and research papers—where deep contextual reasoning over extensive texts is required.

COLT5 represents a groundbreaking improvement in efficient attention mechanisms for increasing the context window. While LongT5 introduced

TGlobal Attention, COLT5 extends efficiency further by implementing compressive memory representations, significantly reducing computational and memory overhead.

With its hierarchical attention approach, compressed token retention, and near-linear computational scaling, COLT5 is one of the most efficient long-sequence transformers, setting a new benchmark for ultra-long document processing.

10.2.6 LongNet: Extending Transformers to Infinite-Length Sequences

While previous models like LongT5 and COLT5 improved attention efficiency, they still face limitations in scaling beyond 50K tokens due to memory constraints. LongNet [9] addresses this issue by introducing Dilated Attention, a novel approach that enables transformers to handle extremely long sequences, even scaling towards infinite-length processing. $\hat{O}_1$ $\hat{O}_2$

LongNet fundamentally redefines efficient attention mechanisms by making attention complexity sublinear, ensuring that even ultra-long documents can be processed without significant memory overhead.

LongNet introduces a novel and highly scalable attention mechanism designed to efficiently handle extremely long sequences without the computational burden associated with full self-attention. Its core innovation is the Dilated Attention Mechanism, which allows the model to skip tokens at fixed, controlled intervals rather than attending to every nearby token. This creates a dilated attention pattern that strikes a balance between capturing local details and understanding long-range context. As a result, LongNet can effectively address both short-term dependencies (such as syntax and phrase-level structures) and long-range relationships (like document-level coherence) without incurring the quadratic computational cost typically associated with traditional transformers.

To further enhance scalability, LongNet incorporates a technique called Hierarchical Scaling, which progressively expands the receptive field of each token by increasing the dilation factor across layers. This hierarchical structure enables the model to gradually integrate information from wider contexts, making it particularly effective for processing sequences that span hundreds of thousands or even millions of tokens.

One of LongNet's key advantages is its compatibility with existing transformer architectures, including models like GPT, T5, and BERT. This means that LongNet's dilated attention mechanism can be integrated into pre-existing models with minimal architectural changes, allowing for long-context processing without the need for a complete redesign or retraining from scratch. This flexibility makes LongNet a practical and adaptable solution for scaling transformer models to handle extremely long sequences. Figure 10.5 shows the architecture of LongNet.

Traditional self-attention has a quadratic complexity of $O(n^2d)$. Here, n is sequence length, and d is model dimension. LongNet's dilated attention reduces this complexity to $O(n.logn.d)$.

Since $logn \ll n$, LongNet achieves sublinear scaling, making it significantly more efficient for long-sequence tasks.

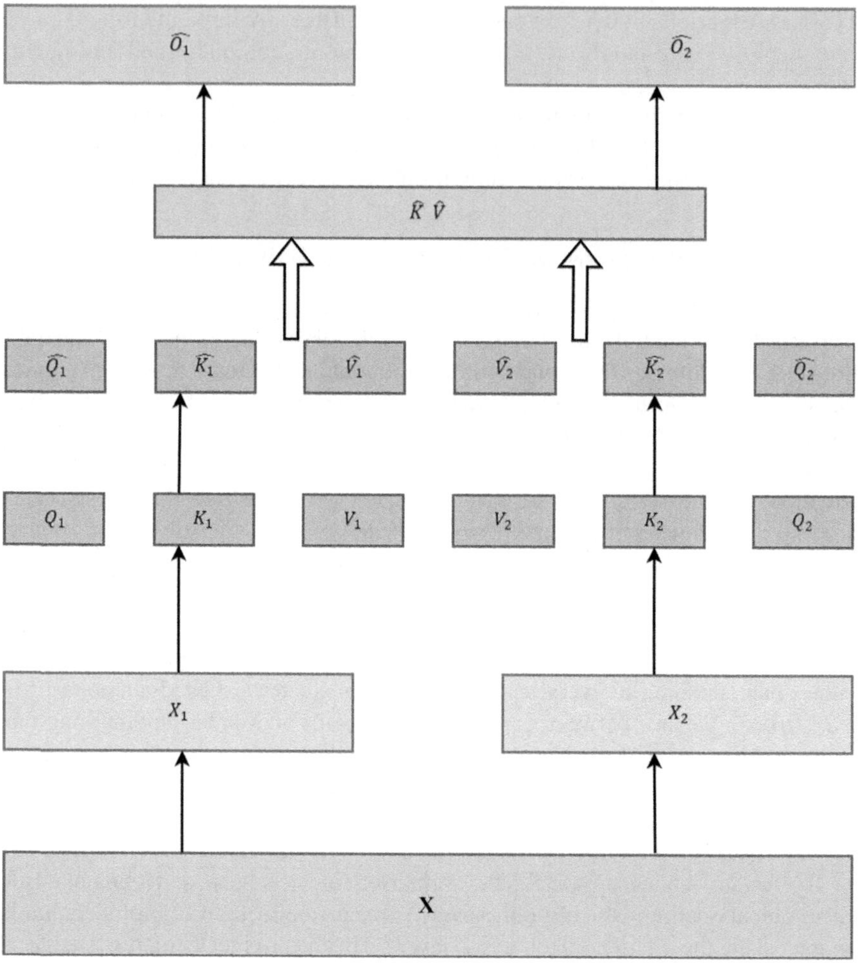

FIGURE 10.5 LongNet.

LongNet represents a significant advancement in efficient attention mechanisms, tackling a major challenge in transformer architectures: scaling to extremely long sequences without incurring high memory and computational costs. Central to LongNet's design is its dilated attention mechanism, which allows the model to skip tokens at controlled intervals. This capability enables it to focus on both local and distant parts of a sequence. The unique structure of LongNet supports infinite-length scaling, theoretically permitting it to process sequences of unlimited length while avoiding the quadratic growth in complexity commonly seen in standard self-attention models.

Importantly, LongNet excels at capturing long-range dependencies without compromising local attention, ensuring a comprehensive understanding of the content. It achieves near-logarithmic complexity in its attention computations, making it considerably more scalable than previous models like BigBird, LongT5, or COLT5, which too rely on sparse or hierarchical attention but still face limitations when dealing with very long inputs.

The practical impact of LongNet is substantial across various fields. In infinite-context language modeling, it enables models similar to GPT to process and generate coherent outputs from inputs longer than 200,000 tokens. This supports applications such as book-length generation or document-level reasoning. In legal and financial analysis, LongNet can efficiently handle large datasets, including legal case records, financial audits, and policy documents, without needing to truncate or split content. Additionally, it shines in the processing of scientific literature and historical texts, allowing for the analysis of entire books, multichapter research papers, or extensive historical archives as continuous sequences. This capability eliminates the context fragmentation issues that often challenge traditional models.

LongNet represents a paradigm shift in efficient attention mechanisms for increasing the context window. Unlike LongT5 and COLT5, which extend attention through compression and sparse mechanisms, LongNet introduces Dilated Attention, enabling sublinear complexity scaling for ultra-long sequences.

By making infinite-length scaling possible, LongNet sets a new benchmark for long-sequence transformers, enabling real-world applications in law, finance, history, and language modeling.

10.2.7 LongRoPE: Efficient Attention Mechanisms in Increasing Context Window

Long-Range Rotary Position Embeddings (LongRoPE) [10] extend traditional Rotary Position Embeddings (RoPE) to efficiently handle extremely long sequences while maintaining computational feasibility. RoPE encodes relative positional information into token representations, enhancing transformer models' ability to generalize over long contexts. However, standard RoPE struggles with extended context lengths due to fixed scaling factors.

LongRoPE overcomes this limitation by dynamically adjusting the positional encoding function to support longer sequences, making it an essential component in improving transformer efficiency for extended context windows.

LongRoPE (Long-range Rotary Position Embedding) presents key innovations in positional encoding, allowing transformer models to effectively handle significantly longer input sequences without sacrificing performance or efficiency. While traditional Rotary Position Embeddings (RoPE) work well for moderate-length sequences, they tend to degrade with extremely long inputs due to fixed-frequency sinusoidal scaling. LongRoPE enhances RoPE by adaptively modifying the position encoding mechanism. This adaptation enables the embeddings to remain stable and informative even at positions far beyond the original design limits, scaling up to hundreds of thousands of tokens.

In addition to its positional robustness, LongRoPE is designed for efficient computational scaling. It reduces the memory and computational overhead typically associated with long-context modeling by avoiding costly architectural changes or the need to recompute embeddings entirely. As a result, models can accurately capture long-range dependencies with minimal performance trade-offs, making LongRoPE suitable for resource-constrained environments.

Another significant advantage of LongRoPE is its compatibility with existing transformer architectures. It can be easily integrated into models such as GPT, T5, and their variants, requiring only minor modifications to the position encoding layer. This backward compatibility allows model developers and researchers to extend context lengths in existing systems without the necessity for retraining or redesigning the architecture.

LongRoPE maintains the same linear complexity as RoPE while enabling scalable long-range token interactions. It reduces the computational overhead of traditional absolute positional encoding techniques while ensuring the model can leverage longer context windows effectively. The computational complexity of standard self-attention is $O(n^2d)$. Here, n is sequence length, and d is model dimension.

LongRoPE optimizes this by introducing adaptive rotary position embeddings, reducing the complexity to $O(nd)$.

This linear complexity enables LongRoPE to scale efficiently beyond 100K tokens, making it significantly more efficient than traditional self-attention mechanisms.

LongRoPE maintains the same linear complexity as RoPE while enabling scalable long-range token interactions. It reduces the computational overhead of traditional absolute positional encoding techniques while ensuring the model can leverage longer context windows effectively.

Mathematically, the RoPE position encoding function is computed using Equation (10.11).

$$\theta_i = \theta_0^{-\frac{2i}{d}} \tag{10.11}$$

where θ_0 is a base frequency, i is the dimension index, and d is the dimensionality of the model.

LongRoPE extends this by introducing an adaptive scaling factor λ and is given in Equation (10.12).

$$\theta_i = \theta_0^{-\frac{2i}{d.\lambda}} \tag{10.12}$$

This modification allows LongRoPE to extend position encoding for sequences significantly longer than the standard RoPE limit.

LongRoPE is a sophisticated positional encoding technique that boosts the ability of transformer models to manage lengthy sequences by efficiently capturing long-range relationships. This enhancement leads to improved performance in large-scale language models that handle long-form text, processing scientific and legal documents, as well as analyzing historical data or books, where preserving context over extensive content is essential. Moreover, LongRoPE contributes to better

TABLE 10.1
Complexity Comparison.

Model	Attention Type	Max Context Window	Complexity
Transformer	Full self-attention	~4K tokens	$O(n^2d)$
Longformer	Sliding window + global	~16K tokens	$O(nwd+O(gnd)$
BigBird	Sparse + global attention	~32K tokens	$O(nwd+O(rd)$
LongT5	TGlobal + local attention	Beyond 32K tokens	$O(nwd+O(gnd)$
COLT5	Compressive attention + memory	50K+ tokens	$O(nwd+O(cd)$
LongNet	Dilated attention	Infinite Scaling	$O(n\log n.d$
LongRoPE	Adaptive rotary positon embedding	Beyond 100K tokens	$O(nd)$

coherence in prolonged conversations with AI and aids in intricate reasoning across multiple lengthy documents or multimodal inputs, making it an essential method for scaling AI applications that necessitate a profound contextual understanding of extensive information.

LongRoPE provides a powerful enhancement to traditional positional encoding mechanisms, making it a crucial component in advancing efficient attention mechanisms for increasing context windows. By dynamically adjusting its positional scaling, LongRoPE effectively balances computational efficiency with the ability to retain long-range dependencies, significantly improving transformer-based models in various long-document applications. Table 10.1 displays the complexity comparison of various models.

10.3 EXTRAPOLATION WITHOUT TRAINING FOR INCREASING CONTEXT WINDOWS

Extrapolation in LLMs [11] refers to the ability to process input sequences that exceed the context length seen during training. Unlike interpolation, which involves predicting within a learned range, extrapolation extends the model's understanding beyond its pretrained limits. This is crucial for tasks requiring long-context retention, such as document summarization, multiturn conversations, and code generation.

10.3.1 Importance in Large Language Models

Expanding the context window of LLMs is crucial for tasks that require understanding and generating long-form content, such as summarizing lengthy documents, engaging in extended conversations, or analyzing comprehensive datasets. A larger context window allows the model to consider more information simultaneously, leading to more coherent and contextually relevant outputs. However, increasing the context window without retraining poses significant challenges, as models are typically optimized for a fixed input length during their initial training phase.

Differences Between Interpolation and Extrapolation

- **Interpolation:** The model makes predictions within the range of known context lengths, ensuring reliable outputs.
- **Extrapolation:** The model generates responses for inputs exceeding its trained context window, often leading to degradation in coherence and relevance.

Limitations of Traditional Models

- **Fixed Positional Embeddings**: Transformers rely on positional encodings that limit sequence length.
- **Attention Complexity**: Standard self-attention mechanisms scale poorly with longer sequences.
- **Loss of Context**: Beyond the trained window, models may ignore earlier tokens, reducing coherence.

10.4 TECHNIQUES FOR EXTRAPOLATION WITHOUT TRAINING

10.4.1 Rule-Based Approaches for Extrapolation Without Training

Rule-based approaches rely on predefined heuristics to process long texts without modifying the model architecture. These methods help simulate longer context windows by strategically splitting, reordering, or compressing input sequences before feeding them into the model. Because of these techniques, LLMs can effectively handle increasing context windows without retraining, ensuring that long-form dependencies are maintained.

10.4.1.1 Sliding Window Approach

The sliding window technique is one of the most common rule-based approaches. It processes long sequences in overlapping chunks, ensuring that the model retains context across windows. This approach extends the effective context window of an LLM by allowing it to process longer inputs without modification.

Given $X = \{x_1, x_2, \ldots, x_n\}$ is the input sequence of length n, W is window size, and S is stride, i.e., step size for moving the window. The overlapping input segments are generated as follows in Equation (10.13).

$$X_t = \left\{x_t, x_{t+1}, \ldots\ldots, x_{t+W-1}\right\}, \quad t = 1, S, 2S, \ldots, n - W + 1 \tag{10.13}$$

where each segment X_t contains a portion of the original input. The stride S controls how much overlap exists between consecutive windows.

Example Calculation

- If we have a sequence of 1000 tokens, a window size $W = 512$, and a stride $S = 256$, the processed chunks will be:
- $X_1 = \{x_1, \ldots, x_{512}\}$

- $X_2 = \{x_{257}, \ldots, x_{768}\}$
- $X_3 = \{x_{513}, \ldots, x_{1000}\}$

Each chunk is passed through the LLM, and outputs are merged to maintain continuity across windows. Because of this technique, the model effectively processes longer sequences beyond its default context length.

The sliding window technique allows models with fixed context windows, like GPT-3.5 and GPT-4, to handle longer sequences by overlapping input chunks, which helps preserve context and reduce information loss without requiring retraining. However, it can become computationally expensive if the overlap is too large and may still struggle to capture long-term dependencies if earlier segments are not effectively referenced.

10.4.2 Zero-Shot Learning

Zero-Shot Learning (ZSL) [12] enables LLMs to perform tasks without explicit task-specific training by leveraging their pre-existing knowledge. In the context of increasing context windows, zero-shot methods allow models to process longer sequences by applying learned patterns to new, extended contexts.

Given an input sequence X with context length C, the model generates an output Y using its pretrained knowledge and is calculated using Equation (10.14).

$$P(Y \mid X, C) = P(Y \mid X) \tag{10.14}$$

This means that the probability of generating output Y remains independent of whether the model has explicitly seen sequences of length C in training.

Example, if a model is trained with a maximum context length of 2,048 tokens, it may zero-shot extend itself to 3,000+ tokens by relying on its internal positional embeddings and learned distributional patterns.

10.4.3 Meta-Learning Methods

Meta-learning [13], or "learning to learn," enables LLMs to generalize across different sequence lengths by learning a common strategy. This approach adjusts model behavior dynamically based on the input length.

Meta-learning optimizes a meta-objective function over multiple tasks and is shown in Equation (10.15).

$$\theta^* = \underset{\theta}{argmin} \sum_{i=1}^{N} \mathcal{L}(f_\theta(X_i), Y_i) \tag{10.15}$$

where, f_θ is the model with parameters θ, X_i *and* Y_i represents input–output pairs, and $\mathcal{L}$ is the loss function.

The goal is to minimize the loss across tasks with different sequence lengths, making the model more adaptable to longer contexts.

For example, if an LLM is trained on multiple context lengths (256, 512, 1024 tokens), it can use meta-learning to generalize to longer contexts like 2048+ tokens.

10.4.4 LM Infinite

LM Infinite [14] is a novel method that extends the context length of LLMs without retraining by modifying attention mechanisms. It introduces:

- Λ-Shaped Attention Mask to selectively focus on important tokens.
- Distance Limit to prevent attention scores from degrading for longer sequences.

The attention mechanism in LM-Infinite is modified as follows in Equation (10.16).

$$A_{ij} = \frac{(Q_i K_j^T)}{\sqrt{d_k}} \, . \, M_{ij} \tag{10.16}$$

where Q_i *and* K_i are the Query and Key vectors, respectively, d_k is the attention head dimension, and M_{ij} is the Λ-shaped attention mask that limits attention distance.

The mask function helps the model focus on the most relevant tokens within a fixed window while also attending to key initial tokens, ensuring that both local context and long-term dependencies are maintained.

Example, using LM-Infinite, a model trained with a 4096-token limit can extend up to 200 million tokens without retraining.

10.4.5 Parallel Context Windows

Parallel context windows (PCW) [15] is a rule-based approach that splits long inputs into multiple smaller chunks and processes them in parallel to simulate a larger context window.

Given an input sequence X_t of length n, divided into overlapping windows W with stride S. Each window is processed independently, and the final output is computed as follows using Equation (10.17).

$$Y = \sum_{t=1}^{T} f(X_t) \tag{10.17}$$

where $f(X_t)$ is the model output for each window, and T is the number of parallel windows.

For a 10,000-token input, splitting it into 1,000-token windows with a 200-token overlap allows models to simulate longer context windows without changing the underlying transformer architecture.

SUMMARY

In order for LLMs to process and reason across considerably longer sequences, this chapter examines methods for expanding the context window. Techniques like YaRN and Giraffe, which modify positional embeddings to scale beyond the initial training constraints, are the first examples of PI. Then, it looks at effective attention mechanisms for long-context management, such as SWA, LongFormer, BigBird, LongT5, COLT5, LongNet, and LongRoPE. These mechanisms offer varying trade-offs between accuracy, speed, and memory use. Extrapolation without training is also covered in this chapter, including rule-based approaches, zero-shot learning, meta learning, and LM Infinite, which expand context capabilities without the need for further correction. In order to get around sequence length restrictions and improve the efficiency and scalability of long-context processing, it lastly presents parallel context windows, a technique for dividing and processing huge contexts concurrently.

QUESTIONS

1. A transformer uses SWA with a window size of 512 tokens. For an input of 4096 tokens, calculate how many sliding windows are required.
2. BigBird reduces attention complexity from $O(n^2)$ to $O(n \times \sqrt{n})$. For $n = 10{,}000$ tokens, compute the number of attention operations in both cases and compare the savings.
3. LongT5 uses a local window of 256 tokens and a global span of 64 tokens for attention. For an input of 2048 tokens, calculate:
   - The number of local windows.
   - The number of global tokens attended.
4. COLT5 achieves a 40% reduction in memory usage compared to a standard transformer with 20 GB memory demand. Compute the memory usage after applying COLT5.
5. A LongNet model can scale context length from 4k tokens to 1M tokens. If training originally required 50 GPU hours for 4k tokens, and compute scales linearly with context length, estimate GPU hours for 1M tokens.
6. Define position interpolation in the context of extending context length for LLMs.
7. Explain the difference between YaRN and Giraffe methods for position interpolation.
8. Discuss how SWA improves efficiency compared to traditional attention. Give a practical example.
9. Compare LongFormer, BigBird, and LongT5 in terms of attention strategy (local, global, random).
10. Evaluate the benefits and limitations of LongRoPE for extending transformer context length.
11. What are rule-based approaches for extrapolation without training? Give one example.
12. Propose a scenario where meta-learning and zero-shot learning can be combined for long-context reasoning in LLMs.

13. **Case Study: Legal Document Analysis with Long Context LLMs**
A law firm needed an AI system to analyze legal case files that often exceed 200,000 words. Traditional LLMs struggled because their context window was too short, forcing the firm to split documents, which led to loss of context and inaccurate summaries. To address this, the firm adopted efficient attention mechanisms like LongFormer and BigBird, which use SWA and sparse global tokens to handle very long sequences. They also applied position interpolation methods such as YaRN to extend positional embeddings and experimented with parallel context windows for better scalability. With these improvements, the LLM could process entire case files in one pass, maintaining consistency and providing accurate legal insights. This saved lawyers significant time and reduced errors in document review. How did efficient attention mechanisms (like LongFormer/BigBird) and position interpolation methods (like YaRN) help the law firm process very long legal documents without losing context?

REFERENCES

[1] J. Su, Y. Lu, S. Pan, A. Murtadha, B. Wen, and Y. Liu, "RoFormer: Enhanced Transformer with Rotary Position Embedding," arXiv preprint, Nov. 2023, arXiv:2104.09864.

[2] B. Peng, J. Quesnelle, H. Fan, and E. Shippole, "YaRN: Efficient Context Window Extension of Large Language Models," in *Proc. of the International Conference on Learning Representations (ICLR)*, May 2024, arXiv:2309.00071.

[3] A. Pal, D. Karkhanis, M. Roberts, S. Dooley, A. Sundararajan, and S. Naidu, "Giraffe: Adventures in Expanding Context Lengths in LLMs," arXiv preprint, Aug. 2023, arXiv:2308.10882.

[4] Z. Fu, W. Song, Y. Wang, X. Wu, Y. Zheng, Y. Zhang *et al.*, "Sliding Window Attention Training for Efficient Large Language Models," arXiv preprint, Feb. 2025, arXiv:2502.18845.

[5] I. Beltagy, M. E. Peters, and A. Cohan, "Longformer: The Long-Document Transformer," arXiv preprint, Apr. 2020, arXiv:2004.05150.

[6] M. Zaheer, W. Song, Y. Wang, X. Wu, Y. Zheng, Y. Zhang *et al.*, "Big Bird: Transformers for Longer Sequences," in *Advances in Neural Information Processing Systems (NeurIPS)*, Jan. 2021, arXiv:2007.14062.

[7] M. Guo, J. Ainslie, D. Uthus, S. Ontanon, J. Ni, Y.-H. Sung *et al.*, "LongT5: Efficient Text-To-Text Transformer for Long Sequences," in *Proc. of the North American Chapter of the Association for Computational Linguistics (NAACL)*, May 2022, arXiv:2112.07916.

[8] J. Ainslie, T. Lei, M. de Jong, S. Ontanon, S. Brahma, Y. Zemlyanskiy *et al.*, "CoLT5: Faster Long-Range Transformers with Conditional Computation," in *Proc. of the Conference on Empirical Methods in Natural Language Processing (EMNLP)*, Oct. 2023, arXiv:2303.09752.

[9] J. Ding, S. Ma, L. Dong, X. Zhang, S. Huang, W. Wang *et al.*, "LongNet: Scaling Transformers to 1,000,000,000 Tokens," arXiv preprint, Jul. 2023, arXiv:2307.02486.

[10] Y. Ding, L. L. Zhang, C. Zhang, Y. Xu, N. Shang, J. Xu *et al.*, "LongRoPE: Extending LLM Context Window Beyond 2 Million Tokens," ," in *Proc. of the International Conference on Machine Learning (ICML)*, Jul. 2024, arXiv:2402.13753.

[11] Y. Li, T. Zhang, Z. Li, and S. C. Han, "A Training-Free Length Extrapolation Approach for LLMs: Greedy Attention Logit Interpolation (GALI)," arXiv preprint, Feb. 2025, arXiv:2502.02659.

[12] M. G. Mohammadkhani, A. G. Mohammadkhani, and H. Beigy, "Zero-Shot Learning and Key Points Are All You Need for Automated Fact-Checking," arXiv preprint,t Aug. 2024, arXiv:2408.08400.

[13] S. Sinha, Y. Yue, V. Soto, M. Kulkarni, J. Lu, and A. Zhang, "MAML-en-LLM: Model Agnostic Meta-Training of LLMs for Improved In-Context Learning," in *Proc. of the ACM SIGKDD International Conference on Knowledge Discovery and Data Mining (KDD)*, May 2024, arXiv:2405.11446.

[14] C. Han, Q. Wang, H. Peng, W. Xiong, Y. Chen, H. Ji *et al.*, "LM-Infinite: Zero-Shot Extreme Length Generalization for Large Language Models," in *Proc. of the North American Chapter of the Association for Computational Linguistics (NAACL)*, Jun. 2024, arXiv:2308.16137.

[15] N. Ratner, Y. Levine, Y. Belinkov, O. Ram, I. Magar, O. Abend *et al.*, "Parallel Context Windows for Large Language Models," in *Proc. of the Association for Computational Linguistics (ACL)*, Aug. 2023, arXiv:2212.10947.

11 Augmented LLMs

11.1 RETRIEVAL AUGMENTED LLMS: INTRODUCTION

Augmented large language models (LLMs) refer to enhanced versions of traditional LLMs that integrate external tools, retrieval mechanisms, or additional processing techniques to improve their accuracy, efficiency, and adaptability. While standard LLMs rely solely on their pretrained knowledge, augmented LLMs can retrieve real-time information, leverage memory, interact with APIs, and refine outputs using external data sources.

Retrieval-augmented LLMs combine retrieval-based and generation-based techniques to enhance the accuracy and relevance of responses. Traditional LLMs rely on pretrained knowledge, which may become outdated over time. Retrieval augmentation allows models to fetch relevant information from external knowledge sources, reducing hallucinations and improving factual accuracy.

Retrieval-augmented language models (RAG LLMs) [1] fuse the generative capabilities of LLMs with the accuracy of external knowledge acquisition, allowing them to obtain real-time information from various sources, including databases, the internet, or curated knowledge repositories. This synergy improves the ability to address domain-specific and fact-heavy inquiries, minimizing hallucinations and boosting contextual relevance. Furthermore, by anchoring responses in reliable sources, RAG systems enhance the explainability, transparency, and trustworthiness of outputs, making them particularly beneficial for applications in sectors like healthcare, finance, law, and scientific research.

11.1.1 Need for Augmenting LLMs with Retrieval

Enhancing LLMs with retrieval functions addresses various significant drawbacks of independent pre-trained models. Conventional LLMs are limited by a fixed knowledge base due to their training cutoff, rendering them unsuitable for tasks that demand current or time-sensitive information. Retrieval augmentation mitigates this issue by enabling models to access and utilize real-time data from external resources such as the internet, databases, or proprietary information repositories. This adaptive strategy greatly minimizes hallucinations—convincing yet incorrect outputs—by anchoring responses in verifiable sources. Furthermore, it boosts scalability by removing the

DOI: 10.1201/9781003650065-11

necessity for regular model retraining since new data can be incorporated through external queries. The accuracy in specific domains is also enhanced, particularly in critical areas like finance, healthcare, and law, where factual accuracy is essential. In addition, retrieval-based systems promote increased transparency and explainability, as they can reference sources, allowing users to trace and validate the origins of the generated content.

11.1.2 Types of Retrieval-Augmented LLMs

Retrieval-augmented LLMs [2] can be classified into three categories based on how they access external knowledge. Retrieval-augmented LLMs leverage external knowledge sources to enhance response accuracy, reduce hallucinations, and improve domain-specific applicability. The *retrieval mechanism* plays a crucial role in selecting relevant information before generating an answer. Table 11.1 shows the various types of retrieval augmented LLMs.

Retrieval mechanisms in LLMs can be categorized into the following types.

- Sparse retrieval mechanisms
- Dense retrieval mechanisms
- Hybrid retrieval mechanisms
- Memory-augmented retrieval mechanisms
- Web-based retrieval mechanisms

11.1.2.1 Sparse Retrieval Mechanisms

Sparse retrieval techniques [3] refer to traditional methods of information retrieval that focus on precise or nearly precise keyword matching through statistical approaches rather than deep learning. These methods depict documents and queries as sparse vectors, predominantly featuring zeros, typically employing models like TF-IDF or

TABLE 11.1
Types of Retrieval-Augmented LLMs.

Category	Type	Example	Use Case
Retrieval mechanism	Dense retrieval	Facebook's RAG	High-precision tasks
	Sparse retrieval	IBM Watson	Large-scale datasets
	Hybrid retrieval	ColBERT	Broad and precise retrieval
Knowledge source	Closed-domain	IBM Watson for Healthcare	Medical diagnosis
	Open-domain	Perplexity AI	General-purpose QA
	Hybrid knowledge	Enterprise AI assistants	Specialized + general knowledge
Integration with LLMs	Single-step	Basic RAG models	Simple QA tasks
	Iterative	REALM	Complex tasks
	Memory-augmented	MemNN + LLMs	Conversational AI

BM25. They are efficient, scalable, and interpretable, making them ideal for large-scale search engines and scenarios where speed and simplicity are paramount. Sparse retrieval is particularly strong in precision for structured or clearly defined queries, particularly when the exact terms are known. However, it struggles to grasp semantic meaning, context, or synonyms, which hinders its ability to deal with ambiguous or natural language queries. Despite these shortcomings, sparse retrieval continues to be a crucial element of numerous search systems and is frequently integrated with dense or semantic retrieval techniques within hybrid frameworks.

11.1.2.1.1 TF-IDF (Term Frequency – Inverse Document Frequency)

TF-IDF [4] is a statistical method that assigns a weight to each term in a document based on how often it appears relative to all documents. It helps rank documents based on their relevance to a given query. The TF-IDF can be calculated using the following Equation (11.1).

$$\text{TF}-\text{IDF}(t,D)=\text{TF}(t,D)\times\text{IDF}(t) \tag{11.1}$$

where TF is the number of times term appears in document D, and $\text{IDF} = log\frac{N}{n_t}$, where N is the total number of documents, and n_t is the number of documents containing term t.

Term frequency–inverse document frequency (TF-IDF) is a straightforward yet effective method for keyword-driven text analysis and retrieval, commonly utilized in search engines and information retrieval systems to rank documents according to their relevance to a query. Its effectiveness comes from its computational efficiency and ability to emphasize significant terms within a document in relation to a broader corpus, making it especially beneficial for tasks such as keyword extraction, content filtering, and document clustering. Nevertheless, TF-IDF relies solely on statistical metrics, overlooking the semantic meaning, context, and relationships between words. It is incapable of understanding synonyms, polysemy, or contextual usage, which restricts its capacity to manage complex language tasks compared to more advanced methods like word embeddings or transformer-based models. Despite these drawbacks, TF-IDF continues to be a useful baseline for numerous NLP applications because of its simplicity, interpretability, and effectiveness in situations where a deep linguistic understanding is unnecessary.

11.1.2.1.2 BM25 (Best Matching 25)

BM25 [5] is an extension of TF-IDF that improves document ranking by considering term frequency saturation and document length normalization. It is a probabilistic ranking function widely used in modern information retrieval systems. The BM25 can be calculated using the following Equation (11.2).

$$BM25(D,Q)=\sum_{t\in Q}\text{IDF}(t).\frac{f(t,D)\ .\ (k_1+1)}{f(t,D)+(1-b+b.\frac{|D|}{avgD})} \tag{11.2}$$

where $f(t,D)$ is the term frequency of term t in document D, $|D|$ is the document length, $avgD$ is the average document length across all documents, IDF(t) is the inverse document frequency of term t, and k_1 and b are hyperparameters controlling term frequency scaling.

BM25 is an advanced ranking function rooted in probabilistic information retrieval and is commonly utilized in search engines like Elasticsearch and Apache Lucene. It enhances the traditional TF-IDF model by integrating term frequency saturation and normalizing document length, which makes it especially effective for retrieving and ranking structured text and concise documents. BM25 evaluates documents based on their relevance to a specific query, striking a balance between the significance of frequently occurring terms while not excessively penalizing longer documents. However, similar to TF-IDF, BM25 is essentially a lexical matching approach—it depends on exact term matches and does not account for semantic connections, such as synonyms or contextual meanings. This limitation hinders its ability to grasp the more intricate subtleties of language, particularly in complex or ambiguous queries. Despite these limitations, BM25 continues to be a solid, interpretable, and widely used technique in conventional information retrieval systems.

11.1.2.2 Dense Retrieval Mechanisms

Dense retrieval techniques [6] utilize deep learning to convert both queries and documents into dense vector representations (embeddings), enabling them to capture semantic similarities instead of depending solely on exact keyword matches. These approaches generally employ transformer-based models (such as BERT or its variations) to translate text into a continuous vector space, where the relevance between a query and a document is assessed using similarity metrics like cosine similarity or Euclidean distance. Dense retrieval is adept at grasping the context, meaning, and intent behind words, making it particularly effective for natural language queries, recognizing synonyms, and handling paraphrased content. It surpasses sparse methods in situations that demand semantic understanding, including conversational search, question answering, and multilingual retrieval. Nonetheless, dense retrieval can be resource-intensive and usually requires substantial resources for both training and deployment, including the necessity for approximate nearest neighbor (ANN) search techniques to efficiently obtain results on a large scale. Despite these obstacles, dense retrieval is vital in contemporary search architectures and is often employed alongside sparse methods in hybrid retrieval systems.

11.1.2.2.1 Dense Passage Retrieval (DPR)

Dense passage retrieval (DPR) [7] is a biencoder architecture that independently encodes queries and documents into dense vector representations, making it efficient for large-scale search applications. The DPR is calculated using the following Equation (11.3).

$$\text{Similarity}(q,d) = \cos(Enc_q(q), Enc_d(d)) \tag{11.3}$$

where, $Enc_q(q)$ is the Query encode (e.g., BERT, RoBERTa), $Enc_d(d)$ is the document encoder and cosine similarity is used to determine document relevance.

DPR is a retrieval approach that employs dual-encoder models, often based on transformer architectures like BERT, to transform queries and passages into contextually rich embeddings within a unified vector space. This facilitates effective semantic matching through similarity measures such as cosine similarity, allowing the system to grasp the underlying meanings of words and adeptly tackle linguistic complexities like synonymy and polysemy. DPR proves especially effective in large-scale retrieval applications like open-domain question answering and intelligent search systems, where relevance encompasses more than mere exact keyword matches. Its capacity to generalize and retrieve semantically related passages renders it superior to conventional sparse methods in intricate language comprehension tasks. Nevertheless, DPR requires substantial training on extensive labeled datasets and involves considerable computational power for both the training and inference stages. Furthermore, efficient large-scale deployment typically necessitates the use of ANN search techniques to sustain real-time responsiveness. In spite of these hurdles, DPR continues to be a fundamental element in contemporary semantic retrieval systems because of its robust contextual comprehension and scalability.

11.1.2.2.2 SBERT (Sentence-BERT)

Sentence-BERT (SBERT) [8] is an enhanced version of BERT that aims to produce high-quality sentence embeddings for effective semantic search and retrieval applications. It operates by transforming both queries and documents into fixed-size dense vector representations through a siamese or triplet network architecture, enabling rapid and precise similarity assessment using cosine similarity. In contrast to traditional BERT, which is resource-intensive and not well-suited for large-scale retrieval, SBERT allows for quicker and more scalable inference by precomputing embeddings and employing mean pooling over token embeddings to create sentence-level representations. This level of efficiency makes SBERT particularly useful for tasks like semantic search, duplicate detection, and question answering, where both speed and contextual comprehension are essential. The sentence embeddings can be calculated using the following Equation (11.4).

$$E = \frac{1}{n}\sum_{i=1}^{n} h_i \tag{11.4}$$

where h_i is the hidden state vector of token, n is the number of tokens in the sentence, and E is the final sentence embedding.

Sentence-BERT (SBERT) is an effective neural retrieval model that produces meaningful sentence embeddings for various applications, including semantic search, document ranking, and question answering. By utilizing a biencoder architecture, it encodes both queries and documents independently, thus enabling efficient retrieval on a large scale through similarity measures like cosine similarity. SBERT provides notable benefits over traditional BERT by minimizing computational load during inference and allowing for precomputed embeddings, making it ideal for real-time use cases. Pre-trained SBERT variants such as SciBERT, BioBERT, and LegalBERT further improve its efficacy in specific fields like scientific literature and legal texts.

However, SBERT depends on pretrained deep learning models, and while it performs efficiently during inference, it may be computationally demanding when processing very large datasets. Moreover, since it employs static embeddings, it fails to capture real-time or newly emerging information unless it is frequently retrained with updated data. In spite of these drawbacks, SBERT continues to be a popular choice for high-accuracy, context-aware semantic retrieval tasks.

For example, a legal research tool utilizes SBERT to retrieve relevant case laws. When a lawyer searches for "precedents on intellectual property disputes," SBERT converts the query and stored legal documents into embeddings and finds the most relevant case studies based on cosine similarity. This makes research faster and more accurate than traditional keyword-based searches.

11.1.2.3 Hybrid Retrieval Mechanisms

Hybrid retrieval mechanisms [9] combine sparse retrieval (e.g., BM25, TF-IDF) with dense retrieval (e.g., SBERT, DPR) to leverage the strengths of both methods. Sparse retrieval is efficient and works well for initial filtering, while dense retrieval captures deeper semantic meaning, improving result accuracy. By integrating both approaches, hybrid retrieval optimizes search precision and recall, making it ideal for large-scale and complex retrieval tasks.

11.1.2.3.1 BM25 + DPR (Hybrid Search)

This method integrates BM25 for fast and efficient sparse retrieval and DPR (DPR) for semantic ranking [10]. The hybrid approach ensures that initial filtering is quick and computationally efficient, while deep learning-based dense retrieval refines results for better semantic relevance.

The hybrid search workflow that combines BM25 with DPR integrates the advantages of both sparse and dense retrieval techniques to improve the accuracy and efficiency of searches. First, documents undergo pre-processing and indexing with BM25, a conventional sparse retrieval algorithm that ranks documents based on term frequency and inverse document frequency, allowing for quick identification of a relevant candidate subset at low computational costs. The top-ranked documents are subsequently fed into a DPR model, which transforms queries and documents into dense vector embeddings using deep learning techniques, capturing semantic meaning that goes beyond mere keyword matches. The DPR model then employs cosine similarity to re-rank the candidate documents, refining the results according to contextual relevance and semantic similarity. This two-step methodology takes advantage of BM25's efficiency for the initial filtering stage and DPR's robust semantic comprehension for accurate ranking, making it particularly effective for large-scale, domain-specific, and complex search situations while managing computational resources and retrieval quality.

The BM25 scoring function is given in Equation (11.5).

$$\text{BM25}(D,Q) = \sum_{t \in Q} IDF(t).\frac{f(t,D)\ .\ (k_1+1)}{f(t,D)+(1-b+b.\frac{|D|}{avgD})} \tag{11.5}$$

where $f(t,D)$ is the term frequency of term t in document D, $|D|$ is the document length, $avgD$ is the average document length across all documents, IDF(t) is the inverse document frequency of term t, and k_1 and b are hyperparameters controlling term frequency scaling.

DPR cosine similarity formula is given in Equation (11.6).

$$\text{Similarity}(q,d) = \cos(Enc_q(q), Enc_d(d)) \tag{11.6}$$

where, $Enc_q(q)$ is the Query encode (e.g., BERT, RoBERTa), $Enc_d(d)$ is the document encoder and cosine similarity is used to determine document relevance.

The BM25 + DPR hybrid search method effectively merges the speed of traditional keyword-based retrieval with the semantic richness of dense neural embeddings, creating a robust and well-balanced retrieval system. BM25 efficiently reduces the document collection by utilizing term frequency and inverse document frequency to rank documents based on precise keyword matches, providing rapid initial retrieval with minimal computational costs. Afterward, DPR enhances these results by transforming queries and documents into dense vectors that capture contextual and semantic intricacies, allowing for more accurate re-ranking based on meaning instead of merely keywords. This combined model improves both precision and recall, making it particularly ideal for large-scale search engines and intricate applications such as question-answering systems where both keyword relevance and deep semantic comprehension are crucial. By integrating these complementary strengths, the BM25 + DPR framework strikes a strong balance between speed, scalability, and retrieval accuracy across various fields.

11.1.2.3.2 Multistage Retrieval (Cascade Retrieval)

Multistage retrieval, commonly referred to as cascade retrieval [11, 12], is a sophisticated search methodology that integrates several retrieval techniques in a sequential manner to enhance both efficiency and precision. In the initial stage, sparse retrieval techniques such as BM25 or TF-IDF are utilized to swiftly sift through a vast corpus, ranking documents based on keyword occurrence and inverse document frequency. This initial filtering drastically narrows the search scope, enabling more computationally demanding methods to concentrate on a smaller, pertinent subset of documents. During the second stage, dense retrieval models like DPR or Sentence-BERT (SBERT) re-evaluate these candidates by transforming queries and documents into neural embeddings, which capture the semantic meaning that goes beyond mere keyword correlations and apply cosine similarity for relevance assessment. Optionally, a third stage may incorporate a cross-encoder model, such as BERT with cross-attention, to execute a more detailed ranking by jointly evaluating query-document pairs for a deeper contextual insight. While this last phase is computationally intensive, it significantly improves accuracy and is generally applied to the top-k documents. This multistage methodology strikes a balance between scalability, semantic depth, and ranking quality, making it particularly effective for intricate, large-scale search and question-answering applications.

Multistage retrieval (cascade retrieval) offers a scalable and flexible approach to handling large-scale document collections by progressively refining search results through multiple retrieval layers. Starting with efficient sparse retrieval methods like BM25 or TF-IDF, it rapidly filters millions of documents based on keyword relevance, reducing the candidate set for subsequent, more computationally intensive processing. The next stage employs dense retrieval models such as DPR or SBERT to capture semantic meaning and context, significantly improving the quality of relevance rankings beyond simple keyword matches. Optionally, a final re-ranking stage using cross-encoder models provides deep contextual understanding by jointly evaluating query-document pairs, further boosting precision for the top results. This layered strategy not only balances computational efficiency with retrieval accuracy but also adapts well to diverse domains—including legal, medical, and financial fields—where precise and relevant information retrieval is critical. By minimizing irrelevant results and focusing resources on the most promising candidates, multi-stage retrieval ensures robust, high-quality search outcomes at scale.

For instance, a medical research assistant utilizes a multi-stage retrieval method to effectively locate relevant research articles within extensive medical databases. The process begins with BM25, which quickly narrows down articles based on keyword matches, followed by DPR that re-evaluates these papers for semantic similarity, capturing subtle meanings even when different terms are employed. Lastly, a cross-encoder model fine-tunes the highest-ranked results to highlight the most insightful and contextually relevant studies. This method allows for rapid initial filtering, strong semantic search capabilities, and an optimized literature review process, greatly improving both the efficiency and accuracy of retrieving medical research.

Although multistage retrieval has notable advantages, it also encounters various challenges. The integration of several models—like BM25, DPR, and cross-encoders—requires substantial computing power, often necessitating the use of distributed systems or GPU acceleration for extensive datasets. Another challenge is the complexity of implementation, as every stage demands careful tuning of hyperparameters and training of models specific to various domains and datasets. Furthermore, the multilayered ranking method can lead to increased latency, which requires a balance between speed and precision, particularly in real-time use cases. Nonetheless, by skillfully combining traditional sparse retrieval approaches with cutting-edge deep learning methods, multistage retrieval provides a robust, scalable solution that is widely used in search engines, academic research platforms, and AI-driven decision-support systems.

11.1.2.4 Memory-Augmented Retrieval Mechanisms

Memory-augmented retrieval mechanisms (MARMs) [13], [14] integrate long-term memory storage with retrieval techniques, allowing models to store, recall, and refine knowledge dynamically. Unlike traditional retrieval methods, which depend solely on external static knowledge bases, MARM enables context-aware retrieval, improving response consistency and personalization.

11.1.2.5 Working Mechanism

Memory-augmented retrieval consists of two key components and is given below.

- **Retrieval Memory Store:** A persistent memory module that maintains structured information retrieved from external sources.

- **Adaptive Learning Module:** Continuously updates stored knowledge based on new queries and user interactions.

In a memory-enhanced retrieval system, the process begins by transforming the user's query into an embedding and searching for relevant past information held in memory. If a similar query is found, the appropriate response is retrieved and revised; if not, the system consults external databases to acquire new information. The knowledge that is retrieved or updated is then incorporated into the model's response, which is later saved in memory for future reference. This dynamic memory updating is regulated by a memory attention mechanism, which is represented by the formula shown in Equation (11.7).

$$M_t = \alpha M_{t-1} + (1-\alpha)R_t \tag{11.7}$$

where, M_t is the updated memory at time t, M_{t-1} is the past memory state, R_t is the retrieved information, and α is the memory decay factor.

MARMs improve the functionality of language models by adding a permanent memory layer that keeps track of and retrieves past interactions, leading to more coherent and context-aware replies over time. A significant benefit of MARM is its capacity to remember conversational history and user-specific details, which greatly enhances personalization and continuity in multiturn conversations. By minimizing the need for repeated external inquiries through the use of memory, it also increases system efficiency and the speed of responses. This enduring context retention enables the model to adjust flexibly to user behavior, preferences, and previous inquiries, making it particularly useful in areas such as virtual assistants, customer support, and personalized search systems.

For instance, a virtual assistant can leverage MARMs to remember a user's previous travel choices and customize its recommendations based on that. By referencing saved interaction history, the assistant minimizes the need for repetitive external searches, resulting in quicker response times. This memory-based method also allows for more tailored and context-sensitive suggestions, improving the overall experience for users when planning trips and making well-informed travel choices.

While MARMs offer various benefits, they also come with certain limitations that can affect their performance and scalability. The need to maintain persistent memory across sessions creates considerable storage and computational demands, particularly as the number of interactions increases over time. Furthermore, if the system is not updated regularly, it may end up providing outdated or irrelevant information, which can diminish the accuracy and reliability of the responses it generates. The deployment of MARM also necessitates a complex system architecture and careful fine-tuning to achieve a seamless integration of memory and retrieval elements, especially when adapting to different domains or fluctuating user contexts. These obstacles require effective memory management solutions and continuous maintenance to ensure that the system stays efficient, up-to-date, and capable.

11.1.2.6 Web-Based Retrieval Mechanisms

Web-based retrieval mechanisms [15, 16] leverage live web sources to fetch up-to-date information dynamically. Unlike static knowledge bases, web-based retrieval ensures real-time accuracy and is particularly useful in rapidly evolving domains such as news, finance, and cybersecurity.

Working Mechanism: Web-based retrieval involves querying search engines, APIs, and online databases to obtain the most recent and relevant information.

In a web-based retrieval system, the process starts with query expansion and reformulation, where the user's input is examined and rephrased into various versions to increase search breadth. These enhanced queries are subsequently sent to external resources, such as web search platforms (e.g., Google, Bing), information repositories (e.g., Wikipedia, PubMed), or specific APIs relevant to the domain during the web crawling and data gathering stage. The content collected is then filtered and ranked using relevance scoring models like BM25 or neural re-rankers to highlight the most pertinent documents. Ultimately, LLMs condense the top-ranked information into succinct, human-readable replies. A frequently utilized ranking formula in this procedure is BM25, which can be expressed as follows in Equation (11.8).

$$\text{Score}(D,Q) = \sum_{t \in Q} IDF(t).\frac{f(t,D)\ .\ (k_1+1)}{f(t,D)+(1-b+b.\frac{|D|}{avgD})} \tag{11.8}$$

where, Q is the query, D is the document, $f(t,D)$ is the term frequency of t in D, and IDF(t) is the inverse document frequency.

Web-based retrieval systems provide considerable benefits by allowing instant access to the latest information from a variety of online sources, thereby preventing responses from being constrained by the static knowledge of previously trained models. These systems offer extensive knowledge coverage by combining data from general search engines, structured databases, and specialized APIs, enabling models to tackle a broader array of subjects and inquiries. Furthermore, web-based retrieval facilitates adaptive search techniques, allowing queries to be dynamically refined based on initial findings to enhance relevance and precision. This adaptability is particularly advantageous for managing rapidly changing information, such as current news, new research developments, or urgent queries, thereby improving both the richness and timeliness of the responses produced.

For instance, a financial AI application can utilize internet-based retrieval systems to gather livestock market information through web APIs and produce contemporary analytical reports for traders. By consistently accessing real-time data, the system provides timely insights into market changes, assisting users in making well-informed investment choices. This method decreases reliance on static and outdated datasets and guarantees that trading strategies are founded on the latest and most pertinent market conditions.

Web-based retrieval systems encounter various limitations, such as increased delays caused by the duration needed for online searches and data retrieval, which can hinder response times. Furthermore, there is a danger of obtaining inaccurate, outdated, or biased information from unverified internet sources, which could jeopardize the quality of the responses. In addition, depending on external APIs introduces challenges related to dependency, as access limitations, rate caps, or service disruptions may affect the availability and reliability of data retrieval. These aspects must be managed carefully to ensure consistency and performance.

11.1.2.7 Knowledge Sources

A knowledge source is a collection of structured or unstructured information that AI systems use to process queries and generate responses. Knowledge sources can be categorized based on their scope and application into closed-domain, open-domain, and hybrid knowledge sources. Each type serves a unique purpose, ranging from specialized information retrieval to general-purpose queries.

11.1.2.7.1 Closed-Domain Knowledge Source

A closed-domain knowledge source [17] is an AI system specifically designed to operate within a narrowly defined field or subject area, enabling it to deliver highly accurate, relevant, and context-aware responses for queries strictly related to that domain. By leveraging specialized datasets, expert knowledge, and domain-specific ontologies, these systems can achieve superior precision compared to generalist models when addressing complex or technical questions. However, their effectiveness diminishes rapidly when faced with queries outside their scope, as they lack the broad knowledge required for open-domain understanding. Mathematically, if Q represents the query space and $D \subset Q$ denotes the closed domain, the system's accuracy $A(q)$ for a query q can be expressed as follows in Equation (11.9).

$$A(q) = \begin{cases} f(q) & if\, q \in D \\ \varepsilon & if\, q \notin D \end{cases} \tag{11.9}$$

where $f(q)$ is a high-accuracy function within the domain, and ε is a low-accuracy baseline outside the domain, highlighting the system's strong domain specialization but limited generalizability.

Closed-domain knowledge sources are specialized AI systems designed with a focused expertise on specific industries or fields, such as healthcare, law, finance, or engineering, enabling them to address domain-specific problems with high precision and reliability. Their narrow scope allows them to leverage structured, expert-driven data—including curated datasets, proprietary documents, ontologies, and established guidelines—which enhances their ability to provide accurate and contextually relevant responses. This domain-specific focus results in significantly higher accuracy compared to open-domain systems, which must handle a much broader range of topics but often at the expense of depth and precision. However, the specialization of closed-domain systems also limits their flexibility, as they typically cannot generalize well to questions or tasks outside their designated area, making them less effective for interdisciplinary or broad queries. Additionally, these systems often require ongoing maintenance and updates from domain experts to keep their knowledge base current with evolving standards, regulations, and best practices within the field.

For instance, IBM Watson for Healthcare serves as an example of a specialized closed-domain AI system focused on the medical sector. It helps physicians by examining patient records, laboratory results, medical literature, and clinical guidelines to enhance the accuracy of disease diagnosis based on the most recent research. In addition to diagnosis, Watson provides personalized treatment suggestions suited to each patient's profile, such as recommending chemotherapy options for cancer patients by taking into account their specific type of cancer and genetic data. Furthermore, Watson supports medical researchers by analyzing vast amounts of scientific literature to reveal insights regarding drug interactions, clinical trends, and the progression of diseases, which speeds up the development of new treatments and boosts patient outcomes.

Closed-domain systems like IBM Watson for Healthcare face notable limitations, primarily due to their restricted scope—they excel within their specialized field but cannot effectively handle queries outside their domain, such as finance or technology questions. Additionally, their performance heavily depends on the quality and comprehensiveness of the training data; if new medical research or updated treatment guidelines are not regularly integrated into the system, the accuracy and relevance of their recommendations may decline over time, risking outdated or incomplete advice.

Closed-domain systems find applications beyond the healthcare sector, tackling specific challenges in diverse fields such as law and finance. For example, legal AI platforms like ROSS Intelligence offer specialized insights into case law, precedents, and regulations to facilitate legal research, while financial AI tools such as Kensho evaluate market trends, asset valuations, and investment prospects using structured financial information. These systems are particularly effective at providing accurate, domain-specific knowledge, thereby improving precision, efficiency, and evidence-based decision-making in vital areas. However, despite their advantages, closed-domain systems are constrained by their inability to manage inquiries outside their established parameters, which limits their functionality to narrowly targeted uses.

11.1.2.7.2 Open-Domain Knowledge Source

An open-domain knowledge source [18] is an AI system engineered to process and respond to queries spanning a broad spectrum of topics without being confined to any specific field or specialization. Unlike closed-domain systems that focus on a narrow domain $D \subset Q$ (where Q is the universe of possible queries), open-domain systems are designed to handle the entire query space Q, providing answers across diverse subjects such as science, history, technology, entertainment, and current events. This wide-ranging capability is typically enabled by leveraging large-scale, diverse training data and general-purpose language models that aim to maximize coverage and flexibility. Mathematically, if Q represents all possible queries, an open-domain system strives for a uniform accuracy function $A(q)$ over Q is given in Equation (11.10).

$$A(q) = g(q), \forall q \in Q \tag{11.10}$$

where $g(q)$ is a generalized function capable of generating relevant responses across varying topics. While this broad approach enables extensive knowledge coverage and versatility, it often comes at the cost of reduced precision and depth compared to domain-specific models, particularly for highly specialized or technical queries.

Open-domain knowledge sources are distinguished by their extensive coverage, allowing them to address inquiries across nearly any topic within their wide-ranging knowledge base, making them ideal for general-purpose uses such as virtual assistants and search engines. They exhibit strong contextual comprehension skills, enabling them to understand and clarify the meanings of words according to different subjects and user intent. Their adaptability allows them to manage various types of inquiries, including factual questions, opinions, and open-ended discussions. Generally, these systems analyze large volumes of unstructured data—such as web pages, books, research papers, and forums—by utilizing advanced natural language processing methods to extract pertinent information and produce coherent, accurate responses.

For instance, Perplexity AI is an advanced open-domain question-answering platform that gathers and consolidates information from various sources to deliver precise and timely answers. In contrast to closed-domain systems that are confined to fixed datasets, Perplexity AI retrieves data from the internet in real time, which allows it to address inquiries regarding current events, trending topics, and the most recent research. Its capability to engage with a broad spectrum of subjects—from science and technology to history and culture—renders it a flexible resource for general inquiries. Moreover, Perplexity AI showcases a strong understanding of context, enabling it to accurately comprehend questions and provide pertinent, up-to-date responses, such as identifying the current president of the United States.

Open-domain knowledge sources function by initially analyzing the user's request through natural language processing methods to understand the intent and context. They then retrieve pertinent information using various techniques, including dense retrieval models that capture semantic meaning and sparse retrieval methods reliant on precise keyword matching. Once the required data is collected, the system compiles or condenses information from various sources to produce coherent, natural language responses, often utilizing advanced AI models such as GPT-4 or BERT. Furthermore, these systems use dialogue management strategies to preserve context throughout multiple turns of conversation, ensuring that replies remain relevant during the exchange.

Open-domain knowledge sources provide notable benefits, including flexibility in addressing a broad spectrum of inquiries across diverse areas like science, entertainment, and general knowledge, which makes them highly useful in various everyday situations. Their capability to obtain up-to-date information from the internet enables them to present the latest news, research findings, and market trends. Furthermore, their user-friendly design is reflected in well-known virtual assistants such as Siri, Alexa, and Google Assistant, which help users with a variety of tasks. However, these systems also encounter challenges: they generally offer lower accuracy than specialized closed-domain models, have difficulty interpreting ambiguous or vague questions that lack sufficient context, and pose a risk of retrieving unreliable or incorrect information due to the inconsistency of their data sources.

Open-domain knowledge systems support a variety of applications, such as virtual assistants like Google Assistant, Siri, and Amazon Alexa, which assist users with different tasks like setting reminders, giving weather updates, and responding to trivia questions. They also form the foundation of search engines like Google, Bing, and Yahoo, which allow users to find information on nearly any subject by indexing extensive amounts of web content. Furthermore, numerous companies utilize open-domain AI in customer service through chatbots and virtual agents that address inquiries across multiple sectors. Although these systems are highly versatile and provide real-time information, they generally lack the specialization of closed-domain systems and may encounter difficulties with accuracy and understanding ambiguous questions. Regardless, open-domain knowledge resources are crucial in general-purpose scenarios, offering easily accessible and up-to-date information to users around the globe.

11.1.2.7.3 Hybrid Knowledge Source

A hybrid knowledge source [19] seamlessly combines the strengths of both closed-domain and open-domain systems, striking a balance between specialized accuracy and broad flexibility. By integrating precise, domain-specific expertise (denoted as K_c) with expansive, general-purpose knowledge (K_o), the hybrid system generates responses R that maximize relevance and accuracy across diverse queries Q. Mathematically, this can be modeled as follows in Equation (11.11).

$$R = f\left(Q, \alpha K_c + (1-\alpha)K_o\right) \tag{11.11}$$

where $\alpha \in [0, 1]$ controls the weighting between closed-domain knowledge and open-domain knowledge based on the query context. This approach enables the system to leverage the high precision and reliability of closed-domain data while maintaining the adaptability and comprehensive coverage of open-domain sources. Consequently, hybrid knowledge sources can deliver more nuanced, context-aware answers that are both accurate within specialized fields and responsive to a wide array of general inquiries, making them ideal for complex real-world applications requiring both depth and breadth of knowledge.

Hybrid knowledge sources are systems that integrate specialized knowledge from fields like healthcare or finance with general information that is widely available, capitalizing on the advantages of both types of knowledge. These systems are context-sensitive, allowing them to transition between specialized knowledge and general knowledge based on the specifics of the question asked. This flexibility enables them to deliver precise and accurate answers to targeted, domain-specific inquiries while also remaining capable of addressing broader, more general questions effectively.

For instance, enterprise AI assistants exemplify hybrid knowledge sources by facilitating a variety of business functions—ranging from customer service to data analysis—through the integration of structured, company-specific information with general knowledge. These systems can offer comprehensive responses regarding internal policies and procedures, such as the process for submitting an expense report or the criteria for project approvals, while also retrieving external information to address broader inquiries such as current trends in project management or strategies for incorporating AI into business operations. This capability to blend specialized internal knowledge with unstructured external data renders enterprise AI assistants both highly relevant and versatile.

Hybrid knowledge systems function through a multi-phase approach that starts with grasping user queries and identifying intents, utilizing natural language processing (NLP) methods to ascertain whether a user's inquiry is specific to a domain or more general. When the inquiry relates to a specialized subject, the system accesses relevant data from internal knowledge assets such as company databases, reports, or documentation. For broader open-domain inquiries, it retrieves information from extensive sources like the internet, public knowledge bases, or general-purpose models. After collecting the suitable information, the system integrates the findings to produce accurate, contextually appropriate responses—often distilling insights from specialized materials or merging them with general knowledge for a more well-rounded answer. During continuing interactions, the system preserves contextual awareness to ensure consistency and relevancy, which is particularly essential in intricate situations like business decision-making that necessitate both specialized knowledge and a wider perspective.

Hybrid knowledge sources provide numerous benefits, such as adaptability and precision, as they merge specialized and general knowledge to generate accurate, context-sensitive replies across various inquiries. These systems excel in problem-solving by combining expertise from specific domains with broader perspectives—for example, assisting an HR manager in understanding internal compensation strategies while also supplying general insights on employee engagement from publicly available information. Their capacity to continuously enhance their knowledge base by integrating internal and external data guarantees ongoing relevance as industries and general knowledge adapt. However, hybrid systems also encounter challenges, such as the technical intricacies involved in merging diverse data sources, which may necessitate advanced data pipelines, API integrations, and mechanisms for real-time retrieval. Furthermore, accessing and consolidating both specialized and general data may lead to performance drawbacks, potentially causing delays in response times. Quality control presents another hurdle, as dependence on unstructured external sources like the internet carries the risk of integrating unreliable or biased information, which can influence the overall accuracy and reliability of the system's outputs.

Hybrid knowledge sources are extensively utilized across diverse fields, such as enterprise AI assistants, healthcare, customer service, and search engines. In corporate environments, they assist employees in finding both company-specific and general information for tasks such as HR assistance or IT support. In the healthcare sector, they merge patient records and clinical protocols with publicly available medical information to aid in clinical decision-making. Customer support systems leverage them to offer precise answers based on internal product information and general resources like frequently asked questions. Search engines may also implement hybrid models to provide results drawn from both proprietary and public databases. By blending specialized and general knowledge, these systems deliver adaptable, context-sensitive, and highly pertinent responses, making them effective instruments in intricate, information-dense settings—though their success can be influenced by technical complexity and possible performance compromises.

11.1.2.8 Integration with Large Language Models (LLMs)

Integrating LLMs, such as GPT-4, with various retrieval mechanisms significantly enhances their capability to handle complex queries, efficiently manage larger datasets, and generate more accurate and context-aware responses. Different approaches to integrating LLMs with retrieval systems can be categorized into single-step, iterative, and memory-augmented mechanisms, with each serving a unique purpose based on the complexity of the task at hand.

11.1.2.8.1 Single-Step Integration (Basic RAG Models)

In single-step integration [20], the process is relatively simple, where the model retrieves relevant information from an external source, then generates a response in a single pass. This method is often referred to as retrieval-augmented generation (RAG), the system follows a straightforward two-step process: first, it *retrieves* relevant information from an external knowledge base or document repository, and then it *generates* a response using that information in a single pass, without any further refinement or iteration. Mathematically, this can be represented as follows in Equation (11.12).

$$Response = G(R(Q)) \tag{11.12}$$

where Q is the user query, $R(Q)$ is the retrieval function that returns relevant documents based on Q, and G is the generation function that produces the final response based on the retrieved content.

For instance, single-step integration works exceptionally well for simple question-answering (QA) tasks where a straightforward answer can be taken from the retrieved data. A common example could involve a user inquiring, "What is the capital of France?" The system fetches a relevant excerpt that mentions Paris as the capital and promptly produces the reply: "The capital of France is Paris." In these cases, retrieval techniques such as Dense Retrievers or BM25 algorithms can effectively pinpoint the most pertinent documents, which the model then summarizes or utilizes directly to create a clear and precise answer.

Single-step integration presents significant benefits such as swiftness, straightforwardness, and effectiveness, making it ideal for queries that are fact-based and have unambiguous answers. Its rapid, one-time retrieval and generation method guarantees prompt replies and straightforward implementation. Nonetheless, it faces challenges when handling intricate tasks that necessitate multistep reasoning or a more profound contextual comprehension, frequently yielding superficial responses that may lack depth or detail.

11.1.2.8.2 Iterative Integration (REALM)

Iterative integration [21] is a multipass approach in which the system refines its response through repeated cycles of retrieval and generation, improving accuracy and depth with each iteration. Unlike single-step models, it uses feedback loops—such as in Retriever-Augmented Language Model (REALM)—to continually enhance the relevance of retrieved documents and the quality of the generated answers. Mathematically, the process involves retrieving documents is given in Equation (11.13).

$$\mathrm{D_t} = \mathrm{R}(\mathrm{Q}, \mathrm{A}_{t-1}) \tag{11.13}$$

Mathematically, the process involves generating updated responses is given in Equation (11.14).

$$\mathrm{A_t} = \mathrm{G}(\mathrm{Q}, \mathrm{D_t}, \mathrm{A}_{t-1}) \tag{11.14}$$

These two processes continue over multiple rounds until a satisfactory answer is produced. This method is especially effective for complex queries requiring multi-step reasoning or synthesis of nuanced information, though it comes with increased computational cost compared to simpler, single-pass models.

For instance, iterative integration is well-suited for complex tasks such as multi-hop question answering or document summarization, where solutions necessitate several reasoning steps across a variety of information sources. When presented with a user query like "What are the key differences between blockchain and traditional databases?", the model initially retrieves pertinent documents on both subjects, formulates a preliminary response, and then gradually enhances its answer by adding more information from subsequent queries. Through an iterative method such as REALM, the model might start by collecting basic information about blockchain and then enrich its answer by incorporating more detailed insights on traditional databases, addressing exceptions, and ensuring a thorough and balanced response.

Iterative integration offers several advantages, including higher accuracy by refining answers through multiple iterations, greater contextual depth for handling complex queries, and improved management of ambiguities by clarifying and correcting responses over successive steps. However, it also has limitations: it is computationally expensive due to multiple retrieval cycles, slower than single-step models because of repeated refinement, and more complex to implement, requiring sophisticated mechanisms to efficiently manage the iterative process.

11.1.2.8.3 Memory-Augmented Integration (MemNN + LLMs)

This method integrates Memory Networks (MemNN) [22] with LLMs to develop a system that retains and accesses past information by keeping records of previous user queries, interactions, or feedback in a memory bank. Upon receiving a new query, the system fetches pertinent past information from this memory and employs it alongside the current input to produce a cohesive response that takes into account the entire conversation history, allowing for context-aware and tailored interactions.

Memory-augmented integration improves system efficiency by utilizing an external memory repository M to keep track of information from prior interactions $\{I_1, I_2, \ldots, I_n\}$, enabling the model to recall pertinent context across multiple stages. In formal terms, at stage t, the system identifies relevant memory entries $M_t = g(Q_t, M_t)$ in relation to the current query Q_t, where f serves as the retrieval function, and merges this with new input to produce a response $R_t = g(Q_t, M_t)$. This method is especially beneficial for conversational AI and tasks that run over an extended period since it maintains the historical context that stateless models would typically lose. By incorporating memory, the system can manage intricate dialogues, track user preferences, and delivering coherent responses throughout lengthy interactions. Furthermore, memory-augmented models facilitate real-time updates to M after each step, allowing for ongoing learning and adaptation, which enhances personalization and performance tailored to specific tasks in areas such as customer service, educational systems, and interactive assistants.

For instance, models that incorporate memory are ideal for conversational AI and personalized support by retaining and retrieving information from past exchanges. When a user inquires, "Can you remind me of my flight details?", the system accesses the relevant travel information stored in its memory to provide a precise answer. Likewise, if the user asks, "What did I mention about the last project I was involved in?", the model retrieves the relevant project details to offer an informed response. By integrating MemNN with LLMs, the system can efficiently remember previous discussions regarding product features, recall customer grievances from past interactions, and provide solutions that are more contextually relevant and tailored to the individual.

Memory-augmented integration provides notable benefits, including the preservation of context for seamless interactions, improving user experience by making the system more tailored and reactive, and facilitating adaptable applications such as personalized suggestions and multi-turn dialogues. Nevertheless, it also encounters challenges, such as the demanding resources required to handle an extensive memory database and the potential for memory overload with unnecessary or outdated data, which can reduce the quality of replies.

11.1.2.9 Retrieval-Augmented Generation (RAG)

RAG [1] is a framework designed to enhance the performance of language models on knowledge-intensive tasks by integrating external retrieval mechanisms into the generation process. This approach addresses limitations of traditional pretrained language models, such as their inability to access up-to-date information or provide verifiable sources for their outputs.

11.1.2.10 Introduction to Retrieval Augmentation

Traditional large pretrained language [23] models store knowledge implicitly within their parameters, enabling them to perform various tasks after fine-tuning. However, they face challenges in accessing and updating specific pieces of information, leading to potential inaccuracies, especially in dynamic knowledge domains. Retrieval augmentation introduces an external, nonparametric memory component that the model can query, allowing it to fetch relevant information as needed. This mechanism not only enhances the model's accuracy on knowledge-intensive tasks but also provides transparency by linking outputs to specific data sources.

11.1.2.11 Need for Augmenting LLMs with Retrieval

The integration of retrieval mechanisms into language models is motivated by several factors and is given below.

- **Dynamic Knowledge Access:** Pretrained models may not reflect the most current information. Retrieval augmentation allows models to access up-to-date data, ensuring outputs are based on the latest knowledge.
- **Parameter Efficiency:** Storing vast amounts of information within model parameters is inefficient. An external retrieval system enables models to access extensive knowledge bases without a proportional increase in model size.
- **Transparency and Verifiability:** By retrieving and referencing specific documents or data points, models can provide evidence for their outputs, enhancing trustworthiness.

11.1.2.12 Architecture of Retrieval-Augmented Generation (RAG)

RAG [24] combines retrieval-based methods with generation to improve the performance and accuracy of LLMs. This architecture involves two primary components and is given below.

- Retrieval Module
- Generation Module

11.1.2.13 Working of RAG

The RAG architecture functions through a multistep approach that first gathers pertinent external information before generating responses that are informed and precise. To start, the user's input query (for example, "What is the capital of India?") is preprocessed by breaking it down into smaller components such as words or subwords, which are then transformed into high-dimensional vector representations through the embedding layer of the LLM. This transformation encapsulates the semantic essence of the query in a numerical form, facilitating efficient processing in the next stages. Subsequently, the retrieval system utilizes this encoded query to search a vast external knowledge base that includes documents, databases, or web resources. There are three main methods of retrieval: Dense Retrieval, which uses embeddings to align queries and documents within a continuous vector space and assesses similarity with metrics like cosine similarity; Sparse Retrieval, which employs conventional keyword-based methods such as BM25 to evaluate documents on the basis of exact term matches; and Hybrid Retrieval, which merges dense and sparse techniques to balance semantic comprehension with keyword accuracy, thereby enhancing retrieval performance for a variety of queries. The system then produces the $top-K$ most relevant documents or excerpts based on these similarity evaluations. After retrieval, the chosen knowledge snippets are integrated as context by concatenating them with the original query and inputting this combined data into the generation module of the LLM. This enables the model to create a contextual representation that fuses both the query and external knowledge, thereby improving the relevance and precision of the output. The generation phase employs this enriched input to generate a coherent response, akin to traditional transformer-based text generation but now anchored in the retrieved external information. Finally, the output undergoes postprocessing to ensure it is clear, coherent, and well-formatted before being presented to the user. This complete pipeline allows RAG to integrate the internal knowledge of the LLM with real-time external data, resulting in answers that are both accurate and contextually pertinent.

The primary advantages of RAG architecture consist of improved accuracy achieved by incorporating real-time external knowledge, allowing models to provide more accurate and up-to-date answers compared to traditional LLMs. It also enhances contextual relevance by utilizing real-world information outside of the training data, leading to responses that are better aligned with user inquiries. Furthermore, RAG provides scalability by enabling LLMs to encompass a wider variety of subjects through external sources, eliminating the necessity for extensive retraining.

This architecture allows for end-to-end training, enabling the model to learn optimal retrieval and generation strategies jointly. Empirical evaluations have demonstrated that RAG models outperform traditional sequence-to-sequence models and other retrieval-based architectures on various tasks, including open-domain question answering and fact verification. Figure 11.1 shows the workflow architecture of RAG.

RAG integrates retrieval mechanisms with a language model to enhance knowledge-intensive tasks. The formulation of RAG involves key components such as retrieval probability, likelihood estimation, and response generation. Below are the mathematical formulations used in RAG models.

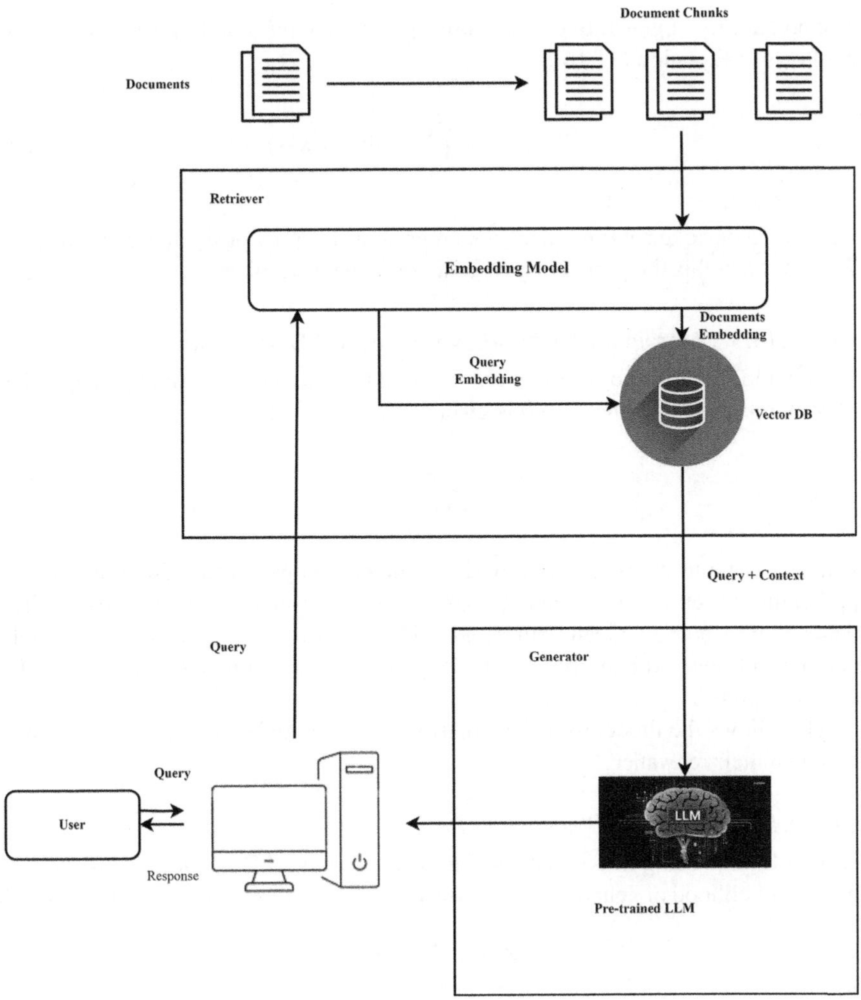

FIGURE 11.1 Retrieval augmented generation.

11.1.2.13.1 Retrieval Probability in RAG

Given an input query x, the model retrieves a set of relevant documents$\{z_1, z_2,...,z_n\}$ from a knowledge source. The probability of retrieving a document z given x is modeled as follows in Equation (11.15).

$$P(z|x) = \frac{\exp(sim(x,z))}{\sum_{z' \in Z} \exp(sim(x,z'))} \tag{11.15}$$

where $sim(x, z)$ is the similarity score (e.g., cosine similarity) between the query x and document z, Z represents the entire corpus from which documents are retrieved.

11.1.2.13.2 Response Generation in RAG

The probability of generating a response y given the input x and a retrieved document z follows in Equation (11.16).

$$P(y|x,z) = \prod_{t=1}^{T} P(y_t|\mathrm{y} < \mathrm{t}, \mathrm{x}, \mathrm{z}) \tag{11.16}$$

where y_t is the token at time step t, y < t represents the previously of generated tokens, $P(y_t \mid y < t, x, z)$ is the probability of generating the next token.

11.1.2.13.3 Marginal Likelihood over Retrieved Documents

Since multiple retrieved documents z are used to generate y, the model marginalizes over all retrieved documents and is given in Equation (11.17).

$$P(y|x) = \sum_{z \varepsilon Z} P(y|x,z) P(z|x) \tag{11.17}$$

where, x is Input query, z is retrieved document, y is generated response, $P(z|x)$ is probability of retrieving document z based on query x, and $P(y|x,z)$ is probability of generating response y given both x *and* z. This equation highlights that RAG models combine retrieval probability $P(z|x)$ with generative probability $P(y|x,z)$ to produce a final response.

This allows the model to weigh contributions from different retrieved documents based on their relevance.

11.1.2.13.4 Training Objective in RAG

RAG is trained using Maximum Likelihood Estimation (MLE), optimizing the negative log-likelihood of generating the correct response and is given in Equation (11.18).

$$\mathcal{L} = -\sum_{(x,y) \varepsilon D} P(y \mid x) \tag{11.18}$$

where D is the training dataset.

11.1.2.13.5 Contrastive Learning for Improving Retrieval

To improve retrieval, contrastive loss is used to separate relevant documents from irrelevant ones and is calculated using the Equation (11.19).

$$\mathscr{L}_{contrastive} = -\log \frac{\exp(sim(x, z^{+}))}{\sum_{z \in \{z^{+}, z_1, z_2, \ldots.\}} \exp(sim(x, z))} \quad (11.19)$$

where z^{+} is a relevant document, z^{-} are irrelevant (negative) documents, $sim(x, z)$ measures similarity.

These mathematical formulations enable RAG models to effectively retrieve external knowledge, inject context into language generation, and improve the accuracy of responses. By optimizing retrieval and generation jointly, RAG surpasses traditional language models that rely solely on pre-trained parameters.

11.1.3 Classification of RAG Models Based on Retrieval Timing

RAG models can be classified based on when the retrieval happens during the response generation process [1, 25]. The four key types of RAG based on retrieval timing are (i) pre-retrieval RAG, (ii) mid-retrieval RAG, (iii) post-retrieval RAG, and (iv) hybrid RAG. Table 11.2 shows the types of RAG based on retrieval timing.

11.1.3.1 Pre-Retrieval RAG (Retrieval Before Generation)

The system retrieves relevant documents first before passing them to the generative model. The retrieved information acts as additional context, improving factual accuracy and reducing hallucinations.

In this framework, a user inquiry like "What are the symptoms of diabetes?" is initially handled by a retriever module, which looks through an indexed knowledge base (for instance, PubMed) to locate pertinent medical documents. These documents are subsequently used as contextual input for a LLM, improving the factual basis of its response. Let Q denote the user inquiry, $R(Q)$ signify the collection of retrieved

TABLE 11.2
Types of RAG Based on Retrieval Timing.

RAG Type	Retrieval Timing	Description
Pre-retrieval RAG	Before generation	Retrieves documents first, then generates a response based on retrieved data.
Mid-retrieval RAG	During generation	Retrieves knowledge dynamically while generating a response.
Post-retrieval RAG	After generation	Generates a response first, then retrieves documents to verify or refine it.
Hybrid RAG	Combination of all three	Dynamically decides when to retrieve information, using multiple retrieval strategies.

documents corresponding to Q and $G(R(Q))$represent the output generated by the LLM utilizing the retrieved context. This process, where $G = LLM(R(Q))$, enhances factual precision and diminishes hallucinations by tying the model's replies to validated sources.

The pre-retrieval RAG is mathematically represented in Equation (11.20).

$$P(y|x) = P(y|x,z^*) \tag{11.20}$$

where $z^* = \underset{z}{argmax} P(z|x)$, z^* represents the highest-ranked document retrieved before generation.

RAG provides various benefits, such as minimizing hallucinations by basing answers on factual information, faster inference thanks to a one-time retrieval process, and strong capabilities in areas like question-answering, summarization, and chatbots. However, its success hinges on the quality of the retrieved materials—if retrieval encounters issues or yields irrelevant or outdated documents, the model may lack adequate context. Noteworthy examples include OpenAI's ChatGPT with web browsing capabilities, Facebook AI's original RAG model, and RAG-based workflows utilizing LlamaIndex and LangChain.

11.1.3.2 Mid-Retrieval RAG (Retrieval During Generation)

Mid-retrieval RAG integrates dynamic information retrieval into the response generation process by interleaving retrieval with generation steps. Formally, given a user query q, the model begins generating a response $y = (y_1, y_2, \ldots, y_t)$ token by token. At a certain token y_k, it performs a retrieval step $R(q, y_{<k})$ to fetch relevant documents $D = \{d_1, d_2, \ldots, d_n\}$ conditioned on the query and current partial output. The model then conditions the next token generation $P(y_k|q, y_{<k}, D)$ on both the original query and the newly retrieved context. This allows real-time adaptation and refinement of the response as new information is dynamically incorporated throughout generation. Mid-retrieval RAG can be mathematically expressed as the following Equation (11.21).

$$P(y_k|x, y_{<k}) = P(y_k|q, y_{<k}, R(q, y_{<k})) \tag{11.21}$$

where retrieval occurs at each step k during response generation.

Mid-retrieval RAG provides a flexible and responsive method for generating replies by sourcing the most pertinent information at each token or generation step, rather than depending exclusively on a single retrieval phase beforehand. This results in outputs that are more contextually aware and precise, which is particularly beneficial in interactive assistants and multiturn conversations where the user's intent can shift. Its capacity to adjust responses in real time leads to greater relevance and a stronger factual basis. However, this method requires substantial computational resources because the need for frequent retrievals at each step of generation increases the processing burden and may result in slower response times. In spite of these challenges, mid-retrieval RAG supports various sophisticated systems, such as T5-RAG from Google Research, which implements iterative retrieval techniques, and real-time

AI search tools like Perplexity AI, showcasing its efficiency in high-performance, content-rich dialogue systems.

11.1.3.3 Post-Retrieval RAG

In the post-retrieval RAG approach, the model first generates an initial response R_0 to a user query Q without accessing external knowledge. Then, it retrieves a set of relevant documents $D = \{d_1, d_2, ..., d_n\}$ to verify or enhance R_0. Using the retrieved information, the model updates its response to $R^* = f(R_0, D)$, where f represents the refinement function that integrates external facts, ensuring the final output R^* is more accurate and reliable. Mathematically, post-retrieval RAG can be represented by the following Equation (11.22).

$$P(y|x) = P(y|x, \hat{z}) \tag{11.22}$$

where, $\hat{z}$ is retrieved after the initial output.

Post-Retrieval RAG offers the advantage of ensuring factual correctness and reducing misinformation by verifying and refining the initial response with retrieved documents. However, it has the limitation of being slower, as the correction process occurs after the initial generation. This approach is employed in fact-checking AI models commonly used for news verification.

11.1.3.4 Hybrid RAG (Combining Multiple Retrieval Strategies)

This approach utilizes a combination of pre-, mid-, and post-retrieval strategies to enhance performance [26]. Formally, given a query Q:

- **Pre-Retrieval:** Retrieve initial background knowledge $D_{pre} = h_{\text{pre}}(Q)$ before generating the response.
- **Generation:** Produce an initial response $R_0 = g(Q, D_{\text{pre}})$ conditioned on Q and the pre-retrieved data.
- **Mid-Retrieval:** If needed, dynamically retrieve additional information $D_{\text{mid}} = h_{\text{mid}}(Q, R0)$ during generation.
- **Post-Retrieval:** Finally, retrieve documents $D_{\text{post}} = h_{\text{post}}(Q, R_0, D_{\text{mid}})$ to verify or correct the output and refine the response as follows in Equation (11.23).

$$R^* = f(R_0, D_{\text{post}}) \tag{11.23}$$

where h_{pre}, h_{mid}, h_{post} are retrieval functions at different stages, g is the generation function, and f is the refinement function.

This hybrid retrieval method combines the advantages of various retrieval approaches—pre-, mid-, and post-retrieval—resulting in superior performance. By utilizing background knowledge prior to generation, dynamically adjusting during the generation process, and confirming or correcting information afterward, it guarantees high levels of factual accuracy, adaptability in addressing a wide range of queries, and ongoing integration of current knowledge. This multilayered strategy enables the system to respond effectively even in situations with uncertain or changing information, making it especially well-suited for intricate reasoning tasks and real-time updates. A notable example of this approach is Google DeepMind's Gemini AI, which employs this multi-stage retrieval technique to improve both the quality and dependability of its outputs.

11.1.4 RAG Models Can Be Classified Based on Retrieval Strategies and Optimizations

RAG models can be summarized as being classified into retrieval strategies (e.g., hybrid search, multi-hop, graph-based, federated, multimodal, personalized) and optimization techniques (e.g., corrective, speculative, fusion, agentic, self, modular, hierarchical, memory-augmented, active learning, contrastive). Table 11.3 RAG models based on retrieval strategies and optimizations.

11.1.4.1 Standard RAG (Baseline Retrieval-Augmented Generation)

RAG is a powerful technique in natural language processing (NLP) that enhances LLMs by integrating external knowledge retrieval to improve factual accuracy and reduce hallucinations. In the Standard RAG framework, retrieval occurs before generation.

Given a user query Q, the retriever module fetches a set of relevant documents $D = \{d1, d2, ..., dn\} = h(Q)$ from an indexed knowledge base. These documents are then provided as additional context to the language model, which generates a response $R = g(Q, D)$. This architecture grounds responses in real-world data, improves transparency by enabling source traceability, and ensures that the model leverages both pre-trained knowledge and real-time retrieval. For example, when asked a medical question like "What are the symptoms of diabetes?", the system retrieves relevant medical literature and generates an informed answer using both the query and the supporting documents.

The standard RAG framework can be expressed mathematically as follows in Equation (11.24).

$$P(y \mid x) = P(y \mid x, z^*) \tag{11.24}$$

where, $z^* = \underset{z}{argmax} P(z \mid x)$, z^* represents the highest-ranked document retrieved before generation. In simple terms, this equation ensures that the retrieved document(s) influence the generated response, making it more accurate and relevant.

Standard RAG provides several important benefits by sourcing relevant documents prior to generating responses. It boosts factual precision by integrating up-to-date external information, minimizes inaccuracies by anchoring outputs in credible data, and enhances comprehensibility through the inclusion of source references. This establishes it as exceptionally transparent and trustworthy across multiple fields, including medical AI, legal AI, education, and research support. For example, in chatbot systems like ChatGPT with web browsing capabilities, when posed the

TABLE 11.3
RAG Models Based on Retrieval Strategies and Optimizations.

RAG Type	Key Feature	Pros	Cons	Use Cases
Standard RAG	Retrieves before generation	Fast, reduces hallucinations	Needs high-quality retrieval	Chatbots, document Q&A
Corrective RAG	Fixes errors post-generation	Ensures correctness	Slower response time	Fact-checking, research
Speculative RAG	Predicts needed retrievals	Faster, reduces retrieval calls	Risk of incorrect predictions	Real-time AI, search engines
Fusion RAG	Retrieves from multiple sources	More accurate, diverse	Expensive, needs ranking	Medical, legal AI
Agentic RAG	AI decides when to retrieve	More efficient	Complex to implement	AI research tools, autonomous agents
Self-RAG	Uses past responses	Improves continuity	Can reinforce incorrect data	Conversational AI, chatbots
Graph RAG	Uses structured knowledge graphs	More reasoning power	Needs graph databases	AI reasoning, enterprise search
Modular RAG	Customizable retrieval and generation	Flexible	Requires manual configuration	Domain-specific AI assistants
RadioRAG	Processes spoken queries	Audio-driven retrieval	Needs high-quality speech models	Voice assistants, meeting AI
Hierarchical RAG	Multilevel retrieval across structured knowledge	More precise context selection	Requires structured dataset	Enterprise knowledge retrieval, hierarchical Q&A
Memory-RAG	Persistent memory for long-term knowledge retention	Improves personalization	Needs advanced memory management	AI tutors, long-term conversation AI
Hybrid Search RAG	Combines dense and sparse retrieval techniques	More balanced retrieval results	Computationally expensive	Research assistants, academic AI
Multi-Hop RAG	Retrieves multiple documents in a step-by-step manner	Handles complex reasoning	Slower due to multi-step retrieval	Multistep reasoning AI, scientific research
Federated RAG	Retrieves data from decentralized sources without central access	Enhances privacy	Requires federated infrastructure	Healthcare, finance, and privacy-sensitive applications

(continued)

TABLE 11.3 (Continued)
RAG Models Based on Retrieval Strategies and Optimizations.

RAG Type	Key Feature	Pros	Cons	Use Cases
Personalized RAG	Tailors retrieval to user history/ preferences	More relevant responses	Requires user profiling	Recommendation systems, AI-driven assistants
Multi-Modal RAG	Retrieves across text, images, and videos	Works with diverse data formats	Needs multimodal retrieval support	AI search engines, AI-powered content summarization
Active Learning RAG	Continually improves retrieval models based on feedback	Adaptive and improves over time	Requires real-time model updates	AI training systems, self-improving chatbots
Contrastive RAG	Uses contrastive learning to improve retrieval ranking	More relevant retrieval results	Needs large datasets for contrastive training	Legal AI, high-accuracy knowledge retrieval

question "Who discovered penicillin?", a non-RAG model might deliver an insufficient or ambiguous answer, whereas a Standard RAG system would state, "Penicillin was discovered by Alexander Fleming in 1928. [Source: Wikipedia]," clearly backed by retrieved information. This document retrieval method is essential to RAG systems and plays a crucial role in delivering accurate, reliable, and scalable AI interactions.

11.1.4.2 Corrective RAG

Corrective RAG [27] is a refined variant of the RAG framework where the model performs knowledge retrieval **after** generating an initial response. Given a user query Q, the language model first produces a response $R_0 = g(Q)$ using only its pre-trained internal knowledge. Following this, a retriever module fetches a set of relevant documents $D = \{d_1, d_2, \ldots, d_n\} = h(Q, R_0)$ from an external knowledge base. A correction function f then evaluates the consistency between the initial response R_0 and the retrieved documents D. If R_0 is verified as accurate, the final output $R^* = R_0$; otherwise, the model generates a corrected version $R^* = f(R_0, D)$. This approach is especially effective for detecting hallucinations, ensuring factual consistency, and improving the transparency of LLM outputs by grounding them in real-world evidence.

Corrective RAG improves the accuracy of AI-generated content by sourcing external documents after the initial response to verify and amend any possible inaccuracies. This validation process that follows retrieval aids in identifying and rectifying misinformation, minimizes hallucinations by corroborating outputs with actual data, and greatly enhances the reliability and transparency of the AI system. It is especially important in critical fields such as journalism, healthcare, law, and education, where accuracy of facts is crucial. For instance, in a news fact-checking context, if someone asks, "Has NASA discovered a new exoplanet?", a standard model might confidently deliver unverified responses. Conversely, a Corrective RAG system would gather credible sources, find no evidence to support the claim, and adjust the response to clarify that there has been no report of such a discovery. This approach ensures that AI-generated responses are trustworthy, current, and responsibly based on verifiable information.

11.1.4.3 Speculative RAG – Predicting Retrieval Needs Before Execution:

Speculative RAG [28] is an advanced technique that improves efficiency by predicting the need for retrieval before accessing external knowledge sources. Given a user query Q, a lightweight predictor model P first estimates whether retrieval is necessary and identifies potentially relevant sources, producing a retrieval plan $S = p(Q)$. If retrieval is deemed necessary, documents $D = h(Q, S)$ are selectively fetched from the knowledge base using the plan S, where h is the targeted retrieval function. The final response is then generated as $R = g(Q, D)$, where gg is the language generation function. This method reduces computational cost and latency compared to standard RAG by avoiding unnecessary retrieval steps, while still maintaining the factual accuracy benefits of grounding responses in external data. For example, when asked "What are the side effects of ibuprofen?", the system may preemptively decide which medical databases are relevant, retrieve only those, and generate a precise, data-backed answer more efficiently. Mathematically Speculative RAG is represented using the following Equations (11.25) and (11.26).

Step 1: Preliminary Prediction Model

$$P(\hat{z} \mid x) = P(x, \theta) \tag{11.25}$$

where, x is input query, θ is lightweight prediction model parameters and $\hat{z}$ is predicted relevant knowledge source.

Step 2: Targeted Retrieval (Conditional Execution)

$$z^* = arg\max_{z \varepsilon \hat{z}} P(z \mid x) \tag{11.26}$$

where, z^* is most relevant retrieved documents, only fetched if necessary.

Speculative RAG enhances response times and lowers computational expenses by anticipating whether and what information needs to be obtained before consulting external knowledge sources. A streamlined prediction model initially identifies which subset of sources is relevant or opts to bypass retrieval if it is confident enough. When it is determined that retrieval is needed, only the chosen documents are gathered, and the ultimate response is crafted based on this focused information. This method boosts efficiency in real-time applications, such as AI chatbots, virtual helpers, and search engines. For example, AI-driven search engines pre-evaluate sources like Wikipedia or scholarly papers to swiftly address inquiries such as "How does quantum computing function?" by retrieving solely the most relevant data. Additional enhancements include using reinforcement learning to improve the prediction model, merging Speculative with Corrective RAG to achieve both speed and precision, and implementing confidence thresholds to omit retrieval only when the model is sufficiently assured, thereby effectively balancing efficiency with factual accuracy.

11.1.4.4 Fusion RAG – Multisource Knowledge Retrieval

Fusion RAG [29] improves accuracy, minimizes bias, and expands information coverage by sourcing and compiling data from various knowledge bases instead of depending on a single one. When a user poses a question, such as "What are the best treatments for diabetes?", the system gathers pertinent documents from a range of databases like PubMed, WHO, and clinical reports. These documents are then evaluated and integrated to guarantee coherence and a fair viewpoint. Ultimately, the AI crafts a thorough response that showcases insights from multiple credible sources, offering a comprehensive and trustworthy answer. Mathematically fusion RAG is represented using the following Equation (11.27).

$$z^* = arg\max_{z} \sum_{s=1}^{n} w_s P(z \mid x, s) \tag{11.27}$$

where, s is the different knowledge sources, and w_s is the weight assigned to each source based on credibility and relevance.

Fusion RAG presents numerous benefits, such as minimizing bias by including various viewpoints, enhancing factual correctness by drawing information from a range of independent sources, and improving domain-specific retrieval which is particularly valuable in areas like medical AI, legal AI, and research applications. For instance, AI-driven medical assistants utilizing Fusion RAG access information from sources like PubMed, WHO, and FDA to respond to inquiries like "What are the latest treatments for Alzheimer's?" by integrating and verifying clinical studies, guidelines, and trial reports to produce scientifically precise summaries that support better medical decision-making. To refine Fusion RAG, methodologies such as AI-based credibility assessments for ranking reliable sources, hybrid approaches that merge Fusion and Speculative RAG to lower retrieval expenses, and context-aware re-ranking through BERT-based models to enhance relevance are implemented.

11.1.4.5 Agentic RAG – AI-Controlled Dynamic Retrieval

Agentic RAG [30] is a dynamic and adaptive retrieval framework in which an AI agent autonomously determines when retrieval is necessary, which sources to query, and how to process the retrieved knowledge for optimal output. Given a user query Q, the AI first applies a decision function $f_{decision}(Q)$ to evaluate whether external retrieval is needed, producing a binary decision variable $R \in \{0, 1\}$. If retrieval is required ($R = 1$), the agent selects an optimal subset of data sources $S^* \subseteq S$ from the available candidates S using a source selection function $f_{source}(Q,S)$. The AI then retrieves knowledge $K = \bigcup s \in S^* K_s$ from these sources and refines this information through a filtering process $f_{filter}(K,Q)$ to extract the most relevant subset K^*. Finally, the AI generates the output O by combining the original query and the refined knowledge K^* through a function $f_{output}(Q,K^*)$ if retrieval was performed, or solely based on internal knowledge $f_{output}(Q)$ if retrieval was deemed unnecessary ($R = 0$). This agentic approach ensures retrieval is used efficiently, reducing redundant calls while improving the quality and relevance of the AI's final response.

Agentic RAG provides multiple benefits compared to conventional RAG techniques by allowing the AI to access information only when required, thus enhancing efficiency and lowering computational expenses through reduced retrieval actions and optimized API usage. This focused method also elevates knowledge selection by concentrating on highly pertinent sources. A significant example of its application is in AI-driven research assistants, where the agentic system independently determines whether to conduct a retrieval—such as looking up databases like ArXiv and IEEE Xplore for recent scientific publications—and subsequently extracts and summarizes essential findings solely when necessary. This leads to effective and precise academic research assistance customized to user inquiries like "Summarize reinforcement learning research."

11.1.4.6 Self-RAG – Retrieval from AI's Own Memory

Self-RAG [31] is a retrieval model that improves AI chatbots by pulling up previous responses instead of referencing external documents, thus fostering long-term memory and better context retention during multi-turn conversations. When a user poses a follow-up question, the AI retrieves relevant prior replies from its memory to formulate effective, context-sensitive answers. This method enables the AI to enhance its responses based on earlier interactions while maintaining coherence and continuity, leading to more natural and efficient conversational experiences without the need for unnecessary external retrieval.

Given a user query Q_t at turn t, the AI retrieves relevant prior responses $M = \{R_1, R_2, \ldots, R_{t-1}\}$ from its memory instead of querying external sources. The retrieval function $f_{mem}(Q_t, M)$ selects a subset $M^* \subseteq M$ of past responses relevant to Q_t. Using M^*, the AI then generates a refined answer $O_t = f_{gen}(Q_t, M^*)$, ensuring the response maintains coherence and continuity with prior dialogue. This method produces efficient, context-aware replies without unnecessary retrieval calls, enhancing the natural flow and accuracy of extended conversations. The mathematical representation of Self-RAG is given in Equation (11.28).

$$P(y|x) = P(y|x,h) \tag{11.28}$$

where, x is current query, h is history of past interactions.

Self-RAG provides multiple benefits by allowing AI to access previous responses stored in its internal memory, which helps maintain the flow of conversation, respond more quickly than conventional external retrieval methods, and enhance personalization by recalling user preferences and past interactions. A significant application of this is in AI-driven customer support chatbots, where the AI can remember earlier conversations to offer more tailored and effective assistance. For instance, when a user inquires, "Can you remind me of my last order details?", the AI can give relevant, context-sensitive information such as, "You last ordered an iPhone 13 on March 5th." This method improves the overall customer experience and optimizes support interactions.

11.1.4.7 Graph RAG – Retrieval Using Knowledge Graphs

Graph RAG [32] is a retrieval approach that extracts information from structured knowledge graphs instead of unstructured text, allowing for more accurate, logical, and organized responses—particularly advantageous for AI models focused on reasoning. When a user poses a question, such as "What role does insulin play in blood sugar regulation?", the AI conducts graph-based retrieval by querying an appropriate knowledge graph (for instance, a biomedical graph) and exploring the connections between entities (like insulin → pancreas → blood sugar). It then formulates a coherent and well-organized answer based on these linked nodes, enhancing both accuracy and interpretability.

Graph RAG is a retrieval framework where the AI sources knowledge from structured knowledge graphs $G = (V, E)$, with V representing entities (nodes) and $E \subseteq V \times V$ representing relationships (edges), instead of unstructured text. This enables more precise, structured, and logically consistent responses—particularly valuable for reasoning-intensive queries. Given a user query Q, the AI maps it to a set of target entities $V_Q \subseteq V$ and performs graph-based retrieval using a function $f_{graph}(Q, G)$, identifying relevant subgraphs $G_Q = (V_Q, E_Q)$. It then uses graph traversal algorithms $f_{traverse}(GQ)$ to trace meaningful relationships among entities (e.g., insulin → pancreas → blood sugar). Finally, the AI generates a structured and explainable response $O = f_{gen}(Q, G_Q)$, leveraging the logical paths extracted from the graph. This approach enhances reasoning, consistency, and interpretability in AI-generated answers. The mathematical representation of Graph RAG is given in Equation (11.29).

$$z^* = arg\max_z P(z \mid x, G) \tag{11.29}$$

where, G is knowledge graph, and $P(z \mid x, G)$ is probability of retrieving node z given query x.

Graph RAG provides numerous benefits by utilizing structured knowledge graphs for information retrieval, leading to responses that are more logical, accurate, and conducive to reasoning. This approach is particularly advantageous for applications in enterprise and scientific fields, such as business intelligence and biomedical research, where precision and clarity are essential. By minimizing ambiguity and focusing on clearly defined relationships between entities, Graph RAG guarantees structured, factually-based answers. A notable application is in drug discovery, where the AI can handle inquiries like "Which drugs interact with metformin?" by navigating a biomedical knowledge graph to gather pertinent drug-gene-disease connections, ultimately aiding in more informed and precise medical decision-making.

11.1.4.8 Modular RAG – A Customizable, Flexible Retrieval System

Modular RAG [33] is a versatile and customizable framework for RAG that permits dynamic configuration of its components—such as retrievers, ranking methods, and knowledge sources—according to specific use case needs. This flexibility allows users to mix different retrieval techniques (like BM25, dense, or hybrid), connect to various data sources (including text corpora, knowledge graphs, structured databases, or APIs), and implement multiple ranking approaches to enhance relevance. When the system receives a query like "What are the latest trends in blockchain?", it conducts dynamic module selection to identify the most appropriate retrieval type (such as graph, text, or audio), followed by choosing knowledge sources, applying custom ranking, and synthesizing a response. This modular design makes it particularly suitable for AI applications tailored to specific domains where adaptability, relevance, and accuracy are essential.

Modular RAG is a customizable RAG framework that allows the AI to dynamically configure its components—retrievers, ranking algorithms, and knowledge sources—based on the user query Q and application domain. Given a query Q, the system selects an appropriate retrieval module $R_i \in R = \{R_{BM25}, R_{Dense}, R_{Hybrid}, \dots\}$ via a selection function $f_{select}^{retriever}(Q)$. It then chooses one or more knowledge sources $S^* \subseteq S = \{S_{text}, S_{graph}, S_{DB}, S_{API}, \dots\}$ using $f_{select}^{source}(Q)$ and applies a ranking algorithm $r_j \in R_{\text{rank}}$ to sort results by relevance using Equations (11.30) and (11.31).

$$K = \bigcup_{s \in S^*} Ri(Q, s) \tag{11.30}$$

$$K_{\text{ranked}} = r_j(K) \tag{11.31}$$

Finally, the response is generated as $O = f_{\text{gen}}(Q, K_{\text{ranked}})$, where f_{gen} synthesizes a coherent answer using the top-ranked knowledge. This modular design enables the system to adapt to different domains—such as finance, healthcare, or tech—by mixing retrieval techniques, integrating heterogeneous data formats, and optimizing for context relevance, making it highly suitable for specialized and evolving AI applications.

Modular RAG provides substantial benefits through its high level of customizability, enabling users to combine various retrieval models, making it suitable for diverse fields such as legal, healthcare, finance, and research. Its design allows for optimization specific to domains by facilitating tailored retrieval processes that meet specialized requirements. For example, in the realm of legal research, a Modular RAG system is capable of addressing inquiries like "Identify a case similar to Roe v. Wade" by utilizing a retrieval module focused on case law (such as BM25), extracting pertinent statutes and precedents, and ranking them according to similarity and jurisdictional relevance. This leads to precise, adaptable, and context-sensitive support for legal research.

11.1.4.9 RadioRAG – Retrieval for Spoken Queries and Audio Data

RadioRAG [34] is a specialized model that combines RAG to effectively manage spoken inquiries by merging speech processing with conventional retrieval methods. It starts by converting the user's spoken input into text through speech-to-text technology, and then it fetches relevant details from audio transcripts, podcasts, or radio archives. The system evaluates and processes the most pertinent sources and produces a brief, contextually suitable spoken reply. This makes RadioRAG especially useful for voice assistants, technology news summaries, and meeting overviews, where smooth interaction between speech and retrieval is crucial.

RadioRAG is a specialized RAG model designed for spoken queries, integrating speech recognition with multimodal retrieval. Given a spoken query Q_{audio}, the system first converts it to text using a speech-to-text function $Q = f_{\text{STT}}(Q_{\text{audio}})$. It then performs retrieval over a corpus $S = \{s_1, s_2, \ldots, s_n\}$ consisting of audio transcripts, podcasts, and radio archives. The AI uses a retrieval function $R(Q, S)$ to gather relevant documents $K = R(Q, S)$, followed by a ranking function $r : K \to K_{\text{ranked}}$ to prioritize sources based on relevance. The final output O is generated as $O = f_{\text{gen}}(Q, K_{\text{ranked}})$, and optionally converted back to speech using $f_{\text{TTS}}(O)$ for voice-based delivery. This pipeline supports applications such as voice assistants, meeting summarization, and spoken news briefings, offering seamless integration between audio input, structured retrieval, and spoken output.

RadioRAG is ideal for applications such as AI-driven meeting summarization, as it effectively processes verbal input and extracts pertinent audio or transcript information. For instance, when a user requests, "Summarize yesterday's team meeting," the system retrieves the relevant meeting transcript, pinpoints key discussion topics and action items, and creates a clear, organized summary. This simplifies meeting documentation and allows for quicker, more efficient follow-ups, boosting productivity in work environments.

11.1.4.10 Hierarchical RAG – Structured Multi-Level Retrieval

Hierarchical RAG [35] is a model for RAG that is specifically designed to handle structured data by executing multi-tiered retrieval across document hierarchies, like sections, paragraphs, or subsections. Rather than retrieving complete documents, the AI analyzes the structure of the document in relation to the user query and selectively pulls the most pertinent sections through a hierarchical retrieval mechanism. It then organizes and filters these segments to produce a clear, structured response. This method is particularly effective for enterprise knowledge bases, allowing for more targeted and contextually relevant answers from extensive, structured sources.

Hierarchical RAG is a structured RAG model designed to operate over multilevel document hierarchies, enabling precise retrieval of relevant sections rather than full documents. Given a user query Q, the system first identifies the hierarchical structure of documents $D = \{d_1, d_2, \ldots, d_n\}$, where each document d_i is organized into levels $d_i = \{s_{i1}, s_{i2}, \ldots\}$ such as sections, paragraphs, or sub-sections. A multilevel retrieval function $R_{\text{hier}}(Q, D)$ selects a set of relevant subdocuments $K = \{s_{ij} \mid \text{relevant to } Q\}$, followed by a ranking function $r : K \to K_{\text{ranked}}$ to prioritize segments. The AI then compiles the top-ranked content to generate a structured response $O = f_{\text{gen}}(Q, K_{\text{ranked}})$.

This hierarchical approach significantly improves retrieval efficiency and relevance in enterprise-scale knowledge systems by narrowing focus to specific content blocks instead of full-document responses.

Hierarchical RAG is especially useful for AI applications in enterprises, particularly for retrieving knowledge from extensive corporate documents. For instance, when a user inquires, "What is our company's work-from-home policy?", the AI employs hierarchical retrieval to pinpoint and extract only the relevant portions of the policy document instead of processing the entire file. This targeted method allows for quicker, more organized, and contextually aware responses, greatly enhancing the effectiveness of enterprise search and minimizing information overload for users.

11.1.4.11 Memory-RAG – Long-Term AI Memory Retrieval

Memory-RAG [36] consistently logs and organizes all previous interactions between the AI and the user into a memory framework that reflects the user's preferences and context. When a new request is made, the system retrieves pertinent past data from this memory and produces customized responses, such as recalling the last book the user inquired about and suggesting relevant follow-up options. Each new interaction updates the memory, enabling the AI to progressively improve personalization and sustain long-term conversational context, leading to more natural and user-focused experiences over time.

Memory-RAG operates by maintaining a memory function M that encodes all past interactions I_t into a context C containing user preferences, queries, and conversation history. When a new user query q_{t+1} arrives, the system uses $M(I_t)$ to retrieve relevant information R, such as the last book queried and its timestamp. This retrieved memory R is combined with q_{t+1} to generate a personalized response $R(q_{t+1}, R)$. The interaction i_{t+1} is then added to the set of past interactions, updating the memory for future use. Over time, as more interactions accumulate, the memory M allows the AI to produce increasingly personalized and contextually aware responses, improving the user experience continuously.

11.1.4.12 Hybrid Search RAG: Combining Sparse and Dense Retrieval

Hybrid Search RAG [37] integrates both sparse retrieval approaches, such as BM25 and TF-IDF, that locate exact keyword matches, as well as dense retrieval methods utilizing neural embeddings and tools like FAISS to discover semantically related content. When a user submits a query (like "What is the impact of AI in healthcare?"), the system initially conducts a keyword-based search using sparse retrieval, followed by a semantic search using dense retrieval techniques. The outcomes from these two approaches are then combined and prioritized based on a scoring method to identify the most relevant results. Ultimately, the AI synthesizes this integrated knowledge to produce a precise and thorough response, harnessing the benefits of both high-precision keyword matching and high-recall semantic interpretation.

Hybrid Search RAG performs retrieval by combining sparse and dense methods to optimize both precision and recall. Given a user query q, sparse retrieval uses a function $S_{\text{sparse}}(q)$ (e.g., BM25 or TF-IDF) to return documents D_s with exact keyword matches, while dense retrieval applies a semantic similarity function $S_{\text{dense}}(q)$, often computed via neural embeddings and nearest neighbor search (e.g., FAISS), yielding documents D_d with semantically related content. The combined candidate set is $D = D_s \cup D_d$. A ranking function $R : D \rightarrow \mathrm{R}$ scores each document based on relevance, producing an ordered list D^*. Finally, the AI generates a response $\hat{r} = G(q, D^*)$, where G synthesizes information from the top-ranked documents to provide an accurate and context-aware answer. Mathematically, hybrid RAG is represented using the Equation (11.32).

$$P(z|q) = \lambda P_{\text{sparse}}(z|q) + (1-\lambda)P_{\text{dense}}(z|q) \tag{11.32}$$

where, q is the user query, z is a candidate document or passage, $P_{\text{sparse}}(z \mid x)$ is probability of retrieval using sparse search (BM25, TF-IDF), $P_{\text{dense}}(z \mid x)$ is probability of retrieval using dense search (Neural Embeddings), and λ is weight balancing sparse and dense retrieval.

Hybrid Search RAG improves AI-d riven legal search by integrating traditional keyword-based retrieval techniques like BM25 with dense semantic search utilizing neural embeddings and FAISS. For instance, when a user types the question, "Find cases similar to Roe v. Wade," the system retrieves both cases with matching keywords and those that are semantically related. These findings are then combined and ranked based on their legal significance, allowing the AI to offer more precise and thorough legal research that encompasses both exact matches and subtly related precedents.

11.1.4.13 Multi-Hop RAG – Step-by-Step Document Retrieval for Complex Reasoning

Multi-Hop RAG [38] tackles intricate inquiries by fetching multiple related documents in a series of steps to facilitate multistep reasoning. For example, if presented with the question "What is the impact of climate change on ocean currents?", the system initially retrieves a general document about climate change, and then it looks for documents that specifically examine ocean currents affected by climate change. By connecting these documents, the AI creates a cohesive knowledge chain, enabling it to generate a detailed and accurate answer. This methodology improves precision and depth, making it particularly useful for scientific studies, legal evaluations, and sophisticated AI reasoning tasks.

Multi-Hop RAG tackles complex queries q by performing sequential retrieval steps to gather multiple related documents $D = \{d_1, d_2, \ldots, d_n\}$. At the first hop, the system retrieves a general document $d_1 = Retrieve(q)$. At the second hop, it uses information from d_1 to formulate a refined query $q_2 = f(q, d_1)$ and retrieves a related document $d_2 = Retrieve(q_2)$. This process continues for n hops, producing a linked chain of documents D. The AI then applies a synthesis function G over the set D to generate the final response $\hat{r} = G(q, D) = G(q, \{d_1, d_2, \ldots, d_n\})$. This multi-hop retrieval and synthesis improves accuracy for complex queries by integrating evidence from multiple sources, enabling multistep reasoning critical for fields like scientific research and legal analysis. Mathematically, multihop RAG is represented using Equation (11.33).

$$P(y \mid q) = \sum_{z_1} P(z_1 \mid q) \sum_{z_2} P(z_2 \mid xq, q) P(y \mid q, z_1, z_2) \quad (11.33)$$

where, z_1 is first hop retrieved document and z_2 is second hop retrieved document (dependent on z_1).

Multihop RAG improves AI-enabled scientific inquiry by tackling intricate, interdisciplinary questions via a step-by-step retrieval of relevant documents. For instance, when posed with the question, "What is the effect of AI on personalized cancer treatment?", the system initially gathers literature on AI in medicine, and then subsequently seeks out studies focused specifically on cancer treatment. By connecting and integrating insights from both areas, the AI produces a detailed and accurate answer, thereby significantly enhancing the quality and depth of AI-assisted medical and scientific exploration.

11.1.4.14 Federated RAG: Decentralized, Privacy-Preserving Retrieval

Federated RAG [39] facilitates the extraction of information from various decentralized sources, improving privacy by retaining sensitive data within local networks, making it excellent for distributed AI applications in areas such as healthcare, finance, and edge computing. When a user submits a query, the AI solicits information from different local databases, with each client carrying out the retrieval process independently. The system then securely combines the gathered information without revealing raw data, enabling the AI to produce a thorough, privacy-protecting response.

Federated RAG retrieves knowledge from multiple decentralized sources $\{S_1, S_2, \ldots, S_m\}$ by having each source independently perform local retrieval $Ri = Retrieve_{S_i}(q)$ on a user query q without sharing raw data. These local results are securely aggregated using a function A to form a combined knowledge set $R = A(R_1, R_2, \ldots, R_m)$, which the AI then synthesizes into a privacy-preserving response $\hat{r} = G(q, R)$. This method enhances privacy and is ideal for distributed AI systems in sectors like healthcare, finance, and edge computing.

Federated RAG allows for the utilization of AI in healthcare while safeguarding patient privacy by accessing data from various hospitals without disclosing sensitive information. For instance, when inquiring about recent developments in diabetes care, the AI gathers research specific to each hospital and compiles treatment results locally, guaranteeing the confidentiality of patient data. This method promotes safe and collaborative healthcare research while upholding rigorous privacy regulations.

11.1.4.15 Personalized RAG – AI That Adapts to User Preferences

Personalized RAG [40] adapts knowledge retrieval by utilizing a user's history and preferences, enabling the AI to gather information that is specifically suited to individual requirements. By modifying responses according to prior interactions and behaviors, it increases the relevance of the retrieved information and boosts user engagement. This tailored approach proves to be especially effective in areas such as recommendation systems and AI-driven personal assistants, where context related to the user results in more accurate and fulfilling experiences.

Personalized RAG customizes knowledge retrieval by incorporating user-specific data such as history, preferences, and past interactions to improve relevance and engagement. Given a query q from user u, the system first accesses the user profile U_u, which may include past queries, clicked documents, and preference embeddings. A personalization function $P(q, U_u)$ adapts the query contextually, producing a refined query q'. The system then performs retrieval $R = Retrieve(q')$, where documents are ranked not just by general relevance, but also by alignment with U_u. Finally, the AI generates a personalized response $\hat{r} = G(q, R, U_u)$, increasing both the precision of the information and the user's engagement. This approach is widely used in recommendation engines, personalized assistants, and adaptive learning systems.

Personalized RAG improves the user experience by gathering information that matches personal preferences and histories. For instance, when a user inquires, "Can you suggest a book on AI?" the system draws on their previous interests—like deep learning or natural language processing—and offers suitable recommendations. This creates more interactive and responsive AI dialogues, since replies are customized to the individual user's profile.

11.1.4.16 Multimodal RAG – Retrieval Across Text, Images, Videos, and Audio

Multimodal RAG [41] enhances conventional RAG by obtaining and processing a range of data types—such as text, images, videos, and audio—to address queries that involve multiple modalities. When a user inputs a query like "Display the newest AI research papers with images," the system conducts multi-modal retrieval across various data sources, then integrates and ranks the results according to their relevance and quality. Ultimately, it produces a comprehensive, multi-modal response that may contain documents, illustrations, and other types of media. This method is crucial for applications such as AI-driven search engines, medical diagnostics, and digital content analysis, where it is essential to comprehend and combine information from diverse formats.

Multimodal RAG extends traditional RAG by processing heterogeneous data types—text T, images I, audio A, and video V—to answer queries that require multiformat knowledge. Given a user query q, the system performs modality-specific retrieval functions $R_T(q)$, $R_I(q)$, $R_A(q)$, and $R_V(q)$, producing candidate sets D_T, D_I, D_A, D_V, respectively. These are fused into a unified ranked set $D = RankFuse(D_T \cup D_I \cup D_A \cup D_V)$ using a relevance and quality scoring mechanism. A generation function G then synthesizes a multi-modal response $\hat{r} = G(q, D)$, which may include text, visuals, or audio content. This architecture enables AI applications—such as search engines, diagnostics, and media analysis—to respond with richer, more informative outputs by leveraging multiple data modalities. Mathematically, the multimodal RAG is represented using the following Equation (11.34).

$$P(y \mid q) = \sum_{z \varepsilon Z} P(y \mid q, z)\, P(z \mid q, M) \tag{11.34}$$

where, M is multimodal data type (text, image, video, audio) and $P(z \mid x, M)$ is probability of retrieving multi modal document z based on input$q$.

Multimodal RAG provides substantial benefits by sourcing and reasoning with various data forms—such as text, images, audio, and video—allowing AI to create rich, multimedia responses. This ability enhances reasoning across different formats, proving particularly beneficial in areas like medical diagnosis, visual searches, and reporting generated by AI. For instance, when a user queries, "Display lung cancer diagnosis cases featuring CT scan images," the AI retrieves pertinent case studies along with medical visuals, then delivers a combined text-and-image response for improved analysis. This approach not only enhances diagnostic assistance but also increases user engagement through interactive, multi-format outputs.

11.1.4.17 Active Learning RAG: Self-Improving AI through User Feedback

Active Learning RAG [42] improves retrieval efficiency over time by integrating user feedback and iterative adjustments into its learning methodology. When a user makes a query (for instance, "Summarize recent AI trends"), the AI fetches and displays an initial group of documents. The user then assesses the response—either through ratings or feedback—which is utilized to dynamically modify the retrieval ranking model. This feedback loop enables the system to enhance its retrieval techniques, decreasing reliance on fixed pretrained knowledge and allowing it to adjust to changing information trends. Consequently, active learning RAG enhances personalization and precision in uses such as chatbots, research assistants, and recommendation systems.

Active learning RAG continuously improves retrieval accuracy by incorporating user feedback into its retrieval model. Given a user query q, the system retrieves an initial document set $D = \text{Retrieve}(q)$ and generates a response $\hat{r} = G(q, D)$. The user provides feedback $f \in F$ (e.g., relevance score, correction, or preference), which is used to update the retrieval ranking function R. This update is formalized as $R' = \text{Update}(R, f)$, where R' represents the refined model for future queries. Over multiple iterations t, the retrieval accuracy improves as $R_t \to R_{t+1}$ based on the accumulated feedback $\{f_1, f_2, \ldots, f_t\}$. This adaptive process reduces reliance on static pretrained knowledge and enables personalized, up-to-date retrieval, making it ideal for dynamic AI systems like chatbots, research assistants, and recommendation engines. Mathematically, active learning RAG is represented using the following Equation (11.35).

$$P(z \mid q, \theta) = P(z \mid \theta_{old}) + \alpha . \Delta_{\text{feedback}} \tag{11.35}$$

where, θ_{old} is previous retrieval model parameters and α is learning rate based on user feedback and Δ_{feedback} is the adjustment based on user feedback.

Active Learning RAG enhances personalized learning platforms by allowing AI tutors to modify content suggestions according to student input. For example, when a student requests, "Can you explain quantum mechanics in simpler terms again?", the AI recognizes from past feedback that its previous explanation was overly complicated. It then alters its information retrieval approach to source simpler, more easily understandable resources for future sessions. This adaptation driven by feedback enables the AI to consistently enhance its educational responses, leading to more effective and tailored tutoring as time progresses.

11.1.4.18 Contrastive RAG – Improving Retrieval Accuracy through Contrastive Learning

Contrastive RAG [43] enhances retrieval accuracy by employing contrastive learning to enable the AI to differentiate between pertinent and nonpertinent documents. When a user inputs a query, the system pulls several potential documents and utilizes contrastive learning by evaluating pairs of positive (relevant) and negative (irrelevant) documents. This method trains the model to more effectively rank documents according to their actual relevance, leading to improved retrieval that eliminates noisy or subpar sources. The AI then leverages the most suitable documents to produce a more precise and contextually relevant response.

Contrastive RAG enhances retrieval accuracy by training the AI to distinguish relevant documents d^+ from irrelevant ones d^- using contrastive learning. Given a user query q, the system first retrieves a candidate set $D = \{d_1, d_2, \ldots, d_n\}$. It then optimizes a ranking model R by minimizing a contrastive loss function L, which encourages the relevance score $s(q, d^+)$ for positive documents to be higher than $s(q, d^-)$ for negative documents. Formally, the model learns to satisfy $s(q, d^+) > s(q, d^-)$ for relevant d^+ and irrelevant d^- pairs. This results in refined retrieval R^* that prioritizes high-quality sources, enabling the AI to generate a more accurate final response $\hat{r} = G(q, R^*(D))$. Mathematically, contrastive RAG is represented using the following Equation (11.36).

$$L_{\text{contrastive}} = -\sum_{(d^+, d^-)} \log \frac{\exp(f(d^+) \cdot f(q))}{\sum_z \exp(f(d) \cdot f(q))} \tag{11.36}$$

where d^+ is relevant (positive) document, d^- is irrelevant (negative) document, and $f(q)$ is query representation.

Contrastive RAG excels in delivering high-accuracy legal research by educating the AI to identify the most relevant legal documents related to a specific case. By employing contrastive learning, the system enhances its capability to assess and prioritize legally significant texts, leading to more precise and legally valid AI-driven research results.

SUMMARY

With an emphasis on retrieval-augmented LLMs, which improve model performance by including external knowledge retrieval into the generation process, this chapter addresses augmented LLMs. After introducing the idea, it categorizes retrieval-augmented LLMs according to three factors: the knowledge source (databases, documents, web content, etc.), the integration method with LLMs (how retrieved data is fed into the model), and the retrieval mechanism (how pertinent information is located). RAG is then covered in detail in this chapter, including its architecture, the timing of retrieval (pre-, mid-, and post-generation), and retrieval strategies with optimization techniques to increase efficiency, accuracy, and relevance. All things considered, it demonstrates how adding retrieval capabilities to LLMs helps them overcome knowledge cutoffs, enhance factuality, and facilitate more context-rich and domain-specific responses.

QUESTIONS

1. Given a corpus of 10,000 documents, if the retrieval mechanism selects the top-k = 20 documents per query, how many documents will be retrieved for 150 queries?
2. A RAG system integrates an LLM with a retriever. If the retriever's recall is 80% and precision is 60%, compute the F1-score.
3. In a knowledge source with 5,000 Wikipedia articles and 2,000 news reports, if the retriever gives preference weight *0.7* to Wikipedia and *0.3* to news, what is the weighted contribution score for each source?
4. If a RAG model retrieves documents *before generation* (pre-retrieval) and retrieves again *during decoding* (dynamic retrieval), calculate the retrieval cost for a query that retrieves 10 docs pre-retrieval and 5 docs per token for a 50-token output.
5. Design a simple RAG retrieval strategy where the retriever first filters by keywords (50 candidates), then applies semantic similarity (top-10). For 100 user queries, calculate the total number of similarity computations.
6. Define retrieval-augmented LLMs and explain their motivation.
7. Differentiate between retrieval mechanisms, knowledge sources, and integration approaches in retrieval-augmented LLMs.
8. Compare the architecture of standard LLMs and RAG models, focusing on the role of the retriever and generator.
9. Critically examine the advantages and limitations of retrieval timing strategies (pre-retrieval, dynamic retrieval, post-retrieval).
10. Propose an optimized retrieval strategy that balances latency and accuracy for a real-time healthcare assistant using RAG.
11. **Case Study:** A healthcare company wants to build a chatbot that can answer doctors' queries about rare diseases. Since the chatbot cannot store all medical knowledge within the model, the team decides to use Retrieval-Augmented Generation (RAG). The system first retrieves relevant documents from a trusted medical knowledge base, then integrates the results with the LLM to provide accurate answers. This helps doctors get reliable information without the model needing to memorize everything. Explain how Retrieval-Augmented Generation (RAG) improves the performance of LLMs in specialized domains like healthcare.

REFERENCES

[1] Y. Gao, Y. Xiong, X. Gao, K. Jia, J. Pan, Y. Bi *et al.*, "Retrieval-Augmented Generation for Large Language Models: A Survey," arXiv preprint, Mar. 2024, arXiv:2312.10997.

[2] S. Gupta, R. Ranjan, and S. N. Singh, "A Comprehensive Survey of Retrieval-Augmented Generation (RAG): Evolution, Current Landscape and Future Directions," arXiv preprint, Oct. 2024, arXiv:2410.12837.

[3] Y. Zhu, J.-C. Gu, Y. Zhu, Z.-H. Ling, and J. Chen, "Accelerating Inference of Retrieval-Augmented Generation via Sparse Context Selection," in *Proc. of the Association for Computational Linguistics (ACL)*, May 2024, arXiv:2405.16178.

[4] B. Das, and S. Chakraborty, "An Improved Text Sentiment Classification Model Using TF-IDF and Next Word Negation," arXiv preprint, Jun. 2018, arXiv:1806.06407.

[5] X. Chen, and S. Wiseman, "BM25 Query Augmentation Learned End-to-End," in *Proc. of the Conference on Empirical Methods in Natural Language Processing (EMNLP)*, May 2023, arXiv:2405.16178.

[6] Y. Ji, Y. Liu, and W. Zhang, "Learning More Effective Representations for Dense Retrieval through Deliberate Thinking Before Search," arXiv preprint, Feb. 2025, arXiv:2502.12974.

[7] V. Karpukhin, B. Oguz, S. Min, P. Lewis, L. Wu, S. Edunov *et al.*, "Dense Passage Retrieval for Open-Domain Question Answering," in *Proc. of the Conference on Empirical Methods in Natural Language Processing (EMNLP)*, Sep. 2020, arXiv:2004.04906.

[8] N. Reimers, and I. Gurevych, "Sentence-BERT: Sentence Embeddings using Siamese BERT-Networks," in *Proc. of the Conference on Empirical Methods in Natural Language Processing (EMNLP)*, Aug. 2019, arXiv:1908.10084.

[9] M.-C. Lee, Q. Zhu, Y. Wang, J. Chen, and C. Faloutsos, "HybGRAG: Hybrid Retrieval-Augmented Generation on Textual and Relational Knowledge Bases," arXiv preprint, Jun. 2025, arXiv:2412.16311.

[10] A. Abdallah, J. Mozafari, B. Piryani, M. Ali, and A. Jatowt, "From Retrieval to Generation: Comparing Different Approaches," arXiv preprint, Feb. 2025, arXiv:2502.20245.

[11] Y. Bai, X. Liu, Y. Chen, and Z. Wang, "Pistis-RAG: Enhancing Retrieval-Augmented Generation with Human Feedback," arXiv preprint, Oct. 2024, arXiv:2407.00072.

[12] J. Huang, Z. Liu, and S. Zhang, "A Comprehensive Survey on Retrieval Methods in Recommender Systems," arXiv preprint, Jul. 2024, arXiv:2407.21022.

[13] H. Qian, Z. Liu, and J. Tang, "MemoRAG: Boosting Long Context Processing with Global Memory-Enhanced Retrieval Augmentation," arXiv preprint, Apr. 2025, arXiv:2409.05591.

[14] W. Liu, Z. Tang, J. Li, K. Chen, and M. Zhang, "MemLong: Memory-Augmented Retrieval for Long Text Modeling," arXiv preprint, Aug. 2024, arXiv:2408.16967.

[15] J.-J. Tian, S. Wang, and H. Ji, "Web Retrieval Agents for Evidence-Based Misinformation Detection," arXiv preprint, Oct. 2024, arXiv:2409.00009.

[16] W. Guan, and Y. Fang, "Optimizing Web-Based AI Query Retrieval with GPT Integration in LangChain A CoT-Enhanced Prompt Engineering Approach," *EAI Endorsed Transactions*, Jun. 2025, doi: 10.4108/eai.21-11-2024.2354589.

[17] F. Ridder, and M. Schilling, "The HalluRAG Dataset: Detecting Closed-Domain Hallucinations in RAG Applications Using an LLM's Internal States," arXiv preprint, Mar. 2025, arXiv:2412.17056.

[18] K. Qian, A. Belyi, F. Wu, S. Khorshidi, A. Nikfarjam, R. Khot, "Open Domain Knowledge Extraction for Knowledge Graphs," arXiv preprint, Oct. 2023, arXiv:2312.09424.

[19] M. Mishra, D. Contractor, and D. Raghu, "Joint Reasoning on Hybrid-Knowledge Sources for Task-Oriented Dialog," arXiv preprint, Feb. 2023, arXiv:2210.07295.

[20] Y. Wang, J. Smith, and L. Chen , "RAG+: Enhancing Retrieval-Augmented Generation with Application-Aware Reasoning," arXiv preprint, Jul. 2025, arXiv:2506.11555.

[21] X. Chen, J. Ge, T. Zhang, J. Liu, and S. Zhang, "Learning from Mistakes: Iterative Prompt Relabeling for Text-to-Image Diffusion Model Training," in *Findings of the Association for Computational Linguistics: EMNLP 2024*, pp. 2937–2952, Miami, Florida, USA, 2024.

[22] Z. Li, C. Wang, and H. Zhang, "MemOS: An Operating System for Memory-Augmented Generation (MAG) in Large Language Models," arXiv preprint, May 2025, arXiv:2505.22101.

[23] S. Gupta, R. Ranjan, and S. N. Singh, "A Comprehensive Survey of Retrieval-Augmented Generation (RAG): Evolution, Current Landscape and Future Directions," arXiv preprint, Oct. 2024, arXiv:2410.12837.

[24] P. Lewis, E. Perez, A. Piktus, F. Petroni, V. Karpukhin, N. Goyal *et al.*, "Retrieval-Augmented Generation for Knowledge-Intensive NLP Tasks," in *Advances in Neural Information Processing Systems (NeurIPS)*, Apr. 2021, arXiv:2005.11401.

[25] Y. Huang, and J. Huang, "A Survey on Retrieval-Augmented Text Generation for Large Language Models," arXiv preprint, Aug. 2024, arXiv:2404.10981.

[26] Y. Yuan, C. Liu, J. Yuan, G. Sun, S. Li, and M. Zhang, "A Hybrid RAG System with Comprehensive Enhancement on Complex Reasoning," arXiv preprint, Sep. 2024, arXiv:2408.05141.

[27] S.-Q. Yan, J.-C. Gu, Y. Zhu, and Z.-H. Ling, "Corrective Retrieval Augmented Generation," arXiv preprint, Oct. 2024, arXiv:2401.15884.

[28] Z. Wang, X. Zhang, and H. Liu, "Speculative RAG: Enhancing Retrieval Augmented Generation through Drafting," arXiv preprint, Feb. 2025, arXiv:2407.08223.

[29] Z. Rackauckas, "RAG-Fusion: A New Take on Retrieval-Augmented Generation," *International Journal of Natural Language Computing (IJNLC)*, Feb. 2024, doi: 10.5121/ijnlc.2024.13103, arXiv:2402.03367.

[30] A. Singh, A. Ehtesham, S. Kumar, and T. T. Khoei, "Agentic Retrieval-Augmented Generation: A Survey on Agentic RAG," arXiv preprint, Feb. 2025, arXiv:2501.09136.

[31] A. Asai, Z. Wu, Y. Wang, A. Sil, and H. Hajishirzi, "Self-RAG: Learning to Retrieve, Generate, and Critique through Self-Reflection," in *Proc. of the International Conference on Learning Representations (ICLR)*, Oct. 2023, arXiv:2310.11511.

[32] D. Edge, H. Trinh, N. Cheng, J. Bradley, A. Chao, A. Mody *et al.*, "From Local to Global: A Graph RAG Approach to Query-Focused Summarization," arXiv preprint, Feb. 2025, arXiv:2404.16130.

[33] Y. Gao, Y. Xiong, M. Wang, and H. Wang, "Modular RAG: Transforming RAG Systems into LEGO-like Reconfigurable Frameworks," arXiv preprint, Jul. 2024, arXiv:2407.21059.

[34] S. T. Arasteh M. A. Akhavan, and P. Kulkarni, "RadioRAG: Online Retrieval-augmented Generation for Radiology Question Answering," *Radiology: Artificial Intelligence*, Jun. 2025, doi: 10.1148/ryai.240476.

[35] H. Huang, Z. Liu, and Y. Wang, "HiRAG: Retrieval-Augmented Generation with Hierarchical Knowledge," arXiv preprint, Jun. 2025, arXiv:2503.10150v2.

[36] H. Qian, Z. Liu, and J. Tang, "MemoRAG: Boosting Long Context Processing with Global Memory-Enhanced Retrieval Augmentation," arXiv preprint, Apr. 2025, arXiv:2409.05591.

[37] B. Sarmah, B. Hall, R. Rao, S. Patel, S. Pasquali, and D. Mehta, "HybridRAG: Integrating Knowledge Graphs and Vector Retrieval Augmented Generation for Efficient Information Extraction," arXiv preprint, Aug. 2024, arXiv:2408.04948.

[38] Y. Tang, and Y. Yang, "MultiHop-RAG: Benchmarking Retrieval-Augmented Generation for Multi-Hop Queries," arXiv preprint, Jan. 2024, arXiv:2401.15391.

[39] D. Zhao, "FRAG: Toward Federated Vector Database Management for Collaborative and Secure Retrieval-Augmented Generation," arXiv preprint, Oct. 2024, arXiv:2410.13272.

[40] M. J. Ryan, D. Xu, C. Nivera, and D. Campos, "EnronQA: Towards Personalized RAG over Private Documents," arXiv preprint, May 2025, arXiv:2505.00263.

[41] Z.-A. Ma, J. Lu, and X. Zhang, "Multi-modal Retrieval Augmented Multi-modal Generation: Datasets, Evaluation Metrics and Strong Baselines," arXiv preprint, May 2025, arXiv:2411.16365v4.

[42] Z. Xu, C. Wang, and J. Zheng, "ActiveRAG: Autonomously Knowledge Assimilation and Accommodation through Retrieval-Augmented Agents," arXiv preprint, Oct. 2024, arXiv:2402.13547v2.

[43] L. Ranaldi, M. Valentino, and A. Freitas, "Eliciting Critical Reasoning in Retrieval-Augmented Language Models via Contrastive Explanations," in *Proc. of the North American Chapter of the Association for Computational Linguistics (NAACL)*, Oct. 2024, doi: 10.18653/v1/2025.naacl-long.557.

12 LLMs-Powered Agents

12.1 LLMS STEERING AUTONOMOUS AGENTS

Large language model (LLM)-powered agents are an advanced class of artificial intelligence (AI) systems designed to process, understand, and generate human-like responses based on vast amounts of textual data. These agents leverage pretrained language models such as GPT, LLaMA, Falcon, and Claude to perform complex reasoning, context handling, and decision-making [1].

With the evolution of AI, LLM-powered agents have become essential across multiple domains, ranging from conversational assistants and automation tools to autonomous AI-driven decision-makers in fields like healthcare, finance, research, and cybersecurity. LLM-powered agents are AI systems built on large-scale neural networks trained on diverse datasets to generate meaningful and contextually relevant text. These agents can perform various tasks such as answering questions, writing content, reasoning, making predictions, and even executing predefined actions via APIs and automation frameworks [2].

These agents exhibit essential traits including natural language understanding (NLU) to comprehend human language, an awareness of context to retain pertinent conversational details, and adaptability for specialization in fields such as law, healthcare, or programming. They facilitate independent decision-making through unified reasoning and planning while also participating in interactive, multiturn dialogues that improve responses based on user feedback. Collectively, these features boost efficiency by allowing for text-based automation, decision assistance, and tailored recommendations [3].

LLMs have transformed AI-powered autonomous agents by enabling them to interpret, reason, and act upon natural language instructions. These agents integrate components such as planning, memory, and tool usage to autonomously perform complex tasks across various domains, including e-commerce, social media management, and real-time coordination.

12.1.1 Core Components of LLM-Powered Autonomous Agents

The fundamental elements of LLM-driven autonomous agents consist of *planning and reasoning*, which facilitate actions and decisions focused on achieving specific

DOI: 10.1201/9781003650065-12

goals; *feedback systems* that assist in enhancing responses and boosting efficiency; *memory* that preserves and applies pertinent information over time; and *multiagent frameworks* that enable collaboration and coordination between several agents to accomplish intricate tasks [4].

12.1.2 Planning and Reasoning in LLM-Powered Autonomous Agents

Planning and reasoning are critical capabilities that enable an autonomous agent to effectively analyze a task, break it down into actionable steps, anticipate possible outcomes, and make informed decisions. These abilities allow the agent to adapt dynamically to new challenges and optimize its responses based on learned experiences [5, 6].

Many LLM-powered autonomous agents use Markov Decision Processes (MDP) for sequential decision-making [7], allowing them to decide optimal actions at each step based on probabilistic reasoning. MDP is a mathematical framework for modeling decision-making problems where outcomes are partly random and partly under the agent's control. It is formally defined as a 5-tuple and is shown in Equation (12.1).

$$(\mathrm{S}, \mathrm{A}, \mathrm{P}, \mathrm{R}, \gamma) \tag{12.1}$$

where S is set of states the agent can be in, A is set of actions the agent can take, $\mathrm{P}(\mathrm{s}' \mid \mathrm{s}, \mathrm{a})$ is Transition probability: the probability of moving to state s' from state s after taking action a, $R(s, a)$ is Reward function: the reward received for taking action a in state s, γ is discount factor: determines the importance of future rewards $(0 \leq \gamma \leq 1)$.

The goal of an agent is to learn an optimal policy π^* that maximizes the total expected reward over time and is shown in Equation (12.2).

$$\mathrm{V}(\mathrm{s}) = \min_{a} \left[R(s,a) + \gamma \sum_{s'} P\left(\mathrm{s}' \mid \mathrm{s}, \mathrm{a}\right) \; V(s') \right] \tag{12.2}$$

where V(s) is the value function, representing the expected cumulative reward from state s, and $\pi^*(s)$ is the optimal policy, mapping states to the best action that maximizes rewards.

For instance, a virtual assistant enhanced by an LLM that is tasked with creating a multistep travel itinerary would have to determine aspects like which flight to select, the most appropriate hotel fitting the user's budget and desired location, the easiest transportation methods, along with appropriate activities and bookings for sightseeing—all while taking into account the user's preferences and aiming to enhance the overall travel experience.

The problem can be modeled as an MDP, where:

- **States (S):** Different stages of trip planning (e.g., searching for flights, selecting hotels, finalizing bookings).
- **Actions (A):** Possible choices at each step (e.g., selecting an airline, booking a 5-star hotel, choosing a rental car).

- **Transition Probabilities (P):** The likelihood of moving to the next stage based on the user's preferences.
- **Rewards (R):** Assign higher rewards for optimal selections based on user priorities (e.g., best price, shortest travel time).

The virtual assistant will iteratively optimize the selections using the MDP framework to ensure that the user's travel plan is cost-effective, convenient, and aligned with their preferences.

Practical uses of planning and reasoning in LLM-driven autonomous agents encompass self-driving cars that assess road conditions and traffic to make navigation choices in real time, AI chatbots that adapt their customer support replies according to the flow of conversation, and healthcare assistants that enhance patient treatment strategies by utilizing medical histories and available resources. By employing Markov Decision Processes, these agents can reason, strategize, and execute intricate decisions with minimal human involvement, facilitating highly efficient automation powered by AI.

12.1.3 Feedback in LLM-Powered Autonomous Agents

Feedback plays a crucial role in refining the decision-making process of LLM-powered autonomous agents. It enables the agent to learn from past interactions, adjust its strategies, and continuously improve performance. Feedback mechanisms allow the system to detect errors, adapt to new scenarios, and optimize responses based on user preferences or environmental changes [8, 9].

Feedback mechanisms can be categorized into several types, including reinforcement learning (RL)-based feedback, in which agents acquire knowledge through rewards and punishments; human-in-the-loop (HITL) feedback, which integrates human input to enhance decision-making; implicit versus explicit feedback, which differentiates between indirect signals from users and direct contributions; and multimodal feedback in physical contexts, which entails analyzing signals from different sensory inputs like sight, sound, or touch.

12.1.3.1 Reinforcement Learning-Based Feedback

Many LLM-powered agents utilize RL, where they receive rewards or penalties based on their actions. This helps the agent gradually learn the best strategy to maximize long-term success [2].

The core mathematical formulation of RL-based feedback follows the Bellman equation, where the updated value function $Q(s,a)$ is given in Equation (12.3).

$$Q(s,a) \leftarrow Q(s,a) + \alpha[R(s,a) + \gamma \max_{a'} Q(s',a') - Q(s,a)] \tag{12.3}$$

where $Q(s,a)$ is expected reward for taking action a in state s, $R(s,a)$ is immediate reward received, α is learning rate, determining how much new experiences influence past knowledge, γ is discount factor, controlling how much future rewards matter, $\max_{a'} Q(s',a')$ is maximum estimated future reward.

For instance, a customer support chatbot that learns on its own improves future interactions by adapting based on user feedback. When a response is deemed helpful, it gets a positive reinforcement (+1), encouraging similar responses in subsequent interactions. On the other hand, if a response is considered unhelpful, it incurs a negative penalty (−1), which motivates the chatbot to refine and enhance its answers for comparable questions. As this feedback-driven learning continues over time, it enables the chatbot to increase the accuracy of its responses and boost user satisfaction.

12.1.3.2 Human-in-the-Loop (HITL) Feedback

In some cases, feedback involves human oversight, where experts validate and fine-tune the agent's decisions. This is particularly useful in high-stakes applications like healthcare, finance, and cybersecurity [10].

HITL feedback [11] incorporates human supervision into the decision-making process, allowing experts to confirm and modify the outputs generated by the agent. This can be mathematically expressed as an optimization process in which the agent's policy $\pi\left(a|s\right)$ is adjusted based not only on rewards from the environment but also on corrections or labels provided by humans. This method proves particularly beneficial in critical fields like healthcare, finance, and cybersecurity, where the consequences of mistakes are significant, and expert contributions enhance both reliability and safety.

For instance, a medical assistant powered by AI might propose treatment options based on a patient's symptoms, which a physician subsequently assesses and amends if needed. The AI gains insights from these expert adjustments, steadily refining its diagnostic suggestions for the future. This ongoing cycle of feedback boosts the system's precision and dependability over time.

12.1.3.3 Implicit vs. Explicit Feedback

Implicit vs. explicit feedback [12] can be formalized within a learning framework where feedback serves as a signal to update the model's parameters θ.

- **Explicit feedback** is represented as direct labels or scores y provided by users, allowing supervised updates via loss functions such as $L(\hat{y}, y)$, where $\hat{y}$ is the model's prediction. Users provide ratings, comments, or corrections (e.g., rating an AI-generated email draft as useful or irrelevant).
- **Implicit feedback** is inferred from user behavior, modeled through probabilistic functions like $P(a \mid s, \theta)$, where the system updates its policy based on observed actions (e.g., clicks, skips, or selections), often using techniques like inverse reinforcement learning or collaborative filtering. The system monitors user behavior (e.g., if a user ignores an AI-suggested route, the system learns to avoid similar suggestions in the future).

This dual feedback mechanism enables the system to adapt by learning both from overt corrections and subtle behavioral cues.

For instance, a customized film recommendation system utilizes explicit feedback when users indicate their preferences with a thumbs up or down on suggested movies, and implicit feedback by tracking behaviors like completing a movie or skipping it. By examining these feedback trends, the AI constantly adjusts its recommendations to more closely match the unique preferences of each user.

12.1.3.4 Multimodal Feedback in Physical Environments

In physical settings, the multimodal feedback for robots and autonomous systems can be represented as a combination of signals $F = \{f_1, f_2, \ldots, f_n\}$ gathered from various sources such as sensors, cameras, and external commands. Each feedback modality f_i delivers input data x_i that the system integrates through a fusion function $g(x; \theta)$, where $x = \{x_1, x_2, \ldots, x_n\}$ signifies the multimodal inputs and θ represents the parameters of the model. This integration allows the agent to more effectively update its state or policy by utilizing complementary information from different channels [13, 14].

For robots and autonomous systems, feedback comes from multiple sources, including sensors, cameras, and external commands.

For instance, an autonomous drone maneuver by gathering multimodal feedback from sensors that monitor wind speed, identify obstacles, and track GPS position. It modifies its flight trajectory in real-time according to these environmental data, and when a human operator steps in to adjust its direction, the drone retains this guidance to prevent similar mistakes later on. This combination of various feedback channels guarantees safe and effective autonomous functioning.

Real-life examples of feedback in LLM-powered agents include search engines such as Google, which modify their rankings based on user click-through rates and feedback; e-commerce sites like Amazon, which enhance product suggestions by analyzing purchasing histories and browsing patterns; and virtual assistants like Siri and Alexa, which enhance their speech recognition and contextual comprehension by learning from user interactions. Feedback—whether obtained through RL, human review, implicit indicators, or multimodal sensing—is crucial for ongoing learning, fostering increased adaptability, precision, and efficiency in these autonomous systems.

12.1.4 Memory in LLM-Powered Autonomous Agents

Memory is a crucial component of LLM-powered autonomous agents, allowing them to retain, retrieve, and utilize past experiences for improved decision-making. Unlike traditional rule-based systems that operate statelessly, memory-enabled agents can adapt over time, enhancing their ability to handle long-term interactions, contextual understanding, and learning from past mistakes [15, 16].

Types of memory [17] in autonomous agents include short-term memory (STM), which supports context awareness during interactions; long-term memory (LTM), enabling learning from past experiences; episodic memory, responsible for retaining task-specific information; and semantic memory, which stores generalized knowledge applicable across different tasks.

12.1.4.1 Short-Term Memory (STM): Context Awareness

STM [20] allows agents to temporarily store recent interactions for maintaining context in a conversation or task. In LLMs, this is often managed by a context window—a fixed number of recent tokens that the model can consider.

For instance, a virtual assistant keeps track of the conversation history throughout a session by retaining details like the user's flight destination. When a user asks to reserve a flight to New York, the assistant retrieves this information in subsequent inquiries—prompting for the date and time—thus ensuring the exchange stays coherent and contextually relevant.

Given a sequence of tokens $\{x_1, x_2, \ldots\ldots, x_t\}$, an LLM updates its state using attention mechanisms and is shown in Equation (12.4).

$$h_t = \text{Attention}(Q, K, V) = \text{softmax}\left(\frac{QK^T}{\sqrt{d_k}} V\right) \tag{12.4}$$

where Q, K, V are query, key and value matrices, d_k is the dimension of key vectors, h_t is the updated context representation.

STM is reset when the session ends, meaning agents with only STM lack long-term adaptability.

12.1.4.2 Long-Term Memory (LTM): Learning from Past Experiences

LTM [19] allows an agent to keep information for an extended period, facilitating personalized experiences and the application of historical knowledge. For instance, a tailored AI tutor recalls a student's previous performances and modifies upcoming lessons based on that; if the student has difficulty with calculus, the AI suggests simpler exercises before advancing. In LLM applications, LTM is usually kept outside the model and is stored in systems such as vector databases (like FAISS or Pinecone) for quick similarity searches, or in knowledge graphs for organized information storage. The retrieval process includes embedding comparisons, where a user query q is aligned with stored memory vectors M_i by selecting $\hat{M}$ and is shown in the following Equation (12.5).

$$\hat{M} = \underset{M_i}{\text{argmax}} \text{cosine\_similarity}(q, M_i) \tag{12.5}$$

where cosine_similarity can be calculated using Equation (12.6).

$$\text{sim}(A, B) = \frac{A.B}{\|A\| \, \|B\|} \tag{12.6}$$

12.1.4.3 Episodic Memory: Task-Specific Retention

Episodic memory [20] stores information for specific tasks and is later forgotten if not reinforced. It is useful for workflows requiring step-by-step tracking.

Episodic memory in autonomous agents can be represented as a time-sensitive storage system, denoted as E_t, that keeps task-specific information for a limited period. At any given time t, the memory state E_t consists of a collection of data relevant to the task, represented as $\{e_1, e_2, \ldots, e_n\}$, which may decay or be eliminated over time unless it is reinforced by a function $R(E_t)$. This can be mathematically formulated as follows using Equation (12.7).

$$E_{t+1} = \begin{cases} E_t \cup \{e_{new}\} & \textit{if reinforced}\left(R\left(E_t\right) = 1\right) \\ \gamma E_t & \textit{otherwise, with } 0 \leq \gamma < 1 \end{cases} \tag{12.7}$$

where γ is a decay factor representing forgetting, and e_{new} is new task-specific information added at time t. This episodic memory enables step-by-step tracking within workflows but allows irrelevant data to fade when not reinforced.

An autonomous coding assistant, for instance, relies on episodic memory to keep track of the order of debugging steps during a single programming session. This capability allows it to assist developers by monitoring their progress and offering pertinent suggestions to help resolve errors more effectively.

12.1.4.4 Semantic Memory: Generalized Knowledge Storage

Semantic memory [18] is the part of memory that holds general knowledge about the world, encompassing facts, concepts, meanings, and relationships that are not linked to specific experiences. In the realm of AI, semantic memory allows agents to store and organize information such as categories, rules, language, and abstract ideas, which they can utilize when reasoning about new situations. This type of memory facilitates general cognitive abilities by enabling AI systems to apply previously acquired principles, definitions, or patterns to new but related scenarios. For instance, if an AI understands the concept of gravity, it can leverage that knowledge to predict the movement of objects in unfamiliar settings. By maintaining a well-structured and adaptable knowledge base, semantic memory improves the flexibility and scalability of intelligent behavior across a range of tasks.

Semantic memory can be expressed mathematically as a structured knowledge base K, which includes a collection of facts $F = \{f_1, f_2, \ldots, f_n\}$ and concepts $C = \{c_1, c_2, \ldots, c_m\}$. In this framework, each fact f_i represents a relation $R(c_j, c_k)$ between the concepts c_j and c_k. This knowledge base empowers an AI agent to engage in general reasoning by utilizing inference rules I, enabling the agent to derive inferences from any input situation S, such that $I(K, S) \rightarrow A$, where A denotes a collection of relevant actions, conclusions, or predictions. For example, if $f = IsA(\text{dog}, \text{mammal})$ and $f' =$ mammals have lungs, the system can deduce that dogs have lungs through transitive reasoning. This formal representation allows the system to extrapolate from existing knowledge to new inputs, facilitating adaptable and scalable behavior.

Memory in agents powered by LLMs enables them to go beyond just reactive behavior, facilitating ongoing personalization and continuous skill enhancement. For instance, self-driving cars utilize semantic memory to remember and enact general traffic regulations, such as halting at red signals, irrespective of their location. To effectively manage memory, approaches like memory pruning (eliminating outdated or less relevant information), reinforcement-based updates (keeping frequently accessed or positively reinforced knowledge), and hybrid memory models (balancing short-term recollection with long-term storage) are applied. These methods enable AI systems to evolve and better their functionality over time. In practical scenarios, memory improves performance in various fields: healthcare AI incorporates patient history for customized diagnoses, finance AI capitalizes on market trends for more intelligent investment decisions, and customer support AI recalls previous interactions to resolve problems more efficiently.

12.1.5 Multiagent Systems in LLM-Powered Autonomous Agents

Multiagent systems (MAS) [21, 22, 23–] consist of multiple independent agents that interact within a common environment to collaboratively, competitively, or coordinatively achieve complex objectives. In the realm of LLM-powered autonomous agents, MAS facilitates intelligent systems to communicate, exchange knowledge, and delegate tasks, leading to improved decision-making and problem-solving efficiency. These agents can be homogeneous, meaning all agents share the same structure and roles—like in swarm robotics—or heterogeneous, where agents have different functions and areas of expertise, such as specialized AI assistants in healthcare collaborating to deliver comprehensive patient care.

MAS can be expressed mathematically as a collection of agents $A = \{a_1, a_2, ..., a_n\}$, each functioning within a common environment E while having distinct states $s\_i \in S$, actions $a\_i\ (t) \in A$, and policies $\pi_i : S \rightarrow A$. In LLM-powered MAS, agents communicate information through communication functions $C: A \times A \rightarrow M$, where M represents the message space, facilitating knowledge sharing and synchronized task performance. Task distribution among agents is characterized by a mapping $T: G \rightarrow A$, where G denotes the set of goals or subtasks. Agents may be homogeneous, which means $\forall a_i, a_j \in A,\ \pi_i = \pi_j$ and $A_i = A_j$, as observed in swarm robotics; or heterogeneous, where $\exists a_i, a_j \in A$ such that $\pi_i \neq \pi_j$ or $A_i \neq A_j$, as is common in contexts like healthcare, where agents undertake specialized functions. This framework facilitates cooperative problem-solving and effective coordination across various environments. Mathematically MAS can be represented as a tuple and is given in Equation (12.8).

$$M = (S, A, T, R, N) \tag{12.8}$$

Where S is Set of states representing the environment, A is Set of actions available to agents, T is Transition function: $T(s, a)$ defines the next state, R is Reward function that evaluates actions, N is Number of agents in the system.

Each agent i follows an individual policy $\pi_i(a \mid s)$ that maps states to actions, enabling cooperative decision-making.

MASs are classified into three categories: cooperative, competitive, and hybrid systems, depending on the interaction dynamics among agents. In cooperative MAS, agents collaborate toward a common objective, coordinating their efforts to enhance overall performance. Competitive MAS feature agents with opposing goals, where each agent seeks to maximize its own benefit, often represented through game-theoretic models. Hybrid MAS integrate both cooperative and competitive traits, allowing agents to cooperate in certain situations while engaging in competition in others. Communication is vital in all categories, facilitating the exchange of information, negotiation, and synchronization of actions to promote more effective and adaptable decision-making within the system.

12.1.5.1 Cooperative Multiagent Systems

In cooperative MASs, agents collaborate to accomplish a shared objective by exchanging information, distributing tasks, and coordinating their actions. A tangible example of this can be seen in AI-driven healthcare systems [24, 25, –26], where various specialized agents work together to improve patient care. For example, a Diagnosis Agent analyzes medical imaging data, including X-rays and MRIs, to identify irregularities, while a Symptom Checker Agent reviews symptoms reported by patients and clinical histories to produce potential diagnoses. At the same time, a Treatment Recommendation Agent applies historical treatment data and contemporary medical protocols to suggest the most effective treatment options. These agents interact and share their discoveries in real time, updating a communal knowledge base K, which enables them to enhance their individual insights and contribute to a more precise and comprehensive diagnostic process. This collaborative strategy not only boosts diagnostic accuracy but also facilitates quicker, more tailored medical decisions. In cooperative MAS, all agents optimize a shared reward function and is given in Equation (12.9).

$$R_{total} = \sum_{i=1}^{N} R_i(s,a) \tag{12.9}$$

where, $R_i(s,a)$ is the individual agent's reward.

12.1.5.2 Competitive Multiagent Systems

In competitive MASs [27, 28], agents pursue conflicting objectives, each striving to maximize its own performance, often at the cost of others. A notable illustration can be seen in AI-powered cybersecurity, where a defensive AI agent and a malicious AI agent partake in a continuous adversarial interaction. The Defensive Agent persistently monitors network activity, identifies anomalies, and implements countermeasures to block unauthorized access. Conversely, the Malicious Agent uses tactics such as exploiting vulnerabilities, conducting phishing campaigns, or avoiding detection through obfuscation methods. Both agents continually adjust their behaviors—utilizing RL or adversarial modeling—to foresee and counter each other's strategies. This relationship constitutes a real-time, evolving rivalry, where each agent learns from previous encounters, refines its policy π_i, and enhances decision-making grounded in observed states $s \in S$ and rewards $r \in \mathbb{R}$. Such competitive MAS frameworks are essential for modeling threat landscapes, evaluating defense effectiveness, and improving the resilience of security systems in high-stakes contexts. In competitive MAS, each agent chooses an optimal strategy, leading to Nash equilibrium and is shown in Equation (12.10).

$$\pi_i^* = arg\max_{\pi_i}\min_{\pi_{-i}} R_i \tag{12.10}$$

where, π_i^* is the optimal strategy for agent i, considering opponents' actions.

12.1.5.3 Hybrid Multiagent Systems

In hybrid MASs [29, 30], independent agents exhibit both collaborative and competitive actions based on their objectives, responsibilities, and the limitations of their surroundings. Collaboration facilitates the exchange of information, task coordination, and the attainment of shared goals, whereas competition fosters innovation, resource efficiency, and strategic choices. This combination of behaviors allows the system to operate more effectively and adaptively in intricate, shifting environments—striking a balance between group efficiency and individual performance.

Let $A = \{a_1, a_2, \ldots, a_n\}$ denote a set of agents operating in a shared environment ε. Each agent $a_i \in A$ is defined by its policy $\pi_i : O_i \rightarrow A_i$, mapping observations O_i to actions A_i.

In a *hybrid MAS*, the interaction between agents combines elements of *cooperation* and *competition*. Formally, this can be modeled as a *stochastic game* $G = (A, S, \{A_i\}, T, \{R_i\})$.

whereSisthestatespace, A_i istheactionspaceofagent a_i, $T : S \times A_1 \times \cdots \times A_n \rightarrow \Delta(S)$ is the transition function, $R_i : S \times A_1 \times \cdots \times A_n \rightarrow R$ is the reward function for agent a_i, $\Delta(S)$ denotes the set of probability distributions over S.

The system is *cooperative* when the agents share a common reward function $R_i = R_j$, $\forall i, j$, optimizing a global objective and is given in Equation (12.11).

$$\max_{\pi_1,\ldots,\pi_n} \mathbb{E}\left[\sum_{t=0}^{\infty} \gamma^t R\left(s_t, a_t\right)\right] \tag{12.11}$$

It becomes *competitive* when each agent maximizes its individual reward, potentially at the expense of others and is shown in Equation (12.12).

$$\max_{\pi_i} \mathbb{E}\left[\sum_{t=0}^{\infty} \gamma^t R_i\left(s_t, a_t\right)\right] \tag{12.12}$$

A *hybrid* setting introduces *subgroups* $C_k \subseteq A$, where agents in the same subgroup cooperate (shared R_i), and different subgroups compete (conflicting R_i). This can be represented as follows in Equation (12.13).

$$A = \begin{cases} \bigcup_{k=1}^{K} C_k \; with \; R_i = R_j & if \; i, j \in c_k \\ R_i \neq R_j & otherwise \end{cases} \tag{12.13}$$

This framework enables the modeling of situations such as mixed-motive games, resource distribution, multiteam RL, and beyond, where agents need to develop strategies that manage both cooperation and competition.

Hybrid MASs demonstrate a dynamic combination of cooperation and competition, particularly noticeable in networks of autonomous vehicles. For example, self-driving cars exhibit collaborative behavior by exchanging information with neighboring vehicles to prevent collisions and enhance traffic flow. Conversely, rideshare AI agents—often representing competing service providers—function competitively, competing for passengers, optimizing their routes, and modifying pricing strategies to increase individual profits. Such systems necessitate real-time role adjustment, allowing agents to seamlessly transition between cooperative and competitive modes depending on environmental factors, system goals, and situational requirements.

12.2 LLMS IN PHYSICAL ENVIRONMENTS

LLMs [31, 32] are progressively being incorporated into tangible physical environments to improve intelligent behavior in systems such as robots and autonomous agents. These applications extend beyond conventional natural language processing tasks, allowing machines to perceive, reason, and act in dynamic and unstructured environments.

In the field of robotics, for instance, LLMs can function as advanced planners that decode human instructions and transform them into actionable objectives. A robot fitted with an LLM could receive a spoken command like "Retrieve the red mug from the kitchen." To accomplish this task, the system must first comprehend the natural language input, utilize computer vision to recognize objects and surroundings, and implement motion planning and control to navigate to the kitchen and grasp the correct mug. LLMs are frequently combined with models like CLIP for visual grounding and with RL policies that manage low-level control.

In navigation scenarios, such as directing a drone or an autonomous vehicle, LLMs can interpret mission directives given in natural language—such as "Examine the area surrounding the fallen tree and return to base"—and convert them into waypoint-based plans, adapting to environmental changes based on sensor information.

These systems typically integrate multiple AI modalities:

- Natural language processing for comprehending user intentions
- Computer vision for identifying objects, scenes, and reference points
- RL or various control algorithms for decision-making and motion execution

Recent research initiatives like OpenAI's SayCan, Google DeepMind's RT-2, and Meta's VC-1 showcase how LLMs can anchor language in real-world physical tasks, enabling robots to execute multistep instructions with impressive flexibility and generalization. This integration signifies a substantial advancement towards creating more intelligent, interactive, and adaptable physical agents.

12.2.1 Manipulation

Manipulation [33] entails the capability of autonomous agents—such as robotic arms, drones, or humanoid robots—to engage with and alter objects in their surroundings, carrying out activities like grasping, assembling, pushing, or repositioning items. Successful robotic manipulation necessitates a blend of perception, control, and reasoning. A key obstacle is perception, which requires accurately identifying and comprehending the characteristics and spatial arrangement of objects by utilizing data from cameras, LiDAR, depth sensors, or tactile feedback. Robots must differentiate between materials, recognize object boundaries, and estimate poses, even in disorganized or dynamic environments. Dexterity presents another significant challenge, demanding fine motor skills and coordination, particularly for tasks such as threading a needle, opening jars, or managing delicate items. This involves accurately actuating multijointed manipulators or robotic hands, often aiming to replicate human-like control. Lastly, adaptability is crucial for functioning in unstructured settings—robots need to generalize across objects with diverse shapes, textures, sizes, and weights, often without any prior experience. Solutions may include real-time learning, tactile sensing, and feedback loops that modify grip strength or trajectory during tasks. Collectively, these challenges render robotic manipulation a complex and continually developing field at the crossroads of mechanics, AI, and perception.

12.2.1.1 LLM-Driven Manipulation Model

Models that leverage LLMs for manipulation enhance the functionality of robots by merging language comprehension with perception, control, and learning. Vision-language models (VLMs) empower robots to discern and establish object references by associating visual data with textual descriptions—such as recognizing "the green bottle next to the red book." RL [34] is applied to refine motion planning and control techniques by gaining insights from previous interactions, enabling the robot to enhance its performance over time through experimentation. Human interaction with LLMs allows users to issue high-level, intuitive commands in everyday language—like "stack the boxes by size"—which the LLM decodes and converts into actionable instructions. Fundamental to these processes are mathematical models such as inverse kinematics (IK), which determine the joint positions required for a robot's end-effector to reach a designated location and orientation in space, thereby ensuring accurate and viable movement. Collectively, these elements empower LLMs to act as an effective bridge between human intentions and robotic execution in intricate manipulation tasks [35, 36]. Here, inverse kinematics helps robots determine the required joint angles to reach a specific position and is formulated as follows in Equation (12.14).

$$\theta = IK(x, y, z) \tag{12.14}$$

where θ is joint angles, (x, y, z) is target position. This equation ensures a robot can accurately move its arm to grasp an object.

In an industrial environment, a factory robot guided by a LLM can assemble electronic parts in response to verbal instructions from humans. When an individual says, "Pick up the resistor and place it on the circuit board," the LLM analyzes the command, while computer vision technology locates the resistor. The robot then utilizes inverse kinematics (IK) to determine the required joint movements to grasp and correctly position the component. Upon finishing the task, the LLM verifies the successful completion and asks a follow-up question like, "Should I proceed with the next step?" This approach fosters smooth collaboration between humans and robots through natural language, minimizing the necessity for manual programming and enhancing efficiency in ever-changing manufacturing settings.

12.2.2 Navigation

Navigation describes an autonomous agent's capability to move intentionally and effectively throughout its surroundings while safely steering clear of obstacles—an essential skill for technologies such as self-driving vehicles, delivery drones, and service robots. Successful navigation involves various interrelated challenges. Path planning entails determining the most effective or safest pathway from a starting location to a target, often utilizing algorithms like A* or Dijkstra's, or employing learning-based methods for mor e intricate, dynamic environments. Obstacle avoidance is about identifying and reacting to unforeseen objects or alterations in the environment instantly, using sensor data from LiDAR, cameras, or ultrasonic devices to avert collisions. Localization is another critical aspect, wherein the robot must reliably ascertain its current location within a known or partially known map via methods like SLAM (Simultaneous Localization and Mapping), GPS, or visual odometry. Collectively, these components empower autonomous systems to navigate intricate and unpredictable settings with limited human oversight, guaranteeing both task efficiency and safety.

12.2.2.1 LLM-Driven Navigation Model

LLMs improve robotic navigation by employing sophisticated methods that merge perception, learning, and decision-making. Neural-simultaneous localization and mapping (SLAM) allows robots to create and update environmental maps in real time while keeping track of their own position, enabling precise navigation in unknown or dynamic areas. RL enhances this by allowing agents to discover optimal navigation techniques through experimentation, thereby refining their ability to choose safe and efficient routes based on prior experiences. Moreover, multimodal AI is essential as it integrates data from diverse sources—such as natural language commands, visual input from cameras, and sensory data like LiDAR or inertial measurements—enabling the LLM to make navigation decisions that are more aware of context and adaptable. This combination empowers autonomous systems to comprehend intricate environments and respond intelligently to both their physical setting and human instructions. A* algorithm is commonly used for navigation, where the cost function is calculated using Equation (12.15).

$$f(n) = g(n) + h(n) \tag{12.15}$$

where $f(n)$ is total estimated cost, $g(n)$ is cost from start node to current node, and $h(n)$ is heuristic estimate of cost to the goal. This ensures the shortest and safest path selection.

For instance, an autonomous vehicle powered by a LLM maneuvers through city traffic by utilizing various AI components to function safely and efficiently. The

LLM interprets real-time traffic information—such as incidents, congestion, or road blockages—to deliver context-sensitive insights. At the same time, the A* algorithm determines the most efficient route to reach the destination, while computer vision systems identify pedestrians, vehicles, and other obstacles in the surroundings. The vehicle continuously modifies its speed and direction in response to evolving conditions, ensuring smooth and secure travel. This combination of language comprehension, planning, and perception promotes more intelligent decision-making and improves overall driving performance in intricate urban environments.

SUMMARY

This chapter examines how autonomous agents are powered by LLMs, which allow them to carry out intricate, goal-directed tasks. Key features like planning and reasoning for decision-making, feedback mechanisms for behavior adaptation, memory for storing and recalling previous interactions, and MASs where multiple LLM-driven agents cooperate or coordinate are described first, starting with LLM-steered agents. The function of LLMs in physical environments is then examined, including navigation (moving through and comprehending physical places) and manipulation tasks (interacting with and changing items). All things considered, the chapter demonstrates how LLMs go beyond text generation to manage, coordinate, and modify intelligent agents in both virtual and physical environments.

QUESTIONS

1. Define LLM steering in the context of autonomous agents.
2. Explain the role of memory in improving decision-making for LLM-driven autonomous agents.
3. Illustrate with an example how feedback mechanisms can enhance planning in an LLM-based navigation system.
4. Compare single-agent systems and MASs in terms of scalability and reasoning.
5. Critically evaluate the challenges of deploying LLMs in physical environments for manipulation tasks.
6. An LLM-driven navigation system receives 12 commands but executes only 9 correctly. Calculate the execution accuracy percentage.
7. If a MAS consists of 5 agents, and each agent exchanges information with every other agent, how many unique communication links exist?
8. A robot using LLM-based planning takes 15 minutes to complete a navigation task. After integrating feedback, the time reduces by 25%. Calculate the new completion time.
9. Suppose a memory-augmented LLM stores 1.5 GB of interaction data daily. Estimate the total memory required for 30 days, and suggest one compression technique to optimize storage.
10. In a physical environment, an LLM-powered robot successfully manipulates 80 out of 100 objects. If a new reasoning strategy improves performance by 15%, calculate the new success rate.

11. **Case Study:** A smart warehouse uses LLM-powered autonomous agents to manage daily operations. The agents are responsible for planning and reasoning (deciding which packages to pick first), using feedback (learning from mistakes like misplacing items), and storing memory (remembering item locations). In addition, multiple agents work together to coordinate tasks. Robots in the warehouse also operate in the physical environment, where they use manipulation (picking up packages) and navigation (moving safely across aisles). This system reduces human effort and improves efficiency. Discuss how the components of LLM-powered agents (planning, feedback, memory, and MASs) support real-world applications like warehouse automation.

REFERENCES

[1] L. Wang, C. Ma, X. Feng, Z. Zhang, H. Yang, J. Zhang *et al.*, "A Survey on Large Language Model based Autonomous Agents," *Frontiers of Computer Science*, Aug. 2023, doi: 10.1007/s11704-024-40231-1, arXiv:2308.11432.

[2] Z. Liu, J. Chai, X. Zhu, S. Tang, R. Ye, B. Zhang *et al.*, "ML-Agent: Reinforcing LLM Agents for Autonomous Machine Learning Engineering," in *Proc. of the International Conference on Learning Representations (ICLR)*, May 2025, arXiv:2505.23723.

[3] M. A. Ferrag, N. Tihanyi, and M. Debbah, "From LLM Reasoning to Autonomous AI Agents: A Comprehensive Review," arXiv preprint, Apr. 2025, arXiv:2504.19678.

[4] L. Weng, "LLM-powered Autonomous Agents," *Lil'Log*, Jun. 2023. [Online]. https://lilianweng.github.io/posts/2023-06-23-agent/.

[5] J. Chen, H. Li, J. Yang, Y. Liu, and Q. Ai, "Enhancing LLM-Based Agents via Global Planning and Hierarchical Execution," arXiv preprint, Apr. 2025, arXiv:2504.16563.

[6] M. Rawat, A. Gupta, R. Goomer, A. Di Bari, N. Gupta, and R. Pieraccini, "Pre-Act: Multi-Step Planning and Reasoning Improves Acting in LLM Agents," arXiv preprint, May 2025, arXiv:2505.09970.

[7] J. He, S. Chen, F. Zhang, and Z. Yang, "From Words to Actions: Unveiling the Theoretical Underpinnings of LLM-Driven Autonomous Systems," arXiv preprint, May 2024, arXiv:2405.19883.

[8] S. Barua, "Exploring Autonomous Agents through the Lens of Large Language Models: A Review," arXiv preprint, Apr. 2024, doi: 10.48550/arXiv.2404.04442, arXiv:2404.04442.

[9] K. Wang, Y. Lu, M. Santacroce, Y. Gong, C. Zhang, and Y. Shen, "Adapting LLM Agents with Universal Feedback in Communication," arXiv preprint, Oct. 2023, arXiv:2310.01444.

[10] P. Kadam, "Enhancing Financial Fraud Detection with Human-in-the-Loop Feedback and Feedback Propagation," in *Proc. of the International Conference on Machine Learning and Applications (ICMLA)*, Nov. 2024.

[11] Y. Emami, L. Almeida, K. Li, W. Ni, and Z. Han, "Human-In-The-Loop Machine Learning for Safe and Ethical Autonomous Vehicles: Principles, Challenges, and Opportunities," arXiv preprint, Aug. 2024, arXiv:2408.12548.

[12] Y. Zhao, B. Wang, Y. Wang, D. Zhao, R. He, and Y. Hou, "Explicit vs. Implicit: Investigating Social Bias in Large Language Models through Self-Reflection," in *Findings of the Association for Computational Linguistics (ACL)*, Jul. 2025.

[13] E. Zhu *et al.*, "MAPS: Advancing Multi-Modal Reasoning in Expert-Level Physical Science," in *Proc. of the International Conference on Learning Representations (ICLR)*, Jan. 2025, arXiv:2501.10768.
[14] G. Dagan, F. Keller, and A. Lascarides, "Learning the Effects of Physical Actions in a Multi-modal Environment," arXiv preprint, Jan. 2023, arXiv:2301.11845.
[15] Z. Xiong, Y. Lin, W. Xie, P. He, Z. Liu, J. Tang *et al.*, "How Memory Management Impacts LLM Agents: An Empirical Study of Experience-Following Behavior," arXiv preprint, May 2025, arXiv:2502.12110.
[16] W. Xu, K. Mei, H. Gao, J. Tan, Z. Liang, and Y. Zhang, "A-MEM: Agentic Memory for LLM Agents," arXiv preprint, Feb. 2025, arXiv:2502.12110.
[17] Y. Wu, S. Liang, C. Zhang, Y. Wang, Y. Zhang, H. Guo *et al.*, "From Human Memory to AI Memory: A Survey on Memory Mechanisms in the Era of LLMs," arXiv preprint, Apr. 2025, arXiv:2504.15965.
[18] B. Yang, L. Xu, L. Zeng, K. Liu, S. Jiang, W. Lu *et al.*, "ContextAgent: Context-Aware Proactive LLM Agents with Open-World Sensory Perceptions," arXiv preprint, May 2025, arXiv:2505.14668.
[19] X. Jiang, F. Li, H. Zhao, J. Qiu, J. Wang, J. Shao *et al.*, "Long Term Memory: The Foundation of AI Self-Evolution," arXiv preprint, Oct. 2024, arXiv:2410.15665.
[20] M. Pink, Q. Wu, and V. A. Toneva, "Position: Episodic Memory is the Missing Piece for Long-Term LLM Agents," arXiv preprint, Feb. 2025, arXiv:2502.06975.
[21] Y. Wang, and X. Chen, "MIRIX: Multi-Agent Memory System for LLM-Based Agents," arXiv preprint, Jul. 2025, arXiv:2507.07957.
[22] Y. Yang, Q. Peng, J. Wang, Y. Wen, and W. Zhang, "LLM-based Multi-Agent Systems: Techniques and Business Perspectives," arXiv preprint, Nov. 2024, arXiv:2411.14033.
[23] C. Jimenez-Romero, A. Yegenoglu, and C. Blum, "Multi-Agent Systems Powered by Large Language Models: Applications in Swarm Intelligence," arXiv preprint, Mar. 2025, arXiv:2503.03800.
[24] L. Yuan, Z. Zhang, L. Li, C. Guan, and Y. Yu, "A Survey of Progress on Cooperative Multi-agent Reinforcement Learning in Open Environment," arXiv preprint, Dec. 2023, arXiv:2312.01058.
[25] A. Mahajan *et al.*, "Generalization in Cooperative Multi-Agent Systems," arXiv preprint, Feb. 2022, arXiv:2202.00104.
[26] Y. Du, J. Z. Leibo, U. Islam, R. Willis, and P. Sunehag, "A Review of Cooperation in Multi-agent Learning," arXiv preprint, Dec. 2023, arXiv:2312.05162.
[27] W. Li, Z. Ding, S. Karten, and C. Jin, "FightLadder: A Benchmark for Competitive Multi-Agent Reinforcement Learning," in *Proc. of the International Conference on Machine Learning (ICML)*, Jul. 2024.
[28] E. Bahceci, R. Katila, and R. Miikkulainen, "Evolving Strategies for Competitive Multi-Agent Search," arXiv preprint, Jun. 2023, arXiv:2306.10640.
[29] T. Enders, J. Harrison, M. Pavone, and M. Schiffer, "Hybrid Multi-Agent Deep Reinforcement Learning for Autonomous Mobility on Demand Systems," in *Proc. of the International Conference on Machine Learning (ICML)*, 2023, arXiv:2212.07313.
[30] E. S. Fraga, V. Udomvorakulchai, M. Pineda, and L. G. Papageorgiou, "A Multi-agent System for Hybrid Optimization," arXiv preprint, Jan. 2025, arXiv:2501.09563.
[31] Y. Son, M. Kim, S. Kim, S. Han, J. Kim, D. Jang *et al.*, "Subtle Risks, Critical Failures: A Framework for Diagnosing Physical Safety of LLMs for Embodied Decision Making," arXiv preprint, May 2025, arXiv:2505.19933.
[32] M. G. Mecattaf, B. Slater, M. Tešić, J. Prunty, K. Voudouris, and L. G. Cheke, "A Little Less Conversation, a Little more Action, Please: Investigating the Physical

Common-Sense of LLMs in a 3D Embodied Environment," arXiv preprint, Oct. 2024, arXiv:2410.23242.

[33] A. Kumar, and H. Lakkaraju, "Manipulating Large Language Models to Increase Product Visibility," arXiv preprint, Apr. 2024, arXiv:2404.07981.

[34] R. Tan, R. Li, and Z. Zhao, "LLM4MAC: An LLM-Driven Reinforcement Learning Framework for MAC Protocol Emergence," arXiv preprint, Mar. 2025, arXiv:2503.08123.

[35] Z. Wang, Y. Du, J. Zhang, J. Bi, H. Chua, T. Wei *et al.*, "LLM-Driven Dual-Level Multi-Interest Modeling for Recommendation," arXiv preprint, Jul. 2025, arXiv:2507.10917.

[36] N. Gao, Y. Chen, S. Yang, X. Chen, Y. Tian, H. Li *et al.*, "GENMANIP: LLM-Driven Simulation for Generalizable Instruction-Following Manipulation," in *Proc. of the IEEE/CVF Conference on Computer Vision and Pattern Recognition (CVPR)*, Jun. 2025.

13 Evaluation of Large Language Models

Assessing large language models (LLMs) is an essential procedure to thoroughly evaluate their performance across various aspects, such as accuracy, efficiency, robustness, and fairness in different natural language processing (NLP) tasks. With the continuous advancement of leading models like GPT-4, BERT, and PaLM, a comprehensive and meticulous evaluation is required to confirm their dependability and effectiveness when utilized in intricate, real-world applications [1]. These applications cover a broad range of uses, including conversational agents, automated code generation, and sensitive fields like medical diagnosis and legal document analysis, where accuracy and contextual awareness are crucial.

An essential skill of LLMs is natural language understanding (NLU), which allows these models to comprehend, process, and extract significant information from textual content. NLU consists of several key elements: semantic analysis, which interprets the meaning and intent behind words and sentences; syntactic parsing, which analyzes the grammatical structure and relationships within sentences; named entity recognition (NER), which identifies and categorizes entities such as people, organizations, and locations; and sentiment analysis, which identifies the emotional tone or opinion conveyed in the text. Collectively, these processes enable LLMs to understand complex language subtleties and facilitate accurate downstream tasks.

The essential elements of NLU [2] consist of several interconnected processes that allow models to accurately interpret textual information. It starts with text preprocessing, which includes tokenization, removal of stop words, stemming, and lemmatization to ready the raw data for analysis. Next, syntactic parsing is employed to examine the grammatical structure of sentences through techniques such as dependency parsing, which helps to clarify how words relate to one another. Semantic understanding is then vital as it identifies context, entities, and relationships within the text, enabling the model to comprehend the underlying meaning. Lastly, contextual comprehension tackles more intricate language traits, including ambiguous expressions, polysemy (words with various meanings), and discourse relations, ensuring that the model can effectively interpret subtleties and the overall flow of conversation or text.

DOI: 10.1201/9781003650065-13

For instance, if the input is "Could you arrange a flight to Paris for me?", the system recognizes "Paris" as a place, understands the user's goal as making a flight reservation, and provides a reply by gathering and structuring the necessary details required to finalize the flight booking.

Assessing LLMs involves several crucial elements: evaluating their performance to ensure they generate high-quality, coherent, and contextually relevant outputs; identifying and addressing biases to tackle ethical issues such as gender, racial, or political prejudices; examining security and resilience by analyzing their vulnerability to adversarial threats, hallucinations, and misinformation; reviewing scalability and efficiency to assess computational expenses and suitability for extensive deployment; and confirming task-specific effectiveness by measuring capabilities in both NLU and natural language generation (NLG) [3].

Important elements of evaluating LLMs involve assessing NLU, which determines how well models grasp text, respond to inquiries, and interpret context, as well as NLG, which measures the fluency, coherence, and relevance of the text produced. The evaluation process also utilizes established metrics such as Perplexity, BLEU, and ROUGE to quantify model performance, while comparison against standardized datasets like SuperGLUE and SQuAD offers a reliable framework for evaluating different models.

13.1 NATURAL LANGUAGE UNDERSTANDING

NLU is a distinct branch of NLP that allows machines to understand and interpret human language in a more sophisticated manner than mere keyword recognition by capturing the intent, context, and meaning of text. It is essential in a variety of AI applications, including virtual assistants like Siri and Alexa, customer service chatbots, sentiment analysis for monitoring social media, machine translation software like Google Translate, and automated text summarization. NLU enables machines to identify the relationships between words and sentences, recognize named entities such as people, locations, and dates, clarify ambiguities in meaning (for instance, differentiating "bank" as a financial institution from a riverbank), and comprehend the underlying intent behind user queries. This is accomplished through several interconnected elements that collaborate to derive meaningful insights from human language.

13.1.1 Syntax Analysis (Parsing)

Syntax analysis [4], often referred to as parsing, entails scrutinizing the grammatical makeup of a sentence to comprehend the connections among words. For instance, in the sentence "The cat sat on the mat," syntax parsing recognizes "The" as a determiner, "cat" as the noun and subject, "sat" as the verb, "on" as the preposition, and "the mat" as a prepositional phrase. Frequently used methods include dependency parsing, which identifies the relationships between words such as subject–verb–object, and constituency parsing, which decomposes sentences into nested subphrases to uncover their hierarchical organization.

13.1.2 Semantic Analysis

Semantic analysis [5] aims to comprehend the meanings of words and phrases, tackling issues like lexical ambiguity—where a word can have various meanings, such as "bank," which may denote a financial institution or a riverbank—and polysemy, where the meaning of a word shifts based on the context, as seen with "run" in "run a marathon" compared to "run a company." It also addresses synonymy, where different terms convey similar meanings, like "big" and "large." For instance, in the statement "I saw a bat in the park," semantic analysis aids in identifying whether "bat" refers to the creature or a baseball bat by examining the context that surrounds it.

13.1.3 Discourse Integration

Rephrased comprehension of context ensures that the interpretation of sentences remains aligned with the larger context of a conversation or written material [6]. For instance, in a dialogue where Person A inquires, "Did you encounter John today?" and Person B replies, "Yes, he was at the office," understanding discourse integration allows the model to recognize that "he" refers to "John." This ability is vital for functions such as coreference resolution, which identifies pronouns and connects them to the appropriate entities, as well as for sustaining dialogue context in chatbots to deliver coherent and pertinent responses.

13.1.4 Pragmatic Analysis

Pragmatic analysis [7] entails understanding language by taking into account context, tone, and the meanings that are suggested rather than stated explicitly. For example, the phrase "Can you pass the salt?" is literally a question that can be answered with yes or no, but pragmatically it serves as a courteous request. This form of analysis encounters difficulties, such as identifying sarcasm and irony, as well as recognizing subtleties like politeness or aggression in discussions, which are crucial for effectively interpreting and engaging in human communication.

13.2 NATURAL LANGUAGE GENERATION

NLG [8] is an essential aspect of Artificial Intelligence (AI) and NLP, enabling machines to generate coherent, contextually appropriate, and human-like text from both structured data (like databases) and unstructured data (such as raw text). It is particularly important for various applications including chatbots, automated report creation, text summarization, and machine translation, where producing fluent and meaningful language is critical. NLG works in conjunction with NLU—while NLU is focused on interpreting and extracting meaning from text input, NLG is tasked with creating well-structured responses that are grammatically correct and logically aligned with the context. For instance, when AI assistants like ChatGPT answer user questions, they utilize sophisticated NLG methods to convert intricate data and insights into clear, engaging, and contextually relevant language, making the interaction feel both natural and informative.

For instance, when an AI assistant like ChatGPT generates a response to a query, it relies on NLG techniques to ensure the text is clear, logical, and meaningful.

NLG consists of several important stages that convert raw data or inputs into text that is clear, coherent, and suitable for the context. The process kicks off with content determination, which entails identifying and selecting relevant information based on the intended purpose—for instance, a weather update might feature only temperature and conditions for a quick summary, or encompass all factors like humidity and wind speed for a comprehensive report. Following this, text planning (or discourse planning) arranges the content in a logical order to guarantee a smooth flow, such as organizing a financial report with a title followed by in-depth explanations. Sentence planning then specifies the structure of sentences, word choices, and tone to enhance clarity—for example, merging raw data points into a refined sentence that describes revenue growth and new product launches. Lexical selection adapts word choice based on context and audience, differentiating between formal business language and casual phrases. Surface realization makes sure that the resulting text adheres to correct grammar, punctuation, and formatting, converting disjointed data into coherent sentences. Lastly, postprocessing and refinement improve readability by eliminating redundancies and enhancing phrasing, yielding concise and naturally flowing output. Collectively, these stages allow NLG systems to generate well-organized, readable, and engaging text across a variety of areas and applications.

The formula for the probability of generating a sequence of words W in NLG is given by Equation (13.1).

$$\mathrm{P(W)} = \prod_{i=1}^{N} \mathrm{P}\left(\mathrm{w_i} \middle| \mathrm{w_1},\ \mathrm{w_2}, \ldots,\ \mathrm{w_{i-1}}\right) \tag{13.1}$$

where $\mathrm{w_i}$ is the word at position i, and $P(W)$ is the probability of generating a sequence of words.

NLG includes various techniques that have continuously evolved to enhance the fluency, coherence, and contextual relevance of the text produced. The basic method is template-based approaches, which depend on established sentence forms and fixed templates for text generation, making them easy to use but constrained in their flexibility and variety. Statistical approaches utilize probabilistic models and language statistics obtained from extensive corpora to forecast word sequences and produce more varied text, often incorporating methods like n-gram models and Hidden Markov Models. With the advent of deep learning, neural network-based approaches have taken precedence, using architectures like recurrent neural networks, long short-term memory (LSTM) networks, and transformers to capture intricate language patterns and dependencies, allowing for the generation of more natural and context-sensitive text. Recently, pretraining-based approaches have transformed NLG by applying large pretrained language models such as GPT, BERT, and PaLM, which are trained on extensive datasets and fine-tuned for particular tasks, leading to highly fluent, versatile, and human-like text generation across a wide array of applications.

13.2.1 Template-Based Methods

Template-based methods [9] in NLG rely on predefined rules and fixed sentence structures to produce text. These methods use handcrafted templates that specify how information should be organized and presented, which guarantees grammatical correctness and consistency in the output. While they are straightforward to implement and useful for generating predictable, domain-specific content—such as weather reports or financial summaries—their main limitation is a lack of flexibility and variability. Because the output is constrained by the templates, these methods often struggle to generate diverse or creative language, making them less suitable for applications requiring natural, conversational, or highly contextualized responses. If $S = (s_1, s_2, \ldots, S_n)$ represents predefined sentence structures, then output T is computed using the following Equation (13.2).

$$T = f(S, V) \tag{13.2}$$

where V is the set of variable placeholders (e.g., names, dates) replaced dynamically.

13.2.2 Statistical Methods

Statistical methods [10] in NLG utilize probabilistic models to generate text by estimating the likelihood of word sequences based on observed language patterns in large corpora. One common approach is the use of *n-gram language models*, which predict each word in a sequence by considering only the previous $n-1$ words, thereby simplifying the complex dependencies in language while capturing local context effectively. The probability of generating a sequence of words $W = (w_1, w_2, ..., w_N)$ is calculated as the product of conditional probabilities of each word given its preceding $n-1$ words, expressed as follows in Equation (13.3).

$$P(W) = \prod_{i=1}^{N} P\left(w_i \middle| w_{i-(n-1)}, \ldots, w_{i-1}\right) \tag{13.3}$$

where $P\left(w_i \middle| w_{i-(n-1)}, \ldots, w_{i-1}\right)$ represents the conditional probability of a word given its preceding words. These models leverage extensive text datasets to calculate probabilities based on observed word occurrences, allowing for the generation of text that is statistically reasonable and locally cohesive. Nevertheless, although n-gram models are adept at capturing short-term dependencies, they face challenges with long-term context and syntactic structures, restricting their capability to create text that is entirely coherent and contextually aware across longer sections.

13.3 EVALUATION METRICS FOR LANGUAGE MODELS

Evaluation metrics for language models play a crucial role in determining how well a NLU or NLG system interprets, manages, and produces language. These metrics offer quantitative assessments of a model's precision, fluency, coherence, and overall efficacy in grasping and anticipating text, which helps researchers and developers evaluate models, recognize their strengths and weaknesses, and inform enhancements.

13.3.1 Accuracy

Accuracy represents the ratio of correct predictions made by a model compared to the total predictions, acting as a key metric to assess its overall performance. It measures how effectively the model classifies or predicts outcomes accurately, highlighting its capacity to apply knowledge from training data to new, unseen instances. Although accuracy is simple and easy to understand, it is particularly beneficial in balanced datasets but may present a misleading picture in situations with imbalanced data, where additional metrics may be necessary to achieve a fuller understanding of model performance. The accuracy is computed using the following Equation (13.4).

$$\text{Accuracy} = \frac{\text{TP} + \text{TN}}{\text{TP} + \text{TN} + \text{FP} + \text{FN}} \tag{13.4}$$

where true positives (TP) refer to cases where the model accurately identifies positive instances, true negatives (TN) are cases where it correctly identifies negative instances, false positives (FP) arise when the model wrongly predicts a positive case, and false negatives (FN) occur when the model mistakenly predicts a negative case.

For instance, if a sentiment analysis system accurately categorizes 90 reviews out of 100, it achieves an accuracy rate of 90%.

13.3.2 Precision

Precision quantifies the ratio of accurately predicted positive cases compared to all instances identified by the model as positive. It showcases the model's capability to minimize false positives by demonstrating how many of the predicted positives are genuinely relevant. High precision is especially crucial in scenarios where the repercussions of false positives are significant, such as in spam detection or medical diagnoses, as it guarantees that positive predictions are trustworthy and diminishes the likelihood of erroneous positive outcomes. Nevertheless, precision by itself does not consider false negatives, so it is frequently assessed in conjunction with recall for a more comprehensive evaluation. The precision is computed using the following Equation (13.5).

$$\text{Precision} = \frac{\text{TP}}{\text{TP} + \text{FP}} \tag{13.5}$$

For instance, if a spam detection model identifies 50 emails as spam, but only 40 of those are genuinely spam, then the model's precision is calculated by dividing 40 by 50, resulting in 0.8 or 80%.

13.3.3 Recall

Recall measures the ratio of actual positive cases that a model successfully identifies among all true positive instances. It indicates the model's capability to recognize as many relevant positive examples as possible, making it particularly crucial in scenarios where overlooking positive cases presents a significant risk, like in disease diagnosis or fraud detection. A high recall indicates that the model reduces false negatives, ensuring that most true positives are identified. Nonetheless, recall by itself does not consider false positives, so it is frequently balanced with precision to offer a more thorough assessment of a model's effectiveness. The precision is computed using the following Equation (13.6).

$$\text{Recall} = \frac{\text{TP}}{\text{TP} + \text{FN}} \tag{13.6}$$

For instance, if a NER model accurately identifies 70 out of 100 real named entities, its recall rate is 70%.

13.3.4 F1-Score

The F1-Score is a metric that integrates precision and recall into a single figure by calculating their harmonic mean, making it a balanced measure. It offers a thorough assessment of a model's accuracy, particularly in scenarios with imbalanced class distribution or when it's crucial to strike a balance between false positives and false negatives. By taking into account both the number of relevant instances retrieved (recall) and the accuracy of predicted positives (precision), the F1-Score provides a more refined evaluation of a model's overall effectiveness, which is especially beneficial in contexts where relying solely on precision or recall is inadequate. The F1-score is computed using the following Equation (13.7).

$$F1 = 2 \times \frac{\text{Precision} \times \text{Recall}}{\text{Precision} + \text{Recall}} \tag{13.7}$$

For example, If precision is 80% and recall is 60%, then the $F1$ is calculated as follows in Equation (13.8).

$$F1 = 2 \times \frac{0.8 \ \times 0.6}{0.8 + 0.6} = 0.6857 \approx 69\% \tag{13.8}$$

13.3.5 Perplexity (for Language Models)

Perplexity is an essential metric that assesses probabilistic language models by evaluating their ability to anticipate a sequence of words. It measures the model's uncertainty in predicting the next word within a sequence, with reduced perplexity indicating superior predictive performance and increased confidence in its forecasts.

In essence, perplexity illustrates how surprised the model is by the testing data—models exhibiting lower perplexity scores are more adept at capturing the fundamental patterns and structures of language, which makes it a crucial tool for evaluating the effectiveness of language models in applications such as text generation, speech recognition, and machine translation. The perplexity is computed using the following Equation (13.9).

$$PP(W) = P(w_1, w_2, \ldots, w_N)^{-\frac{1}{N}} \tag{13.9}$$

where $P(w_1, w_2, \ldots, w_N)$ is the probability assigned by the model to the sequence of words w_1 through w_N.

13.3.6 BLEU (Bilingual Evaluation Understudy) Score

The Bilingual Evaluation Understudy (BLEU) score is a popular metric for assessing the quality of text generated by machines by evaluating its overlap with one or more human-written reference texts through the analysis of n-grams—sequences of words that appear together. It measures the number of n-grams in the generated text that correspond with those in the reference, reflecting both precision and the extent to which the output resembles human language. BLEU is especially beneficial in areas such as machine translation and text summarization, as it offers an objective gauge of how closely the model's output matches anticipated human responses. However, while BLEU is effective at measuring lexical similarity, it does not capture semantic meaning or fluency fully, which is why it is commonly used alongside other evaluation metrics for a more thorough evaluation. The BLEU is computed using the following Equation (13.10).

$$\text{BLEU} = BP \times \exp\left(\sum_{n=1}^{N} w_n \log p_n\right) \tag{13.10}$$

where Brevity Penalty (BP) penalizes shorter output, and p_n is the precision for n-grams.

13.3.7 ROUGE (Recall-Oriented Understudy for Gisting Evaluation) Score

ROUGE (Recall-Oriented Understudy for Gisting Evaluation) is a metric that assesses the quality of summaries generated by machines by comparing them to summaries created by humans. It consists of various types, including ROUGE-N, which measures the overlap of n-grams, and ROUGE-L, which examines the longest common subsequence (LCS) between texts to capture the structure and fluency at the sentence level. NLU is a crucial domain in artificial intelligence, allowing machines to proficiently interpret and process human language through various elements, such as syntax and semantic analysis, discourse integration, and pragmatic analysis.

The formula for ROUGE-N is calculated using the following Equation (13.11).

$$\text{ROGUE}-\text{N}=\frac{\sum_{S\in\text{Reference Summaries}}\sum_{\text{gram}_n\in S}\text{Count}_{\text{match}}\left(\text{gram}_n\right)}{\sum_{S\in\text{Reference Summaries}}\sum_{\text{gram}_n\in S}\text{Count}\left(\text{gram}_n\right)} \tag{13.11}$$

where gram_n is an n-gram (a contiguous sequence of n words), $\text{Count}_{\text{match}}(\text{gram}_n)$ is the maximum number of n-grams co-occurring in both candidate and reference, the numerator sums the count of overlapping n-grams between candidate and reference, the denominator sums the total n-grams in the reference texts.

The formula for ROUGE-L is calculated using the following Equation (13.12).

$$\text{ROGUE}-\text{L}=\frac{\left(1+\beta^2\right)\times P_{LCS}\times R_{LCS}}{R_{LCS}+\beta^2\times P_{LCS}} \tag{13.12}$$

where β is usually set to prioritize recall, P_{LCS} is the precision of LCS and R_{LCS} is the recall of LCS.

13.3.8 METEOR (Metric for Evaluation of Translation with Explicit ORdering)

METEOR (Metric for Evaluation of Translation with Explicit ORdering) evaluates text similarity by considering exact word matches, stemmed forms, and synonyms to provide a more flexible and semantically aware assessment than simple n-gram overlap metrics. The METEOR score is calculated using the following Equation (13.13).

$$\text{METEOR}=F_{\text{mean}}\times\left(1-P_{\text{frag}}\right) \tag{13.13}$$

where P_{frag} is a penalty for fragmentation,

$$F_{\text{mean}}=\frac{10\times P\times R}{R+9P} \tag{13.14}$$

$$P=\frac{\text{number of matched unigrams}}{\text{total unigrams in candidate}} \tag{13.15}$$

$$R=\frac{\text{number of matched unigrams}}{\text{total unigrams in reference}} \tag{13.16}$$

The evaluation of NLU models utilizes several metrics, such as accuracy, precision, recall, F1-score, perplexity, BLEU, and ROUGE, which collectively offer a thorough evaluation of a model's capacity to understand and generate human language.

13.4 BENCHMARKING LLMS

Benchmarking LLMs is essential for evaluating their performance across various NLU and NLG tasks. Several benchmark datasets and evaluation suites have been designed to measure different aspects of LLM capabilities. This chapter focuses on two key benchmarking frameworks: *SuperGLUE* [11] and *SQuAD* [12].

13.4.1 SUPERGLUE

SuperGLUE (General Language Understanding Evaluation) is an advanced benchmark designed to assess the performance of LLMs on a wide range of complex NLP tasks. It was introduced as an improvement over the original GLUE benchmark, offering more challenging tasks that require reasoning, world knowledge, and commonsense understanding.

SuperGLUE is an extensive benchmark created to assess sophisticated language models on a range of demanding NLP tasks, such as reading comprehension, textual entailment, coreference resolution, and sentence completion. It is specifically designed to be more challenging than its earlier version, GLUE, with the goal of pushing contemporary LLMs past simple sentence comprehension. Furthermore, SuperGLUE offers benchmarks for human performance, enabling a realistic evaluation of model abilities in comparison to human-level understanding.

13.4.1.1 Tasks in SuperGLUE

SuperGLUE consists of eight varied benchmark datasets aimed at assessing a wide array of NLU skills in language models. These include BoolQ, which concentrates on binary question answering that necessitates yes/no responses; CommitmentBank (CB), which measures textual entailment with an emphasis on subjective evaluations; COPA, which assesses causal reasoning by requiring models to select from credible alternatives; MultiRC, a reading comprehension task with multiple-choice questions involving several sentences; ReCoRD, which demands reading comprehension that incorporates commonsense reasoning; Recognizing Textual Entailment (RTE), which evaluates the ability to identify entailment relationships among pairs of texts; Word-in-Context (WiC), which tests lexical semantics by determining whether a word carries the same meaning across different contexts; and the Winograd Schema Challenge (WSC), a challenging task for coreference resolution that necessitates pronoun disambiguation and deep contextual understanding. Collectively, these tasks offer a thorough assessment of a model's capability to navigate intricate linguistic phenomena across various domains.

13.4.2 SQUAD (STANFORD QUESTION ANSWERING DATASET)

SQuAD is one of the most widely used datasets for evaluating reading comprehension and question-answering (QA) models. It consists of passages extracted from Wikipedia, along with human-annotated question-answer pairs. SQuAD, which stands for the Stanford Question Answering Dataset, features two primary versions that vary in complexity and difficulty. SQuAD 1.1 includes more than 100,000 pairs of questions and answers where the responses are directly derived from the text, and every question has a definitive answer. In contrast, SQuAD 2.0 presents questions that may not have answers, thus requiring models to not only locate correct answers when they exist but also to recognize and manage questions that cannot be answered based on the text provided, making it a notably tougher benchmark for reading comprehension systems.

The assessment of models using the SQuAD dataset is based on two main metrics: Exact Match (EM) and F1 Score. Exact Match measures the percentage of predictions that precisely align with any of the correct responses, serving as a stringent indicator of precision. Conversely, the F1 Score analyzes the intersection between the predicted and actual answers by integrating precision and recall, delivering a more detailed evaluation of partial correctness and answer quality. Together, these metrics offer a thorough assessment of a model's capability to accurately comprehend and extract answers from the text.

SUMMARY

The assessment of LLMs is covered in this chapter, with an emphasis on evaluating the NLU and NLG capabilities. It describes important language model metrics, such as perplexity to gauge predictive uncertainty, BLEU to compare text generation to reference translations, and ROUGE to gauge text similarity and summarization. The chapter also discusses benchmarking, emphasizing popular datasets like SQuAD for question answering and SuperGLUE for general language understanding. All things considered, it highlights how methodical assessment guarantees that LLMs fulfill performance, quality, and dependability requirements across a range of jobs.

QUESTIONS

1. A language model assigns probabilities:

$$P(''The'') = 0.2,\ P(''cat'') = 0.05,\ P(''sat'') = 0.1.$$

   Calculate the perplexity of this 3-word sequence.
2. A translation system generates:
   - Reference: "The boy is playing football."
   - Candidate: "The boy playing football."

   Compute the BLEU score (precision for unigram and bigram).
3. Given reference summary: "AI transforms healthcare rapidly." Generated summary: "Healthcare rapidly transforms by AI." Calculate the ROUGE-1 precision and recall.
4. A model produces 100 tokens with a cross-entropy of 2.3. Compute the perplexity and interpret what this value indicates about fluency.
5. Given three candidate translations with BLEU scores of 0.55, 0.62, and 0.48, determine which system performs best. Justify mathematically.

6. The SuperGLUE benchmark contains tasks with the following F1 scores: *BoolQ* = 74, *MultiRC* = 65, *ReCoRD* = 68.Calculate the macro-average score and discuss its significance.
7. Define NLU and Natural Language Generation (NLG) with one real-world example each.
8. Differentiate between BLEU and ROUGE metrics. When is each one preferred?
9. Explain how perplexity can be used to compare the performance of two language models.
10. Compare the SuperGLUE and SQuAD benchmarks in terms of evaluation goals and task diversity.
11. Critically assess why perplexity alone is insufficient to evaluate large language models.
12. Propose a new evaluation pipeline that combines BLEU, ROUGE, and human evaluation for NLG systems.
13. **Case Study:** A research team is testing a new Large Language Model (LLM). To evaluate its NLU, they check how well it answers questions in the SQuAD benchmark. For Natural Language Generation (NLG), they measure the fluency of sentences. They use different metrics: Perplexity to see how well the model predicts words, BLEU to check accuracy against reference texts, and ROUGE to compare summaries. Finally, they test overall performance with SuperGLUE, a standard benchmark for LLM reasoning. Explain why multiple metrics (Perplexity, BLEU, ROUGE) and benchmarks (SQuAD, SuperGLUE) are necessary to evaluate the performance of LLMs.

REFERENCES

[1] Z. Guo, R. Jin, C. Liu, Y. Huang, D. Shi, Supryadi *et al.*, "Evaluating Large Language Models: A Comprehensive Survey," arXiv preprint, Oct. 2023, arXiv:2310.19736.

[2] A. Lenci, "Understanding Natural Language Understanding Systems. A Critical Analysis," arXiv preprint, Mar. 2023, arXiv:2303.04229.

[3] E. Reiter, "Natural Language Generation," *Natural Language Generation*, Springer, Oct. 2024, doi: 10.1007/978-3-031-68582-8, arXiv:2502.14437.

[4] Z. Zhang, Y. Hou, C. Gong, and Z. Li, "Self-Correction Makes LLMs Better Parsers," in *Findings of the Association for Computational Linguistics (EMNLP)*, Apr. 2025, arXiv:2504.14165.

[5] B. J. Walton, M. E. Khatun, J. M. Ghawaly, and A. Ali-Gombe, "Exploring Large Language Models for Semantic Analysis and Categorization of Android Malware," arXiv preprint, Jan. 2025, arXiv:2501.04848.

[6] J. Göpfert, J. M. Weinand, P. Kuckertz, and D. Stolten, "Opportunities for Large Language Models and Discourse in Engineering Design," *Engineering Applications of Artificial Intelligence*, Jun. 2023, doi: 10.1016/j.egyai.2024.100383, arXiv:2306.09169.

[7] B. Ma, Y. Li, W. Zhou, Z. Gong, Y. J. Liu, K. Jasinskaja *et al.*, "Pragmatics in the Era of Large Language Models: A Survey on Datasets, Evaluation, Opportunities and Challenges," in *Proc. of the Association for Computational Linguistics (ACL)*, Jun. 2025.

[8] M. M. Maestre *et al.*, "Beyond Generative Artificial Intelligence: Roadmap for Natural Language Generation," arXiv preprint, Jul. 2024, arXiv:2407.10554.

[9] Y. Zhang, "Training and Evaluating Language Models with Template-based Data Generation," arXiv preprint, Nov. 2024, arXiv:2411.18104.

[10] W. Ji, W. Yuan, E. Getzen, K. Cho, M. I. Jordan, S. Mei *et al.*, "An Overview of Large Language Models for Statisticians," arXiv preprint, Feb. 2025, arXiv:2502.17814.

[11] A. Wang, Y. Pruksachatkun, N. Nangia, J. Michael, F. Hill, O. Levy *et al.*, "SuperGLUE: A Stickier Benchmark for General-Purpose Language Understanding Systems," in *Advances in Neural Information Processing Systems (NeurIPS)*, Dec. 2019, arXiv:1905.00537.

[12] P. Rajpurkar, J. Zhang, K. Lopyrev, and P. Liang, "SQuAD: 100,000+ Questions for Machine Comprehension of Text," in *Proc. of the Conference on Empirical Methods in Natural Language Processing (EMNLP)*, Oct. 2016, arXiv:1606.05250.

14 Applications of Large Language Models

Large language models (LLMs) have greatly changed various industries by automating intricate tasks, improving operational efficiencies, and providing intelligent, data-driven insights. These sophisticated AI systems can comprehend and produce language that resembles human writing, making them applicable in a diverse array of fields.

In content creation, LLMs simplify the process of producing articles, marketing materials, video scripts, and social media posts. They support writers by generating drafts, proposing revisions, enhancing the tone, and even tailoring content for different demographics. In software development, LLMs boost productivity by producing code snippets, elucidating algorithms, identifying bugs, and offering immediate assistance in various programming languages. Tools such as GitHub Copilot illustrate how LLMs can function as coding partners, speeding up development timelines and minimizing manual work. In healthcare, LLMs are utilized to assess clinical information, create patient reports, summarize medical research, and aid in decision-making regarding diagnoses. They can also drive virtual health assistants that help patients with scheduling appointments, managing their medications, and accessing dependable medical information. Within the financial sector, LLMs facilitate customer service automation through smart chatbots, analyze market patterns, produce financial summaries, identify fraudulent activity, and help evaluate risks. Their capacity to process extensive amounts of financial information in real time renders them essential assets for traders, analysts, and banking organizations. In cybersecurity, LLMs support threat detection, incident management, and vulnerability assessments by scrutinizing logs, spotting irregularities, and crafting reports. They assist security professionals in staying updated about new threats and automating routine monitoring activities.

14.1 GENERATIVE APPLICATIONS OF LARGE LANGUAGE MODELS (LLMS)

Generative applications [1–3] of LLMs involve producing human-like text, code, and interactive conversations. These models generate coherent, context-aware content for various industries, including writing, programming, and AI-powered dialogue

DOI: 10.1201/9781003650065-14

systems. By leveraging deep learning techniques, LLMs enhance creativity, automate content generation, and facilitate human-machine interaction.

- Text Generation and Storytelling
- Code Generation with LLMs
- Chatbots and Conversational Agents

14.1.1 Text Generation and Storytelling using Large Language Models

LLMs are transforming how text is generated, enabling the creation of high-quality, human-like content across various domains. These models leverage deep learning to analyze vast amounts of text and generate coherent, context-aware, and creative content.

14.1.1.1 Automated Content Creation

LLMs enhance content creation by producing articles, blogs, and reports with little human input, which makes them extremely useful in journalism, marketing, and business communication. These models can generate real-time news summaries by examining live data feeds, create engaging product descriptions, ads, and promotional emails for marketing teams, and support the development of research summaries, white papers, and technical documentation in academic and professional contexts. For example, the associated press (AP) uses AI to automate financial report generation, improving efficiency and consistency, while marketing tools such as Jasper AI and Copy.ai allow businesses to quickly create persuasive advertising content tailored for their target audiences [4, 5].

14.1.1.2 Creative Writing

LLMs are increasingly influential in creative writing, providing support for fiction, poetry, and screenwriting as AI-driven writing partners for authors and content creators. They offer suggestions for plot developments, character creation, and authentic dialogue for stories and novels, in addition to crafting various poetic styles such as haikus, sonnets, and song lyrics. In the film and television realm, LLMs assist scriptwriters in constructing scenes and dialogues for both movies and TV shows. Tools like Sudowrite aid novelists in overcoming creative blocks and improving narrative flow, while initiatives such as OpenAI's explorations in AI-assisted scriptwriting showcase how these models can spark unique ideas for short films and other creative endeavors [6–8].

14.1.1.3 Personalized Content Generation

AI improves user interaction and customization by adapting content to individual preferences across different platforms. It selects news based on reading patterns, provides personalized content suggestions on streaming services such as Netflix and Spotify, and aids in effective communication through tools like Gmail's Smart Compose, which gives predictive email recommendations. For instance, Google

News employs AI to showcase articles that match a user's interests, while Spotify uses AI to create playlists that mirror each listener's distinct musical preferences, resulting in more tailored and immersive experiences [9–11].

14.1.1.4 Dialogue and Role-Playing

LLMs improve interactive storytelling by enabling AI-driven role-playing experiences in games and virtual settings. They power dynamic nonplayer characters in video games, facilitating fluid and responsive dialogue, and also support chatbots designed for role-playing that serve as virtual companions in storytelling [12, 13]. In both entertainment and education, LLMs create engaging, interactive narratives that adapt to user choices in real-time. For example, AI Dungeon provides immersive adventure storytelling where the AI crafts storylines based on player interactions, while Netflix's Black Mirror: Bandersnatch showcases how AI can enable branching narratives in interactive film experiences.

14.1.2 Code Generation with Large Language Models

LLMs are revolutionizing software development by assisting in code generation, debugging, and documentation. These AI-powered models enhance programming efficiency, reduce development time, and provide intelligent code suggestions. They are widely used in software engineering, automation, and AI-driven development environments [14, 15].

14.1.2.1 Automated Code Generation

LLMs are capable of producing functional code snippets, entire applications, and boilerplate code directly from natural language instructions, greatly speeding up the software development process [16–18]. They convert human-written descriptions into runnable code, streamline the creation of standard templates to minimize repetitive tasks, and offer smart code completions and suggestions for more efficient programming. Tools such as GitHub Copilot, which is powered by OpenAI Codex, aid developers by proposing and completing code lines in real-time, while Codex can transform text prompts into code in various languages like Python, JavaScript, and others, enhancing both accessibility and productivity in coding.

14.1.2.2 AI-Assisted Debugging and Code Optimization

LLMs contribute to enhancing code quality by identifying errors, offering solutions, and optimizing performance. They are capable of spotting syntax errors and logical inconsistencies, reorganizing code to improve readability and maintainability, and providing suggestions for increasing execution speed and efficiency. Tools like DeepCode utilize AI to reveal security weaknesses and performance issues, while Tabnine provides smart code completions that assist developers in writing cleaner, more precise code with improved speed and consistency.

14.1.2.3 Code Documentation and Explantation

LLMs facilitate the creation of documentation, enhancing the clarity, accessibility, and maintainability of codebases. They can add explanatory comments to complex code, provide high-level summaries of functions and classes, and transform natural language directives into organized pseudocode to clarify logic and intent. Tools like Codeium aid developers by automatically generating in-line comments and documentation, while Amazon CodeWhisperer offers AI-generated code explanations to assist users in understanding and navigating large or unfamiliar codebases more efficiently [19, 20].

14.1.2.4 AI-Driven Software Testing

LLMs aid in software testing by helping to draft and run test cases, improving both reliability and code quality [21, 22]. They can automatically create unit tests based on the logic of a function, recommend additional edge cases to enhance test coverage, and even employ predictive models to detect potential bugs before they arise. Tools such as Diffblue Cover harness AI to generate unit tests for Java applications, while mutation testing tools use AI to develop test cases designed to expose security vulnerabilities and performance issues, resulting in more robust and resilient software systems.

14.1.2.5 AI-Powered Low-Code and No-Code Development

LLMs make software development easier for those without programming expertise by facilitating coding through natural language and user-friendly interfaces [23, 24]. They empower users to build applications using drag-and-drop functionalities that convert inputs into working code, automate backend tasks with AI-driven app developers, and enable programming via voice or chat where users articulate desired features in simple language. Platforms such as Microsoft Power Automate allow for workflow automation with minimal programming requirements, while tools like Bubble.io offer AI-enhanced, no-code solutions for creating fully functional web applications, broadening access to software development for a wider audience.

14.1.3 Chatbots and Conversational Agents

LLMs have significantly improved the capabilities of chatbots and conversational agents, making them more intelligent, context-aware, and interactive. These AI-powered systems are widely used in customer support, virtual assistants, and personalized user interactions [25].

14.1.3.1 AI-Powered Customer Support Chatbots

Chatbots that utilize LLMs efficiently address customer inquiries, resolve problems, and offer immediate assistance at any time. These AI-enabled chatbots provide prompt replies that cut down on waiting times, utilize contextual awareness by recalling conversation history for more personalized interactions, and facilitate multilingual communication to cater to diverse populations. For instance, numerous companies incorporate ChatGPT-based chatbots to streamline customer service, while banking helpers like Erica from Bank of America assist users in managing their transactions and answering questions, thereby improving the overall customer experience with smart and accessible support [26, 27].

14.1.3.2 Virtual Assistants and Personal AI Companions

LLMs power virtual assistants that aid users in organizing their schedules, setting reminders, and receiving personalized suggestions through voice and text interactions [28–30]. These AI assistants perform tasks such as scheduling reminders, coordinating calendars, and quickly retrieving information, while also connecting with smart home devices for voice-activated automation of IoT systems. Notable examples such as Siri, Alexa, and Google Assistant help with everyday activities, along with Replika, an AI chatbot aimed at offering emotional support and companionship, showcasing the flexibility and convenience of virtual assistants driven by LLMs.

14.1.3.3 AI for Healthcare and Mental Health Support

Conversational agents that utilize LLMs are increasingly being deployed in the healthcare sector for virtual consultations and mental health assistance [28, 31]. These AI tools help users evaluate symptoms and propose potential medical conditions, offer emotional support through therapy-oriented conversations such as cognitive behavioral therapy (CBT), and enhance patient engagement by managing reminders for medications and follow-ups after treatment. Notable examples include Woebot, a mental health chatbot powered by AI that provides therapeutic interactions, and Ada Health, an AI-enabled symptom checker that directs users toward suitable medical treatment, illustrating the ability of conversational agents to improve accessibility and support in healthcare.

14.1.3.4 AI-Powered Business and E-Commerce Assistants

AI-powered chatbots aid customers during their shopping experiences by providing customized product suggestions, streamlining online transactions, and overseeing order tracking and assistance [32, 33]. These intelligent sales assistants evaluate user preferences to recommend pertinent items, create smooth conversational commerce interactions, and automate updates and problem-solving to boost customer satisfaction. For instance, H&M's chatbot offers clothing recommendations suited to personal styles, while Sephora's virtual assistant delivers expert guidance on cosmetics and skincare products, enriching the complete shopping experience through clever, interactive support.

14.1.3.5 AI Chatbots for Education and Learning

Conversational AI assists students by providing personalized tutoring, support for learning languages, and responses to academic inquiries [34, 35]. AI-driven tutors customize educational experiences to meet individual requirements, while chatbots for language learning enable users to practice and enhance their abilities through interactive dialogues. Furthermore, AI tools offer homework assistance and thorough explanations to aid with academic questions. For instance, Duolingo's chatbots act as companions for language learners, and Google's Socratic app employs AI to help students with their homework by producing clear, step-by-step solutions.

14.2 TASK-SPECIFIC APPLICATIONS

Task-specific applications of LLMs [36, 37] involve the use of these models for clearly defined natural language processing tasks that necessitate specialized skills. In contrast to general-purpose language generation, task-specific applications prioritize achieving high accuracy and efficiency in specific areas or functions. Sentiment analysis is a common example where LLMs assess the emotional tone of written content to classify it as positive, negative, or neutral—this is frequently applied in analyzing customer feedback and monitoring social media. Another significant application is summarization, where LLMs condense lengthy texts, such as documents, articles, or reports, into brief and coherent summaries, facilitating quicker information absorption and enhancing knowledge management. Moreover, information extraction focuses on pinpointing and retrieving particular data points like names, dates, or relationships from unstructured text—this is useful in legal document review, healthcare record analysis, and financial reporting.

These specific applications boost automation, lessen manual labor, and enable quicker and more informed decision-making across various sectors, including healthcare, finance, law, marketing, and customer service. As LLMs advance, their capability to adjust to domain-specific tasks with minimal human intervention further increases their significance in operational workflows and data-driven settings.

14.2.1 Sentiment Analysis and Text Classification

Sentiment analysis and text classification [38, 39], driven by LLMs, allow organizations to automatically discern emotions, opinions, and categories within extensive text data. These technologies find broad applications across various sectors to track social media and product feedback, identify hate speech, and detect emotions in dialogues. For example, companies evaluate customer input on platforms like Twitter and Amazon to assess satisfaction and enhance their products, while social media platforms utilize LLMs to locate and eliminate harmful or toxic content. Furthermore, the ability to detect emotions during customer service interactions enables AI systems to identify signs of frustration or anger and respond accordingly, thereby enhancing the user experience. In summary, LLMs improve the real-time comprehension of online conversations, streamline moderation processes, and facilitate data-driven decision-making.

14.2.2 Summarization and Question Answering

LLMs are crucial for summarization and question answering, significantly improving productivity and making information more accessible in research, legal, and business fields [38, 40]. These models have the ability to automatically condense intricate, lengthy documents—such as news articles, academic papers, legal agreements, and financial analyses—into brief, coherent summaries that preserve essential details.

News organizations utilize LLMs to provide concise, easily understandable summaries of breaking news stories, while academic resources like SummarizeBot assist researchers in quickly identifying key points in scientific literature. Simultaneously, AI-powered question answering systems like OpenAI's ChatGPT and Google's BERT can understand user inquiries and produce accurate, contextually relevant answers, making them beneficial for customer service, technical support, and retrieving information. In the legal and financial sectors, companies leverage LLMs to examine and summarize complex regulatory documents, legal judgments, and statements, significantly cutting down review times. For instance, services like CaseText employ AI to create summaries of case law, aiding legal experts in navigating extensive information more effectively. In summary, LLMs facilitate the processing and retrieval of information, leading to quicker decision-making and enhanced access to complicated knowledge.

14.2.3 Named Entity Recognition (NER)

LLMs like BERT, RoBERTa, GPT, and T5 have revolutionized Named Entity Recognition (NER) [41, 42] by shifting from traditional rule-based and superficial machine learning techniques to offering a deeper contextual comprehension of entities. Encoder models such as BERT are particularly effective at token-level classification employing BIO tagging, whereas decoder models like GPT facilitate generative or prompt-based NER, and encoder-decoder models like T5 approach NER as text-to-text problems. These models utilize pretraining, fine-tuning, prompt engineering, and few-shot learning to address multilingual, domain-specific, and even zero-shot NER challenges. Their applications extend across healthcare, finance, law, and business intelligence, though obstacles persist, including hallucination, adapting to specific domains, maintaining labeling consistency, and ensuring computational efficiency. In summary, LLMs have led to the development of more precise, versatile, and adaptable NER systems than ever before.

14.3 MULTIMODAL LANGUAGE MODELS

Multimodal language models [43, 44] are sophisticated AI systems that can analyze and comprehend various types of data—such as text, images, audio, and video—within a cohesive framework. By incorporating different modalities, these models greatly enhance the capabilities of conventional language models, allowing them to interpret visual information, understand spoken language, and create content that integrates multiple data formats. For instance, a multimodal model can evaluate an image and produce a descriptive caption, process spoken queries and reply with text or audio, or condense the information from a video using both visual and auditory elements. This adaptability drives a multitude of applications, including AI-powered content generation (such as producing articles alongside relevant images or videos), smart virtual assistants capable of sensing their surroundings, and educational, healthcare, robotics, and accessibility tools. In the realm of research, multimodal models facilitate intricate tasks such as video comprehension, cross-modal retrieval (like locating an image from a text description), and investigations into human-computer interactions.

In summary, these models signify a significant advancement towards creating more interactive, perceptive, and human-like AI systems by fostering improved context understanding and more natural user engagement.

14.3.1 Vision-Language Models (CLIP, DALL·E)

Vision-language models like CLIP (Contrastive Language-Image Pretraining) [45] and DALL·E [46] integrate textual and visual data by learning joint representations that map images and text into a shared high-dimensional vector space R^d. For example, CLIP uses contrastive learning to maximize the similarity $cos(v_{\text{image}}, v_{\text{text}})$ between paired image and text embeddings $v_{image}, v_{text} \in R^d$, while minimizing similarity for mismatched pairs, enabling the model to understand the semantic alignment between images and their descriptions. DALL·E extends this by using autoregressive transformers to generate images pixel-by-pixel conditioned on a text embedding vector, effectively learning the conditional probability $P(\text{image} \mid \text{text})$. These advances allow AI to perform tasks such as automated image captioning for visually impaired users, where an image I is mapped to a descriptive text T, and text-based image generation, where a prompt T generates an image I. Applications include e-commerce visual search, where a user-provided image embedding v_{query} is compared to product image embeddings to find matches, and marketing, where image content is used to generate personalized advertisements. Furthermore, vision-language models support video understanding by extracting frame embeddings and generating textual summaries S that maximize relevance to the video content V. Tools like Google Lens and AI-generated video summaries exemplify these capabilities, showcasing how vision-language models leverage mathematical frameworks in representation learning and generative modeling to bridge visual and textual modalities for richer, more interactive AI applications.

14.3.2 Audio-Language Integration

Audio-language models integrate speech and text processing by learning joint representations that map audio signals and text sequences into shared vector spaces [47]. Given an audio input signal $x(t)$, a speech encoder f_{speech} transforms it into an embedding $v_{\text{audio}} = f_{\text{speech}}(x(t)) \in R^d$, while a text encoder f_{text} maps corresponding transcripts $s = (w_1, w_2, ..., w_n)$ into embeddings $v_{\text{text}} = f_{\text{text}}(s) \in R^d$. During training, models optimize a loss function such as cross-entropy or connectionist temporal classification (CTC) to maximize alignment between audio and text pairs, enabling accurate speech-to-text conversion $P(s \mid x)$. Similarly, text-to-speech systems model the conditional probability $P(x \mid s)$, generating natural-sounding audio from textual input. These models support applications like live transcription—where continuous audio streams are segmented and transcribed in real time—and assistive tools for speech-impaired users. For podcast summarization, the audio embedding v_{audio} is fed into summarization modules that generate concise textual summaries $\hat{s}$ by maximizing $P(\hat{s} \mid v_{\text{audio}})$. Multimodal virtual assistants combine embeddings from speech and text to handle queries via both modalities, often employing attention mechanisms to fuse information effectively. This mathematical framework allows AI to perform real-time transcription (e.g., Google's Live Transcribe), produce timestamped summaries of long audio content, and enable interactive voice-and-text communication in smart home assistants and chatbots, thereby greatly enhancing accessibility and human-computer interaction.

SUMMARY

The applications of LLMs in many fields are described in this chapter. It starts with generative applications, such as coding generation for software development, text generation and storytelling for creative writing, and chatbots/conversational agents for interactive communication. After that, it discusses task-specific applications including sentiment analysis and text classification for opinion mining, summarization and question answering for information extraction, and named entity recognition (NER) for locating important textual entities. Multimodal language models are also covered in this chapter, with special attention paid to vision-language models such as CLIP and DALL·E, audio-language integration for speech-based tasks, and emerging trends in multimodal AI that integrate various data types for more expansive, flexible capabilities. In general, it highlights how flexible LLMs are when it comes to cross-modal, creative, and analytical activities.

QUESTIONS

1. Given a dataset of 1,000 sentences, design an LLM-based sentiment analysis system and calculate the accuracy if 850 predictions are correct.
2. Define Text Generation and provide one real-world application.
3. Differentiate between Code Generation with LLMs and Text Generation in terms of input and output structure.
4. Explain how Chatbots integrate memory and context to provide human-like responses.
5. If a chatbot answers 80 out of 100 questions correctly, compute its precision and recall assuming it gave 90 answers in total.
6. Compare Summarization and Question Answering as task-specific applications of LLMs.
7. Calculate the BLEU score if the candidate text has 25 overlapping bigrams out of 40 possible bigrams in the reference.
8. An NER system identifies 45 entities, of which 40 are correct. The gold standard has 50 entities. Calculate *precision, recall, and F1-score.*
9. If a text summarization model reduces an article from 2,000 words to 400 words, calculate the compression ratio.
10. Suppose an image-captioning model (Vision-Language Model like CLIP) retrieves the correct caption in 75 out of 100 test cases. Compute its retrieval accuracy.
11. Discuss the strengths and limitations of Vision-Language Models (e.g., CLIP, DALL·E) for multimodal applications.

12. Propose a framework where Audio-Language Integration can be used to improve healthcare chatbots.
13. **Case Study:** A company wants to use LLMs for different tasks. For customer service, they build chatbots that answer questions automatically. For marketing, they use text generation to create ads and stories. In software development, they use code generation to help programmers. The same LLM is also applied in sentiment analysis to check customer feedback, summarization to shorten long reports, and NER to identify names of people, places, and companies. To expand further, they explore multimodal models like CLIP (connecting text with images) and DALL·E (image generation from text). Discuss how LLMs can be applied in both generative applications (like text generation, chatbots) and task-specific applications (like classification, summarization, NER). Give one example of multimodal LLM use.

REFERENCES

[1] D. H. Hagos, R. Battle, and D. B. Rawat, "Recent Advances in Generative AI and Large Language Models: Current Status, Challenges, and Perspectives," IEEE Transactions on Artificial Intelligence, vol. 6, no. 1, pp. 1–18, 2025, doi: 10.1109/TAI.2024.3444742.

[2] V. Koc, "Generative AI and Large Language Models in Language Preservation: Opportunities and Challenges," arXiv preprint, Jan. 2025, arXiv:2501.11496, .

[3] W. Shang, and X. Huang, "A Survey of Large Language Models on Generative Graph Analytics: Query, Learning, and Applications," arXiv preprint, Apr. 2024, arXiv:2404.14809, .

[4] Y. Lee, S. Ka, B. Son, P. Kang, and J. Kang, "Navigating the Path of Writing: Outline-Guided Text Generation with Large Language Models," in *Proceedings of the 2025 Conference of the North American Chapter of the Association for Computational Linguistics (NAACL)*, Feb. 2025.

[5] Z. Xie, T. Cohn, and J. H. Lau, "The Next Chapter: A Study of Large Language Models in Storytelling," arXiv preprint, Jan. 2023, arXiv:2301.09790.

[6] A. Atmakuru, J. Nainani, R. S. R. Bheemreddy, A. Lakkaraju, Z. Yao, H. Zamani *et al.*, "CS4: Measuring the Creativity of Large Language Models Automatically by Controlling the Number of Story-Writing Constraints," arXiv preprint, Oct. 2024, arXiv:2410.04197.

[7] M. Shanahan, and C. Clarke, "Evaluating Large Language Model Creativity from a Literary Perspective," arXiv preprint, Dec. 2023 arXiv:2312.03746.

[8] G. Franceschelli, and M. Musolesi, "On the Creativity of Large Language Models," *AI & Society,* Feb. 2025, doi: 10.1007/s00146-024-02127-3.

[9] S. Woźniak, B. Koptyra, A. Janz, P. Kazienko, and J. Kocoń, "Personalized Large Language Models," arXiv preprint, Nov. 2024, arXiv:2411.02329.

[10] Z. Zhang, Z. Zhang, M. Ding, J. Chen, C. Li, and J. Tang, "Personalization of Large Language Models: A Survey," arXiv preprint, Jul. 2025, arXiv:2411.00027.

[11] Y. Zhao, X. Li, J. Zhang, H. Wang, and Y. Chen, "Amplifying Your Social Media Presence: Personalized Influential Content Generation with LLMs," arXiv preprint, May 2025, arXiv:2505.01698.

[12] M. Tao, X. Liang, T. Shi, L. Yu, and Y. Xie, "RoleCraft-GLM: Advancing Personalized Role-Playing in Large Language Models," arXiv preprint, Jan. 2024, arXiv:2401.09432.

[13] M. Shanahan, K. McDonell, and L. Reynolds, "Role-Play with Large Language Models," arXiv preprint, May 2023, arXiv:2305.16367.

[14] N. Huynh, and B. Lin, "Large Language Models for Code Generation: A Comprehensive Survey of Challenges, Techniques, Evaluation, and Applications," arXiv preprint, Jun. 2024, arXiv:2406.00515.

[15] J. Jiang, F. Wang, J. Shen, S. Kim, and S. Kim, "A Survey on Large Language Models for Code Generation," arXiv preprint, Nov. 2024, arXiv:2411.02636.

[16] N. Ashrafi, S. Bouktif, and M. Mediani, "Enhancing LLM Code Generation: A Systematic Evaluation of Multi-Agent Collaboration and Runtime Debugging for Improved Accuracy, Reliability, and Latency," *IEEE 19th International Conference on Application of Information and Communication Technologies (AICT)*, Al Ain, United Arab Emirates, pp. 1–7, 2025, doi: 10.1109/AICT67988.2025.11268754.

[17] N. Huynh, and B. Lin, "Large Language Models for Code Generation: A Comprehensive Survey of Challenges, Techniques, Evaluation, and Applications," arXiv preprint, Jun. 2024, arXiv:2406.00515.

[18] M. R. Lyu, B. Ray, A. Roychoudhury, S. H. Tan, and P. Thongtanunam, "Automatic Programming: Large Language Models and Beyond," arXiv preprint, May 2024, arXiv:2405.02213.

[19] S. Torka, and S. Albayrak, "Optimizing AI-Assisted Code Generation," arXiv preprint, Dec. 2024, arXiv:2412.10953.

[20] H. Jelodar, M. Meymani, and R. Razavi-Far, "Large Language Models (LLMs) for Source Code Analysis: Applications, Models and Datasets," arXiv preprint, Mar. 2025, arXiv:2503.00481.

[21] F. Dobslaw, R. Feldt, J. Yoon, and S. Yoo, "Challenges in Testing Large Language Model Based Software: A Faceted Taxonomy," arXiv preprint, Mar. 2025, arXiv:2503.00481.

[22] J. Wang, Y. Huang, C. Chen, Z. Liu, S. Wang, and Q. Wang, "Software Testing with Large Language Models: Survey, Landscape, and Vision," *IEEE Transactions on Software Engineering*, Mar. 2024, arXiv:2307.07221.

[23] Y. Xia, Y. Chen, T. Shi, J. Wang, and J. Yang, "AICoderEval: Improving AI Domain Code Generation of Large Language Models," arXiv preprint, Jun. 2024, arXiv:2406.04712.

[24] M. Wang, T. Pfandzelter, T. Schirmer, and D. Bermbach, "LLM4FaaS: No-Code Application Development using LLMs and FaaS," arXiv preprint, Feb. 2025, arXiv:2502.14450.

[25] S. K. Dam, C. S. Hong, Y. Qiao, and C. Zhang, "A Complete Survey on LLM-based AI Chatbots," arXiv preprint, Nov. 2024, arXiv:2406.16937.

[26] W. Li, K. Shi, and Y. Chai, "AI Chatbots as Professional Service Agents: Developing a Professional Identity," in *Proceedings of the 2025 Conference on Empirical Methods in Natural Language Processing*, pp. 12912–12925, Suzhou, China, Jan. 2025.

[27] J. Wei, S. Kim, H. Jung, and Y.-H. Kim, "Leveraging Large Language Models to Power Chatbots for Collecting User Self-Reported Data," in *Proc. of the ACM on Human-Computer Interaction*, Sep. 2023, doi: 10.1145/3637364, arXiv:2301.05843.

[28] J. Mok, I. Kim, S. Park, and S. Yoon, "Exploring the Potential of LLMs as Personalized Assistants: Dataset, Evaluation, and Analysis," arXiv preprint, Jun. 2025, arXiv:2506.01262.

[29] E. Lee, "Towards Ethical Personal AI Applications: Practical Considerations for AI Assistants with Long-Term Memory," arXiv preprint, Sep. 2024, arXiv:2409.11192.

[30] S. García-Méndez, F. de Arriba-Pérez, and M. del C. Somoza-López, "A Review on the Use of Large Language Models as Virtual Tutors," *Science & Education*, Sep. 2024, doi: 10.1007/s11191-024-00530-2.

[31] S. Gabriel, I. Puri, X. Xu, M. Malgaroli, and M. Ghassemi, "Can AI Relate: Testing Large Language Model Response for Mental Health Support," in *Findings of the Association for Computational Linguistics: EMNLP 2024*, pp. 2206–2221, Miami, Florida, USA, Oct. 2024.

[32] H. Yang, H. Lyu, T. Zhang, D. Wang, and Y. Zhao, "LLM-Driven E-Commerce Marketing Content Optimization: Balancing Creativity and Conversion," *in Proceedings of the 2025 2nd International Conference on Computer and Multimedia Technology (ICCMT '25)*. Association for Computing Machinery, New York, NY, USA, pp. 610–615, Jun. 2025.

[33] A. A. Rajasekar *et al.*, "Flippi: End To End GenAI Assistant for E-Commerce," arXiv preprint, Jul. 2025, arXiv:2507.05788.

[34] G. Pitts, V. Marcus, and S. Motamedi, "Student Perspectives on the Benefits and Risks of AI in Education," *ASEE Annual Conference & Exposition* , Montreal, Quebec, Canada, Jun. 2025, 10.18260/1-2--57693.

[35] S. K. Dam, C. S. Hong, Y. Qiao, and C. Zhang, "A Complete Survey on LLM-based AI Chatbots," Nov. 2024.

[36] H. Naveed, A. U. Hassan, S. Aslan, C. Rubio-Campillo, A. M. Qamar, A. K. Al-Makhadmeh *et al.*, "A Comprehensive Overview of Large Language Models," Oct. 2024, ArXiv abs/2406.16937.

[37] F. Chen, L. Zhang, G. Pang, R. Zimmermann, and S. Deng, "Synergizing Large Language Models and Task-Specific Models for Time Series Anomaly Detection," arXiv preprint, May 2025, arXiv:2501.05675.

[38] J. Niimi, "Dynamic Sentiment Analysis with Local Large Language Models using Majority Voting: A Study on Factors Affecting Restaurant Evaluation," arXiv preprint, Jul. 2024, arXiv:2407.13069.

[39] Z. Wang, Y. Pang, Y. Lin, and X. Zhu, "Adaptable and Reliable Text Classification using Large Language Models," *2024 IEEE International Conference on Data Mining Workshops (ICDMW)*, Abu Dhabi, United Arab Emirates, 2024, pp. 67–74, Dec. 2024, doi: 10.1109/ICDMW65004.2024.00015.

[40] N. Sinha, "QA-Prompting: Improving Summarization with Large Language Models using Question-Answering," in *Proceedings of The 5th New Frontiers in Summarization Workshop*, pp. 199–212, Hybrid, May 2025.

[41] F. Villena, L. Miranda, and C. Aracena, "llmNER: (Zero|Few)-Shot Named Entity Recognition, Exploiting the Power of Large Language Models," arXiv preprint, Jun. 2024, arXiv:2406.04528v1.

[42] S. Wang *et al.*, "GPT-NER: Named Entity Recognition via Large Language Models," in *Findings of the Association for Computational Linguistics: NAACL 2025*, pp. 4257–4275, Albuquerque, New Mexico, Oct. 2023.

[43] D. Zhang, Y. Yu, J. Dong, C. Li, D. Su, C. Chu *et al.*, "MM-LLMs: Recent Advances in MultiModal Large Language Models," in *Findings of the Association for Computational Linguistics: ACL 2024*, pp. 12401–12430, Bangkok, Thailand, May 2024.

[44] S. Yin, C. Fu, S. Zhao, K. Li, X. Sun, T. Xu *et al.*, "A Survey on Multimodal Large Language Models," *National Science Review*, Nov. 2024, doi: 10.1093/nsr/nwae403, arXiv:2306.13549.

[45] A. Radford, J. W. Kim, C. Hallacy, A. Ramesh, G. Goh, S. Agarwal *et al.*, "Learning Transferable Visual Models From Natural Language Supervision," in *Proc. of the International Conference on Machine Learning (ICML)*, Feb. 2021, arXiv:2103.00020.

[46] A. Ramesh, M. Pavlov, G. Goh, S. Gray, C. Voss, A. Radford *et al.*, "Zero-Shot Text-to-Image Generation," in *Proc. of the International Conference on Machine Learning (ICML)*, Feb. 2021, arXiv:2102.12092.

[47] H. Wu, J. Chen, W. Chen, X. Li, and L. Li *et al.*, "Towards Audio Language Modeling -- An Overview," Feb. 2024, arXiv:2402.13236.

15 Ethical Considerations in Large Language Models

15.1 INTRODUCTION

Large language models (LLMs) have significantly progressed the domain of natural language processing, powering various applications such as chatbots, translation services, content creation, and data analysis. However, the broad implementation of LLMs presents numerous intricate ethical dilemmas that need to be meticulously addressed to ensure responsible AI utilization. A primary concern is bias; LLMs are trained on extensive datasets obtained from the internet, which frequently harbor cultural, gender, racial, or ideological biases that the models can unintentionally absorb and propagate, resulting in unjust or discriminatory results. Privacy breaches represent another major issue, as these models might memorize or disclose sensitive personal details found in training data, raising concerns about data security and user consent. Moreover, LLMs can be misused to produce misinformation, disinformation, or harmful material, potentially escalating the spread of fake news, hate speech, or malicious propaganda on a large scale [1].

From an environmental standpoint, the considerable computational power needed to train and implement LLMs adds to a substantial carbon footprint, leading to calls for more sustainable practices in AI. Additionally, issues surrounding intellectual property rights emerge when LLMs create content based on copyrighted works, complicating legal and ethical standards. Transparency and explainability are also vital—users and developers require better understanding of how models arrive at decisions to build trust and accountability. Effective moderation tactics are necessary to eliminate inappropriate or harmful outputs without excessively limiting free expression.

To address these complex ethical issues, a comprehensive strategy is crucial. This includes creating fairness-sensitive algorithms, enforcing strong data governance and privacy protections, implementing transparent audit systems, encouraging environmental sustainability through more efficient model designs, and establishing clear regulatory guidelines that balance innovation with social accountability. Cooperation among AI researchers, policymakers, ethicists, and affected communities is essential to ensure that LLM technologies are developed and utilized in ways that are fair, transparent, safe, and environmentally considerate.

DOI: 10.1201/9781003650065-15

15.2 BIAS AND FAIRNESS IN LLMS

Bias in LLMs [2] pertains to the inclination of these AI systems to generate outputs that mirror, reinforce, or enhance prevailing societal stereotypes, biases, or discriminatory patterns. If not addressed, such biases can compromise fairness, negatively impact marginalized communities, and perpetuate inequalities. The origins of bias in LLMs are complex and often interconnected:

- **Historical Data Bias:** LLMs are trained using vast datasets obtained from the internet, literature, news sources, and various other textual materials that inherently contain the historical and cultural biases found in society. For instance, if the training data disproportionately highlights certain groups or includes stereotypes, the model assimilates and replicates these patterns, unintentionally sustaining discriminatory beliefs.
- **Algorithmic Bias:** The mathematical framework and optimization goals of machine learning algorithms can sometimes reinforce biases. For instance, if an algorithm focuses on predictive accuracy without considering fairness metrics, it might unduly favor majority groups with more abundant data, sidelining minority groups.
- **Representation Bias:** When particular demographic or social groups are inadequately represented or inaccurately depicted in training datasets, the model's comprehension of these groups becomes restricted or distorted. As a result, this leads to subpar performance and unfair or stereotypical reactions when the model engages with or discusses these populations.

15.2.1 Examples of Bias in LLMs

- **Gender Bias:** A well-known example involves the stereotyping of genders in professional roles. For instance, when prompted with "A doctor and a nurse walked into a room. Who is the doctor?" many LLMs have historically linked the doctor with being male and the nurse with being female, reflecting societal stereotypes regarding gender roles present in their training data.
- **Racial Bias:** LLMs can produce outputs that tend to associate names or entities tied to particular ethnic backgrounds with negative or stereotypical ideas. Research has demonstrated that AI models sometimes connect specific ethnic-sounding names to criminal behavior or other unfavorable contexts, thereby propagating damaging racial biases.
- **Political Bias:** Because LLMs learn from extensive collections of data that may carry political biases, they can show favoritism in their outputs. For example, models that have been primarily trained on left-leaning or right-leaning sources may lean towards liberal or conservative perspectives when addressing politically charged questions, thus affecting their impartiality.

15.2.2 Mitigation Strategies

Varied and Equitable Datasets: A key method for minimizing bias is the careful assembly of training data that encompasses a wide range of perspectives across various demographic, cultural, and ideological factors. This means proactively seeking out voices that are often overlooked and ensuring comprehensive representation of differing viewpoints to prevent dominance of any single group.

Bias Identification and Rectification Algorithms: Researchers create and utilize specific metrics and tools that assess bias in the outputs of models, such as evaluating differences in error rates or associating stereotypes. These assessments aid in pinpointing harmful behaviors, after which correction methods—such as adversarial training, reweighting, or counterfactual data enhancement—can be implemented to alleviate bias.

Human Oversight and Equity Evaluations: Incorporating human insight throughout the model development process is essential. This includes having diverse teams analyze model performance, performing fairness evaluations that reflect actual scenarios, and establishing governance systems that continuously oversee and rectify biases prior to and following deployment. Open reporting and independent assessments also promote accountability.

15.3 EXPLAINABILITY AND TRANSPARENCY

Explainability [3] pertains to the ability to comprehend, interpret, and convey how a LLM makes its decisions or predictions. It involves clarifying the internal mechanisms of the AI model so that humans can understand which inputs and features significantly impacted a particular output. Conversely, transparency involves the honest revelation of essential details about the model, such as its architecture, the sources of its training data, the methodologies used in its development, and its limitations. Together, explainability and transparency form the basis for cultivating trust, accountability, and ethical implementation of AI technologies, particularly in critical fields such as healthcare, finance, legal services, and public policy, where decisions can greatly affect individuals' lives.

15.3.1 Significance and Illustrations

Loan Approvals: When a financial institution utilizes an LLM-based system to assess loan applications, it is essential to ensure that the reasoning behind decisions is transparent to maintain fairness and adhere to regulations. If a loan application is denied, the system should provide a straightforward and comprehensible explanation—such as outlining aspects like credit score, income, or the debt-to-income ratio—that influenced the final decision. This level of transparency prevents outcomes from being hidden and allows applicants to challenge or enhance their applications based on constructive feedback.

Medical AI Applications: In the realm of healthcare, medical chatbots or diagnostic assistants that rely on LLMs must effectively convey the limits of their knowledge and the origins of their recommendations to prevent the spread of misinformation or misplaced reliance. For instance, if a chatbot proposes a treatment strategy, it ought to reference credible medical literature, clinical guidelines, or peer-reviewed research to substantiate its suggestions. This practice not only fosters trust among users but also aids healthcare professionals in validating AI-generated recommendations.

15.3.2 Strategies for Improving Explainability and Transparency

Interpretable AI Methods [4]**:** Tools such as SHAP (SHapley Additive exPlanations) and LIME (Local Interpretable Model-agnostic Explanations) are commonly employed to offer post hoc interpretations of complex model results. These methods pinpoint and measure the impact of individual input features on a model's prediction, enabling users to identify which words, phrases, or contextual factors influenced the LLM's output. For instance, in the realm of text classification, SHAP values may indicate that specific keywords had a significant effect on the decision.

Confidence Metrics and Uncertainty Assessment [5]**:** By providing confidence or probability metrics alongside predictions, users can gauge how much reliance to place on the model's outputs. For example, a chatbot stating, "I am 85% confident in this diagnosis," conveys information about the dependability of the response and indicates when it may be appropriate to seek human assistance.

Thorough Model Documentation: Transparency is further reinforced by the release of comprehensive model cards or documentation that outline critical information such as the data sources utilized for training, model structure, evaluation metrics, potential biases, ethical issues, and recognized limitations. These documents act as a resource for users, developers, and auditors, fostering informed usage and continuous evaluation.

User-Friendly Interfaces: Creating interfaces that effectively convey explanations, confidence metrics, and caveats in accessible language ensures that non-expert users—like patients, customers, or policymakers—can accurately interpret AI outputs.

15.4 PRIVACY AND DATA PROTECTION

Privacy and data security [6] are paramount concerns during the creation and use of LLMs, as they depend on extensive training datasets that may unintentionally contain sensitive information such as personally identifiable information (PII) and confidential records. This raises the risk that LLMs could accidentally memorize and reproduce sensitive information during user interactions, which has been observed in instances where chatbots provide responses that include fragments of private documents. Furthermore, user engagements with LLM-based applications can reveal private information if adequate security and privacy measures are not in place, leading to potential data leaks. Another major concern is reidentification, where malicious individuals take advantage of the model's ability to memorize training data to extract personal information by formulating specific queries. To address these challenges, various solutions have been suggested and put into practice, including data anonymization methods that remove personal identifiers from datasets prior to model training, thereby decreasing the likelihood of sensitive information being learned or reproduced. Federated learning adds another layer of protection by decentralizing the training process, allowing models to be trained directly on user devices instead of central servers, thus reducing exposure. Moreover, implementing strict user consent procedures and thorough data retention policies promotes transparency and control over the collection, storage, and deletion of user data, helping to protect privacy and comply with legal requirements. Together, these approaches strive to balance the advantages of LLM technologies with the critical need to protect individual privacy and ensure data security.

15.5 MISINFORMATION AND CONTENT MODERATION

LLMs present considerable dangers in producing false information and deceptive content that can quickly circulate on social media, news outlets, and automated messaging systems, potentially leading to widespread negative consequences [7]. For instance, LLMs might generate incorrect or unverified medical recommendations—such as false assertions about vaccine effectiveness—that jeopardize public health, or create realistic-looking fake news articles that can sway elections and manipulate public opinion. To tackle these issues, preventive strategies involve embedding fact-checking and verification mechanisms within LLMs to validate information before distribution, as well as implementing automated content moderation technologies aimed at identifying and flagging misleading or dangerous outputs. Furthermore, including human oversight for sensitive or critical subjects guarantees that expert evaluation supports AI efforts, aiding in the preservation of accuracy, ethical principles, and accountability in content generated by AI. These collective approaches are crucial for reducing the risks associated with misinformation while responsibly harnessing the potential of LLMs.

15.6 INTELLECTUAL PROPERTY AND PLAGIARISM

LLMs present considerable challenges concerning intellectual property and plagiarism [8, 9], as they are frequently trained on extensive collections of copyrighted content and may generate text without adequate attribution, obscuring the distinction between original works and plagiarism. This situation can result in legal conflicts when AI-generated content unintentionally mirrors copyrighted texts, such as producing a passage that is identical to one found in a protected book, or when students submit AI-generated assignments in academic contexts without appropriate citations, raising concerns about automated plagiarism. To address these challenges, solutions like watermarking AI-generated material can aid in tracing their origins and differentiating them from works authored by humans. Furthermore, incorporating citation mechanisms within LLMs can promote the correct attribution of source content. Additionally, the development of new legal frameworks is critical to explicitly outline ownership, usage rights, and responsibilities related to AI-generated intellectual property, ensuring that creators, users, and AI developers function within clear and equitable guidelines.

15.7 ENVIRONMENTAL IMPACT OF LLMS

The environmental implications of LLMs [10, 11] are increasingly worrying due to their high energy usage during the training process, leading to considerable carbon emissions. For example, the energy required to train models like GPT-3 has been approximated to equal the yearly electricity consumption of several hundred households, while large AI data centers collectively play a significant role in the tech industry's carbon footprint. To combat these sustainability issues, researchers and organizations are implementing optimized training methods such as pruning and quantization that lower computational requirements without compromising performance. Furthermore, using renewable energy sources to power AI infrastructure helps reduce the total emissions tied to model development. Efforts are also directed at creating more efficient model designs, which include smaller, specialized LLMs that offer similar functionalities with much lower energy needs, thus promoting AI advancement in an eco-conscious manner.

15.8 REGULATION AND GOVERNANCE OF LLMS

The governance and regulation of LLMs [12, 13] are crucial for ensuring their responsible creation, implementation, and application while addressing significant issues such as fairness, security, and ethical considerations. Strong policies and legal structures are essential for reducing the risks related to bias, privacy, misinformation, and accountability. Key instances include the EU's AI Act, which governs high-risk AI systems by establishing stringent requirements for transparency and risk management, as well as the United States' Executive Order on AI, which prioritizes transparency, accountability, and responsible innovation. To enhance these regulatory initiatives, organizations like the IEEE and OECD have formulated thorough AI ethics guidelines that set industry standards and best practices. Furthermore, independent evaluations of LLM deployments are key to ensuring adherence to ethical and legal norms. Considering the worldwide scope of AI technology, international cooperation on governance frameworks is imperative to align regulations across nations, promote common values, and allow for safe and equitable AI adoption on a global scale.

15.9 ETHICAL USE CASES AND BEST PRACTICES

The ethical applications of LLMs [14] highlight their capacity for delivering positive contributions to society, such as AI-supported medical research that speeds up the evaluation of clinical trials and the identification of new therapies, AI-driven educational resources that provide personalized support to improve learning results, and legal AI tools that aid in contract analysis and document summarization to enhance productivity. To ensure responsible usage, recommended practices stress the importance of educating users about the limitations of AI to set realistic expectations regarding reliability, continuously monitoring for biases in real-time applications to uphold fairness, and offering transparent disclosures in user-facing systems to clearly inform users when content has been generated by AI. Tackling ethical issues like bias, privacy, misinformation, intellectual property, and environmental effects necessitates collaborative efforts among researchers, policymakers, and industry leaders. By employing fairness-aware algorithms, enforcing clear policies, and developing comprehensive regulatory frameworks, society can leverage the advantages of LLMs while alleviating risks, thereby encouraging ethical, reliable, and equitable adoption of AI.

SUMMARY

The ethical considerations in LLMs are examined in this chapter, which starts with an overview of the technological and societal ramifications of their use. In order to mitigate discriminatory trends in model outputs, it addresses bias and fairness and emphasizes the need of explainability and transparency in fostering trust. While misinformation and content moderation emphasize the dangers of producing inaccurate or damaging content, privacy and data protection are addressed in the context of protecting sensitive information. The chapter also discusses the environmental impact of training and operating LLMs, the significance of regulation and governance for responsible oversight, and intellectual property and plagiarism issues. With ethical use cases and best practices in the end, it encourages responsibility, diversity, and sustainability in the creation and use of LLM.

QUESTIONS

1. Define bias in LLMs and explain how it impacts fairness in AI-driven decisions.
2. If training an LLM requires 1200 kWh of energy per day for 90 days, calculate the total energy consumption in kWh.
3. Explain the difference between explainability and transparency in LLMs with suitable examples.
4. A fairness audit found that an LLM has a false negative rate of 10% for Group A and 25% for Group B. Compute the disparity percentage between the groups.
5. Apply the concept of privacy protection by suggesting two techniques that can mitigate risks in LLM-based misinformation detection systems.
6. Analyze the challenges of distinguishing between original content and plagiarized text in outputs generated by LLMs.
7. A privacy-preserving LLM applies differential privacy noise. If the original query frequency is 500 and noise added is 47, compute the noisy output frequency.
8. Evaluate the tradeoff between environmental impact of large-scale LLM training and regulatory governance measures.
9. Propose a framework for best practices in ensuring ethical use of LLMs across healthcare or education domains.

10. Suppose carbon emission per 1,000 kWh is 0.42 metric tons CO_2. Using Q1's energy value, calculate the total CO_2 emissions for training.
11. A content moderation system flags 1,200 misinformation cases out of 1,500 total flagged cases, while 300 were accurate. Compute precision of the system.
12. If an LLM generates 2000 words and 150 are flagged as plagiarized, calculate the plagiarism percentage and suggest a threshold to decide accept/reject.
13. Case Study: Bias and Privacy in a Healthcare Chatbot
A large hospital introduced a healthcare chatbot powered by an advanced LLM. The chatbot was designed to answer patient queries, provide preliminary health advice, and help with appointment bookings. During deployment, two major issues were observed:
    - Bias and Fairness – Patients noticed that the chatbot sometimes provided different health suggestions for men and women, even when their symptoms were the same. This raised concerns about fairness and medical bias in decision-making.
    - Privacy and Data Protection – Since the chatbot required patients to enter personal health information, questions arose about how securely the data was being stored and whether it could be misused or leaked.
    To address these, the hospital formed an Ethics Review Board that focused on ensuring transparency in chatbot responses, protecting patient data, and reducing model bias through diverse training datasets. Based on the above case study, discuss how bias and privacy issues in LLM-powered applications can be mitigated. Suggest at least two strategies for each issue.

REFERENCES

[1] C. Deng, Y. Duan, X. Jin, H. Chang, Y. Tian, H. Liu *et al.*, "Deconstructing the Ethics of Large Language Models from Long-Standing Issues to New-emerging Dilemmas: A Survey," *AI Ethics 5*, pp.4745–4771, 2025.

[2] I. O. Gallegos, R. A. Rossi, J. Barrow, M. M. Tanjim, S. Kim, F. Dernoncourt *et al.*, "Bias and Fairness in Large Language Models: A Survey," *Computational Linguistics*, 50(3), pp.1097–1179,Jul. 2024.

[3] Y. Shanmugarasa, S. Pan, M. Ding, D. Zhao, and T. Rakotoarivelo, "Privacy Meets Explainability: Managing Confidential Data and Transparency Policies in LLM-Empowered Science," in *Proceedings of the Extended Abstracts of the CHI Conference on Human Factors in Computing Systems (CHI EA '25).* Association for Computing Machinery, New York, NY, USA, Article 448, pp.1–8, Apr. 2025.

[4] A. Bilal, D. Ebert, and B. Lin, "LLMs for Explainable AI: A Comprehensive Survey," arXiv preprint, Mar. 2025, arXiv:2504.00125.

[5] E. Becker, and S. Soatto, "Cycles of Thought: Measuring LLM Confidence through Stable Explanations," arXiv preprint, Jun. 2024, arXiv:2406.03441.

[6] B. Yan, K. Li, M. Xu, Y. Dong, Y. Zhang, Z. Ren *et al.*, "On Protecting the Data Privacy of Large Language Models (LLMs) and LLM agents: A literature review", *High-Confidence Computing*, vol. 5(2), 2025, 100300, ISSN 2667-2952

[7] T. Huang, "Content Moderation by LLM: From Accuracy to Legitimacy," *Artif Intell Rev,* 58, p. 320, Jun. 2025.

[8] Y. Zhong, Y. Wen, J. Guo, M. Kafai, H. Huang, H. Guo *et al.*, "Web Intellectual Property at Risk: Preventing Unauthorized Real-Time Retrieval by Large Language Models," in *Proceedings of the 2025 Conference on Empirical Methods in Natural Language Processing*, pp. 17211–17224, Suzhou, China, Jun. 2025.

[9] D. Mondal, and C. Lipizzi, "LLMs Plagiarize: Ensuring Responsible Sourcing of Large Language Model Training Data Through Knowledge Graph Comparison," arXiv preprint, Aug. 2024, arXiv:2407.02659.

[10] J. Morrison, C. Na, J. Fernandez, T. Dettmers, E. Strubell, and J. Dodge, "Holistically Evaluating the Environmental Impact of Creating Language Models," arXiv preprint, Mar. 2025, arXiv:2503.05804.

[11] Y. Wu, I. Hua, and Y. Ding, "Unveiling Environmental Impacts of Large Language Model Serving: A Functional Unit View," in *Proceedings of the 63rd Annual Meeting of the Association for Computational Linguistics* (Volume 1: Long Papers), pp. 10560–10576, Vienna, Austria, May 2025.

[12] W. Pasfield, "Powerin g LLM Regulation through Data: Bridging the Gap from Compute Thresholds to Customer Experiences," arXiv preprint, Jan. 2025, arXiv:2502.03472.

[13] N. Balabanova, A. Bashir, P. Bova, A. Buscemi, T. Cimpeanu, H. Correia da Fonseca *et al.*, "Media and Responsible AI Governance: A Game-Theoretic and LLM Analysis," arXiv preprint, Mar. 2025, arXiv:2503.09858.

[14] H. Gao, M. Zahedi, C. Treude, S. Rosenstock, and M. Cheong, "Documenting Ethical Considerations in Open Source AI Models," in *Proc. 2024 IEEE/ACM 46th Int. Conf. Softw. Eng. (ICSE)*, Lisbon, Portugal, pp. 1–13, Jul. 2024, doi: 10.1145/3597503.3639189.

Index

W

X

Y

Z

"*Dealing* is about learning the hard lessons of life, but more than that, it's a story of redemption, faith, and rising stronger than before. It's for anyone who's been broken, thrown away, then reminded by God that they still matter. Denise and I come from different paths, but we've faced similar struggles and are now in a place to give back by mentoring others, proving that your past doesn't define your future. Through her writing, Denise brings this journey to life in a powerful, unforgettable way. She's a real one, and I feel truly blessed to know her. God is so good."

—Jeremy Meeks

"Denise Fleming's *Dealing* is the real deal. Told in a bold narrative, she brings the '80s alive in a way that makes you feel like you're there. The music, the movies, and the mischief! What an incredible life story always reflecting back to her loving family and unpeeling the layers to her unique tale. Fleming describes her life experience with much candor and honesty. This book is raw and so reflective. I am so impressed with what Fleming has done with her life. An inspirational and keepsake story for readers who are looking for an incredibly cool book."

—Victoria Gotti

"Denise breaks bad and comes clean and you'll never love her any less. In her distinct Cali, cool girl voice, Denise tells it like it is and had me feeling like I was sitting shotgun next to my ride or die on the west coast adventure of a lifetime. With every wrong turn I was yelling, 'Nooo, don't do it!' but holding tight, ready to face the consequences alongside her, knowing Denise would do the same."

—Tara Herrmann, writer and producer of *Orange Is the New Black* and *Glow*

Advance Praise for *Dealing*

"The pages turn themselves as Fleming takes us into the belly of the cocaine beast, with a resting pulse in the mid 2000s. Surprisingly, our paths never crossed during our mutual debouched heydays, and I'm torn between wishing they had—and being really fukken grateful they never did. Denise has a style of polished rawness that finds the humor within the darkness. *Dealing* doesn't pull anything from the bottom of the deck."

—Charlie Sheen

"Man, *Dealing* hit me hard. Denise tells it straight—owns it, no excuses. She never quits, proving that no matter how rough the streets or the prison walls get, you can turn your life around and make something good out of it. That's the heart of a true warrior. And damn, she makes it look good. Proud of you, *mi hermana*."

—Danny Trejo

"Thank you, Denise, for sharing your story. We see in you that it's undeniable that you always have the power to choose yourself, even when you're at your lowest point."

—Jennie Garth

"Whoa, what a ride! Denise's *Dealing* proves that mistakes don't define you. It's not how many times you get knocked down, it's how you get back up. She gives back, inspires others, and reminds us all to never lose sight of who we are. It's real, powerful, and full of heart, just like my lil' homie, Denise."

—Mario Lopez

Introduction

WHEN DID EVERYTHING GO WRONG?

We started out so good—so sweet, so happy.

I don't really know. I'm still trying to figure it out.

This is *that* story.

I was a girlfella—born into a big-hearted Italian family, full of noise, pasta, and drama. I was moonstruck early on by the concept of la dolce vita: Family, good food, and conversation meant everything to me. I was convinced I was in control. I played the game like one of the boys, but with lipstick, attitude, and a small butterfly knife in my purse.

At the beginning, all I could see was the world, dreamy and chromatic. How pretty, alive, and invincible it made me feel. I went screaming wild, pedal to the metal, straight into the fast lane. I took shortcuts left and right, convinced they'd lead me to my destination.

But even a girlfella runs out of luck eventually. And when I did, the fall was fast. Honestly, I didn't think I'd survive.

But I'm living proof that it's never too late to slam on the brakes, whip a sharp U-ey, find a place of self-acceptance, and start over.

Because some of us have to take the long way home to finally arrive.

This is the real story—behind the teased hair, the Madonna bracelets, and the sexy miniskirts. The story of growing up in 1980s Southern California, when the sun was always shining, the parties never stopped, and no one knew how close we were to falling off the edge.

Prologue

Here's the Deal

MAY 1997

A violent lurch yanked me awake, and instantly, everything was wrong.

I wasn't in my bed. I wasn't even in my life anymore. I was in a van that reeked of gasoline and unwashed bodies. I'd been wearing the same thing for days and knew that I didn't look or smell much better than anyone else inside. My wrists and ankles were raw from the metal shackles, which clinked with every bump in the road. I glanced out the window and saw it: Hawaii, in all its lush, postcard-perfect glory. A cruel joke. Paradise on the outside, but I wasn't heading to the beach. I was being hauled, like garbage, to prison.

"Yo, brah! Wake da kine, shoots, we here!" someone shouted.

That was the Hawaiian Marshal's way of saying, "*Wake up the haole chick—we're at the gates.*"

We pulled up to the high-security facility, the kind with gun towers and barbed wire, and that van door flew open. I stumbled out, shackled and sweaty, into a place that would become my home for the next seven years. Seven. Fucking. Years.

I went from zero to drug lord before I even scored a cap and gown. High school dropout turned SoCal coke queen. One minute I was playing

Ms. Pac-Man at the Fun Zone arcade in Newport Beach, the next I was running cash and product like a scene out of *Scarface*. It felt like a game, until it wasn't. Because in the drug world—just like playing a video game in the arcade—you pop in some cash, hope for the best, and play until you lose. And you always lose. I lost everything.

Seven years. Gone.

You wanna know how a sweet sixteen-year-old from Fountain Valley turns into "Flawless," teenage cocaine queen of the OC?

Let me take you back.

Because this wasn't some overnight scandal. This was a slow-motion car crash with the best soundtrack, the hottest guys, the wildest parties, and a broken family. I was raised on Sunday sauce and Sinatra, mob movies and manicures. I had charm, ambition, and zero impulse control. I was destined for something big—I just didn't know it came with handcuffs.

But back then? Before the prison jumpsuit? Before the mug shot?

I was just a girl with a fake ID, a pack of clove cigarettes in my purse, Aqua Net in my hair, and a dream of being adored.

There was beauty, pleasure, and opportunity everywhere I looked. Why shouldn't there be? Like a supermodel in a music video, my world rained party streamers in confetti colors. I was a sweet-faced sixteen-year-old, living the classic *rah-rah-sis-boom-bah* life of an all-American teenager: full of energy, excitement, and, of course, mischief.

Let's start there.

You want to come along for the ride?

I'd say put on your seatbelt—but hell, we never did.

Better to poke your head through the sunroof and scream with joy at the top of your lungs.

It's Orange County, baby. I was young. Invincible.

The scent of sex and Coppertone suntan lotion was everywhere. Blue skies, green palms, and Sting on the radio.

And bodies. Beautiful, lithe, and alive.

And dead. I've got news clippings to prove it.

Chapter One

Sweet Sixteen

SEPTEMBER 1983

I swear, on most days, sophomore algebra was a sedative—Mrs. Lapanee droning on about variables while my eyelids fought a losing battle with gravity. But that Friday afternoon, algebra might as well have been a triple espresso, because burning a hole in my purse were tickets to David Bowie at the Anaheim Amphitheater. I shifted my white leather miniskirt, one leg jittering like a jackhammer under my desk. Five minutes 'til freedom. Five minutes 'til glitter, eyeliner, and loud, unapologetic magic.

Greg, my older brother, had scored me tickets for my sixteenth birthday; I almost peed myself when I opened the envelope. My first concert. Bowie, The Go-Go's, and Madness. The Serious Moonlight Tour. I was electric, alive.

I used to love that jittery, sweaty-palm feeling that came from a dose of nature's speed. All this adrenaline fueled the mischief maker in me. I pulled the rubber band from my ponytail, ran my fingers through my shoulder-length hair, and shot a stinger across the room at the hottest guy in algebra. Darren had that full-on teen heartthrob vibe: brown eyes that could melt you, *GQ*-dark hair perfectly mussed, a lone-wolf slouch, and full, kissable lips. He played the wounded act like a pro. He mouthed,

"Ow!" and I stuck my tongue out. I played the effortless cool girl, like I didn't care, even though every flirtation lit me up inside.

Honestly, boys were easy. According to my dad, I came out of the womb and batted my eyelashes before making a peep. I like to think it's my magnetic vibe, but it's more likely my packaging. I was petite, with Noxzema-clean olive skin, glossy brown hair, bubblegum breath, and pink-polished toes. My Spanish-Italian island roots made me exotic, surrounded by a sea of blue-eyed, blond-haired beach babes.

My best friend Stacy Escobar is one of those.

Stacy and I had been attached at the hip since eighth grade, when she transferred from West Covina to James H. Cox Middle School. I was doodling on my mustard-colored Pee-Chee folder when I first saw her. She stood at the front of Home Ec as Mrs. Woodward introduced her to the class, and I did a quick once-over. She had on the sunshine-yellow high-waisted Ditto jeans I'd been eyeing at the mall for months, but she filled them out in ways I only dreamed of. Her permed blond hair flowed past her shoulders, bangs piled high in perfect layers. But it was more than just her amazing style that intrigued me. It was her confidence. Most new kids come in all shy with their heads down. Not Stacy. She had her chin up and was taking us all in with her sparkly sapphire eyes that said, *Try me.*

Our fate as soulmates was sealed when I saw her after class, full-on assaulting the vending machine to shake loose a bag of chips stuck in the coil.

"Fritos, girl, huh? I'm a Doritos girl, but I don't judge," I said as I threw my shoulder into the machine like I owned the joint. She fished out the rescued chips without missing a beat.

"Saladitos are actually my go-to snack, but you can only get them at 7-Eleven." She tore open the bag and offered me a handful.

"What the heck are those?" I asked, crunching on a corn chip.

"I can't tell you or you'd never try them."

I tried them with her later that day, and if you've never had Saladitos, let me save you a gag. They're salty, dried plums that taste like horse manure and smell like it too. Stacy's not allowed to eat them within ten feet of me—a rule she constantly breaks. That's another reason Stacy's my soulmate: she likes getting into trouble. That same night, we mischievously toilet-papered the houses of all the popular kids in eighth grade. It was hard for us to keep a straight face the following day at school when the wannabe cool kids claimed their homes got hit too. She joined my girl gang along with Kelli, Colleen, Donna, and Julie, but we were each other's ride-or-die from day one. Our friendship defined us—it was like people thought of us as one person: Denise-n-Stacy, or Stacy-n-Denise. I guess these days we'd have a Ship Name like "Stenise." Stacy had a way of making everything more fun. She was louder, bolder than I was, always doing risky things like convincing older kids or random adults to buy us beer while I waited in the car. My world revolved around family, and Stacy thrived on the Trigo chaos. She loved our big family dinners as if they were her own. I couldn't get enough of her.

Now here we were, at Fountain Valley High School (FVHS)—home of the Barons. The campus buzzed with pure 1980s energy, a sea of teens lit by pop culture icons. Madonna wannabes rocked ankle-length leggings, lace, neon, and black rubber bangles, mingling with Duran Duran junkies in styled hair and *Miami Vice* shades. Our campus pulsed with Baron pride, decked out in red, blue, and gold. We were lucky. We had it all: football, basketball, baseball, soccer, wrestling, track, tennis. Athletes ruled the center of the quad, holding court "at the wall," flanked by the cheer squad hierarchies and drill team royalty. The surf team, naturally, claimed the fountain. The stoners wandered off campus to Pup 'N' Taco, the perfect post-high spot to satisfy the munchies.

There was orchestra, marching band, choir, gymnastics, volleyball, and dance—where I spent most of my time. We even had water polo and scuba. Classes were just as electric: driver's ed, auto mechanics, typing, sewing, woodshop, horticulture, cooking. A whirlwind of mullets, mohawks, mods, homework, hickeys, hormones—the whole shebang.

In Orange County—the upper-middle-class enclave of towns hugging the Pacific—we were cool chicks at backyard parties and hot boys in garage bands. Surfers, skaters, musicians. Boy-crazy, girl-crazy. And yeah, most of us got loaded.

Weekends were for drinking games, getting wild, getting high. Sex, drugs, and rock and roll, baby. Drugs were everywhere: teens raided their parents' medicine cabinets, popping pills like M&M's, rolling joints like it was an Olympic sport.

But nothing fired us up like the rivalry with Edison High. The Chargers were sworn enemies, and football games felt like war. After the final whistle, win or lose, everyone flocked to Naugles on Brookhurst. FVHS at one location, Edison at the other. Same street. Different turf. Then we all crashed the Huntington Beach bonfire, right between lifeguard towers three and five.

The week before, I'd decided it was going to be the night I kissed Darren. God, he was cute, and according to the rumor mill, he liked me too. Easy.

It was a hard-fought game, but—annoyingly—Edison handed us another loss.

By the bonfire, Darren handed me a beer, leaning in close, breath warm, murmuring, "Being here with you beats the game any day." My heart skipped, butterflies rioting in my stomach. We kissed softly under the stars, my strawberry lip gloss sweetening the moment. Stacy teased us, breaking the tension, and we laughed, carefree, young, happy. The air was thick with sea salt and woodsmoke, Darren's Polo and my Calvin Klein Obsession blending, while a Sanyo stereo on a beach blanket blasted a new-wave cassette taped off Richard Blade's KROQ-FM.

Later, Darren picked me up to go to the drive-in theater in Fountain Valley. Greg followed us outside and, dead serious, asked to see Darren's driver's license. I was mortified. Greg played the protective big brother—annoyingly nosy about Stacy and me. When we snuck off to Los Alamos Park to secretly puff (and cough our heads off) on a Marlboro Light, Greg would pop around the corner and snap a Polaroid, threatening to tell but never following through.

Another time, Greg was at Naugles when some jock told him I'd gotten drunk and passed out in the back of Stacy's boyfriend's car. Greg pulled me out, drove me home, and carried me through the front door, warning our mom, "Look at your daughter! Put her on restriction. She could have been raped!" What a culo, so damn dramatic. In the end, my mom took away my independence—my white bedroom phone, my prized hotline with a cord long enough to shut the door and still lie on my bed like a teenage queen, free from older-brother snooping—and she disconnected my private number. That hurt big time. I was pissed at Greg, but deep down, I knew he cared.

Through it all, Darren and I kept things simple. At sixteen we didn't overthink; it was just easy days and fun.

"Yo D, your friend wants you," Lucas Jones said, breaking my daydream. Stacy is outside the classroom, waving and grinning like a lunatic. She's coming with Greg and me to the concert tonight. I can tell she's also filled up on high-octane energy when she lifts her neon fuchsia shirt and flashes the whole algebra class, which breaks out in laughter. Stacy bolts, and just as Mrs. Lapanee is about to catch on—*ding!* The school bell. I was so out of there.

In the hallway, I slapped high-fives with everyone—freshmen, seniors, nerds, jocks, stoners, cheerleaders. Somehow, I'd pulled off the impossible, dodging the curse of getting stuck in one clique and shunned by the others.

In the parking lot, Stacy waited by her brand-new white Mazda RX-7 convertible—her sweet sixteen present. We jumped in, blasting our mixtape—Madonna, the Smiths, the Psychedelic Furs—peeling out like teen royalty.

I didn't have my own car yet, but honestly? Riding shotgun in Stacy's convertible with the music cranked and the wind in my hair, I thought, *What's not to love? Let her drive.* I was living.

My sweet sixteen had its own kind of magic. No shiny keys, but a night I'll never forget. Mom took me to the Harlequin Playhouse to see *Grease* live, one of our favorite movies. We'd watched it a dozen times at Edwards Cinema, swooning over Danny Zuko and Sandy. That night, she even got us backstage to meet the cast. All the boys lined up to kiss me. Cheesy, perfect. Totally one of my best birthdays ever.

Less than a mile away was my house, in Fountain Valley, sitting on the corner of a cul-de-sac: two stories, five bedrooms, and a big back yard.

It's the same house we've lived in since my parents were together, but now it's just me, Greg, Jeff, and my mom. Stacy parks and we spring up the sidewalk, past the towering Italian cypress trees lining the path to the front door.

In the white-tiled foyer, we were greeted by two familiar family members: garlic and olive oil, which meant Mom was at the stove. In our house, food was love. My mom, a glamorous Italian-American goddess with heartbreak in her eyes since my dad left, ruled the kitchen like it was her palace. She stood stirring something delicious in the pot with the wooden spoon, equal parts legend and warning. It made the Sunday sauce we craved, but we knew that same spoon could correct your attitude mid-sentence.

Stacy and I beelined for the wet bar in the dining room, stealthily draining Mom's vodka into our flasks and topping off the bottle with water—classic move.

Just then, my oldest brother, Greg, who was twenty, rolled up in his red VW Rabbit convertible, top down, stereo blasting the B-52s loud enough to turn heads. Greg looked exactly like Robert Downey Jr., and he knew it. We heard the front door crack open and shoved the evidence back into the liquor cabinet just in time. Mission accomplished. Greg poked his head around the corner, giving that older-brother look: part suspicion, part smug amusement.

"What are you two hooligans up to?" Greg had assumed the role of "man of the house" since Dad left, which is super annoying. Only four years older than me, he's basically a kid himself.

Stacy smoothly pretended to show me a makeup trick. "See? More of a flick," she said, like she was giving an eyeliner masterclass. Greg raised an eyebrow but let it slide.

"Dinner!" Mom yelled from the sunny kitchen. "Come eat before it gets cold!" Sitting down to eat while the food was still hot was about the only rule my mom ever actually stuck to.

Around the table was the usual noisy circus. Then my other older brother, Jeff—the eighteen-year-old Italian Stallion with dark, curly hair that gave him a young Patrick Dempsey vibe—swaggered in late. He drove a red 914 Porsche he'd busted his ass to buy—delivering newspapers, stenciling and spray-painting addresses on neighborhood curbs, anything. He was a born hustler. Even as a kid, he took money seriously: at our lemonade stand, he'd fill the glasses halfway but charge full price, while Greg gave it away for free, and I sipped profits, with my head tilted toward the sun. That pretty much sums up the three of us, even still today.

Jeff dropped into a chair, drumsticks sticking out of his back pocket, and shot our Bowie plans a look of pure disdain.

"Boring," he muttered, then slid a wrinkled flyer across the table—his band, *The Victims*, was playing a five-kegger at Oscar's house.

I shrugged, but I hated missing it. Everyone who mattered from high school would be there. His legendary house parties were always packed, with cars jammed along the curbs for blocks.

"It's David *Fucking* Bowie!" Stacy retorted, catching herself and apologizing to my mom for swearing, who just laughed.

The truth was, I was proud of my brother's cool status. I loved the way people looked at him on stage—and, by extension, how they looked at me. I was the little sister of a drummer on the rise. That was serious social currency.

Ever since I was little, I remember Jeff being in a band. Our garage was rock 'n' roll central. MTV set vibes. Stacy and I front and center on that peeling brown old leather sofa as VIP fans and occasional roadies. We'd flip on the amp, and the electric hiss would snap every bored teenager in a two-mile radius out of their after-school comas.

But come on—no gig could top tonight's concert.

"Don't let me keep you from happiness. You may be excused."

Stacy and I push away from the table and dart upstairs faster than the Road Runner leaving Wile E. Coyote in the dust.

In my room, I pour us two shots and Stacy cranks up Bowie's "Let's Dance." Getting dressed for a night out is a ritual for us. We've spent hundreds of hours in my bedroom, in front of the full-length mirror, putting together outfits and doing each other's hair and makeup. Orange

County, California, is a stone's throw from the Pacific Ocean, so the mainstream vibe leans on surf culture. Strappy sundresses and skimpy bikinis from OP and Hang Ten dominate our daytime looks. But for a night out, Stacy and I are all about the new-wave rebel punk aesthetic. Think Madonna, Debbie Harry. We worship lace corsets, ripped jeans, and arms stacked with silver bangles. We tore pages from *Vogue* and *Cosmo*, dreaming of strutting like Cindy Crawford in designer wear. Our allowances didn't stretch to Gucci, but we mastered Wet Seal and Contempo Casuals. Finally, we nailed it: tiny sundresses over Dolphin shorts (modesty for wild dancing). Stacy pulls on her black western boots, I tie a blue bandana into a headband, and we hug and scream like two cover girls who just landed a cosmetics deal and became the cover girls of *Sassy* and *Seventeen*.

The amphitheater is buzzing like a live wire. Greg uses his fake ID, allows us one beer, and makes us swear to use the buddy system for bathroom runs. Like we don't already operate as one unit.

Madness kicks off "Our House." The pit of ska groupies goes nuts. Suggs, their lead singer, bounces in his tiny sunglasses and baggy suit. Stacy and I jump in—head-bobbing, marching in circles, arms bent like pistons. Eye candy overload.

Then The Go-Go's take the stage, and all I see is Belinda Carlisle, punk goddess in a metallic rose-colored dress. She sings her heart out, blowing kisses to the crowd, and we scream the "Our Lips Are Sealed" lyrics back.

We completely lose it when The Go-Go's burst into "Head Over Heels." Stacy and I scream every word, gripping each other's hands, hair wild, makeup probably melting.

Bowie appears, and we teleport to the front row. Okay, we elbow, push, and flirt our way there. He's glowing in a gold suit. His alien magnetism pulses through the air. He sings "Space Oddity," and I swear I levitate. For one perfect second, I believe in magic. Stars spin behind him. I feel infinite—my best friend beside me, Greg somewhere nearby, and the world crackles with possibility.

Then Monday comes crashing in like a buzzkill. We're at school, standing by the lockers when Stacy drops a bomb: her parents are separating; she's moving away.

"To Ventura," she says.

Ventura is like a hundred miles from Orange County. She might as well be moving to Japan. I blink, trying to pretend it's just a joke. But her eyes are too serious, too sad. My stomach caves in.

"Wait—when?"

"Next week. It's already decided."

Next week. Not even enough time to fight it. To scheme our way out. To soak up what's left. Just—done.

I nod like I'm cool, like I've got this. But inside, I'm clawing at everything that's about to be ripped away.

She hugs me, tight. "You'll visit. I'll visit. We'll write. We'll call. I swear."

But I already know the truth—some promises have expiration dates.

My parents divorced when I was seven. My memories of them as a couple have been formed from secondhand stories and old photographs, which I've studied over the years like a cop obsessed with a cold case. I needed to keep their love story alive. The images are strung together in my mind like a home movie. It plays as a film noir.

Robert Trigo and Frances met in 1956, and in September 1961, they walked down the aisle to "Ave Maria." My mom was a classic beauty from Brooklyn, a cross between Sophia Loren and Gina Lollobrigida. She wore black capri pants and demure necklines, sometimes letting a bit of her shoulders peek out, paired with classic pumps. Her hairstyles were of the moment—bouffants like Jackie Kennedy's, polished and elegant. My dad is a doctor from Staten Island, handsome, and chiseled, with a natural swagger and Rat Pack charm—sharp in fitted suits when he went to work at his chiropractic office. On his days off, he rocked the "off-duty mobster" look: put together but more SoCal casual, with polo shirts, a black Members Only jacket, and slacks. I idolized them both. She represented romance and glamour, and he was old-school machismo charm.

Together they were like a couple from the golden age of Hollywood. I heard all the stories when they first started dating to prove it: my dad in a suit, slipping the doorman money at the Coconut Grove to get the best seat in the house; my mom in heels, moving across the dance floor, glowing at each other.

They'd been married fifteen years when my dad cheated. The affair was the only reason I was ever given for why my parents broke up. It happened fast. My dad quickly remarried his secretary, Gale. She was a young, blond, hippie-chic, who rocked low-rise jeans, sweet crop tops, and called everything "groovy." Even my dad started saying "bitchin'." Then they adopted a baby boy: Peter. I loved him—he was sweet and always wanted to hold my hand. But I was seven, still holding out hope for that life-size Bugs Bunny my dad used to try to win for me at the carnival. Now it was Peter who got the stuffed animals, the rides on Dad's shoulders—all those little things that used to make me feel special.

Maybe I blocked it out, but I don't remember any Brady Bunch–style family meeting where my parents sat my brothers and me down to walk us through the finer points of divorce. There was never a thoughtful discussion where we kids were invited to ask questions or share our feelings. No, my family dealt with complicated emotions as most did in the seventies: we buried them. Mom, though, bottled up her anger until it exploded in sudden, unpredictable outbursts we never knew how to handle. Meanwhile, Dad just kept living like nothing changed—full throttle, no looking back.

Dad's every-other-weekend visits were always timed around something special, which only pissed Mom off more, because she hated how excited we'd get to see "the cheating bastard." I'll admit, her rants got to me. Sometimes I resented him—because I was the one stuck dealing with the fallout. But deep down, I knew he never stopped loving me—his attention and love were just spread thin across too many people.

Mom did her best and tried to keep traditions alive—Sunday dinners with our loud, loving Italian family, huge bowls of pasta, stories shouted over each other. But her anger had teeth. She was stuck in betrayal, and I felt helpless. Finally, to keep her busy, my aunt Flo gave her what felt like the golden ticket to Willy Wonka's factory: the reins to Café Pasquini, her restaurant in South Coast Plaza—one of the most exclusive malls in the country, tucked between Saks Fifth Avenue and I. Magnin.

The café had a sprawling outdoor patio and a European vibe, long before it caught on as a trend. It looked like a Helmut Newton photo: women in stilettos, ashtrays on every table, the air thick with espresso steam and attitude. People sat for hours in bistro chairs, sipping espresso by day and red wine at night. It was like Harrods in London or Bergdorf Goodman in New York. Mom thrived there, charming customers and making famous friends. I'd see Richard Thomas and Luciano Pavarotti all the time. She even hired our high school friends, including Darren, to work summers behind the counter. The café became our second home, filled with laughter, family, and Mom's newfound confidence.

My Nonna lived right around the corner from the mall and ate lunch at the café every day. Born in Sicily, she looked and acted just like the "Where's the Beef?" lady from the Wendy's commercials—tiny, sharp, and unforgettable. Locals adored her. She was a living legend, keeping us entertained with her no-nonsense wit and deadpan charm. She'd proudly say, "I've never had a drink in my whole life," conveniently excluding the cold beer with her chicken cutlets at lunch or the red wine with her spaghetti and meatballs at dinner.

When I was little, she'd rally the whole family for tomato runs. My parents would drive the RV out to the fields nearby, park on the edge, and she'd send us kids out with laundry baskets, telling us to only grab the ones that had fallen on the ground, as if those fell under some kind of "finders keepers" loophole. She'd wink while she said it. We'd fill the RV up just in time before the police arrived, haul them home, and all get together and turn that bounty into bubbling pots of delicious sauces for canning.

Maybe it was a Sicilian thing—food was sacred, and rules were flexible when it came to feeding people. When the grunions were running, we'd wake up at dawn and head to Newport Beach. Grandpa handed out rags and warned us the fish would slip away if we weren't quick. Sure, it broke the law, but in our house, it felt more like a tradition than a crime. Other than bending the rules when it came to food, Grandpa was straight as an arrow, and Nonna never missed a chance to spread her arms wide and declare him "the best husband in the world."

But it wasn't just about food. It was also about heart, and my mom had the biggest heart of all. She ran the mall, letting old Italian guys play *scopa* and gamble thousands across Carrera marble tabletops like it was Monte Carlo. When Mr. Segerstrom caught wind and shut it down, Mom, feeling bad for them, opened up the café's storage closet instead. My mom was the queen of networking. She bent the rules and kept everyone happy, pouring white wine into paper cups to-go and trading them with the pretty department store girls for expensive cosmetics—luxuries she'd then pass on to Stacy and me. I wasn't raised to live strictly by the book; there's no fun in that. Thanks to Mom, we didn't fuck with Maybelline—we went straight to Estée Lauder, Borghese, and Chanel.

Mom was the heartbeat of the mall. Everyone knew her. Patrons lined up just to get a seat at her table. Watching her hold court at Café Pasquini, radiant, proud, I felt a flicker of hope, a reminder of the warmth and love I'd known as a child. And even then, I missed Stacy. I missed my family before the divorce, before everything shifted.

I could see us all sitting together at the big dining table when Dad was still home, Mom coming out with platters of food, saying, "*Mangia, mangia*!" as Sinatra's "New York, New York" played on the stereo. The sound of laughter was the true background music of our lives.

Those truly were the best times. The Fountain Valley Drive-In was around the corner, where we packed snacks and watched movies together. I could've sworn *Jaws* was an inch away from me. Afterward, we'd head to Bob's Big Boy, climbing onto the statue while Mom shouted, "Get down!" We never listened.

We Trigos were always on the go. We took family vacations in our motorhome, Dad carrying us inside while we slept, waking up surprised at river campsites, Yosemite, or pulling into Circus Circus in Las Vegas. Sometimes he'd take us to Joshua Tree to shoot soda cans off a log, even McDonald's figurines hanging from the trees, with a .22.

Back at home, mornings started with cereal, cartoons, and Flintstone vitamins, then we spent the day outdoors. No smartphones or social media—just swimming, riding bikes, jumping rope, chasing the ice cream truck, hopping on the back of the garbage truck until they kicked us off, running through sprinklers, and drinking from garden hoses that tasted like rubber, dirt, and freedom.

We explored the drainage sewer tunnels beneath the 405 Freeway, our own secret passage. We ran along the edges through the shallow stream of water until the day William Bonin, the notorious serial killer, chased us. We barely made it out alive. To this day, I don't know how we did.

At night, we came home when the streetlights flickered on or Mom hollered, "Dinner time!" Later, the family played board games, laughing through episodes of *Happy Days*, *Laverne & Shirley*, or *Welcome Back, Kotter*, before getting upstairs to bed.

My bedroom was my sanctuary: a frilly canopy bed with a rainbow comforter and pillowcases, posters lined the wall, stuffed animals, and 45s records my mom bought me from Gemco stacked beside the turntable. I listened to soft rock while mom brushed my hair, looping pink hair bobbles into a perfect ponytail.

I loved trying on tube tops, satin bomber jackets, mood rings, and puka shell necklaces. In my closet were brown suede Hush Puppies and black-and-white saddle shoes, polished to erase scuffs. My Dittos and Chemin de Fer jeans were my favorites for roller rink parties.

We played dodgeball, kick the can, ding-dong-ditch, toilet-papered houses, and cracked up over prank calls. Greg and Jeff wore Vans with high tube socks and corduroy OP shorts, running right alongside our friends and me. Wild, unsupervised, unstoppable. Our parents only noticed us if they spotted a mound of bikes on someone's front lawn.

Those were the best days, full of simple magic. Now, Stacy was gone, Dad distant. I wish I'd cherished it more, not realizing how quickly life would start demanding more. Move faster. Be better. Grow up.

Chapter Two

Rebel Yell

OCTOBER 1983

After Stacy abandoned me (sorry, *moved away*), I felt totally adrift, and let me tell you, I am *not* a fan of feeling adrift. I'm a girl who likes to be tethered—preferably to another human—at all times. Call it codependent if you want, but honestly, I think the haters who throw that word around are just jealous they've never felt the kind of soul-bonding love that makes you want to drink someone's blood. Sad for them.

With Stacy gone, the only person left for me to latch onto was my mom. So, every day after school, I'd drift over to Pasquini's, plant myself on a bistro chair, sip my Italian lemon soda, and devour endless, buttery hunks of warm focaccia bread while updating her on every morsel of high school drama. She'd hang on my every word, leaning in close, tossing her dish towel casually over her shoulder, acting like my gossip was national-security-level intel. Looking back, I realize it wasn't the "who kissed who" dirt she loved; it was just having her silly teenage daughter sitting there, happily chattering away, helping her forget life's troubles.

During one of our epic gossip sessions, Julie dropped into our lives like a grenade. She stormed into the café in a rush, all urgency and attitude, asking to use the phone. She wore a tight black tee, faded jeans sculpted to her hips, and badass moto boots—pure East Coast toughness, a look that practically screamed, "I'm here to fuck shit up." Trust me, you don't see a lot of that walking around sunny Newport. Julie didn't walk; she swaggered. She had a tiny waist and boobs so fantastic they should've had their own fan club.

I desperately needed to know her secrets. Whatever conversation she had on the phone clearly wasn't good news; by the end of it, she was in tears. Before I knew it, my mom had her seated at a table with a glass of wine, a bowl of pasta, and a heartfelt offer to move into our house. This was not unusual; my mom had a habit of picking up strays. Once, she brought home a sobbing Scottish woman straight from a bus stop. The woman had just arrived in town, expecting to be picked up by a friend who never showed, and she let her live with us for two months. But Julie was the polar opposite. She was a twenty-three-year-old whirlwind with a wild history of rock stars and famous actors. My mom adored her immediately, probably thinking I needed an older sister figure to keep me out of trouble. Little did she know, Julie was the definition of trouble.

Despite our seven-year age gap, Julie and I clicked. I became her mentee in the fine art of splitting worlds. During the week, she'd be baking cookies, arranging fresh-cut flowers in mason jars around the house, and sipping cappuccinos with me at Pasquini's, teasing my mom about her devotion to celibacy. But come Friday night, sweet Julie became a leather-clad rock goddess, roaring off to LA and returning Sunday with tales so scandalous they should've been fiction.

The first weekend she lived with us, she strutted into my bedroom to borrow hairspray, dressed like Julia Roberts in *Pretty Woman*: thigh-high boots, a leather micro-mini, and a corset top that barely contained her legendary cleavage.

"You're going out like *that*?" I asked, my jaw practically hitting the floor.

"What do you think, genius?" She smirked, shaking her booty at my mirror.

Girls my age weren't exactly taught body positivity in the '80s. Sure, Stacy and I dressed daringly, but we definitely weren't out there openly admiring our own assets like Julie was. She was big hair, big attitude, and all things in excess.

"Take me with you," I pleaded, desperate for a taste of her life, feeling ridiculously childish in my brother's old boxers and oversized tee.

"No chance. You're sixteen and a virgin."

"What does my virginity have to do with it?" I shot back, totally clueless.

"Exactly my point, kid," she said, rolling her eyes. "LA corrupts people."

"Then why do *you* go?"

She laughed, her eyes sparkling. "Honey, I've been corrupted since forever."

After months of begging, pleading, and subtle manipulative warfare, Julie finally broke down. It barely took any convincing to get my mom on board. She trusted Julie would look out for me. Plus, this was the eighties; there was literally a PSA that came on television every night at ten o'clock featuring celebrities looking into the camera and asking America's parents, "Do you know where your children are?" Even with that, most didn't. Parents everywhere were cluelessly optimistic. Julie had only one warning: "Don't embarrass me in front of my famous friends."

"No problem," I promised, secretly praying she wasn't just bluffing about those "famous friends."

That first Friday night, I was dressed to kill: tight pants, a barely-there backless top, sky-high pumps, lots of mascara, and hair teased to astronomical heights, thanks to Julie's endless layers of Aqua Net.

Traffic sucked the energy right out of me, but when Julie turned onto Sunset Boulevard and Def Leppard blasted from the stereo, my blood ignited. I'd been to LA plenty during the day with my parents, but the Sunset Strip at night was like stepping into another universe. We passed the Viper Room (formerly the Central), Whisky a Go Go, and the Roxy, music pumping, lights flashing, a tangible haze of sweat and sex coating everything. Pure eighties decadence.

We bypassed the massive line snaking outside the Rainbow Bar and Grill thanks to Julie's VIP hookup with Tony the doorman. The Rainbow isn't much to look at from the outside—a small, shabby brick building, but inside was rock-and-roll fantasyland. The restaurant had big red leather booths that exuded an old-school Italian vibe. We barely made it a full loop when a guy grabbed Julie from behind and kissed her passionately. He turned to me and grinned.

"Who's this?"

Holy shit. It was Robert fucking Plant.

No wonder he looked familiar; I'd been worshiping his image in magazines and on album covers for years. I listened to "Stairway to Heaven" so much that I wore out the record. Somehow, I squeaked out my name. Julie shot me a look like, *Keep your cool, Denise.* I tried not to faint when he invited us to his table. Celebrities, top models, and rock legends lounged everywhere—Ozzy Osbourne, Steve Perry, guys from Poison, Ratt, Def Leppard, Iron Maiden. The wildest of Jeff's record collection, right in front of me. Julie smirked smugly, clearly saying, *Told ya.*

The night was a haze of Dom Pérignon champagne, pepperoni pizza, casual lines of coke, and rockstar debauchery. I politely passed on the blow, determined to prove Julie wrong about being corrupted, at least not my first night. Whiskey shots felt safer.

After the club closed, we were on our way to the legendary afterhours club Gazzarri's when Robert invited us to an afterparty at a hillside mansion overlooking all of LA. By the pool, naked girls casually lounged, openly making out. A gorgeous blond ran her finger down my arm invitingly.

"Wanna come in the Jacuzzi with me?"

I squeaked out, "Not now, thanks," and quickly retreated, blushing furiously.

I held court with Tommy Lee all night. Stories, shots, and cigarette smoke filled the room. By morning, Nikki Sixx swaggered by shirtless with a half bottle of Jack Daniel's dangling from his hand. I snatched it without hesitation, took a bold swig, and muttered something cheeky. He laughed. Nikki Sixx actually laughed at *my* joke.

From then on, LA became my weekend escape. Eddie Money in a recording studio, Joan Jett private concerts, wild nights with Mötley Crüe.

One night, I met a British post-punk idol with my hands in his bleached hair, tasting his full lips. It was Hot in the City that night.

Julie was right. LA corrupts. And I was loving every second of it, racing headfirst into rebellion at warp speed, fueled by whiskey, hairspray, and pure teenage lust.

Chapter Three

Beach Blanket Bingo!

APRIL 1984

I spent those months in LA hopping rides with older FVHS friends Gwen and Susie, and we danced at the Palace and Odyssey, lost in the rhythm, moving through the smoky air until dawn as DJs spun everything from Duran Duran to Berlin, their synths pulsing like a heartbeat. After the Rainbow, we drifted into places like the Roxy or Gazzarri's, where the danger felt delicious, as my nights blurred together into one neon-lit haze of vodka, bad decisions, and heartbreakingly gorgeous men far too old for me. Like that twenty-four-year-old model from an up-and-coming band who I swore was "the one."

Julie was another whirlwind who disappeared as quickly as she arrived, vanishing to care for her mom. She left me her leather jacket, a half bottle of Aqua Net, and wild memories.

But life has a funny way of making things right again. Stacy moved back, and suddenly the world had meaning. Her mom snagged a little place on Superior Hill in Newport with ocean views, a tennis court, and an abundance of hot surfer dudes as neighbors. Stacy and I reunited like we'd never missed a beat, laughing our asses off when one of us inevitably forgot tennis balls or rackets.

But our bubble burst one afternoon when Stacy broke down courtside. Turns out her parents' divorce was official, and in a fit of cruelty, her mom told her she had to move out. Then, as if that wasn't enough, she dropped the biggest bombshell yet: the man Stacy always called "Dad" wasn't really her father.

"Can you believe that shit?" Stacy sobbed, handing me a crumpled paper with two phone numbers scrawled: her real dad and grandparents she'd never met.

I tried to cheer her up. "Maybe he's super wealthy."

A week later, Greg drove us out to some seedy motel, the kind with dented doors and questionable-looking tenants. Her dad opened the door, a sloppy drunk with Stacy's exact cornflower-blue eyes and heart-shaped face. Within fifteen minutes, Stacy ran out crying.

"He's a total loser," she said bitterly, wiping snot on her Polo sweater. "I'm fucked."

"No St. Tropez shopping sprees from Daddy Warbucks, huh?" I teased gently, pulling her close.

But Greg wasn't laughing. Instead of dropping Stacy off at her grandmother's, he drove right past the bewildered old lady on the porch in her flowered housedress and took us home.

My mom didn't even blink. "Of course you can stay," she said, hugging Stacy tight. Stacy moved in for good.

Meanwhile, Jeff was suddenly rolling in cash. One night, I caught him wrapping thick stacks of bills in rubber bands.

"Did you rob a bank?" I joked.

He dodged my eyes, mumbling something about work. Sure, bussing tables pays—but not *that* well. Soon he upgraded his car, bought a cherry-red Porsche Carrera, and installed a safe in his room. I smelled trouble, but Mom just shrugged it off as "boy stuff."

* * *

Junior year rolled around, and Stacy and I strutted through the halls of Fountain Valley High like goddamn supermodels, rocking oversized blazers, leather pencil skirts, and metallic accessories we snagged from Mom's mall perks. Every morning, Mom left the house early to open the café, and we'd wave goodbye like school was our next stop. Ditching our backpacks, we'd slip into Lycra and blade down the Huntington Beach boardwalk. We meant well, but let's be honest—ambition was easier than follow-through. And sometimes, ditching was a rare stroke of luck. Stacy and I somehow ended up at the scene of a pileup—and there, in the middle of it all, stood my Nonna. Cars crunched, smoke hanging in the air. When I ran up, she locked eyes with me like I was her guardian angel.

"Tell the police it wasn't my fault," she whispered.

So we did—we gave a full report like we'd seen the whole thing. We forged signatures; ditched class for beach days; hosted MTV-fueled ragers, blasting Michael Jackson, the Eurythmics, Cyndi Lauper, and the Smiths; and ran frantic clean-up ops before my mom got home. Every weekend was a fashion show. Every week was another excuse.

By spring break, we were stuck in a vicious cycle. One skipped class turned into twenty, and suddenly, we were so far behind in credits that even summer school couldn't save us. There was no Mr. Hand from *Fast Times at Ridgemont High* coming to my rescue like he did for Spicoli. This was real life. And the craziest part? It wasn't just that I couldn't keep up—it was that no one expected me to. My parents never sat me down to ask what I wanted to be when I grew up. We never talked about college. There was no plan, no push, no pressure. I knew they loved me. I never lacked that. They were just busy trying to navigate their own lives—and they trusted me to do the right thing.

On Monday evening, we hatched a desperate plan as my mom settled down to watch *Cagney & Lacey*, her sacred hour. Perfect timing: after one Harvey Wallbanger, she was usually open to anything.

"We're too mature for high school," I announced dramatically.

Stacy jumped in. "We want GEDs and internships in fashion, to be independent career women like you."

My mom sighed, and I could tell she wasn't thrilled, probably knowing she couldn't stop this runaway train.

"All right," she said reluctantly, "I will buy you girls the study books—but you better actually study."

We hugged and squealed, imagining our glamorous future.

We weren't stupid. But we were lost. Drifting. Looking for something bigger than the suburban dream. Sometimes, that came in the form of a boy.

Enter: Rich.

I met him at a party Jeff took Stacy and me to at a glitzy Newport Beach spot in Fashion Island. Stacy and I had just popped Cheech and Chong into the VCR for movie night when Jeff yelled down, "Hey, you two losers wanna come to a party?"

We ditched Cheech and Chong before they rolled their first joint.

We sprinted upstairs, skipping steps, scrunchies, and oversized Esprit sweatshirts flying.

Jeff poked his head in my room. "Oh, it's kind of fancy, so dress to impress."

Duh.

Stacy hit play on our mixed tape, I plugged in the hot rollers, and we got to work. Stacy, in a glossy vinyl miniskirt and angora sweater, looked effortlessly glam. I finished my sophisticated party-girl look with a gold chain belt, white pumps, frosty rose Borghese lipstick, and a spritz of Coco Chanel—another mall perk.

We climbed into Jeff's cherry-red Porsche 911 Carrera, speeding down the Pacific Coast Highway toward Newport Beach. The sun dipped into the ocean, casting a blood-orange glow. The sound system blasted "The Spirit of Radio" by Rush. Jeff drove like a maniac—horns blaring, drivers swearing. It made me nervous, but not him.

At the elegant French restaurant in Newport, Jeff got swept into the crowd. Stacy and I teetered around, looking for hot guys, when one turned my way.

"Care to smoke?"

Care to smoke? Who is this guy, James Bond?

"Why yes, I'd love to," I said, channeling my inner sexy Bond Girl, taking a hit off his joint and coughing my head off.

Rich had beautiful green eyes and cute freckles on his nose that softened his punkish, I-don't-give-a-fuck demeanor. While everyone else was wearing their rolled-up jeans and blazers, this guy was in a wrinkled t-shirt, shorts, and sneakers. Cool or not? I couldn't decide. He was charming, sexy, and, according to the wad of cash I saw in his wallet when he bought me a drink, loaded. He had me laughing hysterically when he pointed at one woman and quoted the Rodney Dangerfield line from *Caddyshack*, "Bet she got a free bowl of soup with that hat."

We talked the rest of the night, laughing until our jaws hurt. We discussed punk and goth rock bands we loved—Sex Pistols, Bauhaus, Siouxsie and the Banshees, and the Cult.

"But I'm not a punk. I'm an entrepreneur. I plan to make it big early and retire while I'm still young. I don't want to be a slave to the man forever."

I nodded, finding this very deep.

Jeff interrupted us, "I see you met my sister, Denise."

Fuck. Rich was my brother's friend. That's a boner killer. Jeff introduced Rich as a coworker, which immediately raised red flags—Jeff worked at a sports bar, hardly a hub for punk entrepreneurs.

That night, Jeff left with a chick he just met, so Rich drove Stacy and me home in his Volkswagen Karmann Ghia. It was a cute car, but nothing like the flashy coupes in the Newport Beach parking lot. At my house, he waited at the curb until Stacy and I unlocked the door.

He yelled dramatically through the car window, "I'll see you again soon, Denise!"

I met Rich at the beach a few days later. I could tell he had a crush on me, but I refused to engage—I didn't want to date one of my brother's friends. Over the next few weeks, he treated Stacy and me to concerts and dinners. Sometimes the Karmann Ghia's battery died, leaving someone to push the car while the other popped the clutch, until it roared to life—but it was part of the fun.

We saw the Pretenders at Pacific Amphitheatre and Echo & the Bunnymen at Irvine Meadows, and he introduced us to bitchin' venues—Concert Factory in Costa Mesa, the Golden Bear in Huntington

Beach—to watch the Plimsouls. We had fake IDs, so we even went to Vegas and got a suite at the Tropicana. Stacy and I even had our own bedroom. Rich gave us gambling money, bought us dresses, and took us to fancy restaurants. He threw cash around like confetti—yet he didn't have a serious job. When I asked about work, Rich would answer, "Some might say I don't work, per se. Others might say I dabble." Eventually, I started to see the signs clearly. Pagers, running off to the payphones at 7-Eleven in a flurry, whispers behind closed doors. I snuck up and pressed my ear to Jeff's bedroom door. I heard the words *pounds*, *prices*, *shipments*. Beach, blanket, bingo! Jeff and Rich were dealing coke.

I cornered Jeff one day.

"You're dealing, aren't you?"

He flinched, realizing I knew.

"I won't tell Mom," I promised, "but I'm worried."

He assured me everything was fine. I wanted to believe him, because the expensive jewelry, the easy cash, was a lifeline I'd desperately missed since our parents' divorce. But it was scary, too, knowing Jeff was dabbling in something so dangerous. I wanted to believe they'd never get caught. That it was just a phase. That we were too smart, too cool, too charming to let it all fall apart.

But deep down, I felt it: the party couldn't last forever. The crash was coming. We just didn't know when. And that's the thing no one tells you about growing up. You think you're untouchable. Until you're not.

* * *

Mom sensed trouble too but kept herself in denial, awkwardly asking me who Jeff's "friends" were when shady guys visited. Most of the time, I protected Jeff, playing dumb or lying, "Oh, just a friend from high school." Part of me wished she'd see through the lies, so I would challenge her: "I don't know, Mom, what do you think?" Sometimes, she banged on Jeff's door, demanding he open it. He would, but only after hiding his triple beam scale, cocaine residue, and plastic baggies. She eventually set some house rules: no strangers over, and don't lock your door.

Jeff bought my silence with diamond bracelets that came from "tweakers" who traded him hot goods when they couldn't pay in cash—blood money, maybe, but it felt so good to be taken care of again.

I rationalized: I wasn't dealing. I wasn't stealing. I was just accessorizing.

Because, let's face it: We were all living in a material world, and I was a material girl, ready to take whatever life threw my way, no matter the cost.

Chapter Four
Agent 99

SEPTEMBER 1984

It was technically September, but for Stacy and me, life still felt like one long, hazy summer. We were officially "studying for the GED," which just meant we had more hours in our day than dollars in our pockets—and no real idea what to do with either.

Stacy picked up extra shifts at Silky Sullivan's, rocking her high ponytail and flashing that megawatt smile for tips. Me? I was slinging coffee and sass as a server at the café a few days a week. Most days, I felt like Phoebe Cates in *Fast Times at Ridgemont High*—all lip gloss and cool. Inside, though, I was a little lost. At seventeen, I shrugged it off—no one really had their shit together anyway. I lived for the day.

Ten years after the divorce and Dad still wasn't allowed in the house. But his visits were always steady. He took me out on dates—fancy lunches at Reuben's Steakhouse, the kind of place with dark-paneled dining rooms, where you'd get a shrimp cocktail or a wedge salad served on a chilled plate. The waitresses, dressed in crisp black and white, used to flirt with my dad. He'd wink at them or crack some dumb joke, and they'd laugh a little too hard. Annoying. But he and Jeff were thick as thieves, golfing at Driftwood and hunting together. They just got each other.

Jeff would crack open my door. "Dad's outside," he'd say.

And like clockwork, I'd drop whatever I was doing and run out to the sidewalk for one of those big, quiet, lingering hugs, the kind that tried to make up for all the lost time. Then came the move: Dad would reach into his pocket and slide me a folded hundred, like it was some kind of top-secret handoff.

"Don't tell your brothers," he'd whisper with a wink, like I was the chosen one. And for a while, I believed it. But eventually, we all caught on. Dad was handing out hundreds to everyone. No one was being left out.

Mom still handled the basics, and Stacy and I were still getting mall perks from her, high-end perfume and cosmetics. Listen, I was raised at the mall. Not near the noisy food court, but beneath the glittering chandeliers of Cartier and Rolex, surrounded by Lalique glass vases and Williams Sonoma copper tea kettles. One time, someone left a bag at the café—a folded Hermès silk scarf and a jungle-print Yves Saint Laurent cigarette case. Mom waited a month for the owner to come back, but they never did. Then one night, she handed it to me like it was nothing. I wore that scarf like I was on a yacht off the coast of the French Riviera and packed the chic case full of cloves.

We worked for our style. Mom thought we were nuts—and honestly, she wasn't wrong. I must've made a million cappuccinos, just to blow my whole paycheck on one perfect suede skirt. We were just kids, spending whatever we had. And when our pockets ran dry, we figured it out. We always did.

To zen out, we'd toss tuna sandwiches and Pepsi into a cooler, grab a blanket, crank the boombox, and let the ocean do the rest. Sunshine, salt air, Coppertone, and the right Blondie song on full blast—better than any bong hit. Our spot had been the same since eighth grade—between lifeguard towers three and five on the south side of the Huntington Beach Pier, near Main Street shops like Jack's Surfboards and the Golden Bear music club. The End Café sat at the far end of the pier. Surf culture buzzed all around us, prime for people-watching—and being watched. We dressed to dazzle, not to swim. High-cut one-pieces that screamed beach bombshell. Mine was leopard, to match my designer cigarette case, with a neckline that dove low. Stacy rocked zebra stripes, stacked with silver bangles that clinked like she was dining at Studio 54. If no one was gawking, we were doing it wrong. Like the Stray Cats sang, we were sexy, seventeen, and totally electric.

We measured time by our tan lines. Perfectly bronzed o'clock meant it was time to pack up so Stacy could get home and shower before her shift. We were giggling toward the parking lot when a high-pitch engine tore through the air. I shielded my eyes and spotted Jeff in his red Porsche, screeching into the lot by Dwight's. Another Porsche slid in beside him, engine revving. Rich. A classy white 1966 911L. No more Volkswagen. This one commanded respect. It worked. I was impressed.

Drugs were flooding into the US, and while Nancy Reagan lit up the airwaves with her "Just Say No" crusade, the teens in Orange County were saying yes, yes, *hell yes*. Jeff and Rich were deep in it—dealing ounces and eight-balls like candy. Coke was everywhere, tucked in wads of Saran Wrap or hidden in glossy fashion magazine bindles slipped into Levi's back pockets at every high school party. Their clients were all familiar faces—guys in Jeff's band, teammates from Rich's hockey league, and students from FVHS, Edison, and Newport Harbor.

Business was booming, and nobody was saying no. Jeff rocked thick, gold roped-style chains and a diamond pinky ring, pure Italian goombah swagger, like he was channeling my uncles back in Staten Island. Hard to believe this was the same kid who used to wear dorky-ass headgear strapped to his braces. Rich, on the other hand, leaned into SoCal cool. That day he wore a Santa Cruz tee stretched just right across his lean frame. His closet was a shrine to graphic tees—'70s and '80s band logos, surf brands, skate crews—but tees with wacky cartoons was his signature. His real flex? The watch collection: Piguet, Omega, Patek Philippe, Movado. If social media influencers existed back then, they'd have hit as the Bling Guys, raking in followers.

Stacy and I tossed aside our bulky beach bags and cooler as we slinked up to meet them by their cars.

Rich lowered his shades. "What's up, ladies? The beach looks good on you."

"It did," Stacy said. "We're heading out."

"We just got here," Jeff said, frowning.

"Gotta get to work." Stacy shrugged.

"What about you, Denise?" Rich asked. "Can you hang for a bit?"

"Guess so," I said, playing it cool. Stacy took off, and I scooted onto the hood of Jeff's car like I was posing for a cover shoot.

"Don't even think about it," Jeff warned me. "You'll dent it."

"Whatever," I said, rolling my eyes.

"Sit over here," Rich offered, patting his car's hood. "I'm cool with a little damage."

I stuck my tongue out at Jeff and leaned up onto Rich's hood. We hit it off fast, and I could tell by the way his eyes lingered that he wanted more than friendship, but dating a drug dealer wasn't on my to-do list. By then, most teens around me were either selling coke or doing it. I was doing neither. I was just a good girl, along for the ride. Jeff's pager beeped. Back then, having a pager was the ultimate flex. At first, they were for doctors handling emergencies or execs keeping tabs on the office. Jeff and Rich? They used theirs to get orders from clients. Sometimes, we'd page each other just to figure out where everyone was—no Life360, no Snap Map.

If you didn't know how pagers worked, someone would call your number, punch in a callback number, plus a special code to show who was paging you. Jeff's code was 86—after Maxwell Smart from *Get Smart*. I was 99, after Maxwell's saucy sidekick. Greg's was 68, the opposite of Jeff's. Rich? 111 because he was lucky. Mom's pager was 606—that spelled M.O.M. Dad's was 123. And then there was 505, which looked like SOS, the emergency code.

I can't count how many times I sprinted to a phone to call back a 505, only to hear Greg whining, "Will you bring me Naugles? I'd kill for a combo burrito." But the code we all dreaded was 911—that meant trouble with the cops, a warning to lay low.

Jeff got a page and removed his black Ray-Ban Wayfarers to read the number. "I gotta split to 7-Eleven to make this call."

"Oh goody," I said, grabbing my stuff. "I'm starving."

Rich slumped. "You're leaving? What about me?"

"I think you'll survive." I smirked.

Jeff was still on the payphone when I came out of 7-Eleven, crunching on a juicy dill pickle. "I'll give you one day to turn it," he told whoever was on the other end. When he hung up, I handed him a bag of M&M's and a can of root beer. "You better not spill one drop of pickle juice in my car."

"Um, you're welcome," I sassed back.

"Thanks. Let's go. I gotta take care of some business."

"Everything okay?" I asked, catching up to him.

"Alex thinks he deserves a promotion." Alex was a friend from school and one of Jeff's best customers.

"What does that mean?"

Jeff smiled. "You'll see."

Back at home, I sat on Jeff's bed and watched him meticulously weigh Alex's order. When I saw how much product was on the triple beam scale, I understood. Alex was moving from customer to dealer. Jeff had become a distributor. He filled me in. He wasn't just selling coke to users at parties anymore; now those people had their own customers, and Jeff was banking the profits. Jeff explained he was the supplier to Rich. Rich made him the most money because he had a lot of customers. Jeff pitched it like a regular corporate ladder, climbing a legitimate business. His new sales team was upper-class residents of Orange County no one would suspect—the owner of a local jewelry store, the guy selling exotic cars, and a real estate agent. The setup was safer. If he wasn't selling on the street, there was less chance my pager would beep with a 911.

He slid Alex's massive pile of coke off the scale and into a clear baggie and asked if I wanted to tag along on the drop.

I jumped up. "Sure!"

What else did I have to do? An hour later, we pulled up to Naugles to meet Alex. While we waited, I had an idea.

"You should get crafty with this, so it's less obvious you're doing a drug deal. Wait a sec."

I went inside, ordered a large Coke, and grabbed an empty paper cup. Back in the car, I stuffed the baggie inside. *Voila*—coke disguised as Coke. Once Alex arrived, I rolled down the window and handed him his "drink." The whole exchange felt like a thrill ride. I was a smooth operator. Even Jeff was beaming.

"Pretty genius. You might have a future in this business, kid."

My future—now there's something I hadn't thought about in a while. But in that moment, a picture was coming into focus. I was full of hope. Drugs will give you all sorts of illusions, even wrapped in a baggie and taped under your seat. I was soaring above the world.

But that winter, I was soaring for real—above the thick brown smog hugging the city below, winding up into the crisp mountain air of Lake Arrowhead, a resort town a few hours from Orange County, where Dad, Gale, Peter, and Greg had recently moved in. Stacy, Jeff, and I were headed up to spend a few days in the snow.

Leaving Mom behind felt selfish, especially when we were buzzing with excitement about snowball fights and sledding. But she waved us off with one of her guilt-light smiles, already planning Bunco with her friends.

Dad's place was warm and cozy, like a Norman Rockwell painting. He built snowmen with Peter, roasted s'mores in the fireplace, and played the perfect dad. Gale hovered, attentive and nurturing. Dare I say it? They looked like the perfect family. She even cooked well. The only argument I remember was when I was younger—and she wanted me to wear nylons with a dress she'd bought; I refused. Then I cried. Dad, God love him, had my back and took my side. It wasn't even that I really cared about wearing nylons—though, let's be honest, no one cool would be caught dead in pantyhose. It was the principle. She wasn't my mother, and no matter how sweet she was, I didn't want her telling me what to do. Only Mom could do that.

I didn't pull away from Dad on purpose. It just got harder to connect. I got busy, living selfishly like most teenagers, wrapped up in friends and weekend plans. But it wasn't all on me—he's the one who moved a couple of hours away. He didn't push, but he didn't pull, either. We still loved each other. We just weren't as close anymore.

* * *

With my brother Greg out of the house and Stacy working longer hours, Jeff became my main hang. He took me under his wing like I was his intern—eager, loyal, and naive enough to feed his ego while he showed off his new skills. It was only a matter of time before I met his supplier, Shelly. She bartended with Jeff at a dive sports bar called Country Munchkin, a place that smelled like fryer grease and old Coors, with a battered jukebox spinning rad classics like Journey and Van Halen. Jeff picked up a couple of shifts a week, more for the cover than the cash.

Shelly and her husband, Elliot, scored coke from Vinny, her brother-in-law. Family meant loyalty, which somehow made it feel safer. Even though Vinny was fresh out of jail and on probation, he was importing kilos of coke from Peru like business as usual. I knew all of this because, like a good intern, I asked a lot of questions. Jeff answered them all.

When we pulled up to Shelly's small brown house tucked into the bay at Huntington Harbor, I expected someone tough. Instead, she opened the door, and I was floored. Pale blond hair, styled perfectly with a hot curling iron, makeup a dreamy mix of seashell pinks, radiant like Farah Fawcett. She smiled wide, flashing perfect white teeth. I was enchanted.

"Hey, this is my little sister, Denise. My road dog," Jeff announced. God, brothers can really kill a vibe.

Shelly shrieked, still in her pajamas, holding a mug of coffee. "Jeff, why didn't you tell me? I would've put on my best outfit." She chuckled, twirling side to side and taking a bow, showing off her PJs. Shelly hugged me warmly. "Come in, guys. Jeff talks about you a lot." She walked into the corner of the table and giggled again. *This is Jeff's supplier?* I thought. No wonder he wasn't too worried.

Shelly's husband, Elliot, walked in—good build, dark hair, a mustache, genuine smile.

"Want something to drink?" Elliot asked, popping grapes in his mouth.

"Diet Coke," I said. Jeff shot daggers at me. "Actually, I'm good," I corrected.

We all sat down. I learned Elliot was convicted and facing seven years in prison for dealing and possession. His dark chestnut eyes looked hollow. Seven years sounded totally gnarly to me—like a life sentence. I didn't know what to say.

"Sorry to hear you're going to prison. You'll be okay, though, right?"

"My baby will be fine," Shelly cooed, snuggling him on the couch. "You should write him letters."

I'd never met anyone going to prison before.

"Sure, yeah. I'd love to," I stammered.

"I'd like that," Elliot replied gently.

Jeff gave him a brotherly slap on the back. "I'll make sure you get lots of mail, buddy."

Elliot needed someone to help Shelly with the business while he was out of the game, which handed Jeff a golden opportunity. The deal was sealed in the living room with a handshake—no contracts, no lawyers. Just a nod and mutual trust, like an old-school mob movie. I was just a fly on the wall, but I was proud to see Jeff move up the ranks in power.

* * *

Maybe my rebellious streak had always been there—part of my Sicilian blood, part of that Staten Island birthright passed down from Dad. Growing up on the Island, you couldn't help but hear the stories: Guys with thick chains, thicker accents, envelopes passed, favors owed, respect earned. And my father? He had a story of his own. When he was five, he saved an illegal lottery ring during a raid—slipped out with numbers stuffed inside his little jacket. Claimed Lucky Luciano himself gave him a gold coin for being the hero of the day. He had enough cash to buy ice cream for every kid on the block for a week. That kind of story sticks. Becomes a compass, whether you mean for it to or not. Yes, most of my childhood ambitions were variations of Italian-American stereotypes, thanks to a dad and *la famiglia* with deep connections in New York, a background tangled in NYC cops and criminals, and a mom who made a mean Bolognese. I come by my ba-da-bings honestly. I felt destined to become the wife of a made man, surrounded by extravagant gifts and chasing mooching men and children out of the kitchen with a wooden spoon.

Whatever it was, something clicked. The lines between right and wrong blurred until they disappeared entirely. I didn't see anything wrong with using or dealing. It wasn't violence; it was business. Money flowed, people partied, no one seemed to be getting hurt. And me? I was along for the ride—eyes wide open, no seatbelt, no plan to slow down.

The first time I tried cocaine was with Stacy at one of Oscar's epic house parties. Five kegs, Jeff's band covering songs like the Romantics and U2, and the crowd went nuts. His lead singer, Brandy, mesmerized on stage—leaning on one hip, tapping her boot to the beat, belting out "Tattooed Love Boys" by the Pretenders. Sometimes Stacy and I sang backup. That night, just before we took the stage, Brandy asked, "You girls want a bump?" *Are we really doing this?* But before we could answer, she had already scooped a little pile of powder onto a car key and offered it up like it was nothing.

It felt like pure rock 'n' roll—and we were in. Stacy and I sang behind Brandy like she was Joan Jett and we were the goddamn Blackhearts. Unlike alcohol, which left me spinning, coke felt controllable. Too wired? Drink a beer. Edgy? Smoke a clove. Stacy and I were loyal to our Djarums—sweet, herby, moody—and tucked inside my designer case, they made us feel glamorous.

Stacy and I snorted so much blow one night, we decided it would be brilliant to reenroll in high school. After partying all night with no sleep, we hopped on Jeff's moped at sunrise and headed straight to FVHS to meet the principal. My stomach dropped as we approached. I picked up a random rock off the ground. For good luck, I said.

"Good call," Stacy replied.

Inside, we babbled nonstop while Principal Hansen flipped through our dusty files.

"We made a mistake. We should be in school," I said.

"Please, Principal Hansen. We want to graduate and be successful adults," Stacy added dramatically. I squeezed the rock and kissed it. Stacy stretched out her hand. "Give it to me," she whispered. She kissed it too. We stared him down, our hearts pounding as we awaited our fate.

"Hmmm," he muttered, still flipping pages.

"Stacy, pass it." I panicked. That rock felt like the only thing keeping me from flying off the rails.

Stacy handed it back just as she blurted, "Excuse me, Mr. Hansen, we had *so* much coffee. Can we pee? I mean, use the restroom?"

He pushed up his glasses and gestured to a door. "Sure. You can use mine."

Whoa. Private bathroom. Respect. Once inside, Stacy whipped out a baggie of coke, and we lined up rails right there on top of Principal Hansen's toilet. Back in the office, Mr. Hansen gave us the good news: we could return after Christmas break.

Thrilled, we listened as he added, "But you're both too far behind on credits to graduate here. You'll have to transfer to Wintersburg."

I froze. Wintersburg was where the pregnant girls and real burnouts went.

"No way!" Stacy snapped.

"Mr. Hansen," I said, full of wounded pride, "that school's for stoners and losers."

"That's your only option," he said, calm as ever.

So we walked out. Just like that, we gave up on high school completely. We were literally *too cool for school.* Or at least, that's what we thought.

I wish someone had stood in my way, but my family always defended my misbehavior—and that's part of why I love them so much.

Stacy and I were out in the world with no diploma, no GED, and no plan. We should've been scared, but as long as we had each other. Stacy and I—it was us against the world.

* * *

Life only got more chaotic from there. I'd get dressed up every day, zooming around with Jeff and Rich, making deals, dodging cops. It felt like living inside a video game. There's a natural high in sticking it to the system. I wasn't part of the business exactly, but I was driving around with drugs, handing out ounces to friends. Which kinda made me a dealer—just a dumb one, since I wasn't even making money.

Before Elliot began his seven-year sentence, he and Shelly got married to qualify for conjugal visits. Once Jeff was locked in with Elliot's crew, Shelly spent more time at our house. She became part of the family—sitting with us at dinner, chatting with Mom, and showering Stacy and me with attention and compliments.

Shelly mentored Jeff in the drug game, schooling him on the hustle and pushing more product with better price cuts to fatten his pockets. With her by his side, Jeff wasn't messing around—he was in it to save enough money to set himself up for life.

But it wasn't just business. Long hours together, plus Shelly's craving for affection, sparked an affair. The cheating tore Jeff up, and he got jealous whenever she had sleepovers with Elliot at the concrete hotel, otherwise known as state prison.

Still, he was too deep to back out, admitting, "I know I shouldn't be fucking the drug lord's wife, but I love her."

Jeff flexed his hustle constantly, flashing stacks of cash with that big, shit-eating grin. Sometimes he'd swing open the safe in his room just to show the neighborhood kids what "rich" looked like. It was wild. Cruising around in his cherry-red Porsche, music blasting, gold chain swinging—Jeff turned heads everywhere, and the streets started whispering fast: Jeff was dealing blow.

Two figures in the local police department listening were Sergeant Patrick Stevens and Detective Tim Delaney. These guys *lived* to bust dealers. It was peak "Just Say No" America, and they were out to save every "innocent" white teen from the devil's powder. When they caught wind that Jeff and Rich were moving weight in the suburbs, they locked in—this case was personal.

Whenever they tailed us, we'd shake them like a high-speed joyride with the law in our rearview. Caught up in that reckless, teenage adrenaline, we came up with the genius idea to order a pizza to their car—straight out of *Beverly Hills Cop*. Delivery guy sends it over, we stroll past like nothing.

"Really?" Stevens said, grinning. "You kids order pizza to my car? That's your big move?"

"Just making sure you're fueled for the chase," Jeff shot back.

Delaney chuckled, leaning back. "You kids are something else."

They'd shake their heads, half amused, half annoyed.

"That was a good one," Stevens admitted.

We had our share of close calls. They rattled us, but we'd never let it show. It became a game of cat and mouse. They rotated unmarked cars, trying to blend in. Sometimes they left one parked and empty, hoping we'd mistake it for a neighbor's, but we'd just shove a banana in the tailpipe and peel off, laughing all the way to the bank.

And still, we ignored speed limits and rules. Turn up the music, put life on fast-forward—add friends, cars, and drugs. Plenty of drugs.

Chapter Five

A New Sensation

DECEMBER 1984

With too much time on my hands and no clue what to do with it, I was down for anything. So when Shelly invited me to check out the beach house she'd rented right on the sand, I was in. Mom and Stacy were working weekend shifts. Even Jeff was busy bussing tables to keep up appearances. It was the perfect excuse to escape the house and get in a little girl time.

Her place was in Sunset Beach, just a few steps from the water. A light-blue cottage with white window frames and a picket fence. Inside was tidy, lace curtains catching the sun just right. It was the first time in the home of a woman living alone. Sea glass in bowls, shiny black pots with bright-green plants, a huge white leather couch with zebra-striped throw pillows, fresh daisies in a vase on a mirrored coffee table. Fierce, feminine, a little wild. A ceramic tiger lounged in the corner like it owned the place. But the showstopper was the wall art. A massive Patrick Nagel painting, iconic and dripping with luxury.

Shelly looked rad. Baggy white parachute pants, a black t-shirt hanging off one shoulder, oversized hot pink acrylic hoop earrings. She popped in a CD and strolled to the kitchen table. She casually loaded a glass pipe with a bit of cocaine. Jeff had told me that they'd freebased together, only for "special occasions." Shelly turned to me. "Want to try it?" Polite, not pushy.

I wanted to.

I wanted to know what it felt like to live loud—

to be fierce,

to be feminine,

to be *her*.

Shelly was a pro. She heated the powder in the glass pipe until it boiled into vapor, then took a long hit. She held it in before blowing out a thick white cloud. She handed me the pipe. I copied her, feeling grown-up and eager to tell Stacy. The high hit me like nothing I'd ever experienced—larger than life, free, confident. My heart pounded, and I peeled off my jean jacket. The sweet, bitter taste dripped down the back of my throat as I sank into Shelly's white leather couch, staring at the powerful black-haired woman in the avant-garde Nagel painting. Her piercing blue eyes locked into mine, silently saying, *You're just as cool as me now.*

Suddenly, a million loving, creative thoughts flooded my brain. Shelly and I fluttered from room to room like lovebirds, setting up little nests of blankets and pillows. She'd spend ten minutes telling me how amazing I was, then I'd reply, "No, *you're* amazing."

Shelly rifled through her drawers, handing me tops and jeans, and I promised her my studded belt she idolized. It was a full-on love-fest.

A few hours and a couple of beers later, the high faded—and so did the loving thoughts. All those promises? No way I was giving her my belt. I returned the shirts too.

I knew I had to tell Jeff, in case Shelly mentioned it. Only then did I realize how little thought I'd given the whole thing. Jeff might be pissed—at Shelly and me. She'd given his little sister crack, for God's sake!

But when I told him, he barely blinked. It was like I'd told him I tried oysters for the first time. Which, by the way, I hadn't.

Jesus, I was sliding backward, and my brother just shrugged. I thought he'd be disappointed in me, but instead, I was disappointed in him. Eventually I realized Jeff was smoking crack with Shelly all the time. Of course he couldn't protect me from drugs when he was becoming an addict himself.

Grandmaster Flash and Melle Mel were already warning us in "White Lines (Don't Do It)." We just didn't listen.

* * * *

We didn't realize it yet, but we were about to become part of something much bigger. The international cocaine business was booming, flooding the US market with cheap product. Wholesale prices were dropping, and Jeff was ready to take advantage. He showed up to Vinny's with thirteen grand in cash, buzzing with excitement and nerves to buy his first kilo. I swear, he acted like he was buying a house. But Vinny pushed another kilo on him, saying he could pay once it sold. He was taking a gamble, trusting Jeff to handle that much product. Since Vinny knew Jeff was sleeping with Shelly while her husband sat in prison, Jeff was in no position to refuse. He left with two kilos and, at nineteen years old, was thirteen grand in debt to Vinny, a Peruvian drug dealer.

Dividing one kilo on the streets was risky. Two? Straight-up insane. Add in Jeff freebasing, and it was a disaster waiting to happen. His whole vibe flipped. Any cool factor? Gone. He'd buzz around the house, cleaning the toaster, oiling door hinges—anything to calm the paranoia once the high wore off.

Then came a call from a payphone up the street. "There's a helicopter following me," he said, panicked. I figured he was high again. But then Stacy and I looked outside, holy shit—there actually *was* a helicopter circling our house.

"Don't come home!" I yelled and hung up.

Jeff bolted to his bandmate Brandy's house, claiming a blowout with our mom. Later, while she showered he peeked outside, made sure the coast was clear, and snuck the two kilos into her place.

For four days, Jeff sold drugs out of Brandy's. Between customers, he'd step outside, shoot hoops with the neighbor, and glance nervously at the sky. One day, a kid waved up and said, "Hey, that's my dad." The helicopter wasn't after Jeff at all. Just keeping an eye on the neighborhood.

Rich had told me early on that there was one unbreakable rule in the game: *never get high on your own supply.* That's how you get sloppy. And when you get sloppy, you get caught.

Jeff was as sloppy as a melting Bomb Pop in the sun.

His clientele had spilled way past the inner circle, and now he was selling to randos who couldn't keep quiet.

Orange County cops were catching on. Two Newport Beach officers snagged him outside the club in the Déjà Vu parking lot with an ounce of coke—small bags, all individually wrapped. Rookie mistake. Jeff usually dealt in bulk, leaving the small stuff to sub-dealers, but greed got the better of him and now those little bags spelled "intent to sell."

Delaney and Stevens rushed over to interrogate him, pressing for info on Rich, Shelly, and the supply chain. They dangled a deal for info, but Jeff wasn't a snitch. He ended up serving seventy-two days in the Orange County jail, getting out early for good behavior.

As a condition for his early release, Jeff had to go to rehab. Mom visited him almost daily, bringing food from the café, holding his hands, and trying to make sense of it all, but Jeff spun it like a one-time mistake—and she bought it. She even sat through counseling sessions. I tagged along, trying to act normal, but seeing Jeff in that stark, cold place was unsettling. I almost died the day mom broke down crying and shared with the group that she'd fallen asleep on the couch and woke up to a couple of guys in masks holding guns to her face.

"They kept asking me where the money was," she said, looking haunted. "They were screaming, but I didn't know what they were talking about. I just cried and told them they had the wrong house."

Jeff and I exchanged a look. We both knew it wasn't random.

"Anyway," she said, wiping her eyes and looking at me, "you and Stacy were asleep upstairs. I didn't want to scare you. The weird part? Before they left, one of them apologized…and kissed me on the cheek."

After hearing that, I became hypervigilant at home. Doors locked, garage door shut, windows latched. I clocked every unfamiliar car that cruised. If one lingered, I called Rich. He tried his best to calm me, but he was on edge too. The cops were circling, and he knew it.

Ironically, the rehab center was on Newport Boulevard in Costa Mesa, right around the corner from Déjà Vu, the club where Jeff got busted. One night, he called, "Pick me up. Back alley. Nine o'clock." Stacy and I had been living like shut-ins without him, making lasagna with Mom and watching old movies. So, when he asked us to play getaway driver, we were in. At nine sharp, we pulled up behind the rehab in Mom's sedan. Jeff popped out the window, legs dangling, and dropped ten feet to the pavement. He jumped in the backseat, yelling, "Go! Go!"

I looked at him in the mirror. My brother was back.

The laser lights from Déjà Vu pulsed across the sky. We were underage but flashed our fake IDs like pros inside. Shannon's "Let the Music Play" came on and Stacy and I ran to the floor screaming. The DJ kept it rolling. Chaka Khan. Lisa Lisa. Prince. We bumped into Louie Cordero, fresh off Madonna's "Borderline" video. Friends offered us coke. We passed. Jeff did too. Rehab still had him on random tests.

After closing, we boosted him back through the window. Smooth. Until red and blue lights flashed behind me driving home. *Woop-woop.*

I panicked. We'd been responsible. We turned down coke, for God's sake.

The cop said my taillight was out. I handed him my fake ID and stayed calm.

"You're kidding. I just had this serviced."

He let me off with a warning.

The best part? The woman on my ID, Anna Marie Ruiz, was twenty-seven. I was seventeen.

What police academy did this guy graduate from, the movie?

* * *

After rehab, Jeff moved back in with Mom, Stacy, and me. Greg was still with our dad but had started planning a move to Los Angeles to live with our Aunt Flo. She was going to train him at Pasquini Imports.

Before getting into the restaurant business, Aunt Flo and Uncle Angelo imported Italian espresso machines and sold them to cafés and restaurants all over LA, long before Starbucks made cappuccino mainstream. Pasquini was the Rolls-Royce of espresso machines. Hollywood elites had them in their homes. Priscilla Presley. Goldie Hawn and Kurt Russell. Robert Wagner. Even Pam Anderson. She loved hers so much she named her dog "Pasquini."

All my cousins were trained to install and repair the machines. My mom's other sister, my aunt Mary, even ran a competing company called Europa. Espresso ran through our veins, and Greg was on track to join Pasquini's corporate office in downtown LA.

Then my dad called with news that knocked the air out of me. He and Gale had adopted another baby. A girl. Her name was Jenna.

It came out of nowhere. I didn't even know they were looking. What hit harder was the implication. He had a new daughter in his life. Stab me in the heart, why don'tcha?

It was late winter, but the rain had finally stopped, and everything smelled like wet asphalt and new beginnings. Saturday night, Stacy and I saw *The Breakfast Club* with Kelly and Colleen, friends from elementary school, and slept over at Kelly's. We expected an easy, Commodores kind of Sunday. Fluffy pancakes, MTV. Instead, when we walked through our front door the next morning, we stepped into one of Mom's legendary tirades. I figured it was Dad. She had a sixth sense for him—could practically smell if he'd come in to pee or pour a glass of water. "He's been here," she'd mutter, sniffing the air like a divorcée bloodhound. But this time, it wasn't Dad.

"Just tell me the truth," she begged, her voice cracking. "Are you addicted?"

"No!" Jeff said, adamant.

"And what about dealing? Are you dealing?!"

Her hands were shaking. She looked wrecked.

"No!" Jeff said again, just as worn down.

The night before, while she hosted Bunco, two gunmen had stormed in and ordered all the women face down on the floor, hands above their heads.

I glanced down at the carpet, trying to imagine the scene. That morning, my mom had asked me to vacuum. The lines were still visible, and I couldn't help thinking, *Well, at least the carpet was clean.*

The men paced for nearly twenty minutes, waving guns at her friends and demanding to know where the drugs and money were. Somehow they missed the diamond rings sparkling on every hand. Maybe once they realized the women were playing dice and betting pennies, they figured they had the wrong crowd and left.

We called it The Bunco Bust.

For mom, it was the final straw. She wasn't just terrified—she was humiliated.

Jeff knew there was no coming back from this one. He moved into a new apartment a few minutes away.

My mom's reaction? *Good riddance.*

Chapter Six
Déjà Vu

MARCH 1985

Jeff had been living in his own apartment for weeks, but his hustle didn't slow down. Now it wasn't just Mom sniffing around like a German Shepherd on the hunt; it was actual detectives. Stevens and Delaney had become fixtures, tailing him everywhere. They'd pop up at gas stations, beach lots, the mall. Even after Jeff moved, I spotted them parked across the street as I was leaving my house.

Maybe it was my shiny black BMW in the driveway that caught their eye. But it wasn't bought with drug money. I got that ride like any broke teen would, through an insurance payout. I slipped and fell on an oil spill in Jeff's carport. Dad, the chiropractor, racked up the medical bills, called a lawyer buddy, and we sued for poor lighting.

Like a smartass, I flashed the detectives a grin and a wave as I strutted to my BMW in black leather leggings and a white lace corset. I slid in, buckled up, checked my mirrors, and backed out like a model citizen.

I was headed to Jeff's to pre-party before Déjà Vu. Still our go-to. Stacy claimed she was staying home to watch *All About Eve* with my mom. Translation: waiting by the phone for her boyfriend to call. Not me. I was single and ready to mingle. Rich was still around, always good for a laugh, but I was hoping Hassan would show. Smooth. Magnetic. Always pulling me close.

At a red light, I flipped down the visor and touched up my shimmery pink pout. U2's song "Two Hearts Beat As One" blasted from the speakers. I sang along with Bono, head bobbing, one hand drumming the wheel. Window down. Salt in the air. I stomped the gas with my pointy black stiletto and flew down Brookhurst as the sun melted orange.

I pulled up, ready to start the night. "Little Red Corvette" thumped behind Jeff's door. Odd. He usually kept it quiet to avoid complaints, which could bring in the heat. I knocked. No answer.

"Hey! Come on!" I called.

Prince faded into Depeche Mode, then New Order, but I kept knocking. Finally the door creaked open. Jeff stood there, pale, avoiding my eyes. He stepped back, hands on his head.

"Go slow," he said, voice low.

I didn't know what he meant—I stepped inside smiling, until movement caught my eye. Suddenly, I was shoved to my knees.

"What the hell?"

Before I could react, I was face down on the brown carpet, a sweaty hand on my back, cold steel pressed to my skull.

Deep, guttural voices barked commands. One shouted, "The drugs! Where are they?"

His voice was angry and desperate, and the gun pressed harder. Sweat dripped down my face. Tears stung my eyes.

"I don't know. I swear I don't know." He yanked me up by my hair, shoving his foul breath in my face. I gagged. Dirt caked his skin, but what scared me most was the desperation in his eyes. I'd heard the stories—these were professional rollers, tweakers who'd do anything for their next fix. No rules, no limits.

I glanced around—four guys in green camo pants, black tees, and trench coats. A ridiculous thought hit me: Did they coordinate their outfits like seventh-grade girls? Same with their weapons—ancient, rusty machine guns that looked like museum pieces.

One of the men held his gun to me; another pressed his to Jeff's back. The two others guarded the corners, weapons trained inward, eyes scanning the room. Sitting on Jeff's black leather couch was Gwen—a grade ahead of me in school, and the girl who'd stolen my LA boyfriend. Seeing her there, sobbing with wide, terrified eyes, was surreal.

If I'd been a fly on the wall, I might've thought, *Karma's a bitch, Gwen, for sleeping with that model I liked.* But I wasn't a fly. I was caught in the same nightmare, face to face with some kind of fucked up karma of my own.

Another knock at the door snapped everyone to attention. Jeff was forced to open it, a gunman shadowing him. In stepped Marco—our friend—who went pale as a ghost and wet himself on the spot. One thug grabbed Marco by the neck, slammed him to the floor, and shut the door. Marco started shaking so hard I half expected him to break out into "the worm"—he was a killer popper and breakdancer after all. But then, seeing the fear on Jeff's face, he broke down and started bawling instead.

I was shoved back down, cheek pressed into the coarse carpet. The tweaker guarding us screamed in my face, "Where's the stash, bitch? Where is it?"

"I don't know. I don't live here!" I cried, terrified.

"Wrong answer!" the guy screamed, pressing me harder for Jeff's stash. These tweakers were on edge, ready to snap. Too high to care about consequences. Where the hell were Stevens and Delaney when you needed them?

They tore the place apart—ripping cushions, tearing drawers open, hunting every hiding spot. One of them slammed my head against the floor so hard my vision blurred. My heart pounded; I thought I'd pass out. Gwen stayed quiet behind me on the couch, but Marco was the real problem. He kept moaning, gasping for air, then shouting, "Oh, God, please help me! Please!" I wanted to shush the motherfucker up, before he got us all killed, but I was too scared to make a sound.

They forced Jeff down on the floor, facing me. His big brown eyes—usually so confident—were wide with terror, unblinking. The men shouted at him, stomping their boots on his back. One fumbled with his weapon, shoving it against the back of Jeff's head.

"You're a dead man, but you can save your friends. Where is the dope?"

Jeff didn't answer. The music was still thumping. We were about to die while Prince belted out "Controversy."

Asking if I believe in God.

I certainly believed in God, and at that moment, I begged Him to spare my brother's life. I mentally apologized for every sin I could think of.

Then—gunshots. Multiple. I covered my head, certain I'd been hit.

Silence.

Prince's voice floated in the background: I heard *something about dying and being free.*

I opened my eyes. One of them had shot the couch inches away from Gwen. Even the other guys looked shocked.

"What the fuck are you doing? Let's go!"

But Jeff was alive. Everyone was alive. For now.

They screamed for us to get up. Herded us into the bedroom walk-in closet, slammed the door behind us. We scrambled, shoving past sneakers and hangers. Each one of us tried to make our friends into human shields. It was pitch black. No one spoke. We barely breathed.

I accepted I was going to die in that closet.

Time stretched. Could've been minutes, could've been hours. Too quiet outside. Were they gone? No one wanted to find out. But Jeff did. He slowly opened the door and peeked out. The room was empty. We crawled into the hallway on hands and knees, dead silent. They were gone. Gwen burst into tears. Then Marco. Then me. Jeff too. All of us sobbed with relief—it felt like a miracle.

While we tried to collect ourselves, Jeff started surveying the wreckage. Furniture was trashed, drawers dumped, glass shattered. He disappeared into the back room, then came running out, grinning.

"Look what I found!" He held up a wad of cash. "They didn't get the dope either! Can you believe it?"

We just stared at him.

That's when it hit me: *Jeff has changed*. He could've ended it the second they walked in. But the money meant more.

Marco and Gwen tore into him. I stayed silent, embarrassed. The brother I loved was buried under greed and addiction.

We left at warp speed, heading straight to the nearest place with alcohol: the Fountain Valley bowling alley. Jack and Cokes. Lines of blow. Anger softened.

That night was my wake-up call. I loved Jeff, but I needed distance. I kept my promise and didn't tell Mom—what was the point? Then again, maybe I should have. How could she—or anyone—have helped when we were all hiding so much?

* * * *

"*Deniiiiiiiiiiiiiiiiiise*!" My mom preferred screaming my name over climbing upstairs to tell me dinner was ready. That meant come now, while it's hot.

I dropped what I was doing and headed downstairs. If I didn't, she'd just keep going like one of those emergency sirens. It had been months since the night at Jeff's apartment, but I was still rattled.

Mom was setting the table when I walked in, serving chicken cacciatore. I could already taste her special sauce, smoky roasted bell peppers, onions, carrots, and black olives coating the chicken just right.

It was just the two of us at the big table.

"Isn't it good?" she asked, dabbing the corner of her mouth with a napkin. She loved to cook, needed the praise—and by God, she deserved it.

"Mmm-hmm," I said, swallowing hard. I had to say it now, or I'd never find the courage again. "So, I've been thinking.... I want to go to college. In New York." Bam. There it was.

Her fork hovered between her mouth and the plate. "New York?" she repeated, her voice a mix of surprise and concern. "That's really far. And for what?"

Go big or go home, right? I didn't know what I wanted—just that I needed something *more*. "Fashion school," I said. "In New York."

I dashed upstairs, grabbed the pamphlets I'd been collecting, and brought them down. New York had everything—Parsons, the Fashion Institute of Technology. That's where people who were serious about fashion went. That was where *I* could go.

"It'd be amazing," I said, trying to make it real.

She didn't even pick them up. "All the way in New York?" Like I'd said Mars.

"Yeah," I said, almost daring her to argue. "That's where the best schools are. You're from New York."

"But how are you going to do it? Those schools aren't cheap."

I hesitated. She had a point. How *could* I even afford this? Aunt Flo offered to pay for both my brothers' college educations—though they turned it down—but not me. In her world, men provided. Women married, had babies, stayed home.

I wasn't angry. It was just how things were. And to be fair, I never asked for help. She was loving and supportive, and maybe she would've said yes. But I didn't want to feel like I was begging for a handout. Instead, I just felt…defeated. Like my dreams were too big for the life I had.

Even Stacy, my biggest cheerleader, didn't believe in it. I told her we could go together, chase something bigger. She laughed. She was in love now, planning her future around someone else. Her dream had shifted. Mine hadn't.

Mom encouraged cosmetology at the local community college. It was a far cry from hailing a taxi in my stilettos in the busy streets of New York City, but she thought it would be perfect for me.

"Denise, you love looking in the mirror," she'd say, as if that was reason enough to map out my whole future.

With my degree in Bullshit Artistry from the School of Hard Knocks, I sidestepped my way into cosmetology school at Golden West College, not with a high school diploma or a GED, but with charm and grit. And weirdly, I liked it.

I found comfort in my routine. Early mornings. Hot coffee, driving to school, paying attention in class and actually enjoying it. Anatomy was my favorite; it challenged me as a learner. I recruited friends as test subjects, highlighted Rich's and his older brother Mark's hair with the polka-dot cap and crochet hook, and botched a few haircuts that still haunt me. But I worked hard—and pulled off straight A's.

I was certain I'd fail the state licensing exam. The test was heavy on electrical currents and chemistry, neither my strong suit. But anatomy must've carried me through. I drove home blasting Madonna, feeling proud for the first time in a long time. When I walked through the door, Greg handed me a coffee mug that said, "Congratulations!" and smiled. "I knew you could do it."

Mom pulled some strings and got me a job at Aida Grey Salon in South Coast Plaza, two stores down from Café Pasquini and right next to the luxury boutiques. It wasn't glamorous work; I cut hair and covered gray for old-money Newport Beach women dripping in diamonds and dressed to kill. But it was prestigious. I spent my breaks at Café Pasquini—my home away from home. I saw everyone I knew and loved, all the time.

For once, it felt like my life was on track…almost.

Chapter Seven
Busted

MARCH 1986

I'd just rinsed the perm solution and was gently patting my client's curls dry when my pager buzzed. *111.* Rich.

"Hang tight," I told her, handing over a glossy *Vogue*. "Don't move a muscle."

I ducked into the break room and called him back, grateful for a breather.

"Yo!" I said, "You caught me mid-perm. What's up? I've got a minute, but tell me everything."

He laughed. "Not much. yet. You free tonight? Fancy dinner thing, and honestly, the only person I want next to me is you, hot stuff."

"I'll let you know in an hour," I said, playing it cool. Stacy was always my first call, but if she was booked? I was in. A girl likes her options.

I hung up, smiling. Rich always made me feel like the main character. Yeah, he had a thing for me, but it wasn't just flirtation. We had the kind of friendship where if one of us blew a tire in the desert, the other would show up. No questions.

I was upstairs swapping outfits, halfway into a classic black minidress, when I heard my mom and Rich talking in the kitchen.

"Sweet'N Low or real sugar?" she asked, laughing. "Denise uses that fake stuff. Always watching her figure. Something I should be doing."

Then louder, "Want to hear something funny? I pulled in from work and saw Rocky on a skateboard. Midlife crisis or what? I just stood there, praying he'd fall on his ass."

Rich chuckled. "That man's been in crisis mode since the day I met him."

"Oh, you're too much," my mom said, clearly beaming and delighted. I rolled my eyes. Classic Mom—always with the Dad digs. Rich was a sweetheart, and he understood divorced parent diplomacy.

Soon after, Rich and I were cruising down the 91, the Porsche humming beneath us. He turned the music down and started talking business.

"You know, your brother still has steady clients," he said. "Elliot and Vinny are making bank off him. Not that Elliot can enjoy it. But after those tweakers came to the house? I figured Jeff would cool it for a while, lie low." His hands firm on the wheel. "I get it—money's money. But you gotta be smart."

City lights flickering across his face. "You'd be surprised what people'll do for paper."

I could still see the tweakers. Sunken eyes. Jittery hands. I knew exactly what people would do.

I thought Jeff was being careful. He quit working at the bar in HB; he wasn't seeing Shelly anymore. Dad had moved to Tustin to open his own chiropractic practice, and Jeff and Rich invested in high-tech thermo-imaging equipment. Sure, they weren't in the office doing any work like Dad, but they got to say they were in the "medical field."

"Do you think he's in trouble?" I asked, worry creeping into my voice. Rich looked over. "He's all right. But I'm done working with him. I've been looking for someone new. Just in case." He paused. "Found a guy. Juan. From Mexico."

I raised an eyebrow. "Juan?"

"You're about to meet him. Word is, he's a bona fide kingpin. Solid connections, imports direct. And the best part?" Rich smirked. "He's fronting me. No cash down."

That night, I stepped into a mansion in Anaheim Hills—lavish didn't even begin to cover it. I slid into my seat at a black lacquer table, the kind that screamed *'80s drug-lord chic*, with soft under-lighting glowing like we were dining inside a stretch limo. Lobster tails and filet mignon were passed around, but all I could think of was the surreal fact that I was having dinner with serious drug kingpins and their wives.

Juan looked ordinary. Handsome, clean-cut, collared shirt, jeans, easy smile. You'd never guess he moved serious weight. His wife, Silvia, had thick chestnut hair down to her bra strap and sharp green eyes. Though iced out in diamonds, she balanced it all with sensible clothes.

They asked plenty of questions, sizing us up, testing if we were sharp, if we could be trusted. I clicked with the wives right away. They were cool, real-life badass John Gottis. But better. Not just pretty faces—powerful. Of course, they knew the deal. Lavish homes, speedboats, private planes—they don't just appear out of thin air. They come from one thing: expensive, wildly illegal white powder. This was high-level dealing; it would be impossible for them not to notice. Boss wives needed PhDs in denial and poker faces so cold they could bluff a DEA raid.

Their mantra? *What money? What powder? What do you mean, where the fuck is all this money coming from?* They outmatch everyone in confidence and bravado. Who'd dare suggest anything shady? They stood by their men like it was gospel. No questions, no cracks. Solid. They had their man's back, no matter what.

I didn't know if I could trust everyone at that table—but I wasn't looking for friends. Strangely enough, it felt like I had a new kind of family. The kind that, if I ever needed to bury a body, they'd have my back and ask, "Shovel or alibi?" Not many people had that. And it made me feel…powerful.

* * * *

Jeff raised an eyebrow. "You sure you don't wanna come skiing with me, Neise?"

I complained, "Can't. God forbid these rich bitches show up at the Balboa Bay Club with a single gray hair. Plus, my boss is a total loser about time off."

He shrugged. "Eh, all right. See you in a couple of weeks."

I shot him a quick hug. "Okay, enjoy yourself—and try not to break a leg out there, ski bum."

Almost a week later, Greg called with a bombshell. "Neise, Jeff got busted. Sold four ounces to some guy he didn't know. That piece of shit was working with Stevens and Delaney."

I froze, gripping the coiled kitchen phone, heart sinking. Tears came before I could stop them.

"Hey—hey, it's okay," Greg said. "Dad bailed him out. He's already on his way home. But oh my God, the story gets insane."

Then he launched into it like open mic night.

"The cops raided Dad's office—technically Jeff's workplace. Dad had patients in the waiting room when they brought Jeff in, cuffs and all. Hate to admit it, but Dad said the cops were actually being polite. Kept saying, 'I'm so sorry, Doc,' knowing the whole thing looked bad for business.

"And then Dad remembered—he had a gram of coke in his desk drawer. So what does he do? Slips past the cops all polite, 'Excuse me, gentlemen,' beelines to his desk...and swallows the whole bindle."

"You're kidding," I said.

"Swear to God," Greg said. "Forget Wheaties—breakfast of champions."

"Jeff said Dad was higher than Richard Pryor with a blowtorch. But still sharp enough to slide a bag of weed and $1,400 from Jeff's pocket into his sock. They never frisked him. Oh, and he had $10,000 stashed in his drawer...and quickly hid it in a Ficus. The safe? Untouched too. Twenty grand in cash, jewelry, who knows what else—completely missed."

I could just picture Stevens and Delaney expecting Scarface and walking out with nothing but paperwork.

"Anyway," Greg continued, "the cops wanted Jeff to flip on Vinny. He played along, made one phone call to set up a fake deal. But the second he got in his car?" Greg paused. "Jeff floored it like Mario Andretti and ditched them."

My brother. A fugitive.

"He was hiding out in a motel. Me and Dad did food drops. But that couldn't last forever. He went to pull some cash, walked into the bank, and—boom!" Greg yelled.

I yanked the phone from my ear.

"Cops swooped in. Took the nine thousand in his account and impounded the Porsche."

"Noooo, not the Porsche!" I yelled.

"Yep," Greg said. "That gorgeous little baby is G.O.N.E."

I sighed. "You know, Jeff's been talking about becoming a chiropractor like Dad."

Greg's voice dipped. "Well…he's got other plans now."

Before we hung up, he made me swear not to tell Mom. I hung up the phone in a daze. It was hard to believe the same brother who used to steal my Halloween candy and blast his drum set at seven in the morning just to drive me crazy was a wanted man hiding out in a motel.

* * * *

Boy, Jeff had changed.

It was like he was choking down humble pie, bite by reluctant bite. The DA was offering him time like a cop devouring sprinkle-covered donuts—recklessly, without a second thought. Six to ten years, they said. But Jeff wasn't biting. He sat there, stone-faced, like he had nothing left to lose.

Meanwhile, Rich kept a low profile. No more street-level deals. With Juan's help, he shifted to high-volume clients—kilos instead of pounds.

"Great deal," he told me. "Less exposure, more money. Win-win, right?"

I was still nervous. He wasn't delivering pizza. It was drugs and swapping cash. His clients? Addicts, snitches, and assholes who'd flip on their own mother for a cheeseburger and a cigarette. I tried to explain the risk, but Rich wouldn't hear it. He had a plan, and he was locked in.

You'd think he'd learn from Jeff's arrest, but money dulls instincts. Against his better judgment, Rich agreed to a sale with a stranger—something he swore he'd never do.

"But my close friend vouched for him," Rich said. "Swore on his life. I trusted him." So Rich rolled the dice. And lost.

It was a setup.

Cop cars came flying in from every direction. But Rich wasn't going down easy. He still planned to meet up with me—watch a movie, unwind. No flashing lights were ruining that.

He punched the gas in his Porsche and led them on a high-speed chase.

I didn't know any of this yet. I just thought he was running late—until the phone rang.

It was Rich, calling from the giant cell phone he'd just installed in the dash.

His voice came through, fast and clipped.

"Come outside. Now."

I dropped the phone and bolted.

Then I saw him whipping around the corner, nearly flipping the car. He tore down the street—sirens wailing, lights flashing—then screeched to a stop in front of the house. He jumped out, eyes wide with panic, running straight for me.

I froze. My heart thudded in my chest.

Cops were right behind him, guns drawn, shouting, "Freeze!" I thought they were going to shoot him.

But he didn't move.

He stood there, defiant, eyes locked on mine, as they slammed him to the ground, cuffed him on our front lawn, and dragged him toward the cruiser.

He never broke that stare.

It was kind of romantic in a completely fucked-up way. The kind of reckless scene you see in a movie and think, *that could never happen to me*. And then it does.

And just like that…that was it. That's how Rich and I *officially* got together.

If there was ever a red flag flapping in your face, screaming, *run,* that was it. Any normal girl would've. But me? I went all in.

"I love you!" I screamed after him. Not even sure I meant it. But in that moment, it felt real.

I cried as the cops dragged Rich away, but the real gut punch came the next day. They raided Rich's spot at Marina Pacifica—the swanky Long Beach place where he'd been lying low. They found some drugs. What didn't show up on the report? The $30,000 stashed in his tennis racket cover, money I'd seen him hide there myself. The cops knew Rich couldn't explain where that money came from, so they just *took* it. Clean. No report. No paper trail.

That's when I realized the law isn't black and white. No matter how much Purell you use, *all hands are dirty.*

* * * *

I picked Rich up when he made bail, and we had our first kiss outside the Orange County Jail. Real classy, right? He hired a lawyer and vowed to fight this as long as he could.

Our romance became this strange refuge from the chaos. I wore his boxers, his hoodie, all that cliché stuff, because it was *us*, and nothing else mattered. But with our new "status," Rich's problems became mine too. His legal mess—and all the shady stuff tied to it (hello, more red flags)—should've been enough to make me back off. Instead, I dove in deeper. I showed up at every court date, stood by his side, determined to be the loyal girlfriend. I wanted to be like the drug lords' wives—*resilient, commanding respect.* I wanted to be that woman. I was just eighteen, but I could handle whatever came with Rich. I didn't flinch. I stood tall, and people noticed.

Meanwhile, the DA dropped Jeff's offer to five to nine years, but he still wouldn't bite. The good news? Jeff had receipts, invoices, and pay stubs from Dad's office proving he'd worked hard and bought his Porsche legitimately. So, the car was back in his carport, good as new. But in reality? Jeff was a dead man walking, just waiting for the inevitable.

Though Jeff hadn't flipped on Vinny, Vinny wanted nothing to do with him after that phone call. Jeff wasn't looking to deal anyhow. Instead, he enrolled in more classes, determined to prove to the judge that he was a law-abiding citizen and would do everything he could to get a lesser sentence.

* * * *

The Smiths were playing softly in the background, drifting through my room like the soundtrack to a daydream. I was sprawled across his bed—cheeky lace underwear, a tee, and fluffy knee-high socks. Lazy perfection. Deep down, I knew we didn't have all the time in the world. Rich would have to pay the price for his crime eventually.

Maybe that was part of the fucked-up attraction. Knowing he'd have to leave me only made me want him more.

Rich was tracing circles on my back, fingers warm against my skin. "I've made a decision," he said, his voice lazy. "I'm going to have my brother take over the business for a while."

I blinked, twirling a strand of hair. "Are you sure?"

Mark was Greg's age—cute, but a total mess. He helped Rich sometimes, usually causing more trouble than he fixed. Always "losing" product, which everyone knew he was selling on the side to pay off gambling debts. His crew lived for poker games and stand-up comedy marathons. No matter how many times he screwed up, people let it slide. Mark had that kind of charm. We had a saying: if you needed Mark to sell two kilos, you gave him four. Because half would mysteriously vanish into his pockets. Still, Rich always looked out for him.

I got it—family was family. And I loved Mark, but that didn't mean I trusted the plan.

"Denise, Derrick ordered ten kilos. It's a huge payday."

His eyes darkened, like he was doing math in real time.

"And I've got more legal fees coming. I need another chunk of dough for the lawyer."

I nodded, trying to stay cool.

"Okay, I get it—we need the money."

In my head, I ran through the details. That's the thing about me: I don't freeze when things go sideways. Something in me clicks on. I move. I make a plan. Fixing shit for the people I love? It's basically my love language.

First, pick up from Juan in Santa Ana—solid as a rock. He kept a low profile and lived in a modest house to protect his family.

Second, drop off to Derrick in Seattle. Safe—wouldn't hurt a fly. Total weed nerd, running multiple underground grow ops, now branching into coke to build something bigger. Still under the radar. No heat—yet.

I could see it in Rich's eyes: he didn't want to hand this deal to Mark. His fingers drummed the sheets, like he was trying to tap the answer from thin air.

That made me nervous. I didn't want anything to happen to him.

You know how I always felt loved by Dad? Like, he'd bury a body for me, no questions asked? Some send flowers to show they care. In my world, you hang raw meat from your neck and walk into the lion's den.

"Screw it. I can handle it. Leave it to me."

Rich's eyes widened—surprise flickering into something else. Relief. Maybe even pride. A flash of that crooked smile I love. Like this was what he'd been hoping for all along: that I'd step up.

And in that moment, I felt like a badass.

"You sure?"

"Why not?" I shrugged. The words felt natural, like they'd always been mine. Something shifted inside me and settled low in my gut. A strange, calm sense of purpose.

I wasn't doing anything else with my life. The salon gig wasn't enough. Not the kind of money we needed.

And Rich could trust me. I wasn't the scared girl anymore. I'd crossed that line a long time ago.

With Jeff and Rich both fighting cases, I wasn't afraid. If anything, I'd learned from their mistakes. I knew the rules. I knew the players. I knew how to dodge trouble and keep quiet.

I didn't want Rich risking it while out on bail. It was safer—cleaner—if I handled it. I felt ready. Groomed for this. I was built to have my man's back. *No matter what.*

And then finally, a break: the DA dropped Jeff's sentence and offered him two years for possession and distribution in state prison. In state, you serve half your time, so he'd be out in a year. Jeff took the deal. Things were moving. And I was too.

Chapter Eight

Dealing

MAY 1986

The first order of business was picking up product at Juan's. Nighttime seemed like the best time to blend in—under the cover of darkness, no one would see me coming. The hood wasn't exactly the place for a black BMW 320i, especially not for a clean-cut girl like me, but I dressed the part: hooded sweatshirt, matching sweatpants, and my Reebok Freestyles—low-key, street-ready.

To calm my nerves, I cranked up the volume. Eighties energy jolted me awake. I had to stay sharp. This wasn't just a quick pickup; it was about popping my cherry—my first real run in the game. No mistakes.

Juan's block lived up to the Santa Ana hype. Small houses, patchy lawns, streets lined with broken wooden fences. Some had tall, menacing steel gates, like they were hiding something.

I killed the music. The thumping in my chest was enough.

Hands tightened on the wheel, I scanned the street for Delaney and Stevens. Parked a few houses down, the muffler on my Beemer growling louder than I wanted, echoing down the street like a lion's roar in the stillness.

I'm here now, I told myself. *No turning back.*

I wasn't scared—not really—but the weight of it all hit harder than I expected. Just one stop. Pick up the product. Head home. Simple. Right?

I grabbed Rich's hockey duffel bag from the back seat. Gear clunking inside. I pulled out a stick—both as a decoy and for protection. Could I fend anyone off with a slapshot? Still up for debate.

Juan greeted me with a hug. Propped the gate open, and I stepped inside. We sat on his leather couch, but before we talked business, he pulled out some glossy photos.

"My sister," he said, grinning. "She's a Budweiser girl." He was beaming with pride.

I glanced at the photo, taking in her shiny smile. "Gorgeous."

He tucked the photos away and moved to the next part of the show and tell: the merchandise. He peeled back a strip of duct tape on the kilo and handed me a sample. The crystalized cocaine sparkled under the light. I pinched some, rubbed it between my fingers, felt the sticky texture, and slid it onto my upper gums. Perfect.

"Our guys in Seattle are going to love this," I said.

Juan loaded all ten kilos into the duffel. He wrinkled his nose. "Ughhh, man, Rich's hockey gear reeks. Even the dogs couldn't sniff through that."

I laughed. "Gnarly. Doesn't matter how many times he washes it."

He walked me to the car, which was a relief. Nobody in this neighborhood would dare mess with Juan, much less rob me of $115,000 worth of product. Good. Because no matter how much Juan liked me, if I lost the drugs, I'd still owe him that money.

I popped the trunk, threw the bag in, and shut it fast.

I drove like a grandma on the way back. Well, not *my* grandma—she drives faster than most. I went slow. Complete stops. Signaled every lane change. I felt like I was going so slow, I might actually be going backward. Then I gave the engine a little gas or I'd draw attention. It was only a twenty-minute drive, but it felt like it lasted forever. I stared in the rearview mirror the whole way. No music, no distractions. Just the hum of the road…and the weight in the trunk pressing down on me.

I remembered being young in Arrowhead, sitting in church with Dad, my brothers, Gale, and me. Peter, with his classic bowl haircut, was on my lap—too young to read, but I still opened the hymnal. He hummed along to "Amazing Grace," pretending he knew the words. When service ended, we beelined it for donuts, then hit the playground, the air thick with the smell of pine.

That's when he showed up—a boy, maybe a year older, with sandy hair and a wicked sneer. No words. Just a kick to my leg, sending sand flying into my face. He turned and walked off.

My eyes stung, but his words stung worse: "You're just a girl." Like it was supposed to make me small.

Jeff's voice cut through, "Remember what you do to me when you're really mad?" He showed me his fist, hammer-like. "Don't let him talk to you like that."

That was all I needed.

Tears blurred my vision, but I wiped them away and ran after the boy, screaming, slamming my fist into the center of his back. He hit the ground, grasping for air. *Just a girl, huh?* I grabbed a handful of pine needles and jabbed them into his skin while he bawled.

Dad was there in seconds, pulling me off. My family stood over me, proud.

I knew I wasn't just a girl—I was someone who could fight back.

I turned the corner and pulled into Rich's complex in Marina Pacifica.

The dope still needed to get to Seattle. I thought about quitting, but I didn't want to let Rich down. *I've got this,* I told myself. And I did. I was high on adrenaline, like when I kicked that boy's ass. Every nerve alive, every instinct on fire.

Doing the right thing? That shit takes something I wasn't sure I had: the strength to walk away. I was on to something. Maybe it's not about getting it right. Maybe it's just about not getting it wrong too many times.

That short drive felt brutal. I couldn't imagine hauling the dope to Seattle.

"No way am I putting those miles on my Beemer," I told Rich, both hands on my hip. "I've got a better idea. Come on."

"You're the boss," he said.

When I pulled up to Goodwill, Rich gave me a skeptical look.

"Baby, we're not that broke."

"Leave it to me," I said, grabbing a giraffe onesie. Rich raised an eyebrow. "You're kidding, right?"

"Yes, silly. Don't worry." He let out a breath of relief.

"Let's hide the kilos in baby clothes." In my mind, if any of us got stopped, we could deny they were ours. I found a brown tweed suitcase on super sale. Best score of the day.

At the register, the cashier gave us a long look as she rang everything up. "So, when are you due?" she asked, eyeing us a little too hard.

I fought the urge to laugh.

"She's about to pop," Rich said with a grin, nudging me.

I kicked him under the counter.

"Still slim," I said, trying to sound convincing. "We just found out."

The cashier nodded, eyes lingering, judging, like she'd pegged me as some knocked-up teen. *Judge away, lady. If you only knew the truth, you'd be calling security.*

Next stop, LAX. The hour drive was tense. We kept checking the mirrors, watching for tails. At the airport, we bought two one-way tickets in cash. Rich used a fake ID—his photo, a different name. We checked in the suitcase and walked away. We weren't getting on the plane. Derrick would head straight to baggage claim, breezing past TSA—one of the perks of the '80s. No bag checks. No questions.

Once the goods were out of our hands, we waited. Three hours, nervously pacing, until the call came through: all good.

Rich and I exchanged a look—*we'd pulled it off.*

I used to suck at word problems—five apples, one pet monkey, a train going sixty miles per hour, and somehow, you're two-thirds of the way to Grandma's house. I'd be sitting there like, wait. What's the question? Total twilight zone. But figuring out my cut of a deal?

I was freakin' Einstein.

Ten kilos at $11,500 a piece. Sold in Seattle for $25,000 a kilo. After paying my supplier, Juan, back, I walked away with a cool $135,000. Not bad for a nineteen-year-old cosmetologist.

When it was all over, Rich looked at me differently, like he finally saw what I was capable of. After that, he started trusting me with more. And yeah, that felt good. Amazing, even. Being badass at something—and making quick cash while doing it? Totally intoxicating.

We were living our best life, and it felt like things were only going to get better.

Famous last words.

* * * *

The second dinner was ready, Mom turned off the sizzling pots and bellowed our names. We came flying into the kitchen as Sinatra's "Come Fly with Me" blasted from the family record player, filling the house with its familiar warmth.

No matter what craziness was swirling around us, the Trigos—Stacy included—never missed Sunday dinner. She'd even ditch her handsome, twenty-seven-year-old boyfriend to be there. And this guy? He lived in a plush apartment. Unreal views of the Pacific, Balboa Island, and Newport Harbor. Still couldn't compete with Mom's tagliatelle Bolognese.

Halfway through dinner, my beeper buzzed. I whipped it up with attitude—I mean, it's 1986, baby. If you weren't being paged, were you even important?

"Rich?" Mom asked.

"Yeah," I lied. It was Juan. "I'll be right back. Need some privacy."

She raised an eyebrow but let it go. I could tell she was thinking, *Don't let your food get cold.*

"You wild lovers!" Stacy shouted, slurping up sauce. "Tell Rich I said hi!"

I nodded, but I was already elsewhere. Even Stacy didn't know what I was doing. Besides, I didn't plan to stay in the game forever—just long enough to set us all up.

It had only been three days since Derrick picked up the luggage, but I felt the squeeze. Juan wanted his money. Upstairs, I sat on the edge of my bed and grabbed the white rotary phone beside my pink hippo Dad won for me at Circus Circus, back when things were still whole. That stupid hippo always reminded me of how perfect life used to feel.

I pushed that away and dialed Seattle. Derrick answered on the first ring.

"Hey," I said, casual. "I'm seeing you tomorrow, right?"

A long pause.

"Man…I don't think I can make it," he said, laying it on thick. "I'm *reallllly* sick. Caught the flu or something. I—I can't drive eighteen hours like this. I need a few more days…"

Then came the fake cough. So bad it almost impressed me.

I gritted my jaw. What choice did I have? He clearly needed more time to sell.

"Get better. Fast," I said, and hung up.

I called Juan next, knowing checking in minimizes the damage. He wasn't thrilled, but he gave me a few more days.

Back downstairs, Mom smiled that sweet, steady smile. Stacy was showing off a magazine spread,—glamour shots of her draped over a blue Corvette in a red, white, and blue bikini. Still chasing that modeling dream. I felt proud of her. Jeff shoveled food into his mouth, oblivious.

And there I was, nineteen, convinced I had it all figured out. I told myself I was chasing financial freedom, for the right reasons—help Dad's business, get Mom out of double shifts at the café, secure Stacy's future, keep Rich safe.

I was changing. I'd started taking shortcuts left and right, convinced they'd get me to success faster. Not realizing that shortcuts come with detours.

* * * *

It all worked out. Derrick made the drive down with the paper, and Juan got paid back. After that, I was trusted. Which meant I had backing—Juan would fund my startup with whatever I needed.

So, I asked for ten kilos of coke at a time. For me, it was easier to round off numbers.

I wasn't scared of dealers. I was scared of Stevens and Delaney. Of confiscation. Of jail. Of owing Juan $230,000. I still hadn't decided which terrified me more.

I couldn't keep it in the house. I didn't want to see another machine gun or have Stevens and Delaney showing up with a search warrant, but I needed the goods close. Ten kilos meant my ass was on the line.

So, Juan and I built a system.

I'd leave a car unlocked down the street. He or one of his guys would drop the kilos inside. Hours later—once the coast was clear—I'd drive off .

Sometimes, I stashed the kilos—or the money—in bushes just outside my mom's property line. Eventually, I expanded across the neighborhood. At night, I'd wander the block, hands deep into hedges, planting stacks of cash like a blinged-out Johnny Appleseed. I never lost a cent. Not even the gardeners found it.

It was a perfect system. No money or product ever changed hands directly.

At one point, I used the back left tire of my next-door neighbor's Winnebago. I could keep an eye on the stash, and if the cops ever found it? They'd swarm the neighbor's house, not my mom's.

Yeah, I know—what an asshole, right? I was totally out of my mind.

Everything ran smoothly, until the day I tucked three kilos on that tire…and the neighbors decided to take a spontaneous vacation.

That morning, I saw exhaust puff from the tailpipe and nearly blacked out. I bolted over in my oversized Wham "CHOOSE LIFE" tee, no bra, pure panic.

"Denise!" the wife called out, cheerful as ever. I'd grown up swimming in her pool and playing with her daughters. I was the kid my mom dragged next door for coffee, mute except to my mom, which annoyed her. She intimidated me. If she knew what was up, she'd beat my ass. And honestly, she'd be right to.

"Haven't seen you around lately," she said, giving me a once-over.

"I know!" I said, my stomach twisted. "Going somewhere?"

"Yosemite," she said, still smiling, but with an edge. "Figured we'd try to catch a glimpse of the bison." Then she tilted her head. "You out here for something…need anything?"

"Uh, no!" I squeaked. "Just wanted to wish you a great trip!"

She held my gaze a beat too long. The Trigo reputation preceded us. But she nodded.

"Well, aren't you sweet."

The second they turned away, I grabbed the stash just in time. Moments later, they were driving off.

* * * *

We might have messed with Stevens and Delaney, but they weren't idiots. Our landline clicked weird sometimes—clear sign that it was tapped. Even Mom noticed.

"Did someone drop this phone?" she griped. "It's acting funny!"

They showed up unannounced more than once, flashing search warrants, dragging a Doberman through the house to sniff it out. They found a tiny bindle of blow in a drawer—Stacy's stash—and let it slide. They were after something bigger.

"Get that damn dog out of my kitchen!" Mom yelled. Afterward, she'd collapse, crying, then turn her rage on Dad: "Great-white-father," she'd sneered, like he was perched on some throne. "Too busy fucking his young wife while I deal with this bullshit."

She wasn't wrong.

I didn't blame myself. I took no responsibility. I wasn't a dealer—I was the hero. Saving the family. Making money so we could all live happily ever after. Jeff was back at the house, so I assumed he was the one drawing heat. Then Mom found two kilos in the garage. Mine. She almost flushed them. I begged her not to. She handed them back, staring at me like she'd never seen me before, horrified.

"Are you dealing drugs?" she asked, bluntly.

I lied. I couldn't break her heart. She nodded, walked away, and pretended it never happened. I didn't blame her. Sometimes, the ugly truth's too much to deal with. She saw what she wanted to see. When cops came or she found something suspicious, she'd sigh, retreat to her linguini, and block it out.

Soon, home didn't feel safe. I worried the cops were listening. I also worried about the tweakers. I wasn't about to put Mom through another incident like the one at Jeff's. As much as I loved that house, moving out felt necessary. Stacy was practically living with her boyfriend in Newport Beach anyway, figuring out her life, like me.

"We'll still see each other, right?" I asked.

"Of course," she said. "But how are we dividing our clothes?"

We dumped everything into a massive pile on the floor. A full-on fashion standoff. Taking turns picking pieces we bought from thrift stores, Wet Seal, Contempo Casuals, and Charlotte Russe, trying to outdo each other but also being supportive.

"Okay, I know this is mine, but you wear it better," I said, holding up a brown North Beach leather *Top Gun*–looking bomber jacket.

Stacy laughed. "And I could take this strapless Norma Kamali dress, but you'd die without that one."

We nearly ripped a Roberto Cavalli leopard-print silk blouse playing tug-of-war over it. It was ridiculous—but kinda fun.

We thought about renting a pad in Huntington or Newport Beach, but Rich had a better idea. "Let's get out of here," he said. "Clean start, different jurisdiction."

I wasn't sold. Growing up in Orange County was all I'd ever known—my home, the most special place on earth.

And how could I leave that perfect spot between lifeguard towers three and five, where we'd spend summers chasing waves? Stacy and I cruising down PCH to Laguna Beach for Orange Julius. Or South Coast Plaza—I grew up there.

Leaving felt like saying goodbye to my childhood, but Rich convinced me it was for the best.

"We don't want more trouble for your mom," he said.

That got me.

Rich kept postponing his court date. His lawyer said the delays would help show the judge he'd turned his life around. He wasn't ready to face the music. So "stand by your man" became my mantra. I told myself once I saved enough, I'd leave the game and get serious. But now, protecting him was all I knew.

We sped out of the OC, Rich pushing his classic white Porsche to the max, weaving through traffic at ninety miles per hour like we owned the road. A speeding ticket? Didn't even cross his mind. All that mattered was this new life we were chasing.

The Pet Shop Boys' "Opportunities" thumped through the speakers—brains, looks, money. It felt prophetic. I didn't know where we were headed. I just knew we could handle it. Together.

An hour southeast of Fountain Valley, we saw signs for open houses in a gated community called Canyon Lake. Rich had heard it was beautiful—and, more importantly, private. The second we rolled through those gates, it felt like we crossed into another world. Safe. Untouchable.

Rich parked near the realtor's office, popped the trunk, grabbed his skateboard, and cruised the sidewalks while I walked beside him.

"Show us around," he called to the first realtor we saw.

The guy looked us over—Two teenagers? Please.

"I'm, uh, a little busy," the realtor hedged. But Rich insisted. The guy caved.

The neighborhood had different styles—contemporary, colonial, Victorian, Cape Cod, chateaus, Tuscan, Tudor. Rich pointed to a peach-colored Spanish-style Mediterranean hacienda.

"That one," he said. "I want to see that one."

Rich swung open the solid oak door like he already owned it. I stepped inside and gasped. The foyer had soaring ceilings. The master walk-in closet? I could've lived in there. Three bathrooms. *Three.* I was already picturing myself soaking in one of those tubs, bubbles up to my neck, a glass of wine in hand. Rich glanced toward the garage.

"Two-car garage—nice. Room for toys," he said, impressed.

The bottom floor had huge windows with a water view and a deck that led to a wooden dock begging for a boat. And the kitchen. Oh my

God—*the kitchen*. Wide counters, enough space to cook like we were feeding Rome.

Rich turned to the realtor. "I want to make a cash offer. Right now."

The guy blinked. "You want to do *what*?"

"I'll give you a hundred and eighty-five thousand, cash. You know, greenbacks. Right now."

Back then, the laws were loose. No one asked for paycheck stubs or tax returns. No one cared where the money came from. And this guy? He just wanted the sale.

So, we packed up and moved to the suburbs, ready to start playing house.

* * * *

Rich and I were living like we had the world at our feet—unlimited resources, and a brand-new house to deck out however we pleased. Building it felt like playing Monopoly, except the bank had *no limits*. Everything we bought was brand-spanking new.

We hired a landscaper who surrounded the estate with a forest of palm trees—enough to make you think you were in Waikiki. I strung them with tiny twinkling lights because this was *our* paradise. The floors? Sleek salmon pink with white marble swirls. We went for the classy look. It screamed old money—well, old money in the '80s, which really meant *drug lord chic*.

Then, Rich had a wild idea: a massive built-in aquarium spanning an entire wall. Our own private ocean, packed with tropical fish.

The master bathroom? Granite called "blue eyes"—$30,000 worth of sheer luxury, just for countertops. In the kitchen, we laid down white triple-bullnose granite, which basically shouted taste.

A buddy of ours built a gorgeous rosewood bar, because we weren't just living here, we were entertaining. And to keep out the thugs, tweakers, and thieves, we had a massive stone retaining wall built. We weren't just playing house—we were building a fortress.

We turned the four-bedroom house into a five-thousand-square-foot estate with six bedrooms, five baths, and a four-car garage. Rich still rocked t-shirts stained with mustard and ketchup dribbles, wrinkled shorts, and Vans. He even built a half-pipe skateboard ramp on the side of the house where the neighborhood kids would hang out and shred. We were closer in age to the kids than their parents. Maybe the parents suspected something, but we couldn't have cared less.

Naturally, living on a lake, we bought a speedboat—in cash. Sunset cruises became routine. Summer meant parties, water skiing, California wine coolers, loud music, burgers on the grill. We barely left the house, which suited Rich just fine. The club scene wasn't his thing. He preferred pushing a manly cart through Home Depot, picking out things for the house. And on the way home, he'd swing by Taco Bell and threaten to beat the shit out of the poor drive-thru employee, like a deranged suburban dad if he didn't get his taco order right.

"I said *extra* cheese on top!" he'd growl through clenched teeth.

Rich wasn't getting his hands dirty anymore, but he was still the wizard behind the curtain. He'd come a long way from his Karmann Ghia. Now, besides the classic '66 Porsche 911L, we had a black 928 Porsche, a blue '70 911T, and a white Jag XJ6. Rich was obsessed with speed. He raced out the engine to every car he owned and could tell you how fast each one went from zero to sixty. If he wasn't talking about cars or the house, it was hockey—or drugs.

His lawyer kept postponing his court dates, which felt smart at the time.

As for me, I was dripping in gold, frosted in diamonds, feeling like teen royalty in my own kingdom. Still, I tried to stay grounded: visiting Mom, meeting Stacy at the mall, sitting in my childhood bedroom. It was the only place I still felt like myself.

When we weren't smuggling drugs across state lines, we'd unwind playing Super Mario Bros on the massive TV we bought at Circuit City, with the neighborhood kids packed into the living room. It was the biggest screen on the block.

We had one rule: no drugs in the house unless absolutely necessary. Even then, they were gone within hours. Rich didn't use. I barely partied anymore. We were domesticated. I planned dinners—tortellini in fragrant broth, eggplant stuffed with melting caciocavallo. We even got a fluffy white bichon frise and I named her Blondie, after Debbie Harry, because every "it girl" needs a toy dog.

One day, Stacy came over in head to toe white Calvin Klein, looked around, and whistled.

"You're really settling down. It's like you're a grown-up."

I shrugged. "Different. I'm not 'miss limelight' anymore. Rich loves that." Eye roll.

She laughed. "I thought you'd party forever. He tamed you."

"Oh, please," I said. "When I'm all grown up, we'll live together. And when we're grandmas, we'll still be partying."

She smirked. "Uh-huh, but no rocking chairs, right?"

"Deal. No old-lady furniture. Unless it's Chanel."

* * * *

Most women in the drug game were happy spending the money—houses, cars, designer everything—but they didn't get their hands dirty. Not me. I wanted respect. And I earned it by proving I could roll with the big boys.

I knew their interest in me wasn't strictly business, and I wasn't above using that. A little flirting, a well-timed smile—I wasn't naive. If it gave me power or protection, I leaned in. In this world, a reliable ally was worth more than cash. I started with a few of Rich's connections, but over time, I built my own network.

Then, out of nowhere, Juan told me he was heading back to Mexico for a few months.

"You can place one last order," he said. "After that, you're on your own. Or maybe you should get out entirely. A smart girl like you? You could do something else."

I should've listened.

I needed out. But I wasn't ready. I was in too deep, convinced that just a little more time would mean a lot more money. I told myself I owed it to Rich. I owed it to myself. I wanted success. And at the time, success meant money.

Not joy. Not peace. I was all twisted up.

The thing is, I always wanted more. No matter how much I made, it was like Depeche Mode's song; it was never enough. It was like sitting at a blackjack table—chasing the next high, unable to walk away, even when I was ahead. I got hooked. Forgot why I started.

It used to be about outsmarting the system, slipping past the cops, especially Stevens and Delaney. It used to be about protecting the people I loved.

Somewhere in the middle of the hustle, I convinced myself that doing wrong for the right reasons made me a hero. I wasn't just trying to survive anymore. I was trying to get ahead. Win, even if it meant putting all of us at risk. So, I sniffed around for a new supplier. I wasn't just staying in the game anymore.

Hell—maybe I was running it.

Chapter Nine

"D.T."

FEBRUARY 1987

It was a regular Sunday dinner at the Trigo house. Nothing fancy, but it still felt like church. I loved our new home, but part of me would always belong here. The smell alone—olive oil, roasted garlic, sautéed onions—was enough to make my chest ache with nostalgia.

Mom ladled out bowls of *stracciatella* and set down a bubbling tray of baked ziti, browned at the edges. She'd made it with Nonna's sauce—the kind we canned from fresh tomatoes, salt, and basil.

"*Buon appetito*" she called.

We raised our forks with a grin. "*Salud!*" we echoed, clinking glasses.

As a good Italian girl, I greet everyone with a kiss—hello and goodbye—even if it takes hours. I said "please" and "thank you." Maybe that's why I flew under the radar. No one expected me to be anything other than the polite, respectful daughter who showed up for Sunday dinners. That gave me freedom. Power. It was like playing by the rules while quietly breaking them.

For a few hours, everything felt right—familiar voices, good food, that sense of belonging. But the kitchen warmth couldn't cover the cold reality outside.

Rich was still out on bail. Money was draining fast—house, toys, lifestyle. Juan was back in Mexico for who knows how long. If I wanted to keep the dream alive, I had to move fast.

Staying in the game meant a new drug supplier. Fast.

It was easier than I expected. I reached out to Jeff's old supplier, Vinny, who was heading back to Peru. He scribbled a number and told me to call his Colombian buddy, Miguel.

When Rich and I met Miguel, I was surprised by how friendly he seemed—potbellied, dark hair, genuine smile. I hugged him and felt a strange, instant trust. But rumors ran deep. Miguel wasn't a man you crossed. They say the eyes are the windows to the soul; his were pitch black. That smile? Business.

With Miguel supplying, I thought I was in the clear. Then the airlines started cracking down. Random searches, tighter screening, suspicious luggage. Getting product to Derrick in Seattle got trickier.

We had two choices: fly it ourselves or drive.

Derrick and I took turns driving. The drive to Seattle was twenty-one hours, give or take. I kept it light—cruising up Highway 5, windows down, music on, but never too loud. Always scanning for patrol cars.

Sometimes, Camila rode with me. I paid her a few grand per trip to keep me company and take the wheel when I got tired. Sweet deal for her: a paid road trip with a friend. But let's be real—she was risking everything. Trafficking drugs across state lines made her an accomplice.

We'd meet Derrick at the Red Robin in Seattle. I'd forgotten how good-looking he was—dark hair, sharp jaw, one of those faces that turned heads. I was a sucker for a pretty face, and sometimes, I let my mind wander, but I always pulled myself back. Just a friend. Just a partner.

Once the handoff was done, the weight was lifted. We'd usually celebrate—downtown, catching live grunge bands. We'd drink brewskis, move through the crowd, losing ourselves in the energy. Before we parted, Derrick grinned.

"I'll be seeing you soon. Got a friend in Canada helping me move this product quick."

Once Seattle got a whiff of the good stuff, northern buyers followed. Each run introduced more people. Business grew. Then Derrick made a rookie mistake. He broke the golden rule: never introduce your supplier to your customer.

The drug business is really a people business. You've got to know who to trust, and who you can't, and how to make people trust you, even when they shouldn't. There were friends to be made and money to burn—or, in this case, money to be made and friends to burn. It's all about knowing when to step up and when to step back, and how to always keep growing.

So, when Derrick introduced me to his Canadian guy, a.k.a. "Corn Fed" because that's the only meat he demanded at Red Robin, I knew what to do. I liked Derrick, sure. Sweet guy. But I was nineteen, and I was a businesswoman. There's more money to be made cutting out the middleman. Corn Fed was mine now. Derrick would need to find someone new.

Moving product into Canada was trickier. International borders. Mounties and customs. But Corn Fed walked me through his and Derrick's old routes.

Rich didn't lay low like he should've. He used his fake ID, rented cars, and we crossed international borders with coke stashed in door panels and behind bumpers. Every time we hit customs, my heart pounded. But the drug-sniffing dogs, never found a thing. It was a miracle we didn't get pinched. We'd drop the car in Canada and fly home with the cash. Easy.

Back in the States, we weren't sweating Stevens and Delaney anymore. All our business was up north, and the profit was too good to quit. The real problem was money. Too much of it. Since it was all cash, we couldn't stash it fast enough. Even blowing thousands skiing in Whistler or Blackcomb barely made a dent. My purse straps would snap from the weight of it.

Once, I slipped. I'd left my salon scissors in a carry-on. TSA opened the bag and found the stacks. Jackpot. But Rich? Cool as ever.

"Oh my God," he said. "We just got an inheritance. We're flying home with it."

Somehow, they bought it. Maybe it was because we looked like clean-cut white kids. Maybe it was dumb luck. Either way, they escorted us to the plane like VIPs, waiting for us outside duty-free while we shopped.

Honestly, outsmarting the law? That was still part of the fun.

Miguel had started bringing in a much higher quality product—sticky-sweet, pure cocaine that peeled off in thin, opalescent sheets. We called it "Bubble Gum," straight from Colombia. Since this cocaine was exclusive to us, Rich came up with a plan.

"Bubble Gum is the best shit out there, better than anything on the market," Rich said. "But the demand is so high that we can cut it, double our profits, and still have the purest cocaine in the game."

"How do we do that?" I asked.

Rich grinned, that devilish smile I'd come to know too well. "You know how to wash dishes and clothes, right?"

I nodded, annoyed to be slipping from teenpin to housewife.

"Well, now you're gonna learn how to wash cocaine."

Rich had always been a natural at chemistry, and it turned out to be a major asset. At Mother's Market, we walked the aisles, picking fillers, making sure the ingredients were safe.

Then my pager went off. Derrick. Followed by the number seven. Looked like he wanted seven kilos. But the callback number was 714 area code. Orange County. I called from a payphone.

"Surprise, I'm early," he said, high energy in his voice. "You saw my number, yeah? I'll wait. Maybe we can hang out tonight?"

I exhaled, mind racing. "Yeah, I might be busy."

This wasn't a quick exchange. I'd have to cut and wash his coke down first. That took time.

And when it rains, it pours.

Corn Fed called. "Hey, I'm driving to see you," he said. "Traffic's crazy. Ten miles per hour. Ten, ya know? Ten. I'm crawling."

Yeah, I got his code. He wants ten kilos.

Since Derrick was already in town and I hadn't even scored yet, I tried to buy some time.

"Hey, buddy, yeah, I get it—you're only going ten. Listen, why don't you come next week? Traffic's nuts."

"No can do. Just left Whistler. On my way."

I hesitated. "I'll figure it out."

He chuckled. "Of course you will." Then, casually: "All I have to do is get my hair done at this new salon on Sunset Boulevard. They do all the rockstars. Maybe we hit that nice steakhouse before I head home?"

Corn Fed was one of those guys who expected more than just product. He wanted the full experience. To be pampered, wined, and dined like a true customer. Like the talent.

"Sounds great. Can't wait."

I played the game and treated him like the VIP he was.

What I didn't expect was two of my biggest clients ordering at once. It was a sticky situation. I had to get Derrick out of town with his seven kilos before Corn Fed arrived for his ten. Neither of them knew I was supplying the other.

This was like having two prom dates. One limo. Not ideal.

I needed ten kilos of uncut Bubble Gum. Double it to make twenty. After selling ten to Corn Fed and seven to Derrick, I'd have three left to sell on my own.

That would take at least three days of exhausting, nonstop work. And with Derrick already in town waiting, I was behind.

I paged Miguel. "I need ten packs of Bubble Gum. Fast. I'll handle everything after, I promise."

Miguel's voice was calm but firm. "*Mija*, I get it…but right now, the Bubble Gum is in short supply. Very short. Things are complicated. You know how it is."

"You know the pressure, right? I know you can help me, okay?"

A pause. He said, "I'll get some. Might take some time. But don't worry. I've got you. Just…trust me."

The clock was ticking. I borrowed a shitty car from my brother Jeff—the little gray Honda we called "the crack car," a little beater he bought to save miles on the Porsche. It wouldn't draw attention in Inglewood, a few miles north of Compton, where Miguel lived. I avoided wearing red or blue. No gangs colors, no reason to draw attention.

Stevens's and Delaney's faces flashed in my mind. I imagined guns drawn, celebrating my arrest. Ten kilos would make them captains. The thought nearly paralyzed me.

I needed to focus. I rolled down the window, took a deep breath, and flipped through the *Thomas Guide* for Miguel's new address.

When I pulled up to the building, the street was already dark. Trees cast long shadows. Teens stared from the curb. My heart rate spiked. I grabbed my purse and the duffel bag. It screamed "drug deal," but I had no choice. I knocked on Miguel's door. An old woman cracked it just enough to eye me.

"Is Miguel here?" I whispered.

She hesitated, then slowly opened the door. Miguel's wife, Paula, sat on the couch.

"Where's Miguel?" I asked.

Paula smiled sweetly. "Oh, hi, Denise. Miguel had to step out. Don't worry, I'll take care of you. You got the money?"

"No," I said. "Miguel said this was a front."

She gave me a sharp, calculating look. Picked up the phone, spoke rapid Spanish. Her mom glared at me from across the room.

When Paula hung up, she returned with a heavy blue cooler on wheels.

"Can I look?" I asked.

"It's good," she said, waving me off.

My skin prickled. "I want to look."

With a sigh, she took out a razor blade, slicing a "V" into the red duct tape. Out came the coke. "Wanna taste?"

I rolled my eyes. I didn't need to taste it. I could see the product had been stepped on. Dull. No way I could recut.

"These have been repo'ed," I said.

Paula's eyes narrowed. "No way. We have no time to press."

Her mom nodded.

"I can't take them," I said. "Sorry."

Paula leaned in, whispering to her mom in Spanish. Scrambling.

"What if I bring the price down?" Paula offered.

"It's not the price," I said, "it's the quality."

I was paying $10,250 each. And I'd already spent future profits on new jet skis.

I turned and walked. "Tell Miguel to call me."

Outside, I forced myself to breathe. No product. No backup. No time. What the hell was I going to tell Derrick and Corn Fed? My pager went off. Miguel. I pulled off the freeway, found a payphone, fumbled for change. When he answered, I let it rip.

"Are you fucking kidding me? You think I'm going to buy your stepped-on shit? I know what I'm doing, and you've totally wasted my time!"

I heard him laughing. Maybe nobody had talked to him like that before.

"You're in luck," he said. "I'm picking up a new shipment. Meet me at Sears."

I drove deeper into the hood. Sears lot was empty—except for Miguel's car. Miguel stepped out. Respect in his gaze. He wasn't alone. Two men stood beside him. One was Pedro, later called "The Cleaner." I didn't ask why. The other was Marocho, a dark-skinned Colombian who slipped me his number without a word.

"You're a tough one to please," Miguel said.

I hugged him. "Can you just show me what you've got?"

Trunk opened. Real Bubble Gum—sticky, sweet, pristine. Exactly what I needed. The deal went down in the parking lot, like we were buying appliances.

Forget Intro to Drugs 101 or Intermediate Dealing 201. I had just leveled up to You Can't Play Me 301.

Back at the motel, I got to work.

I followed Rich's instructions. It took days. While the batches dried, I tanned by the pool and watched *The Wonder Years*, wondering if Kevin would ever get the nerve to kiss Winnie at the high school dance.

I wasn't much older than those kids, but our lives were galaxies apart.

During those TV binges, I'd glance back at the room. It looked like a war zone: mounds of blow, utensils, colored duct tape, jugs, jars, and triple beam scales. I was responsible for hundreds of thousands of dollars in product. Just me.

How the hell did I end up here?

What the fuck was I doing with my life?

But I kept working—focused, methodical. I added inositol. Rubbing alcohol. Acetone. Watched the mixture settle into perfect white flakes. Then I weighed, bagged, and wrapped.

One kilo became two. Profits doubled.

Tears For Fears' "Everybody Wants to Rule the World" played in the background. And for a moment, I did rule.

I signed each kilo with my initials, D.T, in a black Sharpie, just like all the drug lords did. Why brand something illegal? Same reason they did: pride. This was my work. My empire.

Sometimes, instead of initials, I used the Chanel logo—those sleek, intertwining double C's. It was my way of saying my kilos were the epitome of class, style, and sophistication, pure luxury.

After three grueling days, I made the drops: Ten kilos to Corn Fed. Seven kilos to Derrick. Neither knew about the other. I had three left to move.

Meaning $110,000 in profit.

Enough to cover the jet skis—and then some.

But here's the real story. I was acting like I was successful, but inside, I was a mess. I don't believe in luck; I believe in miracles. It was God intervening. There had to be a reason I was still alive. I wholeheartedly believe that I had angels with me every step of the way, because I could have easily been shot, and my dead body tossed out in the desert. I really have no idea how else I made it through. But I did.

I was proud of the money, but Rich decided what went toward bills, what we spent, and what was reinvested into the business. I was just the good little woman, bringing home the bacon, frying it in a pan, and taking major risks. I'd always been taught men were the providers and women supported. So, it felt natural to hand it all over. For me, it was about having a partner and feeling safe. No blame on Rich. That was how he grew up too, and he was good at managing money. Left to me, I probably would have blown Miguel's money on designer clothes and suffered some major consequences later.

By then, the lifestyle was wearing me down. One weekend, Greg came down from LA. He looked around at the estate, the cars, the lifestyle, and gave a slight nod, like it confirmed something he'd already known.

"Let me in," he said.

"What?" I squinted, pretending not to know.

Greg had never been afraid of work. Two jobs, long hours. But the payoff never seemed to match the effort. He already had a connection through one of Jeff's friends and sold a little on the side, mostly to his jock friends, just to bring in extra cash. In the late '80s, a little dealing on the side was practically normal. Now he was ready to take it seriously.

"The business," he said again.

The idea of working with Greg excited me. I wanted everyone to win. So instead of letting him deal with a crowd of teenagers who could squeal on him, I talked to Rich and we decided he could help with Seattle drives.

The next morning, he dropped the bomb: he was putting in his two weeks' notice at both Pasquini Imports—where he worked on the corporate side of the café Mom ran—and at Tramps, the exclusive nightclub owned by Oscar Lerman, who was married to Jackie Collins.

Tramps wasn't just any club. It felt like a movie set. Hugh Hefner and his Playmates were regulars, as were Farrah Fawcett and Lee Majors, who always managed to get thrown out for being too drunk.

Greg had all the stories, spilling a martini on Prince's leather pants—Prince was cool with it. He passed sarcastic "fuck off" notes between Johnny Carson and Sammy Davis Jr., and even pinched Victoria Principal's ass on a dare. The kicker? Slow-dancing with Tina Turner to "What's Love Got to Do with It" at a "We Are the World" benefit. That was Greg: hustling two jobs by day, rubbing elbows with legends by night.

Still, none of it was enough to keep him around.

"New gig," he told Mom when he quit both jobs. Of course, he didn't bother to mention what that gig actually was.

When Miguel ran short, I'd call Marocho, the same guy from the Sears lot, my new supplier. By now, I was a serious player, deep into international drug negotiations, bargaining with cartel leaders from Mexico, Peru, El Salvador, Colombia, and Bolivia—a teenage girlfella trying to knock down their asking prices like I was running my own version of NAFTA, all while staying feminine in white eyelet shorts and black patent-leather ballet flats.

The supply was coming in so fast that I had to create a color-coded duct-tape system just to keep it straight. Martha Stewart would've been impressed.

Why me?

Why not me?

I'd put in the time, energy, and hustle. I worked my way up the ladder, built an ironclad reputation for paying people back. It didn't matter that I was a teenage girl. What mattered was that I made people rich, and that's the bottom line in any business.

I was a teenage Springsteen. A boss. Born in the USA.

* * * *

That Christmas, Rich gave me a black Mercedes 450SL, complete with a red bow on top. To everyone, it looked like I was spoiled. Like I was lucky to have a boyfriend who gave such lavish gifts. But if they knew how much I'd worked to raise the money *he* used to buy that car, they'd know it wasn't a gift. It was my year-end bonus.

Just a week earlier, I didn't give a shit about another nice car. I was more concerned about how I was going to get *one million dollars* across the Canadian border. Should I throw it in a suitcase and pray?

That morning, I'd sold fifty kilos to a Canadian buyer who managed the entire western half of the country. I'd negotiated the price to $40,000 per kilo. After paying off the drug mules—guys backpacking kilos down through Washington—and the speedboat crews skimming them across the border, hiding behind staged water skiers, I cleared a million in profit.

Now I was standing at the top of Whistler Mountain, pushing off the chairlift in a pink parka and black ski pants, my cool-girl shades on.

I may have looked like a privileged, pampered teenager from Orange County, but I most certainly wasn't. I was Denise Trigo, a nineteen-year-old cocaine boss of Southern California who had successfully made the leap to owning the Canadian cocaine market.

And when it was one of the bosses' birthdays, I didn't just hand over a Hallmark card. I gifted The Royale. What's that, you ask? A $15,000 kilo from Bolivia—the best of the best. Coca leaves had to be processed within two weeks of harvest. Rare. Respected.

You didn't dare cut it. The look on their faces when they unwrapped it? Priceless. Because staying in their favor probably saved our lives more than once.

Meanwhile, my mom was opening the café, making a latte, saving me a seat. I tried not to think about which world felt more real.

Chapter Ten

Desperately Seeking Teenhood

DECEMBER 1987

I walked into Café Pasquini from the December chill in an ivory camisole tucked into high-waisted Levi's, oversized Chanel sunglasses, and a black leather jacket slipping off my shoulders. My black Mary Janes clicked across the marble floor as I passed the espresso bar. Soft waves framed my face, red lipstick. Heads turning.

The moment I saw my mom at her usual table in the center of the café, something inside me exhaled. Like a proper Italian girl, I leaned in for a quick hug and kiss on both cheeks, then collapsed into the wicker chair like I was carrying the weight of the world. I tossed my black studded bag onto the table with a loud *thunk* and let out a long, theatrical sigh—full drama.

She was tying her green apron when she glanced up, her face softening with concern. I breathed in the familiar scent of her Estée Lauder White Linen.

"Is everything okay, Denise?"

I couldn't unload the truth without scaring her to death, so I danced around it. "I guess I just miss everyone. Living so far away with Rich..."

I missed Stacy, my carefree teenage life—the fun, the friends, the freedom. I missed Mom too, watching old Bette Davis movies together.

Mostly, I missed me, the version that felt light and young. I was only nineteen, for God's sake. To make matters worse, Rich always had friends tagging along. I was starting to feel trapped, like Michelle Pfeiffer in *Scarface*, minus the sequined Halston dress and hot sidekick Manny. As much as I loved Rich, the spark in our relationship was starting to fade. Still, I couldn't manage my life without him.

I looked back at Mom. "Rich is in Canada visiting friends." Half true. He was really waiting on money from Corn Fed.

"He didn't invite you?" Her face folded with concern. "Are you two fighting?" Then softer, leaning in, "I was worried it would be hard for you there. It's so new. No city life. Are you coming back home?"

I ran a hand through my hair and shrugged.

She had to know what world Rich was part of. He was Jeff's best friend, and Jeff was counting down the days until prison. Mom sometimes asked if Rich was still dealing.

I lied. I'd say, "He used to, but not anymore."

Mom never judged. Never questioned. Just forgave.

I resented her sometimes for not seeing how lost I was. What if she'd been stricter? More rules. Real consequences. What if she and Dad had talked to me about college, or even just talked to each other? But I was the one lying to the woman who loved me unconditionally. If I'd told her the truth, maybe she could've helped. I never gave her the chance. The only thing Mom was guilty of was believing in me.

It's sad. She always had my back. I never had hers.

I stabbed at my penne *arrabbiata*. After a long silence, she sipped her coffee and met my eyes.

"Take this with a grain of salt, dear, but Richard adores you. He's loyal, Denise. In this world, that's rare."

I wondered if she was thinking about Dad—about the hunting trips that were never about hunting. About Gale. About the humiliation she swallowed whole.

He cheated on Gale too. With a legal assistant named Donna—everyone called her Dee—so his second marriage ended too.

I'd spent mourning what I lost in my parents' divorce. Now I felt another kind of loss—missing the moments with Dad, Gale, and Peter. As much as I craved change, I craved stability more.

Mom was right—Rich was loyal. And to me, loyalty was everything.

Sade sang it best, her smoky voice pleading to hold on to love. And I wanted that. God, I wanted it.

I sipped my Italian soda as my attention drifted back to Mom. She sighed, maybe softening.

"Denise, nobody's going to take care of you but yourself. But you'd be surprised what you're capable of. You're stronger than you think."

Her words landed. She believed in me. And that mattered.

I needed to do something to fix this unhappiness.

* * * *

When Rich got back from Canada, I hit pause on *Dirty Dancing* right before Baby's big lift. I took a deep breath and looked at him.

"I'm done. No more drops. No more scary shit," I said, bracing.

But he surprised me—calm, cool.

"I just want you to be happy."

No arguments. No guilt trip. I was out.

Well, sort of.

I had to train Greg to take over. He was eager, and I showed him everything—including my secret wash method that doubled kilos and the profit.

Before we hit the road to Washington, we stopped by my mom's. Greg leaned in.

"Stevens and Delaney are down the street."

My heart jumped. One of them ducked behind his windshield. We had *three kilos.*

"What do we do?" I hissed.

Rich didn't blink. "Split up."

I jumped in his car, clutching two kilos. Greg peeled off with the third. Tires screeched. We flew in opposite directions. Unmarked cars followed both of us.

"Hold on," Rich muttered, taking a hard right. Still on us. Then: "Watch this." He gunned it south on the 405, exited fast onto Fairview, then looped back north. The tail kept going south—we'd lost them.

Rich's friends came in handy; we stashed the kilos at Rich's number-one clinger's place and waited. But I couldn't relax. Greg was still out there.

The next day, he walked in looking wrecked. "I thought I was toast," he said. "I ditched the car and checked into the Fountain Valley Inn. Figured I'd lay low. But then—"

Rich cut in. "What?"

"They were circling the place. Watching. The manager kept calling my room. I didn't answer—I knew."

I blinked. "So what'd you do?"

Greg rubbed his face. "Taped the kilo to the back of the toilet. Had duct tape in my bag. Just stuck it there."

Rich laughed. "That was your plan? Lowkey genius."

"I walked out, almost like I was surrendering, and then—bam! Cops tackled me. Guns out, cuffs on. And get this: there's a bunch of kids on a field trip to the roller rink watching the whole thing go down." He shook his head. "So damn embarrassing."

I laughed. I always do at fucked-up shit, and this was no exception. "Oh my God, that's kinda funny."

Greg continued, "They tore my car apart, didn't find shit. Just baby clothes. Which they thought was weird."

I chuckled. "And the room?"

"They searched it—*and missed the kilo.* I don't know how. I was sure I was screwed."

I laughed. "Jesus Christ."

Greg grinned. "Guess I got lucky."

I sighed. "We're a day behind. Still gotta get it to Washington."

Greg smirked. "Hey—I'm trained now, right?"

Rich clapped him on the back. “Look at you. Man of the hour.”

Once everything was squared away, we hit the road. Greg’s only rule: “We’re listening to what I want. Peaceful music.”

So, as we pulled out, Joni Mitchell’s voice filled the car. It was a stark contrast to Jeff’s heavy-metal soundtrack—but I loved it all. From Orange County, we shot up I-5, weaving through the Grapevine, dodging snowstorms and big rigs like a video game that hit without warning. Past the vineyards and rolling hills, Wings and other ’70s classics carried us north. We grabbed snacks at a log cabin store in Shasta Mountain, then cruised through Oregon toward Seattle. That’s where I introduced Greg to Derrick and Corn Fed.

On the way back, we coasted down the 101, soaking in Portland’s colorful boats and charm, cut through California’s towering redwoods, and snapped a photo with Paul Bunyan and Babe the Blue Ox in Klamath. Grants Pass felt like stepping into a Gold Rush postcard. We wrapped the run with a stop at the Madonna Inn—because, honestly, the West Coast is the best coast. No debate.

Rich kept making solo runs to Canada. He shouldn’t have been traveling, but kept showing up to court. His lawyer kept postponing his sentencing—only a matter of time.

* * * *

Prison was waiting for Jeff too. No matter how many community college classes he took, he couldn’t outrun the inevitable. He grew out his facial hair, trying to look tougher before turning himself in; he didn’t want to be anyone’s bitch. Eventually, he had to bite the bullet.

I was nervous for him. He tried to act brave, but I knew my brother—he was scared. Mom and I kept encouraging him, reminding him that the only way forward was to get it behind him. One of us Trigos was going to prison. The word alone felt dirty, embarrassing. We didn’t talk about it outside our inner circle. Nobody was allowed to talk shit about my family.

Mom and I drove forty miles to the state prison in Chino every week. We were the only ones who showed up. Greg said, “Prison’s not my thing." Dad wasn't around either. He was off doing humanitarian work—spreading the Calvary gospel, serving as a battlefield medic for freedom fighters in Nicaragua and Honduras. Years later, I learned he'd also worked with the government: smuggling hostages from Lebanon to Israel, falsifying documents, supplying medical aid across Third-World countries.

But while Dad was helping the world, Mom was our world—holding us together. Somehow, I came to love those drives—just the two of us, rolling past hills and grazing cattle, the radio soft in the background, talking and not talking all at once.

The first time we pulled up to the prison, it hit hard. Four massive facilities sprawled across 2,500 acres, all wrapped in barbed wire.

Mom was quiet at first, then the tears came.

"What did I do wrong to deserve this?" she whispered. "Was it because your father and I divorced?" Her voice cracked. Guilt hung in her eyes—like she thought she wasn't enough.

I hugged her. "You're the best mom in the world," I said. And I meant it. I told her, "Jeff was a lost soul." But deep down, I knew that he wasn't any more lost than I was.

Then Jeff appeared—no swagger, no Tigger-like bounce. Just dark raw denim, a light-blue shirt with the top button fastened, and black steel-toed boots. He looked harder, cautious. Surveying the yard filled with broken families, something hit me. I had risked everything—my freedom, my life—for what? Seeing my mom's pain, I silently thanked God I was out of the game. This place was hell.

"Hey, Niese. Mom." Jeff greeted us with a hug and a smirk, like he knew how absurd it all looked. "I'm fine," he said, shrugging. "Not in any cliques. I know how to handle myself." He leaned in. "Keep finding girls to write me. Make sure they send pretty pictures. The guys love that." Then to me, grinning, "I told some of them they'd get letters. They think I'm a player." Clearly, he found his hustle inside.

We laughed.

"Guess what, Mom? I play the drums in the prison band," he added, giving himself some street cred to the yard. Mom brought his favorites from the café, chicken piccata with capers and a prosciutto sandwich, handing them over as if she were trying to bring a little taste of home to that hellhole.

Then Jeff got quiet. "Listen, I need to tell you something. Don't get mad," he said, eyes flicking between us. "But…baby Jenna? She's not Dad and Gale's. She's mine."

I froze. "What? That was over two years ago—how?"

Mom stared straight ahead, stunned and silent.

Jeff explained, "I didn't even know Shelly was pregnant until two days before she gave birth. She barely showed. Denise, you were around her too and you didn't notice. I wasn't ready to be a dad—I was coming here, for Christ's sake. But you know me…. I didn't want to put my baby girl up for adoption either. So, Dad swooped in with a plan."

Mom and I exchanged a stunned look, trying to process.

"Gale always wanted a baby girl," Jeff continued. "So, Dad had Shelly admitted under Gale's name. Easier than all the paperwork. The nurses thought the baby was theirs."

Mom muttered, "Of course, younger girl."

Jeff just nodded, like he couldn't believe it either. "Yeah. The morning Shelly went into labor, Dad drove her to the hospital, pretended to be her husband, and Peter and I cruised the hallways, breaking into operating rooms—you know, Niese, like we always do."

I couldn't speak. Betrayal knotted in my stomach. Mom looked ready to explode.

"I can't believe Gale is raising my grandchild," she said, voice shaking.

I tried to process. "Why now? Why are you telling us this?"

Jeff looked uneasy. "Because now that Dad and Gale are done, she's threatening to take Peter and Jenna and disappear. I'm scared I'll lose her."

When Jeff got out, I wasn't worried he'd fall back into old habits. He'd cleaned up after his arrest, and a year later, he was finally on track. Dad helped him get a job as a thermography tech, working with X-rays and MRIs. He even became a born-again Christian. He still had his quirks, like complaining to Mom when she forgot extra capers, but he was doing better.

And me? I was relieved to be out too. My life finally felt calmer. Clothes everywhere, bouncing between Rich's lake house and my mom's, but moving forward. I started looking for real work, though "teenpin" wasn't exactly résumé gold.

Weekends were for lake life. Glassy mornings turning into afternoon Palm Springs heat. Blue Öyster Cult's "Burnin' for You" blasting. Cold beer in hand, the boat slicing across the water.

"Hit it!" I'd yell, and I'd pop up on the slalom, jumping through the wakes, spraying fans of water on each side. For the first time in a long time, I felt free.

* * * *

Rich and I were lounging on the leather couch, coffee in hand, soaking in the quiet peace of the lake. The phone rang. Rich grabbed it.

"Yo, Jeff," he said, leaning back. "What's up, my man?"

He looked at me, grinned. "Yeah, we're here. Perfect day for skiing. You should come by.... Yeah, sure, bring Marco."

An hour later, we were packed and ready. I tossed extra towels in the boat bag and turned to Jeff.

"It's hot. We need water, wine coolers, snacks. Liquor store run—anyone coming?"

Jeff stretched. "I'll go."

I grabbed my keys, slipped on my flip-flops, and headed out in nothing but my bikini. No need for a cover-up. It was a quick trip. We took off in my convertible Benz, sun blazing, music low. On the way, we caught up.

"I'm so happy you're clean," I told him, meaning it.

Jeff glanced over. "What about you?"

I laughed, light but tired. "So over the bullshit."

We hit the mini-mart, loaded up. Back at the car, I slid behind the wheel—and froze. A black sedan blocked us in.

"Hey!" I shouted, scanning the lot. "Move this!"

Then, everything went wrong. Eight men spilled out of nowhere, walking toward the liquor store, all in white tees and jeans, slicked-back hair, guns drawn. For a moment, I thought it was a robbery.

"What the hell is—" I started, before someone barked, "Get down!"

Before I could move, I was yanked from the car and slammed to the pavement, gun pressed to the back of my skull. Heat blistered through my chest, part sun, part terror. One of them jumped into my Benz and peeled out.

Car thieves?

Another guy hauled me up, dragged me barefoot to a black car, and shoved me in. The door locked. I spotted Jeff—already stuffed in a separate car, speeding off. My stomach dropped. They were going to kill us. The driver climbed in.

"Where are you taking my brother?" I shouted. "What's happening?"

He looked at me through the mirror. "You know what's going on."

But I didn't. I had no idea. Just minutes ago, we were sipping coffee on the lake.

We tore into the desert, the gated calm of Canyon Lake vanishing in the rearview. Sweat rolled down my spine, my skin sticking to hot leather. I clutched the door handle, tried it. Locked. Miles of sand. No help. No witnesses. Just me, half-naked, scared, and silent.

Mexican. Colombians. Peruvians. Bolivians?

Then, a low hum in the distance. A helicopter. It dipped low and landed nearby. The driver got out, met the pilot. He gave me a final glance over his shoulder.

"Don't run."

Where the hell would I run? I spotted a police decal on the chopper. My heart dropped. Cops. That didn't ease the panic. I'd learned not all badges meant safety. The chopper lifted and vanished. The man got back in. Started the car. We drove again. I didn't ask where. But then…the landscape began to shift. Familiar trees. Familiar curves. We were headed back toward home. The car stopped a block away. My Benz—the one I thought they'd stolen—was parked beside a line of police cars.

Then I figured it out: they were after Rich, and even though he'd been out on bail for two years, they were hoping to seize drugs. The driver looked back.

"How many people inside? Any weapons? Drugs?"

"No weapons," I said.

"Don't lie. You want to go down as an accessory? Tell us now."

"There's nothing to tell! If you don't like the answers, stop asking!"

He didn't blink. "Does Rich know we're coming?"

I shook my head. "I thought you were stealing my Mercedes."

Tears burned down my face. His radio crackled: *"Suspect may be armed. If there are doubts, take him down."*

"I just said there are no weapons!" I shouted.

These cops were such dicks. At least Stevens and Delaney had personality. No one cared. These guys were geared up for war. Strapping on bulletproof vests, cocking their weapons, I saw police jackets from six different departments: Newport Beach, Huntington Beach, Fountain Valley, Costa Mesa, Anaheim, and Riverside. Covering over a fifty-mile territory. They were ready to take Rich out. Neighbors peeked from behind curtains. Humiliating. Thank God it wasn't my block. I spotted Jeff again, cuffed, pale. He mouthed, *Anything in the house?* I shook my head. *Are you sure?* Almost sure.

Blood drained back into his face. But I was thinking, even if it were clean, who's to say they wouldn't plant something? Then, it happened. The police charged the house from all angles, an army of DEA agents, detectives, and local officers. Rich was thrown against the wall, cuffed hard.

"No!" I screamed, hating how brutally they were treating him.

Marco had been out back, getting the boat ready. As soon as he saw the cops, he dove into the lake.

"Stop!" they shouted. "Keep swimming and we'll shoot!"

"Okay, okay!" he cried, arms raised. He started sinking.

"Swim back!"

He obeyed, shaking, boardshorts clinging to his body as they dragged him onto the dock. Given his history at Jeff's house with the tweakers, there was a good chance Marco had already pissed himself again.

Inside, we were all handcuffed on the floor as they tore the place apart. Mattresses flipped. Carpets pulled. Drawers emptied and flipped over. Paperwork scattered everywhere.

They collected receipts for everything—jet skis, the boat, cement. Wood. Trees. Title. I was still in my bikini, so I asked to change. The cop smirked and kept walking. If they couldn't get us on drugs, they'd take their thrills where they could.

Hours passed. Tension rose. Different agencies bickered. Some wanted to arrest everyone, others didn't want their names on false charges. Eventually, they let us go. Everyone but Rich.

"I love you, baby! Don't worry!" he shouted as they shoved him into the cruiser. I believed the first part. The second? Not so much.

One officer said he'd probably be released on his own recognizance in Orange County. Maybe. They didn't even know which district would charge him. Jeff turned to me.

"Greg's throwing a party in Costa Mesa. Let's go. We will wait for Rich there."

Greg and Rich's brother Mark shared the apartment. When we walked in, it was wall-to-wall bodies—old high school jocks, random girls, loud music. Greg pulled me aside.

"It's going to be fine," he said calmly. "Rich is smart. He's got this."

I nodded, still jacked up on adrenaline. My body hadn't caught up to the idea of *fine* yet.

Three coked-up cheerleaders jumped onto the coffee table, shouting, "Make that V! Dot that I! Swirl that C.T.O.R.Y—victory, yeah, victory!"

It felt just like high school all over again. I claimed a corner, sipped a beer. I was a ghost in the room, desperately seeking teenhood while real life had already kicked the door in.

My pager buzzed. I ducked into Greg's room and called Rich.

"Where are you?"

"Horikawa," he said, laughing. "No charges. DEA argued for hours—book me or dump me in the desert. I told them, 'At least drop me off near a payphone—and hey, can you lend me a quarter?'" He cracked up at his own joke.

The guns. The cuffs. The raid—none of it had touched him. I was tired—mentally, physically, emotionally.

"I just want to go to Mom's and sleep," I said.

He didn't respond. But I did what a good girlfriend does.

"Okay," I said. "I'm on my way."

Chapter Eleven

Good Cook, Bad Driver

NOVEMBER 1988

It all happened so fast. *Bam*—the wooden gavel hit the desk. Rich was sentenced to eight months. The Marshal took Rich straight from the courtroom. I drove home in tears.

He started out at Orange County Jail in Santa Ana, not far from Juan's place. But OCJ was overcrowded, so they moved him to Theo Lacy, a.k.a. "Camp Snoopy." It was the least awful option. Better food, more yard time, and visits across a picnic table instead of behind thick glass.

Eight months. No sex. No French kissing. No affection. Was that even possible?

The night before, I gave Rich my "scout's honor." Not that I'd made it past Brownies, but I threw in the salute anyway.

Watching someone you love lose their freedom hurts. I felt terrible for Rich. But part of me was relieved. Maybe now, finally, we could move forward—the ultimate reset.

In the meantime, I visited him every weekend. And it was grueling. I had no clout here—no VIP line, no velvet rope. Just hours in line with wives, moms, girlfriends juggling crying babies.

The visits become routine. When my number was called, I'd shuffle in with the others, all of us waiting to see the men we loved. Handholding was allowed. Nothing more. Most of our time was spent saying "I love you," "I miss you," and Rich reminding me to scrub the grout between the marble tiles or warm up the engine of the Porsche 928 *at least* sixty seconds before driving it.

Then, one day, he gave me that familiar grin. "Hey, baby, I've been thinking about making a big change."

My heart soared. *This is it*, I thought. He's finally ready to turn over a new leaf. He leaned in, voice low, glancing around for guards. "I've been meeting some new people in here. Learning some new ideas."

"Like…college courses?" I asked. "You're bettering yourself that way?"

He shook his head. "Nah. My buddies here, these guys know the meth game. And they've been teaching me how to cook it. The profits are insane, babe."

I blinked. "Meth?"

Rich nodded. "Here's the deal, need you to test this guy's recipe. See if he knows what he is talking about."

I almost stood up right there. "No way!"

His face fell. "Come on, baby. I need you to do this for me."

I stared at him, stunned. "Meth? That's disgusting! It's for bikers and tweakers!"

He just shrugged, smiling like it was nothing. "It's not a big deal. If these guys are right, it won't even take an hour to cook. The high is supposed to be insane. This is the future. Profits? Huge."

Again with the money.

I could tell Rich was trying to fit in with his new circle. Despite everything in me screaming, "Run," I heard myself say, "Gross, but okay. I guess I'll try." His eyes lit up. Even though I'd walked away from this life, I still wasn't strong enough to cut ties with Rich. I was still codependent, holding onto him like he was my north star, still believing I was helping him, even from behind bars.

On the way home, I stopped at CVS for supplies. Turning toward Mom's house, my engine roared. Blondie popped her head through the drapes like clockwork. I scooped her up, tucked her under my arm, and drove to the lake house, following the directions Rich had whispered across the picnic table. No labs. No hazmat suit. Just me, in a black polka-dot mini sundress and white sneakers, cranking up *Appetite for Destruction* like it was Sunday dinner and not a felony.

I mixed ingredients in the kitchen, using the insides of a Vicks inhaler and a microwave like a modern-day *I Love Lucy*. Twenty minutes later, I had something white and flaky. Back then, I couldn't just Google "what meth looks like," so I tore a page out of *Vogue*, made a little bindle, and, like a total idiot, brought it with me on my next visit.

At visitation, Rich was amped. "So? How'd it go?"

I glanced around for guards, then casually opened the bindle hidden in my sweater pocket and sprinkled the powder on the table.

His eyes went wide. "*Denise*!"

He brushed the meth off the surface, panicked. The guards didn't notice, but the inmates did. And according to Rich, they couldn't stop talking about me.

"Who's the badass chick who brought drugs to visitation?"

Me. America's dumbest criminal.

* * * *

With Rich in jail, I started going out more—hanging with my girlfriends in Orange County, cruising in his black Porsche 928. I connected with Camila, my old partner in crime, from the Seattle runs, and we made a whole weekend of it. On Saturday, I unwound the garden hose and soaped up the Porsche in my neon-orange Body Glove bikini, while Camila and I took turns posing on the hood like we were in a proper photo shoot. We couldn't wait to drop the disposable camera off at the Kodak shack near my mom's house—one-day photo development felt like magic.

By night, I switched gears—slipped into a tight black off-the-shoulder Betsy Johnson minidress with chiffon leopard ruffles. We pregamed with mini cans of piña colada and strawberry daiquiri, sipping as we cruised to Birraporetti's.

Later, I slid behind the wheel, the souped-up engine purring. I backed out too fast, high on confidence and horsepower. Then—everything became a blur. Sharp turn into my mom's neighborhood, way too fast.

Tires screeched. For a second, I felt like a kid again, skidding my red Big Wheel around the corner, hair flying in the wind, holding tight to the handlebars. Then I hit something—hard.

Through the haze, I saw a neighborhood buddy standing there. For a second, I thought he was a ghost. Was I still alive? His lips moved, then snapped into focus.

"Get the fuck out of here, Denise! Go!"

Camila clutched her forehead, blood trickling down.

"You okay?" I asked.

She nodded, but her eyes said otherwise. I threw the car into reverse, the front end totaled, parts dragging across the lawn. Somehow, it moved.

My neighbors Tom and Mary had their garage door open, so I pulled the Porsche in and scrambled to ditch the evidence—tossed all the cans, hearts pounding.

At home, my mom was still up, glued to the TV, watching *Overboard* on VHS.

"Girls?" she mumbled.

We bolted upstairs, tore off the dresses, wiped off the makeup, and I brushed my teeth. I pulled on sweats, sneakers, and my innocent-looking My Little Pony sweatshirt, figuring it might throw off the cops when they inevitably showed up.

"Shit," I whispered.

"Shit," Camila echoed.

The cops already knew. Oil tracks led straight to Tom and Mary's house. One of the officers cleared his throat.

"Your neighbor's out front, in boxers, yelling about a hit-and-run. Says he chased you down the street."

I blinked. A guy in boxers? Hadn't even registered.

"Yes. I was driving," I said quietly.

My mom stood frozen. I didn't know where the lie came from, but I ran with it.

"He looked angry. I was scared." I just wanted to grab my mom and go back. Then, quieter, "I heard he's an alcoholic and beats women."

My mom, bless her, stayed silent—maybe stunned, maybe just going with it.

One cop softened. "I get it. But you should've left a note. It's the law, and we have to legally take you in."

"No jail time. Just booking," the other officer said.

Jail. Only this time, it was all me.

At the station, I smiled for the mug shot. I gave my best version of the story, even though I didn't remember a damn thing.

I asked to use the restroom. I shoved my fingers down my throat. Coladas, daiquiris, and bellinis—all of it gone. I stood there gripping the sink, staring at myself in that grimy mirror. I could've killed someone. I could've killed Camila. I could've died. What the hell had I become? I splashed cold water on my face and walked out.

Then Sergeant Stevens turned the corner.

"Miss Trigo. How's Jeff? Rich?"

The questioning officer connected the dots.

"Jeff Trigo's your brother?" His face shifted. "I need to breathalyze you. Now."

I didn't know what else to do. "Please!" I begged, almost choking on the words. "I'm not like my brother. He's not even like that anymore. I just want to go home! Please…"

Maybe it was the desperation. Maybe it was the sweatshirt. Maybe he realized he'd missed his window. Either way, he sighed.

"Go. Get out of here before I change my mind."

In retrospect, the way I could wiggle out of legal trouble was wild. In the moment, it felt like a superpower. My mom picked me up at the police station. As we drove, she passed our house.

"Wait, where are we going?" I asked.

She kept her eyes on the road. "I want you to see what you did."

We pulled up to the wreck. A car sat crooked on the lawn, halfway inside the house. My mom stared straight ahead, jaw clenched.

"If that guy hadn't parked like that—" I started.

She cut me off. "Denise, this was all you. You hit a parked car and shoved it into their house."

There was no arguing. I'd turned someone's quiet driveway into a demolition site.

That night, I lay in bed, spinning. How was I going to tell Rich? That car was his baby. He'd rebuilt the engine himself. Made it perfect. The scariest part wasn't the crash. It wasn't the cops, or the damage, or even the lives I'd risked. It was telling Rich.

At the prison, I sat next to his dad—the Porsche was in his name. Rich came in, smiling, clueless. When I told him, my eyes blurred. His jaw clenched. Veins popped in his forehead.

His dad tried to break the tension, and in his southern accent, he said, "Hell, we're all just lucky that feller—the poor bastard—wasn't fixin' to water his lawn, 'cause Denise would've taken him out, bless his heart."

Rich's dad and I laughed. Rich didn't. He stood up and walked away. I cried all the way home.

But maybe that crash was divine intervention. Maybe it was the break I needed to change. I was too young for something this serious. Too broken to see it. But I loved him. Didn't I? A few hours later, the phone rang.

"I could've lost you," Rich said. "I can replace the car. But there's only one Denise Trigo. And she means the world to me."

Relief washed over me.

"I'm really sorry, Rich. I love you too." Any thought of change vanished.

I was a child of the times—blinded by the light.

Chapter Twelve
Changes

NOVEMBER 1989–JANUARY 1991

I've always been a free spirit who loves her independence, but I'm also a natural-born codependent, craving connection just as much as freedom. It's complicated, but maybe that's the best of both worlds—like a crisp salad paired with creamy pasta.

With Rich away, and both of us out of the game, I felt something I hadn't in a long time. Call it freedom. Like Madonna, I got into the groove and hung out with my girlfriends—Stacy, Camila, and Brandy. Because yes, it's true. Girls just wanna have fun.

We'd hit karaoke bars all over the beach cities. I wasn't even using a fake ID. I was twenty-two, totally legit. We'd fill the signup sheet with our picks: Chrissie Hynde, Stevie Nicks, Debbie Harry, Cyndi Lauper, even George Michael and Elton John.

The scene in OC was electric—Margaritaville, Arches, the Cannery, Villa Nova, California Beach, and the Ruben E. Lee a Mississippi riverboat anchored right in the bay. Newport was anything but a sleepy seaside town. Sometimes I'd arrive by Duffy boat, gliding up to the dock as the harbor lights shimmered on the water. Glamorous clubs like Tiffany's, John Dominis, Cano's, and Visions lined the waterfront, pulsing with energy. I flirted shamelessly, basked in the attention, and sometimes even dropped Tommy Tutone's "867-5309" as my number just to be a smartass, but I stayed loyal to Rich. I loved him. That didn't change.

Rich's dad and I met most mornings for breakfast at Mimi's Café before visiting Rich. Those mornings were lovely. But the mix of nightlife and early-morning jail visits wore me down. Visits stopped feeling special; they felt like something I had to do.

Then came the questions: *Where'd you go last night? When did you get home?*

All I wanted was to sleep in, eat pancakes in my PJs, maybe watch *Tequila Sunrise*, *When Harry Met Sally*, or drool over Rob Lowe in *About Last Night* or *St. Elmo's Fire*. Instead, I was up at 6:00 a.m., standing in line outside the jail.

After a while, it felt like I was doing time too.

My dad got me a gig working with him and Jeff at a chiropractic college in LA. I got my phlebotomy license, learned EKGs and other basic medical tests. And, of course, I adored the attention from the cute med students. But I hit the ceiling fast. I was basically Jeff's assistant—he called me "the button pusher" for starting and stopping the machines. He wasn't wrong. The only way up was more school. Doctor. Chiropractor. Crack backs for a living? At five-foot-three? No thanks. Plus, I'd need my high school diploma, and that felt impossible.

I returned to the one job I truly enjoyed: working at a trendy high-end salon at South Coast Plaza called Carlton, assisting a stylist named Marina. Beautiful, with a cool Huntington Beach edge, she felt more like a friend than a boss. Everything felt normal again—well, except the pay. Once you've held hundreds of thousands of dollars in your hands for a few hours' work, no normal paycheck quite cuts it.

Two weeks before Rich was released, I was back in the salon when Marina's new client walked in. Crisp Armani shirt, collar open. Tall, dark, handsome, with a fiery, sexy Latin edge. Full lips, one corner tilted up in an Elvis-like smirk.

We locked eyes the entire time—undeniable chemistry. When Marina finished, he walked over and said, "Lorenzo Estes." And that was it. Okay, I know what you're thinking. I said I was loyal to the bone. It's not like I planned to blow my relationship up. It was like a bag of Doritos—once you taste one, you're never satisfied. You might as well eat the whole bag.

Even though Rich was in jail, the summer of 1990 was one of the best. My cousin Madeline flew in from Staten Island, and suddenly the house was buzzing. It turned into a full-blown cousin mashup: Guido (Aunt Flo's son) and his wife, Stacy; Camila; Marcy; my brothers; and the FVHS crew. We packed into cars, crossed into Mexico, partied in Rosarito, danced on speakers, hit every club we could, and laughed our way through every wild night. For a while, I forgot how complicated everything was. I was just a girl again, acting my age, not somebody's girlfriend, not carrying grown-up choices. Just free.

* * *

The day Rich got out, his dad and I picked him up. I was so happy, but at the same time, nervous. So much had changed. I gave him a long kiss, but it felt different. On the drive to Canyon Lake, I knew—I couldn't go back to playing house. Rich understood I didn't want to give up my job, so he rented a beach house in Huntington Beach. But it wasn't just my job—I couldn't give up Lorenzo either. He lived in Marin County, which made sneaking calls and meetings easier.

One night at Birraporetti's, my mom saw him and burst out laughing like a schoolgirl. She knew—there was no hiding it. When he walked away, I leaned in.

"What is wrong with you?"

She could barely speak. "He's soooo handsome. My God." I opened my mouth to explain, but she waved me off. "Denise, you're not married."

And she was right. Hell, back then you were either dating or married. That was it. So why did I feel so trapped? By my generation's rulebook, dating meant figuring it out. I wasn't a bad person. But I also knew I owed Rich the truth. I just hadn't found the right moment.

To make matters worse, Blondie started having skin issues from the ocean air. She'd pick at her skin, getting bald spots. Rich let his mom take her until it cleared, but she got attached. Suddenly, my dog wasn't mine anymore, and I couldn't even go to her for comfort.

Then one night, I told Rich I was crashing at a girlfriend's place. Instead, I was across from Lorenzo, lost in his dark brown eyes. After dinner, we went to his beach house. Champagne, lines, clothes on the floor—we barely made it upstairs. But the morning after hit like a brick. I woke in a strange bed next to a man I barely knew. Forget smuggling drugs—this was the riskiest thing I'd ever done. Rich wasn't just my boyfriend. He was family. If he found out, I'd lose everything. That thought paralyzed me.

Hungover and panicked, I scrambled out of bed. "Shit, I'm late. I told Rich I'd meet him in twenty minutes for Hapkido class."

Lorenzo just smirked. "Serious? Come back to bed."

I didn't. I raced out the door, chugging water. Pulled over to puke, then took a desperate bump to shake the hangover.

Rich took one look at me. "You look awful. What were you doing?"

"Partied with friends." I shrugged, a lie. He didn't push, but his silence was louder than words. The class was brutal. Kicks, flips, punches. I was dying. But I kept going, powered by guilt, pride, and anger. Not angry at Rich. At myself.

As I hit the bag, it all landed—how deep I'd gotten, how dishonest I'd become. I didn't want to lose Rich. But I didn't want to give up on Lorenzo either. I was spinning, clinging to both. And for what?

It unraveled fast. Rich got suspicious. He quoted what sounded like an Eagles lyric: "Denise got the Mercedes Benz, she got a lot of 'pretty, pretty boys' that she calls 'friends.'" His way of saying he knew something was up. Then came the final blow. I used Addison, a mutual friend, as an alibi. The next morning, Rich was waiting.

"Where were you really?"

"With Addison," I said, too quickly.

"No, you weren't," he snapped. "She called me. Told me what you were doing. She invited me over. I went."

I froze. Rage hit first. "How *dare* you," I shouted, hitting his chest with my fists.

Later, I cornered Addison. She just smirked.

"I'm tired of watching you get everything. Rich is mine now."

Everything? She had no idea what this life really cost. Addison had betrayed me—a dirty little rat, total double-crosser, whose word was worthless. Rich couldn't see clearly, but I knew he would never respect her for that.

"Fine," I said. "You can have him."

And that was it. I was done. Back at my mom's. Addison moved in with Rich. It didn't last. He did it to hurt me, and it worked. It was over.

And even though I was the one who messed things up between us, I was devastated. It felt like the air had been sucked right out of my world. First heartbreak? You're convinced your life is over. But trust me—time has a wicked sense of humor. One day you'll laugh about it. Sometimes you'll even laugh together. And nine times out of ten? They always want you back.

As for Lorenzo, once the dust settled, we talked more, he got comfortable dropping street slang, casually chatting about buying and selling coke. After years in the game, I knew exactly what was up. Lorenzo wasn't just charming and sophisticated with impeccable clothing—he was dealing too. It was 1990, and apparently, coke dealing was still the hottest profession in Orange County.

Like Bowie sang in "Changes," every time I thought I'd made it, it never seemed to live up to what I envisioned. The dream was always sweeter than the reality. So, I did what I had to do. You'd be proud—I broke up with him. Part of me resented him, too, for playing a role in what came between Rich and me. No hard feelings.

"I'm mad at myself, not you," I told Lorenzo, and it was true. I was mad at myself because apparently, I had a type. That type? Yes, you guessed it, drug dealers.

With a smile and a shake of my head, I hit pause on dating and dove into salon life instead.

* * * *

Back at my mom's, something felt different. I was too old to be there, restless in those familiar walls. I longed for my own place, but my assistant job didn't pay enough. Stacy and I had always dreamed of moving in together, but she had her own battles. We kept in touch by phone, sometimes going months without seeing each other, but whenever we reconnected, it was like no time had passed—pure, unshakable friendship.

Stacy, my sister. She knew all my messy history, and lately, I'd been there for her too—holding her hand through heartbreak. She'd gotten pregnant, and Daniel, her boyfriend, made it clear he wasn't ready for a child. With her modeling career slow and no financial backup, she felt trapped. She chose to have an abortion, and I stood by her—no judgment, just love.

She'd moved back to West Covina, trying to repair things with her mom and spending more time with her little sister, Lily. Despite everything, I was glad to see her finding some balance.

That new year, Stacy and I promised it would be our best yet. We kicked it off at Café Pasquini with my mom—old-school style, sharing food, jokes, and homemade Italian lemon sodas. Later, Jeff invited us for a Jacuzzi night. We returned to Mom's house, laughing like teenagers, listening to the Cure, Diet Cokes in hand.

"This place is like a time capsule," Stacy said, her eyes scanning the familiar clutter.

A dreamy Cure song, "Just Like Heaven," played in the background.

"The perfect time for a fashion show," she said, springing up to raid my closet and pick out the silliest outfits. When she spotted my eighth-grade Laura Ashley floral graduation dress, she spazzed out with a joyful squeal.

"Put this on immediately! All you need is baby's breath in your hair and that side bun you wore."

We turned the volume up, letting the Cure's "Lovesong" fill the room. We walked down the hallway like we were on the runway, spinning and laughing without a care. We were home again.

"Classic us," Stacy said with a grin. "Definitely."

The next morning was a different story. I was running late for work, still half-sleep, when groggy Stacy asked me to help find her keys. I needed to leave, but she wanted help. Tensions flared.

"I have to go to work," I said. I couldn't let Marina down or risk losing my job at the salon.

Stacy scoffed, "You're living at home. Your mom'll bail you out, like always."

The words stung. "I need this job."

She dismissed me, and the argument escalated.

"You're being bitchy, Denise."

Then I turned around, grabbed my things, and slammed out the door—finally putting myself first.

We didn't speak for a week. Then, one night, as Jeff and I were heading out, the phone rang. Jeff grabbed the downstairs line; I took the upstairs one.

"Hey, is Denise there?" Stacy's voice sounded light, friendly.

Before Jeff could answer, I cut in, "Jeff, come on, hang up. We have to go."

I heard the surprise in her voice, like she hadn't expected that. "Oh… okay."

I hung up.

A few days later, Joyce called. She urged me to sit down before sharing the news.

My heart pounded. "Why? What's wrong?

She took a shaky breath. "Stacy…had a really bad car accident."

"Oh, God," I whispered, the weight of those words suffocating me. My throat tightened. "Is she okay?"

"She's in the ICU in Palm Springs, sweetheart. They've put her in a medically induced coma. You need to come…the doctors don't know if she'll make it."

Time stopped.

Her words blurred, as though I was hearing them from the end of a long tunnel. Stacy? My brain couldn't process it. Joyce's voice continued, but I could barely register it.

"She was drinking while driving on the freeway. She hit the side of another car, tried to outrun it, then swerved off the road. She wasn't wearing a seatbelt…and was thrown from the car."

I felt a wave of nausea wash over me. "Thrown? How? Oh, God. What? Where is she? What happened?"

"She landed face-first in the desert. A helicopter flew her to Palm Springs Regional…but sweetheart, I need you to prepare yourself. You may want to say goodbye."

I was in a state of shock. My mind couldn't process what Joyce was telling me. I kept trying to convince myself that Stacy would be okay. She was young, vibrant, and strong. She had to be.

Regret hit me like a tidal wave. I dissed her and hung up the phone. That dumb argument that felt so important at the time now seemed so trivial. I was wrong to hold that grudge. I knew it.

And I wondered, if God knew our actions before we took them, if He was in control of *everything*, then maybe He had a sick sense of humor. Why was this the moment I chose to let a petty fight come between us? Was this part of some grand plan I couldn't see, meant to fuck me up for life? Or was I just a lab rat, and someone up above was testing to see if I could survive?

I ran downstairs, panic clawing at my chest. My mom was sitting at the kitchen table, and when she saw me, her expression shifted immediately.

"Mom, it's Stacy!" I gasped. "She's in the ICU at Palm Springs Regional Hospital…there's been an accident. She might not make it."

Her face went pale. She stood up quickly, her voice shaky. "What happened? Tell me everything."

"I—I don't know. She's in a coma. It's bad, Mom. We need to go."

Without hesitation, she grabbed her coat. "Let's go."

Two hours later I was at the hospital. Halfway down the ICU corridor, my legs gave out. I collapsed onto the cold linoleum, hysterical laughter bubbling up from somewhere I couldn't control.

"Denise!" my mom cried with confusion and embarrassment. "Stop, please!"

But I couldn't. I was broken. I couldn't make sense of what was happening.

Then Stacy's mom, Joyce, and her boyfriend, Daniel, appeared in the hallway. Seeing me on the floor, they immediately knelt beside me.

Without a word, they pulled me into their arms, offering silent comfort as my laughter spiraled into uncontrollable hysteria.

"It's okay, sweetheart," Joyce whispered softly.

"Everything's going to be okay," Daniel reassured me.

They helped me to my feet, and Joyce's voice was calm but insistent. "I want to warn you. Stacy looks different because she is swollen, but hearing your voice will help. You have to be strong for her."

I nodded, my heart pounding as Daniel escorted me into Stacy's room. The sight of her, lying there in a coma, stole the air from my lungs. To me, she still looked like Stacy. Her face was swollen, yet there wasn't a single visible mark or scratch. Leave it to her to somehow pull off an angelic look. Daniel leaned down and brushed his lips against her cheek, his voice soft, full of hope.

"Honey, Denise is here," he said gently. Then, glancing at me with sympathy, "I'll give you two a moment. I'll be right outside."

I nodded, unable to speak. My feet felt glued to the floor. I stared at her, not knowing what to say. So much wanted to pour out, but the words wouldn't come. Finally, after what felt like forever, I stepped closer, took her hand, and spoke, voice trembling but determined.

"Stacy, it's me, Denise. I love you so much. I'm sorry. I was so stupid.... I shouldn't have let that little argument get in the way."

Silence. I tried to lighten it, make her laugh. "You're right, I'm a total bitch!"

Nothing. The silence felt deafening. Leaning closer, voice urgent. "Stacy, come on. Fight like you've never fought before. You can't quit on me now. You can make it."

I searched her face for any flicker of recognition, even the smallest movement, but there was nothing. I tried again, hoping to be the miracle that woke her. "You have to fight, Stace.... We don't give up, remember? Never give up."

Still, only silence.

The faint beeps from the monitors filled the room. I waited for a smile, but it never came. Why couldn't I save her? Why couldn't I do anything to fix this? There was a boombox in the room. The doctor had recommended Stacy's mom play music to help her connect with us. While I was there, we listened to Madonna's *Immaculate Collection*. As "Lucky Star" played, I watched Stacy's face, desperate for a sign, hoping the music might bring us back to the Déjà Vu dance floor, where she'd clap to the beat and sing about shining bright, certain everything would be all right. But she didn't move.

I switched to other songs—"Only You" by Yaz and "Total Eclipse of the Heart" by Bonnie Tyler—songs we used to dedicate to each other on the radio when she moved to Ventura. Still, no stir.

"Wake up," I cried. "Please."

Joyce entered. It was time to go. We walked down the hall, and then, tears in her eyes but voice hard as steel, she said, "Denise, the doctors don't believe Stacy will ever live a normal life again. Even if she wakes up from the coma, the brain damage is too severe."

My body went cold. I watched her pause, knowing what was next.

"I'm going to have to decide soon whether to keep her on the ventilator or take her off life support."

I moaned, grabbing her arms. "Please don't. She needs time to get stronger. She'll make a full recovery. She has to. You'll see."

Joyce stayed calm, slowly shaking her head, silently refusing to give me the hope I so desperately wanted.

* * * *

Imagining life without Stacy was unthinkable. We were only thirteen, in eighth grade, when we met, but our connection was instant—fierce and unshakable. It felt like she'd always been there. We were soul sisters. Stacy was a Trigo through and through.

I still see her smile on that first day of school, standing at the front of the class while they introduced her. I remember all the miles we rode our bikes before we had cars. If we added it up, we probably pedaled halfway across the country.

And now, everything had changed. She was in a hospital bed, and there wasn't a damn thing I could do to turn back the clock.

If only I could have frozen us in middle school, preserved that joy and innocence forever. If only everyone could have stayed young, healthy, happy, untarnished by what was coming. We'd all started out so good, so sweet, so full of life.

* * * *

Stacy was on life support for about a week before Joyce made the heart-wrenching decision to take her off. I hadn't eaten in days and could barely walk or talk. The only comfort I found was in sleep, where I could escape the pain. Each time I woke, I called the ICU to check on Stacy, but there was no improvement. The emptiness just crept back in.

Then, on January 25, 1991, the phone rang. It was Joyce. Stacy had passed.

The room spun. The only real friend who ever felt like home—my oldest friend, my safety—was gone. Now, I was alone. People used to say we were one. Losing Stacy felt like losing half of myself. She was only twenty-three. Her death was so sudden, so final, that it didn't even feel real—yet it was.

I believed in the afterlife. I begged, pleaded for one more moment with Stacy. I wanted her to haunt me, visit me in the night, so I could see her face again, hear her tell me that everything would be okay.

I wanted to hold her hand.

I wanted my best friend back—and to undo what I had said, or hadn't said, to change everything.

If the accident hadn't happened, our dumb argument would've been just a blip. Soul sisters like us—we always found our way back. But in that moment, all I felt was guilt.

I attended her funeral, listening as her mom, sister, Daniel, and her modeling agent gave heartfelt tributes to the closed casket. I sat frozen, unable to speak. I stared at a beautiful photo of her in white, surrounded by the scent of peach roses. It felt like Stacy and I were the closest, yet no one asked me to speak. To be fair, I didn't reach out to ask either. I was numb—I felt invisible—and maybe they sensed that. Part of me wished

I'd found the strength to speak, but deep down, I knew I would've just broken down, and that would've only made everything worse.

Months passed. I barely spoke. Barely got out of bed. My mom stayed by my side, helping me through it. I couldn't understand how the world could keep turning without Stacy in it. How could life go on? It felt wrong. I was angry with God. His love felt distant. Why would He suddenly take her from me, especially when we were fighting? It seemed cruel.

I've learned a valuable lesson. Unforgiveness carries a heavy price. These days, I strive to be the first to apologize, to make things right, before life makes the decision for you. Silence costs more than pride ever will.

Eventually, breath by breath, I found a little peace. Instead of drowning in guilt, I accepted that our final chapter didn't define Stacy and me. Our friendship was bigger and stronger than that. What mattered was the love we had for each other. That love will always exist. And it gave me the strength to keep going.

I also learned that life can shift in an instant. First, with Rich. Then Blondie. And now Stacy. Everything I knew had changed. I felt so alone. "Changes" played in my head, Bowie's haunting voice cutting through the silence. Strange, how quickly everything you know can slip away.

The world felt unfamiliar without Stacy. It just kept moving forward, and I had no choice but to move with it, even if I had to do it alone.

And I'd be lying if I said the pain ever truly goes away. The guilt of not talking to Stacy before the accident—it's a cross I'll always bear. Some Madonna songs still bring me to tears, and I still make the same hand gestures to Prince's "I Would Die 4 U," like we're still together on the dance floor—young, thriving, and alive.

What hits hardest now is seeing best friends still growing old together. It reminds me I got ripped off. She left me way too early. If I still have all my marbles when I'm older, there'll be an empty rocking chair next to mine, in her honor. With a Chanel throw draped over it, naturally.

Mom and Dad just married, September 1961.

Mom, Dad, Nonna, and Grandpa.

Gale and Dad.

Jeff in his room, '70s.

Jeff, Greg, me, Peter, and Dad on a weekend visit, '70s.

My little brother, Peter, and I

Greg in our driveway, Fountain Valley, '80s.

Dad at my eighth grade graduation in Laura Ashley.

Denise and Nonna.

Denise and Stacy, Newport Beach.

Newport Beach.

Mom, giving the lawn some love.

Jeff, '80s.

Jeff and Shelly.

Denise and Rich.

Jeff and I in our driveway (the RV is behind us), '80s.

Dad as a battlefield medic in Central America.

The Porsche was so clean, before I crashed it.

Denise, 1987.

Greg on a Seattle run with Paul Bunyan.

Denise, cousin Madeline, and my Benzo.

Jeff on drums, me, and my cousin Madeline from Staten Island.

Denise and Blondie, Canyon Lake.

My kitchen in Fountain Valley with Brandy.

Stacy, always loved, always remembered.

Brandy and Denise.

Lorenzo and Marina.

Lorenzo visiting me from Marin County.

Peter and Dad in Makaha.

Jacob and I at Disneyland.

Please, no more vampires!

O.C.C.C. Module 11 Female Unit. Outside looking in.

Oahu, Honolulu, Federal Courthouse.

SENTENCING TABLE
(in months of imprisonment)

	Offense Level	Criminal History Category (Criminal History Points) I (0 or 1)	II (2 or 3)	III (4, 5, 6)	IV (7, 8, 9)	V (10, 11, 12)	VI (13 or more)
	1	0-6	0-6	0-6	0-6	0-6	0-6
	2	0-6	0-6	0-6	0-6	0-6	1-7
	3	0-6	0-6	0-6	0-6	2-8	3-9
	4	0-6	0-6	0-6	2-8	4-10	6-12
Zone A	5	0-6	0-6	1-7	4-10	6-12	9-15
	6	0-6	1-7	2-8	6-12	9-15	12-18
	7	0-6	2-8	4-10	8-14	12-18	15-21
	8	0-6	4-10	6-12	10-16	15-21	18-24
	9	4-10	6-12	8-14	12-18	18-24	21-27
Zone B	10	6-12	8-14	10-16	15-21	21-27	24-30
	11	8-14	10-16	12-18	18-24	24-30	27-33
Zone C	12	10-16	12-18	15-21	21-27	27-33	30-37
	13	12-18	15-21	18-24	24-30	30-37	33-41
	14	15-21	18-24	21-27	27-33	33-41	37-46
	15	18-24	21-27	24-30	30-37	37-46	41-51
	16	21-27	24-30	27-33	33-41	41-51	46-57
	17	24-30	27-33	30-37	37-46	46-57	51-63
	18	27-33	30-37	33-41	41-51	51-63	57-71
	19	30-37	33-41	37-46	46-57	57-71	63-78
	20	33-41	37-46	41-51	51-63	63-78	70-87
	21	37-46	41-51	46-57	57-71	70-87	77-96
	22	41-51	46-57	51-63	63-78	77-96	84-105
	23	46-57	51-63	57-71	70-87	84-105	92-115
	24	51-63	57-71	63-78	77-96	92-115	100-125
	25	57-71	63-78	70-87	84-105	100-125	110-137
	26	63-78	70-87	78-97	92-115	110-137	120-150
Zone D	27	70-87	78-97	87-108	100-125	120-150	130-162
	28	78-97	87-108	97-121	110-137	130-162	140-175
	29	87-108	97-121	108-135	121-151	140-175	151-188
	30	97-121	108-135	121-151	135-168	151-188	168-210
	31	108-135	121-151	135-168	151-188	168-210	188-235
	32	121-151	135-168	151-188	168-210	188-235	210-262
	33	135-168	151-188	168-210	188-235	210-262	235-293
	34	151-188	168-210	188-235	210-262	235-293	262-327
	35	168-210	188-235	210-262	235-293	262-327	292-365
	36	188-235	210-262	235-293	262-327	292-365	324-405
	37	210-262	235-293	262-327	292-365	324-405	360-life
	38	235-293	262-327	292-365	324-405	360-life	360-life
	39	262-327	292-365	324-405	360-life	360-life	360-life
	40	292-365	324-405	360-life	360-life	360-life	360-life
	41	324-405	360-life	360-life	360-life	360-life	360-life
	42	360-life	360-life	360-life	360-life	360-life	360-life
	43	life	life	life	life	life	life

Sentencing Guidelines—Level 34, Criminal History Category 3, facing 188–235 months (15–19 years).

Makaha Beach Cabanas.

Out on bail on house arrest.

Bojo and Dad.

Credit: Courtesy of Online Wikiwand.
Santa Rita County Jail—the worst place on earth.

Credit: Courtesy of KTVU Chopper.
Oakland County Jail, pink building, Mexicali Rose.

FPC Dublin is in the top right corner with
five white trailers and the track.

Mug shots from all the county jails.

Denise and Sienna.

A moment in the visiting yard, FPC.

My buddy Sienna and I, FPC.

Denise and Nicole, FPC.

San Fransico forty-eight-hour furlough—Jeff, Denise, Greg.

San Fransico forty-eight-hour furlough—
always checking the time.

OC five-day furlough—Darren, Jeff, and I.

Heidi Fleiss and I celebrating Thanksgiving
at Aunt Flo's house in LA.

Mine and Dave's wedding, North Shore, Hawaii, 2005.

My children, my loves—Paloma and Radley.

Mom, Denise, and Aunt Flo on Christmas Eve.

Gina, Mom, Flo, and Mary—my queens.

David and Denise.

Radley and Paloma.

Chapter Thirteen

Fashion, Clubbing, and...Vampires?

JULY 1991–DECEMBER 1994

Losing Stacy didn't just break my heart—it shattered something in me. I was only twenty-three. PTSD doesn't always scream; sometimes it just walks beside you. I moved through life smiling on the outside, but inside, I was numb and drinking to dull the pain, haunted by guilt for living when she didn't.

I resented the salon. If I hadn't been working, I would've stayed home with Stacy. We could've fixed that stupid fight. Instead, I showed up every day, pretending I was okay. It wasn't fair to Marina, and I finally told her.

She didn't ask questions—just nodded, eyes soft. "I get it," she said. "Take the time you need."

"I'll stay until you find someone new," I offered.

She smiled. "I'm really going to miss you."

"Me too." We hugged. Nothing more needed to be said. Marina was one of the good ones.

By then, naps had become my main activity. One afternoon, I shuffled downstairs and grabbed a Pepsi. My mom, cooking for hours, turned off the stove.

"Oh good, you're up. Lunch is ready." Translation: I narrowly dodged her Swiss Alps–mountaintop yell of "Deniiiiiiiiiiiiiiiiiise!"

She'd made her famous *cioppino*: rich seafood broth, chunks of shrimp, Alaskan king crab, and flaky white Chilean sea bass. But I wasn't hungry. I'd lost my appetite after Stacy. Thank God baggy jeans were in style. My waist had vanished, jeans hung loosely on my hipbones, and my mom noticed. She was making all of my favorites lately—her way of trying to nurture me back to life. That's the mama mindset: nurture and nourish. Still, my first spoonful made me swoon.

"Mom," I said, between bites. "Remember how we used to wake up before dawn and drive to Newport Beach for fresh catch?"

She laughed. "You used to freak out over the fish heads."

"I hated their eyeballs. They stared at me—It was so creepy."

We laughed, and then she handed me a hot glazed donut from her friend's bakery near the mall—just like old times. But then, her tone shifted.

"Denise," she said gently, "I still think about my dad every day. I still cry. But it gets easier, sweetheart. You'll always miss Stacy, but you'll learn to live without her. She'll live inside your heart forever."

Tears welled up.

"I believe you can do anything," she continued. "Dream it, and it'll happen. Not like the fairytales I read to you when you were little—this is real life. But your dreams are real too."

Nice words. Beautiful, even. But I was barely holding it together—just getting by, one day at a time. Then things got worse. Rich turned into a full-on dick. He told me I owed him twelve thousand dollars for a paint job on my Benz, a job I didn't even want or need, but he was now demanding the money back.

"You owe me twelve thousand dollars. Pay up."

I panicked. I borrowed the money from Greg, thinking Rich would come to his senses. But Rich found out Greg was using his supplier and cutting him out, selling directly to Corn Fed.

When I asked Rich for the money back, Rich snapped, "Yeah, it was my idea to spend that much on a paint job. I was gonna pay you, but Greg screwed me. Now? No way. You'll just give it to him."

Lesson learned: there are no exceptions in the drug world. Never introduce two people—family or not—who might realize they don't need you. If I'd known the truth, I would've said I borrowed the money from someone else. But I didn't. I had unleashed the Tasmanian devil—my own brother. Turns out, blood may be thicker than water, but cash is thicker than blood.

In the end, I lost out. Heart-wrenching, but eventually, I said, "Fuck it." I sold the black Mercedes convertible from my glory days, paid Greg back, and bought a bouncy white Jeep. I had nothing left—just some expensive jewelry tucked away in a box. The drug money? All gone. Letting go of that Benz hurt. My identity had been wrapped up in that car. I lost everything, but for the first time in a long time, my karma was clean. And that felt good.

Once Stevens and Delaney heard about the breakup, they started showing up at my mom's house. We'd step outside, stare up at the stars, and they'd light a smoke—offering me one—before casually bringing up Rich's new girlfriend and their fancy shopping sprees, trying to get under my skin.

"Nice try, but I'm not the scorned lover type," I'd tell them.

They'd stub out their cigarettes, nodding like they already knew. "Didn't think you'd flip on him," they'd say. "But we had to try. You'd be surprised how many drug dealers go down because of their exes."

I just shrugged. Then I called Rich to give him a heads-up. Our relationship might've been over, but we still had each other's backs. Always would.

It wasn't just the cops stopping by. A couple of heavy suppliers showed up too, testing whether Rich's absence left a romantic opening with me. I shut their little "proposals" down fast. I thought loyalty mattered, but everyone was out for themselves.

I wanted my mom to be proud, but more than that, I was finally ready to make myself proud. Despite everything I'd been through, I decided to chase my dreams. Maybe Stacy was guiding me from somewhere above the blue sky and marshmallow clouds, but I believed in myself. I wasn't at a New York fashion school, but I was determined to break into the industry—for both of us. Life's too short not to go after what you want.

I'm a woman who built an empire on connections, so I did what I do best: I reached out. A friend of a friend had ties in fashion, and I was determined to get my foot in the door. I didn't have a résumé full of experience, but I had passion, drive, and just enough charm to win them over.

Soon, I landed a job at a private-label fashion company designing accessories for major surf brands like Quiksilver, Roxy, O'Neill, and OP. The office sat in Rancho Cucamonga, tucked beneath the San Gabriel Mountains. The two-hour commute? No big deal. I took a cue from the Fresh Prince: I cruised along, leaning back and letting the California sun do its thing.

It's amazing what you can accomplish with a positive attitude. I started as the office secretary, but my work ethic, assertiveness, and confidence quickly made me a valued team member. My coworkers began to trust my eye for trends and I was quickly promoted to assistant designer. Glamorous disco wear and '80s flash were fading; '90s hip-hop streetwear and minimalist, industrial-edge fashion were on the rise. I was proud to be part of the shift, designing accessories like funky bucket hats, beanies, trucker caps with bold colors and contrast stitching, sleek black leather wallets with sterling silver chains, and oversized sunglasses.

The company also sold its own collection, so I started repping the brand at fashion trade shows. And as you already know, sales were my jam. That's how I rolled.

* * * *

Toward the end of 1991, thanks to my new job and better choices, I finally felt like I was getting my life back on track. One afternoon, I called my mom and said, "I think things are going in the right direction." Even though I'd lost Stacy, I could still hear her voice in my head singing "Time After Time" by Cyndi Lauper, reminding me that when I felt lost, I wasn't alone. She would always be near me.

Then something incredible happened. My boss pulled me aside and said, "We're backing you to launch your own clothing line."

I could barely believe it. "Are you sure?" I asked.

He smiled. "We believe in you."

I became my own boss, working from home. No more brutal commutes. With more time on my hands, I reconnected with Brandy from Jeff's old band. She was spontaneous, full of life. When her wealthy husband insisted she bring a friend on one of his business trips, she called me.

"You up for Eastern Europe?" she asked.

Why not? Her husband covered most of the expenses, and my dad gave me seven hundred dollars in spending money. We watched *Thelma and Louise* in a Warsaw theater with English subtitles and rolled the dice at craps tables in smoky casinos—playing lucky charm for the men, and winning money on my own. And yes, we prank-called Rich, just for the laugh.

After Europe, things got wild. I met Jacob—he went to our rival school, Edison. Barf, right? But I didn't care. He was a fashion designer—short, jet-black hair, electric blue eyes, total bad boy with a mischievous sense of humor.

It all happened fast. One night in his room, we racked up lines, drank beers, and blasted Nirvana's "Smells Like Teen Spirit" on the turntable. Later, "Set Adrift on Memory Bliss" by P.M. Dawn came on, dreamy and slow, softening the mood. Our friend was there, but when Jacob and I locked eyes, the rest of the room just fell away. We leaned in and started making out—awkward for our friend, but it felt real.

The best part? Jacob wasn't a dealer—score! He did coke, sure, but who didn't back then? Wild, charming, the perfect mix. He introduced me to the action-sport fashion scene, and soon, we rubbed elbows with the same crowd. He had his own company, which was thriving.

A few months later, I teamed up with a partner who owned a sewing house in Costa Mesa. I dove headfirst into making clothes: fabric, patterns, markers, grading, cutting, sewing—you name it. Before I knew it, I was designing and producing my own women's line—beachwear, flowy floral pants and matching blouses, crop tops, velvet shorts, denim, and knit dresses geared toward teens. Orders came in from around the world.

My business partner and I scored an office with a killer view of Newport Bay. I wasn't about the flashy toys anymore; I was building something real. Fashion was life—trade shows in baggy jeans, hair piled high, a Jean Paul Gaultier blazer, and nights out with Jacob schmoozing. Finally, my partying skills came in handy. I'd party hard but show up early, coffee in hand, ready to hustle. But success brought pressure. Bigger orders meant more cash upfront, and then my backers bailed. I was out.

Did I quit? No way.

I pivoted, grabbed temp gigs as a sales rep for 26Red, an awesome men's clothing brand. Not my dream, but it kept me close to the scene. Then I started assisting the Southern California sales rep for Black Flys Optics, the ultimate '90s brand.

Black Flys wasn't just about eyewear—it was a lifestyle, a Southern Cali cult obsession. I was in the mix, front row to the madness. The fangirls? Total smoke shows—strippers owning the "dancer" label with zero shame. They flew to Vegas, shook it for cash, strutted into afterparties like headliners. It was a fast lifestyle. All about the rush, the high, the adrenaline of being at the center of it all. Promiscuity was the norm. People swapped partners like accessories. No strings, no drama—just heat, freedom, and fun. The guys? Eye candy. Streetwear kings with wild hair—leopard patches, frosted tips, fire-engine red. Tatted, pierced, rich, fearless. They caught colossal waves on lunch breaks, then secured fashion accounts like nothing happened. They stacked cash, slipped bills into lace thongs, cruised around in tricked-out lowriders and monster trucks, and went full-throttle to Catalina in their speedboats.

The '90s in Costa Mesa, Newport, and Huntington? The party never ended; it just changed locations. Clubs to afterparties, oceanfront pads, foam-filled hot tubs, stripper poles in living rooms, drugs, and people hooking up more than anyone could keep track of. No shame. No apologies.

* * * *

Meanwhile, my relationship with Jacob was unraveling. For three years, we were inseparable—weekend camping trips, visiting my dad in Hawaii with Dee and Peter, cruising the harbors on his dad's boat, and spending every night at his mom's house. In the mornings, she'd pour me hot coffee.

"Here, my darling mousey."

"Thanks, Mama Mouse," I'd reply, smiling.

She became like a second mom to me. Did I mention she was Italian? Petite, with that classic Susan Lucci look. You could feel the love in everything she did.

After three love-soaked years of laughter, loyalty, and understanding, things started to shift. Jacob's fashion business hit a rough patch, and his confidence took a dive. Instead of leaning into the support around him, he sank deeper into partying.

At first, I thought it was just a phase. But he stopped hanging with his high school buddies from the fashion scene and me and started spending more and more time with this intense new crowd from downtown Huntington Beach—goths. His new best friend? A guy who drove around in a hearse.

Yeah. A hearse.

I thought it was weird, but Jacob was all in. Then Hearse Guy went and got dental implants to look more like a vampire. Jacob, naturally, announced he was going to do the same.

"Wait, really?" I asked, shaking my head. "Jacob, are you fucking with me?"

Dressing up as a vampire for Halloween? Sure. But living it? That was a whole different level. The guys in this new crew were few but intense—always in black, mostly leather. And the girls? Strippers or cocktail servers at strip clubs. They all had the same look: long, straight platinum blond hair, smoking-hot bodies, fake boobs, and decked out in baby blue or powder pink vinyl. Basically, slutty Barbie…but also very sweet.

From what Jacob told me, they'd pop ecstasy and cruise around in the hearse-slash-tricked-out-limo, complete with a bar and—who knows—maybe even a mini stripper pole. I wouldn't know, because I wasn't invited. Apparently, everyone rolled hard and did whatever felt good. It was hedonism on wheels, and Jacob could hardly keep a straight face as he recounted the previous night to me. He was in heaven.

Sometimes he didn't come home at night. People said they saw him leaving strip bars in the afternoon, walking out of clubs with random girls. When I confronted him, he denied it.

"She's just a friend. I was just giving her a ride," he'd say.

"Yeah, I bet you were" is what I should have said. But back then? I wanted to believe him. Funny how you lie to yourself just to hold on to the life you wish you still had. People kept telling me, "Denise, you need to move on." Eventually, I forced myself to. I stopped calling and kept busy.

I was heartbroken. But "Today" by the Smashing Pumpkins became my lifeline, a reminder to stay present and live in the moment. So I forced myself to go out, even when it felt like the last thing I wanted to do.

Most of the time, I hung out with my new friend Angela, someone I met in the fashion industry. She was a stunning brunette with piercing blue eyes and a body that could rival Pamela Anderson—curves, confidence, and all. But it wasn't just her looks. Angela was wild, spontaneous, unpredictable in the best way. Her boyfriend was great, and his boat and membership in the Newport Beach Yacht Club added a glamorous layer to our adventures.

Sometimes, I'd hang out in LA with my high school friend Marcy, now living on Harper Street. We'd kick off the night sipping free drinks from her charming, very close friend Mark Ruffalo, who was bartending at the Olive. Marcy's roommate was dating David Fincher—the hottest music director in town. Through them, I met Don Henley and Keanu Reeves. The whole constellation. Rob Lowe, my teenage crush, spotted me at a house party in the Hollywood Hills. With that signature smirk, he leaned in, raised an eyebrow, and playfully said, "Double fisted, huh?" I was living the dream.

Weekends in LA with Marcy were never dull. We bounced from Jones to the Roxbury, late nights at Chateau Marmont, everyone in slip dresses and blazers, cigarettes constantly burning. Jacob called almost every day, jealous whenever I started finding my footing. I told myself I didn't care. But honestly, my dumb ass still hoped we would work. I mean, Jesus Christ, it wasn't like he was JFK Jr. In quiet moments, I wondered why he didn't think I was good enough. What did all those other girls have that I didn't? What made me so disposable? It never occurred to me that I had nothing to do with it—that it was Jacob, struggling to figure things out.

But I wouldn't stay home and sulk. I wasn't my mom. With my girlfriends beside me, I'd show up at exclusive Newport Beach clubs in a little black dress, hit the dance floor, and let the music take over.

Then Jacob would reel me back in. We'd flirt, make out, and I'd end up back at his place—caught in his web. He'd express love, I'd fall for it, and then he'd break my heart again and again. I'd move on, be happy, be seen with someone new—and watch him get crushed. Toxic? Sure. But it got better. I thought we'd moved past it all. I was back in the kitchen with his mom, planning a day out on the boat with his dad—laughing about the mess we'd made of each other.

Then one day, I called him at work and heard a girl's voice in the background.

"Who's that?" I asked. He hung up on me.

That was it.

I drove to his studio, ready to confront him, but he wouldn't open the door. Through the window, I saw him standing with a blond in a baseball cap. She tilted her face just enough to stay hidden. I didn't even want a scene—I needed to know if I knew her.

"Who's in there?" I yelled. They laughed.

Oh, you think this is funny?

I snapped, went full gangster. The only thing missing was Metallica's "Enter Sandman" blasting in the background, because I meant *mothafuckin' business.* Fueled by adrenaline, I climbed a tree and leapt onto the roof of his building like a bat hurtling through the night sky. I could've killed myself, but I didn't care—I was mental and on a mission. A fool in love, I marched across the roof in broad daylight, over leaves and twigs, until I reached the big glass window propped open to get fresh air. When

Jacob saw me, his eyes went wide—I thought they were going to pop out of his head. He frantically tried to latch the window shut.

Ha! You think this little latch will keep me out? I thought, wild-eyed, and kicked the window in, glass shattering everywhere.

"Where did she go?" I screamed, scanning the room. She was hiding in the bathroom. "Come out, coward!" I yelled, pounding on the door.

Jacob grabbed me, trying to drag me downstairs, but then my eyes landed on a fancy pair of black Chanel sunglasses. I snatched them and mangled them. Total fashion crime. But fuck her.

You'd think I'd have some dignity left, some self-respect, and just gone home. But noooo—I hid around the corner in his brother's cut-and-sew shop, spying.

Then the cops showed up.

I slipped upstairs to my patternmaker's office. He started pitching a swimwear brand idea that we could collaborate on, and I nodded along.

"Yeah, those A-line dresses are cute. We'll talk swimwear soon," I said. But my mind was on what was happening outside.

"Hey, can I use your phone?" I cut him off before he could say more.

Jacob answered.

"You know you never call the cops, right? I made that clear a long time ago. You know my family won't like that," I warned him. "I'll leave you alone. Just make them go away."

When the coast was clear, I saw Jacob and the blond tramp running out. Did he think I'd give in so easily? Come on, you know me better than that.

So, if all that wasn't enough, I chased him in my Jeep until it started smoking and I broke down right in the middle of the fashion district, and my luck, the owner of Bad Boy Club, I'd been freelance designing for happened to rescue me. Talk about humiliation.

But now? Fuck it, it's a good story. A reminder: never give a man that kind of energy. You're worth so, so much more.

Weeks later, selling Black Flys Optics at the Vegas convention, an acquaintance whispered, "Jacob married some stripper last night—in a drive-thru."

The owner of Black Flys, whom I was casually seeing, saw the shock on my face and placed a hand on my shoulder. "They'll never make it, Denise. He lost a good one," he said, kissing my cheek. I knew he was right, but it still hurt.

That was the death knell.

Then I ran into the newlyweds a few booths over. It was that blond tramp, and they both laughed in my face.

Cold as ice.

On the flight home, I had no tears left. Like the Cars' song, "Bye Bye Love," he was just another broken lullaby. I ended up at my mom's house, searching for comfort. But there was none.

She just shrugged and said, "All men are bastards, Denise. Better to learn that young."

Wasn't that the truth?

Even though I associated my mom's bitterness with weakness, she respected herself. She became independent, loyal to her idea of right and wrong, and brave enough to walk away from a man who cheated and disrespected her. I look up to her for that.

Me? I thought I was being strong by going out and getting drunk. My ego had something to prove, and that was a recipe for disaster.

* * * *

I refused to let him—or anyone—see me break. I went out. Maybe a little too much. I just didn't want to be home alone. I hung out with family as much as I could. My brother Greg was determined to help me meet better people, so he insisted I hang out with his roommate's girlfriend. Through her, Angela and I met Maya in Costa Mesa, at the Shark Club, playing pool.

Maya was a force—thick, long, curly, black hair, a curvy figure, and a shit-ton of confidence. Her magnetic presence and hearty laugh could own any room. But even with all that, she was the first person I knew who used crystal meth regularly. She said it kept the weight off better than cocaine. Despite looking gorgeous, she constantly compared herself to the skinny strippers we were surrounded by.

Hell, even looking at Angela, I caught myself thinking, *I wish I had fake boobs too.*

We were caught up in the superficial, trying to match the glossy image of the '90s, even though we both knew we could hold our own and date any man we wanted. When Maya invited us to a pre-party at Jed's before the club Thunderbird, we went.

The door flew open, and Freddy greeted us like we were celebrities. "Well, hellooooo, ladies! Freddy here at your service," he said with a flourish. "Come on in!"

Inside, the first person I saw was a guy sitting on the couch with his legs crossed like a chick. Blue jeans, black t-shirt, Cubs cap. Freddy led Angela and me over. "This is Philip," he said.

"Hello," Philip said coolly, giving me a limp handshake before turning back to his buddy John, like we didn't even exist. Whatever. We headed to the counter where a cute guy with dark hair pulled back in a ponytail introduced himself as Jed and poured us drinks.

From the living room, Philip called out, "As soon as Lorenzo gets here, we'll head out."

A few minutes later, we walked outside, and there he was. *My* Lorenzo. Hello, rebound. We locked eyes for the first time in years, and that old spark came roaring back. The girls piled into Maya's red Jeep. I touched up my pink pout; I casually mentioned that we used to date.

At the club, I learned Lorenzo still lived up north but came down often for "business." I didn't ask what kind. I didn't care. He gave me the attention I craved, and I let myself fall back into something that felt safe. It wasn't love. It wasn't some epic romance, but we were friends, and the attraction between us was undeniable.

The fast-paced lifestyle of the fashion world was eating me alive, and I needed something—anything—to anchor me. So, I leaned in, sharpened my fangs, and sank them into something sweet.

Chapter Fourteen

This Is Not My Beautiful Life

DECEMBER 1994

Living with your mom at eighteen? Fine. At twenty-seven? Not so much. It felt like failure. I was desperate to turn things around. I still picked up side gigs with a Black Fly Optics rep, but the pay barely covered gas. Not long ago, I was cruising in a Mercedes convertible. Now, I was folding sweaters at Macy's in South Coast Plaza, grinding holiday shifts in DKNY, and wrapping Christmas presents for extra cash. When I wasn't on the clock or at Café Pasquini with my family, I tagged along with Angela, Maya, and her crew—killing time, chasing laughs, and reminding myself I still had a plan.

Sliding into their tight-knit group was easy. Even Philip, who'd been standoffish at first, warmed up. He'd call me over to sit next to him, cracking snide jokes aimed just right to make me laugh. Soon, we were exchanging glances and laughs across the room, already in sync. Rolling our eyes at Fred and newly single Angela, bracing for the chaos, silently roasting Maya's outfit, and noticing girls checking out Duane, like he didn't belong, a grown-up Dennis the Menace awkwardly out of place. It was effortless. We just got each other.

Yeah, they were drug dealers. I knew it. I just didn't care. Who was I to judge? I kept quiet and stayed in my lane.

One January afternoon, Maya and Philip invited me for lunch near the Newport pier. Halfway through, Philip's flip phone rang. He took the call, made another quick one, and went back to eating as if nothing had happened.

I knew the code—meth orders, the kind that needed refining into ice.

For a split second, my old ego flared. I wasn't just some party girl—I'd run crews. But I kept my mouth shut. That was another life.

After lunch, Maya peeled off, and Philip asked, "Hey, you mind giving me a ride to run an errand?"

"Sure," I said. He always picked up the tab and bought drinks at the clubs—it was the least I could do.

In my Jeep, Philip leaned back, elbow out the window, the winter breeze curling around us. He smirked, "So, Lorenzo says you know a lot about coke."

I gave him a side glance. "Yeah, I know a thing or two. Back in the day, I ran it all—house, cars, designer shit.... serious money." I let a little pride slip. "Guess now you're running the show for Lorenzo in the meth world, huh?" I knew exactly what he was doing.

A week later, I was at Philip's place. He and his friend James leaned in, looking for advice.

"We get our goods from one guy now, but we want better quality at a cheaper price," Philip said. "You know anyone who can get meth?"

I shrugged. "Oh, I don't know, maybe. I'm not involved, but I can check with an old connection to see if he knows anyone or would be interested in working directly with you guys."

Honestly, I didn't think much of it. It felt like seeing if Marina, my hairdresser, wanted a new client—only this time, it was a Mexican cartel dealer.

Though I hadn't spoken to him in years, I called Juan. When he picked up right away, I was relieved. Guys like him, you worry.

"Juan!" I laughed, hearing his voice again. "It's been way too long! How've you been?"

He chuckled, jumping right in like no time had passed. After some small talk, I cut to the chase.

"Look, I've got some friends I want you to meet." I spoke in code. "They wash a lot of laundry." Not exactly what we used to do—the harder material, you know.

His tone went businesslike. "For you, low. Five thousand dollars a pound of laundry."

I felt a flicker of pride—anything under $7,500 a pound was what Philip and James wanted.

Juan was quiet for a moment, then said, "I trust you. I'll work with them—but only through you."

I hesitated. "I'm not involved, don't want to get my hands dirty, you know?"

"No shit," Juan said, amused. "We're not rookies, lil homie. My boys handle everything. Don't worry."

"Okay," I said, trying to sound casual. I promised to keep Juan's identity under wraps from Philip and James—loyal to the bone. I hung up, uneasy but knowing I'd just hooked up two guys—and myself—into something none of us fully understood. Not directly involved, not really doing anything wrong. Just helping friends, flexing connections—middleman stuff. Simple enough.

Here's how it worked. Juan's team cooked in Mexico, then got it to Santa Ana. One of his guys would drop it off in an unlocked car near my mom's house. The kicker? Between my old coke-running days and dating Jacob the Vampire, Banana-in-the-Tailpipe Sergeant Stevens had moved in a block away—and we had no clue. The drop-offs were happening right in front of his house. Anyhow, I'd call Philip or James with the location, and they'd pick it up. Philip gave me a cell phone and covered the bill, which I appreciated. I charged no markup—five thousand dollars a pound, the same price Juan gave me. I was just helping friends.

Philip and James sometimes brought reinforcements like Freddy, renting hotel rooms with kitchenettes all over Southern California to cook the meth into ice. It didn't feel like a big deal to me. Maya and I would tag along, pick Philip up to run errands, or swing by In-N-Out for burgers, fries, shakes—just a normal day for me in Southern California.

Maya was an asset in her own way. She put her name on the lease for another apartment in Marina Del Rey for Philip and James, using her credit, helping everyone without a second thought.

Within months, the business exploded. The final product was incredibly pure, and the low price drove demand from Southern California to Arizona, Nevada, Colorado, Washington, Canada, Alaska, Hawaii, and eventually New Jersey and Maryland. I wasn't their only source. The network had grown too wide, too fast for that. Here I was again, a decade later, helping Lorenzo, a guy I liked, increase his profits without realizing it. Unknowingly, I'd set up what became one of the largest methamphetamine operations in the US.

Jed hired more runners. One was Dan—a.k.a. PB, for Pretty Boy—bleach-blond hair, fake tan, flashy Versace shirts. At thirty-four, he and Duane were older than the rest of us. Dan nicknamed me "Flawless," and it caught on.

"Hey, Flawless," Philip would say, shoving a stack of hundreds into my hand after a deal was done. I'd fan it out—usually a couple thousand dollars.

I'd protest, "No, I'm not part of this."

But he'd insist, "Might as well take something," then wink and say, "I know how much you love working at the mall."

I rolled my eyes. "Don't remind me."

He shrugged. "Just a tip. You earned it." Honestly, a tip didn't sound shady. Why not benefit? I kept the money in a Prada shoebox under my bed at my mom's. My family had no clue—because I wasn't technically doing anything illegal.

* * * *

I'd gotten good at avoiding direct contact with the drugs, but that didn't mean I wasn't tempted by the lifestyle. One day, Lorenzo called me—just a casual chat on our cells—and asked if I'd fly to Hawaii with Dan, a.k.a. Pretty Boy, to deliver a few pounds of ice.

"As long as I don't have to carry it," I said.

"No way," he assured me. "It's going in Dan's bag."

I didn't think twice. A Hawaiian vacation? I deserved that. I wasn't touching the product—what was the risk?

"Can I bring Maya?" I asked. Dan was boring, and kind of annoying.

Lorenzo laughed. "Fine. I'll pay for her if it makes you happy." Then, softening, "Wish I was going with you, babe."

So the three of us flew to Oahu. No airport drama. We went straight to Lorenzo's client, Eric, a former football star, paying $25,000 per pound. Lorenzo cleared $13,000 profit on each one. Five pounds meant $65,000—easy money.

Dan left early, but Maya and I stayed all week, soaking up the resort life. Beach, nightlife, great food—exactly what I'd needed.

The only downside? Dan wouldn't stop calling. He had to go to Alaska and wanted me to fly back to LA, grab more product, and return to Hawaii—without Maya. Said Lorenzo would pay well. I still said no. I'd come for a vacation, not to start mulling across the Pacific.

The group's credo was simple: get rich, have fun. But like all highs, the illusion was fading. They were using just as much crystal meth as they were moving, and that never ends well. Everyone was in on the after-hour parties. From Huntington Beach to Laguna, the cool kids, the club rats, the fashion-scene darlings—everyone was drawn in, all of us gravitating toward this wild, fun, party-fueled universe. Even Rich and Jacob floated through now and then. I'd bump into Mariana from the salon, the HB lifeguard with the six pack, even a girl I knew from the mall who showed up in kitten heels and left barefoot at sunrise—classic walk of shame.

The pace quickened. Nights stretched longer. The line between fun and fucked-up disappeared. Alcohol, coke, ecstasy, meth—it wasn't accessories anymore, it was the lifestyle. High on everything, spinning through blackouts, I paused just long enough to look around.

And I realized, this was not my beautiful life.

Dan was getting sloppy. One night before an airport run, we were at Jed's after the club closed. He was sweating, jittery, completely wired from the coke. I pulled him aside.

"Dude, pull it together."

Dan tossed back a shot of tequila like it was water. "You're right, Flawless. I gotta chill," he slurred.

I gave his blinding Versace shirt a once-over. "You're seriously wearing that to the airport?"

He looked down, clueless. "What? It's designer."

"Yeah—and it's screaming, *notice me*."

He shrugged. "I look good."

Idiot. The party had completely hijacked his brain.

The more I thought about it, the more moving to Los Angeles felt right. With the cash I'd saved in my Prada shoebox, I could afford it—if I landed a job. I reached out to Marcy, my high school friend in fashion, to line up interviews. Soon after, I agreed to ride with James to check out his and Philip's apartment in Marina Del Rey to get a feel for rent, space, and maybe figure out my next step.

On the way back, I said, "Hey, maybe we should all take a break or something."

James whipped around, eyes wide with paranoia. "A break? What do you mean? They're onto us. You know that, right? We have to be careful," he said as he merged onto the 405 South.

Philip snapped, annoyed. "Don't talk like that in front of her."

James pushed back. "What? You think I'm wrong? We need to watch our backs. I heard they're looking into—"

"Enough!" Philip cut him off, frustration boiling over. "We don't need to hear this all the time. Can we just get her home?"

Then James dropped a bomb: "Don't worry. I've got a contact…on the inside."

I gave him a blank look through his rearview mirror. "What do you mean, 'on the inside'?"

James grinned like it was a secret. "I made a contact in the FBI. A dirty agent—we call him Agent Blue. He's watching any case they try to build against us." Then he looked at me, serious now. "Don't worry, you don't have an indictment out. Agent Blue checked. And whatever you do, don't mention this to anyone, okay?"

I nodded. My stomach dropped. The car felt smaller suddenly. I didn't want my name tangled in their mess.

When we got out, I turned to Philip. "James's cop talk really spooked me."

"Just ignore that guy," Philip muttered.

After that night, Agent Blue's name came up often. The boys made a big deal—leaving the room, locking doors, whispering like he was the president or something. What had once been a group of fun people was now a bunch of anxious souls, obsessed with the idea of getting caught.

So, I decided I was done. No way I wanted to be mixed up with a dirty FBI agent or drug dealers. I didn't trust any of them.

Fuck this. I just wanted to spend time with my family, the people who actually loved me. And I tried. I really did.

* * * *

It was May—five months since I met James and Philip. I'd cut bait, made up excuses—*Juan's dry, I'm out*—but they kept calling, keeping tabs, making sure I stayed locked in. It felt like I'd joined a gang without realizing it. Tupac's "Me Against the World" came to mind—that feeling of being stuck in the game, forced to fight your way through it. And still, I'd see them out at night, trying to pull me back in.

Their friendship was unraveling. James and Philip leaned hard on Agent Blue, paying him to leak intel. He was supposed to keep them safe, but they didn't even trust each other anymore.

Philip started ranting about people who "needed to disappear." I laughed it off, but inside, the anxiety kept building. Every night felt like a spiritual war. One night, it was like a thousand-pound weight pressed on my chest. I tried to call out for my mom, but could only whisper, "Help." Terrified, I started sleeping with the light on and a Bible by my side.

Then came the dark mass. I squeezed my eyes shut, willing it to go away. That's when I felt a hand grip mine—tight, like it was holding me down. I was too scared to open my eyes. I just whispered, "I'm a child of God" over and over until the pressure finally lifted.

Sleep became impossible. I missed Stacy. The nightmares didn't stop. So I hit every after-hours party in Newport Beach, just to avoid being alone. I got a DUI and hid it from my family. I danced, drank, snorted coke with friends until I passed out. Sometimes I'd do a line of crystal meth—Maya was right: it burned going up, but the high lasted longer.

I was burning through men too—pro surfers, rock stars—it didn't matter. Looking back, I wasn't chasing love. I was chasing destruction. I should've opened the Bible instead of just sleeping next to it. Maybe then God would've filled me with love instead of fear.

I tried to spend more time with my family, but I still saw Maya. Philip always seemed to show up, and I didn't mind. His warmth, his charm, his wit—they were addictive. At the clubs, we'd sit together, bantering and laughing for hours.

James wasn't around much anymore, and thank God for that. No more paranoid rants about who was wired or when the bust was coming. Then one day, Philip found out I had a job interview with Guess Jeans in LA. He asked for a ride.

"Wanna know who I'm seeing?" he asked.

"Who?"

"Agent Blue." The sun glinted off his small oval Ray-Bans. I wasn't sure how to feel. Then, he dropped the bomb: "I told Blue you were driving me. Vouched for you. Said you're someone I can trust." I wasn't thrilled he'd used my name, but it was done.

I pulled up to the Mondrian hotel and let him out. A man nodded at me from the curb. *That must be Agent Blue*, I thought, as his eyes followed my car.

I nodded back.

* * * *

In 1995, Guess was everywhere—glamorous, iconic, untouchable. Billboards across LA featured the era's biggest models, none more striking than Anna Nicole Smith, whose image had become the brand.

And there I was, walking into Guess HQ to interview for *head designer*. I could hardly believe it. The space was sunlit, sleek, buzzing with creative energy. I sat in the airy lobby, nerves on edge. This could be it.

A poised, elegant woman descended the staircase to greet me. She radiated authority—someone who'd seen it all.

I presented my portfolio with quiet confidence. No design school, just raw work and instinct. I didn't get the job, but before I left, she said something I'll never forget.

"Don't quit. I'm surprised you've done all this without design school. If an assistant designer spot opens up, I'll call you."

"Wait, you think my work's good enough for that?" I asked, feeling like Kit De Luca in *Pretty Woman. You think I got potential?*

She smiled. "Yes. If I were you, I'd go to design school. But don't give up."

I didn't get the job, but I walked out of that building lighter. She didn't owe me anything, yet she gave me something real: belief. For someone like her to see potential in someone like me? That meant everything.

* * * *

Turns out there were more secrets in the family than I realized. My brother Greg had married a flight attendant from American Airlines. Now I know what you're thinking, but no, there were no drug runs. She wasn't shady. She was chic. Always up on MAC lipstick trends, knew who wore what before that stuff ever hit a magazine cover. They weren't exactly living together, but they had an arrangement. Greg could fly non-rev anywhere in the world like some kind of first-class aristocrat. Beer in Brussels, chocolate in Switzerland? Why not—the flights cost under a hundred bucks.

When he was in town, we made plans to meet at Mañanas in Fountain Valley, a Mexican joint that felt more like a club than a restaurant. Loud music, strong margaritas, and a crowd dressed like it was Saturday night, even on a Tuesday.

Greg pulled up to Mom's house with Peter in the passenger seat. Peter was turning eighteen, staying with Greg since things got tense at home with Dad's wife, Dee.

As Peter stepped out of the car, he stood straight and proud. Dark hair combed perfectly, sprayed to the side like a *GQ* cover, wearing Greg's black leather moto jacket like it was custom-made.

Greg beamed. "Like my makeover? Tonight, I'm getting Pete a twenty-one-and-over stamp."

"Yeah?" I asked. "How?"

"Easy. My friends are meeting us. Pete walks in next to the hottest cheerleader from Fountain Valley High. Trust me, the guy carding won't even look at him."

And he was right. The cheerleader strutted in with Peter on her arm. They breezed past the bouncer. Hand stamped, no questions.

We grabbed a booth, ordered frozen lime and strawberry Cuervo Gold pitchers, and settled in.

Greg, as usual, was center stage. He told a wild story about getting busted with eleven grams of coke.

"So, the cop pulls me over," he said, eyes wide, waving his hands like he was steering a car through the story. "'You had your hand out the window, acting like it was a flying bird, doing eighty on Adams Street! Then you whip a U-turn into a residential area—what are you high on, young man?'"

We laughed, but I saw the cracks. Greg was bummed. The court date was coming, rehab looming—but he spun it into comedy.

Then, out of nowhere, he pulled a bindle from his pocket, dumped a mound in front of everyone, and snorted a line *right there* at the table.

When he couldn't find a napkin, he grabbed a flour tortilla and blew his nose into it.

I groaned. "Greg, stop."

Peter made a face. "Eww. Just ask the waitress for a napkin, bro."

Greg shrugged. "Let's hope I don't have a random drug test."

And then he launched into a story like it was just another adventure.

"Last time I got called in, I was high in Hawaii, wasn't even supposed to leave the state. Still partying in the plane bathroom, connecting through Texas just to make it in time. I'm sweating bullets, standing in line to piss, trying to figure my way out. Then I spot a bottle of bleach in the cabinet. I tell the cop someone's looking for him. He steps out. Boom—I grab the bleach, fling it into the stall just in time. I'm threatening everyone around me, like, 'Don't say a fucking word.' When it's my turn, I mix it into the piss cup—voilà. Clean test. Freakin' miracle."

That was Greg—our Tasmanian Devil. Pure chaos but somehow looking good and making it all look easy.

And Peter? Watching. Taking it all in. Maybe even admiring it.

That's what I hated most. We Trigos always promised we'd keep him innocent, safe. But in that moment, he was seeing our charm, our recklessness, maybe thinking it was something to aspire to.

Well, that was who we were. A mess of contradictions.

It's hard to explain, but when you're that good at getting into trouble—and even better at slipping out of it—being a Trigo was something to be proud of.

* * * *

By mid-May, I was still planning to move to LA, but nothing was set. Then Philip called.

"Empire Ballroom. Nine-thirty. Bring Angela. No excuses."

I hesitated, saying I had plans with my mom. His tone shifted.

"I need you there. Trust me."

A little demanding, but it was a beautiful night. I figured Philip just wanted to have fun. Like the Beastie Boys' "Fight for Your Right," sometimes you had to stand up for yourself; it's party time, damnit.

So I went. The club was packed and honestly? I had fun. James wasn't there, but that was becoming normal. Rumors and arguments swirled about him—sick, missing, cash gone—but the music drowned it out.

The next day, Maya and I floated on a raft in Huntington Beach, talking about LA and its cool vibe. I loved the apartments with hardwood floors, imagined tons of white candles, and planned to throw endless dinner parties with all my amazing friends I'd have there. I told her I was going to see an apartment that night. She said she'd come.

On the way back, we passed Philip's apartment and stopped, half curious, half worried about James. We knocked. Eventually, Philip opened the door, sweaty, pale, and wearing yellow elbow-length gardening gloves. Bleach clung to the air.

"Where's James?" Maya asked.

"How should I know?" he snapped, trying to shut the door.

"Need to pee," Maya insisted, pushing her luck.

"Not a good time," Philip replied, his eyes cold and distant.

Philip shot me a dead stare like he wanted to kill her. "Hold on a sec," he muttered, clearly annoyed. He slammed the door, and after a minute, he let Maya inside. I waited outside. When she came back, we didn't say a word.

"There were holes in the carpet," Maya finally muttered. "That apartment's in my name."

We were both thinking the same thing, but afraid to say it.

Back at her place, we found police tape. Her next-door neighbor had been shot. No suspects. Was Philip involved?—he'd had beef with Maya's roommate for months. Wrong house? I couldn't stop thinking about James. Was he dead? If so, why? I'd supplied the drugs. Was it my fault? Had he gotten tangled with Agent Blue?

Weeks later, at an after-hours party, I saw Philip again. I sat next to him, half laughing at his cutting jokes. But then the laughter died.

"So…what happened to James?" I asked.

He leaned back, smirking. "Come on, Denise. You already know."

I didn't reply. He mimed yanking a flower from the dirt and placed it gently over my head. A burial. I forced a nervous laugh, trying to convince myself it wasn't real. The look in his eyes said otherwise.

"That's not funny," I whispered.

"Don't tell anyone."

"Who would I tell?"

He just raised an eyebrow. And he was right. Who could I tell? The cops? Please. Even if I tried, Agent Blue would tip him off. I had no choice but to stay quiet.

Rumors spun out—maybe Philip ordered the hit. Maybe Freddy did it to keep his name out of the BNE files. Maybe Duane. Or Agent Blue. No one knew. But someone did. And James was gone. I kept running through scenarios: a silencer in the night? A pillow? Strangling? Blunt force? Where was the body?

Maya kept asking, "Where's James?" I finally told her what Philip implied. She brushed it off. "You're paranoid." Maybe she didn't want to believe it. I barely could.

But I knew I had to pull away. Philip wanted a connection to Juan. I gave it to him, but warned Juan first—it was his call whether to keep supplying. But I was done being anybody's middleman.

I couldn't go to my parents. They thought my life was fine. I didn't exactly show signs of being out of control—no OJ-in-that-white-Bronco moments, no Lisa "Left Eye" Lopes burning down her boyfriend's house. I was polished, presentable, respectful.

Sure, nobody was rigging car bombs like in a Scorsese gangster film, but the Italian mobster rules still applied: if you know too much, you're gonna get whacked. Telling them about the mess I was caught up in would've shattered their hearts—and worse, it would've put them in danger.

Philip kept casually dropping lines like "Agent Blue said this," or "Agent Blue said that." I had no idea who was dirty or clean anymore.

Brandy called. She could tell something was wrong. At lunch at Mrs. Knott's Fried Chicken, she saw right through me. Slowly, I spilled it: the drugs, what Philip said about James, why I couldn't go to the cops. I cried, admitting how scared and trapped I felt.

"Holy shit," she whispered. "Don't worry—we'll figure something out."

Brandy's plan was simple: act normal, party with the crew, then crash at her place on Sunday—off the radar. "No one knows where I live," she added. It wasn't a permanent fix, but I nodded. Some space—that's exactly what I need.

I drove home feeling better. But when I pulled into the driveway, Philip was there—with Maya.

"Let's go out," he said, eyes locked on mine.

I took a deep breath, remembering Brandy's advice. "Okay," I said brightly. "Let me get ready."

We headed to one of LA's hottest clubs. We were loading into Fred's car when he popped the trunk to toss in a jacket. That's when I saw it. The gun. I pretended not to notice. He slammed the trunk shut and looked straight at me, eyes narrowed. For a split second, neither of us blinked. My mind raced. Was that the gun used on James? I kept drinking to steady myself.

As we were driving, Fred started in. "What's with the attitude? Too cool for OC now?"

I grinned. "Stop being a buzzkill."

He leaned forward and snorted a thick rail of meth off the back of his hand. His eyes went glassy. "You're gonna ignore me?" he snapped.

"Dude, get over it," I said lightly.

He caught my eye in the rearview mirror. "Maybe I should pull over and take care of you." Everyone laughed.

"Ha, stop," I said, waving it off. But deep down, I knew he didn't mean a fight.

At the club on Hollywood and La Brea, things eased. "You know I love you, D," Fred said.

Inside, it was packed. I spent the night babysitting Angela; I had to carry her out after she started flashing a famous male pop star. We ended up crashing at a pad in Newport Beach.

Sunday morning, I was at Greg's house. Later, I drove with my brothers to drop him off at rehab, then collapsed onto my bed back at mom's. It was June 18, 1995. I'll never forget that date. Not long after, my phone rang. Lorenzo and Dan were on a three-way. They wanted me to go to Hawaii.

"No," I groaned.

"Come on," Lorenzo said. "A solo white guy flying to Hawaii looks shady. I don't want Dan flagged. Please? Free trip."

"No," I repeated. I was out.

Dan chimed in. "Come on, Flawless. You're the only one I trust."

I rolled my eyes. "Dan, you're relentless. I've said no, like, five times."

Then Lorenzo's tone shifted. "I miss you. Been thinking about us. I want to come to Hawaii too—spend time together. Alone."

I paused. "We need to talk."

My heart pulled. I'd heard he was seeing someone named Melanie, but maybe that was over. Maybe he just wanted a fling. Either way, Hawaii sounded like the escape I needed from everybody in Orange County—a place to gather my thoughts and reset.

Besides, I had to warn Lorenzo about Philip, Fred, Agent Blue, and James. I still cared about him. He had to know.

"I'll go," I said carefully, "but I'm not doing anything shady. I'll walk beside Dan at the airport, but I'm not sitting next to him on the plane. I will not be around any drug deals. I want nothing to do with it. Nothing."

Lorenzo agreed quickly. "Fine. And hey, we'll ride horses on the beach, get you massages. It'll be great, Denise."

Dan jumped in. "Just bring your flawless self. We leave in the morning. More to come."

I smiled. Finally, a break. A chance to breathe.

"Three whole days in paradise," I said, genuinely excited.

Chapter Fifteen
Gangsta's Paradise

JUNE 1995

My alarm went off, and I hopped in the shower before slipping into a gorgeous mint green A-line mini dress, splashed with bold red flowers, the perfect outfit for paradise. My bags were packed. I was just waiting on Dan. No one else was home, so I didn't bother saying goodbye. I figured I'd check in once I made it to Hawaii—it was only a three-day trip.

Dan picked me up at my mom's house, sober and properly dressed now in his "plane traveling" disguise: a casual shirt, shorts, a baseball cap, and a fanny pack slung around his waist. He looked like a creepy version of Chevy Chase from *National Lampoon's Vacation*.

"Hey, Flawless," he said, grinning. "We're running a little late. Not sure we'll make this flight."

"Well, you better drive fast," I shot back as I climbed in.

During the drive to LAX, Dan was on the phone with Lorenzo. At one point, he glanced at me. "Flawless is in a short green dress with flowers on it. Yeah, she sure looks pretty."

Awww, I thought. Lorenzo's thinking about me.

Dan groveled to Lorenzo on the phone. "I know, I fucked up."

After hanging up, he told me, "We missed our flight, but Lorenzo found us another one. We have a layover in San Fran, just enough time to meet him for lunch before Hawaii."

"Works for me," I said, thrilled to see Lorenzo sooner than I thought.

At the airport, I slipped into the bathroom to change clothes. I knew Lorenzo had already seen me in that dress once—that's a fashion crime I wasn't about to commit. When I came out, Dan threw a fit.

"Oh, for the love of God! Why did you have to change clothes?" he wailed.

"Why do you care?" I shot back, annoyed.

That's when I noticed someone following us. I know it sounds weird, especially in an airport, but the guy stuck out. He was holding a big paper tube, like an architect would, and I spotted him at every turn. He was even loitering nearby when I came out of the bathroom.

I mentioned it to Dan, but he brushed it off. "Good eye, Flawless. I like that you're looking out, but he's fine."

Suit yourself, asshole, I thought.

Just before boarding, Dan slipped away, claiming he had to make a quick call to Lorenzo. I had no idea what else they could possibly need to discuss, so I assumed he just wanted an excuse for a quick bump in the bathroom—and didn't want to share his stash with me. Loser.

After boarding, I took my seat and pretended I didn't know Dan when he tried to talk. I was thrilled to be several rows behind him.

We met Lorenzo at the Hard Rock Café, and when he saw us, he stood up. Next to him was a pretty, very pregnant girl. I stopped short. Was this Melanie? Whoever she was, Lorenzo was handing her his napkin and shifting the chair to make sure she was comfortable. I felt a sting of jealousy and a nagging sense that I shouldn't have even come. But the most important thing was warning Lorenzo about Philip. Looks like that would have to wait until Hawaii.

Lorenzo finally introduced me. "Denise, this is Karen. She's my partner Max's girlfriend."

I was relieved but still annoyed that I couldn't sit next to him.

Over lunch, things got weird. Lorenzo asked, "You know Philip, right?"

I blinked. "Um, yeah. You know him too."

He tilted his head, voice too casual. "And…what's his role in the organization again?"

Organization? What were we, a Fortune 500 company? Then he asked if I ever met his brother in Maui.

"Your fabulous younger brother, I have," I chuckled, the memory clicking into place. Lorenzo laughed too—an inside joke from the first time we dated. We had history. I'd stayed at his dad's house, met his dad's girlfriend. We went hiking. I'd eaten at his mom's, stayed there too. We swam in lakes with her near Marin County. We'd shared more than just wild nights. We were close. *Real* close.

Then came the lightning round of names. Guys I'd never heard of. One in particular: the Mechanic.

"Never met him," I said.

Lorenzo grew tense. "You sure? Maybe you just forgot?"

That did it. I stood up. "No, dude. I don't know him." I left for the bathroom.

The pregnant chick hadn't said a damn word all day.

We said goodbye. Plans were set for Hawaii the next morning. Lorenzo kissed me on the cheek. "See you soon," he purred. Despite myself, I melted a little.

"We really need to talk," I whispered. A quick kiss and I was gone.

On the plane, I didn't care about the five pounds of crystal in Dan's luggage. If he got caught, that was his problem. I had one thing on my mind: soaking up some sun and enjoying a few relaxing days without stress.

Just before landing, I checked my makeup. I wanted to look good walking off that plane.

At 8:50 P.M., United flight 49 touched down at Maui Kahului Airport. I struggled to pull my Louis Vuitton down from the overhead. *You overpacked again, girl.* I was ten rows behind Dan, but he waited for me by his seat. Being a gentleman, he took my bag.

"I got it," I said.

"It's okay, Flawless. Looks heavy. Carry this instead," he said, handing me his tennis racket case. Sounded good to me, so I walked ahead of him off the plane.

We passed baggage claim without stopping, and as soon as I stepped out of the terminal, my sundress billowed in the warm tropical breeze. The Hawaiian air hit—thick, fragrant with pineapple and plumeria. Pure bliss.

Then came the sniffing at the curb.

A K-9 assistant. Drug dog.

Two people approached: plain clothes, sharp eyes. "Hello," they said.

"Hi," I said, glancing at Dan. *Why weren't they talking to him?*

"DEA Task Force Agent Josie Adams," the woman said. "This is Mat Johnston, former Honolulu Police Department Narcotics and Vice Division DEA Agent."

"Miss, mind if we check your bags? Just a random check," Adams added.

"No, thanks," I said.

To Dan, they asked, "Sir?"

"Not right now," he replied smoothly. "We've got to go."

"Actually," Johnston said, "it'd be better if we checked both."

I had nothing to hide, but I said no to protect him.

Adams smiled thinly. "It'll only take a moment."

Then it all happened so fast—the cuffs were slapped on, travelers stared, and I was hauled to a small office two hundred yards away. In the office, they split Dan and me up.

Adams entered my room. I panicked. "Can I use the bathroom?" I blurted—the same line I always used when I couldn't handle a situation. When I was younger, it was to escape my mom's fights with my dad. Later, to get away from awkward silences on bad dates, or that uncomfortable lunch at the Hard Rock Café.

But this time, I couldn't get away. She followed me. "Take off your clothes. I need to search you."

"What? You can't do this. I haven't been Mirandized!"

"Take them off."

Humiliation.

Later, back in the room, I noticed a whiteboard. My name. Philip's. Lorenzo's. A map of connections. A web. I was listed at the very bottom. Thank God Juan's name wasn't linked to me. The questioning began. I played dumb.

After hours, Adams said, "If we search your bag and find nothing, you're free to go."

I caved. "Fine. I'm clean." I could already smell the ocean's saltwater and coconut suntan oil. My first umbrella drink was waiting. I was so close to being free.

I signed the search warrant, and the detectives unzipped my bag. When the bag opened, something was very, very wrong. On top of my frayed shorts, bikinis, and sundresses was Dan's white yachting jacket with the words "Nautica Challenge" on the sleeve.

My stomach dropped. Dan must've put his jacket in my bag after he offered to carry it off the plane.

Fuck.

"That's not mine," I said, pointing at the jacket. They pulled it out of my bag. Out fell two pounds of crystal methamphetamine. *Thunk*. I can still hear that sound in my dreams.

I laughed, too loudly.

"Whose jacket is this?" Adams inquired.

I shook my head. "I-I have no idea," I mumbled. I wasn't gonna rat on Dan. It was beyond ironic—after all the crimes I'd gotten away with, I was in trouble for the one thing I hadn't done. "Anyone could've put something in my bag," I argued. "And why would I pack a man's jacket?"

I didn't think the charges would stick. Even if they did, I figured I'd end up in rehab or on probation, like my brothers. All I wanted was to clear up the confusion and go home.

But instead, they pushed harder. "Know the Mechanic?"

I froze; Lorenzo had asked about him. "No," I whispered. "I swear."

Adams and Johnston exchanged glances. They left, and when they came back, they said, "Dan's talking. You should too."

That was the moment.

I could've told the truth, said the drugs weren't mine, said Dan took my bag on the plane and stuffed his jacket inside. I could've told them everything. If I had, I know my life would've turned out completely different.

But there was a real chance I'd end up dead.

It was a fork in the road, and I'll never know which path would've been better. Some days, it's the what-ifs that haunt me more than the life I chose. Instead, I held firm. Said I knew nothing. Protected a man I didn't even like. Because that's how I was raised—you keep your mouth shut.

And so, on Monday, June 19, 1995, I was booked at Wailuku station. In the intake center, they snapped a mug shot of a dazed brunette in a DKNY tee over a see-through sundress, pink lace thong visible underneath, tan legs, and strappy high heels. She looked stunned, bamboozled, overwhelmed—because what the fuck just happened? She had no idea she wouldn't see the beach again for a long, long time.

That night, they threw me into a holding cell. By morning, Dan strolled past, cool as ever, chuckling with the officer—bromance of the century.

Dan leaned in, his voice low. "Just don't say a word," he said.

His whole vibe was off—smug, confident, too casual. Holy shit, Adams had been right. Dan the weasel had been squealing. I was furious. What happened to *omertà,* the code of silence?

"*Vaffanculo*. Fuck you. I hate you," my voice shaking with rage. "You're an asshole." And if he didn't quite get the message, I flipped him off—my last act of rebellion before they dragged me away.

Not long after, I was escorted by a full-blown FBI task force. These were the big guns, units that handled terrorism, organized crime, gangs, bank robberies, and high-level narcotics. Alongside them: special agents, a Hawaiian National Guard sergeant, and Maui International Airport Security.

I was being flown to the federal courthouse on Oahu. Getting cuffed at the curb is one thing. But boarding a commercial flight on Aloha Airlines, shackled like a felon? That was something else.

Steel restraints clamped my ankles. A handcuff belt cinched tight over my dress. They marched me through the terminal like public enemy number one.

On the plane, they sat me next to a vacationing family. The parents shot horrified glances. Their kids stared like I was a sideshow. Anyone walking past to the bathroom slowed down for a long, curious look. Not exactly the kind of attention I was used to. I wanted to cry, but I couldn't. The whole thing felt too unreal. Too humiliating. And weirdly? Almost…funny. Because it was all so *punk rock*.

I kept thinking, *I'd said I wanted nothing to do with this drug deal. I'd been out of the game. I came to warn Lorenzo, to escape Philip. How the hell had it come to this?*

When we landed, two US Marshals met me at the gate.

"Straight to prison," one said.

Prison? Not county jail?

My stomach dropped. Any hope that this might blow over vanished. The van pulled up to the Oahu Community Correctional Center (OCCC). Hawaiian-style huts surrounded by high fences and razor wire. Guard towers peering down, armed officers scanning every corner, making it clear there was no way out.

I was thrown into a small holding cell—just a wooden bench, barely wide enough for one person, and vulgar graffiti scrawled across the walls: crude sketches of vaginas, names, and lewd comments about who "sucks cock."

When the corrections officers from the Arrivals and Releasing Department showed up, they treated me like I'd already been convicted. Their only words came as barked commands: "Get out. Sit here. Arms out." I was dragged out for more mug shots. I stared into the lens, numb. Dead inside.

They fingerprinted me and snapped a red plastic wristband onto my arm, marked with my prisoner number. The digits ended in 022, which flagged me as a "federal case out of Hawaii." The band reminded me of dollar drink nights at the Red Onion or Square Cow with Stacy,

Camila, and Brandy. But this wristband wasn't for a fun night out. This one didn't come off in the morning.

It meant I was in serious, serious trouble.

That's when a tough-looking Hawaiian corrections officer walked in, blue rubber gloves on. "Take your clothes off. Hand 'em to me," she snapped. I didn't understand why she was yelling—I was right in front of her.

She shoved a pair of brown plastic shoes into my hands. I slipped them on, heart hammering. Then she turned on the shower. "Get in." The water hit me like ice. I yelped, but she didn't flinch.

"Use da kine special shampoo," she said casually. "Bugs. You need da medicine for dat." Then she muttered, "My moddah always say, 'When you no wear da shower shoes, you get foot fungus—plus all kine roaches, you know?'" She shook her head, like it was the most obvious thing in the world.

I scrubbed myself in silence, trying to choke down my panic. Then, without warning, she dusted me in white powder. "Lice," she explained, flatly. Next came a hepatitis shot that stung like hell.

"Small-kine," she muttered, handing me a used, dark green two-piece uniform with "O.C.C.C." stenciled across the back. The name "Takahashi" was ironed onto the V-neck top. She passed me stiff white full-bottomed underwear and said, "Keep these on. House rule. My aunty used to say, 'No panties? Spirits get you first. Yeast infection, rash, all kine.'"

Then came the plastic bag of prison "essentials": a bar of soap, a toothbrush, toothpaste, and a comb. "Dis all you need. No more fancy stuff," she grumbled. "Don't matter where you come from. You all gon' learn the same way."

That's how I got booked into OCCC. Just like that, at twenty-seven, my life flipped. As my mom used to say, I was up shit's creek without a paddle. I'd officially lost my virginity to the federal system.

They marched me to Module 11, the only female housing unit. Looking at the modules resembling beach huts, I had a moment of delusion: maybe this wouldn't be so bad. I happened to arrive during a smoke break, so two brute guards shoved me into an outdoor cage with thirty other women. An orchestra of catcalls went up.

"Fresh meat, baby, I get her first," an oversized Tongan woman called out, a cigarette dangling between her lips. Laughter, whistles, like buzzards circling their prey, guards yelling in pidgin, "No make ass!" But I stood tall, chin up, heart pounding. I had no choice—I had to figure out how to survive, and fast.

Inside, the module looked nothing like a beach hut. Cold concrete walls, two tiers of cells circling a central guard station. The officer handed me a cloth name tag.

"Trigo," she said. "No summah fun, eh?" A bunch of fucking comedians.

"Iron last name onto da uniform ova dea," and she pointed to a desk. Then she pointed up. "Your cell stay up dea."

I didn't understand. "Huh?"

She repeated slowly, "Your cell. Top corner."

I begged her for a phone call. "Please. I need to tell my family where I am."

"No mainland calls unless Monday. Gotta sign up one week before. You write da number, da name, pick your time slot. Ten minutes only. If no answer—you wait again."

I was crushed. Back in my cell, I curled up and shut my eyes. I didn't want to be awake anymore.

* * * *

The next day, a guard opened my cell. "Trigo, you got court."

I jumped up—finally. I was sure this was all a mistake. Those drugs weren't mine. I'd explain everything, and I'd be out by sundown.

In court, the US Marshals removed my shackles. I let myself hope. But when the judge read out the charges—"aiding and abetting, possession, intent to distribute five and a half pounds of crystal methamphetamine"—I couldn't follow.

My public defender requested bail.

The judge looked me over, then said, flatly, "Bail is denied."

"What?" I whispered, mascara running down my cheeks.

Back in the Marshal's office, I collapsed on the concrete, sobbing. My body was still in prison, but my mind was shattered somewhere else. I barely remember returning to OCCC—I was a ghost of myself, barely walking, barely breathing.

For two days, I didn't eat or move. I didn't care. They placed a red "Safety Watch" sign on my door, marking me as a suicide risk. And they weren't wrong.

In the dark I just prayed. God help me.

Finally the door buzzed open. A blond girl with a short bob stepped in and sat on the bottom bunk. "Do you mind if I talk with you?" she asked gently.

I barely nodded.

"I'm a federal inmate too. I'm getting out tomorrow, going back to Canada. But I wanted to talk to you first."

Her voice was warm, even cheerful. It didn't match the place at all.

"I know it's hard right now, but you need to get up. If you don't, they'll move you from Safety Watch to Suicide Watch. Once you're there, you're marked. For life. You won't get any privileges. You won't get out of segregation."

She looked at me seriously. "You don't want that on your jacket."

"Jacket?" I asked.

"Your file," she clarified. "The government's file on you."

Her words finally landed. I nodded.

"Look, everything's going to work out," she said, smiling. "God has a plan for you."

I wasn't sure what God's plan was for me, but I listened.

Her words sank in. They gave me a little jolt, a reason to keep fighting. I couldn't help but wonder if God really did have a plan for me, like she said. But I also hoped that plan wasn't for me to just rot in prison.

I tried to make a deal with God in my head. *Please. If I make it out, I'll change—church, no drugs, no dealers.... Whatever it takes.*

I waited for a sign, for some kind of divine answer. I needed help, I needed intervention.

But instead of a voice from above, a correctional officer suddenly barked at me, "Get up. Dis not da Holiday Inn. Take da shower. Eat like da rest a' da girls." She pointed down to the cell down the tier, behind a thick, transparent Plexiglas cell. Inside was a naked girl screaming profanities, groping at herself, with a sign above her cell marked "Suicide Watch." The scene turned my stomach.

"You no mix wit' da others, I put you down there wit' her," the CO warned.

I took the Canadian girl's hand. I got up.

I tried to blend in, but I was battling the language. Everyone spoke Hawaiian Pidgin, fast and full of inside jokes. Half the time, I felt like I'd landed in a foreign country without a map.

Any time I heard anything that even resembled *Trigo*, I leapt up like Pavlov's dog, thinking, *Freedom?*

Instead, they sent me to medical to get my ears checked.

* * * *

Life inside was brutal, but predictable. Brutal, like when a girl mouthed off to a guard, the COs swarmed, pinned her down, and hit her with a needle to put her down like a wildcat. Routine. After breakfast, it was always the same: cell cleanup, inspection. No excuses.

This wasn't my two-story, five-bedroom, three-bath family home. My cell was a six-by-eight coffin: stainless sink, scratched mirror, bolted steel toilet, bunk bolted to the wall. A narrow pane of safety glass gave me a snapshot of other cells, the common area, and the officer's station—if I stood on tiptoe.

The big thrill? Smoke breaks. When a CO hollered, "Aloha! Smoke break!", gold. No money on your books? Stuck inside. No smoke. No sun. No hope. And to have money on your books meant someone knew where you were and loved you enough to send some.

Lucky for me? The inmates were cool. I bummed menthol Virginia Slims just to score ten minutes outside. One hit of sky, sun on my face, head tilted back—I was somewhere else. Like in one of those old black-and-white movies I used to watch with Mom and Stacy. Holding a skinny cigarette, my green two-piece uniform became a tailored suit, my slippers turned into dainty heels. I was Martha from *Who's Afraid of Virginia Woolf?*, channeling Bette Davis, thinking, *What a dump.*

The music saved me too. Inside, the corner TV played music videos on loop, and I watched them like postcards from a better life.

When Janet Jackson's "Runaway" came on, I wasn't locked up; I was barefoot, globetrotting through temples and deserts, free.

Then "Kiss from a Rose" hit, and Seal's voice wrecked me. I'd blink back tears, homesick, praying to hear my family's voices. I thought, *They must be worried—but they'd be even more scared if they actually knew where I was.*

Then came Teresa, my new cellmate. Thin. Twitchy. Eyes darting like she was always hunted. Arms covered in sores. When I offered a hand, she flinched like I'd swung at her.

"What the hell is wrong with you?"

The burly Polynesian guard who locked us in together just laughed. "She stay harmless," he said, grinning. "Brain small kine fried, if you know what I mean."

"How long you been using drugs?" I asked. She sat up straighter, her prison uniform hanging off her like laundry on a wire. Her skin sagged over sharp bones.

"Since I was thirteen," she said, eyes shutting. "Me and my friends used it to lose weight. When we ran outta money, we fucked cops for it." She flashed a sly grin. "But who the fuck wants to know? Betty Ford or what? You one fuckin' cop?" Then she started laughing. And before I could react, she lunged. Scratching, spitting, screaming, "You horny cunt! You're afterbirth running down my leg!" I was repulsed. But now? I got it.

I sold coke for nearly ten years. Helped people move meth. Did I care what it did to people? Nope. Teresa was the result. Right there in front of me. Maybe she wasn't even real. Maybe she was a demon I conjured from my own poisoned karma. She clawed at me again. I kicked her—hard—in the stomach.

She flew back into the wall and started laughing like a maniac. "You worthless cunt."

I banged on the steel door. "Get me out! Please!"

The guard finally wandered over, looked us both over, and grinned. "You two stay gettin' along fine."

But that night I knew. They put her in my cell for a reason. Teresa wasn't just a cellmate. She was the ghost of every deal I ever made. I hadn't cared then. But now I saw. *This*—this was what I helped create. I made *her.*

* * * *

I had to get out of here.

Thank God, a week had passed, meaning my one shot—ten minutes between 1:00 P.M. and 1:10 P.M.—to call the mainland. I hovered near the guard station, nerves buzzing.

"Trigo," the guard bellowed.

"Yes, yes," I said quickly.

She nodded toward a black rotary phone on a desk—straight out of a Hitchcock scene—where my future hung on this one call. "You gotta get da operator first to dial out," she said. "Put yo' index finger in da zero, swipe it all da way around 'til you hear da dial tone. Ten minutes, only." She gave me a look like she meant it.

I immediately started trying but couldn't get a dial tone. Three minutes crawled by, and my anxiety spiked—heart pounding, palms sweating.

"This is crazy!" I snapped. "What the hell?"

It felt like I was trapped in the damn *Twilight Zone*—rotary phones, no dial tone, and my one shot at contact slipping away by the second.

Finally, after what felt like forever, I heard the dial tone with only two minutes left. I swiped in my home number, praying—please, someone pick up. Silence.

No one.

My throat tightened. My mom must still be at the café.

An older guard with a graying beard caught my eye and gave me a look like he wanted to say something. Instead, he just shook his head and muttered, "Stay strong, yeah? You get through dis."

Rules were rules here. When I asked about the next call, he shrugged. "No set day. Nevah know. Mainland call days rotate. You just wait 'til they tell you."

I clenched my fists. This place—this whole system—was built to wear you down, strip away your hope, one rule at a time.

But I wasn't done yet.

The next day, they pulled me into court unexpectedly. That's when I saw him—US Marshal Grant. My Superman: tall, calm, and wearing a flowered aloha shirt—their laid-back uniform. Even though I looked like hell, he treated me like I was still human.

"I hate to see you like this," he said, glancing at my cuffs. "How'd a girl like you get mixed up with these jokers?"

I told him I just wanted to call my family.

And unlike everyone else, he actually did something. He made the calls.

To my relief, Grant was able to reach Brandy. Now it was up to her to break the news to my family.

Until then, every time an agent asked me questions, I gave them nothing.

I stood my ground. I told the truth.

The drugs weren't mine. I was innocent.

* * * *

A day later, I was brought before the judge to see if my bail could be reconsidered. While I waited, a Marshal told me I had a visitor. I assumed it was another fed ready to play bad cop.

They sat me in a cold chair, across a thick glass panel with a small speaker hole. I slumped forward, drained.

Then came a soft knock.

I looked up—and there he was, an angel. My father. My entire world, standing on the other side of that glass like an apparition.

I broke down into tears. "What?" I sputtered. "How?"

"It's okay," he said, his voice gentle. "Denise, it's okay. I'm here. I'm going to do everything I can to help you. I'll clean this up." He looked around. "This is no place for daddy's little girl."

I took a deep breath. "Okay," I whispered, desperate to believe him. "I didn't do this. I didn't know the drugs were in my bag."

I sat shell-shocked, separated by glass, unable to hug him or hold his hand, but his presence comforted me.

"Everybody sends their love, Niesey," he added softly.

"Oh my God, what did they say?" I asked, already guessing the answer in this messed-up situation.

"Jeff wants you to fight it all the way," my dad said. "Greg's in shock. Of course, Fran—your mother—is worried, but she knows I'm here. And Aunt Flo…" He sighed. "She says she is here to help."

That was typical Aunt Flo, so loving and caring.

"I'm just relieved everyone knows where I am," I said, the sadness settling in again.

Ten days after my arrest, on June 29, I faced the brutal truth: I'd spend my birthday in jail. No cake. When I was younger, my mom made the same birthday punch every year—bright, fizzy, crowned with scoops of orange sherbet. She'd drive miles to pick up dry ice, special order it days in advance, and handle it carefully like it was some kind of magic. When she dropped it in the punch, fog would spill down the table like a stage effect. But here, I got nothing. Just cold, gray walls.

I couldn't help but see the absurdity of it all. Lorenzo's birthday was the day after mine, and we talked about a joint party. Now, I was stuck in the joint. My only birthday wish? To get out alive.

Chapter Sixteen

More Than a Feeling

JULY 1995

In prison, stripped of distractions like drugs, alcohol, and messy relationships, things finally started to come into focus. With nothing to cloud my brain, I had to sit with myself. And what I saw wasn't pretty.

I spent hours replaying my childhood: my parents' failing marriage, my growing distance from my dad, and the part I played in letting it all slip. I used to wait for him to make the effort, instead of meeting him halfway. His door had always been open, but I let the miles—and my attitude—do the talking. I traded weekends with him for dumb boyfriends and even dumber choices. Like idolizing Jeff and Rich as my role models. These were lost years, and I hated myself for wasting them.

Over time, clarity came. My dad hadn't abandoned us—he'd simply fallen out of love with my mom. He wasn't perfect, but he never stopped loving us. And now, he was showing it in a way that completely floored me.

He moved to Hawaii to be near me during my case. That's love. He uprooted his life while serving as chairman of the Japanese Chiropractic Association. Hawaii made sense; he knew the Island, had lived there before, and it was a good halfway point for his frequent flights to Tokyo.

Dee, his wife, came too. She was warm, steady, and exactly what we both needed.

In court, my dad's reputation as a doctor and pastor carried weight. His character reference helped me secure another bail appeal, even with the DEA breathing down the judge's neck. They insisted I was a flight risk, thanks to the potential sentence hanging over me. I won't lie, I thought about my options—I daydreamed about bailing to Bali, fishing off some quiet shore, or disappearing to China to write fortune cookies for a living. But my mom's house was on the line.

The judge granted bail—$350,000—with strict conditions: house arrest, random drug tests, and no leaving Oahu. Dad promised to supervise me.

Meanwhile, I stayed locked up while my parents scrambled to raise the money. Mom put our house up as collateral and borrowed from Aunt Flo. I sat in prison, feeling like the biggest loser. With a big capital L. Trapped in a concrete box while my family moved mountains for me. The guilt crushed me. They believed in me, fought for me, when I wasn't even sure I deserved it. The drugs weren't mine, but let's be real—I'd still gotten myself into this mess. Now *they* were paying the price. All I could do was sit there, helpless, ashamed, hoping like hell I'd get the chance to make it right.

* * * *

Meanwhile, now that Brandy knew about my arrest, it felt like I'd been splashed across the *Orange County Register*—tabloid-style. I could almost see the headlines:

FROM VIP TO OCCC: OC PARTY GIRL CAUGHT IN DEA STING

Was she the brains—the bait—or just along for the ride? Full story inside.

God, please let them think I was a clueless party girl.

Because if they thought I was the brains? I was shark chum. Honestly, I was somewhere between the bait and along for the ride. Even I can barely make sense of it.

Philip and the crew were paranoid. Coke-fueled nights, shady moves, Feds closing in—everything spiraling. Philip was desperate to keep me quiet. He knew I could take him down. So, he was cozying up to Brandy.

When I called home, thank God Jeff answered. I heard the love in his voice. "Hey, Niese. Hang in there, road dog." Then his tone shifted. "You're not gonna believe this: Brandy's been hanging with Maya and Philip. I asked her what the hell she was thinking, and she goes"—he dropped into a high-pitched, bratty-girl voice—"'*I'm not stupid, I'm just keeping tabs on him.*'"

I rolled my eyes so hard. Like, *girl*, you are *literally* being played.

Sure enough, a week later, Philip paid cash to send Maya and Brandy all the way to Hawaii, like it was a damn zoo visit to see the caged animals.

I walked into the visiting room. Brandy was already crying. She looked me up and down in my green jumpsuit and smirked. "Honestly, I don't know why I thought you'd show up in some white lace sundress. Guess I'm still in shock."

"Tell me about it," I said, sitting. "Where's Maya?"

She rolled her eyes. "Too spun out from Waikiki partying. Still passed out at the hotel. Total disaster. Full-blown drug addict."

I blinked. "But… don't you two hang out all the time?"

She ignored me. "Angela was wild at the club."

Wait, she's friends with her now too?

"And crazy Fred? That guy's a riot." She lit up, like she was deep in their world. Then, suddenly, "Philip's so evil."

"Why? What'd he do?" I leaned in. She pivoted, like she hadn't heard me. Was she just gossiping, or was Philip sending her to gauge my frame of mind?

Near the end, as an afterthought, she dropped a bomb. "Oh, Lorenzo wants you to talk to the Feds."

I blinked. "What?"

"He called me at the hotel before I came. Said you should cooperate. He really cares about you, Denise." She pouted, selling it. That's when it hit me: Lorenzo was working with the Feds. Why else push me to talk?

Maybe he was flipping on Philip. Or wanted me to flip first and do his dirty work.

I laid it out, but Brandy just looked dazed. "I don't know who to trust anymore." She hesitated.

I pointed at my jumpsuit, the red wristband, the walls. "You wanna end up like me? Get one number?"

She shook her head fast.

"Eh, you bettah get out already," I said. "That party life? Not worth it, Tita." Lockup was rubbing off—I was starting to sound like an islander.

* * * *

A guard finally shouted my name.

"Trigo, roll 'em up! You made bail."

For a second, I swear I could feel sunlight on my face—even inside. It was like the heavens cracked open and church bells started ringing.

I glanced at the pencil etchings scratched on the wall by my bunk. Twenty-two days behind bars. If it hadn't been for those marks, I would've lost all sense of time. Back then, I thought I was some kind of badass, like I'd earned street cred just for surviving lockup. I felt tough, like I proved something. Cool? Please. What a joke. I wasn't tough. I was just lost.

After processing out, I moved into the ninth floor of a high-rise condo at the Makaha Beach Cabanas with my dad. A beachfront slice of paradise on the leeward coast of Oahu on a secluded cove. Crystal-white building. Mountains in the front, ocean in the back.

I knew the place well. Dad had lived there before with Dee and Peter. I'd visited plenty.

From the front, you could see Makaha Valley and Mount Ka'ala, an ancient volcano, rising steep and proud. When it rained, waterfalls spilled down its side and rainbows crowned the horizon. White fairy terns glided through the sky, adding a magical touch to the scenery. Out back, it was ocean as far as the eye could see. Turtles bobbing in the surf. Whales breaching in the distance.

But me? I couldn't even step a toe in the sand.

That LoJack monitor strapped to my ankle barely covered the radius of the cabana. Step out of range, and the box would shriek as if I'd just busted out of Alcatraz. Worse, it was finicky—sometimes that fucker went off for no reason. I kept expecting the Feds to kick down the door, Johnny Utah–style, ready to slap the cuffs on me like I was Bodhi caught chasing one last wave.

I had only three outs: court dates, meetings with my lawyer, and church.

So yeah, I was stuck in paradise. Just a few days into house arrest, out on bail. I was pacing around my dad's cabana, thinking like Tupac—straight up, California dreaming.

Makaha wasn't a tourist spot—it was locals only. No tiki bars, no gift shops. Just Hawaiians with salt-worn faces who didn't have patience for *haoles*. But Dad caught on fast and got tight with Bojo, who lived in the cabana below. Bojo wasn't someone you messed with, and he vouched for Dad early.

"Anybody mess wit' Doc, dey mess wit' me."

After that, Dad wasn't just protected; he earned his place and was respected. As a doctor and a pastor, he volunteered at Calvary Church, helped the community, and slowly became one of them.

Hawaiians are like Italians—when you call someone family, it means something. And Bojo was *ohana*.

Steve, Greg's best friend from high school, lived nearby and would swing by. He and Bojo would sit out on the *lanai* with Dad, smoking *pakalolo* and telling stories like old uncles.

I passed, thanks to drug testing, but if anyone needed a hit, it was me. I wanted to believe Marley's promise though: *that everything is going to be all right.* But nothing felt right. This wasn't the Hawaii I remembered.

Back when Jeff and I cruised Farrington Highway in Dad's surf wagon—windows down, Sting on full blast, sun pouring in. We watched Sunny Garcia crush waves, hit Turtle Bay to visit our friend at the stables, rolled out to V-Land with Squidy, a Wolf Pack legend. Surfed, ate *ono grinds* at Di Amico's, tore through North Shore trails, partied with pro surfers at Sugar Bar. I even hung with my exes on the Island. Rich and I once rented a white limo and danced all night at the Pink Cadillac. Jacob and I stayed in these same condos, hanging out with Dad and Pete on the beach, watching the sun melt into the sea.

That was the Hawaii I remember.

Dad bought me a cassette player. Music became my lifeline.

I'd pop on my headphones, crank up Boston's "More Than a Feeling," and tune out the world, letting my anxiety slip away.

But it wasn't just music that kept me grounded. Dad also brought tapes from Pastor Steven Kirt—sermons by Chuck Smith, the voice of my childhood church in Costa Mesa. Calm. Steady. Reassuring.

Eventually, Dad and I got creative. We rigged the LoJack box to the *lanai* railing facing the ocean. I could sneak down to the sand—but only if I stayed close. The second that monitor beeped, I had to sprint back as if my life depended on it.

And one day, Dad called it. "Too stressful." We settled into a new routine: Quiet moments with him? Golden. Golf on TV, old movie rentals. He loved Errol Flynn—I got a crash course in sword fights. But even in paradise, the storm loomed.

Greg's friend Steve put us in touch with a federal lawyer, Jeremy Easton. That's when reality hit like a tidal wave.

"Wait—so I don't have an out? Like my brothers?" I asked. "This is my first bust. Can't I just go to rehab?"

"You crossed state lines. That makes it federal." Jeremy said.

Translation: I was being charged with aiding and abetting possession with intent to distribute five and a half pounds of crystal meth.

If convicted under the mandatory minimums, I faced 188 months to 235 months in prison.

Fifteen to nineteen years.

I felt like when Jeff used to punch me in the stomach as a kid—only worse. Like the air got sucked out of the room.

Jeremy showed me the sentencing chart. Zone D. Offense level thirty-four. Category III criminal history, thanks to my hit-and-run and a dumb DUI.

I was toast.

"But doesn't it matter that I didn't actually do this?" I asked.

"Not really," he said. "The judge can't reduce the sentence, even if you were a nun."

Still, he had a plan: file a motion to suppress the evidence. The dog wasn't certified. The search was illegal, since I'd made it clear that the jacket wasn't mine.

If we won? Case dismissed.

If we lost? Trial.

There was no way I was flipping. No deal.

But fifteen to nineteen years? That was psych ward–level anxiety.

Then came another gut punch: the US Attorney, Lawrence Brown, told Jeremy I was screwed. Dan had already sold me out, the two pounds of meth, on a prior trip with Maya.

Didn't matter that I didn't carry it.

Only that I knew Dan had brought it.

I went numb. My dad sat beside me, stunned. I felt six years old again—caught with my hand in the cookie jar.

What a big Lu I am, I thought. *Capital L—for loser.*

* * * *

My father took extreme precautions to protect me. Given Philip's paranoia and volatility, he stocked the cabana with guns, just in case any old drug bosses or codefendants decided to go full *Scarface* on us. As surreal and terrifying as it seemed, it was a very real possibility.

Dad and Dee were full-on gun enthusiasts. They kept weapons stashed all over—under their pillows, on top of the bookcase next to *The Life and Times of Jesus the Messiah*. It felt like they were just waiting for the chance to unload on one of Philip's goons. Honestly, I found it a little entertaining, imagining Dee in her red floral muumuu, legs spread, locked and loaded, ready to blow someone's head off. They weren't afraid to use them, either. She used to say it all the time, “Go ahead, make my day.”

Still, even with an arsenal at our fingertips, I felt like a sitting duck. Every knock on the door, every unfamiliar sound, made my heart race. I had recurring nightmares—peeking into Philip’s apartment, that awful stench of bleach, a shadow moving behind me.

One night, Dad found me curled up in the corner of his shower, wearing a tank top and shorts, shaking. The thought of spending fifteen to nineteen years behind bars—or worse, getting murdered—was crushing. I couldn’t fix what I’d done. I couldn’t outrun it.

Dad knelt beside me, resting a hand gently on my shoulder. “Niecy… baby, I’m not gonna let anyone hurt you.”

His voice was so soft, so steady—it cracked something inside me. I started to cry.

“You can’t stop them,” I whispered. “If they come, they won’t stop. Not till I’m dead.”

I looked away in shame. Every choice, every risk, every lie had brought me here, and now, I was dragging my family down with me. For the first time, I saw my own reflection clearly. And I hated it.

Dad didn’t flinch. He held out his hand. “Come on.”

“But what if—”

“No. Denise. Look at me.” His voice sharpened. “Don’t you trust me?”

I looked up at his face and nodded, tears still streaming. Of course I trusted him.

“I made a little bed for you, on the floor by ours. You’ll be right beside me. It’ll be okay.”

I took his hand. He pulled me up and into a tight hug. He always made me feel safe, like nothing could touch me. Even if it was my time to go.

Somehow, the old Blue Öyster Cult song “Don’t Fear the Reaper” drifted through my mind, its words nudging me toward trust instead of fear—even if it was my time to go. That night, I slept beside my dad. I took his hand, squeezing it now and then just to make sure he was still there.

Eventually, I got a small taste of freedom. The view from the cabana was too gorgeous to stay inside forever, so I begged my lawyer to do something. He got the court to approve laundry privileges—yes, laundry—as a way to let me move between floors. The loophole gave me a couple of hours a week of relative freedom.

I made it count. I walked the beach in my white bikini and LoJack, feeling like a ghetto Hawaiian Tropic girl. The water reached my toes—never deep enough to short out the monitor, but enough to feel alive again. I closed my eyes, dreaming of winning my trial, walking free. Sometimes, I pictured the federal courthouse burning to the ground, evidence and all.

My lawyer arranged extra meetings to go over the case, which gave me an excuse to visit his office in Honolulu. Afterward, Dad, Dee, and I would head to the brewery at Aloha Tower for a late lunch. I couldn't touch drugs—not that I cared—but beer was fair game. Those pints of Big Wave Golden Ale and Longboard Lager? Liquid freedom in a glass.

But one day, after a few too many rounds, I left something behind—my federal indictment paperwork. I rushed back into the brewery, flustered.

"Uh, I left some papers at the table—did anyone find 'em?"

The hostess nodded and called over the waiter. He handed them to me with wide eyes.

"Whoa, you're the one? Sweet face and all…that's pretty gnarly, huh?"

I laughed awkwardly.

"Good luck, yeah?" he called as I hustled out.

Yeah, dude, I was gonna need it.

* * * *

Instead of sending a hitman to Hawaii, Philip sent Brandy again to check on me, along with his friend Charles, supposedly to keep her company. That's the story he told her, at least. Call it intuition or gut instinct, but it was more than a feeling. The real reason Philip sent Charles wasn't to be Brandy's companion. No, he was there to scope out the cabanas, case the joint. Philip knew I wasn't talking to the Feds, but he still needed eyes on me—just in case things needed…taking care of.

Brandy came up to the cabana. "Charles is down there. Wave hi."

I peeked over the balcony and saw Charles walking on the beach, clocking the ins and outs of the place. He waved back. I'd always been cool with Charles, but drugs change people, and Charles would do whatever Philip said.

He was cute—dark hair, decent physique—but definitely not Brandy's type. Too immature.

Later, when he came upstairs, I couldn't help noticing their hands intertwined. If Brandy was dating one of Philip's buddies, she wasn't keeping her distance. Clearly hadn't taken my advice to stay away.

But that's the thing about addiction—it sneaks up on you. Brandy liked to party and do cocaine, and with Philip's free supply, she kept sinking deeper.

Charles said he'd wait in the car so Brandy and I could catch up. I figured he was now scoping out the front entrance and trash area—just in case.

I stayed guarded talking to Brandy, knowing everything would get back to Philip. Not that she meant to harm me, but she was like that character busting through the wall in the Kool-Aid commercials: uninvited, making a scene, and drowning in Philip's punch.

And boy, was I right. "You have no idea how our friends miss you… or how much Philip cares," Brandy said, eyes sincere.

I scoffed. "Last time, you told me Philip was evil."

She blinked, then flared up. "You're just jealous I'm close to him now. Must make you crazy that you can't hang with us anymore."

I was stunned. Who was this woman? The old Brandy was gone. I wanted to save her, but she wasn't listening. I had to let her fight her own battle. My own situation was getting more complicated, and I didn't have the energy to focus on anyone else. I had to put myself first.

* * * *

It was August and besides being trapped on house arrest with surprise drug tests, I was constantly being summoned to the federal courthouse. The courts had their claws in me, and Lawrence Brown from the US

District Attorney's office wasn't about to let me wriggle free. He stalked the courthouse like a lion in a suit, and I was the unlucky prey. So when my dad and I stepped into the elevator and saw the DA already inside, I nearly choked.

My spine locked up. There he was—small, bald, smug—holding a stack of files like weapons. He flashed a grin at my dad like they were old golfing buddies.

"Hey, Doc," he said casually, like this was just another day on the green. My dad gave him a tight smile and the kind of nod you give a man you'd rather see dead.

The elevator went silent. You could hear the shuffle of papers as the DA adjusted his grip, pushed up his yellow-tinted glasses, and then turned to me. His voice was calm, but sharp as a blade.

"Denise, you're looking at a lot of time in prison," he said. "Let me know when you're ready to talk."

I cleared my throat, forcing out the line I'd rehearsed in the mirror.

"I wish I could help you. But I don't have any information."

He tilted his head, disappointed but not surprised. "If you say so."

As he stepped out, I muttered under my breath, "Nice glasses, though."

Eye roll. My dad smirked, and we both held in our laughter until the doors slid shut. Petty? Sure. But when the system's trying to crush you, small victories are survival.

* * * *

There were names in my paperwork I didn't even recognize. The web of codefendants was tangled and confusing. I had no idea who half these people were or how they connected to me. I could have crossed paths with some, but never connected the dots. I had no context, no explanation, just paperwork that raised more questions than it answered. Could I have been so naive, not fully grasping the entirety of everything? In time, I would collect more scraps, bits and pieces that might eventually add up to something. But the reality was I was living in the dark.

Still, when things got tight, I picked up the phone and called Philip. He picked up fast.

"Well, aloha," I said, full charm and smartass.

"Nice to hear your voice. How are you doing?" he asked, a little too quickly.

I couldn't resist my dark humor. "Well, ya know. I didn't get lei'd in Hawaii—I got fucked instead."

He laughed, of course. I kept going.

"But hey, my lawyer thinks I might walk if we win the motion to suppress the evidence. That jacket wasn't mine. No right to search it, right?"

He perked up. "Oh yeah—that would solve a lot of problems."

"Exactly. Just gotta hope the judge agrees."

Then my tone got lighter, but deliberate.

"The truth is, I don't know anything. If I did know anything about people selling drugs, of course, I would tell the Feds…but I don't. You're just a guy I hung out at clubs with."

He exhaled. And then his voice dropped, serious.

"You know what happens to people who *do* talk. Lorenzo…he brought up the idea."

I didn't say a word. I just let him talk. Part of me wondered if he *wanted* me to spread that rumor around. If I turned up dead in my cabana, maybe cops would look at Lorenzo instead of him. Classic Philip. Game recognizes game.

"Lorenzo is a dick," he added. "You know he set you up, right? Agent Blue told me so."

You and your Agent Blue, I thought, rolling my eyes. I didn't respond.

Before he hung up, Philip promised to pay Agent Blue to look into my case, to find out what was happening behind the scenes.

"He's gotten rid of charges before," Philip said.

That part was true.

"I'll take care of this mess you got yourself into."

Like I asked for any of it.

He let out a heavy sigh, his voice tightening. "I don't even know why you went to Hawaii in the first place."

Like it was some mystery why I wanted to get the hell out of town—never once acknowledging the fact that *he* went batshit crazy and left behind two unsolved murders, with Agent Blue poking around.

* * * *

As much as I didn't believe most of what Philip told me, he was right about Lorenzo—he started all of this. My lawyer confirmed it. This mess began in Marin County, March 1995, three months before my arrest. After a year-long probe, agents arrested Lorenzo, his brother in Maui, and his old friend and roommate Max, for allegedly running a drug ring. The prosecutor? Then Alameda County Deputy District Attorney Kamala Harris. (Yes, that Kamala Harris. Long before the Senate, before the Vice Presidency.) She offered them ten years. Instead, all three flipped—agreed to give up information to avoid prison. The stupid part? Before my arrest, I was so out of it. I should've seen it coming. He vaguely mentioned he'd gotten into trouble but was "figuring it out," so he wouldn't end up back in San Quentin. I just blinked, wide-eyed and clueless.

"Wait…you were in San Quentin before?"

But what I didn't know was the mess behind the scenes.

Back in March, Max warned Lorenzo not to go through with the deal, but Lorenzo did it anyway—and got them both busted. Max told him, "You got me into this, you get me out." They had a deal, but Lorenzo acted above the law and kept dealing drugs behind the Feds' backs—moving product to his brother in Maui. Lorenzo knew his drug days were numbered. He was just trying to squeeze a few deals through before it all ended. Those drugs were supposed to make it to his brother.

But Max got nervous—Lorenzo was still dealing—and his own ass was on the line. With a baby on the way, Max flipped on Lorenzo, trying to control the fallout and make sure he didn't end up in prison.

The real kicker? Max's girlfriend—the pregnant woman I had lunch with at the Hard Rock Café in San Francisco—started working with the Feds behind both their backs. Wearing a wire under her overalls, she recorded everything. She was the one who *officially* turned me in—to save her baby's daddy from prison. So much for women helping women.

Years later, Max told me, "Lorenzo was looking forward to seeing you in Hawaii. Talked about you all the time." But *was* he setting me up? At some point, he would need witnesses to cut a deal. What were we supposed to be, Bonnie and Clyde turned Hunter and McCall? Some say I was collateral damage. I was. But things still don't add up.

Looking back, the signs were there. Before lunch at the Hard Rock Café, Dan mentioned to Lorenzo what I was wearing to the airport. Clearly, it was for the Feds to ID me. But at the time I didn't put it together. It's clear now, that they were both in on it, feeding information to the Feds. Then right before we boarded, Dan stepped away to make a quick phone call. Updating them on our flight—San Francisco to Hawaii—and my fashion change. Dan sat there through the entire lunch, heard everything, and said nothing. The pieces were there. I just wasn't seeing them.

And remember how Dan said he needed to make a *quick phone call* before we boarded? Probably giving them our updated flight—San Francisco to Hawaii—and what I changed into.

I even told him we were being followed at LAX. He brushed it off like I was being paranoid. But my discovery paperwork proved it—they were tailing us.

My gut says he might've been busted on an earlier run to Alaska. So even if Preggo didn't make the call…maybe Dan would have. Either way, I was pressured into going. Coerced. And now I'm fighting just to stay free.

And this thought would haunt me for years to come…

If I could only turn back time….

I wonder what my life would have been like—who I might've become—if I hadn't gotten on that goddamn plane….

I couldn't believe I'd been betrayed like that. I wasn't some villain—I was just trying to protect my friends, my lover, and myself. But with everyone working their own angles, I never stood a chance.

A few days later, Philip called back. He sounded smug, like he had everything under control.

"I put the pressure on Agent Blue," he said. "Boy, you owe me for this one. I'm a genius." He exhaled like he'd just negotiated world peace. "Agent Blue said your case will be dropped right after jury selection. Be patient until then. I'm buying your way out of this. Just pick the jury."

Despite all the shady shit I knew about Philip, I trusted him. He gave me hope. Funny what and who you'll believe when you're desperate.

* * * *

Still reeling from Lorenzo's betrayal, I clung to one bright spot: my brother Greg was coming to visit. On September 1, he got a hall pass from his rehab facility in Newport Beach and flew to Hawaii to be with me for the motion to suppress evidence.

When I opened the door to the cabana, I shrieked, "It's so good to see you!"

Greg's eyes were wet. "I can't believe you're out on bail, man," he said, voice cracking. "I thought they were going to keep you in."

"I can't believe they let *you* out to come visit me!" I shot back. "We've seen better days, huh?"

He laughed. "You're telling me."

We hugged hard. For the first time in weeks, I felt lighter. We stayed in, talking about everything except court. He told me stories about the rehab—especially the guy who ran it, a total hard-ass.

Greg puffed up his chest and imitated him: "Trigoooooo, what do you think you're doing? Renting out your DVDs? This isn't a damn resort!" He grinned.

I laughed—God knows I needed it.

"Mr. Popular already?" I teased. "Classic Trigo trait."

We talked and snacked on pupus. It reminded me of the old Trigo family dinner table, when that was our safe place. For a while, the storm felt far away.

As the sun went down, Greg hopped in the shower, and my dad and I stood over the stack of movies we'd rented earlier from Blockbuster, debating which one to play first. We had everything from *Clueless* to *Pulp Fiction*, but we never got to pick one. A knock hit the door.

Dad opened it. Detective Adams stood there. Behind her, a US Marshal.

"Miss Trigo," Adams said evenly. "You need to come with us."

My stomach dropped. "W-Why?"

"Another indictment. Out of San Francisco. Conspiracy charges."

The words sank in. "Conspiracy? F-For what?"

The Marshal shifted forward, hand brushing his cuffs. Panicked surged. Adams lifted a hand.

"Those won't be necessary," she said, like routine.

"I need a minute," I whispered, trying to keep it together. My dad looked stunned. Helpless.

I walked to the bathroom. The shower was still running.

"I…I have to go," I called over the water. "They're taking me back."

Greg pulled the curtain aside, water streaming down his face. Confusion. Then Fear. "What? Why?"

"I don't know," I muttered, dazed. "New charges, I guess."

Adams turned to my dad. "She'll be released within the hour," she said, like it was no big deal. But if it wasn't a big deal, why was a US Marshal here? Why were they ready to cuff me?

"Greg and I will follow," Dad said. "We'll take you home when this is over. It'll be okay."

Greg threw on clothes, stepping closer.

"I love you," I told my dad before they led me out.

In the back of the unmarked car, I kept glancing behind us, searching for their headlights. It was the only thing keeping me calm.

Halfway through the ride, Adams turned in her seat. "Just so you know," she said, calm as ever, "Lorenzo Estes was found dead. His body was discovered in a dumpster."

The air left my lungs.

"What?"

And then it clicked. This was Philip. I knew the rules. A snitch talks, and people disappear. But why was I wrapped into this?

"What does conspiracy mean?" I asked.

Adams didn't miss a beat. "Conspiracy means you conspired—"

"Allegedly conspired," I snapped.

She chuckled. "Fair. You *allegedly* conspired to run a drug organization. Had knowledge of criminal activities and participated in a racketeering ring." She paused. Let it sink in. "Oh—and conspiracy adds ten years. On top of the fifteen to nineteen you're already facing."

I did the quick math. Twenty-five to twenty-nine years in federal prison.

Adams wasn't done. "You know, Lorenzo was really upset when you got arrested. I'm not even sure he was going to testify against you."

She caught my eyes in the mirror. I flinched. Did she think I was celebrating his death?

I could feel Adams sizing me up, her eyes narrowing as she considered me. For the first time, there was a flicker of sincerity in her gaze.

"Denise, you need to help yourself right now. Everybody is talking. Don't be the last woman standing. We will convict you."

The heat in the back of the unmarked cruiser felt suffocating, yet goosebumps crawled over my skin. I stared out the window, my thoughts drifting to Lorenzo. The first time I met him at the salon. The instant connection we'd shared. Our passion. I was sad, grieving, and heartbroken, but I couldn't cry. I hated him for putting me in this position. And, if I was being honest with myself, a small part of me was relieved he couldn't testify against me anymore.

And God help me, I thought, *If only Dan would disappear too…maybe I could beat this.*

When we got to the courthouse, I scanned the room, desperate for a familiar face. No Dad. No Greg. They handed me the indictment: conspiracy charges from California. My name was listed with Philip, Fred, Duane, Eric Kekoa, the money man, some of Lorenzo's crew, two strangers, and someone only known as "John Doe." And "the Mechanic." It was all a blur. I assumed they were from other states—Alaska, Arizona, Colorado—all the places the drugs were being distributed. We were all going down. I turned, hoping to see my lawyer. But he wasn't there. Later I found out my dad had been calling him nonstop. No response. Instead, I stood beside a public defender who barely knew my name.

Oh, shit. I was fucked.

Then came the government's motion to revoke my pretrial release—for my "safety," of course. Lorenzo's death changed everything. The DA claimed I was tied to a dangerous network. US Marshal Abigail handed me a plastic bag for my personal items. My chest tightened. I started to hyperventilate.

"Stay chill, Denise," she said. "This doesn't mean anything. It's just in case."

But I knew exactly what it meant. They were locking me up. Again. It was Friday afternoon. No judge would hear another motion until Monday.

No movie night. No dinner with my family. Just another cold bunk. Then the courtroom doors burst open. Dad and Greg rushed in, their faces pale. My father looked like he wanted to tear the courtroom apart.

"No!" he shouted. "If anything happens to my little girl—if she is changed in any way by this experience—I will come after each and every one of you!" He looked at the judge, Adams, the DA. No fear in his eyes. The judge didn't flinch. He slammed the gavel on his Koa wood bench and ordered me into custody.

My dad—my protector, my Army badass, my Doberman—couldn't save me. Adams smirked. That smug, hollow smirk. Something inside me snapped. Fine. It was war. Maybe it was time I dug deep and unleashed the boss I knew I was, the girl who always found a way out of the tightest situations. I wasn't just going to survive this—I was determined to win. If she wanted to play dirty, I'd play smarter. I wasn't going down without a fight. As they led me away, I started making deals with myself.

Okay, Denise. You can do the weekend. You'll come back Monday. You'll win the motion to suppress. You'll survive this. And once the Hawaii charges are dropped, you can deal with the charges in California.

That's how I dealt with everything—I compartmentalized my situation, tackling problems one at a time, like I was standing in the eye of the storm. It was too overwhelming to look at the deadly hurricane surrounding me.

* * * *

The prison phone rang twice before Dad picked up. I pictured him on the *lanai*, coffee mug in hand. It was Sunday. Tomorrow was my motion to suppress.

"Hey, kiddo."

He told me Greg had taken a red-eye back to the mainland. Courtroom stress had been too much. Greg was never one for the hard stuff—especially not jail visits.

"When he got to the rehab facility," Dad said, "they marched him straight into the director's office. And guess who was waiting?"

I could hear the grin in his voice.

"Stevens and Delaney. Practically foaming at the mouth. Figured a package from Hawaii—with everything going on—had to have drugs in it."

"What was in it?"

"A ceramic Precious Moments serenity prayer figurine—Dee sent it," he said, laughing.

I laughed too, even through the pain.

"God, I needed that," I said. "I love that we got them after all these years."

"Dee and I thought you'd get a kick outta it," Dad said, chuckling.

Then, softer, "Dad…I'm sorry. For everything."

He didn't miss a beat. "I know, sweetheart. I love you. Don't worry—God's not done with you yet. This too shall pass."

After we hung up, I lay back on my bunk and stared at the ceiling. Regret consumed me. If I could go back, I'd undo it all—the shame, the recklessness, the hurt I caused my family.

And I couldn't help but wonder how different their lives might be…

…if I hadn't gotten on that goddamn plane….

Chapter Seventeen
High Noon

SEPTEMBER 1995

So, there I was, back at the OCCC. The electric door buzzed.

"Chow time, ladies!" a CO barked. I jumped from the top bunk, stomach growling. Starving. Stress still clung, but I'd made peace with it. Adapt or break.

The chow line crawled. Same menu: kālua pork stew, a scoop of sticky brown rice. My mind drifted to Café Pasquini's lemon chicken, salty capers, buttery cream sauce, cold white wine in a stemmed glass.... My mouth watered.

In the corner, a steel trash can lined with a black Glad bag sat beneath a torn paper sign: "Scraps."

"Grindz you no eat go in da trash marked 'scraps'," one CO said. "For da pig slop."

Translation: leftovers feed the pigs. The pigs become dinner. *The Lion King* skewed that circle of life.

I tried to play it cool. I really did. But when I dumped my tray and the rice ball *launched*—hit the floor and detonated like a starch grenade—panic set in. I froze. Scanned. No eyes on me. *Move.* Head down, I slipped away like nothing happened. Back in my cell. Heart pounding.

Then the voice rang out: "Eh, eh, eh, who the hell wen make dat mess!?" The guard was losing it, shouting in full pidgin fury. "What da F you *tink* you doing, eh? Ho sistah, you bettah get yo ass back ova hea and clean dat shit up before I make you eat da trash!"

I collapsed on the bed, muffling laughter with both hands.

Nikki stared at me like I'd lost my mind. I peeked through the slit in my door. The guard was still at it, sweeping and muttering and cursing under her breath.

"Guess who made that mess?" I whispered. Nikki lost it. For a minute, we weren't inmates. Just girls. Laughing. Alive.

* * * *

Sunday night, the nerves hit. I'd picked out the cutest little pantsuit for court. I was convinced it would win my case—until reality slapped me: drab green uniform, plastic hair comb, no makeup. I stared in the mirror, scowling.

"Ugh, I look horrible!"

Nikki hopped down from her bunk. "Trigo, use dis. Dis how we do it." She grabbed a pencil and Crest toothpaste, mixing them like it was science. "Mascara." Then two colored pencils. "Lipstick, red or pink?" I pointed. She shaved the pink, mixed it with Chapstick, and winked. "You jus' gotta make do, eh?"

I laughed. "Better than nothing."

Nikki slapped her leg, cackling. "Welcome to OCCC Salon! For big hair, use dis." She held up a roll of toilet paper. "Curlers, trust." Then came the final touch: a watermelon Jolly Rancher dissolved in a plastic cup. "Dip your toothbrush, flick it in. Prison hairspray."

"Genius," I said, fluffing my hair. "Not Oribe, but it holds."

Nikki laughed. "Not to da max, eh? But best we got."

That night, the door buzzed for free time, and I went full glam squad. Braiding, twisting, crooked parts—*90210* Kelly and Donna makeovers.

"Trigo, me next!" someone called.

By Monday morning, I was prison chic. Green uniform, DIY makeup. A braid I prayed wouldn't scream *criminal*. I looked in the mirror. No amount of lipstick could cover the shame. Still, I tried to see someone the judge might believe. Sweet. Normal. Worth saving.

In the Marshal van, I stared out the window, praying to a God I'd abandoned long ago. I remembered Makaha. Pastor Chuck's voice on cassette. Silent nights on the *lanai* with Dad stargazing. During the day, we'd watch the clouds drift by, searching for pictures in their shifting shapes. One day, Dad spotted a dragon. I saw the perfect Santa on a sleigh. It was just nice to be together again. All I wanted was that peace. Ocean air. Sky full of hope. Instead, I was headed into battle.

The courthouse felt colder than I remembered. My heart pounded as the guards walked me in—every step a new kind of walk of shame. Inside, Dad waited. Dan was there too. Smug. Ready to testify. I burned with rage, but my lawyer had warned me, "Don't speak to Dan. Don't look. Pretend he's a ghost." They kept me in a holding room while he testified.

Dad later filled me in. Dan was calm. Slimy. He smiled at the judge, like they were old friends. He lied. Said I knew about the drugs in my bag. Said I was a key player in a crime syndicate—our "organization." Gave me codenames: *Flawless. Tristar.* Painted me like I was poison. A threat to society.

"He's a snake," Dad hissed, his fists clenched.

Then it was my turn. To argue the motion to suppress, I had to take the stand. Face the DA, Lawrence Brown. I stuck to the script. Said I didn't know about the meth. Played the OC party girl—too dumb, too distracted, too high to be involved. Brown wasn't buying it.

"Maya Azad—did you smuggle drugs together before?"

"We traveled to Hawaii, yes. But I didn't have drugs."

He smirked. I held my poker face.

He continued, "Okay, Miss Trigo, let me ask you this. Have you accompanied Dan Miller to Hawaii when he was smuggling drugs?"

"Absolutely not," I lied, with conviction. I leaned into the defense: Wrong place, wrong time. No memory. No intent. Just a girl with bad taste in friends. I used every ounce of manipulation I had left.

"I do not recall," I repeated, again and again. The officers? Liars too. Adams claimed she never strip-searched me. Johnston swore the K-9 was certified—"to the best of their knowledge." But who would believe me over them? When it ended, I felt...okay. Not great. But not doomed. Then, the judge spoke.

Motion denied.

Trial next. I went numb. I wanted to disappear. Anywhere else. But there was one small win: I was released on bail. Back to the cabana. Back to the LoJack. Back to the ocean I couldn't swim in. Still, I was home. And I was with Dad. My best friend. And that—at least for now—was enough.

* * * *

I got back to the beach house, knowing the next step was jury selection. I still clung to Philip's promises—Agent Blue would get my charges dropped, but deep down, I was spiraling. Trial loomed. So I did what I'd always done: buried my head in the white sand and told myself it would all magically disappear. Then, I dug into my old church tapes, and slowly, things started to make sense. One thing was clear: I couldn't rely on Philip to save me. Only Jesus saves. Still, I was determined to fight. Those weren't my drugs. I had been set up.

A few days before my trial, Mom and Aunt Flo flew in. Despite feeling undeserving of their love, I felt it like a warm blanket. Family was everything. That...and, well, my freedom, of course.

* * * *

On the day of the big trial, September 19, 1995, I woke up with a pit in my stomach. The stress was crushing. I could barely move. My body hunched over like it was trying to protect me from what was coming. Still, I drew a breath. Told myself: *Hold it together. Just a little longer.* I had to stay strong—for my family, for myself. I braided my hair into a tight French braid and kept the makeup minimal. No glam, no party-girl image. Just Denise: present, awake, sober. I slipped into my red Bebe blazer with the matching A-line skirt and walked into the courtroom, trying to carry dignity with me. But walking into that room felt surreal.

Was all of this really for me?

The courtroom was packed. The witnesses the DA had flown in were staggering. FBI, DEA, Bureau of Narcotic Enforcement officers, members of the Marin County Major Crimes Task Force, the Central Contra Costa County Narcotic Enforcement Task Force, agents from the US Attorney's office. Even a technician from LA Cellular. All lined up to testify against me.

Dan was on the list. So were a bunch of drug dealers and John Does. That pregnant woman from the Hard Rock Café and—somehow—even Mrs. Knotts from Knott's Chicken. She was subpoenaed to verify security footage of me venting to Brandy.

My mother, Aunt Florence, Dad, and Dee were beside me. First time Mom and Dad had been in the same room in years. I knew it hurt her to see him. But she came for me. I think part of her realized that he had shown up for me, and somehow that softened the edges. Maybe even healed a sliver of something.

Still, I would've rather been watching the O.J. Simpson trial on TV. Instead, here I was—center stage in my own real-life legal circus.

I scanned the courtroom: lawyers, witnesses, court staff, and potential jurors. My heart pounded. Trials are unpredictable, no matter how innocent you feel. I tried to read the jurors' faces—blank, cold, unreadable. No smiles. No empathy. Just strangers holding my future in their hands.

The DA had warned my lawyer repeatedly: the federal conviction rate is 98 percent once you're indicted. That wasn't just a statistic—it was my death sentence. I felt like I was walking the plank.

If they found even the smallest shred of evidence that I had knowledge of the drugs, I would get fifteen years, minimum. And even by some miracle, if I beat those odds—the 2 percent who get acquitted—I still had a *second* federal case waiting in San Francisco. Conspiracy. Looking at ten years. Somehow, it wasn't considered double jeopardy. Just another nail in the coffin.

It wasn't me versus a crime. It was the United States of America versus Denise Trigo. Even *Kansas* had a bone to pick with me. As the pressure closed in from all sides, I understood that there was no escape. This was the defining moment of my life. It was time to stop burying my head in the sand, it was time to stand tall and face what was coming, head-on, because nothing was going to disappear. The truth was, once the jury was set, the trial would proceed full speed ahead, leaving no room for a plea agreement. Even though I didn't want to admit it, I knew Philip had been lying to me all along, stringing me along to keep me from testifying against him. And all the while, he was setting me up for up to thirty years in prison if I was found guilty. And *even if* he was dumb enough to believe Agent Blue, that didn't mean that I owed him anything. You can't just go around killing people.

I looked at my dad—his face pale, lips tight, eyes filled with worry. "I'm sorry, Daddy," I whispered.

He nodded. No anger. A silent understanding passing between us. We both knew. This battle—I wasn't going to win it.

My stomach flipped. Nausea rushed through me. My hands were shaking. I leaned into my lawyer, tapped his arm.

"I can't do this," I whispered. "I can't go through with the trial."

He stared at me. "Are you sure?"

I turned one last time—took in the courtroom, the jury, the walls closing in. My family. My dad.

Yes, I nodded. "Yes."

He immediately requested a recess to speak with the DA. The DA verbally agreed to ask for five years or less in federal prison *if* I cooperated fully. *I said I would.*

I'd tell them what I could remember—about me. I wasn't sure what I recalled about anyone else. All I knew was I didn't want to see anyone else rotting in a cell.

Prison is hell. I wouldn't wish it on anybody.

The DA asked the court to dismiss the jury. And just like that, my trial was over. Time to face the music.

I didn't know it at the time, but Judge Enzo had a nickname: "the hanging judge." Zero tolerance for drug dealers. Famous for throwing away the key.

"Miss Trigo, please step up to the bench."

He stared at me, his expression unreadable. "There are risks to a verbal plea agreement," he said, voice steady but hard. "Without anything in writing, you're putting your trust entirely in the DA and his word that he'll push for five years or less."

The words hit like cold steel. But what choice did I have? Jury trial meant gambling everything. I nodded, quietly.

"I understand, Your Honor."

And for the first time in a long time, I felt pride.

I wasn't giving up—I was choosing *me*. My life mattered. To me. To my family. I wasn't going to let it be erased over something I didn't do. So, I pled guilty to a crime I didn't commit just to ensure the shortest prison sentence possible, even though I was *completely* fucking innocent. My stomach churned. But I swallowed it.

Judge Enzo went down his list like a machine.

"Miss Trigo, are you of sound mind?"

The irony nearly made me laugh. *Sound mind? Fuck no*, I wanted to scream. But I smirked instead.

"Yes, Your Honor."

"Have you been coerced into making this plea?"

Inside, I screamed, *Yes. Yes. Hell yes.* All the calls from Lorenzo and Dan, all the pressure, all the lies. But I forced down the truth like poison. I couldn't break in front of the people who still believed in me.

"No, Your Honor."

"Is it true you flew to Hawaii on June 19, 1995?"

"Yes," I said. Voice flat. Disconnected.

"Is it true that you knew you were carrying five and a half pounds of crystal methamphetamine?"

My heart was pounding. My chest tight. I gripped the edge of the table to hold myself upright.

"No, I did not know the drugs were in my bag."

He paused—he didn't like that answer.

"Young lady," he said, eyes narrowing, "you're either admitting guilt today or you're not. I have a busy court calendar."

The heat climbed up my chest, my face. But I wouldn't lie.

"I can't say that I knew the drugs were in my bag. I didn't know." This time, I said it louder. Clearer.

His jaw clenched. His patience thinning. But he moved on.

"Did you know that your codefendant, Dan Miller, was bringing drugs on the plane to Hawaii?"

It was like a slap. "Yes," I answered quickly. "I knew he was committing a crime." I hesitated. "But I didn't realize that by knowing, I was committing one too."

He blinked. For just a second, something in his face shifted.

"A lot of young ladies don't know the law," he muttered.

Maybe it was pity. Maybe just tired truth. But it cut deep. Why didn't anyone teach us this? Why weren't we warned how fast the federal system could devour us? The questions ended. The wheels turned. I was being processed into the federal system, each second dragging me deeper into a nightmare I couldn't wake from.

But the DA wasn't finished. As a final fuck-you, they filed perjury charges for the lie I'd told on the stand during my motion to suppress. When I claimed I hadn't known about Dan. Two more points added to the sentencing.

The math hit like a freight train: 188 to 235 months in prison. Fines ranging from $17,500 to $4,000,000. And don't forget San Francisco, the organized crime charges waiting for me there.

Thirty years in federal prison. It didn't even feel real. I couldn't process it all at once. So I didn't. I compartmentalized it into boxes. *Just breathe. One step at a time.*

Easton worked like hell behind the scenes. He got the fine waived. He even petitioned Judge Enzo to merge the California charges into the Hawaii case. That shaved ten years off my sentence. A tiny win in a storm of losses. But one thing was crystal clear: I was going to federal prison. And there was nothing I could do about it. Bad to the bone?

Maybe. Rock bottom? Nah, I hadn't even seen the full drop yet. This was just the beginning. And I was going to have to fight like hell to survive what was coming next.

* * * *

Adams and DA Lawrence Brown wasted no time escorting me from the courtroom to their office in the federal courthouse. The door shut behind us. Cold air. Fluorescent lights. Adams lit a cigarette, then slid her pack and a lighter across the table to me. I wasn't a smoker, but she didn't ask.

"Here," she said, taking a long drag.

I hesitated, then took it. My hands shook as I brought it to my lips. The smoke burned, but it steadied me.

"I wish you'd talked to us sooner," Adams said, disappointment in her tone. "Could've been a whole different outcome. But here we are." She exhaled slowly. "Let me tell you what we know."

She dropped a thick file on the table and started talking. Dates, names, details—everything I already knew, but more.

"So, what the hell do you want from me then?" I asked, already knowing.

"Just the truth," she said flatly. "Denise, we already have it all. We just need you to admit your part."

Her words landed heavy. I couldn't protect Philip anymore, or anyone tied to James's or Lorenzo's deaths. He deserved prison, sure, but I didn't want them to count on me to do it. Adams seemed to know exactly what I was thinking.

"We have everyone, with or without you. Help yourself—everybody else is," she said coldly.

Then came the questions.

"Was Philip the cook in your drug organization?"

She spread the evidence across the table— witness statements, surveillance, the works. Basically, *he* was cooked. No sense jumping into the boiling pot with him, so I nodded.

"Yeah. He was the cook."

Adams smirked. "Skilled from what I hear. Proud of his work."

I let out a dry laugh.

"Yeah. A good one." I shook my head. What the hell was I even saying?

"Nothing's fly about cooking meth. That's like bragging you're a pedophile. It's filthy."

She nodded, eyes serious now.

"You're right about that."

Brown jumped in, "Do you know someone called 'the Mechanic'? He is one of your codefendants. Hawaii resident. Supposed to receive three pounds from Dan's shipment, twenty-two thousand a pound. The rest was going to Lorenzo's brother."

I shook my head. "No," I said. "I didn't know anything about the drugs you charged me with. Dan's a liar. I didn't even know they were in my bag. I don't know the Mechanic, either."

They barely reacted. They just wanted more.

"Were you involved in Lorenzo's death?" Brown asked. "Who killed him?"

I was exhausted but snapped, "Hellooooo, McFly? I was on house arrest in Hawaii when he was killed."

Thank God. Solid alibi. One thing they couldn't pin on me.

Then Adams shifted. "Eric Kekoa. Bought two pounds from your group in Hawaii. He's in Halawa prison now. Dan's testifying against him."

Of course he was.

"We want you to testify at Eric's trial."

Silence. Eric was not a monster. I did not want to bury him to save myself. Adams slid a stack of evidence toward me. Tapping her finger on Dan's statements, showing I was there when he sold to Eric.

"You're looking at fifteen to nineteen years," she said. "Tell the truth. All of it."

There was no going back.

"Yeah, I was around," I admitted. "But I don't remember much. I was high. *pakalolo*. Hawaiian weed's no joke."

It was the truth. Hard to argue with that.

Brown cut in, "Did Maya know about the sale?"

I paused.

"No. She was too high to know anything."

"You sure?" he pressed. "This could reduce your time significantly."

"I'm sure."

But Brown wasn't done.

"What about Maya? Does she know she is hanging out with drug dealers?"

I shrugged. "We never talked about it."

Everyone in Newport knew. Honestly, they could arrest all of Orange County.

He studied me. Then leaned back. "We'll talk again," he said.

Great. Can't wait.

Back in court, my mom was crying into my aunt's shoulder. Dad sat beside Dee. They looked up when I walked in. Then the shock. Judge Enzo released me to my family for the night. Not common, he said. I had until noon the next day to surrender.

Twenty-four hours. I was still on house arrest, so it wasn't like I could hit up the Mai Tai bar at the Royal Hawaiian, surf Waikiki or work on my tan without a care in the world.

"I think you should see a psychiatrist," Dee said. "Maybe they can prescribe something for the stress."

Sounded reasonable.

Or at least an excuse to get legally high. Maybe she could hypnotize me into thinking prison was summer camp.

So there we were at a psychiatrist's office—me, my mom, my dad, Dee, and Aunt Flo—sitting together for the first time in what felt like forever. My mom locked eyes on Dad's hand, intertwined with Dee's, resting far too comfortably on her leg—I could tell it bothered my mom. *Good Lord.* The psychiatrist looked around the room with her best *calm professional* expression. "So, what brings you all in today?" she asked gently.

I shifted, caught like a deer in headlights. "I'm going to prison tomorrow. Could use something for anxiety."

She blinked. Definitely not the answer she expected. "Would you mind explaining?"

I rambled. Drugs. Wrong place. Wrong decisions.

Then she asked the question I was dying to hear: "Does everyone *need* to be here?"

Mom was ready. "That's my *ex*-husband," she said, pointing at Dad, who shrank into his chair. "He cheated and left me for a younger woman." I could practically hear Dad groaning internally. Then, she gestured to Dee. "And *this* one? His third wife."

Perfect. My last day of freedom, and now we are in post-divorce counseling? I was twenty-seven, facing prison time, and somehow *this* was still the mess I was stuck in.

Eventually, the doctor wrote the prescriptions: Tranxene for anxiety and Ambien to help me sleep. Small mercy.

Back at the cabanas, I hugged my mom and Aunt Flo goodbye, but I kept it together—for them. I wrote letters to my brothers, pretending I was brave. But I was terrified and trying to convince *myself* I'd be okay.

There was no end in sight. I didn't know when I'd be free again. I had no control over my life. It was all gone. I wasn't some badass rebel with a plan. I was just a scared girl with a pen, wishing she could turn back time. I wanted to curl up in my parents' arms and pretend this wasn't real, but they couldn't save me now.

Packing my white bikini, cosmetics, and keepsakes, I felt the weight of the life I was losing. It had been so nice being with Dad here. I'm really going to miss this. Everything felt surreal, like it wasn't happening. But it was.

The next morning felt like my funeral. It was also my aunt Flo's birthday. We went to breakfast. It felt like the Last Supper. I wanted spicy Mexican food, but they didn't serve it until lunch, and I wouldn't be around for that. Instead, I drank a banana shake. Solid food felt impossible.

At the courthouse, I hugged my mom tight. "I love you. I'll be okay. I promise."

I nodded, trying to believe it myself.

She wiped a tear. "Call and write as soon as you can."

I turned to Dee. "Thank you for everything. I'm gonna miss hanging out with you."

She squeezed my hand and smiled, but her eyes were heavy with worry.

Dad pulled me in. "Sweetie, honey, cutie—you got this, Corleone."

I laughed, a broken little sound lodged in my throat. I was dying inside.

Then Aunt Flo took me aside. One last hug. One last truth bomb.

"Not only are you going to get through this," she said, her grip firm, "but you're going to have a better life when you get out."

I nodded, eyes stinging.

"You can handle it. Right? You can handle it!"

I tried to match her energy. "I can handle this!" I said, voice cracking. It felt like a line from a play. But saying it out loud made it real—made it mine.

Maybe it was her birthday. Maybe it was sheer survival instinct. But I stood a little taller, wiped my tears, and turned away without looking back. If I did, I'd never leave.

At noon sharp, I pushed open the courthouse doors and passed through the cold metal detectors. My flip-flops clicked against the marble floor, each step echoing in the emptiness. At the check-in desk, the guard glanced at the two pill bottles in my hand.

"You can't bring those in. If you want one, take it now."

So I did the only thing that made sense in the moment—I took all of them. A full handful of anti-anxiety pills and sedatives, swallowed dry, in one go. *Fuck it.* Given the anxiety I had, it felt like the right dose. And I wasn't wrong.

By the time I was processed and back at OCCC, the best way to describe my state was "really fucking high." Floating. Weightless. Euphoric. I waved at the guards like we were old friends. Said hi to everyone like I was back at FVHS chatting in the quad between classes. The fear? The grief? The crushing unknown? Gone. For now.

The next morning, it slammed back in. Fully aware. I was not going anywhere for a long time.

I stepped into the common area. The air was thick and stale. Girls in cliques, lounging, chatting, passing time. Kind of like happy hour.... Just without the booze and happiness.

Charlotte sat near the back, legs crossed, cool as ever. When she spotted me, she straightened and smirked.

"Look who's finally walking," she called out. "You sure looked good last night." She laughed, eyes gleaming with mischief. "You were so gone, the guard had to send Ava to iron Trigo onto your pocket. You could barely stand."

I didn't remember a thing. I shifted, muttering, "I was…on some pills."

The haze was still thick in my mind. Sitting down, I learned the unspoken rule: federal female inmates were like a bad-girl gang. We stuck together. Guards treated us better—more respect, more empathy—probably because we faced serious time for "high-class" crimes: tax evasion, money laundering, counterfeiting, or the uglier stuff—bank robbery, organized crime, drug trafficking. Anything that digs deep into Uncle Sam's pocket.

I wasn't about to turn down the perks. So, the few federals stuck together, mingling with the pretrial state prisoners, until we got transferred.

Charlotte—calm, respected, and seasoned. Arrested for bank robbery with guns, she faced serious years. She'd done time before and knew the ropes. She took me under her wing, with some tough love. When I complained about the Island, she reminded me it was her home—a place she hoped to return to. She schooled me in respect for Hawaiian culture, the land I'd poisoned with drugs.

My new bunkie, Nicole, was nine years older, infamous for a drug case that rocked the Island. She and her husband were top dogs, about to buy a golf course when they got busted for running a major drug ring—connected to mine. Her operation sold the drugs Philip cooked in California, ordered by Lorenzo, with materials I'd gotten from Juan. We slowly pieced it together. If we'd just cut out the middlemen, we could've been rich bitches on that golf course instead of cellmates in matching green suits.

Time slowed in prison. On Tuesday, October 3—my brother Jeff's birthday—the guards let us out to watch the trial of the century: O.J. Simpson. Before I'd been arrested, I'd track every twist with Mom and Greg. Now, inmates and guards crowded the small TV. When the verdict came—not guilty—the courtroom erupted, and the prison cheered along. O.J.'s smirk was disbelief and triumph. But me. I was bitter. The bloody glove didn't fit O.J.'s hand? Fine. But what about Dan's yachting jacket that was way too big for me? To me, the trial had become a circus of racial politics, not justice. And here I was—in prison—while he walked free.

We were also allowed to write letters to guys we met in the system. Inmate-to-inmate mail, called jail mail. Prisoners passed federal ID numbers around like digits at a bar. You'd think by then I'd start picking better men, or better yet, give up entirely. But let's be real: I was bored, and those were the only men around. Whether it was in passing, on the Marshal's van, in court, or eventually on flights, it was like prison Tinder meets Raya, before apps were even a thing. People took it seriously.

Still new to prison politics, I clung to sassy, fiery Denise—that part of me hadn't been beaten down yet—and yeah, I got into some fights. In prison, you don't fight over big things; you fight over whatever shred of dignity you have left. *That's my shower. That's my pencil. That's my fucking book.* It's meaningless shit that shouldn't matter, but your world shrinks so quickly and so drastically, you cling to whatever you can. So, when a rowdy Island girl named Choy Foo stole my shower, I snapped.

"Idiot," I muttered, ducking into another stall. Bad move.

Next thing I knew, a V05 shampoo bottle clocked me in the head mid-scrub. I whipped around, naked and pissed, and there she was—Choy Foo—towering, furious. She was huge. I grew up with two older brothers, so I knew when I was about to lose. My only goal? Protect the face, save the teeth.

Guards rushed in. She was still wailing on me as I hit the floor, ribs taking the worst of it. Did I mention I was still naked? Humiliation, screaming—and then came the punishment: SHU. The hole. Segregated Housing Unit. But those were the prison rules. It didn't matter if Foo attacked me first; if you were involved in a physical altercation, you got punished, even if it wasn't your fault.

I was terrified. I'd heard stories—cockroaches that looked at you like, *What the fuck are you doing in my space?* Turns out, true. I named a few: Freddy Krueger, Michael Myers.

The SHU cell was the same size but colder, darker. A small window. Books were allowed, but it was a far cry from Rizzoli's—no glossy new releases or bestsellers like you'd find at Waldenbooks, just a steady stream of old Harlequin romance novels. No phone, no smoke breaks, no visits. You could talk to your lawyer, but that was it. Showering meant backing up to the door so guards could cuff you. Then you'd shuffle to a stall with a steel door, get five minutes of warm water, and shuffle back. The whole routine was overkill. I wasn't the Night Stalker. I was just a girl from OC who got in one naked shampoo brawl.

Weeks passed. I lost track of time. I read every romance novel on the book cart. I missed people. I missed the phone, my dad, my mom. Then, finally, they told me I'd be transferred to a county jail on the mainland to await sentencing. The morning of the move, they let me out to shower—and make one last mistake.

As I passed Choy Foo's cell—still locked up—I stuck out my tongue.

"I'm leaving early. Headed to California," I teased, singing like a bratty child, "Na na na na na…" Real mature, I know.

Her eyes narrowed to slits. "I'll see you again, Trigo. And when I do, I'm going to kill you."

Chills. She meant it.

Still, I was glad to go. Even shackled and chained, getting off that island felt like freedom. If I'd stayed, I wouldn't have lasted long. Not with a target on my back.

Chapter Eighteen

The Jailhouse Shuffle

OCTOBER 1995

As I walked between the modules of OCCC, I tilted my face to the sun, soaking in what might be my last bit of warmth and daylight for a while. Just before I stepped into the US Marshal's van, I saw the group I'd be traveling with: all men. I was the only woman.

Back in the day, I never went anywhere alone. I always had a bathroom buddy—someone to stand guard, fix our lipstick, and walk out with a plan. Now I had no one. Just me. *Girlfella.* A girl in a man's world, surrounded by drooling inmates. I guess I asked for this.

At the Honolulu airport, I was shackled and chained to the guys and led through a back security door onto a United Airlines plane. The chains were so heavy I could barely shuffle down the aisle. We took the last rows—a small relief not to be paraded through the terminal like some tourist attraction.

Soon, the plane filled up—families, honeymooners, all blissfully unaware of the chain gang in the back. But once we landed, the Marshals got to work. They unzipped duffle bags, and the loud clank of shackles snapped everyone to attention as we taxied to the gate. My first steps back on the mainland in nearly six months were in perfect lockstep with eight other inmates. It felt like "Back on the Chain Gang" by the

Pretenders. With two Marshals per prisoner, we made a scene striding through San Francisco airport—people stared, mothers pulled their kids away. So much for a triumphant return to California.

I didn't think it could get worse. Boy was I wrong.

I found out I was being transferred to a facility called Santa Rita. According to other Federal Girls, it was the Worst Fucking Place in the Universe. Santa Rita was the third-largest jail in California, fifth in the nation—a mega jail holding more than four thousand inmates across 113 acres. Forty percent were hardened Oakland gang members and street junkies. If I had attracted the worst of affluent Orange County, what fresh hell awaited me here?

Before general population, a heavyset female guard led me into a private room. "Remove your clothing," she ordered, snapping on rubber gloves. Jail had already stripped me down, but this? Next level. I stripped, shivering on the cold linoleum as she inspected every inch.

"Turn around. Spread your legs. Squat," she ordered me. "Wider. Spread your lips. I want to see the pink."

Well, hot damn—did she want to see my ovaries too? Eyes shut, I complied.

"Cough. Arms out. Run fingers through your hair. Show me the bottoms of your feet."

When it was finally over, I pulled on a tattered yellow jumpsuit. They tossed me a pair of dingy granny panties, marked "S" for small in permanent black ink. I prayed they were not used.

As we walked past other inmates, I noticed different uniform colors.

"What do the colors mean?" I asked.

"Santa Rita color-codes by threat level and charges. Blue's medium security, red is for PC or segregation." She looked me over. "Yellow means serious charges or violence history."

I smiled at the absurdity. But at this point, I had to go with it. Part of me registered it as street cred, whether I wanted it or not. The rest of me wanted to disappear.

Clutching my bedroll, I was marched into the night, floodlights making it feel like midday. A monstrous steel door creaked open. Inside, two TVs blared, and inmates whistled. Great. That again. I hesitated. Repulsed, I stepped back. The guard shoved me in. The door hissed shut behind, like a cage locking at the zoo. I climbed a staircase into a massive steel cage: rows of triple-stacked bunks. I searched for my number stenciled on the side of the bunk railings, gagging on the human filth and smell of burnt hair. My bunk was in the middle, sandwiched between metal frames, no room to breathe.

I unfolded my bedding, trying to pick the least disgusting end that I would have to lay my face on. I actually missed Choy Foo's threats and reading steamy Harlequin romances. At least the SHU had privacy. I forced myself to sleep, clinging to the thought of calling my dad. I needed to hear him say, "Everything will be all right, Denise." I had to stay strong for him.

The next morning, loud clanking snapped me awake. The yellow cage door swung open, and we were herded downstairs. Girls rushed to the phones and vending machines. The scene looked even worse in daylight—overcrowded and chaotic. Santa Rita was mostly black and Latino. A few Pacific Islanders. Hardly any white girls. I stuck out like a sore thumb. Normally, I didn't mind, but here, I'd give anything to blend in. Most of the girls were in bad shape—*tore up from the floor up*, as they say. But I was on a mission to find a friend.

Luckily for me, a pretty twenty-two-year-old Latina named Olivia found me first.

"Hey," she said. "Want to borrow some shampoo and conditioner? I'll share till you get commissary."

Now she was speaking my language.

"Thanks, I just got in last night."

"I know," she said, grinning. "I was the one who whistled when you walked in—just messing with you."

"Oh my God, you freaked me out!"

"That was the whole point," she said, smirking.

Olivia and I became fast friends. She showed me the ropes, but she was nothing like my OC girls—she was a straight-up gangster. She spoke the language of prison and the street rules like it was second nature. I respected her instantly; she'd already done two years and didn't even know how much time she was getting.

"I'm probably looking at a dime," she said, like it was no big deal.

In jail, time earns you clout. Long-timers are calm, focused, and drama-free. They've got routines, wisdom, and respect. Rookies and short-timers? Loud, obnoxious, always stirring shit up—the worst dorm-mates imaginable.

Olivia gave me the lay of the land. Women here battled everything from HIV and Hep C to TB. The guards didn't care. They just tossed you in with everyone else. Prostitutes detoxed in their bunks—vomiting, shaking, soaked in sweat. One woman limped past with an untreated bullet wound, oozing pus. Another scratched herself raw from some skin condition.

And the showers? Besides the cold water, let's just say people smuggled in drugs and crapped them out right there—no cleanup crew in sight.

And then there was the food. I didn't need chicken and capers like Jeff, but even OCCC's shredded pork stew was gourmet compared to this. Breakfast was a plastic tray of horrors—two hard-boiled eggs, which I pocketed for later, and a brown lunch sack with green bologna between soggy bread.

God, what I would've given for an Italian sub.

I thought, *I'm going to starve in here.*

Eventually, my parents put money on my books, and I survived on Top Ramen and vending machine candy bars. I love ramen, but living on sodium and sugar is a culinary felony. Whoever ran the Santa Rita's kitchen and commissary? That's the real criminal.

Wearing my yellow jumpsuit, white tube socks, and flip-flops, I spent my days on the front lines, nursing junkies back to life. It made me feel useful. My heart especially broke for Jasmine, "Jazzy," a petite, pretty black woman stuck in the cycle of prostitution and addiction. I found her curled up one day, writhing in withdrawal. Olivia and I got her through it with cold rags, hot ramen, and candy bars to keep her sugar up. Jazzy would always swear she'd stay clean after release. She never did.

She kept coming back—barely alive. Olivia and I would be nursing her again, sending her off with hope, and bracing ourselves for her return.

What got me was the revolving door. Women detoxed, got better, got released...and came right back. Over and over. It made me furious. They got endless chances. It wasn't fair.

God, are you there?

Hello? Can I get just one chance?

But even though I'd never met or sold drugs to these women, I couldn't ignore the bigger picture: I'd played a role in their suffering, and now I had to own it—no matter how hard it was to face.

More federal cases trickled in from Hawaii, and I reunited with Nicole and Charlotte. I also met Lefty—named for always being by your side, a true ride-or-die. She grew up in San Pedro, just twenty minutes north of Fountain Valley. Tough as nails, sweet as pie. We laughed constantly—at ourselves, our situation, the absurdity of it all. *Groundhog Day* in hell. Same wake-up call, different flavor of misery. But they'd say, "Trigo, thank God you're here. I couldn't get through this without you." Guess I didn't get voted "Most Humorous" in eighth grade for nothing. Who knew that humor would make me "Most Likely to Survive" in here?

But inside, I was drowning. The stress was brutal. I didn't know how long I'd be here. Couldn't sleep—too loud during the day, and at night, someone next to me snored like a bear in heat. It was torture.

At first, my jail time turned into a popularity contest back home. If social media had been a thing, I would've gone viral, trending for six months straight. Everyone wrote letters, all desperate to prove they were my ride-or-die, the one who knew me best. But really, it was about who could squeeze the most sympathy out of my loss.

And they weren't wrong. My life was a loss. I might've been walking and breathing, but inside? I felt like the walking dead.

I didn't even realize the seasons were changing. Normally there were signs—leaves turning amber, a sharp bite in the morning air. Outside, the world would've been sliding into the holidays. Department stores would smell like pine and peppermint. The radio would bring back Mariah Carey and Wham!'s "Last Christmas"—my favorite.

Growing up, the holidays were special. The Trigos loved gathering around the TV to watch *Christmas Vacation*, cozy by the fireplace where our stockings hung, stuffed with a Lifesaver hard candy storybook.

The only reminder of the outside came from volunteers singing carols, hoping to lift our spirits. I don't think they knew what they'd signed up for. They could barely get through "Jingle Bells" without crying once they saw us trapped in our cages. Olivia and I just lay back on our bunks and closed our eyes.

And just like that, I was back in my childhood—my large, extended family sitting around tables piled high with food. I could almost taste my mom's lasagna, the crispy breaded chicken Milanese, Romano-and-parsley-stuffed sausages and peppers that Aunt Gina made. Olives, cheeses, and salami on platters next to Aunt Flo's slow roasted lamb. We tore pieces from a rustic Italian loaf to soak up Nonna's bright *salmoriglio* sauce, with mint, lemon, and olive oil. After the adults played chess and cards, we gathered on the green shag carpet beneath the nine-foot flocked Christmas tree, the smell of espresso in the air, eating cannolis, *struffoli*, *sfingi*, and biscotti that Aunt Mary baked while we opened presents.

I chuckled remembering the year Greg got busted on Christmas by Aunt Mary. She found white cocaine residue on top of her toilet but Greg blamed the white powder on her. "Oh that has nothing to do with you walking around in that Santa hat putting powdered sugar on the *sfingis*." Classic Trigo Christmas. My cousins and I couldn't stop laughing.

It hurt to think about my family, but these memories were my lifeline. I couldn't lose sight of the outside world or forget who I was, where I came from, and the people who loved me. Forgetting that would've meant losing hope. I needed to remember home—not just to survive, but to stay whole.

It was a delicate balance—holding on without holding too tight, letting go without getting lost. I was determined not to come out of the system broken. God quietly guided me, giving just enough strength to get through each day.

Holidays stopped feeling like milestones. They all became just another day, time served.

And since there were no classes to take, I dove headfirst into jail mail. Forever boy crazy—of course I did.

Jail mail was like a prison version of the show *Melrose Place*: everyone in everyone's business, full of love triangles and betrayal. Inmates swapped booking numbers like dating app handles, getting hooked up by friends of friends. Soon, everyone had a stack of letters at mail call. Fights, heartbreaks, meltdowns, even marriage proposals—all via letters.

I had a pen pal named Kealii who went full jealous boyfriend mode. He demanded exclusivity. Ha! Not a chance. I dumped him in a letter, asked him not to write anymore. Of course, that backfired. He spread rumors that Hawaiian Marshal Grant and I were having an affair. Then he sent a crude drawing—legs spread, arrow pointing to the slit, captioned: "U.S. Marshal inserts here." Naturally, the rumor spread like California wildfires. Internal Affairs pulled me in for questioning.

Despite how I felt about the government, everyone in there got along with the Hawaiian Marshals. Grant and I having an affair? Ha, no, and Grant didn't get canceled—Kealii did. He got shipped off to Danbury, Connecticut. Bye, island boy. Enjoy the snow.

Jail mail could feel like an endless awkward date—dudes rambling about nothing. Then there was Antonio. He begged me to write back. I finally did and told him I wouldn't respond unless he was a Wall Street mogul caught in an insider trading scandal, a coke-running drug lord or a rock-star rebel. A girl's gotta have standards—even in here.

His reply? One word: *"Bitch."* Honestly? It felt good. Sometimes being a bitch is all you've got to remind yourself who you are. I was still Denise Trigo. I could still get under people's skin.

Eventually, I tuned out the drama and found something real—my homies. We encouraged one another, prayed together, kept each other sane. Friendship turned out to be worth more than any fake jailhouse romance. Even with family in my corner, there was a unique bond among us. We leaned on each other, grounded each other, and reminded each other we weren't alone.

Eventually, I got an "in" with one of the laundry orderlies. My buddy hooked me up with a crisp yellow jumpsuit, fresh sheets, and actual clean underwear—and in those "new" clothes, I felt like a queen. Sure, I looked like Woodstock from Peanuts—a tiny bird in a cage—but at least my clothes were clean. I hand-washed everything in the shower. I would've loved to hang it all on a clothesline, let the California air work its magic. Instead, I draped it over the edge of my bunk and hoped for the best. That bright-yellow jumpsuit was mine, and damn it, I was proud. There wasn't much else to be proud of. And I didn't know when or if I'd ever feel proud again.

* * * *

Surviving on eggs, Snickers, and ramen, I worked out with Olivia in the sliver of space between our stacked bunk beds. No fancy Pilates machines here. Just the old-school "hold-my-ankles-while-I-do-sit-ups" routine. But it was enough.

I talked to my dad every day, caught quick calls with my mom while she worked, and forced myself to take naps when I could. Sounds almost cozy, right? Except for the constant noise, the filth, and sleeping inches from convicted criminals. Then again, I guess I was one too.

One day, my routine got interrupted. I heard my name over the intercom. Released? Family visit? A girl could dream.

Instead, I was led to a small room, where Agent Rick Bloom shook his head and said, "I feel sorry for you, Denise."

Apparently, I looked worse than I realized. I hadn't seen a mirror in more than six months.

Then he handed me a McDonald's Happy Meal. Nice gesture, sure, but I would've killed for a Caesar salad, and a chicken cutlet. Or anything remotely healthy. He skipped the small talk and jumped straight into questions. I stuffed soggy fries in my mouth, answered what I could, and kept the rest to blank stares. I knew better than to say too much.

After what felt like forever, he sighed. "I'll come back later. Try to remember more." Then, almost as an afterthought: "Want me to bring you anything from the outside?"

Where do you even start with that? The list was a mile long. But I managed, "Face moisturizer. That might help me remember things."

He blinked, confused. Thought I was joking. I wasn't.

That's the thing about the Feds—you never get a heads-up when you're being transferred. The DA and the DEA decided it was time to send me back to Hawaii. Fine by me. The repetition was soul-killing. Honestly? Aside from facing that smug DA, I almost looked forward to the travel and the stares. Movement meant stimulation. A reminder that a real world still existed—plants, birds, children, clouds.

After an uneventful journey, a sleepover at OCCC, and a quick aloha smoke break in the sun, the Marshals' van pulled up. There they were—my two favorites, Abigail and Grant.

"Aloha, Denise. Nice to see you," Abigail said.

Grant's eyes softened, the kind that say, "I wish I could hug you." Instead, he said, dead serious, "Hey, D. Don't talk to the prisoner behind you. And whatever you do, don't hit him. You're fucked if you do."

I blinked. "Why? Who is it?"

They exchanged a look and opened the van door.

And there he was—Dan.

The flea on the rat who planted the drugs in my bag. Time slowed. I'd dreamed of this moment. I climbed in, said nothing, and stared straight ahead. The ride was silent. But I could feel him behind me, squirming, trying to find a crack in my armor.

Finally: "I'm sorry, Flawless. I'm so sorry."

Pathetic. Sorry is not good enough.

"You did this to me!" I snapped. "I'm here because of you! You lied and said I *knew* the drugs were in my bag!"

"I thought you knew," he mumbled.

Unbelievable. Even now, he couldn't own it.

"How the hell would I know you put drugs in my bag when I wasn't even there? There's a difference between *thinking* I knew and me actually knowing!" I shook my head, rage giving way to sadness. "I told you I wanted nothing to do with any drug deal."

"I know," he said. "I'm sorry."

I hesitated. "Is it true? Did Lorenzo set us up?"

Dan shrugged. "Kinda, but not really."

When we got out, the Marshals separated us. Abigail came over to my holding cell, eyebrows raised.

"Wow," she said. "Grant and I heard everything. Sounds like you're pretty much innocent, girl. I'm backing Grant—he always defended you. Looks like he was right."

But none of it mattered.

Under federal law, knowing someone is carrying and saying nothing? It's just as bad as carrying it yourself.

Yeah. I'd learned that the hard way.

* * * *

After Hawaii, I was headed back to Santa Rita—not alone. I'd be traveling with Claire, a new prisoner. One of my pen pals was her codefendant and asked me to look out for her—she was struggling. I knew exactly how that felt, so I promised to show her the ropes.

Claire was a quiet, shame-filled Asian girl caught picking up a dope package at the airport. She sobbed hysterically as we shuffled through the airport, wrists shackled and ankles chained. Me? I was used to this shit. I even gave a "whas-up" nod to a cute guy sipping Starbucks and reading the sports page.

The Marshals laughed. "Denise, no shame?"

"What? He was cute!" I said.

But really, it was for Claire, to remind her we're human, even looking like monsters, we had to keep our heads up. I was making peace with my situation—mostly. Didn't stop me from wishing the plane would blow up and spare me another day in Santa Rita.

Others got transferred too—Olivia, Charlotte, Lefty, Nicole—my posse, all waiting for sentencing. Along with them came a message from Choy Foo: "Tell Trigo, I haven't forgotten about her." Great—just what

I needed. Now I have to worry about her mangling my face, the only thing I've got left going for me.

The street junkies called me "Lil Bit," but they knew I didn't take shit. When the gates buzzed and we rushed to the phone, I got to the front by being firm: "I have an important call."

They stepped aside quietly. "Don't mess with Lil Bit, she's crazy," they'd say. Prison was like the streets—I wasn't from Compton, but I ran the OC block, green palms and all.

I tried calling my mom at the café, but the line was busy. It wasn't like back in the late '70s when I could dial the operator and ask for an emergency breakthrough. I always tried to talk to my family. Sometimes I'd make collect calls to the manager at Mossimo in South Coast Plaza, years before Moss and Lori made headlines for that college admissions scandal.

But I wasn't lying back on my bed, gossiping with friends on my white coil phone—graphic tee, knee-high socks. I was in a bright jumpsuit, standing by the cages on the payphone, people glaring over my shoulder. I wanted to scream, *I'm on the damn phone, use another one, bitch!* Instead, I forced a sweet smile and said, "Sorry, it's about my case. I'll be off soon."

Told you—I knew how to handle myself in prison.

* * * *

To understand the people I was mixed up with, I have to tell you what happened while I was on house arrest—the days leading up to Lorenzo's murder.

While plans, paranoia, and cover-ups were in motion, I was stuck at the Makaha Beach Cabanas in Hawaii, staring at the endless blue waves, thinking maybe the worst was behind me and I would win my trial. That was the naïve me. I pieced it all together later. From Brandy, from court documents, from whispers that became testimony.

Here's what I know. Charles called Brandy in the middle of the night to come over.

When Philip opened the door, it wasn't exactly the booty call she had in mind. I could just imagine her thinking *Boooo. No fun. Total buzzkill.*

Philip ordered, "Drive."

They pulled up to the Villa Balboa condos in Newport Beach.

Three cars. Four people.

Lorenzo's body was in the El Camino trunk—wrapped in a tarp, just a few feet away.

Philip threw some luggage in Brandy's car, jumped in the El Camino, and said, "Follow me. Don't lose us."

Weird, Philip never drove.

They crawled along the 405, five under the speed limit, trying not to get noticed, ending up in a Denny's parking lot. Philip told her to wait.

She went inside to use the bathroom, passing two highway patrol officers sipping coffee.

She could've said something. *Anything.*

Instead, she kept going.

Back in the car, Philip was losing it. Screaming, demanding to know who was testifying against me. Wait, I had a hit man in my corner? I would've been screaming across the Pacific, *Hellooo, pick Dan, pick Dan!* But Brandy didn't know anything—how was she supposed to?

Eventually, he threw socks over his hands, handed Charles cash and a bag "to get cleaned," then told Brandy to drive to Maya's place.

When they arrived, Maya took one look at Brandy and asked, "They killed Lorenzo, didn't they?"

Brandy's hysteria began to rise.

Maya shoved her out of her bedroom. "You're gonna get us both killed," she hissed, slamming the door.

Before leaving, Philip put a smaller bag in Brandy's trunk. "Bring it into your house. Don't open it."

Duh, of course she did.

At home, socks over her hands like Philip, she unzipped it.

Inside, a gun.

Panicked, she shoved it in the back of her closet.

A few days later, Charles took it to Newport Beach and paddled out at the Wedge to toss it in the ocean.

Goodbye, murder weapon.

Later, Brandy found a black leather book Philip had stashed in her house. Inside: a $50,000 cashier's check marked "Final payment—Agent Blue," and one of Lorenzo's credit cards.

Lorenzo's DNA was everywhere.

She told Philip's goon, Fred.

Fred naturally told Philip.

Soon, Philip was at her door. "I hear you're having some issues."

She tried to play it cool. "I'm fine."

He didn't buy it.

Ordered her to her room like a child.

She snuck out to the balcony and overheard them talking.

They weren't planning to kill her—yet.

Just keeping her under lockdown.

From then on, someone was with her 24/7.

Philip told Charles to get rid of Lorenzo's designer clothes. Charles kept them.

Later, one of his friends wore Lorenzo's shirt to a club.

Philip lost it, tried to kill Charles by loosening his lug nuts.

Charles caught it before the car crashed—then finally went to the cops.

He offered to testify against Philip, hoping for immunity.

Cops told him he should've come forward sooner.

Now he was facing two and a half years in prison.

Ha. Welcome to the party, Charlie.

By that point, I still didn't know the full story—who, what, or where it all went down. Philip, Fred, and Duane were starting to feel the heat, and the FBI launched a nationwide manhunt. Brandy was done being scared. She was ready to take them all down. Hell, we were all sick of it. Shit was about to go B.A.N.A.N.A.S.

* * * *

Meanwhile, Eric Kekoa was locked up at Halawa Correctional Facility in Oahu. He refused a plea bargain, fighting Dan's claims of drug involvement all the way to trial. As part of my guilty plea, I had to implicate everyone I'd been involved with. So, I was called back to Hawaii to testify against Eric. Dan had already told them I was present when he sold to Eric on that first drug run. *Ugh.*

I went in heavy-hearted. The DA wanted me and Dan to bury Eric. Dan would spill every detail he could remember, or invent enough to nail him. But I didn't want Eric's conviction on my conscience. He was a good guy. If anyone deserved prison, it was Dan.

At the federal courthouse, the US Marshals locked Dan, Eric, and me in separate holding cells. Eric's was next to me; Dan's was across the hall behind a thick wooden door. Between the men's and women's sides was a two-way mirror where inmates could see and quietly talk to each other.

I ended up next to Eric.

"Listen," he murmured, catching my eye in the reflection. "I know Lorenzo started this, and Dan betrayed you. I know you didn't cave at the airport. You fought hard and didn't rat anyone out. I respect that. You've got more balls than any of the men. And I know you gotta do what you gotta do today. It's okay."

I smiled. "Thanks, I appreciate that. Hey, Eric, don't worry. Seriously, everything's going to be okay. Trust me."

Eric took a deep breath, raised his fists, let out a shout, and knocked out ten push-ups. Pure adrenaline, shaking off the pressure.

Then Abigail showed up in a blue flowered aloha shirt and handed me a business card.

"Dan wanted me to give this to you," she said quietly, shaking her head. "He's a real piece of work. Nobody likes him."

The card read: *Join the Dan Miller Prayer Train.*

I laughed and asked the Marshal to pass it to Eric. Then, like it was rehearsed, we started yelling through the wooden door, cussing Dan out and calling him every name we could think of. The only train I was praying for was one that would run him over.

In court, Dan testified. I'm sure he twisted everything to nail Eric. When it was my turn, I started crying so hard I could barely breathe.

The supervising Marshal leaned in, patted my arm. "Just do your best. Say what you know. Don't worry about Eric. Help yourself. You don't owe anybody anything. Nobody would do it for you, Denise. Wise up—you just need to move forward."

I wiped my tears. Game time.

On the stand, I told the truth. Yes, drugs changed hands—but details? Gone. I couldn't remember where it happened—the house or restaurant, how the drugs were carried, a duffel or shopping bag, or where the money went. Dan's fanny pack? I'd been drunk, high, and self-absorbed.

My testimony of guesses didn't back up Dan's story. As a result, Eric was acquitted of all charges. Thanks to my testimony, the DA promised a lighter sentence—eventually.

Eric walked free. I imagined him sipping Mai Tais in the Jacuzzi I'd once sat in. I was happy for him. But dread settled in as I thought about returning to OCCC.

In the end, it felt like a miracle. I had prayed for a reduced sentence without destroying anyone else in the process. I learned God would never leave me, even in my darkest moments.

* * * *

Fate eventually caught up to Philip and Duane. They were tipped off and arrested at a DMV in New Jersey while trying to score fake IDs to flee the country.

Philip's capture made headlines. The Feds, DEA, and district attorneys from both Hawaii and California were on top of it. Robert Mueller, then head of the FBI; Kamala Harris; and the families of victims—James and Lorenzo—were all pulled into the case.

Philip's arrest meant Hawaii's district attorney Lawrence Brown, and California's US attorney Dominic Hayes, would likely call me to testify if the case went to trial, dangling the possibility of a recommendation of five years or less. *Just great.*

Philip faced capital murder charges for the deaths of Lorenzo and James. A life sentence was possible, with a death sentence looming over him.

My lawyer advised delaying my sentencing until after Philip's trial. That left me stuck in limbo at county jail, with no idea when I'd be getting out.

I would have given *anything* to send Philip a message telling him to pick a jury—because after that, all his charges were supposedly going to magically disappear. Agent Blue said so.

I learned not to worry. When anxiety spiked, I called my dad. He and Dee reminded me that 85 percent of what we worry about never happens.

They were convinced Philip wouldn't risk trial and execution. There were too many witnesses against him.

In truth, I was a nobody in this case. So, to avoid getting "canceled" by the Feds, I played the hand they dealt me, figuring I'd find a way to win the game later.

In the meantime, I leaned on God.

Fred, ever the show-off, got arrested too. He landed on *America's Most Wanted* after a customer at a Cuban restaurant in Miami recognized him and tipped off the Feds. When they busted in, Fred couldn't resist the spotlight, cracking jokes as they cuffed him. As they led him out, he looked at the stunned customer and joked, "What? No tip?"

The chatter was nonstop. People were folding, pointing fingers. With mandatory minimum federal sentences, no one wanted to take the fall if they could hand it to someone else. I just prayed Philip would do the same, so I wouldn't be dragged into court.

Meanwhile, Dan the Weasel got seven months and walked free.

Seven months! Just…fucking speechless.

Because there was no federal inmate housing in Hawaii yet, I got shipped back to California. Charlotte, my OG, came with me. We flew the friendly skies on United Airlines with our usual motley crew. By then it was becoming routine. I won't lie, I got used to the attention. Walking through the airport shackled and chained broke up the monotony. My thug parade shocked people. They stared like we were the fucking Beatles. We were so out, we were in. It was rad. The only option was to own it. One shuffle at a time. I wore the steel like a crown.

Chapter Nineteen

Thug Life

JULY 1996–APRIL 1997

The one thing the BOP (Bureau of Prisons) does well is move you around. It's chaotic and disorienting, having to leave behind your friends, your hygiene stash, the comfort of routine, stuffing letters and pictures inside your legal paperwork just to hold onto something, but somehow it keeps you from losing your mind. It's a burst of energy that wakes you up when you least expect it, and if you walk out of the system with your mind intact, you leave with a story worth telling. Which, honestly, I wasn't sure I could pull the whole sane thing off.

Santa Rita County was packed to the brim. There wasn't room for another soul. Unless someone got the bright idea to stack bunks higher than the three already piled up, though I wasn't about to suggest it.

So Charlotte and I were booked into Santa Clara County, a whole new chapter in this prison odyssey. By then, I'd become something of a connoisseur, Santa Clara County looked and smelled different from Santa Rita.

Walking down the halls, I nudged Charlotte and said, "It's not the Royal Hawaiian, but not bad, eh?"

When the glass door to our module swung open, I couldn't believe my eyes. No cages. Single bunks. Lockers just for us.

"Trigo," Charlotte said, eyes sparkling as she pointed to the giant TV in the dayroom, "I think we've hit the Pink Palace. Diamond Head's just over there."

Before I could answer, a guard cut in.

"Watch yourself. It gets rough, lots of fights between the *Norteños* and the *Sureños*."

Another guard added, "This ain't paradise."

Maybe not. But Charlotte and I were still smiling.

Charlotte was old-school Hawaiian, and I'd dealt with drug lords, but this was a different beast. We learned the ropes: the *Norteños* (Northerners, who wore red on the streets) and the *Sureños* (Southerners, who wore blue). Both were rival street gangs, dividing California into hard lines—north and south. They rolled under bigger umbrellas: the Nuestra Familia (Chicano) and the Mexican Mafia. People got hurt. People died.

Charlotte shrugged it off; she was an OG, so I stuck close, copying her mannerisms like it was my full-time job.

I kept out of everyone's business. I was Federal, which made me a boss—someone you didn't mess with. The only time I got confronted was when the girls came to me for advice.

Me, advice?

After nearly a year inside, I must've looked like I knew something. They came with questions about cases, girl drama, and family messes. Some even asked me to pray with them. I became the prison counselor, just without a title.

If I'd played it right, I could've charged candy bars for advice.

But honestly? I never wanted to see another candy bar again.

One morning, I spotted hot oatmeal waiting on my tray and almost squealed with excitement. Charlotte picked up her giant danish, a mischievous grin in place. "I think I can eat this in one bite," she said.

I scarfed down my food like it might vanish. We exchanged a look, faces full of disbelief.

Is this real? We even started teasing friends still stuck in Santa Rita. "How's that green bologna tasting, girls?" we'd call out, laughing at the contrast.

After breakfast, we'd wander to the TV room, quiet enough to actually hear the shows. It became our escape hatch. We lost ourselves in the messy drama of daytime soaps—*General Hospital*, *As the World Turns*, and *One Life to Live*. After lunch, it was nap time or letter-writing; sometimes we'd just lie there, rereading old mail. After dinner and showers, it was time for the "club," pulling up a folding chair in front of the TV to watch music videos. I lived for Tupac and Snoop Dogg's "Gangsta Party," imagining myself in that video: charges dropped, life wide open, wild and free. But that dream was killed in September, along with Tupac who was shot in Vegas. The unit broke out in fights. What a waste of talent. I went back to my bunk, head down, and thought about home.

With the newfound quiet, I dove into personal growth—reading the Bible and books on self-improvement. Even without Louise Hay or Jim Rohn audiotapes, I was learning to stay grounded.

I kept returning to the Bible, sensing a power I hadn't yet understood. I measured my life against stories of men and women who had fallen, and still found purpose. I learned something crucial: believing my past determines my future was a toxic mindset. Yet somehow, I couldn't shake the feeling I was the exception. New days didn't feel like fresh starts. I knew where my past was taking me, and no matter how much I hoped otherwise, I knew I was headed for federal prison.

I wished I could live life over again, knowing what I know now.

Being incarcerated was painful enough, but guilt crushed me. I kept beating myself up over my mistakes. I had a long road ahead, but at least I could recognize that understanding my flaws was the first step toward change. I was learning to trust the wait, embrace the uncertainty, and enjoy the beauty of becoming. When nothing is certain, anything is possible.

I wrote letters to friends on the outside, keeping them light and asking nothing. They weren't really for them; they were for me, a way to remember who I was.

I was surprised I never got a letter from Rich or Jacob, but I hadn't written to them either. I wasn't about to humiliate myself. I'd told Rich through my brother Jeff to keep his distance, just in case he got dragged into my drug case.

Jacob was probably too busy flying with the bats to write. Ah, young love—hormones, oxytocin, dopamine, serotonin, adrenaline, and a little cocaine and alcohol for good measure. It was exhilarating. The sun, moon, and stars all seemed to revolve around the boys I loved. Sitting on my bunk, I realized how foolish it had been. All that time and energy I gave them, like nothing else mattered. I felt like an idiot.

But I was flooded with letters from friends and guys I dated that I hadn't expected. They were full of gossip, life updates, and juicy ex-news. That's how I found out Jacob's marriage had fallen apart. I'll just say karma has a way of handling things. But I won't lie, it was sweet to get the last laugh, though behind bars it didn't feel quite as sweet. I would've preferred to see the suffering in his icy-blue eyes myself. And Rich? He was enjoying his freedom, married with a family, living in the house we had designed together, the simple life I had always wanted. Life sure had a funny way of working out for some while it seemed to keep kicking others when they were down.

* * * *

It was Charlotte's turn to be sentenced, so she had to leave for Hawaii. Saying goodbye was emotional. We clung to the hope that after sentencing she'd return to Santa Clara, but that's the way it goes. She promised to write and keep me updated on her sentence.

Three weeks later, her letter arrived and hit me hard. She'd been sentenced to thirteen years for driving the getaway car in a bank robbery on the Island. It was expected, but the weight of it lingered. She mourned leaving the Island and likely saying a final goodbye to the elders in her life. She mentioned that my shower buddy, Choy Foo, was back in OCCC and waiting to fulfill her promise to me. Panic hit. I knew I'd gotten lucky, but the next time I was in Hawaii, I might run into her. At the bottom of the two-page letter, Charlotte added a postscript: *"Just kidding, D. I talked to Choy Foo and squashed it. Told her you're not that brat that came in. You've matured."* She signed her name with a happy face and a tongue sticking out. I let out a huge sigh of relief.

* * * *

Just as I was getting lost in Luke Spencer's return on *General Hospital*, I heard my name over the loudspeaker: "Trigo, pack it up."

The universe had other plans. My time in Santa Clara was short-lived. Soon, all federal inmates were transferred to Oakland County Jail, which had a new contract with the feds to house those awaiting trial. This meant a reunion with the girls I'd left behind in Santa Rita.

After another mug shot, fingerprints, and a tetanus shot, I was locked into a small cell, an incubation tank before going to general population. The steel door slammed shut behind me, locking me in alone. That's when I truly learned claustrophobia. Instantly, I couldn't breathe, like a rock sitting on my chest, squeezing the last bit of air from my lungs. I searched for any sign of the outside world, but there was no fresh air, no hint of home. It took a few moments for the panic to settle, but I slowly deepened my breaths. It was the only choice I had.

The next day, I was moved to Gen Pop. I was glad to be reunited with Olivia, Victoria, my Filipino friend, and others from Santa Rita. But I quickly learned that in Oakland County Jail, most of your time was spent locked in a small cell. Federal detainees awaiting trial were kept in secure, isolated units, with very limited time outside—about three to five hours a day. That time was mostly for meals, the day room, phone calls, hot water, and showers.

Things went from bad to worse. Oakland County Jail was already overcrowded, and adding federal detainees made it even tighter. Recreation time shrank. Movement restrictions were stricter, and we were always last for outdoor time, which was required by law. Soon, even that disappeared, as the guard said firmly, "The roof is under construction." Just like that, outdoor time was gone. No fresh air. No sunlight.

I spent eight months in solitary. Eight months without sun or rain. Days of pure deprivation. The cell was a cramped six-by-nine. I splashed water on my face to revitalize myself from the tiny spout. I used the small prison-issued bar of white soap and shuddered, thinking about the money I had spent on luxury creams before my arrest.

My electric cell door had a small sliver of glass, just enough to glimpse the pod. If I craned my neck just right, I could sometimes see Olivia, the officer's trustee, swinging a huge mop from side to side, her face intent on the task. On the other side of my cell, a narrow window looked out over the street. Even the briefest glimpse of the outside stirred memories of my old life—freedom. Cocktails. Sex. Sun. Air. Water. Oxygen for my soul.

Sometimes I imagined the cars passing by the wire fences. Did the drivers glance up at the windows, or just shudder and think, *Glad I'm not in there*? The thought reminded me of my mistakes, the countless chances I'd had to leave the drug trade—and the reasons I'd stayed. Reasons I was still trying to understand: loyalty, I guess. Love. Desperation. Confusion.

At night, when I couldn't sleep, I'd close my eyes and find myself in Rich's Karmann Ghia, before everything spiraled out of control. We'd tear through the loud night with Stacy, laughing and swerving and bopping to the music. Simpler times.

And then there were the nights I slept.

In my dreams, no walls held me in. No locked iron gates or leering guards. There was no stench of ammonia or antiseptic used to scrub away urine, shit, and menstrual blood. Awake, the place reeked of filth, but in my dreams, I smelled the sea. I ran, sand shifting beneath me, until gravity yanked me down, and suddenly, I was terrified. I was being swallowed, suffocated by shifting sand. I shot awake, tossing off my itchy gray wool blanket, the pounding of my heart deafening in the silence. I checked my pulse: 197 beats per minute. I took a deep breath, trying to calm myself, using a trick from my dealing days when I controlled my parasympathetic responses, keeping cool so the drug lords I bought from wouldn't see me sweat.

But in solitary, there was only the silence. No noise. Just concrete, regret, and endless hours stretching into eternity. I could handle the regret—or at least, I thought I could. It was the silence that broke me.

Even the sound of the guard's keys against his belt was better than nothing. The oversized clock bolted to the wall was a cruel reminder that I had nothing but time. *Five more hours before I'd be able to mix with humans again*, I thought, as my solitary period neared its end. Many of them were far more fucked up than I was. But at least they breathe, they talk, they swear.

They are human.

Five more hours.

* * * *

I ran a small plastic comb through my hair when Olivia knocked on the steel cell door. She was taking a break from her orderly job. Her black liquid eyeliner was perfect, her lips rosy. Her dark brown hair was pulled back into a thick braid.

"You want to draw today?" she asked.

"Sure," I said. I knew Olivia wanted more than the artwork we made together. She was a master at drawing Latina designs, tough, sexy chola girls surrounded by lowriders, hearts, and barbed wire.

My electronic door buzzed. The bolt popped open. That sound meant hope, anticipation, a flicker of excitement. I threw on my V-neck uniform top over my plain white t-shirt, looked down at my feet, and laughed. High-end Denise, Dolce & Gabbana–Denise, reduced to flip-flops over white tube socks. Prison is a factory for humiliation, designed to tear you down, one razor-sharp cut at a time.

All I had in prison was time. I spent it carefully, picking the few good apples from the rotten bunch. Inside, you don't just want friends; you need them. They are your new family.

That's how I became friends with Lani, a pretty, mellow Samoan girl in for drug trafficking. She kept her head down and stayed away from drama. She taught me how to play dominoes, which we played almost every day during our few hours of freedom. I thought I'd finally found a real friend. Then they transferred her.

Losing friends was one of the hardest parts of doing time. You get thrown into a place full of strangers, find common ground, bond with someone, and then one morning, they're gone. Sometimes it was for good reasons, like being released. Though I only saw that happen once. A girl in the cell next to mine who'd robbed a bank at gunpoint but also survived a commercial plane crash that killed her family. The court showed her mercy and dropped the case.

Most of the time, it was sudden transfers—no warning, no goodbye. Like Victoria and Lani. Shipped off to the feds, the big-girl prison. The real "big house."

I felt like I was always sitting on the bench, waiting for the coach to call my name. Everyone else moved forward, but I was stuck.

* * * *

I was in the middle of my afternoon nap, minding my own business, when *bam*—my door popped open. I jumped up, still half-asleep, trying to process what was happening. A deputy motioned for me to come to the phone in his office.

I'm thinking, *Okay…what's this about? Did something happen to my family?*

"Hello?" I groggily answered.

"Hey, girl!" Victoria's voice crackled through, fast-talking, smart, and sly. "I'm at the FCI, and I tagged in Grant on the other line!"

"Hey, D, how's it going?" Grant's smooth voice came through next.

"Well, you know," I laughed, "just living the dream…or nightmare, I mean."

Victoria cut in, words flying fast. "Just catching up with the guys. Thought I'd throw some fun your way."

"Oh man, I appreciate it. I miss you guys," I said with a grin.

Grant chuckled. "You've been on my mind, D. Hang in there, yeah? When you get out, I'm taking you to dinner."

I smiled, teasing back, "If I ever get outta here…you're on."

Victoria laughed, mischievous. "Better make it worth the wait, huh?"

Grant shot back, "We still talking food here?"

I gasped, laughing. "Oh my God, Victoria, you're impossible."

She cackled. "Just saying!"

Grant chuckled again. Thank God he couldn't see me blushing.

When the call ended, I hung up smiling, still buzzing from the banter. Oakland County Jail had recorded every word. Somehow, Victoria had hacked the FCI phone system and patched it through the US Marshals office. That harmless, flirty call turned into an Internal Affairs questioning.

Now Grant couldn't escort me on transfers anymore. But that call reminded me who I was on the outside.

I still got it, I thought.

Most days at Oakland were monotonous. The TV had three channels: fake wrestling, football, and oddly enough, Riverdance performances. Naturally, I got sucked into football—crushing on the Patriots and ogling players—forever boy-crazy Denise. Mostly, I buried myself in book after book, devouring Jackie Collins and dreaming of Upper East Side lunches at Table 22—then squeezing in what exercise I could in my tiny cell: triceps dips off the bunk, sit-ups on the cold concrete floor.

Phone calls with my family were rare but precious. Usually, I talked to Dad and Dee, who'd moved to Las Vegas with Peter. Sometimes, I reached Mom, who was staying at Nonna's with Greg. She'd sold our family home. She was ready for a fresh start, a clean break from everything the past had brought. The guilt hit me immediately. I still couldn't believe my childhood home was gone.

I heard Greg was still figuring things out. Jeff was in LA, crashing with Aunt Flo and grinding through chiropractic school.

But everyone's biggest worry was Peter, my youngest brother. At nineteen, he got his girlfriend pregnant. Young as he was, he stepped up and married her. They had a baby girl, Ashley.

But it fell apart. Peter was stressed, his wife piling on financial demands. He tried to make it work, but his random jobs couldn't cover everything. Dad and Gale both helped, but Peter was drained, overwhelmed, and just wanted to smoke weed, watch *Star Wars*, and escape. "Niesey," Dad said, "Pete quit a good paying job at a moving company in Vegas, saying he must've breathed mummy dust." We both burst out laughing. But it wasn't funny—Gale, Dee, and Dad decided on tough love. Before we hung up, Dad told me Peter was on the streets. I couldn't help but wonder why life had to be so damn hard.

When the metal door slammed, I shut my eyes and drifted, somewhere softer, somewhere golden, trying to remember if beauty even existed. Mom and Dad, hand in hand on the shoreline in the warm moonlight, reminding me of everything I once belonged to. It felt like a fairytale. A sliver of hope, family waiting for me beyond these walls.

I used to pray for Doc Brown from the movie *Back to the Future* to rescue me in his time machine. I'd imagine him pulling up to the prison gates, hopping out of his DeLorean, and demanding I hurry and get in to zoom back in time. I figured a do-over was my only chance at redemption. I'd set the year to 1973 when I was six, and my parents were still married, and my brothers and I behaved. I'd hug my mom and share a laugh with my dad and there would be a big plate of hot pasta on the kitchen table.

* * * *

It was February 1997, and I was losing my mind in my single-occupancy cell, waiting for sentencing. Sick of bouncing between county facilities the Feds contracted with, I begged my lawyer to get it over with. Anything to get me into a federal prison. More than a year in county was considered psychologically damaging, and I was closing in on two.

Olivia was in the same predicament, stuck with me; sometimes she'd get the guards to play music over the intercom. That music was food for my soul. When Huey Lewis and the News came on, we'd sing the chorus, pointing at each other like idiots.

Other times, the music feels like nails on a chalkboard. Imagine living locked in a closet with dim light and stale airflow. Now, add a nonstop barrage of high-energy Mexican pop. The blaring mariachi trumpets shredded my sanity. The Latina girls' guttural *gritos* went on for hours. Olivia says it made her feel alive. Me? It made my heart race like a Maserati, desperate to escape the suffocating hopelessness, with nowhere to go. No, I was not alive—far from it.

I always imagined rock bottom as a scene from a horror film: a murky swamp, home to decaying, hollow-eyed lowlifes begging for salvation. It was certainly nowhere I ever planned on visiting. Turns out, a rock-bottom existence doesn't need an invite. It just shows up; it comes to you. And it looks just like the real world, only you don't get to control any part of it. Instead, you're dropped into a flat dimension of chaos, where you're lost, alone, and gasping for air. Anything warm or familiar felt so far out of my reach that I began to question if I ever had had it in the first place.

Inside my cell, I spent days without eating, so sick I thought I might die. I wailed for my mom, desperate to feel her warm embrace, to bask in the light of her sunny disposition. But in jail, crying for your mom? That falls under the category of "tough shit." I struggled to silence the negative thoughts spinning in my head like a warped, scratched vinyl record. I was ashamed of how low I'd fallen, of being a disgrace to my family. I felt unworthy of love and compassion.

How does one make sense of this? How does one resurface from a place that low?

By dealing.

Dealing means facing the four-headed demons of shame, guilt, fear, and worthlessness head-on. It's about finding grace in your flaws and accepting the consequences of your choices—owning them without letting them strip away your dignity.

I didn't set out to be bad; I don't believe anyone does. I was sixteen, and everything looked beautiful from where I stood—through the sunroof of my bestie's Mazda RX7, hands in the air, high on freedom, paying no mind to the dangers ahead, clueless that the speedbumps I'd encounter would become detours threatening to shatter my course.

Clawing my way out of that pit of doom wasn't easy.

I had to dig deep within myself just to survive. From the scratched-up window of my cell, I started to see things differently. I could see the streets of downtown Oakland—and most notably, a Mexican restaurant called Mexicali Rose. The sight pulled at my gut—not just for tacos, but also for everything it represented. It was a window into a life I used to know, on Friday nights with my mom, conversations at dinner, the warmth of belonging. From my side of the glass, it looked like another universe. I pressed my forehead to the cold pane and wondered if I'd ever get back there, or if I'd already lost my chance.

But then, just across the street, I saw something else: a homeless shelter. People lined up for hours in the rain, huddled under jackets and plastic bags. Mothers held their babies close, waiting for a warm meal. Men with hollow cheeks—addicts, weary and broken—stood waiting to exchange needles. People poor, desperate, and in bad shape. It was a pivotal moment: for the first time in a long time that I felt grateful for the life I had.

I'd spent so much time trapped in my own pain, but now I saw others surviving their own versions of hell. That's when something shifted. That sliver of connection, that unexpected thread of humanity, was enough to crack the darkness open.

By then, I'd read the Bible cover to cover—searching for comfort, answers, maybe just a voice that could speak to the mess I'd made of my life. Then I found it: John 1:16—grace upon grace. Not the kind my family said before dinner, or the kind handed out for good behavior, but the deep, soul-saving kind. The kind that shows up when you least deserve it but need it most. The kind of spiritual blessing that says, *You can begin again.*

Rock bottom has a way of stripping you down to what's real. Two things define you: your patience when you have nothing, and your attitude when you have everything.

In that silence, between what was and whatever came next, I found something steady: gratitude. It gave me a way to stay present, to let God work in my life.

So, I made the most of it. Ramen noodles became a celebration when dressed up with Slim Jims, gooey cheese spread from the vending machine, and crispy pork rinds from the commissary. Ono-licious! I had stacks of Dean Koontz, Sidney Sheldon, and Michael Crichton to get lost in, and I always had God to speak to. I sometimes even heard God echo love back. I knew then: there's a Heaven for a G. I was Zen in the midst of a shit storm.

I kept rereading the Bible, underlining verses that still guide me today. What resonated most was this: God is loving, merciful, and forgiving. When fear and anxiety creep in, I meditate on Philippians 4:6–7 and feel peace. I turn to Matthew when mourning and seeking comfort. I believed Isaiah 40:31—those who hope in the Lord will renew their strength. And when I was mentally fighting for my life, I leaned into Ephesians 6:10–18, putting on the full armor of God. That step-by-step prayer wrapped around me like my mom's warm chicken soup.

With that foundation of grace and strength, I began facing the parts of my life that needed healing—the pain, the betrayals, and ultimately, forgiving myself.

So much worked against me. Coming from a broken home was hard. Being a latchkey kid in the '70s was fun and free, but by the '80s, it became wild and reckless. My parents trusted me to do the right thing, but with little guidance and the wrong influences around me, I mistook money for security, relationships for validation, control for peace, achievements for worth. Bottom line: I made bad choices—but I was learning from them.

Then there was Stacy—my best friend—who died suddenly, and the guilt I carried for not answering her call. I carried it like a lead weight, numbing myself just to survive.

But the truth is, everyone did the best they could with what they had. It wasn't anyone else's fault that I ended up in this cold, gray cell—it was mine.

I reached a turning point. I had to start letting go, including forgiving the men involved in my case—the hurt, the mistakes, and the consequences. Hate was just another chain, keeping me shackled to bitterness and anger.

And finally, I was ready to be free, not just from prison, but from the things that held me captive inside.

* * * *

After two and a half years in county jail, my prayers were finally answered: my sentencing was set, and I was about to find out how much longer I'd be behind bars. If the DA kept his promise of five years or less, there was a chance I could finally go home. Hallelujah.

I won't lie—just because Jesus and I were now homies didn't mean I didn't have my moments of doubt. Faith needed work, like a muscle. So, between sit-ups and triceps dips off my bunk, I kept praying, hoping, desperate for a shot at going home.

Because of the Internal Affairs mess with Grant, he still couldn't transfer me back to Hawaii, which was a major bummer. But he'd sent a message through Abigail:

"Hey Denise, Grant wanted me to tell you he's going to try and get away to sit in at court to support you at your sentencing."

The thought made me cringe.

"He's so sweet," I said casually. "But can you tell him I'd prefer if he didn't come? I appreciate the gesture."

Abigail blinked, confused. I sighed. "I'm ashamed. I don't want Grant to see me take a beating in front of Judge Enzo."

Fastest way to kill any hope of a dinner date.

Truthfully, I didn't want any guys around—too distracting.

Abigail's face softened.

"I get it," she said. "I'll tell him. And I'm sending you all the luck and aloha." She gave me a knowing smile. "Stay strong." She was the coolest.

It was April 28, 1997. At 3:43 P.M., I walked into the courtroom, praying with every step. Large, intimidating, cold. My heart pounded as the full weight of everything hit me. Then I saw my father's face—and the floodgates opened.

"Dad, I can't believe you're here," I whispered, tears streaming.

"Oh, sweetheart, of course I'm here," he said, his voice thick, eyes wet.

I pulled myself together. I had to be brave. For him. For me. If the sentence was under five years, I might be released this very day. The possibility gave me just enough strength to sit and smile at him.

Then, DA Lawrence Brown entered, ugly glasses and all.

That's when everything went wrong.

He started talking, and my heart sank. The promised five years? Gone. Instead, he asked for thirteen years and nine months. Nearly fourteen *fucking* years? I couldn't believe it. My brothers got rehab for their first bust. Charlotte got less time for armed robbery—and she had priors.

My lawyer, Jeremy Easton, must've seen the shock on my face. "It's the judge's decision, not the DA's," he said gently. "There's still a chance."

Jeremy told the judge I was a high school dropout, easily influenced, lost. But he left out how Dan and Lorenzo coerced me into going to Hawaii, how Dan set me up, or why I couldn't go to the police after James's murder.

But it didn't matter. The judge probably made up his mind before I walked in.

Still, Judge Enzo surprised me. He seemed reluctant. He admitted fourteen years was too harsh. He saw me not as a hardened criminal, but as a girl—naïve, insecure—drawn in by powerful men who used me.

I wanted to snap, "I'm just as powerful as they are," but it wasn't the moment for my dark humor. "Yes, Your Honor," I said.

The judge studied me. "Is there anything you'd like to add?"

I was choked up. I wanted to beg to go home. But I didn't.

"Your Honor, I am extremely sorry for my wrongdoings. I accept full responsibility. I'm ashamed to have been involved with a drug that poisons lives. I'm filled with remorse for the choices I made and the pain I had caused others."

I think he was waiting for more, but I'd already written him a letter. Everything else had been said. Thinking back, I was so strong. Maybe I should've begged. But I couldn't fall apart like that.

And then, the judge spoke again.

"Apparently, your parents put together quite the package. They wanted me to see the real you—the one you were, and the one you'll be again."

He flipped through photos—me in my Brownie uniform, another at church with my mom. Then he glanced at the letters from my extended family, each pleading for clemency. He paused, nodding slightly, as if words were landing.

"I read your letter. I read letters from your extended family—each one full of love, telling me what an amazing, caring person you were. Someone who always puts others before herself." He looked at me, his tone shifting, almost stern. "That, I believe."

"And then there's your dad." His eyes sharpened. "He went to great lengths for you. Collected thousands of letters from his Japanese students—people you worked with—each asking for mercy on your behalf. Not the jokers you ran with," he added softly. "These people…they took the time to write. To speak up for you."

I sat stunned. Strangers I barely knew had fought for me. Believed in me. I couldn't hold back the tears. It must have moved the judge too.

"I feel bad for your family," he said. "I considered them carefully during my deliberations. It's also helped that your father made such an extraordinary effort to support your case. And has done a lot for our country."

I nodded, thoughts a blur. This was like a slow, torturous death. Every muscle wound tight, bracing.

Then, after what felt like forever, he said it.

"You are sentenced to eighty-four months in federal prison."

The gavel dropped.

I blinked, trying to do the math. My lawyer leaned over.

"That's seven years," he whispered.

Seven years. Not five like we'd hoped, but with time served, it meant less than five left. I turned to my dad, gave a small thumbs-up, and forced a faint smile. I could do seven.

Then I thought of Dan again. He only got seven months. Seven. Months. It felt like a punch to the gut.

I took a breath and let the anger wash through me. I chose integrity. I stood tall and owned my part. I didn't run. I didn't name names. Sure, people say the truth will set you free, but in this case, it could have gotten me killed.

I wouldn't trade places with Dan. I'd serve my sentence with dignity. When I got out, I'd have a story to tell with a clean conscience.

I was lucky. I had my family. Their love and support meant more than I could ever put into words.

The DA didn't hide his frustration. He slammed his fist on the table, furious. He'd been counting on a long sentence, thinking it would pressure me into testifying against Philip. But with only seven years, he saw me slipping through his fingers.

I hugged my dad tight, both holding on like we'd never let go. He promised to visit as soon as I landed in federal prison. I called Mom next. She was relieved, and like Dad, promised she'd come see me. I couldn't wait to see her beautiful, kind face again.

It had been two and a half years since I'd seen her. Back in Northern California, I begged her not to come. I couldn't put her through standing on the other side of thick glass, talking through a static-filled phone. The cost alone—a flight, rental car, hotel—for a half-hour visit? Too much. Too stressful.

And what if the facility shut down last minute? That happened sometimes. Jails loved to mess with us like that. That would be my luck.

I did everything I could not to make things harder—for her or for me. I already felt bad enough.

I was leaving the courtroom, and it all sank in: seven years.

Nearly a decade of my life—gone. By the time I was free, most people my age would have degrees, careers, maybe families. I'd be missing it all: birthdays, holidays, memories I'd never make. I'd lost more than time—I'd lost chances.

Tears stung my eyes. As I continued walking, a Hawaiian Marshal leaned in quietly. "Trigo, you're a really good actress. You performed beautifully."

I gave a faint smile. "It wasn't an act."

And it was true. The judge saw me at rock bottom, stripped of everything but hope and faith that maybe, just maybe, I could find my way back home.

Chapter Twenty

I'm on My Way, Making It (Big Time)

MAY 1997

Charlotte and I were transferred from Hawaii to a county jail in Reno, Nevada, to await our federal prison assignments from the Bureau of Prisons (BOP). Now, if you had told me when I was sixteen that someday I would be excited to go to federal prison, I would have taken away your bong. But the reality was, after being held and shuffled through six different state and county jails, I was eager to settle into home sweet prison. When I first landed in jail and heard inmates describe the accommodations in "Fed" as if it were a five-star resort, I found it depressing. They'd brag about microwaves and salad bars like they were luxury cars. I couldn't imagine being that psyched over raw vegetables served under a sneeze guard. But after two and a half years of ramen noodles and vending machine snacks, the novelty of eating like a college freshman had seriously worn off. The idea of anything fresh, even iceberg lettuce, had me drooling.

Once we entered prisoner intake at the Reno facility, Charlotte and I received yet another painful tetanus shot despite telling the medical staff that we had received the same shot weeks prior in Hawaii. Nobody cared. A CO led us into a small incubation cell outfitted with a stainless-steel toilet, a sink, and one stacked bunk bed. While in incubation, we weren't allowed to leave our cell. We couldn't use the phone or watch TV; we had to sleep in the cell, eat in the cell, and, if you haven't already guessed, we had to use the toilet in the cell. I don't care how long you've been locked up; taking a dump in front of someone sitting three feet away never grows on you.

"When do we get out of here?" I asked the CO, who, per usual, was slim on information.

"As soon as I say so," she said smugly before slamming shut the blue steel door.

They put another girl in with us in the middle of the night. I woke up and found her rifling through my court paperwork.

"What the fuck do you think you're doing?" I screamed as I shot to my feet, still groggy.

Charlotte had warned me about jailhouse snitches, women so desperate that they exploit other women. She was looking for information on my case, anything she could turn over to the court in exchange for a lighter sentence. Charlotte slammed her against the cell wall, and I got in her face.

"If you touch my shit again, I will break your nasty fingers."

We were released from isolation a week later and assigned to new separate cells. I was sick to my stomach to leave Charlotte's side. She was my rock. She gave me a big squeeze and told me for the millionth time, "Be strong."

Then I added my part, "Touch no ding-dong."

Usually, Charlotte rolled her eyes at the crass rhyme I made up in defense of the relentless pursuit of male guards coming on to us, promising special treatment in exchange for sexual favors. But this time, she cracked a smile.

I got crammed into a two-person cell as the third wheel. I slept on the floor next to the steel toilet in a bright red, hard plastic contraption that looked like a child's mini kiddie pool they call "a boat." My new roomies shot me dirty looks, pissed off that I was infringing on their territory—as if I wanted to lay my head next to the shitter? After a few sleepless nights, my cell door slid open.

"Trigo, get up. You got two minutes," the CO ordered.

I was on my feet in seconds, slipped on my shoes, and followed the officer down the hall. "You didn't want to bring anything with you?" he asked as I hurried to keep up.

"Why? Where am I going?"

"The Big House; you're being transferred."

"Now? It's the middle of the night."

The CO stopped and crossed his arms. "I'm sorry, are we disturbing your beauty sleep?"

"I just—I thought I would get my assignment and then—"

The CO was losing his patience.

"I need to get my paperwork."

The CO checked his watch. "You've got forty-five seconds."

He took me back to my room, where I grabbed my file, and then it hit me: I was leaving Charlotte, this time maybe for good. I summoned any bit of sexual charm left in me, batted my scraggly eyelashes, and sweetly begged the officer to allow me to say goodbye to my friend. He made a noise like a buzzer.

"Nope. Time's up."

He led me to where I would be discharged. I was sick to leave without telling Charlotte how much I would miss her and how grateful I was for her strength and kindness. My thoughts of gratitude were interrupted when I was handed a plastic bag. Inside were my street clothes from two years ago, inspired by the chic style of Kate Moss. My mind reeled at the sight of them. A white baby tee, a black blazer, a pair of tight jeans, and black leather sandals with a chunky heel and straps that crisscrossed at the ankle. *Do I still have ankles?* I had to look to be sure. They were hairy, but they existed. The smell of stale perfume and cigarettes overwhelmed my senses; I was looking at the clothes of a ghost. Who was the woman who wore these things? I felt woozy and outside of my body.

Slipping on my old jeans, I was brought back into my body in the worst possible way. They wouldn't button. The jeans were extra snug, thanks to my sodium-rich Cup Noodles diet and no access to cocaine. A guard escorted me to a secure area with other inmates who were being transferred. I walked into the room wearing high-heeled sandals and tight jeans, my most stylish outfit in years, and everyone else was in their standard-issue prison uniforms. Plus, they were *all men*. Despite wearing heels, I suddenly felt two feet tall. We were all shackled with heavy chains around our wrists, waist, and ankles.

The officer who attached mine looked me up and down, paused, and said, "Now, that's a look we don't see every day." His casual nature gave me the impression he might answer the question no one else would.

"Where are we going?"

"What do you mean?" he said. "Aren't you headed out on a hot date?"

He and the other COs laughed as they boarded me onto a van going who knows where, full of men convicted of who knows what. They sat me in the front row, saying it was for my safety. Shaking with fear, I imagined Charlotte and tried to emulate how she would act in this situation. I sat up straight, with my shoulders back and eyes trained straight ahead. *Be strong, touch no ding-dong.*

The van hit the road, and the US Marshal riding shotgun (in the most literal sense) turned on the radio. Mariah Carey's "Hero" came on and one of the male transferees began to sing along. He had the voice of an angel. I closed my eyes and asked God to give me strength. I needed all I could get.

My shoulders relaxed a little until the heat-packing Marshal turned to him, saying sternly, "Inmate—"

The man stopped singing, and we all froze.

"You have a beautiful voice. Continue."

This unexpected gift momentarily masked the ugliness of our lives.

Through snippets of conversations on the drive, I learned we were headed to an Air Force Base. *Holy shit.* Was I about to fly on *the* Con Air? I was worried about the plane ride but more about ending up somewhere across the country. Inmates get assigned to prisons nationwide, depending on their security level. If I were to land in Florida or Illinois, it would be challenging for my family to visit. Then another horror crossed my mind: what if I wind up somewhere cold? As a California native, I'm a wussy when it comes to weather. But nothing was in my control, certainly not the weather.

Finally, we pulled into a desolate empty tarmac in the pouring rain. And we waited. Everything about prison is a waiting game. Eventually, the guards escorted me out separately after the men and then chained me back up to them outside of the van. The rain fell hard, and within seconds I was soaked to the bone. Peering through the downpour, I took in the scene. It was like something from a big-budget Hollywood action movie. The aircraft, an imposing Boeing 737, idled on the tarmac along with a fleet of buses and cargo vans. A lineup of fifty heavily armed guards stood before us, all wearing navy hooded raincoats with "B.O.P." in bright yellow letters on the back. They were as badass as it gets.

We were ordered to move. The men, whose legs were almost twice as long as mine, took big strides with ease, but the weight of the chains and the fact that I was in heels made it hard for me to keep up. A tight circle of officers faced outward toward the dark gray sky, with guns drawn in case somebody came blazing through trying to help a prisoner escape. The second inner circle of guards tracked our every move with weapons aimed at the middle of our chests, fingers on the trigger, ready to fire. I was terrified that one of the guys would make a stupid move and I'd get caught in the crossfire. Shackled in heels, taking baby steps like Marilyn Monroe in a pencil skirt, I held my breath and walked as steadily as possible. Never have I wanted to be less feminine.

Guards began calling out last names, and inmates answered with a "Here" before being unshackled and led away. Shivering under the relentless cold rain shower, I finally heard, "Trigo, bus number seven." I was unshackled from the men and directed toward my designated bus—*a bus.* I breathed a sigh of relief; I wasn't flying cross-country.

Standing at the front of the bus, water dripping from my hair and clothes, a puddle formed under my feet. I looked up and met the eyes of two dozen female inmates. Women who were broken and full of despair, the same as me. I had wished to be settled, and now I was on my way. *These are my people now,* I thought as I found my way to an empty seat in the middle. *My people* were all clad in the same beige uniform and were giving me a lot of sideways stares. Teetering on my ridiculous heels, I pulled my blazer closed over my soaked-through white top. One of my greatest nightmares is showing up to an event dressed inappropriately. And here I was, off to the Big House, dressed for a wet t-shirt contest.

A twentysomething blond girl moved from the back of the bus and scooted in next to me. Normally, this invasion of space would have lit my fuse but I felt comforted by her company. Kim had a joyful energy and filled me in that we were headed west of Reno to FCI Dublin. She'd served time at the federal facility in the past and she seemed excited to be returning. I'd met other girls like Kim, whose home situation was so whacked that being in prison was almost preferred. Having a roof over their head and guaranteed three meals daily was better than the situation they were coming from.

The bus's radio must have been broken because the driver had a ghetto blaster resting on the dashboard. As the bus made its way up the Nevada mountainside and the road grew more winding, the ghetto blaster shifted back and forth faster, falling into rhythm with the song playing through its speakers. Robert Plant's "In the Mood." I'd heard the song hundreds of times, but in that moment, I was struck by the purity and rawness of his wailing vocals. To think I met him once when I was still pure and raw myself, felt like a lifetime ago. If Robert Plant could see me now. *Girlfriend, you fucked up your life*. The morning sun rose over the rolling hills of Mount Diablo, casting golden light on the vibrant wildflowers blanketing the hills.

I fogged up the window with my breath and drew a little heart with my finger like I did as a kid, road-tripping with my family. When I was little, like five or six, my dad surprised us with an RV. My brothers and I lost our minds. A house on wheels, what's cooler?

We planned a trip to Yosemite. In the middle of the night, my parents picked us up out of bed, still sleeping, and gently carried us into the RV. I awoke nestled in the top bunk, cozy under a plaid blanket. The RV hummed along the freeway, and our parents laughed and sang along to Neil Diamond's melodies playing softly from the eight-track player.

We were venturing into the great unknown, and I felt completely safe. The day we arrived, my dad was sitting on the bank of the Truckee River when he spotted a tiny baby girl floating by. She had crawled into the water upriver when her parents weren't looking. My dad told the story many times over the years about the baby's big blue eyes, wide with fear as he jumped in and pulled her out. He said it wasn't until she finally took a deep breath that he realized he'd been holding his own. I already held my dad on a pedestal, but he reached superhero status that day.

Kim rattled on about all of FCI's amazing amenities. She explained that there were two units for women, and the main unit was the premier unit.

"Don't be fooled by the one they call 'camp,'" she told me. "It's anything but."

She was a chatterbox, but having served time at FCI previously made her a priceless asset and, therefore, my new best friend. As dawn was breaking, for the first time in a while, I was feeling optimistic.

Chapter Twenty-One

Camp Fed

JUNE 1997

After a butt-numbing journey, the bus grunted to a halt at the entrance of my new home, FCI Dublin. The Federal Correctional Institution is thirty miles east of San Francisco on an active US Army training area. On the compound are three separate correctional facilities. FCI, the main female unit, is classified as low-level security; across the street, the Federal Prison Camp (FCP) houses minimum-security females. Back when the camp housed men, the junk bond king Michael Milken served nearly two years there, and it was currently holding Hollywood Madame Heidi Fleiss. Notorious Dublin alumni include members of the Manson Family, Russian spies, twin sisters who smuggled heroin in dead babies, a woman who attempted to assassinate Gerald Ford, and founding members of the Piru Street Family, which later evolved into the Bloods. Next door is the Federal Detention Center (FDC), which holds adult males in pretrial limbo, including, at the time, Ted Kaczynski, the Unabomber. All three facilities are clustered on the same block, like a deranged Mr. Rogers's neighborhood.

For the umpteenth time in my incarceration journey, I'm put through the booking process: mug shot, fingerprints, urine sample, and squat and cough. I was assigned to FCI along with my new bestie, Kim, and issued a khaki uniform, five pairs of underwear, three pairs of socks, and two white t-shirts. I changed into my new uniform and proceeded to the holding area, where a CO informed me there was a clerical error and that I was being reassigned to FCP, the women's camp. You'd think I would've been happy for the new assignment, given the lower security level, but after Kim had talked up the main unit on our bus ride, I was desperate to live there with her.

"Why?" I asked the CO, incredulously. "I don't want to go to camp! What happened?" I don't advise second-guessing a prison official, but in this case his ego was thrown for a loop. Most people would've viewed this transfer as a godsend. Leave it to me to upend expectations.

He shook his head, opened my file, and said, "You got flagged by Internal Affairs. The BOP missed it. We're supposed to keep you separate from another inmate at FCI."

I knew which inmate he was referring to: Victoria, my matchmaking switchboard operator friend from jail. I hadn't considered the possibility they'd separate us, but considering we pulled off a game of telephone between Victoria in Dublin, me in Oakland, and my dirty-talking main Marshal, Grant, at the Federal Courthouse in Honolulu, it makes sense. Imagine the trouble the two of us could stir up from inside the *same* facility.

I arrived at camp in my crisp new blue uniform and black steel-toed work boots—and was immediately struck by the free-roaming nature of the place. Inmates walked unescorted between outbuildings. The perimeter fence wasn't ten feet and topped with razor wire like I was accustomed. It was a modest brown picket fence, the height you'd see in any suburban neighborhood in America. I asked a CO if there was some underground electrical fence that zaps inmates who go out of bounds. He said no but warned me to think twice before trying to escape.

"The ones who've tried are either spending an extra twenty years in prison or an eternity in hell." Then he made a finger gun, pointed it at my temple, and pulled the trigger.

The CO walked us to a small, unadorned room where Mrs. Burns awaited. A modest gold sign on the door read "Counselor," a title that conjured images of warmth and understanding. That was not Mrs. Burns. She was pale and towering with uncombed white hair and a wandering eye. She looked like a possessed Albert Einstein, and she spoke in a loud monotone.

The first thing she said upon flipping open my file was, "Seven years, that's good. I have no patience for short-timers."

I was earning respect for my lengthy prison sentence; there's something for Mom to hang on the fridge. After that, Mrs. Burns ranted about the rules for fifteen minutes. In the hours since I'd left jail in Reno, I hadn't been given anything to eat or drink. The first time I was allowed to go to the bathroom was during my piss test. My head was pounding, and my stomach ached with hunger pangs. Then I noticed something on Mrs. Burns's desk. The holy grail. The prison commissary list.

The prison commissary is a small market, like an off-brand 7-Eleven, where inmates can purchase authorized items like shaving kits, snacks, candy, and, at that time, cigarettes. I'd already planned my wish list based on intel I gathered from friends in jail. Whenever I met someone who'd spent time in Fed, the commissary was the first thing I'd ask them about. Commissary inventory differed from prison to prison. Most carried standard essentials like shampoo, conditioner, and toothpaste. But the commissary item I wanted more than anything was a Sony Walkman radio and headphones. Music was my escape plan. I would drown out the cacophony of prison with familiar melodies, the songs like conversations with old friends. Walkman radios were rare, and I was dying to know if it was on the list.

"Hello…Trigo? Do you understand?" Mrs. Burns's one eye was glaring at me, and I wasn't sure how long I'd been staring at that coveted list.

"You can count on me, ma'am," I bluffed.

Temporarily satisfied, Mrs. Burns permitted one quick phone call "on the house." If I wanted to make any calls after that, I'd need money on my books.

Getting money on your books was no easy task. First, you needed someone on the outside who was willing to send it. The system to transfer funds in prisons has changed in today's digital world, but in the nineties, it was like dealing with something from the Dark Ages that might have included a carriage ride for as long as it took for the money to arrive. I'd been transferred to different institutions so often that the funds my parents sent by check took an eternity to process, leaving me waiting far too long for basic hygiene supplies and ramen. At least I was lucky to have parents willing to send funds; most inmates don't.

On my way out to make my phone call, Mrs. Burns handed me a copy of the commissary list. I quickly scanned it, and there it was, listed between religious prayer oil and watch batteries, a Sony Walkman radio and headphones. Soon, I would have music and crack-free lips. But first I needed money.

I called home, and my brother Jeff answered; his voice stirred so many emotions in me that I immediately burst into tears. "Denise," he asked, "is that you? Where are you?"

"I'm chillin' in the Bahamas." I sniffled. "It's beautiful, I wish you were here." Jeff laughed. "Tell me everything," I said, starved for a slice of home. "Where are you? Who else is home? What are you doing?"

He said he was alone in the kitchen, eating leftover chicken parm. I could see him at the grand oak table, where we gathered for family dinners and blew out birthday candles a few times a year. When everything seemed perfect.

"Are you using a plate?" I asked him.

"Nope, I'm eating it straight from the Tupperware."

The tears came again. "Calm down," Jeff urged. "Where are you?" I told him that I had just arrived at FPC in Dublin. "Take a breath, it's gonna be okay. You gotta try and relax, especially on your first day." Jeff had served time in Chino State about a decade earlier, so he knew what was at stake. "You don't want to wind up someone's bitch."

"You would know," I shot back. For a moment, I wasn't just a prisoner—I was a person loved and cared for. A sister, a best friend. I told Jeff to tell everyone hi and to send money. Jeff assured me they'd send money and visit soon. Hanging up, I felt momentary relief before more tears started flowing. Mrs. Burns came around the corner, like she'd been anticipating my breakdown.

"Why are you crying?" she shot. "Are you a mental case? I hope you're not a mental case." She grabbed my file again to make sure.

I found my way to C Blocks, the converted Army barracks that made up camp. In the yard, an asphalt track surrounded some rusty old exercise equipment. Flanking the yard were five two-story buildings, well, trailers, containing administrative offices, a kitchen and cafeteria, a commissary, medical, classrooms, and housing. It looked like a quaint college campus, except you'd be shot if you tried to leave.

I entered building C4, my assigned housing unit, and was welcomed with the traditional evil-eye stares and deranged catcalls inmates give to newcomers.

Then someone called out, "Yo, Trigo!"

It was Lani, my Samoan friend from Oakland County Jail. Seeing a familiar face, I lost all sense of time and place and ran over and gave her a big hug. In return, she handed me a cigarette, the prison equivalent of the flower lei a tourist receives in Hawaii. I followed Lani to an area in the yard with picnic tables where we smoked, and I listened as she gave me the lowdown on the place, beginning, first and foremost, with breakfast.

"The eggs are decent, not that powdered crap," she said. "Sometimes we get fresh cinnamon rolls. There's always cereal available, and fresh fruit." Then she got a tad more direct. "It's served from five-thirty to six-fifteen. You snooze, you lose."

Lani told me it was essential that I report to the officer's station on time at eight-thirty the following morning to get my job assignment.

"Landing a decent job is clutch," she said, "so you don't want to piss off the assigning officer by showing up late."

We finished smoking, and Lani showed me to my bunk. On the way, she gave me a fresh pack of cigarettes. She knew it would be a while for my money to arrive, and cigarettes were currency I could use to trade for shampoo or toothpaste if things got desperate. I thanked her as we rounded the corner into the dormitory and found my bunk.

"You know who's right across from you?" Lani didn't wait for my response before blurting out, "Heidi Fleiss!"

The sensational story of the infamous Hollywood Madam Heidi Fleiss captivated me. Her trial was global news as prosecutors angled to reveal the contents of her "little black book." Prominent men, handsome Hollywood movie stars like Charlie Sheen, and dignitaries were all shaking in their Prada loafers at the threat of being singled out as clients. Salacious photos of Heidi and her cadre of badass women jet-setting around the world and sunbathing topless by the pool at her Beverly Hills mansion were splashed on the covers of tabloids and high-brow magazines. Many people gave her lifestyle a thumbs down, which she returned with a middle finger up. That's the part of her story I loved most; the woman lived balls out. I knew she'd been convicted on counts of tax evasion and money laundering and sentenced to serve time in prison, but I never imagined my bunk would be right next to Heidi Fleiss.

Heidi wasn't in her bunk when Lani said goodbye. It was 7:00 P.M., and I was exhausted. I made up my bed and lay down, and the next thing I knew, it was morning. The dorm buzzed with women dressing for work and chomping on apples and bananas. A Sony Walkman moved to second place on my commissary list, replaced by an alarm clock. It was eight o'clock. I rushed to get dressed and make it to the officer's station for my work assignment on time.

"You're all on probation for the first few days," the hairy-chested lady officer explained to a few other newbies and me.

On probation in prison, isn't that a bitch? It meant that we'd be rotated from crap job to even crappier job before landing a permanent position. She handed us what looked like a two-pronged fork, marched us out to a path leading up to the cafeteria, and ordered us to pull all the weeds from the cracked concrete.

"What concrete?" I asked.

The officer got in my face. "I don't tolerate humor. Get to work."

I wasn't even trying to be funny. The pathway was made up entirely of clovers and dandelions.

I yanked weeds in the boiling sun for an hour before finally saying, "Screw this," and sat down to smoke a cigarette. Some of the girls joined me; others just stared at us wide-eyed. One by one, they gave up, too, and soon, we were all smoking and swapping stories like a chain-smoking chain gang. Eventually, a CO shouted at us to get back to work. I sighed, snuffed out my cigarette, and half-heartedly pushed weeds around like a child with a plate full of peas. I hoped Lani would have pity on me and offer me a line of credit for cigarettes because I was going to need a lot of them to survive the next two weeks.

My temp gig the next day had me trading my fork in for a broom and a standing dustpan. I walked the grounds all day, sweeping up cigarette butts (many of them probably mine) and other random scraps of trash. Inch by inch, I swept, sweating my tits off in the ninety-degree desert heat. My new blue uniform had gone from crisp to soggy, and the requisite steel-toed boots that had me feeling like a gangster at first now felt like a gangster had strapped cement blocks to them to feed me to the fishes. I was on broom duty for two days before receiving my permanent placement in landscaping.

Landscape didn't sound too bad. I always loved foraging for ripe tomatoes and clipping fresh basil and mint back home in Orange County for dinner. My Sicilian grandfather had planted lemon and apricot trees in our backyard and a small vegetable and herb garden on the side of the house. In the front, we had these massive rose bushes that bloomed in a soft lavender hue. My mom took great pride in our yard. She'd come home from the café, still in her green work apron, and water the lawn wearing flip-flops. My Italian garden fantasies were dashed when I was handed a pair of goggles and a weed whacker.

"What do you want me to do with this?" I asked Bruce, the landscape foreman.

"Whack the weeds," he answered dryly, shrugging.

The closest I had come to a weed whacker was when my brother taunted me with one in our garage, pretending to be a psycho killer in a horror movie. The one I now held wasn't powered on, and I was still terrified. Halfway into whacking whatever was in front of me, including plants I wasn't supposed to touch, I told the foreman I wanted to quit. He gave me a crooked smile and told me I had to wait two weeks to apply for a job transfer.

The most coveted job among many inmates was with UNICOR. The government corporation contracted with the federal prison to employ hundreds of inmates to manufacture custom draperies, parachutes, and disaster blankets, and repair USPS mailbags. The inmates working for UNICOR had the same air of sophistication as someone who attended a college on the East Coast. Even though they stood on their feet for long hours doing incredibly tedious work, they had a cult-like devotion to the job and their foreman, Kurt. It was also the best-paying job in the entire prison. They made a whopping twenty-three cents an hour, but compared to my hourly wage of eight, it gave girls without family or financial support a chance to put some money on their books. They hustled, and I respected that.

At the end of the workday, I was tired and filthy.

I collapsed onto my bunk when someone behind me asked, "Bad day?"

I answered with bitchy sarcasm, "No, I love doing mindless work on the face of the sun."

I sat up to find Heidi Fleiss, laughing. Her friend June wasn't.

"Sucks to be at the bottom," June retorted.

Then she took Heidi by the arm and pulled her out of the bunk. It wasn't the fabulous introduction to Madam Fleiss that I'd hoped for, but I was too exhausted to care. My head hit the pillow before I'd even kicked off my work boots.

The next day, Foreman Brian barked out commands while presenting me with another terrifying piece of equipment from the shed: a lawnmower.

"Trigo and Gomez, take your mowers across the road and cut all the grass from the front gate to the back."

I looked across at the main FCI grounds; by my best guesstimate, the area measured somewhere around…fucking enormous.

I turned to Gomez, my new work colleague, to make sure I heard the foreman correctly and asked, "We're supposed to mow all of that, just the two of us?" Gomez was already halfway across the street.

I tilted the clunker of a machine on its back two wheels, like I'd seen my dad and brothers do a hundred times, and pushed it to catch up. Gomez fired hers up right away.

"How'd you do that?" I asked.

She shrugged and started mowing.

"Hey," I yelled over the sound of the motor, "shouldn't we split up the territory or whatever, so we don't double up work?"

Gomez ignored me and plowed straight ahead. She was either an incompetent teacher or a lousy peer. I tried my hardest to start it, but I couldn't get the thing to budge. When it didn't comply a twelfth time, I lit up a smoke far enough away from Brian's prying eyes. After a while, I asked Gomez for help and to show me how to pour gasoline into the machine. When she got it started, I pushed the thing around as best I could. It must have weighed as much as I; my whole upper body was vibrating. Thankfully, it kept breaking down. Can you guess what I did then? Yep, I lit another smoke.

"This lawn looks like it's been mowed by a drunk driver," a CO yelled, exiting the FCI building like his hair was on fire.

I didn't disagree with his assessment. I assured him I'd do better, and I did by convincing Gomez to do it for me. She was an easy sell, as she was trying harder than I was to please our foreman. I didn't care if my request got me in trouble; I'd take time in the hole over mowing for one more second. By day's end, I overheard Brownnoser Gomez complaining about me to Brian, but before she could truly paint a portrait of my incompetence, I cut her off.

"Gomez was such a huge help today! I don't know where I'd be without her," I bragged. "She works so hard and really knows her stuff!"

In an instant, Gomez's demeanor melted, and she even managed to push out a smile. I learned later that not only was she trying to flatter Brian to make good on her work detail, but she also had a huge crush on him, so I had done her a solid.

Back at the bunks, I entered the center hallway, where the industrial floor fan was switched to high speed. I kicked up my pace, looped my t-shirt through my bra, and strutted like a supermodel walking the runway. I got a bunch of dirty looks from inmates, but I had zero shits to give. I walked within a foot of the fan, let the wind rip through my hair, and then whipped it around like Beyoncé in concert. Heidi Fleiss came around the corner and busted up laughing at me. I kept going; it felt so good that I couldn't stop. Breathless, I gave one more stripper-esque hair flip and skipped to my bunk. Heidi was still cracking up when I arrived.

This was my first time taking her in, and I was immediately smitten. Her dark, intense eyes peered out over high cheekbones and a tough-as-nails jaw. Her raven-colored hair was cut just above her shoulders, enhancing her elegant posture. Her complexion was fair and dewy.

"You had those girls drooling," she said through a laugh that was warm and wicked all at once. Getting a laugh from Heidi did more for my self-esteem than her compliment. She asked me where I was from.

"I say Los Angeles for people who don't know about Orange County, where I'm really from."

She grinned. "Orange County, huh? You know Johnny Drama?"

"Fuck yeah, I know Johnny! Shit, me and Johnny, we've had some *nights partying*."

Heidi and I reminisced about the LA club scene and house parties. It turns out that when I was partying with Julie at the Rainbow Room, Heidi was throwing parties next door at the Roxy. We discovered we knew a bunch of the same people: drug dealer/high-profile escort…the Venn diagram is pretty obvious. Our conversation was peaking when Heidi's friend Sienna walked in. Sienna was striking too, with long legs and straight, sandy hair that stretched to her waist like a prison Barbie. Her presence was commanding. Heidi introduced me.

"Bud, this is Denise, she's from LA. You two will get along great. She's in for dealing too."

I greeted Sienna with a friendly smile, but she didn't return the gesture. Instead, she tugged on Heidi's arm, saying, "Buddy, come on. Let's go." She gave me a dismissive once-over, making it clear I wasn't welcome in their plans.

Heidi sighed. "Okay, Bud, okay."

On their way out, Sienna turned to me and stuck out her tongue. I want to tell you that I ignored the catty middle-school behavior, took a hot shower, and went to bed, but what's the fun in that? If continuing my friendship with Heidi, who provided me a much-needed connection to home, meant competing with snotty Sienna, then I was up for the challenge.

Game on, bitch.

Chapter Twenty-Two

Broken Pieces

AUGUST 1997

The next morning, as I walked through the cafeteria-style kitchen line, Heidi, dressed in white with a hairnet, handed me a piece of fruit and flashed a smile.

"Ready for landscaping?"

"Kill me now," I muttered.

She leaned in. "I'll talk to the food service supervisor. See if I can get you a job with me. Just stick it out for now, okay?"

"I'll try," I said, grateful she cared.

"Trust me," she said with a grin. "She hates everyone, but worships me."

At lunch, I looked for Lani, but she was already surrounded by her Unicorn crew. Heidi was with Sienna, so I sat alone, feeling like the new kid on the first day of school with no clique to join.

Heidi waved me over. As I walked toward them, I caught Sienna's glare from across the room.

"I worked my magic in the kitchen," Heidi said, flashing a smug little grin. "Got you a gig, if you can get out of landscaping."

Sienna shot Heidi a look. The smile she gave was razor-thin. "Wow. That's *really* nice of you, bud."

Heidi, unfazed and cool as ever, tossed it right back. "Yeah, buddy. Landscaping's the worst. Come on."

"Bud" and "buddy." Their thing—their private little code. The kind of best-friend language that says, *You're not in this club.*

Sienna's eyes flicked to me, flat and unreadable. But I caught it. That tension. She hated this. Hated Heidi pulling me into her orbit.

I knew I shouldn't, but Sienna wasn't nearly as scary as Choy Foo. So, as Heidi turned her attention elsewhere, I couldn't help myself—I stuck my tongue out at her.

I'm from the OC. I know how to play the bratty bitch game better than most.

I walked away with a smug grin. Now, all I needed was a brilliant plan to pull this off—and maybe a backup plan for when it blew up in my face.

When Bryan strapped that damn motorized backpack on me, reeking of gasoline, and barked at me to start blowing leaves in the outside visiting area, I nearly fainted. That was it. The thought of that buzzing in my ears for hours was a slow and torturous death. Survival mode kicked in. No plan, just instinct. I tore the blower off my back, found the nearest tree, and rubbed pine needles up and down my arms until they were red and welted. It hurt. Good. That was the point. Honestly, I'd rather chew off my own arm than do landscaping.

Then I told Bryan I needed to see the nurse. The rest of the day crawled by while I waited for a five-minute check-up, but I pulled it off. I convinced the nurse I had sun poisoning. She wrote up my job transfer, and just like that, I was in my food service whites, chopping fresh vegetables in the kitchen with the Hollywood Madam.

I didn't need to make friends with anybody. I got along with everyone, and I knew that I came into this place alone—and by God, I'd be leaving alone too.

But Sienna? She was different. There was no reason for her to treat me like competition. I mean, can't we all just get along? We're all locked up in prison together, for fuck's sake—capisce?

One day, I finally got my shot.

After dinner—steamed vegetables nuked in the microwave—Heidi, June, Sienna, and I headed back to the dorm, and Sienna and I stood up at the same time to smoke. Heidi and June didn't smoke, so when Sienna and I both stood up, it was awkward, but we walked out together and lit up.

She let her guard down when she spotted Mrs. Burns in the distance. "That old hag is something else," she said, shaking her head.

"Yes! She asked me if I was a mental case when I first got here." I laughed.

Sienna chuckled, then launched into a story about her first phone call home. "Dude, I saw this place and totally freaked out. I begged my mom to put a thousand bucks on my books for commissary. Mrs. Burns was listening, of course, and she started screaming like a total nut job. 'No drug money! Don't you dare bring drug money into my prison!'"

We both cracked up.

Turned out we had a dozen stories like that. Like the time Sienna was separated from all the other inmates on a transfer bus and locked in a cage—just like Hannibal Lecter.

When we came back from our smoke break, her animosity toward me had melted.

Life in A.M. food service was routine. Heidi and I had to be in the kitchen for the 5:00 A.M. count, prepping breakfast by 6:30 A.M. Every day, we ate the same thing: bran flakes with banana slices.

Ms. Valentine, the supervisor who hired me because I was Heidi's friend, ripped on the other inmates, but she was always kind to me.

After a few months, my sleep schedule was wrecked. Lunch shift ended at 11:30, and I lived for my afternoon naps.

There was another supervisor, this Italian guy who flirted with me, talked about God, and kept telling me to stay positive. But my favorite was the officer who thought he was a gangster. He'd roll an onion past us just to watch me scream, thinking it was a mouse. In return, Heidi and I would tease him, asking if we could take a giant cucumber back to the barracks for "girl time." His face would go bright red every single time.

It was all about humor—Heidi and me, making the best of it. She even slipped sometimes, calling me "bud" or "buddy," but never in front of Sienna. She'd freak.

Nights were mail call, social hour with cigs, walking the track, or flopping on our bunks. That's when Heidi started opening up about her notorious black book—her celebrity clients, what they paid for sex, and their kinks and their wild fetishes. You think Denise Trigo was gonna get close to the Hollywood Madam and *not* hear the juicy details? C'mon, you know me better than that. Hanging with Heidi was always a blast—sharp, confident, and full of stories from a life most people only dream about. She made it all sound so effortless.

"You know, Denise, I only hire beautiful women," she said, scanning me with a grin. "It's an honor to be one of Heidi's girls. I would've made a lot of money working with you. When you get out, hit me up. I'll send you to the South of France. You'll make money and get a free designer wardrobe."

I wasn't a prostitute, but I couldn't help feeling a little honored. Travel, sex, money, and clothes? Sounded like a fucking dream job to me. Instead, I was stuck with more grueling kitchen work.

As a condition of my sentencing, Judge Enzo ordered me to take GED classes. Time to bite the bullet. After a week in the classroom, Mr. Wilson, our teacher, scheduled tests for a few students who'd been studying. I was too new, he said. He was pale, polite, always in khakis. The girls never listened to him—talked over his lessons, passed notes, cracked jokes. Sometimes he'd just stand there, hands on his hips, like he was thinking, *What am I doing here? I should've been a doctor.* Yeah—don't we all have regrets.

I didn't listen to him either. I pushed back. I wanted to see just how badly I'd bomb. Then I'd pick through the shrapnel and figure out my next move.

A few days later, Mr. Wilson stood at the front of the classroom, holding the test results. "Only two people passed," he announced. "Joci...and Denise."

I blinked. "Me?"

He nodded, eyes wide behind those thick glasses. "You passed. The whole thing."

I sat there, waiting for the catch. It never came.

Some of the women who'd been grinding at this for years stared down at their desks. I felt bad, like I'd crashed their party at the last minute and snagged the hottest guy.

I couldn't help but think it was Stacy's divine intervention, because honestly, I still didn't have a freakin' clue about the two cars moving at different speeds traveling the same distance but different start times and who was going to make it to the destination first—and frankly, I didn't give a damn. What I cared about was that I had just dropped the limiting beliefs I had put on myself. It also made me realize something else: Stacy and I could've passed years ago if we'd only believed in ourselves. Why hadn't we? We were so sure we'd fail. If I'd had even a sliver of that confidence back then, maybe I could've pulled Stacy along. Maybe she'd still be here. Maybe I wouldn't be in prison.

But I couldn't rewrite the past. All I could do was stay present and not let old ghosts steal this win. I silently thanked God, then called my mom with the good news.

To celebrate, Sienna, Heidi, and June threw me a little graduation party. The best part? They officially inducted me into their "high society prison sorority"—a.k.a. the Bud and Buddy club. Now I was a full-fledged member. That night, lying on my bunk, I pictured us all at some future reunion, ten years down the line. Where would we be? Who would we have become? Would we still be buds—or just memories in each other's rearview?

* * * *

It had been more than two years since I'd seen my brother and mom. Crushing, I know. So when Jeff drove my mom to visit me, it was a huge deal.

When they walked in, Mom was hysterical—tears streaming down her face.

"What happened?" I asked, heart pounding.

Jeff tried to calm her down, hand on her shoulder. "It's okay, Mom, breathe," he said, but I could see that look in his eyes, like, *Girl, you have no idea....*

We headed outside to the picnic table. The sun was warm, but it didn't ease the tension.

Jeff sat, rubbed his face, and said, "We almost didn't get in. The guards turned us away—Mrs. Burns hadn't finished the paperwork and had already left for the day."

Mom broke down again, shoulders shaking.

"She's been like this for hours," Jeff said, voice thick.

I squeezed Mom's hand, trying to be strong. "It's okay, Mom. I'm here. So good to see you."

She looked up, face snuffling. "Thank God Jeff is here; he marched across the street and demanded to see the warden."

I teased Jeff, but couldn't hide my thanks. "Yeah, Jeff, you really know the system. Look at you, Chino, taking no crap."

He grinned. "Chino no more. But I don't take shit from the po-po. The fuzz. The heat. Them pigs. Donut lovers."

I laughed. "OMG, I miss donuts." I rolled my eyes. "How's the café, Mom?"

Mom just nodded, like all was fine. To lighten the mood, I teased her, copying Jeff's diva demands from Chino State. "Next visit, bring me chicken piccata—extra capers, don't forget!"

"I should've dumped it on his head," Mom said. We all burst out laughing.

Years ago, I watched Mom lose it like this when Jeff was in Chino. But seeing her daughter in prison? Had to be worse. I'm glad I told her not to visit me in those county lockups; the thick glass between us would've been brutal.

Here in federal prison, I could look her in the eye and hug her tight. We held each other for what felt like forever, hands locked, words spilling out—apologies, reassurances, love.

"I'm so sorry, Mom," I choked out. "I never meant for any of this."

She shook her head. "Don't be silly. How many times are you going to apologize? I'll always love you." And I felt it. All of it.

But then she looked worn down. "I'm sorry, too," she whispered. "Being a single mom, raising three kids wasn't easy."

"I know, Mom. You were amazing. It's not your fault."

"No," she said, voice cracking. "I could've done better. But I love you more than life."

Meanwhile, Jeff, the smooth talker, flirted with my friends in the visiting yard. Bragging about almost being a doctor—*eye roll.* But he promised to visit every school break and write letters. And he did. These visits and letters were lifelines.

Despite the support and mindset shift from Oakland, I was still wrestling with the trauma. I cycled through the stages of grief—shock, denial, depression, testing, and bargaining. But then came anger.

One day, I dropped my tray in the garbage and just said, "Fuck it. Why get my hands dirty?"

That's how the movement started. Heidi, June, and Sienna followed—bing, bang, boom—one by one, their trays hit the garbage too. We giggled, walking away, hearts racing. Harmless, right? Wrong. In prison, nothing's harmless.

That spark lit a wildfire. We went from rule breakers to full-on vandals. Like rock stars trashing hotel rooms, my girl squad ripped screen doors, tore down "No Smoking" signs, and kicked over trash cans. Zero fucks. We even made a point system—one point per piece of government property destroyed, like frat boys keeping conquest scores.

Sienna upped the ante; she ripped down a curtain rod, leaving it dangling like some avant-garde art. Ten points for that one.

We knew the risks—transfer to high-security, no furloughs, longer sentences. But the adrenaline hit? Worth it. The more we broke, the more it felt like we were taking back control from a system designed to break us.

No doubt, we were worse together—egging each other on—but swinging back to "old Denise" felt damn good.

The one rule? Fire extinguishers. That was Sienna's turf. Our "prison Barbie" had the cushiest gig: roaming all three facilities (FCP, FCI, and the Men's FDC) with a clipboard, checking extinguishers, and occasionally killing ants. We wouldn't mess with her hustle.

But things escalated fast. The warden called an emergency town meeting. Mr. Martinez, the Prison Administrator, took center stage.

Short, stocky, usually chill. That day? Bright red and furious, waving the curtain rod.

"Whoever did this, step forward, you sicko!" he barked.

No one moved. Heidi and I lost it—snorting, laughing, and bolting back into C4.

"Buddy, he's so mad," Heidi gasped, breathless with laughter. I leaned on the wall, wheezing.

Then June got caught. She smeared marshmallow fluff on a woman's locker and the woman ratted her out. Next thing we knew, June was handcuffed in front of the lunch line.

Mr. Martinez sent her straight to the SHU at FCI. Honestly, cuffs were a bit overkill, but then again, nothing screams "you really screwed up" like handcuffs in a place where everyone's already locked up.

Since June was our best electrician, Heidi and I tried to get her back by jamming carrots in the fridge fan, figuring they'd have no choice but to call her in. Instead, a wave of carrot mush blasted us. Imagine us laughing, trying to clean up that disaster before we got caught. We even messed with a fire extinguisher—crossing our own line—just to make it look like they nailed the wrong girl. Still, no dice.

We finally gave up on getting June back. Then Heidi got denied boot camp (her shot at early release); it pushed Heidi over the edge. So when a guard told her to move her locker, she snapped. She *hurled* a chair at her—*Take that, bitch!*—like she was running the show and didn't give a damn. After all, she was used to calling the shots.

Heidi got arrested for attempting to assault a CO and was sent to the SHU at FCI.

From solitary, Heidi sent me messages, daring me to stir up trouble and get transferred too. But I had to focus on getting out—not moving up. We made a buddy pact instead: to meet in LA—someday.

* * * *

Finally, after what felt like forever, I was eligible for the five-hundred-hour drug program. The best part? Graduate, and they knock a year off your sentence. Officially, it was called the Residential Drug Abuse program (RDAP), designed for inmates with a diagnosed drug disorder. But here's the thing: you didn't actually have to be an addict. Just a drug charge would do.

Since RDAP inmates were housed together, I moved to C2. I ended up with three roommates, and we clicked right away. My bunkie, whom I called Bae, was pregnant and about to pop—she didn't work. One of the others, an older woman, worked food service at the FCI docks, and the last hustled at UNICOR. All were sharp, chill, and for the most part, drama-free. It felt like a little oasis compared to the madness of C4.

For whatever reason, I'd always been good at making connections. High school, the streets, prison—it didn't matter. I could blend into any crowd. I became a chameleon again, kicking back on the track with everyone: Asian, white, Black, Hispanic, you name it. We debated politics, traded poetry, and talked art and philosophy. I "talked stories" with the Islanders, played spades with the grandmas, soaked up gang-life wisdom, sang hymns, prayed with the Jesus freaks. Hell, I even had deep convos with the COs. The Feds don't discriminate—young, old, rich, broke, Black, Brown, white, disabled, gay, straight, or ginger—if you caught a federal charge, you were in. I found my way into every clique with ease. And yeah, I missed Heidi. But I knew we'd reconnect—eventually. Time was just the middleman. Time—my worst enemy—slowed to a crawl, like a snail on Valium.

Still, my main one was Sienna, my ride-or-die. We didn't room together, but we both lived in C2. Every day we hit the track or worked out to those cheesy aerobic *Bodies in Motion* VHS tapes by Gilad. We watched CNN and *60 Minutes* to see what was going on in the world. Mail call? Together. Meals? Together.

Then came some good news: my old friends Lefty and Nicole transferred in from FCI. My Hawaii 022 girls were back. I had my own little bad-girl posse again, and it felt like things were finally falling into place.

I also started going to church services. In here, your mindset can make or break you, and I needed peace. The volunteers were full of love and light, always finding me in the back of a crowded service to lay hands on me and tell me God had a plan. That He'd never left me. I wanted to grow. And I wanted to lift others while I did.

Next step in the glow-up? A new job. I was burning out in the kitchen, but it had its perks. The foreman played music while we worked, and one day the Goo Goo Dolls came on. Johnny Rzeznik belting out "Name." It cut straight through me—all those lost dreams that were tossed away. Shit, it was deep.

But what I still needed was a change of pace. Up before dawn and worn out by lunch prep—I'd never worked that hard in my life. Some days I broke down crying. The foreman would shake her head and say, "Trigo, get outta here. Go rest."

Eventually, I scored a transfer to bottom C2 bathroom orderly. In layman's terms? I became the janitor. I swept, mopped, cleaned toilets, scrubbed showers, and restocked every stall with toilet paper. I cleaned piss, shit, blood, and hair, but honestly? It was a win. Took me about an hour a day. After that? Free time. I'd hit the track with Sienna, grab lunch, nap, read, and sit under the old-fashioned hairdryer with deep conditioner in and a *Cosmopolitan* magazine in hand, daydreaming about the OC life. It gave me space to breathe, think, and just be.

I was in the best shape of my life. I'd daydream about wearing a bikini, strutting down Huntington Beach with Stacy between lifeguard towers three and five. Sometimes I was nine again, zinc on my nose, belly-boarding until I wiped out. Other times, I was building sandcastles with my brothers.

BEEP—BEEP—BEEP

"Inmate Ramirez, report to the officer's station. Inmate Ramirez."

Just like that, the ocean was gone. It was hard to dream without the smell of Coppertone or the salty ocean breeze, but Sienna and I made do, working on our farmer tans by rolling up our sleeves and shorts as high as we could. Sometimes, we'd get "shots" from the COs for showing too much skin, but whatever. The risk was always worth it. Girl's gotta live, skin's gotta tan.

Honestly, I was just making up for lost time—and lost sunlight. Nothing felt better than lying out in the yard, listening to '90s R&B on my Walkman, letting the music melt the bars away for a few minutes. But the reality always crept back in: the barbed wire, the "toxic" barrels next to the track, the endless shouts from COs. It never let you forget where you were.

* * * *

By March of 1998, there was a chance to leave the prison camp and work outside the facility for a week. I jumped at it, found someone to cover my janitor shift, and climbed into the prison's white work van.

As we pulled away, I couldn't believe how big the world looked.

The first time out was electric—just seeing the vast stretch of the bay made me feel alive. Ten of us were driven into San Francisco, and our job? Scraping bird shit off the roof of Alcatraz. I'm not even kidding. After janitor and gardening duty, it didn't faze me. No job was too gross.

Another time, we painted a house—way better than bird crap. I got to see the Golden Gate Bridge glowing orange, white sailboats skipping across the bay, couples walking into seafood restaurants. Bicycles. Dogs. Flowers. Life.

And honestly? It was fucking depressing.

I know, I know—it should've been a reprieve. But all it did was remind me of what I didn't have. So, I decided: if I couldn't be out in the world, I'd bring the outside world to me.

Step one? I needed real cosmetics—none of the bullshit they sold on commissary. I wanted name brands. No, I'm not talking Chanel luxury skin moisturizers or La Prairie caviar eye cream, for fuck's sake. Just something from CVS…okay, and maybe MAC. I was in desperate need of some MAC lipstick.

Who better to pull off a little smuggling operation for Agent 99 than my Maxwell Smart brother, Jeff? On school breaks, he'd visit and, when no one was watching, toss a tube of Russian Red MAC lipstick over the fence. Easy. When the perimeter truck was gone and the guards were distracted, a rolled-down window and—*whoosh*—that's all it took.

And even though I was a "holy roller," I convinced Jeff to pack the lipstick tube with pot. Yep—weed. We took our chances. We loved the thrill. Bad girl turned good girl gone bad again—I wasn't blind to the risks. Smuggling was my way of saying "screw you" to the whole system. I needed to feel like *me*—a natural-born rebel. Being good all the time was impossible.

The hardest part? Sharing. One puff never got anyone high enough to forget their problems, but it was enough to get them "dirty" if they were called for a random drug test. That meant SHU, a transfer to the FCI across the street, and a year added back onto your sentence. Same went for the homemade hooch. It gave us a buzz, but there was no such thing as happy hour in prison.

And here's the kicker: I hadn't even graduated from the drug program yet.

When you've lived fast, prison slows you down so much it mocks you. The hours drag on, and the boredom turns into rebellion. You take chances just to see the cause and effect. You take chances just to feel alive again. I ran the track, listening to "Mo Money Mo Problems" on my Walkman and laughed—because here I was, an OG now, whistling catcalls at newcomers and running things inside just like I had outside in the OC. So, I leveled up.

I was importing luxury—designer soaps, real shampoo, legit skincare, nail polish, and cosmetics—you name it. Anything to feel human again. My prized possession? A pair of white Keds with a one-inch platform. Prison chic.

It took time. Good thing I had plenty. I studied routines, mapped the patterns, and soon I had a system.

Trisha, a little blond Latina and the prison's town driver, was my key. People on the outside deposited cash into her mom's account. On her runs around the Bay Area, she'd buy what I needed and stash it in a trash bag near US Army Camp Parks, a mile from the FPC.

From there, my UNICOR roommate—who operated a forklift—picked it up, hid it with UNICOR materials, and got it to the FCI dock. Lani, a food services worker and fellow 022, brought it into our camp on yet another forklift.

Then Bae—my pregnant roommate and tight with Lani—waited at the dock for the drop. When Lani made the pass, I called in Kay, who handled the trash. She'd roll a gray barrel to lower C2, where I, the janitor, waited. Circuit complete. I got the goods but everyone got a cut.

Whether it was coke or conditioner, I knew how to move product.

The hardest part wasn't hiding it from the guards—it was the inmates. Snitches were always watching. The drug program had that "keep out of trouble" clause hanging over my head. And you know the drill—SHU, an added year on my sentence, regret, shame. So, I got creative.

Face creams went in the outside vents. Nail polish in the rafters, MAC makeup tucked into the curtain hem in my cell. I swapped cheap shampoo for the good stuff. I wasn't just surviving; I was running an underground Sephora.

Yes, it was risky, but the smuggling ring made prison exciting—*that* rush. The same rush that had gotten me locked up in the first place. But I knew living on the edge was the only way I'd survive the next few years.

Because here's what I learned: drop Denise naked in the middle of the desert, and she'll walk out the other side clothed, healthy, and rocking MAC lipstick.

Still, officially, I was part of the five-hundred-hour drug program. The teacher was chill; he let us joke around and always talked about how weed should be legal. We laughed. Legal weed? Back then, it sounded absurd.

He didn't bother teaching us about drugs—we already knew all that. Most of us had used, dealt, or made them. Instead, he focused on addiction, behavior patterns, and how to avoid bad influences. Did I learn anything new? Not really. But that wasn't the point. It was the year off your sentence that made it worth it.

* * * *

Four years in, I was craving a new thrill, so I opened a body piercing shop out of my cell. It was nothing like the Electric Chair on Main Street in HB, where I got my belly ring back in the day. But piercings were still hot and we were bored, so inmates were booked out for months. There was something satisfying about pushing a needle through someone's skin. No ice, no numbing—just thread the hole and tie it off until I could smuggle in real jewelry. But it wasn't about the pain—it was about giving others a sense of identity, a way to feel like themselves again inside a system built to erase it. In return, they cleaned my bathrooms, cooked my meals, and saved front-row seats for movie night.

I was running the joint.

When my pregnant bunkie, Bae, went into labor, I wasn't about to play midwife on a concrete floor, so I stayed up all night with her, raising hell until they agreed to take her to the hospital. They kept stalling, obsessed with whether she was fully dilated.

She gave birth in the hospital, cuffed to the bed. Then they brought her back, babyless. I stayed by her side, helping her through it the only way I could.

To distract her, we needed entertainment. In prison, that meant endless talking dog movies. After the thousandth one, we were all on the edge. That's when Sienna convinced her guard friend to sneak in real movies—*Boogie Nights*, *The People vs. Larry Flynt*, stuff we weren't supposed to have. We'd steal TVs from the chapel or lower C3, smuggle them into our cells, and watch between inmate counts. It wasn't Netflix and chill—it was nerve-wracking and illicit—but it gave us a little thrill. A little life.

They don't call FCI and FPC the "rape prison" for nothing. A lot of shady shit was going on. If you wanted anything, you had to play the game. I didn't kiss ass like some girls. I ignored the guards. Treated them like total dorks. It worked. The more indifferent we acted, the more desperate they were for our attention. Soon, they were breaking rules *for us*, just to prove they were cool.

We had guards—male and female—wrapped. One even let me on the main prison computer, the one with private info on all sixteen of my codefendants. A goldmine. There's nothing like researching your codefendants, especially the ones who've snitched on you. I knew everything: their release dates, transfer locations, all of it. Turns out, my case involved charges against sixteen different codefendants.

But here's the thing: sometimes the inmates didn't get what they thought they wanted. No matter what we asked for or what we thought we needed at the time, we were still powerless. Still down and out, and the guards took full advantage. They held the power over us, and they used it against us.

* * * *

Then—finally—I caught a break. I got approved for a thirty-six-hour furlough. Within one hundred miles only, and you had to have at least eighteen months left. But still. A real bed. Real food. Family. So, I planned to spend my time with my family in San Francisco. The next furlough would be a five-day one, and if I made it to six months left, I'd be allowed to fly back to my hometown. This was the government's way of pretending to "reacclimate" us. Honestly, it's *all* bullshit.

But still, to me it was a dream come true.

I woke up buzzing on March 31, 1998. I expected a rifle to be aimed at my back the moment I stepped out of camp. But instead, there was Mom and Jeff waiting, and I slipped quickly into the car. As we drove into San Francisco, I couldn't stop staring out the window, spellbound. The city was alive, and for the first time, I was part of it.

We got to the hotel—more like a cozy house, with a kitchen and everything. Dad, Dee, and Greg were waiting. Their hugs were real, tight, full of love, which meant everything. I needed that reminder of who I was, where I came from, and where I belonged.

"Hey, kiddo!" Dad grinned, pulling me into a bear hug. "We missed you."

"I missed you too," I said, my voice thick.

They'd set the big wooden dining table—kinda like the same one I remembered from better days, where we'd sit for hours talking, laughing, arguing. This wasn't some Sunday feast straight out of *Goodfellas*, but a simple, healthy breakfast. Fresh-squeezed orange juice, bagels, eggs, seedless grapes bursting with sweetness. Prison food didn't stand a chance.

I went to scoop some scrambled eggs onto my plate, but somehow half of them ended up on the table. Greg chuckled, leaning back in his chair. "You stunads…some things never change."

I laughed, shaking my head as I scraped up the egg. "Guess I'm consistent," I said. For a brief moment, I felt relaxed.

Greg hadn't seen me since the Marshals picked me up and told me Lorenzo had been found dead. Visiting was "too hard" for him, which stung, but whatever—everyone deals differently. Peter didn't come either. He was figuring out his life in Vegas with Greg and was still not on good terms with Dee, so he wasn't welcome on this trip. I was bummed, but there was nothing I could do.

Mom was on her best behavior, sitting with my dad and Dee, trying to keep things smooth. My two brothers were playful, cracking jokes, but even in the comfort, sadness hung in the air. We all pretended everything was normal, but it wasn't. This was a countdown. I kept glancing at the clock.

We all got ready to see the city. I changed into jeans and a t-shirt—no fashion statement. I just wanted to fit in. At Union Square, I stood frozen at the MAC counter, overwhelmed by lipstick options. I'd dreamt of this moment. Now, I couldn't move.

A saleswoman hovered. "Need help, honey?"

I shook her off. "I'm fine."

My mom came over, gentle. "Do you want anything?"

"No," I muttered. There were too many choices, and I was afraid of making the wrong one. I was overwhelmed. Also, after what I put my family through, I didn't feel worthy of anything. I just wanted to leave. I had no idea who I was anymore. Being thrown into a cage changes you.

We cruised the city, but I couldn't relax. I felt like everyone knew, like I had "INMATE" stamped on my forehead. And it didn't help that Jeff nudged me in the side with a smirk and said, "Where you wanna go next, Dublin?"

"Ha ha, very funny, Chino," I shot back, matching his grin. But even though I was surrounded by love, I felt like a visitor from another planet.

At Fisherman's Wharf, the menu had too many choices. My mom looked worried. "Denise, are you okay?"

Then my dad joined in, his voice full of cheer. "'Niesey, have anything you want. Lobsters? Clams? Both? Live it up!"

I couldn't take it. "Just order anything," I choked out, then bolted to the bathroom.

At the sink, I stared at the automatic faucet like it was a puzzle. The world had changed and moved on without me. Why couldn't I turn the damn water on?

I forced myself to pull it together. I had to enjoy this time—*had to.*

The rest of the night was a blur. Before turning myself back in, I bought a bunch of products from CVS—stuff the girls had requested—and tossed them into a garbage bag. We dumped it a mile away from camp at the Army barracks. My smuggling ring would retrieve it later.

On April 1, stepping back through the prison doors, I felt more comfortable inside than I was out there. The April Fool's joke was on me.

I thought of Tupac and how he always talked about surviving the bullshit, and it made me smile.

* * * *

I stayed busy with routine, worked during the day, drug program at night. Then one night at mail call, the news hit. Frank Sinatra was gone. I cried. He was my youth, my family, my Sunday dinners. Everything I'd left behind. But I kept moving. That's all I could do. Through all the shenanigans and close calls, somehow, I graduated. After completing the drug program, we all got a year knocked off our sentences, which meant some of the girls walked out free.

I still had a year left. As happy as I was for them, I couldn't shake the feeling of loss—especially my roommates, whom I had grown so close to and loved. It was bittersweet. Just when you get comfortable, just when you start to build a family in a place where family should never exist, it gets ripped away again.

We threw a big party for the girls finishing the five-hundred-hour drug program. It was tradition for their families to send outfits—no one wanted to leave in prison sweats. Some asked for cheesy club wear, others for tea dresses or slouchy gangbanger style. I found it all fascinating, especially since I loved fashion. We came from different worlds—different ages, classes, beliefs, and zip codes—but I started to see our sameness more than our differences. Selling drugs, robbing stores, violence on the streets—we made excuses that crime was the only way we knew how to survive, but despite the differences in our stories, our frameworks were one and the same. The narrative of crime is a narrative about acceptance, of craving it so much that you'll do anything to be seen, heard, and understood. You'll lie, hustle, and cheat your heart out just to feel like you belong. Money and success are merely side effects of a larger epidemic.

It hurt watching them leave. They were my prison family. Still, I had Sienna, Nicole, and Lefty. And we always reminded ourselves: We don't belong here. We come in alone, and one day, we'll leave alone.

Just when I thought it was smooth sailing, things shifted. A tough-looking Mexican girl who used to tell me I was pretty and funny suddenly decided I'd given her a dirty look during a movie. It was probably just my RBF (Resting Bitch Face), but she took it personally, and now she wanted to beat me up.

Every time I passed her, she hissed, "Trigo, don't even look my way, cuz I will beat ya, you hear?"

It was a constant stress. "You think you're better than all of us? You think you're so cool?" If she lost her temper and hit me, I'd lose my year off. Even though I'd graduated, they still held that over me.

Sienna kept advising me, "Just ignore her, buddy. She's a total loser." The irony of someone in prison calling someone else a "loser." Ha.

Walking the track one day, Sienna grinned, nudged me, and said, "Buddy, your song is on!" Whether it was "Graduate" or "Losing a Whole Year" by Third Eye Blind, she'd sing along like they were written just for me. We laughed at the absurdity—because who knew if I was actually going to graduate…or lose a whole year.

As much as I didn't want to fight, I couldn't let her punk me out. If I did, I'd be a punk-ass bitch, and everyone would take advantage. So, to save my prison rep, I went full Orange County valley girl on her. I'd mouth off "Loser," making an "L" with my thumb and finger on my forehead, praying she didn't snap. After all, she had something to lose too. If things went sideways, she'd be sent to the FCI too.

Since I wasn't in the drug program anymore, I had to move out of C2. I could either live in an empty bunk next to the Mexican girl, or I could move into the open-floor dorm in C4—no privacy, just dorm-style living.

I begged Burns for another option, but she wouldn't budge. So, back to C4 I went, the place where I first met Heidi. It felt like ages ago. The place was off the hook—loud, dirty, and stank from girls hoarding food and never throwing out trash.

And to make things worse, a new prison administrator, Ben Arnold. Blond hair, short man's complex, and a real dick. He treated us like workhorses. He even stressed out Sienna, waking her at all hours to spray for bugs. It brought me right back to Santa Rita.

I was at my wit's end. The prison was falling apart—always running out of toilet paper, power outages, fire alarms in the middle of the night. Hours stuck outside in the rain waiting to be counted. And the food? Desert Storm leftovers from the Gulf War. Horrible.

One night, Sienna's bridge partner had had enough. She just said, "Fuck it," and escaped right after the 4:00 P.M. stand-up count. We cheered her on, but after an all-nighter filled with sirens and SWAT teams, we went back to our misery. At least she never got caught. She was a legend.

Not like the '86 escape when some guy landed a stolen helicopter in the FCI exercise yard and swooped up his lover. They got away—only to be found ten days later buying wedding rings at the mall. Still, you had to admire the heroism of armed air piracy and the romance of it all. No, I didn't think he was Prince Charming, but I had to respect how much he sacrificed for his lover. It made me think about how much Lorenzo had sacrificed—me.

Chapter Twenty-Three

Life Goes On

MARCH 1999–OCTOBER 1999

In March 1999, I got the good news: I was eligible for a five-day furlough. This sorry-ass bitch was heading back to the OC, baby.

I was at the weight pile, crushing leg-press sets with Sienna and Nicole, but today I was floating somewhere over the rainbow. Just like Dorothy on her way outta Oz. I repeated, "There's no place like home, there's no place like home, there's no place like home," clicking the heels of my Keds together like they were ruby slippers.

Sienna grinned at Nicole. "Dude, she's lost it."

Nicole snorted. "That's old news."

I smiled. "You both love my twisted mind."

Sienna chuckled, but I saw the sadness behind her smile—a sting of jealousy I understood all too well.

"I'm happy for you, buddy. First it's a furlough, then freedom. You're gonna get out soon and forget all about us losers in here."

"Not a chance," I said. "But I might forget we're living next to that toxic barrel. Breathing those chemicals all this time? By the time we get out, it won't matter. We'll all be dead anyway."

Sienna rolled her eyes. "Right! Did you see the guys in hazmat suits? No one knows what's in that thing. No wonder it's here."

"Perfect way to get rid of prisoners," I said, trying not to laugh. "Plus, no chance of getting pregnant. So there's that."

Letty, working out nearby, jumped in. "True that. It's the government's way of wiping out lowlifes." She smirked, then on a serious note added, "Forget all that. See you when you get back. Enjoy your furlough—and don't think about us for one second."

"Yeah, enjoy, Denise," Nicole said with a smirk. "Don't do anything we wouldn't do."

I shot back, "You mean commit a crime? Not without you guys."

In the counselor's office, Mrs. Burns handed me my instructions. "Trigo, a cab will pick you up and take you to the BART."

I blinked. "The BART?"

"It's a train—Bay Area Rapid Transit. Take it to the airport, then catch a flight to John Wayne Airport in Orange County."

"Did my family send my ticket?" I asked, hoping for a good old-fashioned paper stub.

"It's paperless, Trigo," she said. "Show your prison ID—that's your ticket."

I stared at her, lost. "Don't you need an actual ticket to get on a plane?"

Mrs. Burns snapped, "Are you ready to go home or not?"

I nodded slowly, trying to act like I got it. But in my head, I was already picturing myself accidentally boarding a flight to Mexico and starting this whole disaster over again.

The morning of my furlough, just as I stepped into the cab, Mrs. Burns stopped me cold. Her look could've frozen lava.

"Don't miss your flight. No drinking or drugs—we'll test you. And by God, don't do anything stupid, like commit a crime. Be on time. I'll be waiting outside."

I nodded, trying to process it all. As the cab pulled away, wearing my gray sweats, I felt completely out of place. The fearless me—the one who'd crossed borders without a second thought—felt like a ghost. I was sure they wouldn't let me on the plane without a paper ticket, but somehow, I made it through. Confused? Definitely. Scared? Absolutely. But I pushed forward.

On the plane, my seatmate leaned over with a smile.

"Have you ever been to Orange County? I haven't. My daughter just had a baby. I'm going to help out."

"Yeah, I live there…used to," I said, my mind elsewhere.

She nodded. "Where are you coming from?"

I was too tired to lie. "Prison. I'm on a five-day furlough to see my family."

Her eyes widened. For a second, she didn't say anything. Then, quieter, "What happened?"

I gave her the short version. "Flying to Hawaii with a guy. He hid drugs in my bag. I knew he was carrying, didn't know he'd planted them on me. He got seven months. I got seven years." She blinked, then softened. "That's rough. I'm sorry."

I just shrugged. "*C'est la vie.*"

We didn't say much after that. She wished me luck, and the silence settled in—loud and heavy.

Was she judging me?

Or was that just me, judging myself?

As I stepped off the jetway stairs, a blast of warm air hit me, thick with the scent of jet fuel and sunscreen. Orange County. Jesus Christ. I'm finally home.

Inside the terminal, my feet moved on instinct, like they remembered the way better than I did. I couldn't believe I was finally here.

The memories clawed at me, it had all started in an airport just like this one. But I pushed them aside. That "vacation" ended up being a prison sentence. Years I'd never get back.

But this wasn't about the past. Not now. Not with five days ahead of me.

I didn't even glance at baggage claim. God, could I ever travel with luggage again? The thought felt absurd. I was already moving, weaving through families and business travelers like a woman possessed.

I needed one thing.

One person.

Mom.

Seeing my mom in her car on the curb made my heart surge. She stepped out of the car, and we hugged—tight. That embrace felt like it lasted forever.

On the drive to her new place, I hesitated before asking, "Mom, can we drive past the old house?" She sighed, eyes on the road. Then she nodded.

We sat in silence in front of my childhood home. I took it all in—how Dad had carefully laid thick squares of El Toro Zoysia grass, and Grandpa's cypress trees still stood, guarding the lawn like soldiers. The cracked sidewalk where I chalked hopscotch and played jacks with neighborhood girls. The spot where our old lemonade stand used to be, just to the left. The stained-glass window on the side, still catching the light.

I would've given anything to go inside. To stand in my room one last time. To say goodbye. I wanted to peek over the fence just to glimpse the lemon and apricot trees, to see the backyard patio, and breathe in all the childhood memories that kept me alive when I was alone in a cell.

This is why I hadn't given up—because life was once so sweet, and the thought of that sweetness made me believe there was still something worth fighting for.

Honestly, they'd probably have to call Stevens and Delaney to drag me out. Too much left unsaid. My mom gave me a knowing look.

"I know, honey. It's hard."

I mourned my life all over again.

It felt like yesterday when Stacy and I popped in our perfect mixtape. We'd dance around in our socks, shouting lyrics from the Go-Go's and laughing like the world couldn't touch us. Getting ready for nothing and everything.

But it also felt like a lifetime ago.

Now Stacy was gone. My home was gone. And the life I once knew? Gone.

Life doesn't hit pause when you step away. It holds two fingers down, hits record, and keeps playing forward—without allowing you to rewind—whether you like it or not.

Finally, Mom broke the silence. "Come on, sweetheart. Let's go have some fun." She drove me to her new condo. It felt strange, like someone else's—but I tried to settle in.

No girlfriends showed up. No welcome committee. No friends holding up colorful banners spelling out *Welcome Home.* Nothing like what I used to imagine from my bunk at night. I could've picked up the phone. But too much time had passed. No one was coming. And there was no one I wanted to call. It wasn't about friends anymore—it was family.

I had no clue where Angela and Maya were. My LA friend Marcy, solid as ever, had moved to New York, and Brandy and I hadn't talked since she visited me in Hawaii. The only thing I got from her after my arrest was a letter with the lyrics to Candlebox's "Far Behind," a haunting reminder of loss and the distance that grows between people. Not a simple Hallmark card with a cat dangling from a tree saying, "*Hang in there.*"

But she'd been through her own kind of hell too.

Charlotte warned me back in '95, "You'll be lucky if even one or two friends stick around by the time you're out."

Did I believe her? Not then.

"Jeff should be here any minute," Mom said. "He cleared his schedule to spend time with you."

I couldn't believe it. He'd be graduating in three months—soon officially a doctor. I was so proud of him.

"So, what do you want to do first?" Mom asked.

No-brainer. "The café. I'm dying for real food."

Just then, Jeff walked in. "What's up, gangsta?" He pulled me into a hug. "Let's eat. I'm starving."

"Yeah, let's do it."

Back at Café Pasquini, I sat outside in a bistro chair and devoured everything the chef brought out. First, a Caprese. Then a crisp, tangy Caesar. We shared the famous Grand Prix sandwich and a slice of pepperoni pizza, but it was the pasta al Pomodoro—kissed with Calabrian chili—that fed my soul. I laughed, watching Jeff chase capers across his chicken piccata, wishing this moment could stretch on forever.

Not just to be a rebel, but knowing it was safe, I broke the prison's no-drinking rule, sneaking a glass of Cabernet. It'd be out of my system before check-in. We snapped a photo, but I swapped my wine glass with Mom's Coke—no evidence.

The next morning, Jeff drove me to the salon where Marina worked. My roots were desperate for help. The second I saw her, time froze. She put down the blow dryer and walked over, cool as ever, and hugged me tight. "It's so good to see you! I'm almost done," she said, running her fingers through my hair. "You're still gorgeous. But this hair? Definitely needs help." She winked. "Don't worry, it'll be as beautiful as you when we're done."

As I sat in her chair, we slipped right back into old rhythms. She brought up one of her old clients—my ex, Lorenzo.

"I can't believe all that happened."

"I know," I said quietly. "Hard to believe he's really gone."

"God, he was hot." She laughed, giving me a playful smack.

"I know. I miss that." We both cracked up.

And just like that, we were gossiping again.

As I sat under the dryer, flipping through an old issue of *InStyle,* I thought about the rusty dryer back in prison, and my mind drifted.

People had written to me—some out of love, some out of curiosity. But a lot of the messages from old girlfriends were different. Mean-spirited, heavy with gossip and cheap shots. A few mentioned nonchalantly that they'd gone on vacation with guys I used to date, like that wouldn't sting. One even asked my brother if I'd "lost my looks" in prison—if I was fat now, or if my hair was short. It was strange.

But Dad…Dad's letters were different. He never missed a week. Just steady words of hope and faith. Said he prayed for me every day. Those were the ones I folded up carefully and read over and over. They reminded me I was still worth loving.

Marina worked her magic, washing out the brassy CVS box blond and leaving warm brown tones with sun-kissed caramel streaks.

That night, Jeff and I went to Birraporetti's, our old Irish-Italian bar. Peach bellinis, like always. I wasn't out to get wasted or drinking to numb anything. I just wanted to feel normal. Free.

Then Darren walked in—my high school boyfriend. Like some movie moment.

We sank into the red leather booths and traded stories—my prison tales, his screwups. There was no judgment. Just love. We howled, remembering Stacy, how she got her fingers stuck in the driving simulator and the firemen had to weld her out. Instant freshman legend. Only Stacy. For a minute, I was back at a bonfire on Huntington Beach, someone's mixtape blasting '80s tunes, the warm crackle of the fire, and that sweet, careless freedom of being teenagers. On a higher level, I think God sent him. I couldn't have picked a better person to walk through that door.

The rest of the days blurred together. My dad, Dee, Greg, and Peter all visited.

"Glad mummy dust didn't get to you, and you were able to make it," I teased Pete.

Dee rolled her eyes, and Greg grinned. "Yeah, Pete—lucky you dodged more mummy dust, or we'd have to put you in a pyramid and lay you to rest."

Pete smirked, shaking his head, and Jeff gave him a playful smack on the back. Laughter rippled through the room. It felt good, the Trigos together again, like nothing had changed. For a moment, it almost felt like everything was normal. Then, just when I started to believe it, reality hit. It was time to go back.

I wasn't free. Not yet.

Eleven more months in prison.

Six months in a halfway house.

Five years of probation after my release.

So basically, six and a half more years of this bullshit. The neverending punishment.

* * * *

When I got back to prison, slipping into the routine was easy. That July, one of the guards broke the news. JFK Jr.'s plane went down. "No," I said. "That can't be true." But it was. All on board, gone. Even behind bars, a girl's allowed to mourn the most beautiful man who ever lived. But by October of '99, the place was a complete disaster. The short-timers were the worst. For them, this was just a stint, not home like it was for the rest of us. They did dumb stuff just to piss people off: leaving clothes in the washer and walking off, screwing up the whole system. We'd end up folding their crap just to wash our own.

Sienna and I couldn't even watch the news anymore. We had no idea what was happening in the world, and the girls couldn't care less. At lunch break, they claimed the TV, glued to *Jerry Springer*. At night, we were also outnumbered, so we couldn't watch any political shows. Picking a fight wasn't worth it. I knew the cost: one wrong move, you're in the SHU, with a fresh year tacked on.

The place was crawling with rookies too—new guards with zero respect and no clue how to handle us. But hey, one win: the hothead Mexican girl got into it with a short-timer and got shipped across the street. No more worrying about her screwing up my release date.

I had four months left before they'd send me to a halfway house. I was officially a short-timer now. But once I got a taste of that Orange County air, I knew—I was born for freedom. I didn't need to take this shit anymore. It was time to play smart, fight back, and beat the system at its own game.

And I came up with the perfect plan.

My lawyer had retired, so my dad connected me with Simon Fujimori, a sharp public defender in Hawaii. I laid it out for him: the DA wanted me to testify against Philip, who was facing life and kept delaying his trial. Simon saw the play: file a motion for sentence reduction, knowing the DA plans to call me in for testimony. I might as well reap the benefits. We both knew the trial was never going to happen. This was leverage. I'd use the system against itself.

Simon promised if the court approved, I could skip the halfway house. This wasn't just about getting out early. I could wait. Easy. This? This was about *winning*.

I told Sienna I might see her at the track next week—worst case, a round-trip in shackles. I gave her everything in my locker, introduced her to Candi, fresh in from Malibu on a drug charge. I wasn't about to leave Sienna hanging without a new buddy.

Letty and Lani had been released; Charlotte was still at the FCI.

Me? I wasn't sticking around a minute longer. Came in alone. I'd leave alone.

But one last thing: Mrs. Burns.

She had a file on me. SIS had been sniffing around, digging into rumors about our relationships with corrupt guards. Sienna had cracked, spilled to Mrs. Burns, and begged for protection. That set off alarms. If Burns narc'd on the guards or us, my release was toast.

But she didn't. "Don't say another word," she told me. "I protect my long-timers. Short-timers? Not so much."

I didn't ask questions. I just kept moving.

On October 24, 1999, I was called to R&D—Receiving and Discharge. The US Marshals walked me out of the Federal Prison Camp just as Internal Affairs rolled in, ready to hook me up to a lie detector and press me about dirty guards.

But I was already gone.

I slipped out calm as hell, like Neo and Trinity in an action movie—walking in slow motion as everything behind me exploded.

This flight back to Hawaii was different. I didn't pray for the plane to nosedive into the Pacific just to end it all. This time, I wanted to live.

When California handed me over to the Hawaiian Marshals, Abigail greeted me with that familiar grin.

"You look good, girl," she said.

I gave her the quick rundown on the 022 girls. "Thank God Nicole made it to the camp. She makes killer kimchi. Her husband still writes her love letters and she just laughs at him for being sentimental. *Ohana* for life, that one."

Abigail chuckled. “Send her my best. Yeah, she’s a real one.”

Back at OCCC, they placed me in a new module—Module 11—and it felt different. The guards didn’t yell. They handed me smokes, let me step outside. The inmates waited their turn, showed respect. Word had gotten around—I’d been down a long time. *I felt different too.*

I came back stronger. Wiser.

At dinner, it was kālua pig and rice—same as always. But this time, I tasted it. Smoky. Tender. Like it had been slow-cooked in an *imu*, backyard luau style. And for once, I didn’t just eat—I appreciated it. The food, the land, the people, the deep-rooted traditions that made Hawaii more than just a place. It felt like something I was part of.

Church services were called. I found a quiet moment with a volunteer and told her, “I’m going to court tomorrow. I might be getting released.” I didn’t ask for prayers for myself; I asked for my family. “I know I’ll be okay,” I admitted, “but they have their hopes up. I don’t want to let them down again.”

She held my hand and prayed. When she finished, she looked me in the eye and said, “God says you’re getting out. But you might not like everything the judge has to say. He’s doing it for a reason.” Then she added, “Don’t rush into a relationship. God has someone special for you—someone to build a family with.”

I smiled, hoping she was right. And hoping he was wicked hot.

That night, I smoked my last cigarette under the stars. The Hawaiian trade winds brushed my face as I stared past the barbed wire, imagining freedom.

Fear whispered, *Could I make it on the outside?*

Monday, October 25, 1999. I stood before Judge Enzo again. This time, he didn’t seem so intimidating. The courtroom was nearly empty—just Bojo sitting in the back, grinning. His smile calmed me.

The DA, Lawrence Brown, and US Attorney Dominic Hayes from San Francisco were on my side now. They wanted my testimony, and they knew better than to piss me off. I could always come down with a sudden case of “amnesia.”

The judge hesitated. "I can't just release you after all this time and let you walk the streets with nowhere to go."

Bojo jumped up. "Dr. Trigo wen wire money for one ticket. I'll drive her to da airport, no worries!"

I felt the corners of my lips turn up. After a brief pause, Judge Enzo ruled for early release. My heart swelled.

But then came the condition: the judge ruled I'd live with Dad in Vegas—not California. He feared Philip might come after me if I stayed in OC. A chill ran through me. I remembered the church volunteer's warning. But I wasn't about to show fear. I spoke up, steady and clear:

"I'm not scared of him."

Enzo laid out more conditions. "Young lady, I'm ordering you to continue your education—and I don't mean art school. And you'll be drug tested. For five years."

I groaned silently. I had just served five years, and now I was being told where to live, that I had to go to school, and *art* didn't count?

Now came the fatherly speech. "You spent your time with the wrong crowd," Enzo said. "You know better now, Miss Trigo. You're smart, you're astute, you're an attractive young woman. There's absolutely no reason why you needed to be here in the first place."

"I understand that too," I said, cutting in.

Bojo shot me a sharp glare, silently telling me to knock it off.

Judge Enzo continued, "And there certainly isn't any reason why you need to come back here. You still have time to make something of yourself. You're not too old to start a family and make a life. There's just no reason in the world why you can't have a good life. Your life isn't over. It's just starting again. And you've just got to put these characters you were hanging around behind you once and for all."

It was surreal, hearing so much kindness and concern from the same man who had sentenced me to seven years in prison.

"I'd like to see you again, but when I see you again, I'd like to see you with a good education, a good job, possibly with a family, and not in a green prison suit. You understand?" Enzo concluded.

I nodded. Court recessed at 8:33 A.M.

The release process took almost as long as intake. When we finally finished, the Marshal opened a huge clothing trunk and pulled out a few random items. "Sorry," he said, shrugging. "Slim pickings right now." I couldn't have cared less. I would've run down a Paris runway in a clown suit during Fashion Week if it meant getting out. And what I got wasn't far off: slipper shoes three sizes too big, an oversized plain white t-shirt, and my old green prison pants with OCCC stenciled in white down the leg. I looked so fly.

I will never forget the day I walked out of federal prison: October 25. As I descended the courthouse steps toward Bojo's car, I kept glancing over my shoulder, half-expecting someone to call out a mistake and drag me back inside. Instead, I looked up at the gorgeous Hawaiian sky, threw my arms wide, and yelled, "Woohoo! Yessss!" I was overwhelmed. Grateful.

I was free.

Bojo laughed but motioned for me to tone it down—he was definitely not in the mood to draw more attention. On the steps, I noticed a young man speaking with his lawyer. They smiled at me, but I saw the tension in this guy's eyes—eyes that had just seen the inside of the system. My heart ached.

"Good luck," I told him. "You'll get through this. I promise you."

He exhaled sharply, as if holding his breath all along. "Thank you, and congratulations," he said, standing a little taller. His lawyer gave me a thumbs-up. Small moment. Huge meaning.

Bojo opened the car door for me. As I fastened my seatbelt, he ran around to the driver's side. Before starting the engine, he cleared his throat.

"D, Pops called. I didn't have time to make one stop. Cool if I drop off smoke, eh?" He looked sheepish. "It'll only take a second."

I blinked. Not even ten minutes out of prison, and I was about to commit a crime again? So what did I do? What anybody in my position would: get the hell out of there. "Dammit, Bojo. Do what you gotta do, but step on it. Let's get the hell out of here," I snapped, already trying to put as much distance between me and the courthouse as possible. So yeah, we drove off with a pound of weed in the back seat—exactly the kind of behavior my drug program warned against. My heart thudded. I kept glancing in the rearview, sure the cops were tailing us. How ironic would that be? Survive prison only to get caught on release day—*thug life*.

Our first stop? Ala Moana Mall. No, not for MAC. I darted into a surf shop, grabbed a pair of Roxy trunks and a tank top, changed in the bathroom, and tossed my prison rags in the trash where they belonged. "Good riddance, girlfriend," I muttered.

While Bojo wrapped up his deal (which, for the record, I wanted no part of), I sat on the beach. Half an hour later, Bojo scooped me up and asked if I wanted to be in *Baywatch*. Said he knew someone on the crew, the same guy he'd just sold weed to. I passed. I could already hear the director: *"Cut! Who's the chick with the farmer's tan?"*

After that, we went to Bojo's house. His family welcomed me with open arms—no questions, no judgment, just love. His wife served the most delicious Huli Huli chicken I'd ever tasted, and his daughter handed me a pair of white denim pants and a sweatshirt for my red-eye to Vegas.

That was healing. That was *ohana*.

Later that night, Bojo drove me to the airport. Once we got there, we hit the airport bar. Before I was even off the Island, I broke the law for the second time that day and got completely wasted on Mai Tais. I downed that sweet, dark rum like it was Hawaiian Springs water. Honestly? I felt like I'd earned it.

Was I supposed to drink? No. Call me a rebel, but I've got a little outlaw in my DNA—and that's something I love about myself.

When I landed in Las Vegas, Dad and Dee were waiting. It felt like a scene from a rom-com reunion: no luggage, just me sprinting into their arms. I broke down sobbing, ugly crying into Dad's shoulder. Joy. Relief. Exhaustion.

He pulled me back, eyes misty.

"Niesey, you did it. You're free."

Then, softly, he quoted *Ben-Hur*:

"Row well and live, 41."

My tears turned into laughter. It's one of the movies we watched at the Cabanas while I was on house arrest. If you haven't seen it, Charlton Heston's character is chained to a Roman galley, forced to row as a slave. His number was 41. That became my dad's nickname for me while I was locked up. His way of saying, keep rowing, keep pushing forward—you'll make it.

Chapter Twenty-Four

Freebird

OCTOBER 1999–PRESENT

There were plenty of loose ends after my release. Not long after, I was ordered to fly to San Francisco to meet with Dominic Hayes, the District Attorney. It was time to talk about Philip's trial. Hayes was working alongside Robert Mueller, the former FBI director and special counsel known for his high-profile investigations. Mueller was pushing for the death penalty and a capital murder charge for Philip.

When I met Hayes, he gave me a quick once-over and said, "Freedom looks good on you."

I was dressed in a sleek charcoal gray blazer and matching trousers—sharp and put-together, the kind of outfit that said, *Nobody better fuck with me.*

Hayes raised an eyebrow. "Before we get started, I need to address something," he said, his tone shifting. "The day you left Dublin Federal Prison Camp, Internal Affairs wanted to talk to you about alleged misconduct, sexual acts, and corruption involving the guards."

I played dumb. "Oh really? Huh."

"They called me," he went on. "Asked if anything happened."

"No, not at all," I said, firm and without hesitation.

He gave a dry smile. “Right. Of course not.”

I was hesitant about answering any questions Robert Mueller asked me in the grand jury. I’d already done my time, and most of it was a blur. The whole scene felt surreal—one of the main counsels sitting next to Mueller actually fell asleep in his chair mid-proceeding. Nobody batted an eye. It was so bizarre. I was *this close* to leaning over and yelling, “*BROOOOOOO WAKE UP!*” Still, I told them what I remembered, which wasn’t what they were looking for.

One thing I did know, Philip didn’t stand a chance of escaping his charges. Too many people were lined up to testify against him. But I didn’t feel sorry for Philip. You can’t just go around ordering hits on friends—or merely moving around dead bodies.

To avoid the death penalty and a life sentence, Philip was forced to reveal his involvement. His testimony implicated Fred and Duane, leaving those two goons standing with their dicks in their hands. I’m not sure if Fred and Duane had joined forces, but a private investigator they hired was blowing up my phone, asking, “Denise, could I get a statement from you? I’d like to call you in to testify for their defense, to claim Philip is a liar.”

Yeah, I wasn’t doing that, not even for those “stand-up” guys. Finally, the PI called again. “Can’t we just meet? I’ll take you to lunch.”

What is it with these guys thinking they can bribe me with food? Ha. I finally decided to fuck with him. “Sure, I’ll meet you. Get a pen and write this down. Ready? Go to the intersection of Main Street and PCH. Got it?”

He hummed. “Um, okay.”

“Now go to the pier and keep walking. Just keep walking,” I repeated.

It took him a moment, but finally, he got it. “Ha. That’s a good one.”

“Listen, I don’t want to be mean, but take a walk off the pier, buddy. As far as I’m concerned, my court days are over. I have no intention of ever setting foot in a courtroom again. Not even for a speeding ticket.”

He laughed again and said, “I understand. Denise, good luck with your life. You really didn’t deserve all that time.”

The same went for Internal Affairs. They left me messages, but I ignored them. Eventually, they stopped calling. I mean, get a life, will ya?

Consequently, Fred and Duane were forced to negotiate their own deal with the DA. Once the Feds catch people, it's survival of the fittest, every man for himself.

In the end, Fred admitted to killing James, and Duane killed Lorenzo.

The *San Francisco Gate* headline read, "Guilty Plea in S.F. Drug Dealer's Death."

Ultimately, this meant Philip wouldn't go to trial, and I wouldn't be called to testify.

Hallelujah, thank you, Lord Jesus!

Testimony stated that Duane had snuck up behind Lorenzo and shot him point-blank in the back of the head, execution-style. Fred stripped Lorenzo's body, stuffed him into a sleeping bag, and threw it in the back of the El Camino. Then they hid the car inside a storage unit. The El Camino drove to Oceanside, a place chosen for its high murder rate.

They stopped for breakfast, leaving the body in the truck bed with a tarp over it while they ate eggs. After paying the bill, they drove across the street from the IHOP to a parking lot. They tossed Lorenzo's beautiful, lifeless body in the dumpster, throwing several garbage bags on top of him. Still hard to believe, Lorenzo, my ex-boyfriend, was found two days later by a homeless man rummaging for cans.

* * * *

Returning home after prison was hard. I thought I'd reached the finish line, only to realize I was standing at the starting line of a whole new life.

Some nights, I'd break down because I knew nothing would ever be the same. I was changed, trying to navigate a world that had moved on without me.

Then came the diagnosis: PTSD. Great. Now what?

On top of everything, I had to fight to stay out of prison. Probation officers made it nearly impossible to hold a job—random drug tests, constant check-ins, officers popping up unannounced. The testing centers were packed with people who knew they'd fail but showed up anyway, hoping to dodge the system. Some even called in bomb threats to shut the place down. One morning, I pulled up and the building was in flames. Through it all, my father would just pat my arm and say, "Denise, this too shall pass."

I prayed he was right.

Then the whole world lost its mind over Y2K. Dad had been stockpiling canned goods since the seventies, always prepared for destruction. Me? Just my luck the computers would crash and every prisoner would walk free right after I'd finished my sentence. I held my breath hoping probation would at least disappear in the glitch. No such luck.

* * * *

In March 2000, I finally got approval to move back in with my mom in Orange County. Once settled, I headed straight to the beach between lifeguard towers three and five. I sat on the shore, watching the sky fold into the waves, wondering what my life might have been if I hadn't gone to prison. Would I even be alive? Or maybe I'd be a posh mom in a Central Park penthouse. A doctor in Newport Beach. Anything.

I thought about the women I left behind—trapped by federal mandatory minimums, robbed of their futures. Some would never raise their kids or chase their dreams. My heart broke for the innocent souls serving life or sitting on death row, powerless to fight back.

I thought about all the betrayal I'd endured and wondered if I'd ever trust anyone again. Then there was my family, the house we grew up in, gone. That still takes my breath away.

I wasn't behind bars anymore, but I wasn't free. Shame, guilt, self-doubt, and broken confidence—they built their own prison. On good days, I could breathe. But thoughts of Stacy always pulled me back. She didn't survive. I did. She missed everything—the pain, yes, but also the hope and joy that came after.

That truth became a turning point.

I sat with it. *Dolce far niente.* The sweetness of doing nothing. Just me, the waves, the quiet, and God. Alone in my thoughts, finally able to recharge.

Just like in that Oakland cell, I realized I had a choice: stay stuck in the past, or shift my mindset. God and the scriptures weren't just words. They were light cutting through the dark, guiding me step by step toward wholeness.

Time to dream again. To build. To trust. To love. I could have the career and family I'd always wanted. I am worthy of God's love simply because I exist.

I could've buried the past, pretended it never happened. But that would've been the real loss. Every choice, every mistake, every fight shaped me. Now I could use my experience to help the next girl coming up behind me.

So yeah, I fought like hell to take back what's mine. I deserve to smile. To laugh, to love, and to hold my head high.

And if the enemy whispers that it's too late? That I missed my shot?

I smile.

And I say, "*Just fucking watch me!*"

Epilogue

The events in this story aren't just about me. They're about everyone who shaped my life—and everyone I affected. Not everyone made it out alive, but those of us who did were forever changed. After experiencing the devastation of drugs, living only for the moment, and our all-consuming self-involvement, nearly every step forward became an opportunity for reflection. At least it was for me. Even for the most self-aware, you are who you are. Amid all the corruption, extortion, and coercion swirling around us, I was almost invisible, a background blur to the bigger picture. Some escaped the fallout, some got off easy, and some landed hard. Here's how that played out for my cast of characters.

Dad: I was devastated when my dad passed away from pneumonia—ironically, in the same ICU in Palm Springs where Stacy died. Dee has since moved on. I really miss what we all had.

I'm grateful we had time to grow close before he passed. I miss him more than words can say, and I believe he's on a spiritual journey now, watching over me and guiding me. He visits in dreams and sends signs. Through God's grace, I've been given proof that life doesn't end here. We shall meet again.

I remember him so vividly. Screaming in the courtroom. Threatening the judge and the DA as they led me away in handcuffs. He said if I came out damaged or changed in any way, shape, or form, he was coming after every single one of them—*the motherfuckers.* That's my dad.

Fearless. Protective. All heart. I did my best to stay sane for his sake. But no one goes through the prison system untouched. *No fucking way.*

Mom: She still has that incredible sense of humor. Laughing with her through life's ups and downs has been one of my greatest blessings. She has never held my past against me. She sees only my innocence and beauty, always reminding me of my wholeness and purpose. That kind of love leaves space for a person to change, and that's what makes her the greatest mom in the world. She adores her grandchildren and was my lifeline when my now-teenagers were babies. And no one cooks like Mom—her meals aren't just food; they're a safe space for swapping stories, leaning in, and making everyone feel seen and heard. Her love and support have shaped my life in more ways than I can count. She's my treasure, and I can't imagine life without her.

Greg: Greg and I are cofounders of Love Me Nutrition, a wellness brand centered on supplements that gives back, grounded in messages of self-acceptance, confidence, and self-love. Entrepreneurial in spirit, we're always collaborating on media projects and creative ideas.

Jeff: Jeff has four children, including Jenna, who made him a proud grandpa. He continues his work as a chiropractor, having opened his own practice in Huntington Beach. He hasn't lost his rock 'n' roll spirit. These days, he's playing drums again, this time for a Christian band at his church.

Aunt Flo: My Aunt Florence's beautiful soul has flown to the heavens to find rest. Before she passed, I held her hand, giving her strength just as she once gave me before I walked through those steel prison gates. As I played Luciano Pavarotti softly in the background, I encouraged her to let go, reassuring her she would come out stronger on the other side. Her courage and love will stay with me always.

Philip: Philip pled guilty in federal court to two counts of soliciting murder, a move that spared him the death penalty for tampering with—and ultimately killing—a government witness, Lorenzo Estes. He also admitted to arranging the murder of his best friend, James Ellenberger, which earned him a forty-year sentence. Still protesting his innocence, he took the deal—it was that or face lethal injection. He has since been released.

Fred and Duane: Fred pled guilty and took a plea deal from Mueller, receiving a twenty-five-year sentence in federal prison. He admitted to killing James. Duane claimed he wasn't mentally competent to stand trial—ha, I agree with that—but received the same twenty-five-year deal and admitted to shooting Lorenzo. I'm not one to say who ordered the hits, whether it was Philip, Agent Blue pulling strings, or just their own hot-headed impulsive behavior. Either way, they're all squirrely.

Dan: Seven months to my seven years still hits hard. My bet is Dan had been working both sides of the law long before we got arrested in Maui. I learned to forgive but come on. I still think he's a punk-ass bitch.

Pregnant Chick: I only had contact with her that one time at lunch at the Hard Rock Café. Her baby's daddy, Max, Lorenzo's partner, told me her actions haunted her. She carried heavy guilt for setting me up—and even more for possibly playing a part in Lorenzo's murder by going undercover. She turned to pills and alcohol for solace, and her addiction eventually killed her. Max also assured me Lorenzo would never have testified against me. He was playing both sides of the law, was planning to meet me in Hawaii, and regretted asking me to accompany Dan. *Yeah, whatever.*

Agent Blue: Agent Blue was, in fact, a government informant, posing as a corrupt FBI investigator to James and Philip in exchange for confidential information. Lorenzo trusted him. That trust cost him his life. It became clear why the DA's office didn't want to charge me in California—they feared uncovering a Pandora's box of FBI corruption. The *San Francisco Chronicle* ran a story about Agent Blue. The headlines read, "Defense in Murder Case May Implicate State/Dealer Lured to His Death by Informant." The government acknowledged they had failed to investigate allegations of law enforcement complicity and corruption. Instead, Blue made a deal, never served time, and walked away with a $40,000 reward from the Bureau of Narcotic Enforcement. Thank God this girlfella didn't count on him to make my charges disappear.

Robert Mueller: Robert Mueller did not follow up on any leads against Agent Blue. At the time, he was focused on climbing the political ladder. After this case, Mueller left San Francisco in September 2001 to head the FBI in Washington, DC. Later, as Special Counsel, he led the investigation into Russian interference in the 2016 US elections and related matters.

Peter: Then there's my little brother, Peter. He struggled with bills and self-doubt, convinced he could never be independent. Those beliefs led him to be homeless. We all tried to help, housing him, encouraging him, loving him until he was ready to try again. Through it all, Peter never lost the most essential part of himself: his kindness. Even in the darkest moments, he smiled and made others feel lighter. Eventually, a minister in Los Angeles took Peter into a sober house. He became the minister's poster child, and together they worked to serve the homeless community. I was so proud—it felt like Peter's time to shine. But just when you think your karma's clean, life stares you back in the face and says, "Fuck you! I'm not done with you yet!" Peter, who never used hard drugs, tried what he *thought* was coke or meth—it was Fentanyl. One hit. That's all it took. On May 4, 2018, a *Star Wars* fan to the very end, Peter fell to his knees. His last words were, "Am I moving forward or falling backward?" I like to believe he was moving forward. Every time I hear "The Man" by Aloe Blacc, I see Peter—standing tall, facing the sun. And to Bojo, who died suddenly in Hawaii. Same way. Gone too soon. Fuck drugs. Have I mentioned how much I hate them? How much they ruin lives? I'm with Nancy now, just say no. Drugs aren't what they used to be. One mistake—and you're gone. No second chance.

Denise: In a lot of ways, I *did* live happily ever after. I came to realize the warmth and security of my youth was the high I'd been chasing all along—not money or success or forbidden love. All I ever wanted was to feel safe within my own skin, to navigate the world without constant self-doubt. Ultimately, it was about finding a home in myself, loving who I am, flaws and all.

I am cautious to think (or declare) that I have it all figured out. Listen, I'm not here to teach any lessons (don't look at my paper if you want the test answers). I can only attest to my experience. But I hope that by sharing it, I might connect to someone struggling to find the light. Or that even if the light in your life is luminous and unyielding, you'll find comfort in knowing that there is a land between sin and salvation and that those who walk through it are neither doomed nor enlightened. They are simply human.

Every decision shaped the woman I became, and I'm grateful for that.

Shortly after my release, I broke the law to spend time with Heidi. We reclaimed stolen time at Hollywood parties, and at one of them, I met David, a wicked cool Bostonian whose humor and unwavering positivity became an anchor in my life. Somewhere that night, with the Goo Goo Dolls' "Iris" playing in the background, our souls recognized each other. He would later become my husband, and we've been married for over twenty years.

Around that same time, I got jobs in the entertainment industry and hustled my way back. Eventually I returned to fashion and producing, using everything I knew to build a successful fashion PR firm and tell stories that mattered. God has been so good.

But the most extraordinary role of my life is motherhood. My son, Radley, and my daughter, Paloma, are my greatest story. Every day they teach me joy, presence, and unconditional love. Radley, my sweetheart, kills it on the drums, and Paloma, my mini me—the better version of me—is a force of nature who lights up the universe with her smile. Within a year of each other, both got into Northeastern University, and I couldn't be more proud of the people they are becoming. Life with them is complete. They are my best friends, and everything feels brighter with them in it.

I honor the traditions that once made me feel loved growing up. Big Sunday dinners, laughter around the table, and recipes passed down through generations. Dishes like fresh *linguine alle vongole* that transport us to summer days along the Italian coast, or slow-simmered meat sauce rich enough to rival any scene Paulie cooked in *Goodfellas*. My mother was right. Meals are not just food; they're belonging, love, and home.

I'm still a girlfella—a girl who came up in a man's world. But now I understand that real wealth isn't money. It's gratitude. It's faith, freedom, time, and good health. It's God, family, and friends who love you for exactly who you are.

That's legacy. That's Baller Rich.

Today, I share my story with inmates across Southern California. It has healed me in ways I never expected. I recontextualized my larger-than-life past and saw it for what it was: a series of mishaps and accidental discoveries, abounding in contradictions. I was the life of the party, but I also knew a kind of loneliness few can imagine. I'm a wife and mother living in the Hollywood Hills, but I spent seven tough years in prison. I've been called an airhead, but I ran a multimillion-dollar international business. I'm virtuous, but I broke the law. I made some epic mistakes. And I got back up, anyway.

So, I stand in front of youth in prisons where I was once starved, beaten, and thrown in a hole. I reach out to inmates wearing uniforms with numbers above their pockets, searching for something salvageable, some hope or yearning in their eyes that suggests they haven't given up. I tell them what my father once told me: *this too shall pass.* Nothing is permanent. Not even rock bottom. Then I tell them, "Hi. For the new ones who don't know me yet, my name is Denise Trigo Fleming. We're a lot alike. I've seen light in the darkest places. I learned that even in the hardest moments, there's a way forward. That spark—the grace of God—lives inside you. It will always lead you home."

It's never too late to look in the mirror and decide you're worth fighting for. Like Sinatra, I also did it "My Way." I took detours, wrong turns, and yes, the scenic route, but every mile shaped me.

So, if you're lost, struggling, and heading in the wrong direction, come back to yourself—whip that U-ey. Roll down the windows, turn up the music, and notice the beauty around you. Better yet, poke your head through the sunroof and scream with joy at the top of your lungs.

I took the long way home.

But I made it.

And so can you.

Acknowledgments

This book exists because I did not walk this road alone. I drew strength from the people I love—those still here, and those watching over me. Writing it meant facing my past and confronting pain, doubt, and fear head-on. There are people not mentioned here whose presence is deeply valued. And there are others who became part of my story in ways I never would have chosen—yet their roles shaped the path that led me here.

To my husband, Dave: What a beautiful life. Words cannot capture the depth of my love and gratitude for you. Twenty-three years, Hawaii, Italy, and every adventure in between—thank you for your optimism, believing in me, and for giving me the space and freedom to chase a dream until it became real. For raising two beautiful children together, you've been an angel. I am honored to share this life with you, my soulmate, my best friend.

To my parents, Mom and Dad, my two heroes: Thank you for the foundation you gave me and for loving me unconditionally. Your love has always been my constant light, guiding me back to who I am and where I come from. Your smiles, your hugs, your laughter, and the forgiveness and safety you gave me—these are the things that carried me through. You are my north stars. *I love you both deeply.*

To my brothers, Greg and Jeff: Thank you for the shared history, the laughs, the fun, the wild chaos, and the understanding only siblings can provide. You are my ride or dies. That will never change. I love you both so much.

To Peter, Aunt Flo, and Stacy in heaven: Thank you for your love, guidance, and laughter. I feel you all with me every step of the way.

Peter, my sweet little brother—your kindness was your superpower. You faced more than most and never lost your smile or your lighthearted nature. You touched so many lives. Until we meet again, Sweetheart. I love you always.

Aunt Flo, your strength carried me. Your famous "you can do it" speech meant more to me than you can imagine, and everything you taught me in the kitchen lives on in every meal I make.

And Stacy, my best friend, save me a dance to "Lucky Star" on the dance floor.

To Aunt Mary, Aunt Gina, Uncle Michael, and the only cool cousins—you know who you are: I loved growing up with you all. Thank you for every holiday feast made with love, and every adventure along the way. I carry your recipes and your hearts with me always.

To my literary agent, Noah Ballard: Thank you for championing this book and for believing in me from the start. You not only helped turn a dream into a reality, you pushed me to bring the pages to life. I'm forever grateful.

To Post Hill Press: Thank you for taking a chance on me and helping bring this book into the world.

Book Cover: Jonathan Mannion, thank you for your guidance and for connecting me with Rebecca Meeks. Rebecca, your creative vision is fire. I felt the love in every detail.

To those who offered writing encouragement along the way: Andrew Lewis, Sue Carswell, Sheila Hamilton, Sara Shepard, Jessica Jones, with a special thank you to Matthew Daddona and Tara Herrmann. Your conversations, shared stories, and friendship reminded me that my voice mattered and that I wasn't alone.

To everyone struggling: Lean into God; that light will guide you home. Don't give up. Have faith that a beautiful life is waiting for you, and trust that God will finish what He has started in you.

My homies: To those I served time with (not the annoying ones): you lifted me, made me laugh, and walked beside me in the trenches. I got nothing but love for ya.

And to my homies that I met on the outside, I'm so grateful for our connection. You make me feel like I'm not alone. Especially the ones that I work with inside prisons, sharing our stories, mentoring, and giving hope to those who need it most. Let's remind each other what we do matters. Keep showing up.

And finally, Radley and Paloma: My breath of life. I hope this journey shows you that what you focus on becomes your reality, and who you become is entirely up to you. Trust God and follow your passion—the rest will find you. Thank you for loving me unconditionally and for being so ridiculously cool and fun to be around. You've given me more laughter and joy than I ever thought possible. Remember, family is everything, so stay close and look out for each other. Through it all, stay grateful—that's where the magic is. You are truly my best friends. But you know that already.

I love you, always and forever. Mom.

About the Author

Denise Trigo-Fleming is a California native, prison reform advocate, media producer and founder of Girlfellas Studios. She is also CEO of Look Los Angeles, a fashion public relations and marketing firm, and owner of Love Me Nutrition, a supplement company that promotes wellness and gives back to the community. Denise resides in the Hollywood Hills with her husband, talent manager Dave Fleming, and their two children, Radley and Paloma. She enjoys traveling and cooking recipes that transport her to summer days on the coast of Italy with her family. *Dealing* is her first book.

About the Author